State and Business in Tanzania's Development

It is widely accepted that countries' institutions play a major role in their economic development. Yet, the way they affect, and are affected by, development, and how to reform them are still poorly understood. In this companion volume, *State and Business in Tanzania* diagnoses the main weaknesses, root causes, and developmental consequences of Tanzania's institutions, and shows that the uncertainty surrounding its development paths and its difficulty in truly 'taking off' are related to institutional challenges. Based on a thorough account of the economic, social, and political development of the country, this diagnostic offers evidence on the quality of its institutions and a detailed analysis of critical institution- and development-sensitive areas among which state-business relations rank high, even though the institutional features of land management, civil service and the power sector are shown to be also of prime importance. This title is also available as Open Access.

François Bourguignon is Emeritus Professor of economics, Paris School of Economics and School of Advanced Studies in Social Sciences (EHESS), Paris. He is Former Chief Economist and Senior Vice President of the World Bank and the Co-Founder of the European Development Network. His awards include the Dan David Prize and a silver medal from the French National Centre for Scientific Research (CNRS).

Samuel Mwita Wangwe is Chairman and Consultant of Daima Associates and Principal Research Associate with the Economic and Social Research Foundation (ESRF) and Research on Development Policy Institution (REPOA). He has published sixteen books and over eighty articles and was awarded the 1988 Elgar Graham Prize. He also frequently serves as an advisor to the Tanzanian government.

The Institutional Diagnostic Project

A suite of case-study monographs emerging from a large research program on the role of institutions in the economics, and the political economy of development in low-income countries, supported by a synthesis volume of the original case studies. This program was funded by the United Kingdom's Foreign and Commonwealth Development Office during a period of six years, during which program researchers had regular interactions with its staff, either directly or through Oxford Policy Management (the lead managing organisation).

Books in this collection:

François Bourguignon and Jean-Philippe Platteau *Institutional Challenges at the Early Stages of Development: Lessons from a Multi-Country Study*

Selim Raihan, François Bourguignon and Umar Salam (Eds.) *Is the Bangladesh Paradox Sustainable?*

António S. Cruz, Ines A. Ferreira, Johnny Flentø and Finn Tarp (Eds.) *Mozambique at a Fork in the Road*

François Bourguignon, Romain Houssa, Jean-Philippe Platteau and Paul Reding (Eds.) *State Capture and Rent-Seeking in Benin*

François Bourguignon and Samuel Mwita Wangwe (Eds.) *State and Business in Tanzania's Development*

State and Business in Tanzania's Development

The Institutional Diagnostic Project

Edited by

FRANÇOIS BOURGUIGNON
Paris School of Economics and EHESS, Paris

SAMUEL MWITA WANGWE
Daima Associates

CAMBRIDGE
UNIVERSITY PRESS

Shaftesbury Road, Cambridge CB2 8EA, United Kingdom

One Liberty Plaza, 20th Floor, New York, NY 10006, USA

477 Williamstown Road, Port Melbourne, VIC 3207, Australia

314–321, 3rd Floor, Plot 3, Splendor Forum, Jasola District Centre, New Delhi – 110025, India

103 Penang Road, #05–06/07, Visioncrest Commercial, Singapore 238467

Cambridge University Press is part of Cambridge University Press & Assessment,
a department of the University of Cambridge.

We share the University's mission to contribute to society through the pursuit of
education, learning and research at the highest international levels of excellence.

www.cambridge.org
Information on this title: www.cambridge.org/9781009285797

DOI: 10.1017/9781009285803

First published 2023

A catalogue record for this publication is available from the British Library

Library of Congress Cataloging-in-Publication Data
NAMES: Wangwe, S. M., editor. | Bourguignon, François, editor.
TITLE: State and business in Tanzania's development : the institutional diagnostic project /
edited by François Bourguignon, Paris School of Economics and EHESS, Paris,
Samuel Mwita Wangwe, Daima Associates.
DESCRIPTION: Cambridge, United Kingdom ; New York, NY :
Cambridge University Press, [2023] | Series: Institutional diagnostic project |
Includes bibliographical references and index.
IDENTIFIERS: LCCN 2023037474 | ISBN 9781009285797
(hardback) | ISBN 9781009285803 (ebook)
SUBJECTS: LCSH: Economic development – Tanzania. |
Institutional economics – Tanzania. | Business and politics – Tanzania. |
Tanzania – Economic policy.
CLASSIFICATION: LCC HC885 .S73 2023 | DDC 338.9678–dc23/eng/20230816
LC record available at https://lccn.loc.gov/2023037474

ISBN 978-1-009-28579-7 Hardback

Contents

Figures

Tables

Boxes

Contributors

Paschal Assey is a retired Civil Servant, with more than 30 years of diverse experiences including policy analysis, development planning, developing monitoring systems, and managing development projects. He served in different capacities including Deputy Chief Executive Officer – Millennium Challenge Account Tanzania, Director for Poverty Eradication – Vice President's Office of the Government of Tanzania, National Coordinator of The Poverty Eradication Initiatives Programme, and Principal Economist of the Planning Commission of Tanzania.

He obtained BA Economics from University of Dar es Salaam, MA in Public Administration from Carleton University Canada, and National Accountancy Diploma from the National Board of Accountants and Auditors Tanzania.

François Bourguignon is the director of studies at the Ecole des Hautes Etudes en Sciences Sociales (EHESS) and Emeritus Professor at the Paris School of Economics, where he previously held the position of a director. From 2003 to 2007, he was Chief Economist and Vice President of the World Bank. He was also Chairman of the Institutional Diagnostic Project.

He has vast experience in advising governments and international organisations. In addition, he is the author/editor of numerous books and articles in international economic journals: his work, theoretical and empirical, focuses mainly on the distribution and redistribution of income in developing and developed countries. During his career, he has received several scientific distinctions, such as the Dan David Prize in 2016.

Klaus Deininger (discussant) is Lead Economist in the Sustainability and Infrastructure Team of the Development Research Group at the World Bank.

His areas of research focus on income and asset inequality and its relationship to poverty reduction and growth; access to land, land markets, and land reform and their impact on household welfare and agricultural productivity; and land tenure and its impact on investment, including environmental sustainability. His works also account for capacity building (including the use of quantitative and qualitative methods) for policy analysis and evaluation, mainly in the Africa, Central America, and East Asia Regions.

Antonio Estache (discussant) is Professor of Economics at Université libre de Bruxelles and a researcher at the European Centre for Advanced Research in Economics and Statistics (Belgium). Since 2008, he has also been Policy Advisor for all major multilateral development agencies and various governments and parliaments. Prior to that, he spent 25 years at the World Bank working on the restructuring and regulation of infrastructure services, on public sector reforms (including decentralization, budgetary processes, and tax reform) as well as on the macroeconomic modelling of their economic and social impacts. He has also published extensively on these topics.

Catrina Godinho is Climate Change Specialist at the World Bank, a fellow of the Energy for Growth Hub and Agora Energiewende, and former OIES-Saudi Aramco Fellow at the Oxford Institute of Energy Studies. Her research focuses on the political economy of climate change and energy sector reform and governance. At the time of writing, Catrina was Research Associate at the Power Futures Lab at the University of Cape Town.

Hazel Gray (discussant) is Director of the Centre of African Studies (CAS) at the University of Edinburgh. She previously worked at the Ministry of Finance in Tanzania from 2000 to 2004, and she was a lead author of the UNDP Human Development Report for Tanzania in 2014 and 2017. She is the co-chair of the journal *Critical African Studies*. Her research interests cover the political economy of development and industrial change in Africa, the political economy of institutions and social provisioning, and heterodox economics. Her monograph 'Turbulence and Order in Economic Development: Institutions and Economic Development in Tanzania and Vietnam' was published by Oxford University Press in 2018.

Jan Willem Gunning (discussant) is Emeritus Professor of development economics at the Vrije Universiteit Amsterdam. He has also been a staff member of the World Bank and Professor at Oxford, where he was Director of the Centre for the Study of African Economies. He has long been active in the African Economic Research Consortium in Nairobi. Gunning was a co-founder and the first president of the European Development Research Network (EUDN). He is a member of the Royal Netherlands Academy of Arts and Sciences (KNAW) and has served as the Academy's general secretary. He received an honorary doctorate from the University of Auvergne for his role in research on African economies.

François Libois is a research fellow of the *Institut national de recherche pour l'agriculture, l'alimentation et l'environnement* (INRAE) and Associate Professor at the Paris School of Economics (PSE). He obtained his PhD in 2016 from University of Namur and consecutively worked as post-doctoral fellow for the "Economic Development and Institutions" program under the guidance of François Bourguignon.

By training, François Libois is an applied microeconomist mostly working on topics at the intersection of development, environmental and institutional economics. In general, he is particularly interested by the role of intermediary institutions in the process of development and, in particular, when it deals with natural resource management. He has several pieces of work on biodiversity conservation, fisheries, forests, and access to energy.

Dr. Servacius Likwelile (late) doubled as Senior Lecturer in the Department of Economics at the University of Dar es Salaam Tanzania and Advisor at the Research on Development Policy Institution (REPOA). In his career, he served in various positions including Permanent Secretary Treasury and Paymaster General – Ministry of Finance and Planning Tanzania, Alternate Governor – African Development Bank Group and World Bank; Executive Director of Tanzania Social Action Fund (TASAF), Director for Poverty Eradication in the Vice President's Office of the Government of Tanzania, and Head of the Economics Department – University of Dar es Salaam. He obtained BA, MA, and PhD (Economics) from University of Dar es Salaam.

Sist J. Mramba is Lecturer at the Law School of Tanzania, an advocate, and an expert of experienced environment, land, natural resources, and common lands and forestry.

He is specialised in the economic issues related to forests, common property resources, and rural land use in Tanzania, as well as transfer of public land to private use. He is the author of several articles and books – including Land Law Manual for Learners and Practitioners. In addition, he has authored several official reports on institutional arrangements and land policies, especially in Tanzania.

Rwekaza S. Mukandala is Professor at the University of Dar es Salaam (Tanzania), where he served the role of Vice Chancellor from 2006 to 2017. Furthermore, he is Chair of the Research and Education for Democracy in Tanzania (REDET) and the Tanzania Election Monitoring Committee (TEMCO). He has also been President of the African Association of Political Science (AAPS) and Chair of the Organising Committee for the XIX World Congress of the International Political Science Association (IPSA) in Durban (South Africa) in 2003.

Rwekaza S. Mukandala has published 15 books and more than 60 articles in international and local journals. He has carried out research on politics, aid and donors, and governance in many African countries. He has also consulted widely on these and other related issues for the Government of Tanzania, International Organisations, and donors.

Jean-Philippe Platteau is Co-Director of the Institutional Diagnostic Project. He is Emeritus Professor at the University of Namur (Belgium) and an active member of the Center for Research in Development Economics (CRED). He is the author of numerous journal articles and several books. Most of his work has been devoted to the study of the role of institutions in economic development and the processes of institutional change. He has always paid particular attention to informal institutions such as social norms, informal markets, and the rules of village societies, leading him to take an interest in the influence of non-economic factors and in problems located at the frontier of economics and other social sciences. His latest work focuses more specifically on the role of culture and religion.

Samuel Mwita Wangwe obtained a PhD at the University of Dar es Salaam (Tanzania) and has over 40-year experience as an economist, policy researcher, and analyst, as well as an economic advisor to the Government of Tanzania. He has authored/co-authored/edited 15 books on development and economic management and over 80 published articles in journals and edited books.

Currently, Samuel M. Wangwe is Consultant and Chairman at Daima Associates, a private consulting firm based in Dar es Salaam, and is Principal Research Associate within the Economic and Social Research Foundation (ESRF) and the Research on Development Policy Institution (REPOA).

The Institutional Diagnostic Project: Presentation

François Bourguignon and Jean-Philippe Platteau

This study of Tanzania is one of four case studies in a research project whose final aim is to devise a methodology to establish an 'institutional diagnostic' of economic development in a particular country. The objective of such a diagnostic is to identify the institutional factors that may slow down development or reduce its inclusiveness or sustainability, the reforms likely to overcome these weaknesses, but also the political economy that may prevent or facilitate such reforms. These diagnostics must thus rely on a thorough review of economic development and institutional features of countries under analysis, which is the content of this volume on Tanzania. As a preamble, the following pages offer a general description of the whole diagnostic project.

I 'INSTITUTIONS MATTER'

'Institutions matter' became a motto among international development agencies in the late 1990s, when it became clear that structural adjustment policies (SAPs), themselves based upon the so-called Washington Consensus and their emphasis on markets, were not delivering the growth and development that was expected. The slogan sounded a note of disappointment for those liberalist reformers, sometimes jokingly called the 'marketeers', who promoted reliance on market mechanisms and the pre-eminence of private actors so developing countries could get out of the crises of the 1980s and restore long-run growth. Giving more space to the market was probably justified from a theoretical point of view. Practically, however, it was another story. What the 'marketeers' had not fully realised was that a well-functioning market economy requires regulating institutions, public goods, and non-market services that most often were missing or deficient in the economies being considered. Under these conditions, liberalising, privatising, and deregulating might in effect prove counterproductive without concomitant institutional changes.

Nowadays, the 'institutions matter' slogan appears as a fundamental truth about development, and it is indeed widely shared by the development community, including international organisations. Equally obvious to all is the complementarity between the market and the state: the economic efficiency expected from the former requires some intervention by the latter through adequate policies, the provision of public services, and, more fundamentally, institutions able to impose rules constraining the activity of various economic actors, whether public or private. Practically, however, the institutions of a country are the outcome of history and specific events or circumstances. Therefore, they are not necessarily well adapted to the current economic context and to the modern development challenge. This raises the issue of how existing institutions can be reformed.

That 'institutions matter' has also long been evident for those academic economists and political scientists who kept stressing that development is the outcome of the joint and interactive evolution of the economy and its institutional setup, with the latter encompassing not only state and political agencies but also cultural and social norms. As a matter of fact, the study of the role of institutions has a long history in the development economics literature, from the very fathers of the discipline in the post-Second World War years and their emphasis on development as a structural and cultural transformation, as for instance in the writings of Peter Bauer, Albert Hirschman, Arthur Lewis, and Hla Myint, to the New Institutional Economics as applied to development issues, in particular the work of Douglass North, to the institutional political economy approach put forward nowadays by social scientists such as Mushtaq Khan, to the more formalised school of political economics pioneered by Daron Acemoglu and James Robinson.

II HOW INSTITUTIONS MATTER IN DEVELOPMENT POLICY TODAY: THE ROLE OF 'GOVERNANCE'

Faced with the disappointing performances of the so-called Washington Consensus, which governed the market-oriented SAPs put to work in developing countries at the time of the macroeconomic crisis of the early 1980s, international organisations and bilateral development agencies switched to what was called the post-Washington consensus. This extended set of principles was seen as a way of compensating for the neglect of institutional considerations in the original set of policies. Market-oriented reforms had thus to be accompanied by other reforms, including the regulation of various sectors, making government more efficient, and improving human capital formation. Most importantly, however, emphasis was put on good governance as a necessary adjuvant to market-led development, especially in its capacity to protect property rights and guarantee contract enforcement. With time, governance then became a key criterion among donors for allocating aid across low-income countries and monitoring its use.

It is fair to say that, practically, governance is defined and evaluated in a rather ad hoc way, based on some expert opinion, firm surveys, and simple economic parameters such as the rate of inflation or the size of budget deficit. The relationship with the actual nature and quality of institutions is thus very indirect. This still seems the case today, even though the recent World Development Report by the World Bank, entitled 'Governance and the Law',[1] intends to go deeper by showing how governance, or policy making in general, including institutional reforms, depends on the functioning of institutions, the role of stakeholders, and their relative political power. Practically, however, there remains something rather mechanical and schematic in the way institutions are represented in this report, which is actually more about effective policy making than the diagnosis of institutional weaknesses and possible avenues for reform.

If there is no doubt that institutions matter for development, the crucial issue is to know how they matter. After all, impressive economic development achievements have been observed despite clear failures in particular institutional areas. In other words, not all dimensions of governance may be relevant at a given point of time in a given country. Likewise, institutional dimensions that are not included in governance criteria may play a decisive role.

There is admittedly limited knowledge about how institutions affect development, how they form, and how they can be reformed in specific contexts. Despite intensive and increasing efforts over the last few decades, the challenge remains daunting. The difficulty comes from the tight imbrication of the way the quality of existing institutions affects the development process, including policies, the political economy context that conditions possible institutional reforms, and the influence that the pace and structure of development exerts, directly or indirectly, on the dynamics of institutions.

III SEARCHING FOR EVIDENCE ON THE RELATIONSHIP BETWEEN THE QUALITY OF INSTITUTIONS AND DEVELOPMENT

Three approaches have been followed to help in the identification of development-hindering or promoting institutional features, and of their evolution over time, whether autonomously or through discretionary reforms. All three approaches have their own drawbacks.

The first approach consists of historical case studies. These are in-depth studies of successful, or unsuccessful, development experiences, and their causes and processes as they unfolded in the historical past or in the contemporary world. The formation and success of the Maghribi trading networks in the eleventh-century Mediterranean basin, the effects of the Glorious Revolution in Britain, the enactment of effective land reforms in Korea and

---

[1] World Bank (2017b).

Taiwan after the demise of Japanese colonial rule, and the implementation of
the Household Responsibility System in rural China are all examples of institutional changes that led to vigorous development, whether state-led or resulting from decentralised initiatives triggered by external factors. On the other
hand, violent fights for the appropriation of natural resource rents in several
post-independence African states illustrate the opposite course of blocked
development under essentially predatory states. Studying such events is of
utmost interest insofar as they highlight rather precise mechanisms susceptible of governing the transformation of institutions, often under the pressure
of economic and other circumstances, sometimes prompting and sometimes
hampering development. In their best-selling book *Why Nations Fail*, for
instance, Acemoglu and Robinson (2012) masterfully show the role of institutions in several historical and contemporaneous experiences of sustained
or failed development. In particular, they stress the critical role of inclusive
institutions as compared with predatory ones, and most importantly the role
of favourable political conditions in changing institutions and sparking development. The most serious problem with this approach, however, is that the
experiences thoroughly analysed in the history-based empirical literature are
rarely transferable in time or in space and are not necessarily relevant for
developing countries today.

Under the second approach are cross-country studies pertaining to the contemporaneous era. They rely on indicators that describe the strength of a particular set of institutions or a specific aspect of governance in a country, for
example, the protection of property rights, nature of legal regimes, extent of
democracy, strength and type of controls on the executive, extent of corruption, and so on – the issue being whether there is a correlation between these
indicators and gross domestic product (GDP) growth or other development
outcomes. These institutional and governance indicators are generally based
on the opinion of experts in various areas evaluating, on a comparative basis,
countries on which they have specialised knowledge. They are thus based on
largely subjective grounds and lack the precision needed for statistical analysis.
If correlation with development outcomes is sometimes significant and often
fits intuition, the use that can be made of them is problematic as they essentially refer, by construction, to an abstract 'average country' and may be of
little use when focusing on a particular country. Most importantly, they say
nothing about causality and still less about the policy instruments that could
improve institutions under consideration. Corruption is generally found to be
bad for development, but in what direction does the causality go? Is it true in
all countries and all circumstances? What about the cases where corruption
'greases the wheels' and reintroduces economic efficiency in the presence of
too-stringent administrative constraints? And if it is to be curbed, what kind of
reform is likely to work?

Cross-country studies are a useful approach, provided that they are considered as essentially exploratory. They need to be complemented by more

country-specific analyses that can detect causal relationships, shed light on dynamic processes at play in key sectors of the economy as well as on their interactions with institutions and the political arena, and inform on potential ways of conducting reforms.

The third approach exploits the fact that some sorts of institutional weaknesses or strengths are readily observable, such as the delivery of public services such as education or health care. For instance, the absenteeism of teachers in public schools reveals a breach of contract between civil servants and their employers and/or a monitoring failure by supervisors. There are ways of incentivising teachers so that they show up at school, and numerous experimentations, rigorously evaluated through randomised control trial (RCT) techniques in various community settings, have successfully explored the impact of such schemes in various countries over the last two decades or more. Identification of similar institutional weaknesses at the micro-level and experimentation on ways to remedy them have sprouted up in the recent past, so much so that the field has become the dominant subject among researchers in development economics. Inspired by the RCT methodology and its concern with causality, a new economic approach to history has also blossomed in recent decades. This literature exploits so-called natural experiments and intends to assess the impact of institutional changes that exogenously emerged in particular geographic areas in the past, the outcomes of which can still be observed and compared with otherwise similar neighbouring regions today. These outcomes can be of an economic, social, or political nature.

A major limitation of the third approach is that it generally addresses simple cases that are suitable for experimentation. Identifying more macro-level institutional failures and testing appropriate remedies through the RCT method is much less easy, if not impossible. In addition, successful testing of reforms susceptible to correcting well-identified micro-level institutional failures does not mean that the political will exists, or an effective coalition of interest groups can be formed, to fully correct the detected inefficiency. Thus, in the example of teachers' absenteeism, there is no guarantee that the state will systematically implement the incentive scheme whose impact has been shown to be the best way to improve school performance. The institutional weakness may thus not be so much in the breach of contract between teachers and their public employer as in the incapacity of the latter to design and implement the right policy. As this example shows, an in-depth understanding of macro-political factors is needed to reach a proper assessment of the feasibility of reforms and the conditions required for their successful implementation.

These empirical approaches leave a gap between an essentially macro-view of the relationship between institutions and development, whether it consists of stylized historical facts or cross-country correlations between GDP growth and governance or institutional indicators, on the one hand, and a micro-perspective on institutional dysfunction (e.g. the observation of absenteeism of civil servants or corrupt tax inspectors) and possible remedies, on the other hand. Also note that, in most cases, these approaches permit identification of relationships between institutional factors and development outcomes but not the mechanisms responsible for them. In economic modelling parlance, they give 'reduced form' rather than 'structural' evidence about the institution–development nexus. Filling this twofold gap requires a meso-approach based, as much as possible, on structural analysis conducted at intermediate levels of the social and economic structure of a country, including economic or social sectors as well as key groups of actors and official decision-making or monitoring entities.

Awareness of these drawbacks of the standard analysis of the relationship between institutions and development and, therefore, of the need for a more structural, sectoral, and political economy approach to that relationship has motivated the exploratory research undertaken within the present Institutional Diagnostic Project.

IV INSTITUTIONAL DIAGNOSTIC AS A NEW APPROACH TO INSTITUTIONS AND DEVELOPMENT

The Institutional Diagnostic Project research programme aims at developing a methodology or, rather, a framework that allows the identification of major institutional weaknesses or dysfunctions that block or slow down economic growth and structural transformation, and/or make them non-inclusive and non-sustainable, in a given country at a given stage of its development process. The diagnostic is also intended to formulate a reform programme and point to the political stakes involved in its implementation. In other words, it should contribute simultaneously to a better understanding of the specific relationship between institutions and development in the country under consideration, to a more complete stocktaking of policies and reforms likely to improve the development context, and to characterising the political barriers that might obstruct these reforms. It is a country-centred approach that differs from historical case studies in the sense that the focus is not on a particular event, circumstance, or episode in a country but on the overall functioning of its economy and society. It also goes beyond the mere use of governance or institutional indicators that appear much too rough when dealing with a specific economy. On the other hand, it makes use of micro-economic evidence on institutional weaknesses and dysfunction in a country and, when available, on whatever lessons can be learned from experimental works that may have been conducted in the area concerned. It thus makes use of the various methodological approaches to the study of the institution–development relationship, but goes beyond them by embedding them in essentially a structural approach adapted to the particulars of a country.

A priori, it would seem that institutional diagnostics should resemble the 'growth diagnostics' approach developed by Hausmann, Rodrik, and Velasco around 2005 to identify the binding economic constraints to economic growth.[2] The resemblance can only be semantic, however. Practically, if the objective is similar, the difference is huge. Most fundamentally, the growth diagnostics approach relies explicitly on a full theoretical model of economic growth based on the accumulation of means of production and innovation in the private sector, the availability of infrastructure, financial facilities, the control of risk through appropriate insurance mechanisms, and the development of human capital. Constraints in one of these dimensions should logically translate into a high relative (so-called) shadow price paid for that resource or that facility, that is, the actual cost paid by the user of that resource, which may differ from its posted price. The observation of those prices should then allow the analyst to identify the constraints most likely to be binding. No such model is available, even implicitly, in the case of the relationship between institutions and development: there is no shadow price easily observable for the availability of a fair and efficient judiciary, an uncorrupted civil service, an effective regulatory agency, or a transparent budget. Another, more heuristic, approach needed to be developed.

In the exploratory attempt of the Institutional Diagnostic research programme, we decided to avoid designing a diagnostic framework *a priori*, testing it through application to various countries, and then revising it progressively in light of accumulated experience. Instead, our preference is a more inductive approach consisting of exploring the relationship between existing institutions and the development process in a limited number of countries. On the basis of these in-depth country case studies, the idea is to draw the contours of an institutional diagnostic framework destined to be applied to other countries. The purpose of this framework is to identify pivotal and dysfunctional institutions, understand the causes of the dysfunction, and suggest feasible ways of correcting them in the particular social and political context of a country. In short, the elaboration of the diagnostic methodology has proceeded quasi-heuristically, from a few exploratory yet detailed attempts to understand the role and the dynamic of major institutions in a country, as well as their interactions with the local environment, including the society, the polity, and the geography.

A requirement of the UK Department for International Development, now the Foreign and Commonwealth Development Office, that funded this research project was to focus on low-income and lower middle-income countries. Accordingly, and in view of available resources, the following four countries were selected: Bangladesh, Benin, Mozambique, and Tanzania. The rationale for this choice will be provided in the individual case studies. At this stage, it will be sufficient to emphasise that, taken together, these four countries exhibit the diversity that is needed in such an exploratory exercise, diversity being understood in terms of geography, population size, economic endowments, historical and cultural legacy, or development strategy. Despite that diversity,

---

[2] Hausmann et al. (2005).

however, the fact that they often face similar economic and institutional challenges in their development suggests there may be common lessons to be drawn from the in-depth study of these challenges.

V STRUCTURE OF CASE STUDIES

Before presenting the structure of the case studies, it is worth defining more precisely what is meant by 'institutions'. In the present research programme, we use a definition derived from North (1990) and proposed by Baland et al. (2020, p. 3) in the recently published *Handbook of Institutions and Development*:

[Institutions are defined] as rules, procedures or other human devices that constrain individual behaviour, either explicitly or implicitly, with a view to making individual expectations about others' behaviour converge and allowing individual actions to become coordinated.

According to this definition, laws and all that they stipulate are institutions, insofar as they are commonly obeyed. Even though often appearing under the label of governance, democratic elections, the control of the executive, and the functioning of public agencies are institutions too. But this is also the case for customary law, even unwritten, and common cultural habits. Institutional failures correspond to situations where a law or a rule is inoperant and contraveners are not punished. Actually, this situation may concern large groups of people such as when, for instance, several laws coexist, or a law cannot be enforced on the whole population for lack of resources. The formal production relationship between employers and employees or between firm managers and the state through tax laws are institutions that govern modern companies in developing countries, but the existence of informal production sectors results from the inability of the state to have labour and tax laws enforced throughout the whole production fabric, especially among micro- and small enterprises. Yet implicit rules govern the relationship between informal managers, their clients, and people who work for them. As such, production informality may thus be considered as an institution in itself, which coexists with formal labour laws. The concept of institution also applies to laws and customs that rule social and family life. Here, too, informal institutions such as religion and tribal tradition dictate behavioural rules that differ from secular laws, for instance in areas such as marriage, divorce, or inheritance. However, note that, because the focus is on economic development, most institutions and institutional weaknesses considered in the Institutional Diagnostic Project generally refer to those likely to have a significant impact on the economy.

Equipped with this definition, the in-depth study of the relationship between institutions and development in a country and the identification of institutional impediments to long-term inclusive and sustainable development will proceed in three steps. The first one is mechanical. It consists of reviewing the economic, social, and political development of a country, surveying the existing literature, and querying various types of decision makers, top policymakers, and experts about their views on the functioning of institutions in their country. The latter can be done through questionnaire surveys or through focused qualitative interviews. Based on this material, some binding institutional weaknesses around economic development may be identified and hypotheses elaborated regarding their economic consequences and, most importantly, their causes.

This direct but preliminary approach to the institutional diagnostic of a particular country is also expected to point to several thematic areas where critical institutions seem to be at play. Depending on the country considered, some of the areas obviously deserving scrutiny could be the following: modalities of state functioning, that is, the bureaucracy and the delivery of basic public goods such as education; tax collection; economic regulation and the relationship between private business and political power; land allocation system and property rights; or decentralization.

The second step consists of a thorough analysis of these critical areas in order to precisely determine the modus operandi of relevant institutions and the sources of their inefficiencies, ways of remedying the situation, and the most important challenges posed by the required reforms. Are the observed institutional inefficiencies caused by a lack of competent civil servants, their tendency to shirk or get involved in corrupt deals, the excessively intricate nature of the law or administrative rules or their undue multiplication and mutual inconsistency, or bad organization? Moreover, why is it that reforms that seem adequate to correct major institutional inefficiencies have not been undertaken, and why have important reforms voted for in parliament not been effectively implemented? Who would be the gainers and the losers of particular reforms and, therefore, who is likely to promote or oppose them?

Based on these detailed analyses of key thematic areas, the third step of the case studies, and the most challenging task, is to synthesise what has been learned into an articulated view of the main institutional problems hindering progress in various areas, their negative consequences for development, and, most importantly, their causes, proximate or more distant, as well as their susceptibility to reforms. This is the essence of the diagnostic that each case study is expected to deliver.

It bears emphasis that this exercise is a diagnostic, not a reform, agenda. Because there are gainers and losers from most reforms, political and economic circumstances will determine whether they can be undertaken or not. This needs to be thoroughly discussed, but it must be clear that no firm conclusion about the political feasibility can be reached without a precise evaluation of the distribution of political power in the society, something that goes beyond the contemplated diagnostic. From the strict standpoint of the diagnosis, however, its critical contribution is to expose the nature of the institutional dysfunction and highlight possible reforms as well as the stakes involved. In other words, the diagnostic must eventually make all key actors aware of the implications of the needed reforms, and of the expected collective gains and the possible losses they would entail for some groups in the population or some categories of key economic and political actors.

Preface to the Tanzania Study

François Bourguignon and Samuel Mwita Wangwe

Why was Tanzania chosen as a case study of the relationship between the quality of institutions and development, and why is it a good candidate for diagnosing institutional obstacles to development? First, because it is a peaceful country with a stable political regime and very limited ethnic rivalry in a sub-Saharan African context. In that way, it was thought to be easier to relate development issues to the functioning of institutions without interference from latent conflicts of a purely political nature. Second, this is an economy that has gone through major institutional reforms. It attracted world interest in the late 1960s and was exemplified as an ambitious attempt at socialist development under the direction of the founder of the nation, Julius Nyerere. In the midst of the global crisis of the early 1980s, and possibly the relative failure of the previous model, it then went through a drastic transition to a full market economy under the firm guidance of international financial institutions. It is thus interesting to check whether there are still some remnants of that difficult transition in today's economic institutional framework and their implications. Third, it had been a fairly fast-growing economy between the early 2000s and the COVID crisis, and some observers feel growth could accelerate further in the future. On that ground, it is likely that institutions are stabilising themselves, making them easier to observe and analyse. Finally, Tanzania is a country that has been studied by various eminent scholars in economics and political science, so it is possible to rely on solid expertise in many areas.

Overall, there is a lack of clarity about what Tanzania's development path should be. GDP growth has been satisfactory at 3.4 per cent per capita since the turn of the millennium, in part because of high world prices of commodities until the mid-2010s. Yet growth is presently slowing down, whereas the sectoral structure of the economy is increasingly moving towards non-traded goods, generally not a powerful growth engine, rather than manufacturing or agro-industry.

The uncertainty surrounding the choice of a development path and the reason Tanzania has not yet succeeded in truly 'taking off' may be related to several institutional challenges scrutinised in this volume. Among them, the complex and volatile relationship between the state and big business, including foreign companies, plays a dominant role. Big business enjoys considerable economic leverage with the government, directly through its weight in employment and major contribution to GDP growth, and indirectly through its influence on some members of the dominant political party. Its objectives are not necessarily aligned with those of the government and the community, though. Combined with the lack of regulatory power of the government, weak state capacity, and generalised corruption, such a situation considerably weakens the capacity of successive governments to impose and implement effective development strategies. Another major institutional constraint on development lies in the extraordinarily complex and rent-generating land management system that prevents the exploitation of particularly favourable agro-industrial opportunities.

Unlocking constraints for sustained faster economic development in Tanzania requires institutional reforms in several areas, the feasibility of which may depend on changes in the political and political economy contexts that are discussed at the end of the volume.

Before getting to the crux of the matter, however, an important warning is necessary about the period covered by this diagnostic.

The Tanzania case study was launched in the last quarter of 2016. Opinion and expert surveys were run in January and February 2017, and a workshop on the first draft of the whole case study took place in Arusha in January 2018. Finally, a complete first version of this volume was posted on the Economic Development and Institutions website in September 2019. At the time of publication, the three-year delay since raises a difficulty.

The problem is that most of the initial analysis was conducted at a time when the administration of John Pombe Magufuli, who came to power practically at the beginning of 2016, had less than two years of experience. The institutional and economic changes intended by the new president, and particularly their sustainability over time, were, in those days, far from clear in the opinion of the public, analysts, and key decision makers. Moreover, data that would have permitted evaluation of the first reforms and current policy making of the new administration were simply missing.

At the time of final publication, considerably more information is available about the first term of the Magufuli administration – the second term was aborted by the death of the president in March 2021. A choice thus emerged about whether some substantial rewriting should be undertaken to make sure that the diagnostic would incorporate the experience of Tanzania during the Magufuli years, or whether things should be left unchanged with possibly an afterword that would simply address those elements of the diagnostic that would need to be modified or nuanced in view of the information available since the end of the study.

As it would be extremely onerous to ask all the authors and discussants to revise their contributions, we opted for mostly the second solution, except for some updating that was felt to be necessary in some chapters authored by the two editors of this volume. Other chapters have been left virtually unchanged. This also holds for the final chapter on the institutional diagnostic. However, an afterword now explicitly deals with the lessons to be drawn from the Magufuli administration and, especially, whether they confirm the existing diagnostic or lead us to amend it in a few directions.

Acknowledgements

Many people helped us in completing this institutional diagnostic of Tanzania by giving us advice on how to proceed, hints on some key issues, and comments on various drafts of the study. However, two of them deserve special mention both because of their contribution and their unexpected deaths during the COVID-19 pandemic.

First, we would like to pay tribute to Benno Ndulu, former governor of the Bank of Tanzania and member of the scientific committee of the Economic Development and Institutions (EDI) research programme, who suggested that Tanzania could be the pilot study of the Institutional Diagnostic Project. He accompanied us throughout the whole study with his support, advice, and comments. Benno was a major figure among African economists. He was also a dear friend of the two editors of this volume. We are sorry he is not with us at the time this volume is published.

Second, we would like to honour the memory of Servacius Likwelile, former finance permanent secretary, who was also an early supporter of the Tanzania Institutional Diagnostic and co-authored one of the chapters. It was a continuous pleasure to work with him, and we are sad he will not be with us to share the satisfaction of the final publication.

We next need to acknowledge the precious help the editors and authors of this study received from many friends and colleagues. First, we would like to thank Katie McIntosh, who was the representative of Oxford Policy Management (OPM) in Dar es Salaam at the time this study was started and followed it on behalf of OPM from the beginning to the very end, not only making sure that drafts were handed over in time and organising meetings, workshops, and seminars, but also reading the various chapters and making judicious comments on them. This study would not have been completed without Katie's professionalism, devotion, and friendliness. Thanks again, Katie.

Another special debt has to be addressed to Honourable Judge Joseph Warioba, former prime minister and vice president, whose guardianship of and advisory role on this work ensured it was of high quality, informed by a diverse set of viewpoints, and situated in the reality of the Tanzanian context.

The members of the Scientific Committee of EDI's institutional diagnostic research activity, the late Benno Ndulu, Louis Kasekende, Lemma Senbet, Célestin Monga, Romain Houssa, Ravi Kanbur, and Umar Salam, as well as EDI's co-research director Jean-Philippe Plateau, must also be acknowledged for the crucial role they played in critically challenging the process and conclusions of the study, pushing authors to produce meaningful, high-quality research.

We must also acknowledge the EDI team members who contributed valuable insights and a management function to the process, including Mark Henstridge, Yasmina Yusuf, Benjamin Klooss, Vinayak Uppal, Stevan Lee, Rachel Smith- Phiri, Umar Salaam, Tatiana Goetghebuer, and Ombeline de Bock. We would specifically like to acknowledge Kaley Milao for her coordination support to the team of authors and organisation of key events, including the Arusha workshop in January 2018.

Policy Research for Development, and specifically Cornel Jahari and Abel Kinyondo, must also receive a very special acknowledgement for partnering with the EDI programme on the implementation and analysis of the Country Institutional Survey, which is featured in Chapter 2.

There remain a few individuals whom we must single out for their contributions to the thinking and analysis underlying the Tanzania Institutional Diagnostic. We would like to acknowledge Godson Nyange for his support in facilitating key meetings and providing valuable advice and reflection throughout the study. Josaphat Kweka and Donath Olomi must be acknowledged for providing valuable reflections on the design and analysis of the survey, as well as Tausi Kida and Moses Kusiluka for their contributions to the Arusha workshop discussions in January 2018. We are also grateful to Andrew Coulson, the author of several books on the political economy of Tanzania, for insightful comments on a former version of this study.

We are extremely grateful to all those who met us along the Tanzania Institutional Diagnostics journey to provide their reflections and challenge us to consider a variety of issues. We would like to express a special thank you to former presidents Benjamin Mkapa and Jakaya Kikwete for their insightful reflections on Tanzania's development, particularly during their years in the presidency. We are grateful to past and present government officials who made time to speak with us, including Philip Mpango, Servacius Likwelile, Omari Issa, Neema Nduguru, Alphayo Kidata, Lordship Othman Chande, Mussa Juma Assad, Valentino Longino Mlowola, Adolf Mkenda, Wilfred Mbowe, Felix Ngamlagosi, Godfrey Chibulunie, Msafiri Mtepa, Mathias Kabunduguru, Maduka Kessy, Matern Lumbanga, Stephen Wasira, and Pius Msekwa. We acknowledge Zitto Kabwe and Ibrahim Lipumba for their comments.

We thank members of the private sector who contributed to a diversity of viewpoints, including Leodegar Chilla Tenga, Ali Mufuruki, Mohammed Dewji, Shabir Abji, John Wanyancha, and Patrick Rutabanzibwa.

We are grateful to a large group of researchers, academics, and others whose critical challenge function must be acknowledged. This includes Donald Mmari, Kasim Kulindwa, Vincent Leyaro, Jehovaness Aikaeli, Joseph Semboja, Dennis Rweyemamu, Issa Shivji, Ringo Tenga, Alphonce Tiba, Remidius Ruhinduka, Brian Cooksey, Aidan Eyakuze, Kees de Graaf, Risha Chande, Alex Makulillo, Richard Sambaiga, Bruce Heilman, William John, Bashiru Ally, Wilfred Kahumua, Stephen Kiraura, and Onejumo Selijio.

Finally, we must acknowledge the representatives from international organisations and donors in Tanzania who provided useful insights along the way, including Bella Bird, Yutaka Yoshino, Denis Biseko, Vel Gnanendran, Thomas Allan, Jean-Paul Fanning, Nick Lea, John Wearing, Francis Samba, Thomas Baunsgaard, and Virginie Ruyt.

This project was funded with aid from the UK government.

Abbreviations

ARIMO	Ardhi Institute Morogoro
ARITA	Ardhi Institute Tabora
ASDP	Agricultural Sector Development Programme
ASDS	Agricultural Sector Development Strategy
BEST	Business Environment Strengthening
BOOT	Build, Own, Operate, and Transfer
BRN	Big Results Now
CCM	Chama Cha Mapinduzi
CCRO	Certificates of Customary Rights of Occupancy
CEPII	Centre for Prospective Studies and International Information
CIS	Country Institutional Survey
CMI	Chr. Michelsen Institute
COMESA	Common Market for the Eastern and Southern Africa
CPI	Consumer Price Index
CRO	Customary Right of Occupancy
CSRP	Civil Service Reform Programme
CUF	Civic United Front
CVL	Certificate of Village Land
DARESCO	District Electric Supply Company
DED	District Executive Director
DLHT	District Land and Housing Tribunal
DRC	Democratic Republic of Congo
EAC	East Africa Community
EDI	Economic Development and Institutions
EPA	External Payments Arrears
EPP	Emergency Power Producer
EPZ	Export Processing Zone
EPZA	Export Processing Zones Authority

ERP	Economic Recovery Programme
ESAF	Enhanced Structural Adjustment Facility Programme
ESDP	Education Sector Development Programme
ESIRSR	Electricity Supply Industry Reform Strategy and Roadmap
ESRF	Economic and Social Research Foundation
EWURA	Energy and Water Utilities Regulatory Authority
FCDO	Foreign and Commonwealth Development Office
FDI	Foreign Direct Investment
GDP	Gross Domestic Product
GRO	Granted Right of Occupancy
HBS	Household Budget Survey
HRD	Human Rights Defender
HSRP	Health Sector Reform Programme
ICT	Information and Communications Technology
IDA	International Development Association
ILFS	Integrated Labour Force Survey
ILO	International Labour Organization
IMF	International Monetary Fund
IPD	Institutional Profile Database
IPP	Independent Power Producer
IPTL	Independent Power Tanzania Ltd
IWGIA	International Work Group for Indigenous Affairs
JICA	Japan International Cooperation Agency
kWh	kiloWatt hour
LGA	Local Government Authorities
LGAF	Land Governance Assessment Framework
LGRP	Local Government Reform Programme
LNG	Liquefied Natural Gas
LSRP	Legal Sector Reform Programme
M&E	Monitoring and Evaluation
MEM	Ministry of Energy and Minerals
MITI	Ministry of International Trade and Industry
Mha	Million hectares
MLHHSD	Minister of Lands, Housing and Human Settlements Development
MTEF	Medium-Term Economic Framework
MW	MegaWatts
MWI	Ministry of Water and Irrigation
NACSAP	National Anti-Corruption and Action Plan
NAFCO	National Agricultural Food Corporation
NBS	National Bureau of Statistics
NDC	National Development Corporation
NEC	National Executive Committee
NESP	National Economic Survival Programme

NMC	National Milling Corporation
NORAD	Norwegian Agency for Development Cooperation
NSC	National Sports Council
NSIC	National Small Industries Corporation
OCGT	Open Cycle Gas Turbine
ODA	Official Development Assistance
OECD	Organisation for Economic Co-operation and Development
OPM	Oxford Policy Management
OPRAS	Open Performance Appraisal System
PAC	Public Accounts Committee
PAP	Pan Africa Power Ltd
PCCB	Prevention and Combating Corruption Bureau
PFMRP	Public Financial Management Reform Programme
PMO-RALG	Prime Minister's Office – Regional Administration and Local Government
PMS	Performance Management System
PO-PSM	President's Office – Public Service Management
PO-RALG	President's Office – Regional Administration and Local Government
PPA	Power Purchase Agreement
PPP	Public–Private Partnership
PRSP	Poverty Reduction Strategy Paper
PSM	Public Service Management
PSRC	Parastatal Sector Reform Commission
PSRP	Public Service Reform Programme
PV	Photovoltaic
QoG	Quality of Government (database)
RCT	Randomised Control Trial
REA	Rural Energy Authority
REB	Rural Energy Board
REPOA	Research on Development Policy
RSDP	Roads Sector Development Programme
SACMEQ	Southern and Eastern Africa Consortium for Monitoring Educational Quality
SADC	South African Development Community
SAGCOT	Southern Agricultural Growth Corridor
SAP	Structural Adjustment Programme
SASE	Selective Accelerated Salary Enhancement Scheme
SBF	Sun Biofuels Africa Ltd
SDI	Service Delivery Indicator
SEE	Survey of Employment and Earnings
SGFSRP	Second Generation Financial Sector Reform Programme
SGR	Standard Gauge Railway
SIDA	Swedish International Development Cooperation Agency

SIDO	Small Industries Development Organisation
SIDP	Sustainable Industrial Development Policy
SME	Small or Medium-Sized Enterprise
SOE	State-Owned Enterprise
SPILL	Strategic Plans for the Implementation of Land Laws
SPP	Small Power Producer
SWOT	Strengths, Weaknesses, Opportunities, and Threats
TAA	Tanganyika African Association
TANESCO	Tanzania Electric Supply Company
TANU	Tanganyika African National Union
TASAF	Tanzania Social Action Fund
TDCU	Tanga Dairies Cooperative Union
TDV	Tanzania Development Vision
TEA	Tegeta Escrow Account
TIC	Tanzania Investment Centre
TNBC	Tanzania National Business Council
TRA	Tanzania Revenue Authority
TZS	Tanzanian shillings
UK	United Kingdom
USA	United States of America
USAID	United States Agency for International Development
WDI	World Development Indicators
WEF	World Economic Forum
WGI	Worldwide Governance Indicators
WRI	World Resources Institute
WSDP	Water Sector Development Programme

PART I

THE POLITICAL, ECONOMIC, AND INSTITUTIONAL FEATURES OF TANZANIA'S DEVELOPMENT

This first part of the volume reviews the economic, social, political, and institutional development of Tanzania. The first chapter focuses on the political history of the country since independence, whereas the second evaluates its economic development achievements and, most importantly, the challenges ahead. The third chapter focuses on the possible obstacles to development arising from weak or failing institutions, as perceived by various types of decision-makers, top policymakers, and experts.

I

Tanzania in a Geographic, Demographic, and Historical Perspective

François Bourguignon and Samuel Mwita Wangwe

Embarking on a study of a country's economic development requires having clearly in mind its main geographic and cultural aspects as well as a precise vision of its history and the main features of its current political context. Such is the objective of this first chapter.

1 THE NATURAL AND HUMAN CONTEXT OF DEVELOPMENT IN TANZANIA

With almost a million square kilometres, Tanzania is by far the biggest country in East Africa and even in Southern Africa, excluding South Africa. It borders the Indian Ocean over 1,400 kilometres and extends some 750 kilometres west inland at its larger width. It shares borders with eight countries: Kenya and Uganda to the north; Rwanda, Burundi, and Zaire to the west; and Zambia, Malawi, and Mozambique to the south. Today's United Republic of Tanzania also includes several islands off its Indian Ocean shore, including the island of Zanzibar.

Just a few degrees below the equator, Tanzania's climate is essentially tropical, although it is temperate in the highlands. Much of the country outside the coastal area is above 900 metres. It consists of extensive rolling plains interrupted by the Great Rift Valley, which cuts the east of the African continent from north to south. The Rift crosses the western part of Tanzania, where it is interspersed by Africa's three great lakes: Victoria, Tanganyika, and Malawi (or Nyasa), whose shores are shared with neighbouring countries. The country offers a wide variety of landscapes: from coastal swamps to rain forests, and from savannahs to plateaus and mountains. Four major ecological regions are usually distinguished because of highly differentiated climates. The mountain lands in the north and south-west receive generous amounts of rain, and the same is true of the lakeshore regions, especially Lake Victoria's; high plateaus that fill the centre of the country are semi-arid, whereas the coastal area is both hot and humid.

Overall, however, the country enjoys high agricultural potential, which presently is under-exploited. It is estimated that land suitable for cultivation amounts to 44 Mha, of which only 30 per cent is presently cultivated, most often under harsh conditions, and is rainfed with irregular precipitations and using traditional techniques. Numerous rivers and lakes represent a huge potential for irrigated agriculture, however. As much as 7 Mha are considered to have medium or high irrigation potential, out of which only 5 Mha are actually under irrigation.

Tanzania's subsoil is rich in minerals and fuel resources. Minerals include gold, iron ore, nickel, and uranium, whereas fuels include coal and natural gas, mostly offshore. Gemstones are another important resource, most notable diamonds and a local stone called tanzanite. Altogether, mineral and fuel exports represent 45 per cent of exports.

The beauty of its mountainous, sea, and savannah landscapes along with its world-famous reserves of wild animals is another of Tanzania's resources. Year-round, tourists flock to the numerous reserve game parks at the foot of Mount Kilimanjaro and to the resorts on the Indian Ocean coast in Zanzibar and neighbouring islands. Tourism revenues represent more than 25 per cent of exports of goods and services, even though they contracted sharply in 2020 owing to the COVID-19 pandemic.

Moving on to population characteristics, Tanzania shelters some 60 million people. Given its size, however, it is relatively sparsely populated. Its population density is the lowest in East Africa. However, as in most African countries, its population grows very quickly, presently at an annual rate of around 2.8 per cent, and density increases at the same pace. It more than doubled over the last twenty-five years. Even though urbanisation progressed during that period, it had only a small impact on the rise in population density in rural areas. This densification of the country would look even more impressive if the comparison were to be made with that seen in the mid-twentieth century at the time of independence. Population density then was only eleven inhabitants per square kilometre, a figure that is found today in desertic countries such as Libya, Mauritania, and Australia. In the opposite direction, the present size of the population and its rate of growth is sometimes worrying when one thinks about the future. By 2040, the Tanzanian population will reach more than 100 million, which may raise serious issues of employment, individual livelihood, and pressure on the provision of public goods and services.

This low population density is a reminder of the conditions of the early peopling of the geographical area that became Tanzania and the human landscape found by the colonisers in the late nineteenth century that then shaped the context of early development after independence. It can be summarised in two words: ethnic diversity.

It is estimated that there were 120 different ethnic groups in Tanzania, most with their own language, customs, and political systems, and kingdoms or chieftaincies at the time of independence. This state of affairs raises two important issues: (1) Why did no single groups or coalitions impose or at least repeatedly try to impose its rule over the others, as was seen in various other instances in Africa, in particular among neighbouring countries such as Kenya or Uganda? (2) To what extent was this conspicuous ethnic diversity a decisive factor in the development path that Tanzania followed after independence and is still following today?

There may not be a decisive answer to these questions. But it is tempting to imagine that the extension of the area that would later become Tanzania and the diversity of its habitats are the cause of the relative fragmentation of ethnic groups since the early days of the peopling of the country. In his chapter on the history of Tanzania, J. Sutton insists that until the fifteenth century, the peopling of Tanzania by successive arrivals of new tribes proceeded more by assimilation than by the conquest, extinction, and acculturation of existing tribal groups by others.[1] Even though conflicts and struggles erupted afterwards, with some groups trying to appropriate the land of others, as explained by Kimambo in another chapter of the same volume,[2] no big kingdom was ever formed that would be able to conquer a significant portion of the territory. Also, it took a long time before tight links were established between the coastal area and the interior of the country, and they were more commercial – in particular, through caravan trade – than bellicose. Today, the largest ethnic group, the Sukuma, represents only 13 per cent of the population, whereas the second largest group, the Nyamwezi, is four times smaller. This contrasts with other East African countries, where the largest groups are of comparable size or where there are essentially two groups of unequal size that are strongly rivalrous.

The lack of rivalry among ethnic groups and the rather common front opposed to the German colonisers at the time of the Maji-Maji uprising (1905–1907), which some consider to be a founding event of the Tanzanian nation, explain the lack of a strong power struggle at the time of independence, which was doubtlessly gave Tanzania a decisive advantage over other countries where internal fights for the control of power have wasted time and resources that could be put towards development. It is also argued that Swahili developed rather early as a kind of lingua franca for communication among groups and played the role of a unifying factor.

Another kind of human differentiation with some importance in Tanzania's history is the racial discrimination explicitly introduced by the colonial powers on the basis of the origin of the population. Strong differences were thus made between Europeans, Arabs, Asians, and Africans. Even though Africans were over-dominant from a demographic point of view, economic power was in the hands of the others. Europeans lost importance when most left the country at independence. But Arabs and Asians, mostly Indians, remained powerful.

[1] See Sutton (1969).
[2] See also Kimambo et al. (2017).

The former owed their economic power to the conquest of Zanzibar by the Oman Sultanate in the late seventeenth century and the Arab domination over trade along the East African coast and between the coast and the interior. Even though they were a tiny minority, they were able to maintain their influence throughout the colonial period and after Zanzibar united with the mainland after independence. Indian merchants had always been part of the trading network along the African shores of the Indian Ocean. Some Indians were also hired as civil servants by the Oman Sultanate in Zanzibar. In colonial times, a sizeable number were brought in by the British to build railroads in the region. Many of them decided to stay. As they could not access land cultivated by Africans, they specialised in retail and wholesale trade in the interior of the country and later in light manufacturing. Both groups failed to integrate with the African population. They remain small minorities today, but their early business specialisation in the pre-colonial and colonial economy gave them an economic power that was not in proportion to their demographic weight. Their social distance from Tanzanian Africans is still quite detectable.

A last source of human differentiation to be stressed concerns religion. Christianity was introduced in the sixteenth and seventeenth centuries in the coastal area and progressively spread to the interior of the country through numerous missions. Today some 60 per cent of the population is Christian, half of it Roman Catholic and the other protestants of various denominations. Being 30 per cent of the population, Muslims are far from being a minority. They are mostly Sunni, but Shia are also present. Given the strong historical influence of Arabs in Zanzibar and along the coast, Muslims tend to be concentrated in those areas. A rather tiny minority of Tanzanians are animists or without religion. Traditionally, religion was not a source of friction in Tanzanian society. On the contrary, tolerance on both the Christian and the Muslim sides has been the norm. Lately, however, following the rise in Islamist activism in the world, some tension has occasionally appeared.

Such is, in a few words, the natural and human context in which Tanzania's history unfolded throughout colonial times and after independence, and which has influenced and continues to influence its economic development today.

II A SHORT ACCOUNT OF THE POLITICAL HISTORY OF TANZANIA

Two features are apparent in the short history of Tanzania since independence.[3] The first is the extent to which it is intertwined with the economy. The course followed by Tanzania was strongly influenced by economic

---

[3] This short historical account relies heavily on several key references, in particular, Edwards (2012, 2014); Coulson (2013); Lofchie (2014); Ndulu and Mwase (2017); and Shivji (2021) for the fifth phase.

events, most noticeably the serious balance of payment crisis of the early 1980s, but the country's course also had a huge impact on the economy itself, in particular the early choice of a socialist development strategy. The second feature is its clear periodicity. Unlike many African countries, politics in Tanzania have been fairly peaceful and respectful of the constitution. History since independence divides itself logically into four periods, each corresponding to a different personality in the presidential seat – hence the organisation of the brief summary that follows, after a short reminder of the colonisation period.

The African Association, which became the Tanganyika African Association (TAA) after splitting from Zanzibar, initially had weak political ambition. Yet a land dispute between settlers and natives in two Meru villages in the 1950s led the local TAA secretary, Kyrilo Japhet, to launch a vigorous anti-government campaign and to seek support from the Trusteeship Council, which was responsible for the supervision of territories under mandate in the United Nations. This triggered the politicising of the TAA.

Julius Nyerere, who had studied in the United Kingdom and was one of the early Africans in Tanganyika to get a university degree, accelerated this process when he became the president of TAA in 1953. He transformed it into a real political party with local bases throughout the territory and links with trade unions, cooperative societies, and tribal unions. The explicit goal of this newly labelled Tanganyika African National Union (TANU) was independence.

A Independence

Independence was obtained in a peaceful way after TANU won practically all the seats of the Legislative Council that were open to election in 1958, and then again when all the seats in the Council were open to election in 1960. The British colonial secretary then acceded to African demand for a 'responsible government'. One year later, independence was declared, with TANU as the party of government and Nyerere as prime minister.

Three years later, the new Republic of Tanganyika united with Zanzibar, where a violent revolution against the Arab minority that was ruling the islands had just brought to power an African-dominated party. Together the two countries formed the United Republic of Tanzania, with Julius Nyerere as president and Abeid Amani Karume from Zanzibar as vice-president. Tanzania is one state and a sovereign united republic. Nevertheless, the new country was a union, with two governments, the Union Government (United Republic of Tanzania) and the Revolutionary Government of Zanzibar as an autonomous government. The size imbalance between the two members of the union was the main reason for this structure of governance. The population of Zanzibar never represented more than 3 per cent of the whole population of the united republic.

B Forging a Nation: The Nyerere Socialist Era

Although Nyerere had been at the helm since 1961, it was not until 1967 that his strategy for the development of Tanzania was made explicit. A first five-year development plan with emphasis on private sector development, poverty reduction, and agricultural development proved disappointing. The resulting frustration, as well as the views about development that Nyerere developed during the time TANU was preparing for independence and that he shared with some other African leaders, led him to elaborate a new strategy. It was very much inspired by the experiences of socialist countries such as the Soviet Union and China, which were to be adapted to fit the African context. The full strategy was exposed in the Arusha Declaration, which is still very vividly recalled today not so much because of its economic aspects but because it was in some sense foundational for Tanzania as an independent nation.[4]

The Arusha Declaration announced a socialist-oriented development programme adapted to the African context under the label of 'Ujamaa', or 'family-hood', in Swahili. It comprised three dominant strategies: first, emphasising the agricultural sector and the urgent need to improve its productivity, most importantly through regrouping dispersed subsistence farms; second, ensuring state control of the means of production and exchange, and thus nationalisation of part of the non-agricultural sector; and third, addressing social demands in terms of education, health, equality, and participation in public decision making.

The implementation of the programme sketched in the Arusha Declaration was quick in terms of nationalisation of banks, import–export companies, and several major industries. It was slower in agriculture, where the gains in productivity as well as generalised access to social services, including education and health, were supposed to go through 'villagisation' and, in part, collective farming. The Ujamaa villages undoubtedly represented the most original part of the whole development strategy put forward by the Nyerere government. Yet some resistance grew against the villagisation process in various parts of the country, and in several cases it became necessary to move people by force.

The results of the strategy spelled out in the Arusha Declaration were far from spectacular. In a rather candid evaluation ten years later, Nyerere himself gave a lukewarm account of it, acknowledging that growth had slowed since the new development strategy had been put in place, and results in the agricultural sector were particularly disappointing (Nyerere, 1977).

Nationalisations did not hold on to the Arusha promises. In fact, they led to disastrous results a few years later, very much because of mismanagement by bureaucrats, interference from politicians, weaknesses in technology management, slow human resource development, limited commercialisation, and corruption at the head of nationalised companies. Even the most obvious

---

[4] See Nyerere (1967), United Republic of Tanzania (1967).

economic strengths of Tanzania, like sisal exports, progressively weakened, a drop that was aggravated by falling world prices and that led the economy to the edge of bankruptcy.

Results were especially bad in the agricultural sector. The villagisation programme seems to have badly disrupted production processes. The outcome of villagisation as a basis for harnessing economies of scale proved disappointing, as collective farms were not as productive as envisaged – for example, productivity on farms under the villagisation programme was lower than that seen on private peasant farms in the 1970s.[5] If overall productivity gains had been obtained in the extensive cultivation of some export cash crops such as tea and tobacco, this had been at the expense of food crops. In a few years, Tanzania had gone from being a net exporter to a net importer of food, the progress in export crops being insufficient to cover the cost of imports. Without the aid of the World Bank and the International Monetary Fund (IMF), the country would have been bankrupt and doomed to famine. While some scholars such as Edwards (2014) interpret this failure as the result of Nyerere's socialist policies, other scholars argue that it does not necessarily reflect the failure of this strategy but rather the failure to involve people in the whole Ujamaa initiative.[6] Key social groups such as mass organisations had either been weakened or co-opted into the single party system or into the ruling bureaucracy and were not truly representing and acting for the people.[7]

After slowing down, gross domestic product (GDP) per capita started to fall after 1976, at the same time as severe balance of payment problems developed. Nyerere refused the conditions imposed by international financial institutions for helping the country out of its foreign payment difficulties. A National Economic Survival Programme (NESP) and then a home-grown Structural Adjustment Programme (SAP) were launched in the early 1980s. However, they came too late and failed to get the economy out of the crisis. After having expelled an IMF mission in 1981, Nyerere was finally forced to accept a stand-by agreement with that institution in 1985. This agreement was a preliminary step towards an SAP to be signed with the World Bank, the aim of which was to move the economy back to a market-led economic system and, as a matter of fact, to undo much of Nyerere's effort to build a socialist economy. He left power in 1985, leaving to his successor the task of managing this change in economic regime.

If the economic achievements of the Nyerere era were disappointing, the same cannot be said of the non-economic sphere. A key success, and a consequence of the villagisation process, has been to promote participation

---

[5] See Collier and Wangwe (1986).
[6] See Nyerere (1968), United Republic of Tanzania (2017a, pp. 54–6).
[7] For instance, the state machinery made the decision to ban the Ruvuma Development Association, which is regarded by some scholars as having been a genuine socialist organisation emulating members' participation in its development affairs – see Ibbott (2014).

in development activities and decision making. The nation-building project Nyerere embarked on – which included disbanding chiefdoms and promoting the Swahili language – brought national unity and cohesion. This was reinforced by investments in education, the schooling system, literacy, and health programmes. In comparison with many other African countries, Tanzania is exceptional in the political stability it has shown since independence, under the influence of Nyerere's probity and respect of constitutional rules. Both legacies are closely linked, for political stability would have been difficult to achieve in the presence of tribal rivalry.

Another aspect of Nyerere's actions that made him a major political figure in Africa was his pan-Africanism and his view that African states were most often too small to develop in an autonomous way. Here, too, however, he was unsuccessful, at the level of both the continent and the region. As far as the latter is concerned, he was a strong promoter of the East Africa Community (EAC) that would federate Kenya, Tanzania, and Uganda. Yet, after some years, Western-oriented Kenya's leadership sought to isolate itself from the socialist regime in Tanzania, whereas Uganda, under Amin Dada, aggressively invaded the northern region of Tanzania in 1978. Nyerere chased the invaders and then entered Uganda, where he was able to oust Amin Dada after a long war, the cost of which was sizeable for Tanzania and was aggravated by the consequences of the breakup of the East African Community. Rising oil prices also contributed to an economic situation that was already difficult. These circumstances ultimately led to the end of Tanzania's socialist era.

C The Difficult Transition to the Market: 1980–1995 (Nyerere-Mwinyi)

Ali Hassan Mwinyi, who was the vice-president of Tanzania and also the president of Zanzibar, was elected president in 1985 with the explicit support of Nyerere, who was still in control of the Chama Cha Mapinduzi (CCM) party that was borne from the merger of TANU of Tanzania Mainland and Afro Shirazi Party of Zanzibar in 1977 and that is constitutionally the single political party in Tanzania. His objective was quite explicitly to re-establish the primacy of market mechanisms and to put the Tanzanian economy back on a positive growth path. This was done in a somewhat disordered way over his two presidential mandates under the strong influence of bilateral donors and the Bretton Woods institutions, though there was some domestic resistance.

The first set of reforms consisted of trying to align prices to supply–demand conditions so that they would give the right incentives to economic agents. Agricultural marketing, including the supply of agricultural inputs, was liberalised, prices and wages were deregulated, the currency was massively devalued, and import tariffs were rationalised. Initially, growth reacted positively to the reforms, mostly because of the release of aid resources that had been withheld by donors because of friction with the Tanzanian government in the last years of the Nyerere era and because the agricultural sector recovered some dynamism after years of paralysis. However, growth then stagnated, as it was becoming obvious that several institutional factors were preventing it from really taking off.

Another set of structural reforms was launched during the second mandate of Mwinyi from 1990 onwards, the most important one being dismantling and privatising the numerous state-owned companies that ran the economy during the socialist era and were still operating. Other reforms included opening the financial sector to private domestic and foreign actors, concentrating tax collection within a single Tanzanian Revenue Authority,[8] dismantling monopolies in the agricultural output trade, and reforming the civil service with the aim of reducing the number of civil servants and making them more effective.

Other reforms were undertaken in the political sphere. Constitutional changes had been passed in 1985 that defined more precisely the prerogatives of the president and limited his mandate to two five-year terms. Most importantly, a multi-party system was established in 1992, formally ending the legal monopoly of the CCM party, the so-called party of the revolution. Consequently, the political scene became much more active, and the Tanzanian people's political unity began to weaken as the 1995 general election approached.

The end of Mwinyi's second term was marked by various corruption scandals, the most notorious of which was revealed by the World Bank in November 1994. The embezzlement, amounting to some 3 per cent of annual GDP, involved senior officials in the Ministry of Finance and caused donors to temporarily stop all disbursements.[9]

This event was the culmination of a rampant crisis between the executive branch and the donors that ran throughout practically the whole Mwinyi presidency. Its root lay in the fundamental opposition of a large part of the Tanzanian elite, including in some instances cabinet ministers, to moving away from the socialist regime. Some held such a view for ideological reasons, but others clearly tried to protect the rents they were able to create during the socialist era. As a result, the reforms imposed by the international financial institutions slowed down and had little impact on the economy. Corruption was rising, whereas growth would not take off. The crisis that culminated in donors withdrawing a significant part of their aid in 1995 was finally overcome thanks to the work of a consultative group, which was able to pacify the donor–recipient relationship.[10]

It is hardly surprising that such a transition from socialism to a market economy was so difficult and conflictive, both with donors and within Tanzania. It is not surprising either that corruption practices spread in such a period of disruptive reforms, especially starting from a regime where corruption was

---

[8] Implemented under President Mkapa in 1996.
[9] See Lofchie (2014, pp. 127–8).
[10] See Edwards (2012, pp. 27–40), Lofchie (2014, Chapter 4).

already widespread among the elite. Some time was necessary for the economy and society to stabilise and growth to pick up. Quite revelatory in this respect is the 'Mzee Rukhsa' or 'Everything goes' nickname given by Tanzanians to the Mwinyi era. Although this occurred some twenty-five years ago, it will be seen that this period left durable marks on society and the economy.

The economy and society started to settle down and growth started to pick up under the presidency of Benjamin Mkapa, the first president elected in multi-party elections.

D The Marker Era: 1995–2015 (Mkapa-Kikwete)

The evolution of Tanzania over since the early 2000s under the successive presidencies of Benjamin Mkapa and Jakaya Kikwete may be described as the actual implementation and deepening of the reforms passed under the presidency of Mwinyi. Despite the underlying tension mentioned earlier, this took place with remarkable political stability, at least on the mainland, owing in part to the single party (CCM) that had ruled the country since independence remaining the dominant party after the move to a multi-party system. In fact, it took some time for the opposition to strengthen and it is only recently that it has started to represent a possible threat to the CCM, at least on the mainland.

The same cannot be said of Zanzibar, where the confrontation between the CCM and the local opposition party (Civic United Front, CUF) and later ACT has been extremely conflictive, with several upsurges of violence. Rigged elections, a partisan electoral commission, harsh repression of protests, and reneging on union government commitments created a climate of mutual distrust that proved difficult to calm down. A constitutional reform of the relationship between the two members of the United Republic of Tanzania that could reduce the intensity of the confrontation has been considered for some time, but it is presently at a stalemate.

Another prominent feature of the last two decades is the frequency of major corruption scandals, which suggests that corruption is indeed rooted in society and the economy. Several cases came to light under both Mkapa and Kikwete, which every time led to ministers and high-ranked officials being dismissed and led to donors temporarily suspending aid disbursements. Since those days, Tanzania has found itself systematically rated very low in the corruption rankings published by Transparency International and comparable organisations. Donors repeatedly conditioned their aid on efforts being made to curb corruption, and successive governments have committed to act in this area. Their impact has been limited, though. Inherited from the socialist era and the disordered period of transition towards a market economy, corruption is a plague that now seems extremely difficult to eradicate.[11]

---

[11] The current president, J. P. Magufuli, was elected on a very strong anti-corruption platform and has sent strong signs of his determination in this area since taking office in 2016.

Some other noteworthy political developments are worth stressing. One is the inflow of refugees owing to conflicts in the neighbouring Democratic Republic of Congo (DRC), Rwanda, and Burundi since the mid-1990s. At some stage, there were around 700,000 refugees hosted in Tanzanian camps who were supported by international organisations and the Tanzanian government. Another development was the re-launch in 2000, twenty-three years after its collapse in 1977, of the East African Community. Initially revived with its three founding members (Tanzania, Kenya, and Uganda), the EAC was enlarged to include Rwanda and Burundi in July 2009.[12]

On the economic side, the progress towards an all-market economy proved to be slower than anticipated. The number of parastatals or state-owned enterprises (SOEs) still active in 1995 was considerable – that is, more than 300. It took time to privatise them, to merge them in joint ventures with the private sector, or simply to dismantle them. There was concern that the privatisation programme did not give adequate opportunity for local private entrepreneurs to participate. One factor that contributed to this outcome was the failure to operationalise the Privatisation Trust Fund established by the Privatisation Trust Act of 1996. It also took time for the public mindset to change with respect to the role of the private sector in development. It was only during the second term of Kikwete's mandate that policies aimed at creating a favourable climate for the private sector were explicitly adopted.

Still on the economic side, the last twenty years have seen significant progress towards macroeconomic stability but relatively little towards the 'self-reliance' goal pursued since the Nyerere era. Since independence, donors have generously supported the development of Tanzania. They have sometimes suspended their aid after corruption scandals or in times of disagreement about the policies to be implemented, but they have always been present when their help was crucially needed. It cannot be denied that, at least over the last twenty to twenty-five years, Tanzania has been an 'aid darling'.

In any case, the recent period has been rather favourable on the economic growth front. Considerable acceleration took place during the second term of the Mkapa presidency. With an average GDP growth rate of 6 per cent between 2002 and 2015, Tanzania is among the African champions. As in other countries, however, it is difficult to say how much of this is thanks to domestic reforms and how much to a favourable international context.

E The Fifth Phase: November 2015–March 2021

On 5 November 2015, the fifth president of Tanzania was elected. John Pombe Magufuli's nomination within the dominant CCM party was the result of a difficult process, as he was a kind of outsider with respect to influential groups within the party. He won the nomination, and then the election, very much

---

[12] And, more recently, South Sudan.

on his anti-corruption platform and his well-recognised personal probity, a quality he had shown as the minister of Public Works in the previous administration. For the first time since the advent of multi-partyism, however, the opposition showed real strength, getting a little more than 40 per cent of the votes in the run-off ballot.

One of the factors that contributed to his rise to power in spite of his limited record as a player in the ruling party is the manner in which the credibility of the dominant party, CCM, had been eroded by a series of corruption scandals and a general perception that corruption had been on the rise in the country.[13] In this regard, the main opposition party, Chadema, made considerable political gains in society by launching an anti-corruption campaign that contributed to eroding the credibility of CCM. This may have been one of the factors that led to dropping Edward Lowasa from the CCM candidacy, even though he was rated as highly popular among the candidates within CCM. The decision to drop his name is likely to have been influenced by the fact that he had been mentioned in a recent major scandal and had then been attacked by Chadema in their anti-corruption campaign. The ruling party, CCM, and its leaders had been so maligned and marred by allegations of corruption that it is likely this situation enhanced the chances of nominating for the presidency a candidate who was not identifiable with the party and its heavyweights – that is, a relatively clean person. Ironically, when Lowasa was dropped by CCM, he was nominated by Chadema as their presidential candidate. It had ben hoped that this candidate, perceived to be popular in CCM, would move to Chadema with a substantial group of CCM members. In any case, he moved with a handful of CCM members. The nomination of Lowasa as Chadema presidential candidate had a major paradoxical effect on the choice of campaign agenda on both sides. Chadema dropped the anti-corruption agenda, presumably because earlier they had tainted Lowasa as a corrupt person, and the CCM candidate picked the anti-corruption agenda and campaigned on that ticket, often putting CCM on the back burner. This change of roles in the agenda put forward, and shifting agenda so easily, may be an indication of the ideological shortcomings of both parties. Magufuli won with 58 per cent of the vote, mainly on his anti-corruption platform.

It may be too early to evaluate the full consequences of Magufuli's actions, as the outcomes were still unfolding in terms of institutional diagnostics when he died in March 2021, after just more than five years in office. Yet it will be useful for the analysis in this volume to mention their main original features.

---

[13] Numerous scandals struck under Magufuli's predecessors. Three major ones strongly impacted public opinion: (1) side payments in the tendering of an energy project to a foreign company that proved unfavourable to Tanzania; (2) more recently and still in connection with this tender a scandal stuck because of fraudulent payments to CCM politicians out of an escrow account opened by the National Electricity Company (TANESCO); and (3) fraudulent payments involving high-ranking politicians and bureaucrats made from an external payment arrears (EPA) account set up at the Central Bank to help service the balance of payments.

President Magufuli entered office as a popular leader largely on account of the promises he made about fighting corruption, cutting down on unnecessary public expenditures, checking the waste of public resources, identifying as a man of action (he was nicknamed the 'bulldozer'), and caring for the downtrodden (*wanyonge*). These promises were appealing because they came at a time when corruption scandals had been rampant, poverty and unemployment were still major concerns, and the ideological direction of CCM was being questioned because of what Shivji calls the consequence of CCM having been disarmed ideologically and organisationally over a generation.[14] His popularity was enhanced by the perception that he was a leader who could get things done. This was appealing because the Kikwete administration had increasingly gained a laissez-faire reputation and because of the perception that 'law and order' had been eroded while transparency – which he promoted – was perceived as not being accompanied by accountability. This perception planted seeds of what was later to manifest as high-handed actions to return the country to order and get things done, even if it meant taking shortcuts involving autocratic means. Indeed, he did get things done, confirming his nickname 'bulldozer', but, as some have said, he was more of a supervisor than a political leader.[15]

President Magufuli identified the concept of development with accomplishing major infrastructure undertakings. Huge projects were thus launched, including the hydroelectric dam across Stigler's Gorge (Nyerere Hydroelectric project), the Standard Gauge Railway from Dar es Salaam to Kigoma and further west, and many miles of tarmac roads across the country. These projects will yield development returns in the future, possibly helping industrialisation, another of Magufuli's priorities (Tanzania ya viwanda). However, he did not really define the kind of industrialisation he stood for, nor the way it could trickle down to agriculture, the sector where the majority of the poor (wanyonge) are found. The industrialisation drive remained unplanned and confused, and the youth still have not seen the level of job creation that they had hoped for. The animosity that often tinted the relationship between the president and big business did not help to carry forward the industrialisation agenda.

Under President Magufuli, efforts were also made to get the most out of Tanzania's natural resources to benefit the people of Tanzania. He effected a piece of legislation called the Natural Wealth and Resources (Permanent Sovereignty) Act that was passed in 2017 and that asserted the Tanzanian people's sovereign ownership and control over natural resources. He took on Barrick, the multinational gold company, and stopped containers full of mineral sand from being exported while he formed a local team of experts to check the mineral content of the sand. He also worked on other forms of

[14] See Shivji (2021).
[15] See Shivji (2021).

revenue generation from minerals. However, these efforts fell short in two areas. First, building the human and institutional capacity for managing natural resources along the long-run lines was not accorded priority, contrary to recommendations that had been made by civil society organisations such as Haki Rasilimali – the Tanzanian branch of the 'Publish What You Pay' international non-governmental organisation (NGO) – about extractive industry governance. Second, the regime did not effectively engage in formulating and strengthening policy frameworks for managing natural resources.

On other fronts, the president boldly moved against grand corruption in both the political and business spheres. For what this kind of study is worth given the difficulty of evaluating corruption, a 2020 report by the Tanzanian anti-corruption agency, the Prevention and Combating Corruption Bureau (PCCB), revealed that corruption had declined during his administration. In education, he abolished primary and secondary school fees, and accelerated the building of classrooms and the provision of desks. On health, investments in new facilities and equipment were enhanced, and health insurance coverage was extended at a cheap premium to almost one-third of the population. He was also in favour of less informality in the economy but did not have a clear strategy for formalisation besides issuing street vendors and kiosk-owners with identity cards at 20 shillings that would free them from further tax payments and harassment by law enforcement personnel.

Magufuli wanted to see results fast. His strategy fits the saying 'If you want to go fast, go alone; but it you want to go far, go together'. He chose to go fast and obtained some results. But, breaking very much from his predecessors, he ruled in a rather authoritarian and personalised way.

If Tanzania continued to be a relatively stable and peaceful polity during his mandate, this stability was superficial, and continuity was illusory (Shivji, 2021). To some extent stability and peace were induced by fear and the narrowing of civic space. Political rallies were banned, and opposition leaders were openly harassed by the police and implicated in numerous court cases. Space for civil society organisations and NGOs was severely restricted. Many organisations and civil society actors were subjected to all kinds of intimidating demands from state authorities, but print and electronic media bore the brunt of the repression. Some journalists and opposition leaders were taken to jail or even assaulted. Ironically, while the mainstream media was undergoing censure, a small pro-Magufuli media house emerged, introducing itself as an independent advocate that supported him. Its newspapers and TV defamed prominent people, including former secretary generals of the ruling party who were perceived to have fallen out of favour. The media house abused Magufuli's critics and pursued opponents and foes without hindrance. Of course, no disciplinary action was taken against it by either regulatory bodies or media watchdogs. After Magufuli died, however, the organisation was taken to court and convicted for defamation. This story illustrates the fear inspired by Magufuli's authoritarianism in the whole state apparatus, including the closest circle around him, as well as many private actors (Shivji, 2021).

This state of affairs made people unhappy and frustrated as they were not able to hold their government accountable. Instead, 'people were expected to be accountable to the government'.[16] Magufuli's domestic popularity started very high as measured by the annual TWAWEZA poll. His posture as a 'man of integrity', determined to go against the status quo, and able to sometimes take spectacular measures initially pleased public opinion. Over time his popularity started to fall, however, to such an extent that the 2018 TWAWEZA poll showed a rate of approval only moderately above 50 per cent. TWAWEZA got into trouble with the Magufuli government, and no more poll results have been published since then.

In two elections (local government elections in 2019 and the general election in October 2020) when people could have openly expressed their views, there were rampant claims of unfair treatment of the opposition. In the local government elections of 2019, the opposition felt so mistreated that they opted out of the elections, which led Magufuli to observe that opting out was a democratic decision too. In the general election of October 2020, Chadema presidential candidate Tundu Lissu drew such large crowds during the campaign that the winner of the election appeared increasingly uncertain. However, Magufuli, the CCM presidential candidate, and CCM parliamentary candidates won with such a large margin that opposition cried foul, accusing CCM of malpractice supported by the police. Indeed, Magufuli won with 84 per cent of the vote, and CCM won all parliamentary seats except a couple. However, for the first time since the beginning of general elections in 1965, no election petitions were filed. By itself, this was not only a telling critical comment on the 2020 general elections under President Magufuli's watch but above all a veiled pointer to the loss of people's trust in the impartiality of the judiciary. In the *Journal of Democracy* in July 2021, Dan Paget argued that with brutal resolve, the ruling party sought not merely to win an election, but to annihilate the opposition. According to other observers,[17] the flawed 2020 Tanzanian elections are blamed on an authoritarian turn instigated by Magufuli, although focusing exclusively on Magufuli obscures the authoritarian foundations of CCM rule and the strategies used by CCM to maintain political control, albeit in a more subtle way.

The stand Magufuli took on COVID-19 is another sign of his distrust of others' opinion as well as a mind that could at times be seen as both obsessive and self-contradictory. He denied the existence of the pandemic while sometimes acknowledging its reality. He thus publicly claimed that Tanzania had eradicated COVID-19 through three days of prayer, but is also reported to

---

[16] Conversation with Dr Kitima, a priest, vice chancellor of the University of Dar es Salaam, and member of the Tanzanian Academy of Science, in his personal capacity.

[17] See Cheeseman et al. (2021).

have played down the pandemic and denounced vaccines as a Western conspiracy against Africans. Under his administration Tanzania suspended updating its COVID-19 cases and deaths to the World Health Organization and communication on the pandemic was prohibited, even though there were clear indications that the number of admissions at hospitals of patients exhibiting respiratory symptoms consistent with COVID-19 was increasing. Although still unofficial, he may have been one of them when he died in March 2021, a few weeks after starting his second presidential mandate. Despite, or possibly because of, his persistent denial of the virus, the US State Department diplomatically remarked after his passing that the United States remained committed to continuing to support Tanzanians 'as they work to combat the COVID-19 pandemic'.

The history of President Magufuli's administration underlines the risks of viewing leaders through rose-tinted glasses. Charismatic individuals can claim the reformer's mantle, but giving them too much credence before structural reforms are implemented sells democracy short and increases the risk of authoritarian relapse.

F The Beginning of the Sixth Phase

President Samia Suluhu Hassan was sworn in as the new president of the sixth-phase government on 19 March 2021 following the death of Magufuli. Several new developments and notable changes in policies on several fronts have already been observed.

Freedom of the media and of speech has been one immediate change from the Magufuli regime. Social media immediately became vibrant in the first week of the sixth phase. Print and electronic media are operating freely, and some of those that had been closed have been restarted. There is freedom of the opposition parties, and President Samia has openly spoken in favour of bringing unity and peace between CCM and the opposition parties. There are clear signs of departure from authoritarianism.

President Samia has demonstrated that observance of the rule of law is being restored. Several businesspeople who had been arrested and stayed in custody without being charged and those who had been charged falsely for money laundering have been released. Those who had been close to Magufuli and broke the law with impunity have been taken to court and charged.

There are encouraging indications of an improved business climate. The relationship with the business sector has improved, as indicated by frequent meetings with sections of the business community and resumption of dialogue between government and the private sector in the Tanzania National Business Council. President Samia has been accompanied by business representatives in her state visits to other countries (Uganda, Kenya, Rwanda, Burundi, and the United States), an indication that she is determined to improve relations with the private sector. President Samia has liberalised several policies politically and economically and in terms of economic diplomacy, as indicated by mended relations with several foreign governments and international financial institutions, notably the World Bank and the IMF. The policies and procedures related to issuing permits to investors have eased, and permits for foreign experts have been made more liberal and efficient. Investors are facilitated more efficiently in terms of the time it takes.

G Final Remarks on Political History

Numerous major events have occurred over the last fifty years or so that have oriented Tanzania in various, sometimes opposing, directions. In the first stage, post-independence Tanzania continued colonial trends, with essentially an outward market orientation. Then came the turn to socialism and the attempt at creating a self-reliant African socialist society. This second period lasted seventeen years, during which huge and sometimes violent reforms took place at the same time as mindsets were deeply modified. Then a new period came that started to reverse the previous order, trying to instil in society the seeds of a market economy and a multi-party democracy. Ten years later, this new regime is more or less in place, but the old order has not completely disappeared in the minds of civil servants and the employees and managers of SOEs. Also, such a succession of reforms and the difficulty of monitoring them in a rigorous way has generated specific mindsets, especially regarding corruption, that will take time to be modified.

Most importantly for the present study, it is difficult to imagine that such a contrasting evolution in such a short time span has had no impact on the institutional context in which present and future development must take place. It is the purpose of this study to identify precisely which institutions are the most likely to be obstacles to that development. Before focusing on institutional issues, however, it is necessary to review the main features of the development process in Tanzania.

2

Features and Challenges of Economic Development

François Bourguignon

Tanzania graduated in 2020 from low-income to lower middle-income status in the country classification used by international organisations. This means that its national income per inhabitant is now just above USD 1,025 at the current official exchange rate. This was celebrated as an important achievement, even though such a nominal concept that does not take into account the purchasing power of the population is of dubious significance. After correcting for this factor, it turns out that the average Tanzanian citizen lives on USD 2,700 at the present purchasing power of advanced countries. Although higher in absolute terms, this figure is still less than a sixth of the world average and ranks Tanzania only slightly above the bottom 10 per cent threshold in a world ranking of countries. Despite graduation, Tanzania is still a poor country where economic development is as urgent today as it has been since independence.

As noted in Chapter 1, the country has gone through difficult times with the severe crisis that ended Nyerere's socialist experiment and the painful transition to a modern market economy under the control of donors and international financial organisations. It is only since the end of the 1990s, that is almost forty years after independence, that the country has seen steady growth. Progress since then has been impressive. Yet, with still almost half of its population below the international poverty line of USD 2.15 a day at international prices, there is still a very long way to go before it will have completely eradicated poverty, fast population growth making this even more challenging.

This chapter analyses the economic development obstacles that Tanzania faces today and is likely to face in the future on its way to full poverty eradication. It starts with a review of the evolution of key economic indicators and its main causes with a focus on the most recent period and the factors that may presently be constraining further or faster progress. The spotlight then moves to social issues, where results appear significantly less remarkable than could be expected given the economic achievements. The chapter ends with a summary of the main economic and social development challenges faced by Tanzania in the early 2020s. More detailed aspects of the economic as well as institutional context of Tanzanian development are considered in subsequent chapters.

I THE MAIN FEATURES OF TANZANIA'S ECONOMIC DEVELOPMENT

The short economic history of Tanzania has been chaotic. It is only during the last twenty-five years or so that economic development has proceeded at a steady pace, and this is the period the following review will mostly focus upon. Yet it is also important to sometimes refer to the preceding period, that is the socialist development era and the difficult transition to a full market economy, to put the recent period in perspective.

The following review of economic development in Tanzania is organised around four major sets of issues that, directly or indirectly, have all to do with the determinants of the pace and structure of economic growth. The first set is concerned with the gross domestic product (GDP) growth rate and the way it can be explained by changes in the sectoral structure of the economy and/ or productivity gains within sectors. The second set of issues has to do with capital accumulation as an essential factor of growth, and more generally the division of national income into investment and consumption expenditures. The third set involves the role of external trade, a major factor in all contemporaneous development histories. The last set is about the financing of the economy and especially foreign finance flows, including official development assistance (ODA).

A Pace and Sources of Aggregate Growth

Growth has closely followed the changes in political and economic regimes that have characterised Tanzania since the end of the Nyerere era. Growth was fast following independence but slowed down a bit after the implementation of the socialist Ujamaa strategy, and then fully collapsed when the destabilisation caused by the latter combined with adverse external conditions to produce a severe economic crisis in the mid-1980s. A long period of stagnation followed as the transition back to a market economy took place under strict macroeconomic and structural adjustment constraints imposed by the International Monetary Fund (IMF) and the World Bank. It was only in the late 1990s that GDP per capita started to grow vigorously again, after almost twenty years of stagnation. Since then, progress has been dynamic, to such an extent that Tanzania's development has often been called a 'success story' – masking earlier difficulties. GDP per capita has grown on average by 3 per cent and total GDP by around 6 per cent a year over the last twenty years or so. As can be

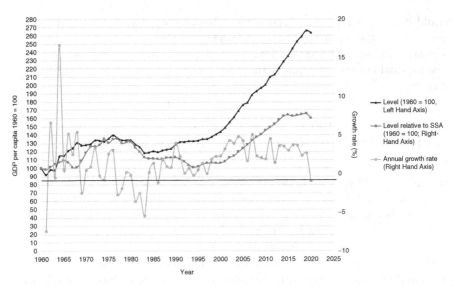

FIGURE 2.1 Tanzania's GDP per capita (absolute and relative to sub-Saharan Africa) and growth rate, 1960–2020
Source: Penn World Tables 9.1 1960–2009; WDI 2019–20

seen in Figure 2.1, GDP per capita has practically doubled over that period, a rather impressive performance in comparison with earlier decades and with the whole of the sub-Saharan region.

That overall evolution of growth since independence in Tanzania is far from unique to the region. Most sub-Saharan countries have gone through the same sequence of booms and busts, although with different intensity: fast growth after independence, recession and severe balance of payment crises in the early or mid-1980s partly because of unfavourable external contexts, structural adjustment programmes (SAPs) forced upon them by the IMF and the World Bank, and exit from this long stagnation in the mid- or late 1990s. Compared with the whole of sub-Saharan Africa – excluding South Africa – Tanzania did better in the post-independence years, then worse in the early 1970s, at the time of Ujamaa. It then performed on a par with the region, recovered earlier from the long stagnation of the 1980s and early 1990s, and then performed significantly better over the last two decades. Over the last sixty years, Tanzania's growth of GDP per capita has outperformed the average sub-Saharan country by 50 per cent.

The comparison is less favourable with other developing countries. In the early 1980s, countries such as Bangladesh, Cambodia, India, Laos, and Vietnam had a GDP per capita lower than Tanzania in international purchasing power parity. Today, it is 30 per cent higher in Bangladesh and Cambodia and more than twice in the other countries.

1 The Sources of Growth: Structural Change More Than Productivity Gains
Analysis of changes in the structure of the economy and productivity growth
since independence is made difficult because of a lack of homogeneous series
over the whole period. The Groningen Growth Development Centre (GGDC)
provides data on sectoral components of GDP and employment that result
from a careful analysis of all existing sources of data – especially on employment – and reasonable inter- or extrapolation when data are missing. The
problem is that the GGDC changed definitions and price corrections in its
most recent release for the 1990–2018 period, thus making it not directly
comparable with the previous release, which covered 1960–2011. Rather than
trying to build artificially homogeneous series covering the whole economic
history since independence, we use the two sources as follows: the initial series
for the 1960–97 period, that is the independence period followed by the long
recession that ended in the late 1990s, and the most recent dataset since 1997.

Tables 2.1a and 2.1b describe respectively the evolution of the structure
of the economy over these two periods. Figures for 1997, which appear in
both tables, thus refer to two different sources that differ on the one hand in
the definition of sectors and on the other hand in the base year for constant
price GDP series. Differences are noticeable. Reassuringly, however, it turns
out that the two data sets are roughly consistent with each other in describing
the changes in the structure of employment and GDP over periods common to
the two sets, although this convergence is not explored further here.

The story told by Table 2.1a on the earlier period fits the growth account
presented earlier. It breaks down into a rather dynamic time from independence
to the mid-1970s and then a long regression until the late 1990s. Structural
changes are noticeable – from 1977 to 1997 – with the GDP-share of agriculture
falling rapidly in favour of manufacturing, utilities, and government services.
Changes on the employment side are more limited,[1] the dominant feature
being the loss of agriculture mostly to the benefit of trade and hospitality, with
a pronounced drop in both sectors in relative productivity, that is the ratio
of sectoral productivity to overall (GDP) productivity. On the GDP side, the
second subperiod – from 1977 to 1997 – witnesses structural changes that go
in the opposite direction, with agriculture regaining weight at the expense of
manufacturing and other sectors, whereas labour movement from agriculture
to the rest of the economy continues at the same slow pace.

Structural changes shown in Table 2.1b for the last two decades resemble
the post-independence period in the preceding table, with fast and accelerating
progress of aggregate productivity and a quick decline in the GDP share for
agriculture. Sizeable relative gains are observed in construction, whose share

---

[1] They are also imprecise outside big sectors such as agriculture, manufacturing, and government
services. This may be seen from abnormally high relative productivity in the low employment
sector in 1960. For instance, the sectoral productivity in the construction sector would be halved
if its share of employment were 0.4 instead of 0.2 per cent, although this is a tiny difference.

TABLE 2.1a *Evolution of the sectoral structure of employment and GDP, 1960–97 (GGDC Release 2014, GDP at constant 2005 prices)*

(%) Year	1960			1977			1997		
	GDP	Empl.	R. Prod[a]	GDP	Empl.	R. Prod[a]	GDP	Empl.	R. Prod[a]
Agriculture	45.0	91.7	0.5	33.0	88.5	0.4	39.7	85.3	0.5
Mining	3.8	0.1	27.9	1.2	0.6	2.0	1.6	0.5	3.4
Manufacturing	6.9	1.07	6.4	12.4	1.6	7.7	8.5	1.5	5.7
Utilities	0.8	0.0	29.9	1.5	0.1	18.9	2.6	0.2	14.8
Construction	7.2	0.2	42.2	8.7	0.7	11.9	7.3	0.6	11.2
Trade and hospitality	17.7	1.0	18.3	16.2	3.9	4.2	15.9	6.1	2.6
Transport, storage, and communication	6.3	0.2	26.9	9.0	0.8	11.6	7.0	0.7	9.6
Finance, insurance, real estate, and business services	2.6	0.1	27.9	3.4	0.2	20.1	4.8	0.2	23.8
Government services	9.2	3.5	2.6	13.8	2.2	6.2	11.6	3.1	3.7
Community, social, and personal services	0.5	2.1	0.3	0.8	1.4	0.6	1.0	1.8	0.5
Total	100	100	80.1	100	100	108.8	100	100	100
GDP and GDP/worker (1997 = 100)	27.6			60.6			100		

[a] Sectoral productivity relative to overall productivity at the bottom of the column (1997 = 100), i.e. GDP divided by Empl. column

Source: Author's calculation from Groningen Growth Development Centre database.

TABLE 2.1b *Evolution of the sectoral structure of employment and GDP, 1997–2018 (GGDC Release 2021, GDP at constant 2015 prices)*

(%) Year	1997			2007			2018		
	GDP	Empl.	R. Prod[a]	GDP	Empl.	R. Prod[a]	GDP	Empl.	R. Prod[a]
Agriculture	39.7	84.4	0.5	32.2	75.3	0.4	27.9	69.7	0.4
Mining	2.8	0.6	4.6	4.7	0.6	8.5	4.4	0.8	5.6
Manufacturing	6.9	1.8	3.9	7.9	2.7	3.0	9.1	3.2	2.8
Utilities	1.9	0.2	11.3	1.6	0.1	15.2	1.3	0.1	10.2
Construction	6.1	0.8	7.5	9.4	1.2	7.9	14.7	1.9	7.9
Trade and hospitality	13.1	6.4	2.0	11.7	10.4	1.1	11.4	14.2	0.8
Transport, storage, and communication	8.2	0.7	11.0	7.9	1.6	5.1	8.3	2.1	4.0
Finance, insurance, real estate, and business services	10.6	0.4	24.6	12.7	0.8	16.7	12.2	1.1	11.1
Government services	8.5	3.3	2.6	10.2	3.2	3.2	9.3	3.7	2.5
Community, social, and personal services	2.3	1.4	1.7	1.7	4.2	0.4	1.4	3.2	0.4
Total	100	100	100	100	100		100	100	
GDP and GDP/worker (1997 = 100)	100	100		180	132.5		356	198.6	

[a] Sectoral productivity relative to overall productivity at the bottom of the column (1997 = 100), i.e. GDP divided by Empl. column

Source: Author's calculation from Groningen Growth Development Centre database.

more than doubled, mining, and, to a lesser extent, manufacturing. It is interesting that these changes look to be continuous throughout the whole timespan, the structure of GDP in 2007 being intermediate between those observed at the beginning and end of the period. For employment, the same migration phenomenon as before is present, although much enhanced, between agriculture and the trade sector. Employment movement towards the latter sector is so strong that its productivity relative to that of the whole economy is more than halved over the whole period – which implies a slight decline in absolute terms.

Focusing on the periods of fast growth, it is tempting to conclude from these tables that Tanzania's engines of economic growth stood in those sectors whose GDP share benefited most from the decreasing importance of agriculture. They comprise manufacturing, transport, and government services in the post-independence years, and essentially construction, mining, and manufacturing in the last twenty years. Such a reading of the preceding tables would be misleading, however. First, engines of growth in a small open economy such as Tanzania are almost necessarily located in sectors that produce tradable goods. Growth in other sectors reflects the dynamism of the demand side of the economy or its consequences rather than being the cause of overall growth. Thus, mining and manufacturing are sectors that might possibly qualify as growth engines, but not construction, which essentially responds to the demand arising from growing public infrastructure investments. Second, true engines of growth are unlikely to be sectors whose labour productivity lags behind that of the whole economy while their employment share rises, as has been the case for the trade and hospitality sector in Tanzania. Either those sectors are sheltering surplus labour or their development concentrates in sub-sectors with lower productivity, an unlikely trend.

The case of the manufacturing sector is of particular interest owing to the emphasis presently put by the Tanzanian government on the need for the economy to industrialise. It can be seen in Table 2.1b that the manufacturing sector has grown somewhat faster than total GDP over the last twenty years, without its share in GDP ever reaching the level achieved by 1977 before the long recession. Assuming that part of that growth was a response to the increase in demand originating in the rest of the economy, the other part can be seen as truly autonomous and directed towards exports – or substituting for imports. It is indeed the case that manufacturing exports grew quite substantially during the 2000s, as emphasised for instance in MacMillan et al. (2017, pp. 155–60),[2] suggesting that this sector has the potential to grow independently of the rest of the economy, a feature that is expected from a genuine growth driver. Yet the contribution of the manufacturing sector to the overall growth of the economy is presently limited by its size. It is easily calculated that the 2 per cent GDP-share increase in Table 2.1b is responsible for only 10 per cent of overall growth over the last two decades.

[2] See also World Bank (2014a, pp. 33–5).

An unexpected feature of the evolution of the manufacturing sector over that period is the drop in its productivity relative to that of the whole economy – see Table 2.1b – which seems to contradict the capacity of this sector to play the role of a growth engine, even as a side influence rather than the main driving factor. The point is that this concept of relative productivity may be misleading, and the comparison with the growth of overall productivity may hide the true contribution to overall growth of the productivity gain arising within a sector.

The reason for this ambiguity lies in the key role of structural change, that is the reallocation of labour across sectors, in overall labour productivity gains. When workers leave agriculture, they move away from a sector where labour productivity is among the lowest – as can be seen in Tables 2.1a and 2.1b – and move to sectors where the productivity is higher. By itself, this restructuring of employment thus raises the overall labour productivity in the economy. This would be the case even if no productivity gain were taking place within sectors. When comparing the change in the productivity within a specific sector to overall productivity, it must thus be taken into account that the latter includes this structural change effect. Productivity may well increase in the sector under consideration, but may be less than the overall productivity gains due to structural change.

The decomposition of the change in overall productivity into its structural change and its within-sector components shown in Table 2.2 for the two pre- and post-1997 periods is quite instructive. The striking feature is the importance of the structural change component. Until 1997, gains in overall labour productivity – and roughly speaking in GDP per capita since employment may be assumed to be approximately proportional to the population – were essentially due to structural change, whereas the within-sector productivity gain was negative. Roughly speaking, this can be interpreted as the result of workers moving from agriculture to sectors with a higher productivity but contributing at the same time to lowering productivity within the latter. This is exactly the way the increasing employment share and decreasing GDP share of the trade sector, the main destination of the net flow of workers out of agriculture, can be interpreted in Tables 2.1a and 2.1b.

Things change drastically after 1997, however. First, the structural change effect tends to weaken, mostly because the productivity gap between agriculture and the trade and hospitality sector shrinks. Second, the average within-sector productivity increases, especially after 2007.[3] Over the most recent sub-period, the within-sector productivity component is even slightly bigger than the structural change effect. It thus looks as if some deep change had taken place in the Tanzanian economy. Coming back to the issue of the contribution of the manufacturing sector to growth, it can be seen in the Appendix that its contribution to the growth of overall productivity is definitely more through its

---

[3] The same decomposition for Tanzania's productivity growth for the period 2002–12 can be found in McMillan et al. (2017), with results intermediate to those for the periods 1997–2007 and 2007–18 in Table 2.2, that is a strongly positive structural change effect and a much smaller (positive) effect for the within-sector productivity component.

TABLE 2.2 *Decomposition of the change in overall labour productivity into structural change and within-sector productivity effect, 1960–2018*

(Percentage points)	Structural change	Within-sector productivity	Total
(GGDG Release 2014, GDP at 2005 prices)			
1960–77	68.7	–32.8	35.9
1977–97	7.9	–14.7	–6.8
1960–97	85.2	–42.7	42.5
(GGDG Release 2021, GDP at 2015 prices)			
1997–2007	25.7	6.8	32.5
2007–18	22.3	27.5	49.9
1997–2018	53.7	36.2	89.9

Source: Calculation in Appendix

autonomous increase in productivity than its participation in structural change through faster employment creation than in the rest of the economy.

What should be concluded from this review of the changes in the structure of the Tanzanian economy and in sectoral productivities in terms of sources of growth? A first conclusion is the importance of the sectoral reallocation of labour as the main source of growth from independence until today,[4] except, of course, during the long recession of the 1980s and 1990s, a period of more than fifteen years over which both overall growth of labour productivity and its structural change component have been close to zero. A second conclusion is the negative overall contribution of changes in within-sector productivity from independence to the mid-2000s. It is only over the recent past that productivity gains acquired a dynamic role in Tanzanian growth. Interestingly, it will be seen later that this coincides with a sustained high level of capital accumulation, as not experienced in Tanzania since the socialist era. Causality is not granted, though, especially because much of the gross capital formation seems to have taken place in infrastructure, as may be guessed from the surge of the construction sector, which produces a type of capital whose impact on productivity generally takes some time to become visible.

The rather satisfactory rate of growth that Tanzania has enjoyed over the last twenty years or so is good news. That it cannot be attributed to the

---

[4] This conclusion may seem to contradict the widely publicised view in McMillan et al. (2014) that structural change had a negative impact on sub-Saharan growth. Tanzania may be an outlier. However, note that McMillan et al.'s estimate is for the period 1990–2005, which includes part of the long recession that hit the whole region. In Tanzania, the contribution of structural change to growth was indeed close to zero, if not negative, during that period, but the country got out of stagnation before the rest of the region and then grew faster.

autonomous growth of a specific sector progressing on international markets or competing with imports is more worrying. The reallocation of labour from low-productivity agriculture to a slightly less low-productivity trade sector cannot be considered as a sustainable engine of growth. At some stage, employment in higher productivity sectors, especially in tradable goods and services, will have to expand. It is not clear this is about to happen. Even though more dynamic lately, the manufacturing sector is presently not big enough to be more than a side engine of growth. As noted in Chapter 1, the agricultural sector is home to the natural comparative advantages of the Tanzanian economy. Until now, however, these have not been exploited and agriculture lies largely behind the growth of the rest of the economy. Mining is the last tradable sector that could be an autonomous source of growth, but this would be more through favourable international prices, and therefore its positive impact on the demand side of the economy, than through enhanced production on the supply side, unless of course a flow of new resources were to be discovered in the coming decades.[5]

II INVESTMENT AND THE STRUCTURE
OF AGGREGATE SPENDING

Even though the growth performance of the Tanzanian economy has been reasonably high over the last twenty years, and especially the last decade, it is not to be ignored that it was largely demand-driven rather than the produce of a clearly identified autonomous growth engine in tradable sectors. This would be the case, for instance, if a significant improvement in the terms of trade or important foreign resources grants had fed private and public domestic demand, fostering activity and possibly investment. It will be seen later that such an improvement in terms of trade occurred at around the turn of the millennium. In the future, however, a way has to be found to maintain and enhance the progress observed lately in the productivity, and therefore competitiveness, of key tradable sectors, manufacturing in the first place, but possibly also agriculture and the agroindustry. This requires keeping investment at a high level and making it more effective.

The evolution of the domestic expenditure counterpart of GDP is shown in Figure 2.2 from 1985 to 2017. Earlier data are not available or are not comparable, whereas data after 2017 are still provisional and likely to be affected by measurement errors. The dark curve that describes the evolution of the GDP-share of gross capital formation exhibits an interesting shape. It surged in 1990 and reached a level close to 40 per cent for a few years. It then fell sharply until 2000, before progressively getting back to its previous maximum over the last ten years or so. Such an evolution raises two sets of questions. First, what explains such fluctuations and what made, and is making possible today, such

---

[5] The recent discovery of sizeable offshore fields of natural gas is discussed below together with foreign trade issues.

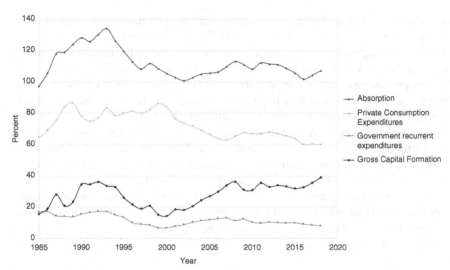

FIGURE 2.2 Absorption and expenditures on GDP, 1985–2018 (percentage of GDP)
Note: Because of a shift in the base of Tanzanian national accounts in 2015, the IMF
today reports only data after 2012. Figures for the period before 2012 are taken from
previous 2005-based national account series after adjusting them proportionally so that
they coincide with the new definition in 2012
Source: IMF, International Financial Statistics

a high rate of investment in a country that has just graduated from low-income
status? Second, are the rate of growth of the economy and its productivity
gains consistent with its investment efforts?

The evolution of investment in the first half of the period shown in Figure 2.2
closely follows the economic history of Tanzania. After Nyerere's resignation
in 1985 and the concomitant shift to a market economic system under the pressure of donors, and in front of the dismal situation of the economy, ODA flows
surged while new ambitious development programmes were launched. These
included huge investment efforts that were essentially financed externally;
hence the high level of absorption – that is, total domestic expenditures including investment – observed in around 1990, a period during which domestic
spending overcame GDP in some years by as much as 35 per cent. But donors
did not want to keep Tanzania permanently on a drip and started reducing
aid. After a short rebound in the early 1990s, growth slowed down, and so
did investment. As the share of private consumption in GDP kept constant, it
turned out that the brunt of the drop in absorption caused by the decline in aid
was borne by investment and government recurrent expenditures.

The recent, more progressive surge of investment is a different story. First,
growth accelerated in the 2000s, partly because of foreign financing and partly
because of improving terms of trade. This triggered a rebound in investment.

Second, the share of private consumption in GDP started to decline, thus providing space for additional investment expenditures. The economy then gradually settled into a new rather favourable kind of equilibrium, with an investment rate a little below 35 per cent of GDP and private consumption around 60 per cent, but also with a need for foreign financing to fund a level of absorption still above GDP.

There are several explanations for the decline of the average household propensity to consume that permitted the sharp increase in investment. The first is the change in the share of agriculture in total income. The propensity to consume is known to be higher from agricultural income, if only through subsistence farmers consuming most of their own produce. As seen earlier, the share of agriculture in GDP fell drastically at the turn of the millennium, thus bringing about a drop in the average propensity to consume in the economy.[6] In addition, the propensity to consume has likely decreased owing to various other causes, including an increase in taxation in the early 2000s, a slower inflation of consumption prices relative to the GDP deflator, and rising income inequality, as will be discussed later.

In view of the decomposition of changes in labour productivity in the preceding section, one may ask whether the evolution of the investment share in GDP is consistent with it, and thus check the role of capital accumulation as a key determinant of Tanzanian growth. Interestingly, the profile of the investment ratio over time explains why growth has long been driven essentially by structural change while within-sector productivity was falling, a feature that changed only during the last decade. Indeed, the slow pace of capital accumulation observed before the late 2000s was barely enough to cover more than the capital needs arising from depreciation, demographic growth, and the extra capital required to equip the net flow of agricultural workers moving to higher productivity and therefore more capital-intensive sectors. This explains why no gain was recorded in within-sector productivity in earlier periods. As the investment rate rose, a threshold was then passed such that the investment rate is able not only to cover all these needs but also to increase the capita–labour ratio, and therefore productivity within sectors of production. Apparently, the threshold was passed in the late 2000s, before the investment rate reached a plateau at around 35 per cent of GDP. Growth proved to be the result of both structural change and within-sector productivity gains.[7]

---

[6] Although data may not be as precise, the opposite evolution seems to have taken place in the 1980s and early 1990s, when the GDP-share of the agricultural sector was increasing and the economy was in a deep recession.

[7] With a capital-output ratio of 2.5, a depreciation rate of 4 per cent, and a population growth rate of 3 per cent, maintaining the overall capital-labour ratio requires an investment rate of 17.5 per cent. However, this figure becomes higher when it is assumed that most capital is used outside agriculture and the non-agricultural sector must absorb a net flow of workers out of agriculture. A net flow equal to 1 per cent of the labour force is equivalent to employment having to grow by 4 per cent a year on top of demographic growth outside agriculture. Then a 27.5

This rather favourable evolution nevertheless leaves open the question of whether these productivity gains are efficient or whether the pace of capital formation would allow for faster gains. Answering this would require a detailed analysis of the conditions of production sector by sector, even though the World Bank enterprise surveys suggest several common factors that limit productivity, such as insufficient and irregular power supply or the lack of skilled manpower. A rough calculation shows that the observed average productivity gain across sectors in the 2007–18 period could probably have been substantially higher in view of existing estimates of the productivity of capital.[8]

Not only the volume but also the composition of investment matters for growth. In this respect, the low level of the stock of infrastructure in Tanzania needs to be emphasised. In most enterprise surveys, managers report the low volume and quality of infrastructure as one of the factors that most constrain production and competitiveness. This is particularly true in the field of electricity, Tanzania being among the countries where the consumption of electricity is the lowest in the world. But this is also true of port facilities and the road network. Efforts are being made, as can be seen from the surge of the construction sector over the last two decades, but needs are huge.

If it proves possible to maintain such a high volume of investment as the present one, the prospects of the Tanzanian economy would seem promising. Two downsides must be mentioned, however. First, this requires that external funding remains available. It can be seen in Figure 2.2 that, even though lower than in the early 1990s, the absorption rate is still above 100, which means that the economy relies on foreign financing to cover part of its expenditure. This need was on average around 8 per cent of GDP over the last ten years. Second, outlets for production from new private investments must be available, which raises again the issue of the nature of the growth engine. This is not granted if growth is mostly demand-driven, as suggested earlier for the last two decades, unless the source of growing income behind demand has some permanence. If this is not the case, the high level of investment and growth can only be maintained through an expansion of tradable sectors and progress being achieved in terms of international competitiveness. This is the issue we now turn to while focusing on external trade.

A External Trade

The evolution of trade between Tanzania and the rest of the world has been extremely variable over time. Data series for foreign trade since independence

---

per cent overall investment rate would be needed to absorb the net labour flow from agriculture without changes in sectoral capital-labour ratios.

[8] Using the same assumptions as in the preceding footnote, an investment rate of 35 per cent as observed in the recent years would permit a 3 per cent annual increase in within-sector productivity instead of the observed 2.2 per cent. This estimate would be higher if, of course, it was assumed that some capital is used in agriculture, unlike in the preceding footnote.

do not seem very reliable, nor do they always fit national accounts. What seems certain is that the share of exports in GDP was around 30 per cent at the time of independence and had practically collapsed by the time of the dramatic balance of payment crisis that triggered the SAP in the mid-1980s. It was then as low as 5 per cent to a large part because of a dramatic drop in the production of export crops. It had recovered a little by 1990, and then exports surged for a short while before falling sharply again, in both instances mostly for climatic reasons and fluctuations in international prices.[9] They have gradually regained lost ground since the turn of the millennium and seem to have now stabilised at around 20 per cent or so over the last years. Yet their composition was drastically modified, with traditional exports crops losing weight in favour of mining and, to a lesser extent, manufacturing products.

Notwithstanding these fluctuations, and taking the late 1990s as a point of departure, exports have been extremely dynamic over the last twenty years, to such an extent that they may have been a significant contributor to the overall growth of the economy during that period. If their volume has grown on average only slightly faster than GDP, their unit value has significantly increased both with respect to imports – as can be seen from the terms of trade graph in Figure 2.3 – and domestic goods. As exported and domestically consumed goods and services can rarely be substituted for each other, exports have directly contributed to the growth of overall production roughly in the same proportion as their share in GDP, that is around 13 per cent over the last two decades. However, because of very favourable terms of trade – a 40 per cent increase since 2000 according to Figure 2.3 – they raised the purchasing power of the economy and exerted positive pressure on growth through the domestic demand side of the domestic economy. These effects are part of the implicit demand-driven component of recent growth mentioned earlier in this chapter when reviewing growth performances and their determinants.

The overall growth of exports hides a substantial diversification of exported products. Figure 2.4 shows that merchandise exports were essentially agricultural products in the mid-1990s and, as such, subject to fluctuations in climatic conditions as well as price variations in international markets. In a few years in the early 2000s, mineral exports and especially gold and precious stones became dominant, with a share of total exports slightly above half. Agricultural products now represent less than 20 per cent, less than manufacturing products. For both groups of products, it should be noted that present trends may be stronger than it appears in the chart. In 2018, gold exports have been negatively affected by a ban agreed by the government of Tanzania, which was accusing foreign mining companies of cheating on the gold content of exported auriferous sand, whereas agricultural exports suffered from a row between the government and foreign buyers of cashew nuts whose price was found too low. The 2019 figures may not be completely back to normal.

[9] On export fluctuations and their causes during this period, see Kweka (2004).

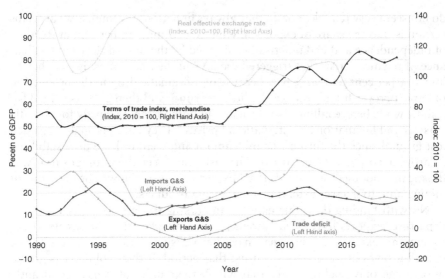

FIGURE 2.3 Foreign trade and terms of trade, 1990–2019 (shares of GDP or 2010 based indices)
Note: The real effective exchange rate is defined as the ratio of the price of domestic over foreign goods. It is obtained by dividing the consumer price index in Tanzania by the product of the exchange rate (in Tanzanian Shillings per dollar) and the mean GDP deflator of partner countries. Trade partners were identified by the mean share of merchandise exports and imports across the two sub-periods 1997–9 and 2013–15. Only partners with shares above 2 per cent were considered. The resulting list of countries is, in order of importance, India, South Africa, China, Kenya, Japan, UK, Saudi Arabia, Germany, UAE, Switzerland, Netherlands, USA, and Belgium
Source: Author's calculation from World Development Indicators (see figure note)

The manufacturing sector has also been a driver of export growth. Its share in merchandise exports doubled in the last fifteen years and now represents a fifth of total exports. It was mentioned that the growth of the manufacturing sector being faster than of GDP could mean that an increasing share of its output was directed towards foreign markets or was substituting imports. Figure 2.4 confirms this view on the export side. It is also quite striking that the surge in manufacturing exports coincided with a steady and strong real depreciation of the currency – see the real exchange rate chart in Figure 2.3.[10] After a big depreciation in the early 1990s followed by an equally rapid re-appreciation, the real effective exchange rate declined continuously between 1998 and 2006, at roughly 4 per cent a year. That simultaneity between manufacturing export growth and the real exchange rate fits the view famously put forward by Rodrik (2008) about the favourable development impact of

[10] Recall that the real exchange rate is defined there as the price of domestic over foreign goods.

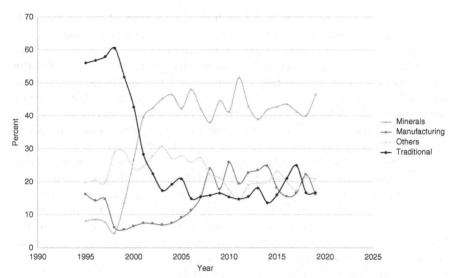

FIGURE 2.4 Composition of merchandise exports, 1995–2019 (shares of total)
Source: Calculation from Bank of Tanzania annual reports (1995–2019)

the undervaluation of the local currency on development.[11] Tanzania could thus be another example of the favourable consequences of currency undervaluation on industrialisation and growth, although it might be better to refer in this case to a move away from overvaluation rather than an undervaluation strategy. Note also that the argument does not apply to mineral exports, whose price is set on international markets rather than by domestic production costs.

The preceding remarks refer to merchandise exports, thus ignoring exports of services. The latter represent between 50 and 60 per cent of merchandise exports, and no noticeable change has taken place in this ratio over the last two decades or so. Service exports primarily include transports of goods between landlocked neighbour countries and domestic seaports, and, most importantly, tourism receipts. If they contributed to the dynamism of exports in the early 2000s, the latter have now stabilised and represent a little more than 4 per cent of GDP.

There is no doubt that the development of exports, particularly during the 2000s, largely contributed to the growth performances of the Tanzanian economy. The issue, however, is whether such a dynamism is sustainable in the long run. Commodity exports, mineral or agricultural, are determined by foreign demand and their price is set on international markets. Their revenue is thus uncertain, even though the relative diversification of Tanzania's commodity exports attenuates that uncertainty. The same can be said of the transport services that depend on the trade activity of neighbouring countries – a business

---

[11] See also Eichengreen (2008).

likely to increase within a few years with the completion of the railway link with Rwanda and Burundi. Overall, then, the manufacturing and tourism sectors represent the only truly autonomous factors of growth. They are also labour-intensive, unlike other non-agricultural exports, a key issue for the inclusiveness of growth, especially in view of the fast population increase. As seen earlier, however, they are presently too limited – roughly 6 per cent of GDP altogether – to be a real growth engine of the Tanzanian economy.

One word must be said about the huge offshore resources of natural gas discovered in Tanzania since 2011. The dependency on foreign prices is at its strongest here since projects are currently on hold in view of international liquefied natural gas (LNG) prices being much lower than the estimated cost of extraction.[12] Estimates of potential revenues vary depending on the expected overall cost of extraction. Revenues amounting to 1.2 to 1.5 per cent of GDP seem reasonable estimates.[13] Of course, this would be a real bonus for Tanzania and might be managed without too much negative spill-over of the 'natural resource curse' type. However, it is unlikely to drastically change the long-run economic prospects of the country either.

Another factor that may have contributed to the dynamism of Tanzanian exports that is worth emphasising is the change in the relative weight of destination countries. Exports towards China have surged over the last two decades, reflecting both the expansion of China as a trade partner of sub-Saharan Africa and the fast growth of its economy. But trade has also grown very fast with two African countries that have become major trade partners: Kenya, another member country of the East African Community, and South Africa, the dominant economic power of the region.

On the side of imports, the most noticeable fact over the preceding few decades has been their explosion in the early 1990s, when import licensing was almost completely abolished as a final step of the transition towards a market economy. They then fell against GDP partly because they were reverting to a more normal level and partly because of the real depreciation of the currency. Since the beginning of the century, the GDP share of imports has surged again under the pressure of accelerating growth, increasing investment, and a stable real exchange rate, before declining, possibly because of the real depreciation of the national currency over the last five years or so.

As far as the composition of imports is concerned, the most noticeable change is the sizeable drop that has occurred in the share of consumer goods – from 36 per cent in 2000 to around 25 per cent in 2016. It may result from two circumstances: the drop in the share of private consumption in GDP and

---

[12] This remains true despite the increase observed since the mid-2020s.

[13] A report by NRGI, a New-York-based non-governmental organisation specialising in advice on natural resource policies, estimates the Tanzanian revenue of the Lindi LNG gas project to be 1.2 per cent of GDP, if the project goes ahead (Olingo, 2017). Henstridge and Rweyemamu (2017) assume lower extraction prices that would make the investment profitable. Yet their detailed calculation leads to actual revenues of around 1.5 per cent of GDP in the twenty years following investment – at least five years or more from now.

the real depreciation of the currency. It is unlikely that the former can explain all the observed drop, so some import substitution has probably taken place,[14] which might have reinforced the impact of exports on the development of the domestic manufacturing sector.

Trade policy in Tanzania is constrained by its simultaneous membership in the East Africa Community (EAC), in the South African Development Community, and the Common Market for the Eastern and Southern Africa. The most developed agreement is with the EAC. It includes free trade among members (Burundi, Kenya, Rwanda Tanzania, and Uganda) as well as a common external tariff; yet some freedom is left to members to depart from common tariffs through 'stays of application' or duty remission on imported intermediate products. It turns out that the number of such exceptions has swelled over recent years in Tanzania. According to a recent report, it increased from 7 in 2011 to 100 in 2018, mostly being aimed at protecting domestic production and encouraging exports – through duty remission.[15] This may be another explanation of the slowing down of imports over the recent years. On the other hand, the rent-seeking aspect of some of these trade measures should not be ignored. For instance, such a suspicion of corruption has arisen with respect to the 100 per cent tariff on sugar imports.[16]

It is fair to say that the value of imports is structurally higher than export revenues in Tanzania, which is another aspect of absorption being higher than GDP or domestic savings not covering investment expenditures. The deficit reached alarmingly high levels at the time of the liberalisation of imports at the turn of the 1990s, and when exports had not yet fully recovered from their collapse during the crisis of the 1980s. It was still high until a few years ago, averaging more than 10 per cent of GDP between 2005 and 2015. It has got close to zero over the last few years, but it is still too early to know whether this is the result of structural changes, temporary policies, or favourable trade circumstances.

B The Financing of the Economy and the Key Role of Foreign Aid

A thorough appraisal of the way Tanzanian development has been financed over time is a difficult task because of the lack of mutual consistency of the data sources to be used – that is, national accounts, balance of payments, and general government accounts – and, sometimes, the lack of time consistency within some of these sources, an example being the recent change of base in

---

[14] As the GDP share of consumption in 2000 was around 80 per cent and that of imports was 13 per cent, the 36 per cent share of consumption goods in exports corresponds to an average household propensity to consume imported goods of (0.36 × 0.13/0.80 = 0.06). Assuming this propensity remained constant, the 20 per cent drop in the GDP share of household consumption between 2000 and now would have generated a drop of 1.2 per cent in the GDP share of imported consumption goods, or 6 per cent of imports in 2018–19 instead of the observed 11 per cent (i.e. 36–25 per cent).

[15] See WTO (2019, p. 270).

[16] A detailed analysis is provided by Andreoni et al. (2020).

TABLE 2.3 *The financing of the Tanzanian economy, 2010–18*

(% of GDP, period averages) Period	2010–12	2013–15	2016–18
Domestic flows			
Domestic savings	22.3	23.8	30.5
Central government	–0.8	0.2	4.0
Private sector[b]	23.1	23.6	26.5
Gross fixed capital formation	33.1	33.0	35.8
General government	6.3	4.5	6.3
Private sector[b]	26.8	28.5	29.5
Need for funding	10.8	9.2	5.3
Government: deficit excluding current foreign grants	7.1	4.3	2.3
(Deficit including current foreign grants)	4.2	3.0	1.6
Private sector[b]	3.7	4.9	3.0
Foreign financing			
Primary and secondary income in current account[c]	–0.9	–0.6	–0.9
Official development assistance	7.8	6.1	4.6
Foreign direct investment	4.6	3.5	1.7
Foreign inflows accounted for	11.5	9.0	5.5
Outstanding debt	28.7	30.3	33.2
Of which			
Public and publicly guaranteed	18.3	21.0	22.9
Other	10.4	9.3	10.3

[a] Government account indicators are defined over the fiscal year from 01/07 to 30/06;
accordingly, GDP, savings and investment figures have been transformed into 2-years
averages for consistency
[b] Including non-government public entities
[c] Excluding foreign grants included in Official Development Assistance
Source: Author's calculation from IMF, Government Accounts and Balance of payments
data in annual reports of the Bank of Tanzania.

national accounting. It is only recently that it has become possible to make
these various sources mutually consistent. Results appear in Table 2.3, which
shows the evolution of key indicators since 2010 on a three-year average
basis.[17] Inconsistencies are still apparent when comparing the 'total' row in
the foreign financing section of the table with overall needs for funds in the
domestic section. The former exceeds the latter in 2010–12, which seems odd,
even though not impossible. Fortunately, the discrepancy is limited.

The very acute need of the Tanzanian economy for foreign financing was
already apparent in the absorption figures shown in Figure 2.2. By definition, the

[17] Averaging partly eliminates year to year variations in the need for external funding that arise
from the volatility of changes in inventories.

gap between this aggregate indicator and GDP is the overall need of the economy for external funding. It averaged 13 per cent of GDP in the 1990s, but this average hid a strongly declining trend that even reached zero for a short while in the early 2000s. Since then, however, the need for external funding has increased again, and was still around 10 per cent in the mid 2010s. Table 2.3 shows that it then halved thanks to a noticeable increase in the domestic saving rate, but the question arises whether this change is permanent or results from specific circumstances.

A second noticeable feature of the table is the difference between the public and the private sector. In the early years of the 2020s, as practically all the time during the one or two decades before, the main financing difficulty of the Tanzanian economy clearly arose in the government. Its current savings, that is the difference between its current revenue and recurrent expenditures, were negative or close to zero. In other words, government revenues barely covered current spending, so that all public investments, and often more, had to be financed by foreign or domestic private agents. The reason for such a state of affairs was not so much because of abnormally high recurrent expenditures, but rather the relatively low tax revenues. With an average tax/GDP ratio of around 11 per cent, Tanzania lies behind all East African countries and substantially below the average sub-Saharan country.

It is only in the last few years that the government has adopted a more rigorous fiscal policy consisting of a slight increase in revenues, not more than half a percentage point of GDP, though, and a pronounced drop in current expenditures – a little more than 2 per cent of GDP. This has allowed the government to cover a substantial share of public infrastructure investments and to significantly reduce its budget deficit. Yet the social cost of the cut that took place in recurrent spending should not be ignored. If it was not fully compensated by efficiency gains, it must have affected some services delivered to the population.

On the foreign financing side, most of the funding needs of the Tanzanian economy are covered by foreign aid. Although its volume declined substantially with respect to GDP, it remains substantial, and the sign of a high degree of dependency on foreign donors. At a little less than 5 per cent of GDP, today's volume of aid represents a quarter of the government's budget.

Given its importance, the ambiguity of the role of ODA in the development of the Tanzanian economy must be stressed. Tanzania may need foreign aid to provide basic public services and infrastructure, but it may also be the case that it is the availability of foreign aid that has led in the past to low savings and inefficiency in the public sector as well as to price distortions, through 'Dutch disease' effects,[18] as the ongoing debate on aid effectiveness emphasises.[19] It is

---

[18] The so-called Dutch disease arises in the presence of sizeable foreign currency inflows that do not result from a rise in exports or import substitution. They make non-tradable sectors relatively more attractive to investors, thus undermining the industrialisation potential of the country.

[19] See, for instance, Deaton (2013)'s indictment of foreign aid, and in the specific case of Tanzania Edwards (2014).

difficult to analyse in detail the causality relationship between foreign aid and the need for external funds or the trade deficit because of very special past circumstances. These comprise the whole transitional period towards a market economy when donors provided resources the economy could not produce, or donors' debt relief policies directed towards so-called Highly Indebted Poor Countries from the late 1990s to the mid-2000s. In Tanzania, as in most other poor countries, aid flows observed during this period include debt service moratoria and debt cancelling operations that do not bear much relationship to the actual funding needs of these countries.

If these problems have largely disappeared in the recent period, the issue arises of the meaning of the concomitance between the recent drop in trade deficit – and the need for external funds- and in ODA, as observed in Table 2.3. For some time, there have been talks among donors about progressively reducing aid flows to Tanzania, the present volume being often held up as a possible hindrance to the autonomous development of the country. In several instances, the Tanzanian government has openly concurred with such a view. There may thus have been something like a tacit agreement between donors and the Tanzanian government that aid flows need to be scaled down, with the latter correctly anticipating this trend and making policy decisions to adjust to this situation. It may also be the case that the reduction in foreign aid flows is the consequence of various crises during which donors have effectively put off disbursements or reduced their commitments because of major corruption scandals involving the government. This occurred in 2014 after the USD 180 million escrow scandal, in which an escrow account at the Central Bank was unlawfully emptied, itself the last episode of the Richmond scandal that a few years before had involved an overcharging private power provider and caused the resignation of several members of the government, including the prime minister. More recently, donors have threatened again to hold onto aid disbursements because of what they saw as violations of human rights by the government. Domestic policies behind the observed drop in external funding needs, including reining in public spending and letting the currency devalue in real terms, may be a kind of response to these repeated frictions with donors.

Several episodes of severe tensions between Tanzanian governments and donors have taken place in the past that could have led to a rupture. One took place at the end of the socialist period at the middle of an acute macroeconomic crisis when Nyerere was resisting the IMF's conventional and potentially socially costly adjustment measures. After a few years of tension, other donors finally imposed their view that transformative reforms were needed. Another crisis developed in the mid-1990s. On one side were the donors, exasperated by various corruption affairs, the ineffectiveness of financial management, and the lack of results of the programmes they were financing. On the other side, the Tanzanian government was complaining about the cost of dealing with all the monitoring procedures imposed by donors and its lack of autonomy in deciding the use to be made of aid. A special commission appointed by the Danish aid agency wrote a report with inventive suggestions about reforming the cooperation between the Tanzanian government and donors. This largely anticipated reforms that would become current practice in the development community a few years later, including part of aid being provided as general budget support, and therefore at the full discretion of the recipient country.[20]

Remembering these episodes is important because it shows how important foreign aid and donors have been in the development of Tanzania, practically since independence. By and large, aid may have been the engine of growth that seems to be missing in the domestic economy. By allowing investment to gain 5 to 10 per cent of GDP, it may have been responsible for two to four additional percentage points of annual growth. However, such a high volume of aid may also have had negative effects on other aspects of the economy, whether on savings, the efficiency of government machinery, the degree of corruption, or the democratic functioning of society – as forcefully argued by authors such as Easterly (2006) and Deaton (2013).[21] The volume of aid soon recovered its pre-crisis level after both the crises just mentioned, so that, even though modalities had changed, the country somehow remained as aid-dependent as before, at least in terms of a large part of capital accumulation that was directly or indirectly financed by aid. Now that a trend has appeared that tends to lessen this dependency, the question arises whether the policies meant to address this new situation, including the drop in recurrent expenditure, is sustainable. In any case, at close to 5 per cent of GDP, foreign aid remains sizeable and a pillar of Tanzanian economic growth.

Foreign direct investment is another source of investment funding. It amounts to roughly a sixth of the overall capital formation. As a percentage of GDP, it has been roughly constant until recently. The drop observed during the last few years may only be the reaction of foreign investors to the dispute alluded to earlier between the Tanzanian government and a gold mining company, and more generally to the suspicious attitude of that government towards foreign companies. The new government seems to have a more friendly attitude towards foreign companies. It should be noted, though, that direct investments in Tanzania are heavily concentrated in mining, a sector less transparent to domestic authorities than manufacturing, which accounts for only 15 per cent of foreign investments.[22]

---

[20] On the first crisis, see Catterson and Lindahl (1999) and Helleiner (2002a); on the second, see Furukawa (2014) and Helleiner (2002b). Helleiner was the chair of the reconciling commission appointed by Denmark.

[21] A detailed analysis of these issues in the specific case of Tanzania's development is provided by Edwards (2014).

[22] Besides mining (50 per cent), other major sectors of foreign investment include financial services (11 per cent) and power generation (8 per cent). These proportions refer to 2013 (NBS, 2015) and may have changed since then, despite referring to stocks rather than flows of foreign investment.

It would be wrong to consider that Tanzania's increasing indebtedness results from a gap between the needs for external funds on the one hand and foreign aid and direct investment on the other. As illustrated in Table 2.3 indebtedness has increased since the mid-2010s despite funding needs being almost exactly met by aid and direct investments. The point here is that foreign aid comes under the form of grants and concessional loans, with the latter contributing to increasing the level of debt. The Highly Indebted Poor Countries initiative permitted to reduce Tanzania's debt to 22 per cent of GDP by 2006. It had gone up to 33 per cent by 2018, with practically all that increase concentrated in the public and publicly guaranteed debt. It has further increased since then. Concessional loans contribute to reducing the debt burden but their share seem to be falling.

III SUMMARISING THE DETERMINANTS OF
AND CONSTRAINTS TO GROWTH

Many other aspects of economic development in Tanzania could be analysed, including monetary policies, taxation, infrastructure capital, and social sectors. The latter will be considered explicitly in the second part of this chapter. The others will be dealt in one way or another in subsequent chapters. At this stage, however, it is useful to summarise what has been learned from the preceding review about the determinants of and constraints to economic development in Tanzania.

The main conclusion is without any doubt the uncertainty that bears upon what could be a sustainable engine of growth in the Tanzanian economy. Growth has taken place, and substantially so, but it seems to have been more demand driven than resulting from the autonomous development of a few sectors oriented towards export or import substitution. It is true that exports have been a driving force for a while in the last two decades, but this has in large part been thanks to mining, especially gold, and thus has been highly dependent on foreign demand and world prices. Manufacturing exports have also played a role, but a minor one, and the whole sector is still too small to be a true driver of development. Instead of an autonomous supply side drive, it thus seems that it is domestic demand, pulled by purchasing power increases arising from gains in terms of trade and foreign aid, that have fed growth throughout the economy, especially in sectors highly dependent on public spending and investment.

This situation raises an issue of autonomy and sustainability in Tanzanian economic development. Dependency on foreign demand for commodities, on prices on international markets, and on foreign aid is the opposite of truly autonomous development that would result mostly from efforts by domestic agents to expand production through enhanced productivity and competitiveness. The present development strategy is in some senses passive. This does not mean that domestic agents lack dynamism, only that they mostly respond to domestic demand stimuli that often originate outside national borders.

This model may not be sustainable if drastic changes take place within the foreign context, such as a lasting contraction of commodity prices or a further reduction of foreign aid. In addition, the mineral natural resources exported by Tanzania will be depleted in the foreseeable future: gold reserves, for instance, represent only thirty years of current exports.

Overall, Tanzania has done well in productively exploiting favourable opportunities that have arisen in its foreign environment. It may now be time to consider a more autonomous strategy, and it is the task of subsequent chapters to reflect on the institutional factors that may influence or constrain this choice. However, the present review of Tanzania's development achievements and challenges would be incomplete without an examination of its social aspects, in particular its inclusiveness.

IV SOME SOCIAL ASPECTS OF TANZANIAN DEVELOPMENT

This review of the main features and evolution of the Tanzanian economy has essentially been conducted at the macro-level. It is now time to see what has happened at the level of individual households and the extent to which the overall progress of the economy has been reflected in individual welfare. Three dimensions of welfare are briefly reviewed in what follows: income poverty and inequality, education, and health.

A Poverty and Inequality

Figure 2.5 presents some summary statistics on poverty, inequality, and household consumption expenditure as estimated in the five national Household Budget Surveys (HBS) taken since 1990 and compares them with relevant national account indicators. Two sets of poverty headcount estimates, both based on the HBS, are shown. The National Bureau of Statistics (NBS) uses a poverty line based on the value of the food basket consumed by the poorest half of the population deflated by the share taken by food in the budget of these households. The poverty line is updated from one survey to the next through specific food price indices – which differ substantially from the consumer price index (CPI) or the deflator of consumption expenditure in national accounts. The methodology to compute the poverty line and even to collect data on the consumption of food products seems to have been changing over time, so there is some imprecision on the estimated evolution of poverty across the five surveys. The other set of estimates is taken from the World Bank Povcalnet database. It is based on the international poverty line, set to USD 1.9 per person – at 2011 purchasing power parity – and per day, and the same household survey sources as the NBS but made comparable over time through the CPI.[23]

---

[23] Differences in the methodology of the two sources have been discussed in some length in various papers (Hoogeveen and Ruhinduka, 2009; Mkenda et al., 2010; Atkinson and Lugo, 2014).

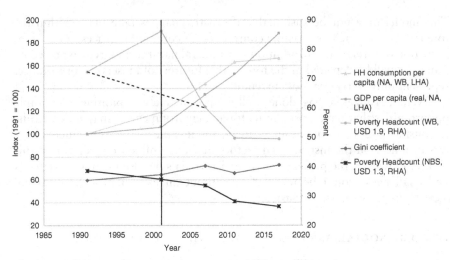

FIGURE 2.5 Consumption per capita, poverty and inequality, 1991–2017
Source: HBS (since 1990), NBS data (1991–2017), World Bank Povcalnet database (1991–2017)

According to the NBS estimates, the proportion of poor people in Tanzania has regularly declined over the last thirty years or so, even though the estimated drop is anything but impressive in view of the change that took place in GDP per capita or even household consumption per capita. Indeed, the poverty headcount fell from 39 per cent in 1991 to 26 per cent in 2017, whereas GDP per capita nearly doubled, an elasticity much lower than commonly observed. The picture painted by the World Bank estimates is quite different. First, the poverty headcount is approximately double, reflecting a discrepancy between the two sources in the definition of the poverty line. Second, poverty would have surged, rather than slowly declined, between 1991 and 2001. Accordingly, the acceleration of growth in the 2000s would have caused a sizeable drop in poverty from 2001 to 2007. The drop is still sizeable between 2007 and 2011, but no significant change has occurred since then.

Clearly, the 2001 estimate by the World Bank is wrong and inconsistent with other data sources such as consumption per capita as recorded in the national accounts. It is thus better to ignore it – as is done with the dashed line in Figure 2.5. After 2001, the two sets of estimates show a roughly consistent evolution of poverty given their implicit difference in the poverty line and the resulting value of the headcount.[24] Both show an elasticity of poverty with

---

[24] Another data source on poverty is the National Panel Survey (NPS) designed to track people and analyse individual poverty dynamics. In contradiction with data from the HBS used both by the NBS and the World Bank, it shows an increase of poverty between 2008 and 2013. Belghith et al. (2018) show that the discrepancy is due to the NPS and NBS estimates using different price indices to compare real expenditure over time.

respect to GDP per capita around unity for the 2001–11 period, an order of magnitude commonly found in sub-Saharan countries.[25] However, things seem to have changed over the recent period, since both sources show some stickiness of the poverty headcount between 2011 and 2017 despite sizeable growth of GDP per capita. It is also reported that poverty might even have slightly increased in urban areas (World Bank, 2019a, p. 7).

The main conclusion to be drawn from this discussion of poverty estimates, besides the need for more clarity in the way the poverty line is set, is that there seems to be a real challenge in Tanzania in transforming GDP growth into poverty reduction. In other words, growth has not been inclusive enough over the last twenty-five years, this being especially the case in the recent past.[26]

This conclusion is reinforced by the observed change in the degree of inequality of distribution of per capita household expenditure. Figure 2.5 shows an increasing trend in the Gini coefficient, the most usual measure of inequality, since the early 1990s, although a short-lived reversal seems to have taken place between 2007 and 2011 – which, coincides with the acceleration of poverty reduction noted in Figure 2.5. Over recent years, however, inequality has reverted to its previous rising trend. Even though Tanzania's level of inequality would probably stand below average by sub-Saharan African standards, the change that has taken place since the early 1990s is far from negligible. Economic development in Tanzania has favoured relatively more the upper part of per capita consumption scale, especially the top decile. Decile shares available in the Povcalnet database suggest that as much as two-thirds of the increase in consumption expenditures of the whole population went to the top 10 per cent. This is twice its share of total consumption. Such a situation would quickly become worrying if it were to last.

As an important footnote to the preceding discussion of inequality, it must be stressed that the inequality of consumption expenditures as recorded in household surveys is most likely underestimated. People at the very top of the distribution of living standards are unlikely to be covered in HBS, and if they were, they would most likely under-report their expenditures. Moreover, inequality of consumption expenditures is known to be substantially lower than income inequality. In the case of Tanzania, the huge discrepancy between the growth of GDP and that of consumption expenditures in the national accounts – see Figure 2.2 – suggests that the difference may be quite significant. In addition, incomes from illegal activities or corruption, judged to be substantial, escape measurement. This is where the most important source of

---

[25] See Arndt et al. (2017a). A unit elasticity was also implicit in the evolution of poverty projected by the National Strategy of Growth and Reduction of Poverty, locally known as MKUKUTA – see United Republic of Tanzania (2005, pp. 35–9).

[26] Arndt et al. (2017b)'s estimate of change in poverty through five deprivations (water, sanitation, housing, education, and TV/radio) recorded in various editions of the Demographic and Health Survey is also worth mentioning. Over 1992–2010, they find that poverty has unambiguously diminished.

inequality may lie, and it may have a sizeable impact on the economy overall depending on the use made of it by those to whom it accrues. Unfortunately, not much is known about it and about its evolution over time.[27]

B Education

The educational level of the population has enormously progressed in Tanzania, as in the rest of the sub-Saharan African region over the last two or three decades. According to the Barro-Lee database, the mean number of years of schooling in the adult population has increased from less than four years in 1990 to six and a half today. Likewise, the proportion of the population without education and who were therefore illiterate was around 15 per cent by 2015,[28] down from 27 per cent in 2000. The mean number of years of schooling has followed the sub-Saharan average, whereas the proportion of adults without education is lower in Tanzania.

If human capital in a country were measured by the number of years of education of its whole population, then it would have grown at roughly 4.5 per cent since the beginning of the millennium, less than GDP and less than the physical capital stock, but enough to contribute to productivity gains. However, looking at the performances of the education system today leads to a more nuanced view about the efforts made in the country to improve its stock of human capital.

On this account, Tanzania does not seem to be doing that well. With respect to education, the recently developed Human Capital Index by the World Bank ranks it in the bottom 10 per cent of countries ordered by increasing 'expected years of schooling' and 'learning-adjusted years of schooling'.[29] However, this does not mean that no effort is being made in the country to improve the coverage of its schooling system; quite the contrary. The difficulty would rather seem to lie in the quality of the schooling system.

As in the whole sub-Saharan region, primary school enrolment has made huge progress in Tanzania, although with pronounced fluctuations and a somewhat surprising reversal over the last few years. As can be seen in Figure 2.6, enrolment increased very rapidly after independence before receding at the time of the macroeconomic crisis and adjustments in the 1980s, and then stagnating for the next ten years. It then surged again with the launch of the 'Education

[27] Yet see Atkinson (2011) for a historical estimation of top incomes in Tanzania. According to his estimates, based on income tax date, the top 0.1 per cent was earning 5 per cent of total personal income in 1970 – declining since colonial times. This figure is comparable to the concentration of income at the top in the United States today. The publication of income tax tabulations in Tanzania was disrupted in 1970.

[28] This is the last year recorded in the Barro-Lee database.

[29] The expected number of years of schooling is the number of years a child is expected to stay in school, and it is approximated by the sum of age-specific enrolment rates. The learning adjusted years of schooling is obtained by multiplying the preceding number by a harmonised test score.

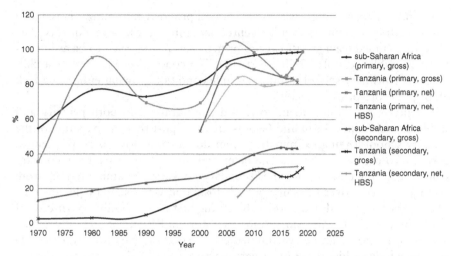

FIGURE 2.6 Primary and secondary school enrolment (gross and net) in Tanzania and the sub-Saharan region, 1970–2015 (per cent)
Source: UNESCO, WDI and NBS

for All' programme under the aegis of UNESCO and the UN's Millennium Development Goals initiative in the early 2000s. This major increase in enrolment, which resulted from the international initiatives just mentioned, and also from Tanzania's economic recovery as well as policies such as the abolishment of tuition fees, could not be sustained. After having practically become universal in the mid-2000s, enrolment had fallen back by twenty percentage points by 2015, a drop possibly underestimated according to Joshi and Gaddis (2015, p. 2). Since then, the situation has somewhat improved, but the gross enrolment rate is just below 100 per cent, whereas universal enrolment would imply a rate above that threshold: net enrolment has not recovered.[30] This trend is confirmed by the direct observation of school attendance in the national household surveys taken by the NBS.

The progress in secondary education has been steadier, although Tanzania is lagging behind regional averages. Enrolment increased from 5 per cent in 1990 to 31 per cent in 2010. Since then, it has stagnated, after sliding a bit in 2015, as for primary. Furthermore, the gap with respect to the sub-Saharan region has become larger, although a kind of plateau seems to have been reached there too.

[30] The net enrolment rate is defined as the ratio of children of official school age who are enrolled in school to the population of the corresponding official school age, whereas the gross enrolment rate would include all children in school. The gross enrolment rate is the ratio between all students enrolled in primary education, regardless of age, and the population of official primary education age.

Pre-primary schooling has also made rapid progress, and Tanzania is ahead of other African countries. Yet high enrolment rates may hide low quality. The pupil to qualified teacher ratio at pre-primary level is reported to be as high as 169:1 in public schools (UNICEF, 2017). The consequence is that most children enter primary school in unfavourable conditions, owing either to a lack of, or poor, pre-primary facilities.

Quality is also found to be low, and deteriorating, in both primary and secondary schooling. Joshi and Gaddis (2015) report that the pass rate of the primary school leaving examination went down from close to 70 per cent in 2006 to 30 per cent in 2012. The deterioration is even worse for secondary schooling, as the pass rate for the Secondary Education Examination fell from 90 to 30 per cent over the same period (Joshi and Gaddis, 2015, Figure 1.1). The deterioration is already noticeable in the first grades. Only 10 per cent of grade three students can read a grade two story in Kiswahili, and only 30 per cent have mastered grade two numeracy. In addition, this low average performance hides a high level of disparity across geographic regions and social backgrounds.

Even though Tanzania does better than most other east and southern African countries in the educational achievement tests conducted under the Southern and Eastern Africa Consortium for Monitoring Educational Quality, the drop in performance is worrying. At primary level, a possible cause may be the overcrowding of schools, partly due to the surge in enrolment in the early 2000s. The average number of pupils per teacher in primary schools closely followed the enrolment rate. It went from 45:1 in 2004 to 58:1 in 2007. The number of students per classroom increased accordingly. It is thus no surprise that the quality of schooling worsened during that period and that parents were disincentivised to send their children to schools that they knew were overcrowded (Ponera et al., 2011). However, another cause of low and falling performances in both primary and secondary schools is teacher absenteeism. Surprise inspections suggest that one out of four teachers is not in school when supposed to be there, and more than half of teachers are not in the classroom when they should be teaching. It has been estimated that students in primary school are taught for 2.4 hours a day on average, instead of the scheduled five hours. As can be expected, all these ratios are much worse in rural than in urban areas (Wane and Gaddis, 2015). Teacher absenteeism has apparently gone down since 2010, but it remains extremely high.[31]

As diagnostics for the educational sector date back to 2015, things may have changed for the better. Yet changes are known to be slow in this area. On the other hand, some indicators may have worsened. For instance, the number of primary education teachers is reported to have reduced by 5 per cent since 2016, whereas the population of children has increased by around 10 per cent.

---

[31] See Han and Peirolo (2021).

On average, the number of pupils per teacher might have increased by 15 per cent over recent years.[32]

There is most likely a direct relationship between the observed drop in primary enrolment and the deterioration in the quality of schooling, with the relationship self-reinforcing over time. Primary school overcrowding and the subsequent lowering of school quality may have disincentivised parents, as mentioned earlier, but overcrowding itself and the lack of resources in general may have disincentivised teachers, causing a further drop in quality.

A possible cause of that evolution may be the recent drop in the share of public expenditures from GDP. It was already the case that education's share in the budget had fallen by the mid-2010s, even though it was still increasing in real terms. It is too early to say, but this might not be the case in recent years, thanks to the recent tightening of expenditure, thus aggravating existing constraints on progress in the public delivery of educational services.

C Health Care

The diagnostic of the healthcare sector in Tanzania is mixed. On the one hand, some input and outcome indicators show satisfactory results, while others have evolved less favourably. On the other hand, a recent evaluation suggests important quality issues in health care delivery. In addition, the funding of the sector strongly relies on foreign assistance, and this shows no sign of decline.

Figure 2.7 shows various indicators that illustrate the contrasting performances of the health sector. Under-five mortality has undoubtedly made considerable progress since the turn of the millennium, most likely in connection with the launch of the Millennium Development Goals. This indicator went down from 148 for 1990–5 to 67 in 2010–15.[33] Thus, Tanzania was very close to achieving Millennium Development Goal number four, which was to reduce infant mortality by two-thirds between 1990 and 2015. Present trends also seem promising in view of the third Sustainable Development Goal, which requires reducing under-five mortality below twenty-five per thousand.

It is not coincidental that the fast drop in infant mortality after 1995 took place at the same time as health care expenditure per capita was growing at an accelerated pace. What is more surprising, however, is the sudden pause in that progression and the stagnation of both public and total health care spending

---

[32] The first figure is derived from information collected by UNESCO, whereas the second one is based on demographic growth estimates. To this estimate should be added the effect of the recent rebound in gross enrolment. UNESCO reports an increase in the pupil–teacher ratio in primary schools from 42:1 in 2016 to 56:1 in 2019.

[33] These figures are drawn from the various Tanzania Demographic and Health Survey reports. Note that they refer to a period extending to up to five years before the survey.

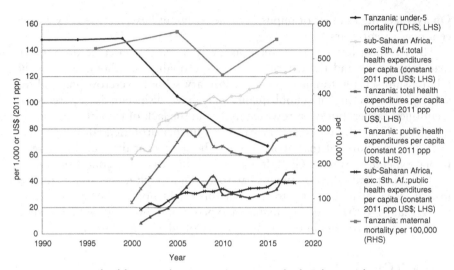

FIGURE 2.7 Some health care indicators in Tanzania and sub-Saharan Africa, 1990–2018
Source: WDI and Tanzania Demographic and Health Survey (DHS)

after a small drop in 2010,[34] a stagnation that might be related to the slowing down of progress on the child mortality front. Over the last ten years or so, the share of health expenditures in GDP has fallen, a trend that can also be observed more recently at the regional level. The gap between Tanzania and the average sub-Saharan country in real health care expenditure is striking. The fact that it essentially comes from private spending may suggest a deficit in health care infrastructure, including professionals, needed for the private provision of health care.

With essentially a flat long-run trend, the evolution of maternal mortality is less satisfactory than child mortality.[35] This seems to contradict the substantial increase documented in the Tanzanian Demographic and Health Survey in skilled delivery assistance as part of the Strategic Plan to Accelerate Reduction in Maternal, Neonatal and Child Deaths launched by the Ministry of Health and Social Security in 2008 (United Republic of Tanzania, 2016b, p. 172).

This last observation suggests that there may be some skill deficit in the provision of health care. It is not clear whether this may apply to maternal mortality, but the 2014 Health Service Delivery report by the World Bank points to such weaknesses when concluding that the 'major challenge for Tanzania's health sector is the shortage of skilled human resources for health'

---

[34] The surge in expenditures in 2006 and the following two years may be explained by the severe drought that hit the country at that time and had serious consequences for the nutrition and the health of the population.

[35] It is not certain that the fluctuation shown for 2010 is statistically significant.

(World Bank, 2014a, p. 9). The report also insists on possible gains in efficiency through increasing the caseloads of health personnel, currently low by international standards, and reducing absenteeism, although, at 14 per cent, it is much less pronounced than in the education sector.

On the financing side, a major cause of concern is the importance of foreign assistance. The share of expenditure financed by external sources has averaged 45 per cent since 2006, which suggests a serious problem of sustainability in the long run. If progress in health outcomes is to continue at the same pace as in previous years, funding will have to keep increasing faster than GDP, unlike what is being observed today. More funding will thus be needed domestically. This might come from the higher formalisation of the economy, leading to more people being covered by health insurance programmes paid for by employers through the National Social Security Fund, or, in the informal sector, from expanding the coverage of the Community Health Fund, a voluntary insurance programme. However, it is unlikely that with a premium of less than USD 10 per household and per year, the latter could become a significant source of funds for the health care system, especially given its complex decentralised governance. Further progress in health care will have to come from more resources being made available at central government level or through the cross-subsidising of health care in the informal sector by the health insurance system in the formal sector.

This expansion of health care funding and service provision is still more necessary given that large disparities are observed in most health indicators between geographical areas and, within areas, between households with different socio-economic characteristics. From that point of view, the cheapest progress in health care in Tanzania may come from extensive rather than intensive strategies – in other words, more people being covered rather than more risks being covered.

V CONCLUSION: THE MAIN ECONOMIC CHALLENGES OF TANZANIAN DEVELOPMENT

Tanzania started its independent existence with considerable economic dynamism, until it was hit on the one hand by the consequence of an ill-prepared transition towards socialism, which made the economy increasingly inefficient, and, on the other hand, by the global development crisis of the early 1980s. There followed a long and painful period of slow growth, caused by a grim international economic environment and a difficult adjustment back to a market economy. The growth acceleration observed over the last twenty years is all the more spectacular. At the current rate of growth, GDP per capita will double in twenty years, and the country has just graduated from the low-income tier of World Bank classification to become a middle-income country.

This does not mean there is no cause for concern about the long-run sustainability of the present pace and structure of economic growth. The main challenges identified throughout this chapter are listed next, before they are compared to former diagnostics about Tanzanian development, and finally a few remarks on the likely consequences of the COVID-19 crisis that recently affected Tanzania, as the rest of the world.

A Main Causes for Concern about Tanzanian Development

The first cause for concern is the uncertainty about what could be Tanzania's long-run engine of growth. To a large extent, growth during the last two decades has been pushed by the demand side of the economy, itself relying on increasing export revenues and foreign financing. Such a model is quite different from the industrialisation model that has been experienced over the last few decades in Asia, or in Latin America in the 1960s and 1970s. To be sure, the Tanzanian manufacturing sector has not underperformed; it has even been able to significantly expand exports and substitute some imports. The problem is that it is presently too small to pull the economy forward thanks to its sole area of development. Although manufacturing exports have done well, they remain a minor fraction of total exports, and it is the other fraction that has driven recent growth. The problem is that this component is essentially exogenous, depending on international prices and the foreign level of activity, and is therefore unable to feed a pace of growth faster than that of the global economy. More is needed for Tanzania to continue reducing its income gap with the rest of the world. On the other hand, circumstances may become less favourable than they have been since the turn of the millennium. A priori, there are fewer external constraints in manufacturing, agroindustry, or tradable services such as tourism. How to enhance their development?

A second cause for concern is how to sustain and, more importantly, to enhance the within-sector productivity gains observed in the last decade or so. Maintaining the investment rate at a 35 per cent level is a challenge in itself. At the same time, there are indications that such a high rate of capital formation may not be fully exploited. Moreover, there may be untapped efficiency gains that could improve productivity and competitiveness. Agriculture, for instance, has often been mentioned as under-performing in comparison with other countries in the region and the continent,[36] possibly because the difficulty in establishing firm land rights disincentivises innovation and investment.

The third source of concern may be the most serious one. It is the strong dependency of the Tanzanian economy upon foreign financing. It is true that, for several reasons, the gap between absorption and national revenue has been scaled down in recent years. However, it is not clear whether this is due to domestic structural factors and policymaking or to decisions made by foreign

---

[36] See for instance Benin (2016, Chapter 2).

donors. In any case, even during recent years, dependency has remained high. Excluding foreign grants, the deficit of the current account was still above 4 per cent of GDP on average between 2015 and 2020. ODA itself still represented more than 5 per cent of GDP over the same period, a little more than a quarter of the government budget and practically all of the public investment in infrastructure. What would happen if, for some geopolitical reason or unexpected development, this flow was to dry up? It is most unlikely that the current growth trend could be maintained.

An important unknown for the economic development of Tanzania is what will happen with its offshore natural gas reserves. These are sizeable and could provide Tanzania with substantial additional revenues for the twenty to thirty years after a five-year investment period. This would require that the international price of gas stays at a much higher level than observed throughout the 2010s. It has been seen that extraction costs are high. At this stage, it is therefore not clear whether the discovery of these reserves truly modifies the prospects of the Tanzanian economy in the reasonably near future.

A final source of concern is on the social side. Poverty is receding slowly, certainly more slowly than if the real income or consumption expenditure of all households was growing at the same rate as GDP per capita. That growth has not trickled down more systematically to all segments of the population since its acceleration at the turn of the millennium is a problem, and a challenge for the future. The reason why growth has not been inclusive lately is unclear, but action should be taken so this situation does not persist. Increasing inequality may indeed have adverse effects on future development through the demand side of the economy, by reducing the aggregate propensity to consume, and more fundamentally by undermining the social and political climate. The same applies to the stagnation of school enrolment below universal enrolment in primary school and the low quality of the educational system in general, which may put future growth, poverty reduction, and the social equilibrium at risk. More is to be done to ensure more inclusive growth and more dynamic investment in human capital.

The preceding review of the economic development challenges faced by Tanzania was essentially factual. Little was said of policy choices or the behaviour of major economic actors. Only the consequences of their actions, rather than their decisions and their behaviour, were analysed. The way in which the economic decision makers, public or private, interact and generate specific economic outcomes, including obstacles to development, depends on the complex set of rules that govern these interactions. These rules constitute the institutional framework in which development takes place. Beyond the pure economic facts reviewed in this chapter, a deeper analysis of development challenges thus requires identification of the institutional challenges causing them. This will be the task of the rest of this volume.

B Convergence with Former Diagnostics of Tanzania's Development

Several former attempts have been made in the last ten years to diagnose the main obstacles to faster economic growth in Tanzania, so it is worth checking whether they agree with the analysis in this chapter, even though the latter relies on more recent data.

A first diagnostic was undertaken in 2010 under the auspices of both the Government of Tanzania and the US government, the latter as part of the Partnership for Growth initiative (Partnership for Growth, 2011), following the methodology proposed by Hausman et al. (2005). It subsequently influenced the reflection about national development strategies, including the 'Vision 2025' report.

A similar, although more focused, exercise was undertaken two years later by the Organisation for Economic Co-operation and Development (OECD) as part of its 'Investment Policies Reviews' aimed at recommending measures to improve the investment climate and attract more foreign investors (OECD, 2013).

Finally, a more recent study is the World Bank 'Systematic Country Diagnostic', entitled 'To the next level of development', completed in February 2017. This document comprises a review of Tanzania's development since the mid-2000s similar to the one undertaken in this chapter. However, because it relies on data that do not go beyond 2015 and in some cases stop before then, it misses some important recent changes, especially with respect to the evolution of productivity, poverty, and income distribution.

Overall, the diagnostics brought forward by these various studies are convergent and very much overlap with the analysis in the present chapter. Yet their main objective is to identify possible economic and, in some cases, institutional bottlenecks for development rather than more structural factors that slow down or threaten future development as attempted earlier in this chapter. Institutional issues and some of the bottlenecks pinpointed in these growth diagnostic studies will be considered in more detail later in this volume. For further reference, however, the priority policy areas they single out are the following – with the agency supporting them noted in brackets:

- infrastructure, especially power supply and spatial integration (United States–Government of Tanzania, OECD, World Bank);
- lack of vocational, technical, and professional skills (United States–Government of Tanzania, OECD, World Bank);
- appropriability of returns: insecurity of land rights (United States–Government of Tanzania, OECD), high and volatile tax rates (OECD);
- lack of access to finance for small and medium-sized enterprises (SMEs) and agriculture (United States–Government of Tanzania, OECD, World Bank);
- disorganised regulation of business (OECD);
- low quality of civil service and delivery of public goods (World Bank);
- weak institutional capacity to manage natural resources (World Bank);
- mobilisation of government revenues (World Bank).

C The COVID-19 Crisis in Tanzania

Clearly, the recent past has been very much influenced by the COVID-19 crisis, and this is why the review in this chapter stopped before 2020. Because it may influence future development, a word must be said about its impact on the economy and the population.

It is difficult to get a clear idea about the health impact of COVID-19 in Tanzania because of the denial of the existence of such a pandemic by the then president, John Magufuli. As soon as May 2020, President Magufuli lifted the few restrictions initially set on public gatherings, schools, and universities, and declared the nation free of COVID-19. He eschewed lockdowns, discouraged the use of face masks, and banned the release of infection data. Information about the spread of the pandemic was tightly controlled. Talking publicly about signs of the pandemic, as for instance the rising frequency of burials, was strictly prohibited.

It is unclear why President Magufuli adopted such a posture and went as far as advising sick people to go to church to be cured. He always wanted to appear as a man who was inflexible about work and did not take sickness as an excuse. A few days before getting sick himself, he inaugurated a new road in Dar es Salaam, and congratulated the contractor and the workers for completing the work in time and for 'no-one [having] used corona as an excuse to delay it'. His government had become more and more authoritarian over time, and he handled what he saw as essentially a distraction from work for the whole population in the same imperious way he handled other affairs that he thought could threaten the country's development. Of course, such an attitude denotes a worrying denial of reality and a complete lack of a sense of responsibility, which indeed characterised some aspects of management throughout his mandate.

Meanwhile, hospitals were crowded and were rejecting patients, oxygen was becoming scarce, and funeral announcements were multiplied by three to four times. Several high-ranked politicians or policymakers are known to have died from COVID-19, including the author of one of the chapters in this volume. President Magufuli himself died in March 2021 officially from a heart attack, but many suspect this was COVID-19. He was replaced by the vice president, Samia Suluhu Hassan, who immediately reverted to an open and effective treatment of the pandemic.

Estimates of the impact of COVID-19 in Tanzania are still imprecise. According to (still provisional) national accounts, GDP growth receded to 2 per cent in 2019 from roughly 6 per cent in the preceding years. The order of magnitude of the economic cost of the pandemic would thus have been around 4 per cent of GDP. Such a recession meant that GDP per capita went down for the first time since the 1990s. At less than 1 per cent, the drop is limited, though. It is lower than in other sub-Saharan countries that imposed severe lockdown on their population. In Rwanda, for instance, GDP is estimated to have fallen by as much as 3.5 per cent. At the same time, the health casualties may have been lower there than in Tanzania, precisely because of the measures taken to prevent the spreading of the virus. Without reasonable estimates for Tanzania, it is difficult to say.

The 2020 slowdown in GDP was caused by a drop in traditional exports and tourism owing to the COVID-19 crisis in the rest of the world, and also because of precautionary behaviour by the population in light of the diffusion of the virus – and possibly some proportion of the population being infected and becoming temporarily sick. During June and July 2020, the World Bank ran a survey covering 1,000 SMEs to measure the impact of the pandemic. It was found that as much as 140,000 formal jobs, or roughly 5 per cent of total formal employment, were lost, whereas 2.2 non-farm informal workers, roughly one-third, suffered income losses. However, it is difficult to go from such observations at one point in time to estimates of the overall impact of the crisis upon poverty. Estimates have been circulated according to which the poverty headcount went from 26.1 per cent in 2019 to 27.2 per cent at the end of 2020.[37]

As far as the future is concerned, GDP growth is forecast to be around 4 per cent in 2021, below the trend over the last ten years or so. Huge vaccination efforts are presently being made and improvements in health services are being implemented to increase the capacity of the system to deal with possible new waves of infection. Tanzania was also provided with emergency loans by the IMF and is expecting more aid from other donors to address the consequences of the COVID-19 crisis. This makes the prospects for 2022 look a bit more favourable.

APPENDIX

A.1   SECTORAL DECOMPOSITION OF CHANGES
IN OVERALL LABOUR PRODUCTIVITY

This decomposition is based on the following identity behind that decomposition as follows:

$$\Delta \frac{Q}{L} = \sum_i \left(\frac{\overline{Q_i}}{L_i} \right) \Delta L_i + \sum_i \overline{L_i} \Delta \left(\frac{Q_i}{L_i} \right)$$

where Q_i and L_i stand for GDP and employment in sector i, and Q and L for the same at the aggregate level. The upper bar notation stands for averaging across the initial and final period.

The first term corresponds to structural change, the reallocation of labour, whereas the second stands for the within-sector productivity effect. The figures in Table 2.A.1 correspond to the terms in the preceding equation after dividing both sides by the initial labour productivity, Q/L.

The same decomposition for Tanzania's productivity growth for the period 2002–12 can be found in McMillan et al. (2017).

---

[37] All the preceding figures are from World Bank (2021). Nothing is said there about the way the poverty estimate was obtained.

TABLE 2.A.1 *Full decomposition of overall labour productivity growth into structural change and within-sector productivity components, 1960–2018*

(%)	1960–1997 (GGDC release 2014, GDP at 2005 prices)		1997–2007 (GGDC release 2021, GDP at 2015 prices)		2007–2018 (GGDC release 2021, GDP at 2015 prices)	
	Structural change	Within-sector productivity	Structural change	Within-sector productivity	Structural change	Within-sector productivity
Agriculture	-3.5	8.0	-4.7	7.6	-2.9	12.5
Mining	5.6	-7.4	-0.4	3.8	2.0	-0.1
Manufacturing	2.8	0.9	3.6	0.1	2.0	3.7
Utilities	3.5	-1.1	-1.0	1.2	0.4	0.0
Construction	13.5	-11.5	3.3	3.0	6.8	5.9
Trade and hospitality	54.9	-52.8	7.0	-4.6	4.4	0.9
Transport, storage, and communication	9.7	-7.2	7.3	-5.0	2.8	1.7
Finance, insurance, real estate, and business services	3.2	0.3	7.6	-1.5	5.7	-0.1
Government services	-1.3	6.6	-0.2	5.2	1.7	2.1
Community, social, and personal services	-0.1	0.8	3.2	-3.2	-0.6	0.9
Whole economy	88.3	-63.4	25.7	6.8	22.3	27.5
Overall change	24.8		32.5		49.9	

Source: Author's calculation from Groningen Growth Development Centre database.

3

Gathering Evidence on the Quality of Institutions

François Bourguignon and François Libois

The objective of this chapter is to collect insights from different sources and different people about institutional features that may slow down economic development in Tanzania or threaten its sustainability and inclusiveness.

It essentially follows three approaches, and these are presented in separate sections. First, by exploiting the numerous institutional indicators available in international databases, insights were collected about the quality of Tanzanian institutions in comparison with a set of relevant countries. Insights aim to identify those institutional features that may possibly differentiate Tanzania. Second, an original questionnaire survey was undertaken among various types of decision makers operating in Tanzania. The survey asked them about their own perception of how institutions worked there and how they affect development. Finally, the analysis was enriched by the summary of the main points that arose in a large set of open-ended interviews with top policymakers of the country about the same questions. The final section concludes.

I INSTITUTIONAL INDICATORS: HOW 'DIFFERENT' IS TANZANIA AMONG DEVELOPING COUNTRIES?

The development community has long known that institutions matter for development, and several country-level indicators describing various aspects of institutions, especially those that have to do with governance, have developed over time. They are meant to facilitate cross-country comparisons and to correlate, in a rough way and most often on a cross-sectional basis, institutional or governance quality with growth or other development indicators. Many such international databases now exist. They either focus on a specific institutional area – democracy, corruption, ease of doing business – or cover a wide range of themes. The Worldwide Governance Indicators (WGI) provide synthetic indicators obtained from extracting from these datasets some common factors in pre-defined institutional areas.[1]

Quantitative indicators reported in these cross-country datasets generally reflect expert opinion on some specific aspect of institutions in a country. They may not coincide with the way people within a country perceive them. This is the reason why this analysis of the specificity of Tanzania in the space of cross-country institutional indicators is extended to more specialised and more pragmatically oriented databases that are not included in the WGI. This is the case of the World Bank enterprise surveys that collect the opinion of firm managers or the African Barometer, which surveys the public on some more focused institutional issues.

A How Different Is Tanzania Using the Synthetic WGI?

Figure 3.1 compares Tanzania with two sets of comparator countries and according to the six synthetic indicators present in the WGI database for 2018. The six indicators refer to the following institution-related areas: 'Control of corruption', 'Government effectiveness', 'Political stability and lack of violence', 'Regulatory quality', 'Rule of Law', and 'Voice and accountability'. Comparator countries are of two types:

- *Neighbour countries* may share a close history, similar environmental conditions, comparative advantages, or political and economic organisations. The issue is thus whether such a common background does exist and, most importantly, whether Tanzania departs in any way from it, or on the contrary conforms with it. This group includes the East African community (Burundi, Kenya, Rwanda, Uganda), to which we add three countries on the southern border of Tanzania (Malawi, Mozambique, and Zambia).[2]
- Another natural set of comparators are those countries that were at the same level of development, as measured by gross domestic product (GDP) per capita, as Tanzania twenty or thirty years ago and have done better since. These *outperforming peer countries* are all in Asia: Bangladesh, Lao and Vietnam have gained between 60 and 150 per cent in GDP per capita over Tanzania since 1990, and Cambodia substantially less (30 per cent). The issue is whether these outperformers present institutional features significantly different from Tanzania, which might explain their better performance or be a consequence of faster growth.

Before discussing the charts shown in Figure 3.1, a word must be said about the WGI database and the way these indicators are measured. As mentioned, each

---

[1] The methodology used in the construction of these synthetic indicators may be found in Kaufmann and Kraay (2002), whereas the datasets of individual expert-based institutional indicators utilised are listed in WGI-Interactive Data Access on WorldBank.org.

[2] South Sudan and Democratic Republic of Congo were not included owing to a lack of data.

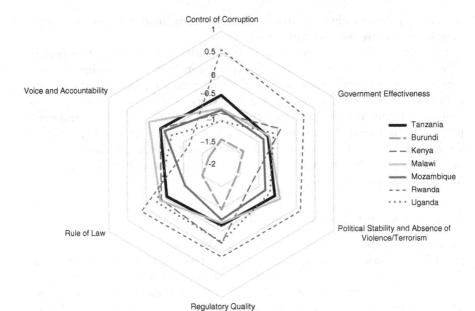

FIGURE 3.1a WGI: Tanzania and neighbour countries, 2018

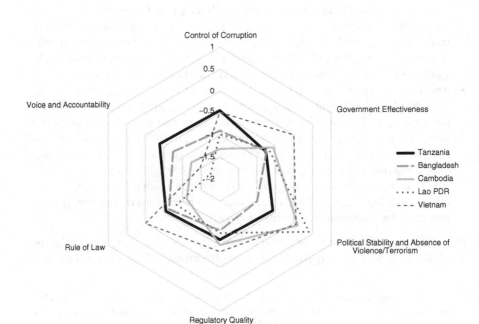

FIGURE 3.1b WGI: Tanzania and outperforming peer countries, 2018

synthetic indicator results from the combination of those individual indicators in the original datasets that belong to each institutional area being considered – corruption, regulation, rule of law, and so on. Synthetic indicators thus capture the common information in the underlying set of individual indicators; that is, how they differ across countries. They are normalised with mean zero and unit standard deviation. As their distribution across countries is not far from being normal, their value, between –2 and +2, indicates where a country ranks in the global ordering according to a particular synthetic indicator. Roughly speaking, 0 would correspond to the median and –.5, around which most countries in Figure 3.1 tend to concentrate, would roughly correspond to the third decile from the bottom. Thus, most countries in the figure are in the middle part of the lower half of the global ranking – which comprises more than 200 countries.

A striking feature of Tanzania, taken in isolation, is the relative balance that is observed among the various indicators. If it were not for 'government effectiveness', its radar chart would be an almost perfect regular hexagon. An obvious conclusion is thus that most institutional areas described by the WGI in Tanzania are weak by international standards – that is, at the limit of the bottom third of the global ranking – but government effectiveness is a bit weaker than the others.

The comparison of Tanzania with neighbour countries shows both convergence and divergence. On the one hand, there are clearly two outliers in the region: Burundi with uniformly extremely weak WGI scores and, at the other extreme, Rwanda with scores high enough to reach the sixtieth global percentile in all institutional dimensions but 'voice and accountability', a clear reflection of its rather autocratic but otherwise effective leadership regime. On the other hand, Tanzania's institutional profile turns out to be very similar to that of the other countries in the region. In Figure 3.1, Tanzania generally lies in the middle of the range defined by its neighbours – Uganda, Kenya, Mozambique, Malawi – in all areas except the control of corruption, where it apparently does less badly. Overall, if it were not for the very peculiar institutional quality profile of Burundi and Rwanda, two countries deeply marked, in opposite directions, by what has probably been the most tragic ethnic conflict in the history of the African continent, the left-hand chart of Figure 3.1 would suggest a rather homogeneous and moderately weak institutional quality profile for Tanzania and the Eastern Africa region.

When comparing Tanzania with outperforming peer countries on the right-hand panel of Figure 3.1, four features are noticeable: (1) the superiority of Tanzania over all countries in 'voice and accountability' and, to a lesser degree, the 'control of corruption'; (2) the neat dominance of Vietnam in all other dimensions; (3) the relative disadvantage of Tanzania in the area of political stability – which is a bit surprising given precisely the stability of its democracy until quite recently; and (4) the similarity between Tanzania and other better performing countries in other areas. The main point, however, is that, despite those outperforming countries having grown considerably faster than Tanzania from the late 1980s to the mid-2010s, no strong differences seem to be present in their institutional quality profile, except for the superiority of Tanzania on the democratic front and the outstanding performance of Vietnam. Therefore, with the exception of the latter, growth does not seem to have brought a significant institutional advantage to the other outperformers. It is striking that Tanzania even dominates Bangladesh in all areas.

One could object to the preceding comparison with the outperforming peers that it should be carried out not in the most recent period but in the past, when income per capita in those countries was actually overtaking Tanzania's. Figure 3.2 is the equivalent of Figure 3.1 for 2005. On the basis of the right-hand panel, it certainly cannot be said that outperformers were institutionally dominating Tanzania; it might even have been the contrary. However, what is striking is that, when comparing 2005 with 2018, all outperformers have substantially improved the quality of their institutions whereas little has changed in Tanzania, except for a slight improvement in the control of corruption, most likely the result of President Magufuli's anti-corruption campaign, and a more sizeable worsening of government effectiveness. Faster growth among outperformers is thus associated with institutional improvement over time rather than some initial institutional advantage, which is an interesting observation.

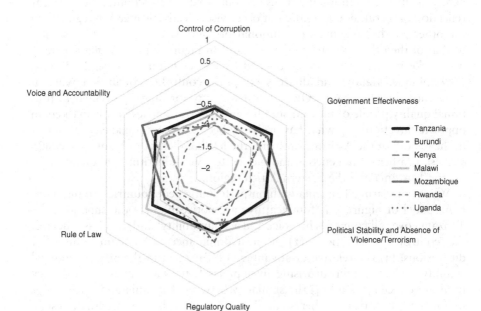

FIGURE 3.2a WGI: Tanzania and neighbour countries, 2005

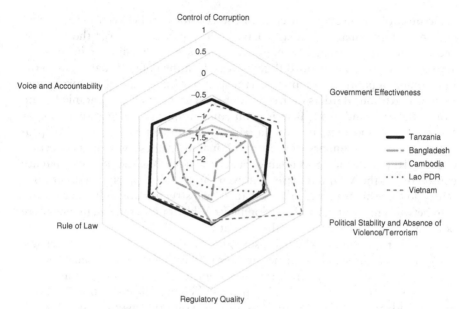

FIGURE 3.2b WGI: Tanzania and outperforming peer countries, 2005

    The same can be said of the comparison between the left-hand panel of Figures 3.1 and 3.2. It appears there that neighbour countries in general have witnessed some improvement in the quality of their institutions, whereas this is not the case of Tanzania. As a matter of fact, it is noticeable that Tanzania practically dominated Burundi, Kenya, Rwanda, and Uganda in almost all areas in 2005, whereas it only dominates Burundi in 2018. It can thus be said that, in relative terms with respect to its neighbours and outperforming peers, the quality of institutions in Tanzania has somewhat deteriorated – except in the control of corruption – even though its ranking in the international scale may not have significantly changed.

B Exploring Alternative Synthetic Indicators

The conclusions from the comparison of WGI between Tanzania and comparator countries are interesting, and should somehow contribute to the institutional diagnostic of Tanzania: relative homogeneity of institutional quality at a low-middle international level across WGI areas, convergence with neighbour countries except Burundi and Rwanda, progress in the control of corruption, which may turn out to be less of a problem than in most comparator countries, less political stability but more democracy than outperforming peer countries, and limited improvement of institutional quality over time with respect to comparator countries. Yet the issue arises whether these conclusions may depend on the specificity of WGI synthetic indicators, in particular the way they are obtained from a variety of individual indicators and the fact that they are defined across the whole range of world nations.

Because of the growing interest in the relationship between development and institutions, many databases have been put together over the last few decades that rely on expert opinion to compare the quality of institutions across countries and in many different areas, be it the Polity IV database on the functioning of political institutions, Transparency International on corruption, Reporters without Borders on freedom of speech, the World Economic Forum Competitiveness index, the Bertelsmann Foundation Transformation Index, or Varieties of Democracy, to quote a few. As mentioned earlier, the WGI provides a statistical summary of those individual indicators found in a collection of these datasets, which presumably are related to each of the six areas that are considered in the WGI database. But even though they clearly make intuitive sense, do these areas provide the best analytical structure to study the relationship between institutions and development? Why not other areas, maybe more political or sociological, or possibly sub-areas?

The other question is whether a statistical summary based on the heterogeneity observed among all countries in the world is the best instrument to study the way institutions may affect the development process among countries at an early stage of economic development. Differences in institutional quality between advanced countries and low-income countries may not be of much relevance when trying to understand how institutions may be an obstacle to reach lower-middle income status. Would the synthetic WGI in the six institutional areas defined in that database be the same if they had been built on a sample of developing countries only?

To answer these questions, the Institutional Diagnostic Project has explored a set of alternative indicators based on developing countries and endogenously defined institutional areas. These are based on the Quality of Government (QoG) database managed at the University of Goteborg, which functions as a kind of repository of all databases gathering expert opinion in institutional areas (Teorell et al., 2022). They boast today more than 2,000 individual indicators covering more than seventy years and most countries of the world, even though, of course, not all indicators are available for every year and every country – very far from it. Only a subset of developing countries and indicators were selected so as to avoid missing data and to strictly focus on institutional characteristics. As a result, the size of the country sample and the set of individual indicators were severely reduced, even when working on a single year.[3]

Instead of predefining categories of individual indicators related to a single theme such as the control of corruption or the rule of law in the WGI database, a statistical procedure was used to regroup individual indicators by their informational proximity, or more precisely by their capacity to rank countries in roughly comparable order, while maximising the difference in rankings

---

[3] Unfortunately, the collection of datasets in the QoG database changes over time, which makes comparability over time difficult, or applies constraints when working on the limited number of datasets available over the time span being studied.

produced by distinct synthetic indicators. Each group or category of individual indicators is then summarised by a single synthetic indicator, in the same way as the synthetic WGI summarise all individual indicators behind 'regulatory quality' or 'government effectiveness'. A statistical pseudo-cluster analysis permits us to endogenously define an arbitrary number of such categories with a methodology that is somehow equivalent to minimising the country-variability of individual indicators within categories and maximising differences between them.[4] To get a set of categories comparable with the WGI, it was arbitrarily decided to define six categories.[5]

The novelty of this procedure lies in the statistical categorising of individual indicators based on how similar their variation across countries is, while not paying attention to what they represent. With the procedure used to summarise the informational content of all individual indicators in a category, the method extracts maximum information from the overall set of individual indicators in the database through a small arbitrary number of synthetic indicators.

The drawback of this methodology, compared with the WGI, is to make the labelling of categories less intuitive. As variables are grouped in an agnostic way, as a function of their informational content but not of their labelling, it may not be obvious a priori to find a common label. The intuition, however, is that, if the informational content across countries is similar, they must be related to some common institutional area. Experience shows that commonalities among indicators belonging to the same group are sufficient to encapsulate them under a single theme.

In our comparison of Tanzania with other countries, 160 individual indicators were selected from the QoG covering forty-five developing countries with no missing information. The preceding methodology was then applied to this subset of the QoG database, and resulted into six categories of individual indicators, each one being summarised by a synthetic indicator. Table 3.1 presents these six indicators, reporting the number of variables falling in each category and the common approximate theme they seem to cover. When needed, and to differentiate these indicators from the WGI, they will be labelled 'QoG-DGC' synthetic indicators (DGC for developing countries) in what follows.[6]

It is interesting that this purely statistical categorisation of indicators led to a grouping that is not very different from the a priori grouping used by the WGI mentioned earlier. Yet there are noticeable and interesting differences. For instance, administrative capacity – or government effectiveness – and

<hr/>

[4] For a similar cluster analysis approach, see Chavent et al. (2011).

[5] A statistical test permits us to check how significant it would be to further disaggregate the set of individual indicators. It would have been possible to go beyond six categories, but with the risk of finding an increasing number of categories comprising a restricted number of individual indicators.

[6] These synthetic indicators are also sometimes used in companion case studies within the Institutional Diagnostic Project.

TABLE 3.1 *The six QoG-DGC synthetic indicators*

Group	Number of indicators in the QoG database	Label
G1	15	Corruption
G2	20	Administrative and regulatory capacity
G3	29	Conflict and violence
G4	14	Competitiveness (World Economic Forum)
G5	24	Democracy and accountability
G6	56	Voice and civil society

regulatory capacity are now a single indicator, suggesting that both are some-what correlated across the developing countries in the database. This was not the case with the WGI. The same is observed with the control of corruption and the rule of law, which are now amalgamated as the issue of corruption. On the opposite side, voice and accountability in WGI are now separated into 'voice and civil society' and 'democracy and accountability'. 'Voice and civil society' groups variables with a societal content. 'Democracy and accountability' describes more specifically the way political institutions work.

Overall, it is rather satisfactory to see that the institutional areas thought to be important play an important role in differentiating developing countries, and also that nuances need to be introduced, which are not present in the a priori categorisation used in WGI. That it is difficult to distinguish corruption and the rule of law, or that it makes sense in developing countries to distinguish between the autonomy of civil society and individuals on the one hand, and indicators describing the functioning of the parliament or the relationship between the executive and the judiciary on the other are useful warnings when embarking on an institutional diagnostic of a country.

Figure 3.3 is the replica with QoG-DGC indicators of Figure 3.1 built around the WGI. Both charts refer to 2018, and it can be seen they are convergent. The same regularity among the six axes is observed for Tanzania with some more weakness in 'administrative and regulatory capacity'. In the comparison with neighbour countries, Tanzania still dominates Burundi but is close to other countries, except Rwanda – excluding 'civil society and voice' – a feature that was already present in Figure 3.1. As before, Tanzania does better than all countries but Rwanda in the control of corruption. When compared with outperforming peer countries in the right-hand chart, Tanzania appears a bit stronger than in Figure 3.1. It dominates Bangladesh – as before – but still appears weaker than other countries with respect to administrative and regulatory capacity and conflict and violence. Thus, the conclusion obtained earlier that institutional quality in outperforming peer countries was not over-whelmingly above that of Tanzania, and that Tanzania clearly dominated in terms of political institutions – that is, 'voice and accountability' in Figure

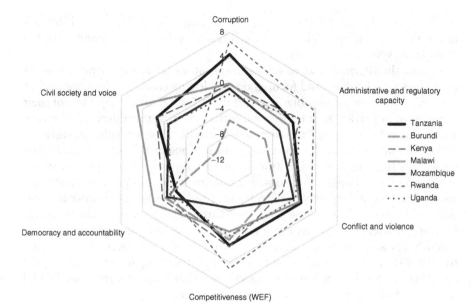

FIGURE 3.3a QoG-DGC synthetic indicators: Tanzania versus neighbour countries

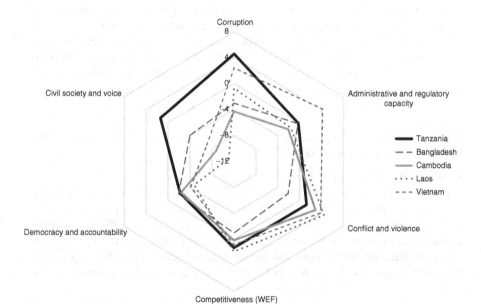

FIGURE 3.3b QoG-DGC synthetic indicators: Tanzania versus outperforming peer countries

3.1, 'civil society and voice' in Figure 3.3 – is maintained. The main difference lies in the evaluation of Vietnam, which is relatively less favourable with the QoG-DGC synthetic indicators.

In sum, the alternative set of synthetic indicators derived in the present study from the QoG database and focused on developing countries does not lead us to modify the conclusions obtained with the WGI. This is clearly a test of their robustness. In particular, it is remarkable that ignoring the differences between advanced and developing countries, which are likely to strongly structure the WGI, does not really modify the relative institutional profile of Tanzania when set against those of the comparator countries considered in the present study. One could have thought that some institutions would differ across countries mostly because of the gap between advanced and developing countries but that this would matter less among the latter. Corruption may be a case in point. It clearly matters a lot when examining differences among all countries, as it is much less acute among advanced countries. It was not necessarily expected to be a differentiating feature when restricting the comparison to developing countries. It possibly reflects the importance that experts behind individual indicators put on that specific institutional feature.

C Tanzanian Institutions According to Other Indicators

Individual indicators in the databases used to build synthetic institutional indicators often originate from experts who presumably have inside knowledge about the way institutions work in a country and are able to make cross-country comparisons. Views may be different among people who are more directly exposed to the functioning of a country's institutions, as citizens or firm managers. As a complement to the preceding analysis of synthetic expert indicators, this section compares Tanzania with the same set of countries using two surveys that are representative of users of institutions: the World Bank Enterprise Survey,[7] and the Afrobarometer (for the sub-Saharan comparator countries).

• World Bank Enterprise Survey
The Work Bank Enterprise Survey is a firm-level survey based on a representative sample of private firms, which collects the opinion of entrepreneurs on their working conditions and their daily experience with the institutional fabric of the country, including the government and public agencies. Their concerns are thus as much about the functioning of some particular institutions (law, regulation) as about the availability of key inputs or infrastructure. The

---

[7] One may wonder why no direct use was made of the Country Policy and Institutions Assessments published annually by the World Bank for low and lower-middle-income countries. The point is that this dataset, as well as its equivalent in other multilateral development banks, is already included in the datasets that the WGI are based upon.

survey asks, among other things, whether business owners and top managers identify a given topic as a major constraint.

Unlike the situation with the synthetic indicators reviewed earlier, the Tanzanian institutional context of firms is felt to be very constraining. Figure 3.4 shows how various areas are felt as more constraining by firms in the same set of countries as earlier. Firm managers in all neighbour countries but Burundi feel much less constrained than in Tanzania. Compared with out-performing peers, the difference is even more striking. Less than 15 per cent of firms feel constrained in those countries, except in Bangladesh where, as in Tanzania, corruption and electricity shortages appear to be a major constraint for more than half of the firms.

The perception of Tanzanian entrepreneurs, however, appears more negative than their actual experience. If corruption is reported as a major constraint by almost half of firms in Tanzania, only a fifth effectively experience the payment of bribes, a value substantially lower than the sub-Saharan average (a quarter) and lower than Burundi (almost a third), or Kenya and Malawi (around a quarter). The dimension in which Tanzania clearly underperforms is in the share of firms that expect to give gifts to secure contracts with the government. On this specific question, two-thirds of Tanzanian firms answer positively, much more than in neighbour countries but at a level comparable with Cambodia, Laos, and Vietnam. It suggests that in some contexts corruption is institutionalised in such a way that firms fully internalise it and do not perceive it as a constraint, while they are more perceptive in other contexts where corruption looks more like rent extraction.

The relatively pessimistic perception of firms in Tanzania and the contrast with their practical experience appear again in the relationship of firms with the tax administration. Senior Tanzanian managers report that, on average, they spend 2 per cent of their time dealing with the tax administration. This is below most of the comparator countries. Still, it translates into the worst perception of the tax administration compared with all other countries. The length of procedures may explain these differences. Interaction with public officials might not be that costly in monetary terms or in actual time spent, even if things do not move forward.

An interesting conclusion that comes from this brief review of the World Bank Enterprise Surveys in connection with the deeper analysis of synthetic institutional or governance indicators made earlier is that the context in which people assess the quality of their institutional environment matters. Experts may be right that, practically, corruption and rent-seeking in Tanzania tend to be milder than in other developing countries since Tanzanian entrepreneurs altogether seem to pay fewer bribes. Yet entrepreneurs may be more sensitive to the fact that some of them make such payments. Whether facts or perception matter more for development is an open question, but perception does drive actual behaviour, at least partially.

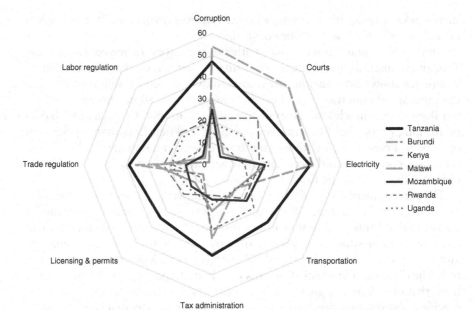

FIGURE 3.4a Perceived constraints in World Bank Enterprise Surveys: Tanzania versus neighbour countries

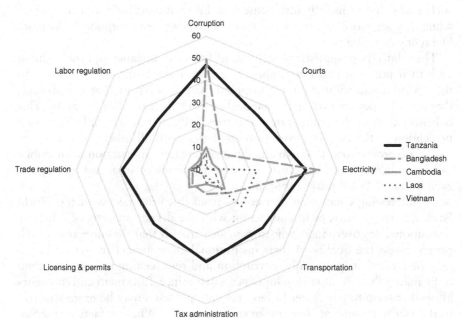

FIGURE 3.4b Perceived constraints in World Bank Enterprise Surveys: Tanzania versus outperforming peer countries

• **Afrobarometer**

The Afrobarometer is a representative sample survey that aims to collect attitudes of African citizens towards democracy, governance, living conditions, civil society, and related topics. It is managed by a network of think-tanks in Africa and presently covers thirty-five countries.

When comparing Tanzania with neighbour countries,[8] the striking institutional feature observed in the 2012 wave of the Afrobarometer is doubtlessly the relative lack of trust of its citizens.[9] Tanzanians do not trust their governments very much, but they are also reluctant to trust their friends and relatives. They also report being dissatisfied with the functioning of their democracy, despite their democracy being stronger than elsewhere – as expert-based synthetic indicators analysed earlier strongly suggest.

Their comparatively limited trust of the state apparatus is surprisingly not related to major differences in how Tanzanians evaluate the performance of their government. If anything, Tanzanians are slightly more satisfied than their neighbours in terms of the delivery of public goods – education, health, possibly water. One potential explanation of this apparent contradiction may be a higher level of expectations. Independently of other considerations, it seems only natural to them that their government delivers in terms of public services.[10] This is surprisingly in stark contrast with neighbour countries.

Another factor correlated to the low level of trust in Tanzania is probably the perception of high-level corruption. A third of survey respondents think that most people in the office of the prime minister and the president were corrupt. This figure is two times lower in neighbouring countries, even accounting for the fact that Burundi pushes the average upwards. For members of parliament and government officials, Tanzania is ranked the highest in perception of corruption. Still, when people are asked about the actual corruption that they directly experience, the picture is more nuanced. Mozambique and Kenya show a lower frequency of bribes than Tanzania, whether it is to get documents, secure access to water, health, and education services, or to avoid trouble with the police, whereas the opposite is true of Uganda, Malawi, and Burundi. However, one type of side payment is three times more frequent in Tanzania than in neighbouring countries: it consists of compensatory gifts, whether food and money, in return for votes (27 per cent versus 9 per cent).

---

[8] Owing to data availability, neighbour countries include Burundi, Kenya, Malawi, Mozambique, and Uganda. Rwanda is not among them because the government did not authorise the Afrobarometer surveying of the population.

[9] The Afrobarometer survey is taken approximately every four years, but the 2016 wave was very much influenced by the recent election of President Magufuli with a rather disruptive platform. The 2012 wave seemed more typical of the pre-Magufuli era, which is the main focus of the present study.

[10] This is the interpretation given by a large majority of Tanzanians choosing statement b) from between the two following statements (question 21): a) The government is like a parent. It should decide what is good for us; b) The government is like our employee. We are the bosses and should tell government what to do.

Tanzanians also express rather different views from their neighbours on democracy and the way it is supposed to work. Half of the surveyed people think that their country is not a democracy, or that it is a democracy with major problems. Again, these figures reflect the perception of citizens about their institutions and not the hard facts about how institutions work. They substantially differ from the expert opinion reviewed earlier and depend a lot on respondents' reference points or hopes for their country. Still, digging further, Tanzanians also complain about not being able to say what they want (55 per cent in Tanzania versus 14 per cent in neighbouring countries) and not being free to join political organisations (69 per cent versus 10 per cent). More than two-thirds of Tanzanian citizens call for a more accountable government, even at the cost of slower political decisions.

As an intermediate conclusion, it is important to put these perceptions in perspective. Among the six neighbouring countries being compared, Tanzania ranks second in terms of GDP per capita (purchasing power parity corrected) and growth rate. If Kenya is slightly above Tanzania, the other four countries are way below. Despite this good relative performance, only one-fifth of Tanzanians assess the economic performance of their country as fairly good or very good, while one-third of the neighbouring populations do. Actually, Tanzanians may display a negative bias in making judgements about their country, an attitude that may reflect high expectations and not necessarily unsatisfactory achievements.

This bias is even more striking when comparing the 2012 and 2016 waves of the Afrobarometer. Abrupt changes are observed. The perception of corruption is then on a par with neighbour countries, if not below, whereas trust in the government and state apparatus rises above most neighbour countries. Of course, this sudden and abrupt change in perceptions should be taken with care – on the one hand because actual behaviour has not changed as much, and on the other hand because the 2016 Afrobarometer wave in Tanzania was clearly very much affected by the recent election of a rather disruptive candidate to the presidency on a rather aggressive anti-corruption platform. To conform with the focus of the present study on the pre-Magufuli period, the preceding discussion of the Afrobarometer results refer to the 2012 wave.

D Insights Gained by Comparing Tanzania with Other Countries

The main conclusion from the comparison of Tanzania with other countries is that Tanzania does not show any clear specificity in terms of institutional quality among neighbouring countries when obvious outlier comparators – that is, Burundi and Rwanda – are ignored. This conclusion has several possible explanations. One is that the indicators used in the comparison are too vague and too aggregate to show how specific the institutional landscape may be in a given country. More detailed indicators could show deeper differences, but, by their construction, they would refer to one, possibly limited, side of the landscape. The comparison with those countries that outperformed Tanzania's growth does not show a clear institutional disadvantage of the latter in recent years. However, it is clearly the case that outperformers have been able to substantially improve their institutional quality in the last fifteen years – that is, between 2005 and 2018 – whereas Tanzania did not in any significant way. Neighbour countries also improved, albeit by less than outperformers – Rwanda being from that point of view a clear outlier.

Representative surveys conducted among firm managers and citizens yield additional insights. More than in the case of expert-based synthetic indicators, however, the problem of the reference point emerges when comparing countries. It is not clear whether differences between Tanzania and comparator countries are driven by intrinsic differences in institutional quality or by distinct reference points among respondents living in different environments. Both the World Bank Enterprise Survey and the Afrobarometer suggest that Tanzanians are more demanding of their formal institutions. This could ease up institutional reforms but does not say much about how constraining the quality of institutions may be for development.

A last remark is in order about the comparison exercise conducted in this section, in the spirit of so many studies of this kind. As already mentioned, the choice of comparator countries is crucial. Observed differences may possibly reveal a particular challenge in a country, which then needs deeper investigation. In the present case, however, care must be taken because comparator countries as well as Tanzania have in common an institutional context of relatively low quality. It is not because the control of corruptions is estimated to be slightly better in Tanzania than in the comparator countries used in the present analysis that corruption may not be detrimental to its development. In other words, the often-heard argument that corruption or another symptom of institutional deficiency 'is as bad here than among neighbours or even outperformers' in no way reduces their deleterious potential impact on development.

II THE COUNTRY INSTITUTIONAL SURVEY: TANZANIAN DECISION MAKERS' OPINIONS ON THEIR INSTITUTIONS

The Country Institutional Survey (CIS) is a sample survey tool developed as part of the Institutional Diagnostic Project.[11] It aims to identify institutional challenges as they are perceived by people most likely to confront them on a

[11] At this stage, the authors would like to acknowledge the role of the Research on Development Policy (REPOA) in completing and analysing this survey. REPOA appointed and trained enumerators, contacted respondents, and administered the survey. Abel Kinyondo provided detailed comments on the questionnaire and then on responses that greatly improved the analysis of the results, although he may not agree with all of the conclusions stated here. Last but not least, Katie McIntosh, then from Oxford Policy Management (OPM), dedicated very much of her time to the supervision of the survey. Her role has been crucial for its satisfactory completion.

regular basis. Given its broad sample of respondents, CIS intends to yield more diverse views and deeper insights into the way institutions work than expert-based institutional indicators in international databases.

The pilot CIS, carried out in Tanzania in early 2017, targeted individuals who had been or were in a first- or second-tier decision-making position in business, public administration, academia, non-profit organisations, or local branches of development agencies. They daily interacted with Tanzanian institutions, and possibly also affected the way they functioned as part of their activity. They were thus expected to have a better knowledge of the country's institutions, their strengths and weaknesses.

The remainder of this section is organised into six sub-sections. The first describes the design of the questionnaire. The second explains how the survey was implemented. Results are then discussed, with emphasis first on how development-constraining institutional areas are perceived by respondents in the third sub-section, and then on perceived specific institutional strengths and weaknesses in the fourth. The fifth sub-section is devoted to the way respondents see future institutional changes engineered by a disruptive president completing his first year in power. A final sub-section puts the survey in perspective and concludes.

A The Survey: Design of the Questionnaire

The questionnaire has four intertwined components: (1) the personal characteristics of the respondents; (2) institutional areas perceived as the most constraining for the development of Tanzania; (3) the perception of the functioning of institutions; and (4) current (at the time of the survey) institutional developments in the country.

The questionnaire first collects information about personal characteristics of the respondents, including nationality, gender, level of education, place of birth. In a final part, it gathers more sensitive information on the past and present occupation of respondents as well as on their political affinity.

The second section of the questionnaire enumerates ten broad institutional areas listed below in Table 3.2 and respondents were asked to select the three areas that, according to them, most constrain development in Tanzania. Respondents then had to allocate twenty points among these three areas – the higher the number of points, the more detrimental the area for development. The selected areas are important for the analysis but also for the subsequent part of the survey because they determined the set of questions presented to the respondent in the main part of the survey.

The core section of the CIS comprises 345 questions on the perception of institutions. All rely on a Likert scale, ranging from 'Not at all' and 'little' to 'moderately so', 'much', and 'very much'. Responses are then converted into discrete numbers, ranging from one to five, for the analysis. The questionnaire is inspired by the Institutional Profile Database (IPD), an expert

TABLE 3.2 *Definition of institutional areas in the CIS survey*

Institutional area	Sub-areas
Political institutions	Functioning of political institutions and political life; participation of the population; civil liberties; transparency and accountability; corruption; state capacity; interference of non-state organisations in policy making; recruitment of politicians
Law and order, justice, security	Rule of law; functioning of the judicial system; protection of civil liberties; control of violence; supervision of public companies; business law and its implementation
Functioning of public administrations	State capacity; transparency of economic policies and reporting; corruption; public procurement; supervision of public companies; geographical coverage of public services; relationship with business sector; regulation; decentralisation
Ease of doing business	Relationship with public administration; privatisation; public procurement; price controls; competition regulation; foreign direct investments; functioning of the credit and capital markets; litigation procedures; labour market regulation; role of trade unions; recruitment of business leaders
Dealing with land rights	Access to land for business purposes (urban and rural); role of local communities; role of public administration; security of property rights (or equivalent in view of the state property principle); conflict settlement and functioning of land courts
Long-term and strategic planning	Ex-ante and ex-post evaluation of policies; communication on economic policy; capacity to coordinate stakeholders; long-run and strategic vision of development; obstacles to public action; decentralisation
Market regulation	Capacity to regulate market competition; regulation of utilities; regulation of foreign direct investments; regulation of the financial sector; regulation of the labour market; quality of the system of information on firms
Security of transactions and contracts	Security of contracts and property rights; insolvency law; litigation procedures; business laws and business courts
Relating to the rest of the world	Trade openness; financial openness; relationship with neighbouring countries; attitude towards foreign direct investments; ease to start a business; land tenure security, relationship with donors;
Social cohesion, social protection and solidarity	Participation of population to policy debate; civil liberties; access to the justice system; sense of national identity, discrimination practices; geographical coverage of public services; instruments of social protection; traditional solidarity

survey conducted jointly by the Economic Services of the French Embassies, the Centre for Prospective Studies and International Information in Paris, and the University of Maastricht (Bertho, 2013). The last wave of that survey taken in 2012 covered 143 countries in 2012. Respondents were staff members of the Economic Department of French Embassies or country offices of the French Agency for Development. The CIS questionnaire differs in several dimensions, mostly because many questions were adapted to the Tanzanian context. Yet about 40 per cent of the CIS questions remain similar to their IPD counterpart.

From a practical point of view, administering the whole questionnaire was not an option owing to its length. To shorten the time needed to complete the questionnaire, every question was associated with at least one of the ten general institutional areas in Table 3.2, and respondents were asked to answer only the questions related to the three institutional areas they selected in the previous step of the questionnaire, as well as questions related to a fourth area, randomly drawn from the remaining ones. This original feature of the questionnaire guaranteed that all institutional areas are at least partly covered at the end of the survey. In practice, respondents had to answer around half of all questions, as some questions appeared under several institutional areas.

Because the survey was taken only a year after the election of a new president whose mandate had been announced as rather disruptive, respondents were explicitly asked to answer the questionnaire as if no change had yet taken place in the institutional framework of the country. Enumerators were specifically trained to convey that message to the respondents. As institutions are persistent, there is little doubt that answers to the survey describe the way in which decision makers of various types in Tanzania perceived the institutional landscape that prevailed before the election of President Magufuli and the kind of influence it had exerted on the development path of the country.

Because of this potential disruption in some institutions or in the perception of them, a last section of the questionnaire was devoted to the most recent institutional changes. Respondents were asked to identify the questions to which they would have answered differently if they had been about the recent past or the near future of Tanzania. In this open-ended part of the questionnaire, respondents also had the possibility to mention institutional features that they thought were important for development and were not covered in the survey.

B Execution of the Survey

The Tanzania CIS survey was conducted between the end of January and early February 2017 in a collaborative effort between Institutional Diagnostic Project researchers, OPM, and REPOA, a Tanzanian think-tank. A total of 101 individuals were sampled in a purposively stratified sample aimed at collecting the views of people involved in, or in close contact with, institutions. Respondents had been or were in first- or second-tier positions in the decision-making structure of public, private, or civil society organisations. Their selection followed two steps.

First, survey designers defined sample strata in terms of occupation, position level, geographical constraints, and, tentatively, gender balance. By design, half of the sample were surveyed in Dar-es-Salaam, with the remaining half divided into five major cities: Dodoma, Morogoro, Mwanza, Mbeya, and Arusha. The sample also had to include a quarter of respondents from economic spheres, another quarter from the political sphere, a third quarter from the civil society in a broad sense, and the remaining quarter from various areas including the donor community, diplomats, the police and military forces, or the judiciary.[12] Note, however, that many respondents occupied other positions in the past and thus had experience in more than one area.

It must be stressed that the CIS survey sample design had no intention to be representative of any particular population, a fortiori of the whole population. From that point of view, it is not an opinion survey, as for instance the Afrobarometer could be. People with direct experience of the way institutions work in Tanzania were targeted, and a stratification was built in within that population so that a diversity of viewpoints could be obtained. The reason for that choice is that the goal of the CIS survey was to learn from the experience of people with knowledge of the state of institutions in Tanzania rather than what a majority of these people would think about the functioning of the judiciary or the work of the auditor general.

As we targeted top-tier decision makers, they turned out to be different from the standard profile in the whole population. They were older and more educated than the general population. A majority of respondents were in their forties, eighty of them had a university degree, while twenty-nine reported to have studied abroad. Almost all of them lived in urban areas, but half were born in rural areas. Even though not in the sample stratification procedure, political diversity was achieved: eighteen respondents declared a political affinity with the ruling party, seventeen with the opposition, and forty-five reported no political affinity.[13] Such a diversity is reassuring as it avoids excessively laudatory or critical views in questions addressing the role of the government.

C Critical Institutions for the Development of Tanzania

Figure 3.5 shows the institutional areas most frequently mentioned by respondents as constraining development. Institutions behind public administration came first and political institutions second. Business-related institutions were in third position. On the other side of the spectrum, only four respondents chose 'security of transactions and contracts', possibly because this area was considered to be more specific and technical than others. Similar conclusions

---

[12] See details in Table A.2 in the appendix.
[13] Twenty-one explicitly preferred not to answer the question.

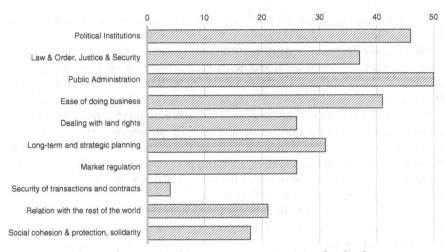

FIGURE 3.5 Choice of institutional areas as most constraining for development

are obtained when taking respondents' weighting into account, yet political institutions then rank first.

A framing bias could partially drive the ranking of the areas, with the first areas in the list appearing more often among the choices of respondents. Still, the allocation of the twenty points by respondents over the three selected field is less sensitive to this sorting as respondents have to focus on three fields only when they allocate the points. It has remarkably little effect on the ranking. Last but not least, qualitative insights collected in the preparation of the survey and described in the next section are very much in line with the current conclusions.

Critical area choices vary by the characteristics of respondents and yield contrasting stories. For instance, female respondents gave very little weight to political institutions, but they consider that social cohesion and protection, solidarity, and relations with the rest of the world matter more for development than do the male respondents. Political affinity also played a role, with respondents closer to the ruling party, CCM, emphasising the difficulties arising from land rights, while the opposition stressed the constraints related to political institutions and to the public administration.

The choice of the top three constraints to development, according to respondents' opinions, is a piece of information in itself, but it also determines most of the questions asked of each respondent. Areas that were not chosen by many respondents may actually work well, or they may work imperfectly without constraining development. The fourth area, randomly selected among the remaining field and imposed upon the respondents, permits an examination of that issue. Indeed, the less critical institutional field, namely 'security of transaction and contracts', ended up being covered by a fifth of respondents. There is thus enough statistical power to understand why this area was considered as less critical by respondents.

D The Perceived Functioning of Institutions in Tanzania

Within and across areas, the CIS aimed to identify, as precisely as possible, which specific institutions were perceived as constraining by respondents. The subsequent analysis first evaluated questions by their mean response on a scale ranging from 1, 'most negative', to 5, 'most positive'. For questions asked in a negative way, the Likert scale was inverted to make sure that a higher value always meant a better perception. Questions were then ranked according to the top weaknesses and strengths of Tanzanian institutions. The last part of the analysis explored the heterogeneity of answers across sub-samples and tried to determine whether the perception of institutional weaknesses was correlated with some salient characteristics of respondents.

As in many opinion surveys, there was a mass of answers around the central position, which may reflect the default choice of respondents if they were unsure about their position. It is therefore more relevant to look at the tails of the distribution, namely questions with clearly positive or negative answers. Forty-six questions – or 13 per cent of all questions – had an average score below 2.5, while only twenty-seven scored above 3.5.

An alternative to asking respondents which were the problematic institutional areas is to look at the proportion of low-score answers among all questions that fell under that area. This is equivalent to comparing the distribution of low-score answers by institutional area to the distribution of all questions as done in Figure 3.6.

The first part of the graph shows the distribution of all questions across the ten areas.[14] For instance, the first bar in Figure 3.6 shows that 15 per cent of the 345 questions of the CIS fall under 'political institutions'. The first bar in the second group reports that 13 per cent of the forty-six questions with a score below 2.5 are related to political institutions. In the third group, which plots the distribution of questions with an average response above 3.5, 14.8 per cent of questions are part of the political institutions cluster. Not all areas exhibit such a balanced pattern, however. 'Public administration', 'ease of doing business', and 'land rights' are largely overrepresented among low scores, which suggests that they comprised relatively more obstacles to development than others. This conclusion agrees with the identification of critical areas in Figure 3.5. This is not the case for land rights, of which treatment was almost unanimously perceived as unsatisfactory. On the other side of the spectrum, the 'social cohesion, social protection, and solidarity' area represents 20 per cent of all questions, but only 4 per cent of low-scores and 48 per cent of high scores.

A closer look at the questions that collected the lowest average scores permits us to bring more precision to the identification of institutional weaknesses by respondents. In this perspective, issues related to land come at the

---

[14] It sums to more than 100 per cent as some questions are, by design, relevant for several institutional areas.

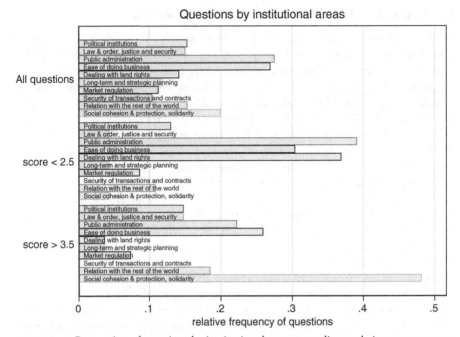

FIGURE 3.6 Proportion of questions by institutional areas according to their average scores

forefront. What comes out of detailed questions is that land laws do not seem well understood at the local level, and at this level it is common to have operations outside the legal framework, with limited transparency, and eventually involving corruption. Respondents qualified land tenure as insecure, leading to frequent land disputes and eventually feeding open conflict. Overall, the unequal and fractionalised distribution of land was often found to be a constraint for development.

The second most cited negative item is corruption. This is thought to permeate many institutions of the country, whether at the political level or in the relations between the bureaucracy, the citizenry, and business. The delegation of missions by the state to public monopolies such as electricity production and distribution (the Tanzania Electric Supply Company, TANESCO) or natural resource extraction (gas) is found to be not very transparent. Corruption in the privatisation process of public companies that took place in the recent past is also denounced. Respondents estimated that transfer prices were too low and that promised gains in efficiency were not achieved. These points remain relevant in the current management of natural resources and respondents anticipated that they will be so in the future. On a smaller scale, the role of corruption in increasing the cost and the hardship of starting a business was also mentioned.

In the agricultural sector, respondents complained about low price levels and their volatility, which they imputed to the role of intermediaries. Access to physical and financial inputs was also felt as being restricted. Both were thought to constrain the development of the agricultural sector.

Other weak points reported are more scattered, including the absence of independent trade unions, the non-indexation of wages on inflation, the low prospect of university graduates getting a position in line with their training, and the dependence of Tanzania on foreign stakeholders.

Strengths are also worth mentioning. Respondents praised the limited discrimination based on geographical origin, religion, and ethnicity, for instance, in access to public services such as school and education. More generally, the sense of Tanzanian identity appeared to be quite strong. These positive statements should, however, be put into perspective. First, given the peculiar format of the questionnaire, less than a third of respondents had to answer these questions. Second, the risk of internal conflict based on regional differences, religion, or ethnic lines is nevertheless seen by respondents as moderately high, which seems somewhat contradictory. In a different perspective, respondents consistently emphasised the feeling of security. They were also satisfied that people were free to form associations of a varying nature, violence against political organisations was limited, and the executive had strong control over the police.

Although respondents complained about the role of foreign stakeholders, they underlined the positive role of foreign aid. It was widely recognised as a source of funding for infrastructure and a driver of improvements in the health and education sector. However, its impact on corruption was also emphasised.

At the grassroots level, respondents underscored the traditional solidarity links (family, neighbours, associations, religious organisations, etc.), which provide support to those in need, as well as the role of informal microfinance institutions such as rotating saving and credit associations. On the other hand, respondents were confident that formal social protection mechanisms, such as the Tanzania Social Action Fund, would act as a complement to rather than as a substitute for informal instruments.

Perceptions of institutions varied across groups of respondents, as evidenced by an analysis of the heterogeneity of answers. For instance, women, who, in our sample, disproportionally came from the civil society, criticised the Tanzanian state for discriminating along gender, religious, ethnic, and regional lines in terms of access to the judicial system, health care and administrative services. They were also more concerned about the influence of interest groups in the design of policies.

The same disaggregation was implemented in many subgroups. It yielded results that fitted expectations. Respondents who positioned themselves closer to the opposition party had rather negative perceptions about the independence of the judiciary, the army, and the police. They also felt civil liberties were restricted. Unsurprisingly, being close to the ruling party yielded opposite views. Respondents who studied abroad were more sensitive to matters related to trade and to the influence of foreign stakeholders in national policies. They perceived Tanzania as being very exposed to competition from foreign firms, whether from neighbouring countries, other developing countries, or advanced economies. They were also concerned by the fact that foreign firms, governments, and multilateral organisations are an obstacle to the implementation of autonomous policies and reforms.

Being involved in business raised the awareness of respondents about foreign firms having an easier time establishing themselves in Tanzania and gaining access to funds from local banks. Despite being active in the private sector, these respondents found that access to information about the ownership structure of large firms was quite difficult. Overall, business managers were rather pessimistic about the progress of the middle class and considered that networks were important for accessing top official positions, compared with merit-based promotion.

E Prospective Assessment of Institutional Changes

It should be kept in mind that the CIS survey intended to capture the perception of institutions as they operated during the five to ten years prior to the time of the survey, which was about one year after President Magufuli was sworn in with an ambitious reform programme, most importantly concerning corruption. The timing of the survey is therefore quite interesting for gaining some insights into the respondents' anticipations about the new regime. At the end of the interview, respondents were thus asked how Tanzanian institutions had recently evolved and whether their answers to the questions on the core part of the questionnaire would have been different if reference had been made to the recent past or the near future of Tanzania. In total, 90 per cent of the respondents wished to express their opinion, even though in some cases very briefly.

As many as 28 respondents explicitly mentioned a fall in corruption and increased transparency and accountability as major recent changes in the Tanzanian institutional landscape. They explained that civil servants abided by the law more, and side payments and bribes had been drastically reduced. If questions had been about the recent past and not on a longer timeframe, most felt that corruption would probably be less frequently mentioned as a major institutional weakness.

A corollary of the reduction in corruption was the improvement of tax collection. Fifteen respondents said that the recent surge in tax collection efficiency would have changed the way they answered the core part of the survey. They felt that taxpayers had a harder time bypassing their tax duties. According to a few respondents, changes in tax collection had pushed some businesses into financial trouble. They mentioned that some firms had to close operations, that many of them faced liquidity constraints, and that it had become harder to make money. On the public spending side, more effective tax collection was viewed as raising the capacity of the state to accomplish its mission. It was expected that, combined with greater accountability, this would be a guarantee of better use of public resources. Eighteen respondents mentioned that public service provision was improving, especially in the dimensions related to education, health, and infrastructure. A few of them thought this was the result of a change in the work spirit of civil servants and would eventually lead to more equal coverage of public services, to less discrimination, and to less importance of social networks when applying for a position in the public service. Clearly, however, these perspectives of a more equal and meritocratic society were aspirations and hopes, rather than what respondents had already experienced. In effect, some respondents questioned the depth and sustainability of current changes, and whether they could alter the development path of the country.

These positive prospects were somewhat counterbalanced by concerns about the transparency and accountability of the new regime. More than 10 per cent of the sample explicitly pointed out that it had become hard to express views challenging the government, although free press, free media, and even free demonstrations were essential for the accountability and transparency of public affairs. The independence of the judiciary system was also mentioned as crucial for the credibility of the executive towards citizens and firms, a view that was not limited to respondents aligned with the opposition. Actually, several respondents expressed their fears that the new administration could depart from these principles. The risk of an autocratic drift was even mentioned in a few cases.

F Discussion and Conclusions

From the CIS, a broad consensus emerges pointing to several institutional challenges. As far as general institutional areas are concerned, the major concern is about political institutions, public administration, and the ease of doing business. The judiciary system comes just afterwards. Other areas are further down, but one may also consider that they are included in the areas at the top – for example, land right management may be covered by public administration and security of contracts by the judiciary. The problem here is that it is difficult to define institutional areas that do not overlap with each other. To a large extent, this difficulty is also present in the definition of synthetic institutional indicators. It is unavoidable when institutional areas are defined in too broad a way, but breaking them down would lead to a large number of sub-areas among which it would be difficult to decide which is more constraining than others for the development of the country.

As general as it is, the institutional decomposition used in the CIS survey and the ranking given by respondents is nevertheless instructive, even though it clearly requires further analysis to grasp its meaning and its implications. In a way, this will be done throughout the rest of this volume. At this stage, it is worth stressing the convergence of the CIS-survey and the analysis of synthetic indicators in pointing to administrative capacity as a major obstacle to faster development in Tanzania, and to the lack of competitiveness of the production sector that is potentially due to a suboptimal business environment.

Individual questions in the core part of the questionnaire yield more precise insights about respondents' perception. Summarising them leads to the following list of consensual institutional challenges:

- the management of land rights and, more generally, the allocation of land;
- corruption at the level of both politics and the public administration;
- the regulation of the economy, in particular of infrastructure;
- the lack of transparency and accountability of the state.

Note that these challenges fit in their own way the ranking of broad institutional themes by respondents. Corruption, and the transparency and accountability of the state clearly affect how the functioning of both political institutions and the public administration are perceived. On their side, the management of land rights and the regulation of the economy also cut across broad themes such as public administration and the ease of doing business.

On the strength side, the survey again shows some consensus around the sense of national identity and security, which implicitly seems to point to political stability.

The open-ended discussion with the respondents at the end of the interview made it possible to check that the recommendation to complete the questionnaire bearing in mind the institutional Tanzanian context during the last five to ten years had been complied with. This did not prevent optimistic expectations and hopes about the way the new administration would address some of the preceding challenges.

Stepping back from the analysis of results, the question then arises of whether a survey which relies on the country's political, economic, and social decision-making population leads to a different evaluation of institutional quality than the expert-based institutional indicators found in international databases. As a way of testing this, use has been made of the fact that many questions in the CIS overlap with the IPD questionnaire submitted to some French diplomats posted in Tanzania. Based on common questions between the two questionnaires, it is possible to measure the degree of correlation between the opinions of a sample of 100 economic, administrative, or academic actors in Tanzania and those of a few close foreign observers. There is some convergence between the two surveys, but it is very partial.

If we select the 130 questions that are identical in the CIS and the IPD, the correlation of answers between the two surveys is only 0.30.[15] On the same set of questions but within the CIS, the correlation between Tanzanian respondents and foreigners is also limited, reaching 0.5. This rather low degree of

---

[15] The IPD was conducted in 2012 and asked questions on the prevailing institutional conditions at that time. The CIS was carried out in 2017 but covered institutions in the previous five to ten years, creating a large overlap between the two surveys.

correlation, combined with the heterogeneity analysis, shows the importance of the identity of respondents to this type of survey. Many studies rely on few respondents per country, who often share a similar position in society. They have their own view of institutions, which may not be shared by Tanzanian or even other foreign diplomats active in Tanzania (the correlation between French diplomats and foreign respondents is only 0.22).

By enlarging the sample of respondents, the CIS survey is innovative and offers a more diverse view on institutions. Within broad areas, the CIS yields more precise answers on what is found to go wrong and for whom. Most importantly, it allows us to analyse the diversity of perceptions across population groups in the society, which is essential in interpreting sample averages. From that point of view, the Tanzanian experience suggests that a substantially larger sample of respondents would have yielded more precise estimates of cross-averages.

III OPEN-ENDED INTERVIEWS WITH TOP DECISION MAKERS AND POLICYMAKERS

In addition to formally surveying a large number of private and public decision makers and observers of political, social, and economic life in Tanzania, several experts, some of whom are or had been at the highest level of responsibility in the country, were also interviewed on an open-ended basis. They were not asked to complete a questionnaire, but were simply invited to share their thoughts about the binding institutional constraints in Tanzania. Other issues came up in the general discussion. The main points drawn from these interviews from the perspective of an institutional diagnostic of Tanzania are summarised after briefly introducing the respondents.

The experts who were interviewed were not representative of any specific population sub-group. They were simply people who, because of the responsibility they currently had, or had in the past, as political leaders, top civil servants, business executives, non-governmental organisation (NGO) directors, or researchers, had been led to deeply reflect on Tanzanian institutions, their potential role in slowing down economic development, and possible directions for reform. Yet, in approaching them, care was taken to have as much diversity of viewpoints as possible, either in terms of occupation – that is, the various occupations listed above – or in terms of perspectives on the Tanzanian economy – for example,. ruling party versus opposition. One may thus say that, taken together, the opinions of the personalities who were interviewed made up a sample of the way the various components of the elite think about the nature of Tanzanian institutions and their potential role in preventing faster development. It can be seen from the list of people who were interviewed – see appendix – that they were fairly diverse, from think-tank directors and academics, to leading business leaders, to personalities at the very top of the state hierarchy, including two past presidents, the Chief Justice and the Controller Auditor General at the time the study was completed.

The first question asked as an introduction to the discussion was: 'In your opinion, which kind of institution, formal or informal, is preventing economic development in Tanzania from accelerating?' Then an open, mostly informal, and definitely 'off the record' discussion followed, very much led by the person being interviewed. The following paragraphs offer a synthesis of what could be drawn from these very rich interviews for the present study. They cannot do justice to the richness of about fifty fascinating hours of discussion and the deep insights they provided for the pursuit of this institutional diagnostic exercise.

The four areas most intensively discussed directly or indirectly have to do with the management of the state and civil service. More precisely, they are: (1) the issue of corruption; (2) the functioning of the civil service, including the issue of decentralisation; (3) the regulation of public and private firms; and (4) land use rights. All these areas are closely related, as it can be seen that corruption is the natural consequence, and at the same time the cause, of a dysfunctional bureaucracy and/or badly coordinated regulations. Likewise, it is the multiplicity of regulations and laws that makes civil service inefficient. Finally, the management of land use rights, which was almost systematically cited as a major obstacle to development – both in agriculture and in urban areas – may be taken as a good example of the effect of weak capacity and corruption in some parts of the bureaucracy and a partial understanding of a well-crafted but complex law.

Three other general institutional areas were stressed, but with less frequency and less strength, by the personalities being interviewed. The first one was the issue of political checks and balances, or more generally the actual functioning of the political system; the second one was the mindset of the population, including that of the public bureaucracy; the final one was the capacity and functioning of the judiciary system.

Corruption was uniformly seen as both a widespread evil and a fundamentally deleterious factor for development in Tanzania, even though the point was sometimes made that Tanzania is not necessarily worse than its neighbours in East Africa or even than better performing countries in terms of economic growth. However, corruption undoubtedly plays an important role in public opinion and is a central issue in election times. As was explained in Chapter 1, it arose around the end of the socialist era and grew more rapidly under President Mwinyi's mandate at the time of the transition towards a market economy. President Mkapa was elected on the basis of an anti-corruption platform and commissioned Judge Warioba to produce a report on corruption, which revealed how widespread it was and proposed some corrective measures. Yet major corruption scandals have taken place during each presidential mandate ever since President Mwinyi. President Magufuli was elected in large part on his reputation of high integrity and his anti-corruption platform.

The causes of petty and grand corruption may be different, but they are seen as equally detrimental to development. Corruption is often attributed to the relatively low level of income of politicians and civil servants in comparison with the private sector and, for politicians, in view of the uncertainty of their position. Yet 'needs' is only one part of the story. Greed and a mindset that does not consider paying or accepting bribes as dishonest is the other part of the story. Moreover, the lack of coordination of regulations, administrative rules, and laws offers numerous rent-seeking opportunities in the various layers of the bureaucracy. Raising salaries – and, for high-level politicians, creating compensation that facilitates life after leaving office – may be part of the solution to reduce corruption to a tolerable level. Reforming the organisation of the state by coordinating laws and rules so as to eliminate rent-seeking opportunities is equally important. Yet publicly identifying and formally prosecuting those found guilty of corruption, whether as a corruptor or a person who is corrupted, is central to any anti-corruption strategy.

Even though some of the personalities interviewed tended to minimise the consequences of corruption, most stressed the development costs arising from the misallocation of resources involved in grand corruption, the undermining of the profitability of some investments through import smuggling (e.g. sugar, rice), bribes to acquire business licences, land use rights or trade permits, and, most importantly, the loss of tax revenues leading to inefficient, and ineffective, higher tax rates.

The *inefficiency of the civil service*, stressed by most interviewees, has very much to do with corruption, but, as suggested earlier, both find their root cause in the way the state bureaucracy functions. A weakness frequently pointed to was the multiplicity of regulatory bodies, ministerial bureaus or public agencies that have their say in specific areas. One expert mentioned that the production and commercialisation of a new food product would require twenty-two authorisations from different administrations. Another reported that the farming sector was administered through fifteen different public entities. Others mentioned the frequent discrepancy between local government decisions and rules enacted by the central government. Of course, the problem may not be the number of public entities having a say on some aspect of the economy, but the lack of coordination among them, leading to ineffectiveness and rent-seeking opportunities for bureaucrats who have the power to short-circuit the whole system. A good example of a reform aimed at simplifying things was the creation in 1995 of the Tax Revenue Authority, which centralised tax collection operations formerly under the responsibility of various decentralised administrative entities. Another more recent example of the need for coordination among public entities is the creation of the President's Delivery Bureau, in charge of coordinating efforts to reach the National Key Result Areas through the monitoring and evaluation of various administrations.[16]

Another weakness of the civil service stressed by a number of experts was the low capacity of the bureaucracy. This might be due as much to insufficient

---

[16] These areas correspond to the implementation of the BRN (Big Results Now) initiative by President Kikwete to accelerate progress towards the 2025 Tanzanian Development Vision, including the status of a middle-income country.

human capital at all levels as to excessive movements of bureaucrats caused by political cycles. There seemed to be a consensus that it was at the local level that the bureaucracy was the least effective. In particular, the point was made that the poor understanding of laws by the public gives undue power to local bureaucrats, which they use for inefficient decisions and, often, their own profit. More generally, the question was raised as to the efficiency of the way decentralisation is being implemented.

The *regulation* of production activities is of utmost importance for economic growth as it affects the competitiveness of the production apparatus and the investment climate. It is judged to be deficient in Tanzania in several ways. First, companies that are still state-owned, after the wave of privatisation that took place throughout the 1990s and early 2000s, were reported by some experts as inefficiently managed or inefficiently regulated. The most obvious case seems to be that of TANESCO, the public company responsible for the distribution and most of the production of electrical power – an area where Tanzania appears to be lagging behind most African countries. It was reported that its regulatory agency, the Energy and Water Utilities Regulatory Authority (EWURA), maintains a cap on the price of electricity, which essentially makes TANESCO unprofitable, increases its debt burden, and prevents it from investing in a badly needed expansion of coverage. It was also reported that several public–private partnerships in power generation failed because of inadequate tariffs and uncertainty about potential nationalisation. A major reorganisation of TANESCO has recently been confirmed, which consists of breaking the company into various functional entities – that is, 'unbundling' – and issuing shares to the public. How regulation will be modified is not yet clear. Other state-owned companies that have been found to be underperforming include the telephone company Tanzania Telecommunications Company Ltd and the petroleum company Tanzania Petroleum Development Corporation.

It is worth stressing that interviewees with a deeper knowledge of the energy sector pointed to a rather different diagnostic about the difficulties of the power sector. It was pointed out that the agency, which had been operating for a relatively short period of time but enjoyed international recognition for its professionalism, was making rigorous recommendations and followed world best practice in this area. The interpretation was therefore that political pressure often meant their recommendations were being imperfectly and incompletely implemented.[17]

With regard to state-owned companies, it was also fairly surprising to learn in one of the interviews that many of the numerous privatised state-owned companies were no longer functional. This suggests that those parastatals were indeed extremely inefficient and were bought essentially for their equipment

---

[17] The head of EWURA was replaced by the president shortly after he had recommended a tariff increase that followed agreed pre-defined rules. The tariff increase was not implemented. This occurred a few weeks after he was interviewed with his management for the present study.

and buildings, rather than their activity. It is also possible that the private management of these companies did not benefit from the same competitive advantages as when they were state-owned.

Concerning the private sector, the complaint most often heard was that too many regulations are a strong disincentive for investment, whether domestic or foreign. In natural resources, the view was that capital, knowledge, and know-how are needed but that foreign investors still fear the risk of nationalisation – despite a foreign direct investment act explicit in dismissing that risk. In manufacturing, the opinion was that domestic firms prefer investing in trade than in production, subject to more and heavier regulation. Foreign direct investments are more oriented towards the exploration and extraction of natural resources, telecommunication services, and tourism, all sectors where regulation is apparently also heavy.

The excessive number and complexity of regulations were also mentioned as the main reason why small and medium-sized enterprises are not formed. A more fundamental reason, not mentioned by the respondents but well established in many other developing countries, might also be that the actual gain of creating formal enterprises is small. This may also be the case in Tanzania.

The management of *land use rights* is the best example of the consequences of an inefficient and sometimes corrupt bureaucracy and a legislation that is complex and thus not well known or understood by the public. The uncertainty on land rights is very often cited as a real handicap in developing the agricultural and agro-industrial sector, and in some cases even industrial projects in urban areas. As far as the latter are concerned, a frequently cited example is that of the two to three years it took to get the land use right needed to construct a liquefied gas terminal on Tanzania's coast. In agriculture, everybody seems aware of the long delays investors face in acquiring land rights and the bribes they end up offering to shortcut cumbersome processes whether at the local or the national level. Land is the subject of the second largest number of judicial cases, often with individual investors confronting the local or regional authorities responsible for the allocation of land. Many disputes also arise from farmers squatting or claiming back land allocated to investors but not fully utilised.

Land is the property of the state in Tanzania, and was actually collectivised during the socialist era. After a long maturation process, a Land Act was passed in 1999 to codify the operations on land use rights, in particular to facilitate investment. It is considered to be a good law, but its implementation at lower government levels is said to be problematic because of the lack of capacity of local bureaucracies and a poor understanding of the law by villagers. There also seems to be little accountability of the civil servants responsible for land operations with respect to both investors and the local population. Records of these operations are also said to be badly managed.

In a country where land is abundant and agriculture has great potential, such ambiguity around land use rights is unfortunate. It also has negative consequences in urban areas.

The functioning of the political system naturally came up in the interviews. The main issue was the accountability of the government and the nature of *checks and balances* on the executive. Emphasis was put in particular on the key role of the Controller Auditor General and the need for the content of his annual report to be better publicised and publicly debated, and for the auditing of public entities to go beyond official accounts. The view was expressed that parliamentary debates should receive more space to review the government's actions. This seemed to several experts all the more important in a country where the president enjoys considerable power, and until recently was able to control the entire bureaucracy and to some extent the legislature. Things may be changing as the opposition and political competition are rising. The relationship between the two members of the Tanzanian Union – that is, the mainland and Zanzibar – was also seen as a sensitive issue that has now been discussed for some time in relation with a reform of the constitution.

The *judicial system* would seem to be the main instrument to fight corruption. The interviews emphasised its lack of resources. At present 16 per cent of the 180 districts do not have a court and a third of the regions have no high (i.e. appeal) court. The judicial system is thus in a constant state of congestion. Corruption is also present among the staff, in no small part because of outdated information technology that generates frequent involuntary (or deliberate?) losses of key pieces of evidence.

Although on the edge of institutional issues, the *mindset* of the population with respect to specific issues was frequently mentioned in the interviews as being responsible for slowing down economic development. Several experts indeed thought there was still a suspicion with respect to the private sector in the civil service and possibly in public opinion, which somehow acted as a brake on development. The lack of a true culture of business was also emphasised, with evidence for this perhaps lying in the disproportionate number of non-indigenous among entrepreneurs, the opposite being true in the political sphere.

IV CONCLUSION

It is striking to see that, altogether, the three preceding approaches to the quality of institutions are convergent on the likely constraints that Tanzania's institutions enact on economic development, independently of the capacity of the country to devote the resources necessary to key development functions. By the very nature of the analysis, conclusions are less clear in the case of the institutional indicators, in part because they combine many different dimensions of institutions and in part because they result from a comparative exercise that is somewhat arbitrary – that is, weaknesses may be the same in Tanzania as in the comparator countries, including the highly performing ones. Even in that case, however, there is clearly some convergence among the various approaches in pointing damaging weaknesses in administrative and regulatory capacity, or 'government effectiveness'.

What emerge more precisely from the three exercises, as well as from the institutional implications of the growth diagnostics briefly reviewed in Chapter 2, are the following themes:

• land issues featured very clearly in the CIS survey, and the limitations due to the uncertainty surrounding land use rights;
• the regulation of firms, in particular the electricity company, TANESCO.

Corruption was mentioned in practically all approaches, but, as mentioned earlier, corruption is a symptom, the cause of which has to be found in the poor functioning of several institutions. From that point of view, the open-ended interviews with top decision makers, as well as the institutional indicators, unambiguously point to:

• the organisation of the civil service; and
• the coordination between state entities – in particular, the relationship between central and local governments.

These various themes are analysed in-depth in the second part of this volume.

APPENDIX

APPENDIX A.1: STRATIFICATION OF THE CIS SAMPLE

TABLE 3.A.1 *Stratification of the CIS sample*

Sphere of influence	Occupation type	Number of respondents
Economics	Foreign companies	5
	Trade unions	6
	Farming representatives	6
	Small entrepreneurs	5
	Business leaders	6
Politics	Government executives and senior bureaucrats	15
	Politicians	8
	Retiree statesmen	5
Law and order enforcement	Police	2
	Military	2
	Justice	4
Civil society	Media, chief editors	4
	Religious	4
	Civil society organisations	4
	Top academics	8
	Development NGOs	5
International stakeholder	Donor community	8
	Diplomats	3

APPENDIX A.2: LIST OF KEY INFORMANT INTERVIEWS

- Shabir Abji, executive director, New Africa Hotel
- Bashiru Ally, lecturer, University of Dar es Salaam, before being appointed secretary general of the ruling party, CCM
- Mussa Juma Assad, controller and auditor general
- Mohammed Othman Chande, chief justice of Tanzania
- Brian Cooksey, independent research professional
- Mohammed Dewji, billionaire businessman and former politician
- Aidan Eyakuze, Twaweza
- Omar Issa, chief executive officer of the president's Delivery Bureau,
- Zitto Kabwe, member of parliament (Opposition)
- Maduka Kessy, executive secretary, Planning Commission
- Alphayo Kidata, Tanzania Revenue Authority commissioner
- Jakaya Kikwete, former president of Tanzania
- Ibrahim Lipumba, former member of parliament and national chairman of the opposition Civic United Front
- Matern Lumbanga, chairman, Public Procurement Regulatory Authority
- Alex Makulillo, professor, Faculty of Law, Open University of Tanzania
- Philip Mpango, minister of finance
- Valentino Longino Mlowola, director general of the Prevention and Combating of Corruption Bureau
- Benjamin Mkapa, former president of Tanzania
- Adolf Mkenda, permanent secretary Ministry of Industry, Trade and Investment
- Wilfred Mbowe, manager, Central Bank
- Pius Msekwa, former vice chairman of the ruling party Chama Cha Mapinduzi
- Ali Mufuruki, businessman, founding chairman of CEO Roundtable of Tanzania
- Msafiri Mtepa, principal economist at Energy and Water Utilities Regulatory Authority,
- Benno Ndulu, governor, Central Bank
- Neema Nduguru, independent consultant
- Felix Ngamlagosi, director general, EWURA
- Patrick Rutabanzibwa, country chairman, PanAfrican Energy Tanzania
- Richard Sambaiga, senior lecturer in sociology and anthropology, University of Dar es Salaam
- Joseph Semboja, former CEO of UOGONZI
- Issa Shivji, professor, University of Dar es Salaam
- Leodegar Chilla Tenga, chairman of the National Sports Council
- Ringo Willy Tenga, Law Associates Advocates
- Alphonce Tiba, senior environmental management officer
- John Wanyancha, director of Corporate Relations at Serengeti Breweries Limited
- Stephen Wasira, member of parliament (CCM)
- Joseph Warioba, former prime minister and vice president

Conclusion of Part I

The first part of this volume has sketched the main political, economic, and institutional features of Tanzania's development, emphasising on the one hand the economic challenges the country is likely to face in trying to sustain and accelerate its pace of economic growth, and on the other hand, the possible institutional obstacles to meeting these challenges, as perceived by decision-makers and observers. The brief account of Tanzania's political history has also shown the key role played by the structure of political power, the business elite, and the way they interact.

To understand better the nature of the institutional obstacles to the acceleration and sustainability of economic development now requires going beyond this rather general characterisation and mostly macro approach. Corruption, the land laws, the organisation of the state, or the quality of the civil service may all be unanimously perceived as major handicaps for development in Tanzania, but an institutional diagnostic requires characterising more precisely the constraints they raise for development, and, more fundamentally, the nature of the institutional dysfunctions behind them. Petty corruption does not have the same economic consequences and the same causes as grand corruption between top politicians and big business. Land laws may be more problematic in some transactions and for some aspects of development than others. If the state proves unable to perform some tasks satisfactorily, why is reforming it so difficult or even unfeasible? It is only by getting into the analysis of such detailed issues that one may hope to get into the reality of the institution-development relationship in a particular country, rather than loosely relate aggregate economic performances on the one hand and perceived dominant institutional weaknesses or failures on the other, even though a helpful first analytical step.

We proceed with such a detailed analysis in the second part of this volume through a small number of thematic studies, chosen on the basis of the most salient points arising from our economic diagnostic of Tanzanian development and the opinions we gathered on the quality of institutions, especially from key informants.

PART II

FIVE CRITICAL INSTITUTIONAL AREAS FOR TANZANIA'S DEVELOPMENT

This part of the volume delves deeper in the relationship between institutions and development by focusing on five thematic areas, expected to be of much relevance for the understanding of the way institutional dysfunctions may raise obstacles to development whether its pace, structure, sustainability, or inclusiveness.

The following five areas have been selected.

- The relationship between the state and business
- Strengths and weaknesses of the civil service
- Fiscal decentralisation as an example of institutional ineffectiveness
- The land right laws
- The elusive reform of the power sector

Available resources did not allow to cover more ground.

All studies have been written by Tanzanian authors with expertise in the related domain. Their aim has been to identify the way institutional factors hinder development in their particular field, the institutional reforms that could improve the situation, and the political economy feasibility of such reforms. In all cases, their study is supplemented by the opinion of scholars with a broader view of the area being covered and thus able to reflect on what Tanzanians could learn from other countries' experience. Their comments also point to the similarities and differences between Tanzania and countries at comparable levels of development.

4

Politics and Business

An Ambiguous Relationship

Samuel Mwita Wangwe

I INTRODUCTION

The relationship between government, or more generally the political elite, and the business world, in particular 'big business', is a key determinant of development. A government may want to pursue policies that favour some specific activity, exploit some comparative advantage, generate both employment and foreign currency, and lead to a satisfactory rate of growth. However, in a market economy, business interest has no reason to be automatically aligned with such views. Then a kind of game takes place between business and the political elite, by which one side tries to impose its views on the other side. One example is when the former (business) has captured the latter (political elite) through sheer corruption. The development of the country then depends on the interest of incumbent big firms, which has no reason to automatically coincide with that of the national community. Another example is that of a neutral government whose action is primarily in the national interest, with its actions primarily limited to providing a favourable environment, or 'business climate', including, presumably, transparent regulation rules for all producers irrespective of their size or influence.

The real world is more complex, exhibiting competition within the business elite for gaining support from politicians, and competition among politicians for accessing, or maintaining themselves in, power. The latter may take place through voting but also through power struggles within political parties. The strategy of politicians in power may also be to attract the support of the public by ostensibly staying away from business influence, thus getting close to the neutral case mentioned earlier. These relationships are examined in this chapter in the context of Tanzania.

State–business relationships in Tanzania have been changing over time, and this chapter sets out to make a contribution to the interpretation and understanding of these changes. The extent to which the government has been effective in its intervention and the extent to which it had roots in society ('embeddedness') and the power to impose its own will on the private sector and the rest of the society needs to be examined. In this context, this chapter addresses the kinds of developments that influenced the extent to which the state and politics were able to impose a vision that is compatible with underlying social and economic forces. In addition, it addresses the extent to which the state became a vehicle for furthering the interests of powerful sections of business as opposed to furthering national interests.

The nature of the prevailing ideology about development has been an important factor in influencing the political economy surrounding Tanzania's development. Since independence in 1961, the economic development of Tanzania went through four stages of very different nature, and a fifth and sixth stages were not completed yet at the time of writing. In order to capture the characteristics and influence of these stages, this chapter takes a historical perspective. In this regard, it is organised in six sections representing four periods and attempting some speculation on what kind of equilibrium is likely to emerge in, or be associated with, the fifth- and sixth-phase governments. However, prior to addressing the six periods, after this introduction, the theoretical framework and methodology that has guided the rest of this chapter is presented in Section II. This is followed by sections that coincide with the six periods. Section III examines the first period from independence to the Arusha Declaration (1961–6) and represents the initial conditions that largely set the stage for the Arusha Declaration of 1967. Section IV examines the second period, from the Arusha Declaration to the economic crisis (1967–85). During this period, the policy framework was essentially addressing the socioeconomic challenges as seen in the initial post-independence period. Section V addresses relationships in the third period (1986–95), which is characterised by policy reforms that changed the relationship between politics and business. In this period, Tanzania was implementing a series of economic recovery programmes primarily determined by the international financial institutions. Section VI examines politics–business relations during the fourth period (1996–2015). This is essentially characterised by initiatives taken by the government to consolidate reforms and define its own development agenda, in which the integration of business with politics was progressively institutionalised, while in an informal setting corruption was going on between sections of business and sections of the political elite. Since the fifth-phase government came into office in November 2015, the relationship between politics and business has changed considerably. Although the period was rather short (up to March 2021), it may be necessary to preliminarily discern the characteristics of the equilibrium that was emerging. The changes in this period are examined in Section VII, which identifies the signs that the country was showing the will to make a substantial shift from the prevailing equilibrium and adopt a new one, which was still in the making. Section VIII discusses the sixth-phase government under President

Samia Suluhu Hassan from March 2021. Although she has not been president long enough to make conclusive statements, there have been notable changes in policies on several fronts that point in the direction of improving politics–business relations. Finally, Section IX brings together these developments in politics and business relations into a conclusion.

II THEORETICAL FRAMEWORK AND METHODOLOGY

This analysis of politics and business aims to contribute to an understanding of how positive institutional change can be achieved, as well as to the design of an institutional diagnostic tool that would permit policymakers to identify weak institutional areas that constrain development and appropriate directions for reform. This institutional diagnostic tool focuses on the institutional (formal and informal rules of the game) weaknesses possibly responsible for economic constraints. It is expected to enhance the understanding of a body of evidence and provide insights into what practicable actions produce institutional changes that improve economic outcomes, increase growth, and enhance industrialisation for socioeconomic transformation.

The theoretical framework that is adopted in this chapter will enable a better understanding of what is at stake in terms of institutions and what action should be taken, if politically feasible. The theoretical framework adopts a political economy analysis that is dynamic, representing the interests of various groups that may also change over time. The framework puts the lessons from experience in context and takes into consideration changes in the political economy. The analysis of the political economy will bring out the relationship between politics and business over time, with analytical interpretation of ideological evolution and socioeconomic development and special reference to the context of promoting industrialisation. The relations among politics, business, and institutions is traced from independence onwards, in terms of the institutionalisation of political power within the ruling party, and the changing distribution of power among groups of classes within the state and groups within business.

The theoretical framework that is adopted here considers the alternatives between a state that negotiates with the business sector to get the best for the public while satisfying constraints inherent to business, and a state that is 'captured' by a business elite and makes decisions that are in the interest of that business group rather than of the public. The latter case may manifest a kind of capture equilibrium. This capture equilibrium may occur when a group of big firms with some converging interests hold the government or the political elite 'captive' through providing political goods or services (campaign financing, job creation in constituencies, income addition, etc.). This situation makes the state take decisions in the interest of big business most of the time, while often partially converging with public interest by justifying that such decisions favour employment, the interests of the poor such as the promise of affordable prices of imports brought in by traders (who may be the majority), or some other public economic goal through allowing some big companies to pursue their interests. What they do not make clear is the kind of advantages they grant at the same time to those companies and the kind of benefits they themselves get in the process. This equilibrium situation permits some firms to make more profit, while politicians (or their parties) may maintain themselves in power as they increase their probability of gaining political capital and winning the next election, as well as accessing resources for personal gain. The existence of competition among the business elite gives more freedom to the government in choosing what is best for the country. However, in cases where corruption prevails, the choice of what is best for the country may be distorted. At a certain level of corruption, the state may even create its own channels for accumulating personal wealth through private business, which may not necessarily be big business, but it may be convenient for the government to accumulate wealth through such business. The state identifies a business entity to work with in order to syphon public resources. The selected business may be prominent or otherwise, provided it has the trust of the political players. The state's real situation may lie in between the two extremes of a free and a captured state. It is likely to vacillate between these extremes over time, and this equilibrium is likely to be maintained until it is disrupted.

One source of disruption could originate from exposing the relationships and deals, making them public knowledge. Thus, the media is one institution that could disrupt by exposing deals, provided they are not controlled themselves by the business or the political elite. Civil society organisations may also play this role, as can opposition parties or other organised social groups. However, depending on the degree and nature of capture of the political elite by business, it is quite possible the political elite could find it difficult to act, especially if those who are supposed to take action to rectify the situation are the ones who are being exposed. Captured by business links, and by the structure of political power within the dominant party, the political elite may find it difficult to make decisions, as the inclination to maintain the *status quo* may be overwhelming. This is a case of the presence of transparency without accountability.

Another source of disruption of the equilibrium could originate from the dynamics of changes in the overall economic context, such as changes in foreign prices, technological development, and various changing business opportunities, making some businesses lose while others gain over time, or some political factions gain while others lose power. What would be observed in that case would be a particular equilibrium, which could be modified owing to some exogenous change in the distribution of political power or business opportunities. This could be the rising of the opposition against the historically dominant party, or simply the personal will of a president, given the considerable power granted to the president by the constitution. Exposure such as that caused by the media and other players in the civil society can modify the relative power of some politicians or conflicts within the political elite, making it possible for one side to denounce the corruption of the other even when they themselves may be engaging in corruption.

Another view of the relationship between business and politics, through which state capture may be manifested, is the concept of rent and rent management. The capture view and the equilibrium distribution of rents are two ways of describing the same thing. In a seminal discussion of rents and rent-seeking, Khan (2010) distinguishes between different types of rents. Some of these are value-reducing and some value-enhancing, and some can be either depending on context. The manner in which economic rents are managed and oriented towards the short- or long-term horizon is important in influencing the extent to which rents may be value-enhancing. There are several types of rents, for example monopoly rents, natural resource rents, rent-like transfers, Schumpeterian rents, rents for learning, and rents for monitoring and management. Access to these rents by businesses can be politically driven, influenced by the relations between politics and business. Political decisions may transfer rents to business groups through direct transfers of assets or funds such as foreign aid, the transfer of publicly owned assets through privatisation or allocation of land, transfer of subsidies such as through utilities, or transfers in the form of election spending, and various forms of corruption can be influenced by the behaviour of the political elite (Cooksey and Kelsall, 2011). The extent to which rents are value-enhancing is determined in part by the extent to which benefits go to the general prosperity of the private sector or are reinvested locally for the good of the economy. Management of rents and the degree of centralisation can influence the benefits accruing to business as a community and the time horizon of its outlook.

The methodology that has been adopted in this chapter follows the nature of the business–state relationship and its evolution through the history of that relationship in Tanzania since independence. This methodology has been preferred in order to take fully into account the dynamics of the relationship. The information that has been used has been collected through a desk review of the relevant literature and personal interviews with selected political and business leaders.

III THE EARLY INDEPENDENCE PERIOD, 1961–1966

A The Situation at Independence

The early independence period from 1961 inherited effects of the colonial period, whereby local development initiatives had been interrupted, and accumulation processes had been countered by colonial government policymaking processes. This period inherited the colonial creation of social differentiation and compartmentalisation of society along racial lines (Rweyemamu, 1973). Europeans in business and the civil service were at the top, followed by Asians in trade, industry, and commercial agriculture, and at the bottom of the ladder were Africans. These classes were reinforced by economic and social discrimination. This situation was consolidated through discrimination in the issuance of business licences along racial lines, which had become institutionalised. The task of the newly independent government was to try to redress this discrimination in the issuance of business and trade licences.

B Origins of the Position of Asians

The origins of Asian business can be traced to the beginning of the twentieth century. Immigration of Asians, also referred to as British Asian subjects, began when some came to East Africa to construct the East African Railways, and others to start a network of commerce in the region (Mkapa, 2005). Those who were in trade had connections with the commercially active on the Swahili coast. Those who were engaged in internal trade were largely active in buying crops (maize, paddy, cassava, millet, sunflower seeds, groundnuts, beeswax, and honey) from peasants and selling manufactured goods (textiles and garments, soap, and cooking oil) in return. Over time, some of them turned commercial capital into industrial capital, mainly through agricultural processing such as rice and flour milling, oil processing, and soap. In the struggle for independence, Mwalimu Nyerere's visionary leadership took on board supportive Asians and Europeans.

C Development Initiatives in the Early Post-Independence Period

On gaining independence in 1961, Tanzania was a poor agricultural economy, with small mining and commercial sectors, and an expanding state bureaucracy assisted by foreign aid and loans. The guiding policy framework in the early post-independence period emanated from the World Bank and Arthur D. Little reports of 1961, which emphasised private sector development without questioning or specifying the ownership and product mix. The policy and strategy arising from these reports was expressed in the Three Year Development Plan (1961–3) and the First Five Year Development Plan (1964–9). The two plans essentially left the economy in the hands of the private sector, which was largely foreign (non-indigenous), relying on foreign aid and foreign direct investment (FDI). These development plans were geared to gradual growth by building on the basic structures of the colonial economy, encouraging agricultural modernisation, and stimulating private investment in industry and commerce.

The ownership structure of industry during the first years of independence remained primarily the outcome of colonial restrictions that had reserved certain industrial activities for British firms, and barriers to indigenous investors were removed (Silver, 1984). Industrial policy was geared to basic import-substitution industrialisation, with support to protected industry via tariffs (thereby creating rents, which were either of learning or monopoly character). There was little incentive to encourage learning and the infant industries did not grow to maturity as expected. This resulted in learning rents turning into monopoly rents. Members of parliament lacked personal power bases (Bienen, 1970), a phenomenon that was reinforced by tight vetting of candidates and election regulations prohibiting use of private funds in campaigns (Barker and Saul, 1974). In the industrial sphere, a mini-industrial investment boom that began in around 1955 continued until the mid-1960s. The main investors were East African Asians (the Chandes, Madhvanis, and Chandarias), settlers, traders, and multinationals. These groups were attracted to Tanzania because they were uncertain about political stability in Kenya and Uganda, about the future of the East African common market, and because the government gave them the right signals. These investments were probably as much as Tanzania could expect, and the period should be viewed as reasonably successful in terms of creating value-enhancing economic rents (Cooksey and Kelsall, 2011).

The investment programme that was proposed in the early 1960s built on the inherited structure from the colonial period and was expected to be implemented through the encouragement of local and foreign private investment. The accent here was on using foreign capital to solve what was seen as the problem of scarcity of capital. In spite of all the incentives provided for in the Foreign Investment Protection Act of 1963, the response from the private sector fell below expectations. In addition, the absence of any significant local entrepreneurial class posed a problem of how to gain local control of the development process.

During this period, the country was very rural, with about 95 per cent of the population residing in rural areas, where poverty was rampant largely owing to low productivity in agriculture. Efforts towards agricultural transformation in the absence of a significant business class in agriculture started with various initiatives and programmes to support agriculture productivity growth and rural transformation. In the first five years of independence, the government adopted a transformation approach on the recommendation of the World Bank (World Bank, 1961). This involved moving some of the farmers from their traditional villages to new villages or settlement schemes to fast-track the introduction of agricultural transformation, on the assumption that smallholder farmers were poor because of lack of capital and technology. The rationale for the transformation approach was to transform agriculture by introducing the technical, social, and legal systems that allow the use of modern agricultural techniques meant to achieve high productivity, based on investment of capital (Bank of Tanzania, 1982, p. 76). The assumption was that a business class could be created in agriculture driven by technology. The improvement approach based on demonstration effects from progressive farmers also did not yield the expected outcomes, owing to a lack of participation from the peasants themselves. This approach to agricultural transformation failed because of the cost of replicating it in the country (Cliffe and Cunningham, 1973).

D Continued Concern over Social and Economic Differentiation

Clearly, in the early 1960s, little was done to cultivate a healthy relationship between politics and business, since business was dominated by foreigners and alien Tanzanians. This kind of domination had political sensitivities after independence. In the absence of any significant local (African) entrepreneurial class, reliance on the free market and private sector-led development was risking the continuation and even consolidation of distorted economic and social structures. This situation posed the political problem of how to gain local control of the development process. These initial conditions in the early post-independence period exhibited social and economic differentiation in the business sector and political concerns over the control of business by non-Africans. This situation continued to influence relations between politics and business into the subsequent periods.

These considerations influenced the timing and content of the Arusha Declaration. This was a decisive factor in disrupting the equilibrium that had essentially persisted in the early post-independence period.

IV THE ARUSHA DECLARATION: BUSINESS AND POLITICS RELATIONS, 1967–1985

A The Arusha Declaration Response

The Arusha Declaration in 1967 was a response to the challenges of the early post-independence period. It made an ideological shift and enunciated the principles of socialism and self-reliance to address concerns about the initial conditions at independence. In the theoretical framework of this chapter, the Arusha Declaration represents a disruption of the equilibrium that was prevailing in the early independence period. Enshrined in the Arusha Declaration was the concept of people-centred development, which became a running theme through the post-independence Nyerere period. This concept was interpreted broadly to include social and economic liberation with human dignity, equality and freedom of the individual, equality of opportunity across all races, and commitment to reduce income and wealth differentials in society. Implementation of the Arusha Declaration started with nationalisation of the major means of production at that time, such as large industries, commercial farms, banks, and large wholesale and retail trade establishments. One consequence was the change in the ownership pattern whereby the major means of production were nationalised, and most major subsequent investments were made in public enterprises. This situation led to the emergence of a public business through parastatal sector development. The nationalisations soon devolved into a three-tiered structure of parastatal investment banks, holding companies for productive enterprises, and the enterprises themselves. The Arusha Declaration precipitated and shaped the different type of relationship between politics and business that followed.

B Emerging Public Sector Business Leaders

In order to curb the growing relationships between politics and business, the Arusha Declaration introduced a Leadership Code that prohibited politicians and public servants from engaging in private business as shareholders or directors. It was hoped that this move would curb the practices of capitalist accumulation that had started to emerge in the business and politics relationships. The appointees to leadership positions in the parastatal business sector fell into three groups of managerial staff. The first group was appointed from the category of politicians: mainly nationalist organisers in the struggle for independence, such as George Kahama and Paul Bomani, who had organised farmers in the independence struggle through cooperatives in the Lake Region in Kagera and Mwanza, respectively. The second group were young, educated Africans. Most of these young managers were sent to study abroad, mainly at the Arthur D. Little School for training professional managers and Williams College, both in the United States. Although qualified, they had little experience. Therefore, they were subjected to learning by doing and gaining experience running large-scale operations on the job. The third group was expatriates who were engaged to fill positions for which Tanzanians were not available.

The appointments of top managerial staff favoured consideration of 'political commitment, ideological orientation and patriotic pretensions', rather than training or professional competence (Cooksey and Kelsall, 2011, p. 17). This is one indication that the choices that were made about management and mode of operation were more driven by politics than value-maximisation. The interaction between politics and business changed with the adherence to state control of the major means of production.

C Initiatives to Promote Indigenous Business Sector

Initiatives were taken to try to move the business sector from being predominantly foreign and non-indigenous Tanzanian owned towards increasingly indigenous private business owned. In this context, the most important initiative was to promote small businesses to support empowerment of the majority of the indigenous entrepreneurs. In order to ensure that small businesses were supported to engage in industry and to spread out to the whole country, in 1966 the government established the National Small Industries Corporation (NSIC) under the National Development Corporation (NDC). In 1973, the NSIC was hived off from NDC and transformed into the Small Industries Development Organisation (SIDO), with a vision of being a leading business support organisation in Tanzania, providing quality services efficiently and effectively in a business-like manner that would unlock potential for the growth and competitiveness of small and medium-sized enterprises (SMEs) in rural as well as urban areas.

The central purpose and role of SIDO was to create and sustain an indigenous entrepreneurial base through promotion and support of SMEs by providing them with business development services and specific financial services on demand. The strategy that was adopted was to facilitate capacity building and capacity development of small enterprises through technology development, transfer and provision of technical services, training, consultancy and extension services, marketing and information technology programmes, and financial advisory and credit services. For over a decade following its establishment, SIDO played an important role in facilitating growth of the small-industry subsector and operated within the framework of a centrally planned and state-controlled economy. The impact on indigenous private sector development was at best quite modest is not insignificant. However, among the private businesses that were either not nationalised or were established after the nationalisation phase of 1967–8 was over, the foreign and non-indigenous Tanzanian private sector continued to dominate the industrialisation scene.

D Initiatives to Promote Parastatal Sector Business

The parastatal business sector was the real hope for changing the dominance of non-indigenous private sector business by facilitating the expansion of the parastatal sector. It is for this reason that parastatal sector expansion was accelerated through a series of favours in resource allocation. Favours took the form of import licences, foreign exchange allocations, credit allocation, and human resource allocations. The emerging new equilibrium in the relationship between politics and business in the new environment was manifested through new institutions such as parastatals, villagisation, import licensing, foreign exchange controls, credit control, and price controls. Protection through tariffs and other means was negotiated between investors and the government rather than through a cohesive industrial strategy (Rweyemamu, 1979), a situation that ensured that rents were accessed. These institutions provided rents to the parastatal business sector. The types of rents available to industrial parastatals included direct state subsidies, access to finance directly from state-owned commercial banks, foreign concessional financing by donors for specific projects, and rents originating from tariffs and exchange rate policy (Bigsten and Danielson, 2001). Price controls based on the cost-plus principle guaranteed rents for the parastatal business enterprises.

The politics of the extension of state control was increasingly vested in an expanding group of ruling party, bureaucratic, and management officials (Shivji, 1976). However, some of the private businesses developed relations (formal and informal) with the state. It is important to understand these relations, how they changed over time into the liberalisation era, and their implications for privatisation, institutional reform, and corruption. The foreign private sector players were incorporated into nationalised companies as managers, through management agreements, as suppliers of equipment, and as minority shareholders.

E Public–Private Business Relations

In pursuit of national unity, during this phase the space for key stakeholders to articulate their interests was curtailed. Private sector business was not organised and did not have a forum for dialogue except the various chambers of commerce. However, private investment continued to grow as parastatal investments were increasing.

The question is to what extent the political elite promoted the domestic business sector. The NDC was mandated by the government to set up large-scale industrial enterprises with the state holding majority shares. In practice, the minority shareholder acted as supplier of equipment and provider of management and technical advice. Choice of technology for the projects was left to the foreign partner as the Tanzanian state had little access to global information on the sources and comparative costs of technology (Barker et al., 1986). Most of the directly productive parastatals were turnkey projects engaging foreign partners and expatriate management. Rather than engaging in joint ventures with the domestic business sector, the parastatals often engaged foreign-owned companies in joint ventures in consideration of supply of technology, equipment, and management. The desire to show results quickly induced NDC to set up enterprises in the shortest possible time. It is for this reason that NDC was quite happy with turnkey projects offered by the foreign partner (Barker et al., 1986). The large number of joint ventures with foreign capital weakened state control in industry, and over-reliance on expatriates and foreign technical assistance left little space for building up technological expertise among nationals and in the process the domestic private sector was not promoted.

The preference for foreign partnership on the grounds of technology transfer and technical assistance meant that the potential of partnership with the domestic (Tanzanian or East African) private sector was not fully harnessed. In this regard, Barker et al. (1986) have examined the production processes of enterprises established by East African Asian capital and concluded that they stood a better chance of achieving sustainable accumulation because they obtained their profits through simpler management organisation, using equipment closely tailored to their needs, with relatively low capital costs and low maintenance requirements, which was more amenable to local manufacture and maintenance. The implication is that the assumption by government that local entrepreneurship was not available to provide technical assistance to parastatals and therefore led to reliance on foreign technical advice and management agreements may not have been correct in all cases. The reasons may have been political, considering that the dominance of non-indigenous private business and racial inequalities had been a major concern in the post-independence period.

The relatively large local private business sector did not enter into joint ventures with parastatals except in a few cases, such as the LONRO-controlled MTAVA (a vehicle assembly plant set up in 1965), where the shares were 50 per cent LONRO, 23 per cent Cooperative Union of Tanzania, 23 per cent Mwananchi Development Corporation (the economic wing of TANU, the ruling political party), and 4 per cent Barclays. In 1975, the structure had basically remained the same, except NDC had taken over the shares of Mwananchi Development Corporation. The parastatals were not only government owned, but also took shares of the ruling party lines of business. The line of business between government and the ruling party (TANU) was basically blurred, presumably because at that time the political environment was that of a single party regime.

Mwalimu J. K. Nyerere appointed some Asian businesspeople to the boards of parastatals. For instance, J. K. Chande from the Asian business sector was appointed chair of the board of the National Museum and also joined the board of the TANESCO). His milling business was nationalised along with others in 1967, he was made general manager of the National Milling Corporation (NMC) until 1975, and he continued to be a member of parastatal boards for many years.

F Performance of Parastatal Businesses

The rapid investments carried out by parastatal enterprises resulted in an increasing burden on the budget and foreign aid dependence as the performance of the parastatal business sector deteriorated. Parastatal performance has been shown by several researchers to be weak. Coulson (1979) examined several parastatal projects (e.g. fertiliser and bakery projects) and found their performance weak, riddled with bureaucracy and inefficiency. Productivity in parastatals was found to be low (Shao, 1978; Barker et al., 1986). Clark (1978) finds that large parastatals had low profit rates, at only a quarter of the profit rates of smaller private companies in 1971. Shao (1978) finds that output per employee was higher in Asian-run enterprises (e.g. textiles, grain milling, and sawmills) than in parastatals. Although labour productivity grew up to 1973, mainly as a result of rapid capital investment, this growth could not be sustained (Szirmai and Lapperre, 2001). Most interestingly, employment in industry increased nearly threefold over the same period – an indication of falling labour productivity (Bank of Tanzania, 1982, p. 114). Jedruszek (1979) finds that productivity in industry declined by 14 per cent between 1967 and 1977. Manufacturing productivity was below average over the period despite large capital investments. Jedruszek suggests that productivity was low because managers had no incentive to control production costs and promote efficiency and productivity while workers exercised their rights and not their responsibilities.

The weak performance of the parastatal enterprises can be interpreted as reflecting limited technological learning, a process that was inhibited by several factors: first, management agreements between government and foreign companies meant that top management was predominantly foreign. For instance, in their survey Barker et al. (1986) found that three-quarters of top management in parastatals was foreign. Tanzanian management was found to be less experienced and mainly occupying positions of general manager and personnel manager rather than technical and production management. The foreign managerial staff were skilled and experienced but found it difficult to initiate adaptations to Tanzanian conditions. Second, graduate education emphasised theoretical and administrative knowledge, and training was largely for administration. The exception was the Faculty of Engineering, which turned out its first graduates in 1977. Skill development at middle and lower levels was weak, with few opportunities for advancement through in-plant training, or training in other local institutes or abroad. The technical colleges were relatively theoretical and skilled workers accumulated some skills in repair and maintenance but not innovation, design, and manufacture. The strong technical division of labour between mental and manual labour was not conducive for effective technological learning and productivity increase.

From the end of the 1970s, the state tried to reduce the growing cost of subsidisation through a rationalisation programme that involved splitting up existing parastatals into smaller units and attempting to cut down on the overall number of parastatals. These initiatives were largely subverted from within as managers made deals with supportive politicians and bureaucrats within line ministries to expand by establishing new subsidiary parastatals, starting new branches or new areas of activities (Mukandala, 1988).

Poor productivity and lack of financial control led to widespread losses. By 1985, 165 of 354 parastatals had net losses: in output–labour ratio, private firms out-competed parastatals by a factor of two (Bryceson, 1993, p. 17). The government promised that it would close down loss-making parastatals, and yet this became politically difficult. The government continued to grant them bank overdrafts. Between 1973 and 1982, bank lending to agricultural marketing parastatals grew from 31 to 61 per cent of total lending (Bryceson, 1993, p. 21). Although parastatals were supposed to make profits, in reality they were subject to a variety of political directives, among which profit-worthiness was not a prime concern. In 1983, a government commission recommended the liquidation of poorly performing parastatals, together with other cost-cutting measures (Bryceson, 1993, p. 23).

G Political Elite–Parastatal–Private Business Relations

Politicians and employees began to plunder the parastatal sector partly through the manner in which parastatal businesses related to private businesses. While parastatal businesses were favoured in terms of allocation of resources, the private sector enterprises positioned themselves to access some of these resources through the black market. Dealings in the black-market trade earned rents for many private operators. The central leadership group around President Nyerere remained committed to a long-term socialist vision and industrialisation, but rent management was increasingly beyond their control.

At all levels of staff, parastatal resources were being used for personal gain. Corruption emerged and grew in allocating parastatal goods and services. Public vehicles were utilised for private business. Funds were misappropriated or embezzled, and records were falsified. A large proportion of the parastatal business sector had accounts permanently in arrears and unprofessional practices on the part of staff were smoke screened. (Bryceson, 1993, p. 21)

Despite the apparent formal political centralisation of power endowed by the dominance of party institutions within the state, the managers of parastatals were able to maintain their hold on state-created industrial rents even when their performance was poor. Systems of performance management and accountability were weak. Managers of parastatals were very much part of the cohesive intermediate class group that ran the single ruling party, TANU (Shivji, 1976; Mukandala, 1988).[1] However, the party was not able to discipline this group as it was able to make coalitions with supportive bureaucrats and politicians, especially ministers, to maintain rents despite poor performance (Gray, 2013).

J. K. Chande (2005) suggests that his experience in running NMC showed that income and wages policy and sometimes the erratic price interventions (e.g. putting a cap on the price of rice for NMC) negated the market forces, precipitating damaging effects. Interference by ministers and lumping unrelated economic activities in one parastatal company, such as bread with wine, complicated the management of parastatals even further. Observing how most parastatals were run, Chande notes that there were not enough entrepreneurs willing to work in the parastatal system, which was dominated by the cautious, doctrinaire, and anti-enterprise line driven by innate suspicion of the market and mistrust of any deals that seemed to be yielding rapid profit. Many businesspeople (Africans and Asians) fell victim to the practice of privileging political doctrine over sound economics and business (Chande, 2005). The economy was not geared to making surplus.

H Decentralisation of Management of Rents and Loss of Political Control

The stable and inclusive coalition within the ruling party gave the overall appearance of strength, but central control over the constituent parts was actually quite weak. Parastatal managers increasingly engaged in illegal activities to bolster their falling incomes and racketeering in the form of trading goods illegally at high prices based on their monopoly status (Gray, 2013). There were clear signs of loss of control and legitimacy as the shortage of goods was threatening erosion of political support. The shortage of goods was becoming severe.

By the mid-1980s, the political consensus on industrial policy slowly consolidated around the conclusion that state-led industrialisation was under threat

---

[1] TANU of the Tanzania mainland was united with the Afro-Shirazi party (ASP) of Zanzibar to form the Chama Cha Mapinduzi (CCM) party in 1977.

from weak performance and accountability systems, corruption, market distortions, and the absence of appropriate incentives to encourage reaping of learning rents or Schumpeterian rents. Industrialisation efforts were further frustrated by failures in agricultural production and low productivity in manufacturing' (Coulson, 1982, pp. 194–5; see also Svendsen, 1986).

Some political leaders were outspoken in their condemnation of these activities but were relatively powerless to stop them (Maliyamkono and Bagachwa, 1990). Initially it was diagnosed that shortages were caused primarily by hoarding by private traders. In 1983, Operation Economic Saboteur, championed by Edward Sokoine, the popular prime minister, led to the imprisonment of thousands of Tanzanian-Asian shopkeepers, but did not affect those who had links to the party (Maliyamkono and Bagachwa, 1990). The difficulties that were exhibited in the crackdown and the failure to stop shortages of goods in the market influenced the decision by government to adopt partial trade liberalisation in 1984. Under the government's own funds import scheme, businesses were allowed to use their own foreign exchange, no questions asked, for importing certain categories of goods, which went a long way to ease some of the economy's crippling shortages. The shift towards liberalisation culminated in the adoption of the structural adjustment programme (SAP) sponsored by the International Monetary Fund (IMF) in 1986. The adoption of the SAP marked the formal abandonment of the socialist strategy in industrialisation.

In 1985, Julius Nyerere stepped down as president and was succeeded by Ali Hassan Mwinyi, who as president of Zanzibar already enjoyed a reputation as an economic reformer. His election paved the way for a deal with the IMF, a new policy direction, and an evolution in the main types of rent creation and rent-seeking. The shift was made by the Mwinyi government and endorsed by the ruling party with Mwalimu Nyerere as chairman. It was essentially in reaction to an acute economic crisis and the conditionalities of the IMF and the donor community. This marked the beginning of the equilibrium disruption that had prevailed during the 1967–85 period. The emergence of a new equilibrium was in the making.

V POLICY REFORMS: OPENING UP SPACE FOR BUSINESS, 1986–1995

A Reforms as Response to the Crisis

Generally, the reform and SAP period (1986–95) started with the first generation of reforms essentially focusing on 'getting prices right'. Macroeconomic policy reforms included reforms in trade policy, exchange rate devaluation, removal of price controls, and removal of subsidies. The adoption of SAPs was perceived as a defeat of Ujamaa ideology, marking the shift towards a more market-oriented and private sector led economy. The SAP policy package aimed to promote efficiency in the productive sectors.

The second generation of reforms focused on the country's institutional framework for managing development in the context of the market. Emphasis was placed on the institutional framework conditions of public service reform and privatisation that were deemed necessary to support and facilitate the efficient working of the market.

Public service reforms took place partly against the backdrop of maladministration and partly as a result of political patronage having contributed to the bloating of the civil service. Public service reforms had the objective of organisational restructuring, reviewing the management of civil servants, improving the conditions of service, and improving their attitude towards providing greater support to the private sector.

B Privatisation and Politics–Business Relations

An important component of reform was divestiture of public enterprises. Privatisation was conceived as an opportunity to get rid of the burden of parastatals on the budget and to strengthen the private sector. The privatisation programme involved the transfer of assets from the public sector to the private sector. However, the pace of reform was extremely slow (Tripp, 1997, p. 91). Parastatal managers fought with reformers in the government to keep them (the parastatals) under state control (Fischer and Kappel, 2005). However, the soft budget constraint was tightened up (Bigsten and Danielson, 2001, p. 72), and many enterprises were divested. The fiscal deficit declined 'substantially and rapidly' after 1988 (Bigsten and Danielson, 2001, p. 33). However, in the majority of cases parastatals lost their dominance.

Some parastatals, such as the General Agricultural Export Corporation, were simply wound up. Others, including Tanzania Breweries and Williamson Diamonds, became joint ventures with the private sector. Some of these did very well after privatisation, examples being the sale of NMC to Bakhresa and the acquisition of the Minjingu Fertiliser factory and salt mines by Mac Group.

Debates in the Tanzania Chamber of Commerce, Industry and Agriculture, which were predominantly indigenous, warned against changing ownership in some parastatals in the direction of joint ventures with foreign firms. Such outcry could be an expression of patriotism, but it is also quite likely that the existence of some parastatals benefited the private sector – by operating as a weak competitor by selling inputs at low prices, for example.

A few companies saw management or employee buy-outs, such as Katani Ltd in the sisal industry. In these cases, former managers became owners without paying a fair price. This can be seen as the price of facilitating the development of indigenous entrepreneurs. The approach was one way of promoting ownership by the former managerial group. It may have been an opportunity to reward and promote those few with experience and the knowhow to run the enterprises. It was actually a way of deploying the pool of industrial managers who could use their experience of the industrial process and their political power within the state to manage the industrial activities as private sector operations.

The privatisation programme provided support to domestic indigenous private sector development. In response, an initiative was taken in the early 1990s to form a privatisation trust, which would take care of the interests of indigenous Tanzanians in the privatisation exercise. However, in practice, the trust was not provided with the necessary funding and so it was not operationalised. Although indigenous manufacturing did expand after liberalisation in very small-scale manufacturing, as pointed out by Tripp (1997), this was not an outcome of privatisation. The privatisation process did not promote indigenous entrepreneurs in medium- and large-scale manufacturing. Tanzanians of Asian and Arab origin secured most of the gains, while a small African business class of traders was also beginning to emerge (Havnevik, 1993; Tripp, 1997). The opportunity created to benefit indigenous domestic private sector development was not harnessed as expected to address the imbalances that had precipitated the Arusha Declaration. This was a missed opportunity of promoting indigenous capitalism. Indeed, in some cases privatisation returned most of the medium- to large-scale industrial activities.

A considerable number of the privatised manufacturing firms were actually sold back to their pre-nationalisation owners (Waigama, 2008). For instance, Aluminium Africa, which produced roofing sheets, was sold back to Chandaria Group (Kenya), which had been the former owner (Gibbon, 1999). The fact that the privatisation process reinforced the ownership of non-indigenous and foreign capital suggests that the concerns that had led to the Arusha Declaration were not addressed in the privatisation process.

The choice was sometimes between granting ownership to local owners and selling the enterprises to higher bidders who were foreigners or other local alien groups in society. The latter group won the bids most of the time as the privatisation trust was not funded adequately to facilitate indigenous Tanzanian owners. The bidding process was decided on the basis of politics, with various factions of the political elite supporting bidders who had sought their support. The possibility of corruption cannot be ruled out even if concrete evidence is not available.

C The Balance between Industrialists and Traders

For years, government subsidies and the opportunities for selling in a controlled market afflicted by acute shortages had been a major source of rents, which some state managers were keen to preserve. Those rents were increasingly threatened since most of the parastatals that survived faced increased competition. The commercial sector was to a large extent let loose during the Mwinyi era, the result of his policy of permissiveness, or *ruksa*. Many formerly outlawed activities were made legal by the reforms, but that did not necessarily lead to a decrease in smuggling. Critics argued that the measures were stimulating importers to earn easy foreign exchange by smuggling prohibited exports such as minerals and wildlife products (Tripp, 1997). Whatever the truth of the matter, the Mwinyi era was a period in which traders (importers and exporters) made large profits. Traders were in a more favourable position than industrialists and other long-term investors. Some enterprises abandoned industrial production and were turned into godowns (warehouses) for traded goods. For instance, the Tanzania Shoe Company was turned into a godown for stocking imports, including shoes. This is a manifestation of the response to the influence of trade liberalisation on the balance between traders and industrialists. The trade liberalisation favoured traders and importers in particular at the expense of industrialists. The surge in the import/GDP ratio, which reached almost 50 per cent in the early 1990s, is a manifestation of this imbalance (Bourguignon, Chapter 2, this volume).

The implications for industrialisation deserve to be reflected upon. An implicit assumption of economic reforms and industrial restructuring was that enterprise-level inefficiencies are a reflection of distorted or inappropriate macroeconomic policies. It was suggested that if appropriate adjustments could be put in place at macro-level, enterprises would receive the right signals through the market. In response to these signals, enterprises would restructure appropriately (World Bank, 1981, 1987). Various industrial studies have revealed that restructuring the industrial sector entails much more than macroeconomic management. Studies of the industrial sectors in several African countries (UNIDO, 1988, 1990) have confirmed that the problems of industry cover all levels (macro, sectoral, and plant) and all aspects of performance (including economic, financial, managerial, technical, and marketing). In his study of the performance of the Tanzanian textile sector, Peter de Valk has demonstrated that performance of enterprises is determined not only by macroeconomic factors, but also by international factors, sectoral policies, and characteristics at firm level, and that all these levels interact in a complex way (Valk, 1992).

However, in Tanzania, proactive trade liberalisation was so rapid that the assumption that economic reforms and industrial restructuring would occur at enterprise level did not hold. Although much inefficiency may have been a reflection of distorted or inappropriate macroeconomic policies, macroeconomic stabilisation was not sufficient to enable enterprises to respond and adjust accordingly. Instead, many enterprises closed. This phenomenon has been known as deindustrialisation. However, the experience of Vietnam, for instance, shows that it is possible to undergo reform without experiencing low growth and deindustrialisation. Having introduced reforms in 1986 – the same year Tanzania adopted the SAP package – Vietnam's annual rate of GDP growth over the period 1990–2000 was 7.9 per cent, which was exceeded only by China's 10.6 per cent (Thoburn, 2013). The main challenge is that the Tanzanian political elite did not balance appropriately the interests of industrialisation and trade. Trade was favoured, while industry experienced deindustrialisation.

D Political Elite Engagement in Business

Many members of the political elite had been running private businesses on the sly for years, circumventing the leadership code under the Arusha Declaration. However, this was legitimised in 1991 by the Zanzibar Resolution, which overturned the Arusha Declaration's Leadership Code (Gibbon, 1995, p. 14). Those with political connections fell over themselves to acquire land, the assets of former parastatals, and seats on private enterprise boards, and to generally use their public positions to make private gains in any way they could. The political elite engagement in business became more significant during this period, with political positions being increasingly associated with corruption in political elections and the peasants and workers representation progressively being squeezed as it was becoming costly to seek votes for political leadership positions because of the increased amounts of money involved in campaigns (Gibbon, 1995, p. 13). The use of money increasingly became an important factor in ascending to political leadership positions.

This period witnessed more open participation of the private business sector in the policymaking process. The private sector revived its representation in the form of specific trade and industry associations. However, these associations were still weak and most of the business deals were arranged and negotiated between individual businesses and the political elite. Big corruption scandals, especially those associated with natural resource rents, emerged on a wide scale. The Mwinyi era witnessed unprecedented scandals. In the most notorious instance, improper discretionary tax exemptions originating in the Ministry of Finance in 1993–4 led to a large fiscal deficit and the freezing of much foreign aid (Bigsten and Danielsson, 2001, p. 20). There were equally massive abuses of a government import financing a counterpart funds scheme. Another example was the notorious so-called Loliondogate scandal, which concerned the lease to an Arab general of a crucial section of the Ngorongoro game reserve for hunting (Gibbon, 1995, p. 16). But there were many others. The outbreak of the aforementioned tax exemptions scandal in the Treasury and misuse of import support funds suggested that even the Treasury was not successfully centrally controlled. It is in the context of these new heights of corruption that the use of the anti-corruption campaign slogan by the CCM presidential candidate in 1995, Benjamin Mkapa, was attractive to the electorate.

VI INITIATIVES TO CONSOLIDATE REFORMS AND DEFINE THE DEVELOPMENT AGENDA, 1996–2015

A Long-Term Development Agenda Revisited

The fourth period consisted of consolidating reforms and (re-)establishing a developmental state in the context of a full market economy. Growth had been fast at the beginning of the socialist period. After a long period of crisis and adjustment, it returned to its post-independence level, and has been fluctuating at around 6–7 per cent since 2000.

From the mid-1990s, the government started to rethink the short-term recovery programmes and decided to revert to addressing the long-term development agenda. The Sustainable Industrial Development Policy (SIDP, 2020), spanning 1996–2020, and Tanzania Development Vision 2025, spanning 2000–2025, were formulated in this spirit. The twenty-five-year SIDP 2020 was designed to initiate the process of structural transformation through industrialisation and enhancing sustainable development of the industrial sector. It would formally recognise the private sector as the main vehicle for making direct investments in the sector, while the government would provide an enabling environment and investments that crowd in (invite) private sector investments. The main contents of SIDP 2020 were later subsumed in the development of Tanzania Development Vision (TDV) 2025, the main guide to national development frameworks in Tanzania, envisioned as a middle-income country with a strong, diversified, and competitive economy.

According to TDV 2025, the private sector was to be given greater space in development, with special attention to empowering the relatively weak indigenous private sector. The disadvantaged position of the majority of the indigenous population and other vulnerable groups in society was to be addressed through economic empowerment by undertaking affirmative action programmes to empower these groups. It is in this context that the National Economic Empowerment Policy and Strategy were formulated in 2004.

What is striking, however, is that despite the formulation of SIDP 2020 and TDV 2025 envisioning the realisation of a semi-industrial economy by 2020/2025, growth during this period relied relatively less on industrialisation than during the socialist period in the 1970s. Growth in the post-1996 period was driven more by construction, telecommunications, and trade than by industrialisation. Although slowly increasing, the GDP share of manufacturing has not changed much since the late 1970s. This is an issue of concern, as the present long-run development plans of Tanzania are expected to rely heavily on substantial progress in labour-intensive industrialisation.

B Industrialisation and Politics–Business Relations

This raises the issue of the obstacles to industrialisation. There is an inadequate business climate – weak infrastructure, cumbersome administration, and corruption – which prevents entrepreneurs developing manufacturing and other long-term investments. The informal relations between the political elite and some big businesses undermine efforts to achieve a generalised improvement in the investment climate. The business elite is attracted by other activities, such as trade, that are more amenable to negotiation of taxes paid, and in which the payback period is relatively short, consistent with the election cycles. More generally, the imbalance between industrialisation and trade has continued to favour trade. Experience has shown that imports of some agricultural products based on low tariffs, such as rice and sugar, make local production less profitable and prevent long-term investments that are required to realise the development of the domestic agroindustry. In short, the Tanzanian economy has done rather well since the turn of the century, but it could do better, in particular by giving more weight to industrialisation, possibly in connection with agroindustry.

The question is whether the obstacles to moving in that direction can be found in pure government failures, that is, wrong allocation of public investments and low state capacity, or in the lack of appetite of local entrepreneurs and the lack of attractiveness of Tanzania to foreign investors. In this regard, the argument developed earlier in this volume (Chapter 2) that transport, communication, and construction cannot be powerful engines of growth because their growth depends on the domestic demand side of the economy is relevant. There is a need to develop the tradable sectors, such as industry and agriculture. Agriculture, for instance, would produce raw materials for industry as well as exports to earn foreign exchange needed for industrialisation.

The Agricultural Sector Development Strategy (ASDS) was developed in 2001 in order to address the constraints/challenges facing the sector in a holistic manner.[2] The vision of the ASDS is to have an agricultural sector that by the year 2025 is '*modernized, commercial, highly productive, utilizes natural resources in an overall sustainable manner and acts as an effective basis for inter sectoral linkages*' (URT, 2001, 32). Commercialising the predominant smallholder agricultural subsector and accelerating its growth rate are critical in achieving the noble goal of pulling the majority of the rural poor out of abject poverty. The question remains as to what kind of business–politics relation is more likely to result in the development of these productive sectors.

It is also possible that there is an issue of competitiveness in the Tanzanian manufacturing sector and the kind of support by the government given the bad experience with the parastatals, or the suspicion that the private sector will divert that support for its own use.

Successful development needs to have the right political base to influence implementation of the developmental policies. The relative power of groups within the private sector, such as traders and industrialists, has continued to favour traders. Tariffs to protect domestic industry are in place and are generally sufficient during this phase. However, effectiveness in implementation continues to be low, largely because of corruption, and tax assessment continues to be characterised by corruption, extortion, and arbitrariness.

A survey of fifty large industrial companies found that twenty-nine had their origin in the domestic private sector, while twenty-one firms were set up by foreign firms and/or the government (Sutton and Olomi, 2012).

---

[2] The ASDS covers crops and livestock production and immediate agribusiness-related activities, but excludes fisheries, forestry, and hunting.

A number of firms that had been involved primarily in trading activities during the socialist period bought up industrial parastatals. The survey by Sutton and Olomi (2012) found that, out of 50 large enterprises, 12 were trading ventures that had shifted to industry, having used the capital accumulated in trade to finance industrial enterprises. It also found that they had benefited from transferring a well-functioning medium-sized organisation (organisational capability) and access to markets and knowledge about markets. The likes of Bakhresa and Mohammed Enterprises belong to this category. This process of transforming commercial capital to industrial capital is a positive sign towards industrialisation. Mohammed Enterprises, which is active in textiles, beverages, edible oils, soap, agro-processing, grain milling, food, bicycles, energy, and petroleum, was founded as a trading company. The firm's move from trading to industrial processing came in 1998, when it established several businesses in agribusiness and manufacturing. The trading division remains the largest business within the group, dealing with the import of over twenty industrial and consumer commodities. The Murzah Group started as a trading activity, and from 1997 diversified into industry, establishing an oil manufacturing plant and producing cooking oil and soap for the local market. The plant operation draws on technological expertise from Alfa Laval (an Indian firm), supported by technology from Tetra Laval (of Sweden). Motisun Holdings, which has interests in steel and assembly, engineering, plastics, paints, beverages, hotels, and real estate, originated as a trading enterprise in the 1970s and diversified into manufacturing. MM Integrated Steel Mills Ltd has entered into a joint venture agreement with the National Development Company Ltd for mining of iron ore and coal, with forward integration into sponge iron in southern Tanzania, with a view to making Tanzania only the third country in Africa to produce its own iron ore.

The privatisation process of the 1980s and 1990s facilitated the rise of industrialisation through the private sector. For example, Mohammed Enterprises expanded its manufacturing activities by buying up industrial parastatal assets. Bakhresa grew from a small firm in the 1970s, acquired NMC, and diversified around food processing. In 1988, the government decided to sell a flour mill (NMC) as part of its privatisation programme. The enterprise invested in more modern technology, raised the mill's capacity from 50 metric tons (mt) per day to 240 mt per day, and has continued to diversify into other industries such as bottled water in 1988 and fruit juices in 2006. Mac Group, which had started as a trading company before independence, diversified into industry in 1976 and continued to expand and diversify (Sutton and Olomi, 2012). It benefited from the privatisation of the salt mines and Minjingu mines but kept on investing to stay competitive. Tanzania Breweries, which had been nationalised in 1967, was privatised in 1993, with 50 per cent sold by the government to SAB Miller Africa and 5 per cent sold to the International Finance Corporation. Since then, it has been modernised and expanded.

There are industries that started before independence, were not nationalised, and have continued to expand until now. For instance, Sumaria Group began as a small general trading business in Kenya in the 1940s, extended to Tanzania in 1957, and continued to expand, starting with plastics and diversifying into other industries through the period. Since 1975, the company has established or acquired some twenty-five companies in the areas of plastics, pharmaceuticals, clearing and forwarding, food processing, edible oils, soaps, cement, wheat flour, confectionery, textiles, real estate, soft drinks, dairy, and sisal. It has grown into a widely diversified multinational firm in the process (Sutton and Olomi, 2012). Sumaria Group aims at world-class manufacturing and service standards by developing strategic partnerships with leading regional firms.

There are cases where industrialisation through cooperatives has been a viable option. For instance, Tanzania Instant Coffee Company was established by the government, and from 1966 to December 1982, foreign experts appointed under a management agency contract manned the factory. Since 1982, the company has been managed by Tanzanians. In 2005, the ownership was diversified, with the majority ownership changing hands from the government to Kagera Cooperative Union, which has a 54 per cent share. Other shareholders include Karagwe District Cooperative Union, Tanzania Federation of Cooperatives, the government, and the firm's employees (Sutton and Olomi, 2012). The company operates the only instant coffee factory in East and Central Africa, for which it has won international awards on several occasions. A key milestone was the organic certification of its products. Another cooperative enterprise is Tanga Fresh, which is a leading dairy foods company created through a Dutch–Tanzanian bilateral programme. It began in smallholder dairy extension services in 1985, leading to the formation of the Tanga Dairies Cooperative Union (TDCU) made of thirteen primary societies. In 1996, a group of Dutch farmers entered into a joint venture with the TDCU to establish Tanga Fresh, which began in 1997 with a modest processing factory and continued to expand and diversify beyond fresh milk and fermented milk into plain and flavoured yoghurt, mozzarella cheese, butter, and ghee (Sutton and Olomi, 2012).

Promising industrialisation initiatives have taken place. The question is whether they are likely to continue and be sustainable. The shift in the pattern of industrial ownership from state to the private sector did not insulate industrial subsidisation from the types of corruption that were seen to have hampered industrialisation under socialism. The manner in which the formal and informal relationship between the political elite and business evolves will be determinant. During this phase the persistence of corruption is likely to have reduced the speed of industrialisation, and, unless it is checked, implementation of the industrialisation agenda is likely to be hampered.

C Formalisation of State–Private Sector Relationships

Liberalisation heralded the development of more open relationships between domestic capital and the state. The resurgence of the private sector was accompanied by a gradual inclusion of businesspeople within the formal framework of the ruling party. Formal institutions linking the private sector and the state were established, such as the Tanzania National Business Council (TNBC), constituting both private sector and government officials and chaired by the president.

The engagement of businesspeople in politics was enhanced by formalisation of the Zanzibar Resolution (1991) by removing the leadership code, and one response to it was the increasing number of CCM members coming from the private sector (Mmuya, 1998). The informal relations that had been constructed between state and capital through clientelist relations towards the end of the socialist period grew stronger. The implication is that corruption became increasingly apparent in this consolidation period. In his campaign, Benjamin William Mkapa promised to fight corruption. In 1995, President William Mkapa was elected and by January 1996 he appointed a presidential commission against corruption to assess the state of corruption in the country. Known as the Warioba Commission, this produced the Warioba Report in November 1996. In its analysis, the report distinguished grand corruption and petty corruption and areas/environments where corruption was occurring. The report also revealed the mechanisms (e.g. regulations and procedures) that facilitated corruption. Despite the commission's findings, numerous cases of grand corruption came to light over this period and were reported in the media. These were indicative of the close informal relations between the political elite and key business figures (Gray and Khan, 2010).

D Politics of Indigenous and Non-Indigenous Business

An issue that was not resolved by privatisation was the political economy concern relating to the dominance of non-indigenous Tanzanians in the industrialisation process, an issue that had contributed to the timing and content of the Arusha Declaration. By 2002, Tanzanian Asian capital accounted for around 26 per cent of all manufacturing firms (Chandra et al., 2008). Out of the fifty large enterprises that were surveyed by Sutton and Olomi (2012), only one, Bonite Bottlers, was found to be owned by an indigenous Tanzanian (Reginald Mengi). Bonite Bottlers is part of the IPP group of companies and produces Kilimanjaro Drinking Water, the leading bottled water in Tanzania. The IPP group has diversified into other areas, such as mining and the media sector.

The difficulties of imposing discipline on the political elite's rent-seeking networks seem to be insurmountable. Mushtaq Khan has recently argued that the ruling party, CCM, does not take advantage of its favourable political stability and strong organisational capacity to pursue a broad-based capitalist growth strategy because of the weakness of African capitalists. The more capable capitalists in Tanzania were, and remain, of Asian, Arab, or European origin, and, he argues, placing them at the centre of a growth strategy would be politically contentious. So far, capable Africans have been more interested in capturing political rents and rents from investments in real estate and short-term earning services than creating industrial ones. While single deals with short-term payoffs are possible, 'a long-term relationship between individual capitalists and political patrons is necessary for black African capitalists to emerge and grow' (Khan, 2010, p. 125). As a possible solution, Khan advocates formulating an active industrial policy for an indigenous business class. In the 1970s and 1980s, SIDO nurtured indigenous industrialists into relatively successful enterprises such as Northern Electrical Industries. These indigenous industrialists emerged from targeted potential industrialists who were supported with capital, training, technology and markets. The successes that were recorded suggest that a proactive empowerment programme stands a chance of supporting and nurturing indigenous industrialists.

E Politics and Foreign Business Relations

FDI into industry expanded under liberalisation. By 2008, the manufacturing sector accounted for around 21 per cent of total FDI in stock. In addition, FDI in the mining sector accounted for around 28 per cent of total FDI. However, the ability of the state to manage FDI has been limited. As a result, it has added little to new industrial capabilities and its contribution to manufactured exports has been even less successful (Bank of Tanzania, 2009). Industrial deepening did not happen through inviting FDI, as had been envisaged. This may be explained by the fact that FDI came predominantly to firms where capabilities had already been established during the previous period of state-led industrialisation, rather than to establish new industrial activities. The explanation for this outcome could be twofold. First, FDI was invited for its promise to bring in capital with no specific strategic requirement for technology transfer and technological capability building. Second, FDI was not strategically invited into priority sectors where technological capability building was most needed. In the absence of strategic policies to guide FDI into technological capacity-building activities, FDI caught the low-hanging fruit and had no incentive to invest in more technologically oriented sectors.

Promotion of industrial exports has been expressed in the form of Export Processing Zones (EPZs). However, industrialisation under EPZs has faced challenges of implementation. After the first zones had been established, the total number of firms operating inside the physical EPZs remained very low. A World Bank survey of EPZs in Africa identified that the clearance times within Tanzanian EPZs were actually worse than for manufacturing firms outside EPZs (Farole, 2011). Another challenge associated with developing industrial exports through EPZs is the management and implementation of incentives provided to ensure that firms in EPZs are fulfilling their export requirements.

F Corruption: Informal Politics–Business Relationships

Corruption can also be an inhibiting factor in industrialisation, especially in changing the relationship between industrialists and traders in favour of industrialists. Corruption in Tanzania has been widespread, and can be broken down into the categories of looting, and predation and rent-seeking.

1 Looting Involving Government Monies

Looting involves the *theft* of government monies. Two examples are presented here for illustration purposes: the External Payments Arrears (EPA) account and the Tegeta Escrow Account (TEA). The EPA scandal dates back to the 2005/6 financial year,[3] when a lump sum worth TZS (Tanzanian shilling) 133 billion (USD 116 million) was misappropriated to twenty-two company accounts by the Bank of Tanzania, and a concern was raised by the international auditors (Deloitte and Touche) in September 2006. The anomaly occurred between May 2005 and March 2006 (around election time) from the EPA account. The recipients of EPA money were mostly bogus companies set up for the purpose of emptying the EPA, an old commercial debt facility transferred from the Ministry of Finance to the Bank of Tanzania. When the case was exposed and pressure built up, the governor of the Bank of Tanzania was sacked by President Kikwete. Several Bank of Tanzania officials and EPA recipients from the business community were arrested and charged. An unusual aspect of EPA is that it was claimed that large amounts of money had been returned to the government under an informal amnesty agreement (Cooksey and Kelsall, 2011). This is a case of transparency without accountability.

The second case, TEA, demonstrates that, apart from looting public funds, one effect of corruption is that it undermines implementation of the officially declared development agenda and policy. The agreement to build a gas pipeline and power station according to the energy policy was pitched to compete with the independent power plant (Independent Power Tanzania Ltd, IPTL), which was not consistent with the national energy policy. Some sections within the political elite argued against IPTL on the grounds that the gas project (Songas),

---

[3] The EPA account was originally set up by the government to help service balance of payments, whereby local importers would pay into the account in local currency, after which foreign service providers would then be paid back by the Bank of Tanzania in foreign currency. However, owing to poor foreign currency reserves in the 1980s and 1990s, the debt within the account accumulated, leading to efforts under a scheme known as Debt Buyback – which involved some debt cancellations. Despite these efforts, unscrupulous officials and businesses were able to take advantage of one of the plans devised to reduce the account debt, under which a creditor could endorse debt repayment to a third party. (Reported in *Daily News*, a government newspaper in Tanzania.)

which was consistent with the energy policy, was already in the pipeline. This faction argued that IPTL used technology that was not consistent with the energy policy, constituted excess capacity, and was highly overpriced. Despite this opposition, IPTL obtained government agreements, tax exemptions, and other requirements in record time.

When details of the deal were leaked out by the mass media, there was a public outcry, and President Mkapa took steps to allow the contract to go to international arbitration. The tribunal found that the project was significantly overpriced, but evidence of bribery – which, if proved, would have invalidated the contract – was not presented in time to influence the tribunal's ruling that the Power Purchasing Agreement should proceed, with a reduced tariff. Both IPTL and the natural gas agreement were finally signed on the same day in 1999. Thus, Tanzania was burdened (belatedly) with the cost of two projects when it only needed one and entered into an agreement that directly contradicted the 'least-cost' policy option. TANESCO's subsequent financial difficulties have required bailouts from the government and an emergency power project loan.

When a dispute arose as to the level of capacity charges that IPTL was charging TANESCO, it was agreed that the funds arising from the charges should be kept in a special account (TEA) pending settlement of the dispute. TEA had been opened in 2006 when IPTL was liquidated and bought by Pan Africa Power Ltd (PAP). However, by the time the International Centre for the Settlement of Investment Disputes made its decision in favour of the claim by TANESCO that IPTL had overcharged TANESCO, the funds in the TEA had been transferred to the PAP account that claimed to have bought IPTL.

Top political leadership claimed that the funds were private and not public funds. Although the president praised the Parliamentary Public Accounts Committee (PAC) for standing against evil, and sacked some key players in the saga, he still went on to claim that the funds were private money. On the contrary, some sections of the political elite argued that the funds were public money.

The businessman who facilitated this huge loss, Harbinder Singh Sethi, was hardly a significant businessman in Tanzania before the scandal, although he had been a key player in facilitating deals with the political elite in Kenya and South Africa and has been a player in real estate in New York (Policy Forum, 2014). This is an indication that his skills in facilitating deals and the trust he had from sections of the political elite had a proven record and were possibly more important than his prominence or performance as a businessman. This is the case of a businessman who was 'created' by trust to play the role of syphoning public funds to the pockets of sections of the political elite in collaboration with a section of the business community. It indicates that Tanzania has not yet developed inclusive political institutions that can constrain the appropriation of public resources by the ruling elite (Policy Forum, 2014). This case demonstrates the presence of transparency without accountability.

2 Predation and Rent-Seeking

A slightly different but equally lucrative area of corruption can be referred to as predation. Logging and hunting are good examples. In the first, under-valuation and non-taxation of forest products in Tanzania led to huge revenue losses. An estimated 90 to 95 per cent of potential revenue from the forest sector is lost to illegal logging. Fishing and hunting licensing and regulation are other sources of major natural resource rents that are captured by officials and private business actors. In a recent case, forensic auditors concluded that the Ministry of Natural Resources and Tourism had misused half of the Norwegian-funded Management of Natural Resources Programme, worth about USD 50 million over ten years. In an unprecedented move, the Norwegian government requested the government of Tanzania to return the missing money. The government challenged the audit findings, 'errors' were discovered in the report, and Norway eventually agreed to the reimbursement of a token amount (Jansen, 2009).

Predation also occurs in the field of procurement, which accounts for around one-third of all government expenditure. Procurement creates rents when the government procures goods or services from the private business sector at either an inflated price or inferior quality. Sometimes, officials and politicians operate on both sides of the deal, and intermediaries broker the deals.

G Transparency without Accountability and Erosion of the Ruling Party's Credibility

During this period, institutionalisation of transparency was enhanced and institutions of governance were created, but accountability challenges persisted. While macroeconomic management continued to be consolidated, management of government expenditures and off-budget resources permitted a large share of the rents to be appropriated as corruption, primitive accumulation, or patronage spending (Cooksey and Kelsall, 2011). Indeed, a lack of discipline with respect to grand corruption was quite apparent. This situation is not consistent with successful implementation of a long-term development agenda and industrialisation in particular. The opaque relationship between politics and business aimed at maximising the profits of the latter became more transparent, but the top political leadership did not support accountability wholeheartedly.

The several cases of corruption, the exposure that followed, and the little action that was taken eroded the popularity of CCM, the ruling party. For example, Twaweza's 'Sauti za Wananchi' (Twaweza's 'Voice of the Citizenry') surveys indicate a drop in approval of the performance of public leaders, with the president's approval ratings falling from 45 per cent in 2012 to 31 per cent in 2014, and similar or more dramatic falls in the approval ratings of the prime minister, MPs, and village/street chairpersons and councillors. The situation even threatened the chances of CCM winning the next elections in 2015.

This erosion in popularity of the ruling party was felt by party members. This situation is demonstrated by four developments. First, the TEA saga resulted in the PAC (with majority CCM members) putting pressure on the Executive. Although the Executive was not willing to be held accountable, a few members of the Executive were sacrificed through sackings and forced resignations. Second, in the elections of councillors in 2014, the TEA scandal and other corruption incidents were widely used to discredit CCM as a corrupt party. CCM lost more seats than ever before. Third, during the screening of CCM presidential candidates in 2015, corruption became an important consideration for decisions within CCM. Although reasons for disqualification of some prominent candidates were not given explicitly, it is widely believed that this was because of corruption. Fourth, the CCM presidential candidate, Dr John Magufuli, made anti-corruption a main campaign slogan. In his campaigns, he emphasised what he would do to fight corruption rather than what CCM would do about it. The opposition candidate Edward Lowasa, who had crossed from CCM to Chadema, was silent on corruption in his campaigns, possibly because he had resigned as prime minister in 2006 on allegations of corruption, which had an effect on how the electorate was perceiving him.[4] These developments all marked the waning of the kind of relationship between business and politics that had prevailed for three decades. That equilibrium was coming to an end and a disruption was imminent, either by CCM losing the elections or by CCM making decisive changes internally. The latter option was taken.

VII FIFTH-PHASE GOVERNMENT: FIGHTING CORRUPTION AND CHANGING RELATIONSHIPS BETWEEN POLITICS AND BUSINESS

The foregoing analysis has shown that, although the political elite monopolises the main forms of rent creation, rent management within the political system is decentralised and not effectively coordinated by a single individual or group at the apex of the state.[5] The result is damaging to the effective implementation of a long-term development agenda. Throughout the 1960s and 1970s, Julius Nyerere took great pains to centralise rent management, using a variety of means, including his own charisma and personal authority and the powers of the president as per the constitution. However, the collapse of the formal economy in the late 1970s disrupted that equilibrium. Since then, the following three governments under Mwinyi, Mkapa, and Kikwete have not been sufficiently daring to restore that system. The fifth-phase government, led by President John Pombe Magufuli from November 2015 to March 2021,

---

[4] A few months before he crossed from CCM to the Chadema party, he had been branded as corrupt and his name had been placed on the list of shame. This information was widely known.
[5] Some of the arguments in this section have been supported by Shivji (2021).

showed the beginnings of disrupting the equilibrium that has prevailed for three decades, distinguished itself with a high level of commitment to fighting corruption, putting off unnecessary government expenditure, and announcing the intention to industrialise Tanzania.

However, it takes considerable personal authority and time to disrupt that equilibrium and establish a new system. The fact that President Magufuli had not been an insider in CCM, the ruling party, and had campaigned on the anti-corruption ticket may have been an advantage. In one of his speeches to the business community, he challenged the sector's members by pointing out that he had not been brought to power by their money, a situation that was very different from how his predecessor had come to office. At the same time, his lukewarm relationship with business leaders was a problem, because he needed them. In this regard, his statements in the TNBC meetings of May 2017 and March 2018 had mixed messages. On the one hand, he expressed a conciliatory tone, expressing recognition of the role of the private sector in development and the willingness of government to support private sector development. On the other hand he pointed out on several occasions how members of the private sector had engaged in acts of corruption and other malpractices. This perception of the private sector prevailed during this phase. The discussions in the TNBC were not particularly constructive. In fact there were no more TNBC meetings after 2018 although TNBC is supposed to meet the president twice a year. This was a sign of deteriorating relations between the president and the business community.

The ascendance of President Magufuli and his campaign slogan against corruption was influenced by the falling popularity of CCM because of the corruption scandals that had been exposed, but little accountability followed. Magufuli had an opportunity to influence the manner in which the political elite interacted with business to take advantage of favourable political stability and the strong organisational capacity of CCM, to pursue a broad-based development strategy driven by the private sector. He had the opportunity to pursue a more active industrial policy that could support industrialists and rectify the bias in favour of traders. His concern over economic empowerment of the vulnerable groups in society could have formed the basis for promoting indigenous Tanzanian industrialists and inclusive industrialisation, an issue of major concern in the initial conditions at independence and as reiterated in TDV 2025 and in the National Economic Empowerment Policy of 2004. The concerns over these issues were (and are) real and have not gone away. However, during this phase, public investment was preferred to private investment to the detriment of the latter. It was common for public investments to crowd out the private sector. Activities that were earlier being performed by the private sector were transferred to the public sector such as insurance to National Insurance Corporation and construction to Tanzania Building Agency and JKT. The orientation was to encourage public sector institutions to procure their products and services from other public sector institutions. The private sector was accorded low priority. Private businesses faced harassment from the Tanzania Revenue Authority (TRA) and what came to be known as the Tax Task Force consisting of TRA, police, security and Prevention and Combating Corruption Bureau (PCCB) officials. The list of unbailable offences under the notorious Money Laundering Act was extended to cover even such offences as tax evasion and business-related offences. Closure of bank accounts was generously applied to business based on all kinds of demands from revenue authorities. The president's harsh interventions against the private sector prevented pursuit of a broad-based development strategy driven by the private sector.

President Magufuli demonstrated the will and reputation to impose a new discipline in CCM, by going over the heads of the party and engaging directly with the masses in his own terms. This enhanced the chances of taking a new direction towards an inclusive development strategy. The fifth-phase government showed that there is an opportunity to address collective action problems within CCM, short-termism driven by periodic elections, and corruption in elections. If this had happened successfully, there was a chance of facilitating the development of an anti-corruption regime that could create a long-term transformative development strategy through industrialisation. These long-term development concerns, including industrialisation, were pillars during the 1967–85 period. There were signs that under the leadership of President Magufuli several elements of these pillars had a good chance of being revived. However, the president's unrelenting industrialisation drive gave jobless youth little relief as it hardly dented unemployment figures. His idea of industrialisation lacked consistency, coherence and was not guided by clear policy and strategy. It did not show consistency with a broad vision of building a nationally integrated economy in which industry, agriculture, and services would be mutually reinforcing. Agriculture received little attention and private investment in the economy faced hostility from the Magufuli government. Major emphasis was placed on investments in infrastructure. This presented an opportunity for facilitating private investment, provided other business environment conditions were put in place.

Implementation of a long-term development agenda and industrialisation in particular faced two challenges. First, the institutional environment and the political structure of CCM needed to reform in order to cope with this requirement of long-term development and transformation. As president and chairman of the ruling party, Magufuli did not institutionalise the party and make it fit for the task. CCM was not structured for political mobilisation that addressed the set of rules, organisations, and norms that would constrain the behaviour of the political elite and make them accountable to the citizens of Tanzania. The ruling party did not seize the opportunity to explain, discuss strategies, and promote ownership of the development agenda and strategy among the key actors. Second, the president put emphasis on hard work as a main contributor to development and self-reliance, but this was not accompanied by capacity building and incentives. Instead, salaries and promotions of public servants were frozen for his presidency as priority was accorded to public investments in large infrastructures. Public service performance management and the associated incentives were not institutionalised. Public service support for businesses deteriorated and the business climate weakened, as indicated by declining rankings reported by the World Bank.

The fifth-phase government put emphasis on the prudent use of natural resources for the development and benefit of the people. This was a fight against scooping rents through corruption and other ways. It is in this context that a progressive piece of legislation called Natural Wealth and Resources (Permanent Sovereignty) Act was passed in 2017 recognising the sovereign ownership of the people of natural resources. However, there was little space for private investment in general and little appreciation of private investment, either FDI or private domestic investment. A notable attack on FDI was the taking on of the multinational gold company Barrick when the president stopped containers full of mineral sand from being exported by Acacia, a subsidiary of Barrick, for smelting. He formed a local team of experts to investigate the mineral content of the sand. Simultaneously, the Tanzania Revenue Authority slapped on the company a huge bill of unpaid taxes amounting to USD 190 billion. Eventually the parties struck a deal under which Barrick would pay USD 300 million in settlement of the tax dispute and give Tanzania a 16 per cent stake in a new company, Twiga Minerals, which would operate Barrick's three mines. This may have appeared as victory, but there are two challenges here. First, the message that the saga sent to other private investors was negative, leading to the risk of scaring away investors and reducing the credibility of contracts that the government entered into with them. Second, the process of negotiating with investors of this kind was not institutionalised. The local team that was formed to negotiate was not followed by creation of the local human and institutional capacity to carry out negotiations with private investors on a continuous basis.

The earlier Kikwete administration, which had promoted transparency with little accountability, shifted towards a higher level of accountability with reduced transparency. However, accountability of the top leader to the constitution and to the people he was leading was reduced while subordinates became accountable to one person at the top with little institutionalisation. Magufuli did not make himself accountable to the business community and ruled by fiat, legitimising his approach by material measures in the interest of the downtrodden or oppressed (called *wanyonge* in Tanzania) to the detriment of private investment and private business in general. Autonomous institutions of democracy such as parliament and the judiciary were stripped of their content so they existed in name only, going through the rituals of elections, law-making, and judicial decision making, which means little in practice. In terms of relations between politics and business, this situation introduced little transparency and a low level of certainty in the policies that influenced business decisions.

In conclusion, while it is appreciated that corruption declined and investment in infrastructure increased, economic prosperity suffered. Too much attention went to infrastructure and little went to boost the economy of private sector actors. Agriculture and participation in the global value chain was not accorded priority although the livelihoods of over 60 per cent of the populations is derived from agriculture, and public investment often crowded out private investment. The regime was not friendly to business and the private sector development that the third-phase government under Mkapa had started and was built further by the fourth phase government under President Kikwete. The private sector suffered in the hands of the fifth-phase government. Lack of participation in public affairs made people unhappy and dissatisfied, and they could not hold their government accountable. Business with other countries and international relations deteriorated. Weak institutions for holding the leadership accountable were the main cause of this situation. It has been argued that this underlines the risks of viewing leaders through rose-tinted glasses: Charismatic individuals can claim the reformer's mantle, but giving them too much credence before structural reforms are implemented sells democracy short and increases the risk of authoritarian relapse (Cheseman et al, 2021).

VIII SIXTH-PHASE GOVERNMENT LED BY PRESIDENT SAMIA SULUHU HASSAN, MARCH 2021 TO DATE

Magufuli died on 17 March 2021, and Samia Suluhu Hassan was sworn in as the new president of the sixth-phase government. Although she has not been president long enough for conclusions to be drawn, there have been notable changes in policies on several fronts.

First, freedom of the media and freedom of speech have been an immediate change from the Magufuli regime. Print and electronic media are operating freely and some of those that had been closed have been reopened. This is positive for transparency. Second, there is freedom for opposition parties and President Samia has openly spoken in favour of bringing unity and peace between CCM and the opposition parties.

Third, the relationship with the business sector has improved, one indicator being the resumption of dialogue between government and the private sector in the TNBC. Within 100 days in office, President Samia chaired a TNBC meeting, meetings that had not been held since 2018. Since then TNBC has been holding meetings twice a year. President Samia has also met sections of the business community on several occasions. In her state visits to other countries (Uganda, Kenya, Rwanda, Burundi, and the United States), she has taken members of the business community with her. All these are positive signs that the relationship between politics and business are likely to improve under President Samia.

Fourth, President Samia has liberalised several policies to make them business friendly. She is more liberal politically and economically and more friendly to the outside world, from neighbours in the region to Western governments. She is already opening up to the outside world. She has paid state visits to Uganda, Kenya, Burundi, Rwanda, and the US. She has mended relations with the World Bank and IMF.

Fifth, President Samia has demonstrated that observance of the rule of law is being restored. Several businesspeople who had been arrested and remained in custody without being charged and those who had been charged falsely for money laundering have been released. Those who had been close to Magufuli and broken the law with impunity have been taken to court and charged. A former District Commissioner for Hai District who was breaking the law with impunity, claiming that he was doing so under the orders of Magufuli, was jailed in October 2021. Cyprian Musiba, whose media house was known for defaming and relentlessly humiliating former leaders, has now been taken to court; two recent cases have been won and he has been fined heavily. His media house is not functioning anymore. Upholding the rule of law is likely to enhance the certainty of the environment in which business operates.

Finally, there are encouraging indications that the business climate is improving. The policies and procedures for issuing permits to investors have eased and permits for foreign experts have been made more liberal and efficient. Investors are assisted more efficiently in terms of time. The TRA has been instructed to act with fairness and promote compliance with competence instead of force. More processes for handling investors have been digitalised and delays have been reduced.

IX CONCLUSION

This analysis of politics and business relations has shown that there are weak institutional areas that constrain development and appropriate directions for long-term development through industrialisation. The political economy analysis that has been adopted in this study has demonstrated its dynamism in the sense of representing interests of various groups that have been changing over time. This framework has put the lessons from experience in context and has brought out the relation between politics and business over time. It has been shown that, in the first two phases (1961–67 and 1967–85), the state was able to relate to business with a view to getting the best for the public, while satisfying constraints inherent to business. However, the equilibrium that had prevailed through this period was disrupted in the following phases. During the third and fourth phases (1986–95 and 1996–2015), the relationship between politics and business changed quite substantially. It gave space for a business elite to negotiate with sections of the political elite in ways that resulted in decisions in the interest of business groups that also benefited respective sections of the political elite. This equilibrium permitted some firms to make more profit and politicians (or their parties) to maintain themselves in power. At a certain level of corruption, the state could even create its own channels for accumulating wealth through private business, which may not necessarily have been big business but were convenient and trusted. These confident businesses facilitated the accumulation of wealth by opening channels for syphoning off public resources. This equilibrium prevailed in the third phase and was consolidated in the fourth phase. The fifth phase, led by President Magufuli, showed signs of disrupting the situation. The source of this disruption was simply the personal will of the president, given the considerable power granted to him by the constitution. However, the change was not institutionalised, and in many ways business was disrupted.

One major lesson to draw from all regimes is that although the ruling party has not changed since Independence, the polity in Tanzania remains fragile, institutions remain weak, and the masses are disorganised. Therefore, the polity in Tanzania is vulnerable and amenable to the rise of individuals who are able to make changes that are not institutionalised. Under the circumstances, organisation-building and institution building remains foremost in the design and implementation of the long term development agenda.

The analysis has also shown that the political elite has the opportunity of monopolising the main forms of rent creation and rent management. These were centralised within the political system and not effectively coordinated in the first and second phases, thereby degenerating into a decentralised rent management system in the following two phases. In the fifth phase, Magufuli tried to reverse the decentralised rent management system to a centralised rent management system. Throughout the 1960s and 1970s, Julius Nyerere took great pains to centralise rent management, using a variety of means, including his own charisma and personal authority and the powers of the president as per the constitution. However, the collapse of the formal economy in the late 1970s disrupted that equilibrium. Since then, the political leadership in the third- and fourth-phase governments restored that centralised system of rents. Although the long-term development agenda was defined during this period (1996–2015), its implementation faced considerable challenges arising from the nature of the politics and business relations. The institutional arrangements that were put in place during the fourth phase (1996–2015), such as PAC, the Controller and Auditor General, and the PCCB, enhanced transparency. It has been shown that transparency improved but accountability fell short. It indicates that during this phase Tanzania did not develop inclusive political institutions or a strong top leader who could constrain the appropriation of public resources by the ruling elite. The fifth-phase government led by President John Pombe Magufuli from November 2015 showed the beginnings of disrupting the equilibrium that had prevailed for three decades. However, this was done by weakening institutions. This factor, however, makes it relatively easy for President Samia to make several reversals within a short time.

The question of whether the relationship between politics and business is likely to facilitate improvement of the investment climate and create conditions for capital accumulation and industrialisation continues to be relevant.

Throughout the 1960s and 1970s, President Julius Nyerere centralised rent management and implementation of the long-term development agenda took shape. However, this situation was reversed in the following phases. The fifth-phase government under President Magufuli attempted to reverse decentralised rents towards centralisation, and channels of syphoning rents for personal gain were curtailed. However, preoccupation with the drive towards personal rule and the further weakening of institutions undermined the implementation of a long-term development agenda.

A key criterion, it seems to us, is that the high political elite of the CCM should recognise that the current situation emulating short-termism is unsustainable. Organs such as the Central Committee of the party could then conceivably be used as monitoring mechanisms for mutual discipline of the elite, helping steer rent-seeking into more developmental areas. When introducing the Arusha Declaration in 1967, President Nyerere and the chairman of the ruling party TANU asked the question as to whether the existing TANU internal political structure was capable of implementing the Arusha Declaration. Nyerere argued for reform of the party in order to cope with the demands of the Declaration. A similar question is relevant today in a different context. It is whether the current internal political structure of CCM is capable of disciplining the elite and steering rent-seeking towards a truly developmental state that can facilitate capital accumulation and industrialisation. This chapter has shown that the business and politics relations are important determinants of the investment climate and national policies that are crucial factors in driving capital accumulation and industrialisation.

The fifth-phase government under President Magufuli took initiatives to disrupt the equilibrium constructed on the tradition of inaction from the top political leadership when it comes to corruption. President Magufuli demonstrated a sense of new discipline in CCM and government, discipline in expenditure management, fighting corruption with vigour, staying above capture by sections of the business community, and declaring commitment to industrialisation, though without coherence and consistency. The challenge continued to be a move in the direction of personal rule and the weakening of institutions. The relations between politics and business in the fifth phase government were so tense and businesses were disrupted to the extent that they could not effectively facilitate capital accumulation and industrialisation. This is the task that President Samia Suluhu Hassan has to grapple with. It will depend on how the internal power structure within CCM plays out.

Good leadership needs to be sustained over a long period of time, as it has been in the case of countries such as China, Korea, Indonesia, Malaysia, and Singapore, which have undergone transformation over decades. Tanzania would require at least two or three decades to realise meaningful socioeconomic transformation through industrialisation. The Growth Commission led by Michael Spence (World Bank, 2008) took stock of the state of theoretical and empirical knowledge on economic growth with a view to drawing implications for policy for the current and future policymakers. On the role of leaders in successful development, its report concluded that leadership could be the main determinant of success. Fast, sustained growth requires a long-term commitment by a country's political leadership, a commitment pursued with patience, perseverance, and pragmatism. Successful cases share an increasingly capable, credible, and committed government. Good and visionary leadership has to communicate the chosen development goals to the public and convince people that the future rewards are worth the effort and sacrifice. Leadership is essentially a team effort involving multiple players with complementary roles, all behind a clearly defined development agenda. While individual leaders can make a significant difference in transforming the institutional structures and their outcomes, there is a need to reflect further on how to nurture leadership and its team effort, both within each phase and across phases.

Discussion of 'Politics and Business: An Ambiguous Relationship'

Discussion by Hazel Gray

I INTRODUCTION

This chapter is a timely contribution to debates on economic development in Tanzania, both for reasons that are specific to Tanzania and because of the rethinking about frameworks for understanding state–business relations that is going on in international policy circles. For a country with ambitious plans for industrialisation, understanding the dynamics of state–business relations over time is critical in order to shed light on key political economy constraints on effective policymaking and implementation. Research on the relationship between politics and business in Tanzania is relatively sparse. On one level this is unsurprising, given that the size and importance of formal businesses to the economy overall is low as a proportion of total output and as a proportion of total employment. Nevertheless, the role of big business in influencing the effectiveness of policies of economic development has implications that go beyond the relatively small number of firms that make up the formal business sector, permeating every aspect of economic activity. Research has also been hampered by the surprisingly common idea that state–business relations emerged out of a tabula rasa after market reforms from the mid-1980s. In fact, relations between some key private sector businesses and politicians have much deeper roots and extend across the period of socialist economic policy of the 1970s. The regional scale of many of Tanzania's largest businesses also often goes unexamined.

A further constraint is that institutional approaches for understanding these relations have been mainly developed in the context of industrialised countries that bear little resemblance to Tanzania. This chapter breaks through some of these constraints with an analysis that reaches beyond standard analysis of the institutional constraints on economic development. In particular, it does an excellent job of highlighting the historical roots of today's industrialists and in emphasising the links within parts of the ruling party to sections of the business community. The chapter is also very useful in providing unique insights into Tanzania's most recent phase in the evolution of state–business relations under President Magafuli, and makes concrete suggestions about the internal governance mechanisms of CCM that go beyond the standard policy recommendations of development partners. The comments that follow address some areas that I think merit further reflection.

II THEORETICAL FRAMEWORK

The theoretical starting point of this chapter is that politicians and business interact along a spectrum between a state that negotiates with business and produces a win–win of public benefits and a situation of state capture. Where the state is captured, interests of the state have converged with a set of narrow aims of big business to maintain their size and profitability. The framework assumes that politicians will systematically favour the interests of large firms because they provide specific material or political benefits – such as campaign finance, job creation, and lower prices for products. Thus, an equilibrium can emerge between political and economic actors that will lead to poorer economic performance over time. This is in contrast to the counterfactual of an uncaptured state that can incentivise and discipline big business in the best interests of sustainable economic development. State capture is manifested in the way that institutions operate and in the type and effectiveness of economic policies adopted by the state. The characteristics of state–business relations can therefore mainly be read by examining the evolution of institutions and policies.

The idea of the captured state has become very influential in explaining the political economies of African countries. It became particularly popular in South Africa, where the debates over Jacob Zuma and the influence of the Gupta family were presented as an archetypal case of state capture. Lofchie (2014) also adopts a state capture lens to understanding Tanzania's political economy. However, the concept has some limitations when applied as a framework for understanding state–business relations in Tanzania. This is because state capture is a rather blunt tool for understanding certain aspects of Tanzania's political economy, in particular the fissures within the ruling party that shaped the outcome of a number of areas of policymaking in the 2000s and 2010s. In Tanzania, the ruling party and bureaucracy was significantly fragmented both horizontally, within the elite, and vertically, with significant differences in the nature of state–business relations at different levels within the ruling party and across the country. As set out in this chapter and elsewhere (Gray, 2015, 2018), in the 2000s some groups within the ruling party had very close relations with parts of the business sector, but the other issue that needs to be emphasised is that others within the ruling party strongly opposed these links. Thus, the successes and failures of various economic policies were a result of both the close relations between certain factions within the ruling party and the opposition from other factions for more open support towards these same groups within the private sector. For example, while one factor in the lack of impact of the EPZ programme in the early years of its operation was the problems in effectively enforcing export quotas, the scheme was also hampered by a lack of sufficient investment in the scheme in the first place. This led to delays in vital infrastructure and insufficient learning rents to allow domestic firms that were quite far from achieving international competitiveness from acquiring the technologies and skills that could have allowed them to break into global export markets. An important reason for this is the limited political saliency of providing transparent industrial policy rents to a group of mainly Tanzanian-Asian industrialists. Thus, a nuanced approach to the idea of capture is needed; one that can explain why the state in Tanzania has exhibited hostility and suspicion towards the private sector, while at the same time explaining clientelist relations between factions of the ruling party and segments of the private sector.

III ACCUMULATION OUTSIDE MARKET INSTITUTIONS

Economic institutions in Tanzania have gone through a profound transformation since the 1980s with the process of economic liberalisation. In thinking about the nature of state–business relations in Tanzania, it is also important to recognise the fact that interactions between the state and the private sector were occurring within a context of enormous institutional transformation. Key institutions of a market economy, including an array of institutions setting rules and standards for market-based interaction and discipline, were hardly operational for much of the period under scrutiny – accounting frameworks, financial sector regulation, competition regulation, commercial courts, and so on were in a construction phase for much of the last thirty years. This meant that significant areas of economic activity and accumulation were occurring with minimal effective regulation. Within this institutional hiatus, personalised and clientelistic relations may actually have played an important role in facilitating the path of firm growth and diversification, rather than causing a blockage to economic development. This is not to say that clientelist state–business relations are sufficient or desirable for economic development, but that, in Tanzania's recent economic history, economic success and failure has occurred within a context of personalised relationships between business and the state. Much of the accumulation that went on in Tanzania in the era of high growth occurred outside formal market processes. These forms of accumulation exacerbated social differentiation, and also generated new economic actors as well as enriching existing powerful elites.

This observation also suggests that we need to be cautious about explaining changes in state–business relations through a chronology of policy changes.

There were clearly very important policy shifts, as set out in this chapter, but these did not immediately filter through to changes in state–business relations. This is because the distribution of power between different social groups and networks tends to be more enduring than institutions and policy frameworks. In many of the approaches to state–business relations, there is an explicit or implicit assumption that groups that hold power will be able to influence the structure of formal institutions and policy frameworks over time (in the work of Acemoglu and Robinson (2012), and in Douglass North's last works (2009, 2012)). It is assumed that where the distribution of benefits provided by institutions and policies is not in line with the distribution of power, powerful groups will push for institutional changes that benefit them. However, where such groups hold limited popular legitimacy, their influence over the path of institutional development and policy approaches can be quite marginal. This disjuncture between the pattern of benefits produced by institutions and the actual distribution of power can be sustained over long periods of time when informal networks and redistributions that occur outside institutional rules meet the demands of powerful groups.

This observation is particularly important for understanding state–business relations in Tanzania. Significant sections of the private sector hold limited public legitimacy as a result of the influence of socialist ideology, but also because of the racial structuring of the economy that was established during the colonial period. This means that it has often been difficult for the state to create effective and open policies to support the domestic private sector. At the same time, many of the industrialists who held significant informal influence over the implementation of economic and trade policy have held power informally across the policy eras, and despite the approaches to constraining the growth of the private sector in the 1960s and 1970s. This is important for understanding the challenges that face President Magafuli in supporting the development of a private sector that has limited public legitimacy, and also helps to explain the growing influence of state and party-owned enterprises working within the private sector.

IV STATE–BUSINESS RELATIONS AT DIFFERENT SCALES

One of the key points stressed in this chapter is the importance of the Tanzanian-Asian business class in the private sector in Tanzania. The chapter does a very good job of outlining the historical origins of this group of Tanzanian-Asian large businesses that have played a key role in industry and trade since independence. A historical perspective is important in explaining the tenacity of their businesses in the face of significant policy shifts. This chapter emphasises the clientelistic relations between certain Tanzanian-Asian industrialists and the ruling party in the 2000s that were identified in a number of grand corruption cases that occurred in the era. These close clientelist relations are described as being a cause of policy failure. However, as explained in the previous section, despite the wealth and economic power of this group, it is a group that has held quite limited political legitimacy, and this lack of political legitimacy has also shaped the way in which economic policies have been implemented over time. This is the reason why, despite the economic importance of this group of firms, there has been little policy discussion on how to include this group positively into Tanzania's vision of economic development. Large firms can play an important role in sustainable economic development, particularly in terms of their role in enhancing domestic technological capabilities through research and development, and can play a key role in expanding employment. Economies where large firms are owned by minority groups face a particular political economy challenge. However, there are examples of countries that have successfully included large businesses into their development vision. For example, in Malaysia the ruling party was able to negotiate a relatively successful distribution of rents and incomes between the Chinese-Malay business sector and the state. The challenge is to create policies and targeted rents that overcome market failure and address collective action problems, while at the same time disciplining rent recipients in order to ensure effective use of policy rents. Solutions to this challenge may not come from sweeping institutional reforms but from a more targeted agenda of support and monitoring of firms. In Tanzania, targeted industrial policy and competitions policy could help tie large firms into a more productive path of economic development, but this would need to be accompanied by a politically viable strategy underpinned by building a more inclusive constituency in support of industrialisation through linking social, industrial, and economic policy more closely.

The other approach would be to invest much more heavily in SMEs and engage in a more radical transformation of the ownership structure of the industrial sector. It should be noted, however, that this has been on the agenda of the ruling party for many years (including in the 1996 industrial policy) with minimal success (Gray, 2018). This is partly because the scale of investment and support that would be needed to really develop the SME sector in Tanzania has not been recognised or addressed in existing policy mechanisms. A starting point would be to develop industrial policies that were more explicitly differentiated in terms of the size of target firms, allowing for strategies that addressed the different needs and power of large, medium, and small firms. In contrast, the recent response to these political challenges of supporting domestic industrialists has been a return to the development of state- and party-owned firms (Jacob and Pedersen, 2018). This has become an important part of President Magafuli's strategy to overcome the previous links between factions of the ruling party and large firms in the private sector that have been important in supporting the ruling party. If these state and party firms are successful, this could shift the nature of state–business relations in important ways over the next decade.

V GRAND CORRUPTION

This chapter outlines a number of grand corruption cases that have become pivotal to understanding the 'black box' of state–business relations in the 2000s. These cases provide the evidence of close clientelist relations between the ruling party and powerful private sector actors (Aminzade, 2014; Gray, 2015). While these cases clearly led to a number of very poor deals for the country, there are a set of complex economic consequences of such deals that need further analysis. For example, grand corruption often relates to strategies of forging political stability between elites. Focusing on the role of particular individuals rather than the structural drivers of such types of corruption can be misleading. I explain some of these wider implications in Gray (2015). At the end of that article, I argued that it would be possible for CCM to clamp down on the networks that underpinned these particular corruption deals in the short term, where there are shifts in the distribution of power, but that successful anti-corruption agendas can be attached to many different kinds of political and economic strategies. This appears to be the case with President Magafuli, whose anti-corruption agenda has been attached to a political and economic agenda that is very different from the 'good governance' and liberal economic approach advocated by development partners. He has been initially successful in clamping down on particular networks and in centralising power within the ruling party. Short-term reduction in corruption is much easier to achieve than long-term shifts as these also depend on changing the distribution of political and economic power over time. The success of his strategy therefore depends on how successful the ruling party is at building up new economic power bases or in re-forging relationships with powerful economic actors in ways that allow both for support to domestic industries and for effective monitoring and disciplining of firms receiving industrial policy rents.

VI THE WAY FORWARD

Tanzania has returned to a more active approach to industrial and economic strategy, but to be effective this needs to go hand in hand with an analysis of the changing relationships between the state and the private sector. These relations are dynamic, but they also have deep roots that do not necessarily change with the announcement of new policy agendas. Research on state–business relations in Tanzania has focused on the long-standing and complex relations between Tanzanian-Asian businesses and the ruling party. A neglected aspect of these relationships is the regional scale at which many of these firms operate and hold power. At the same time, the influence and role of state and ruling party firms has not yet received sufficient attention and should be a major area of future research. Such analysis should be grounded in a detailed understanding of the structure of Tanzania's economy and in histories of particular firms and sectors.

Understanding state–business relations requires an analytical lens that goes beyond the codified rules to examine the deeper relations and distributions of power that shape how institutions actually work. This chapter highlights the informal and clientelist relations that were key in the 2000s and 2010s, and ends with some suggestions about the need for internal changes within the ruling party. The current strategy on clamping down on clientelistic state–business relations focuses on changing the internal balance of power within the ruling party by shifting the composition of the Central Committee and building up loyalty to the president through selection processes. It is clear that this strategy has been quite successful in shifting the internal distribution of power within the ruling party from a fragmented equilibrium towards a more centralised and hierarchical control under the president. A number of institutional theories discussed in this chapter suggest that centralisation is necessary to generate a long-term approach to developing the economy. However, I would argue that the success of such a strategy cannot be taken for granted. It requires effective internal feedback mechanisms between different parts of the state about the successes and failures of different policy choices. It also raises challenging questions about the fact that centralisation of power can consolidate behind oppressive political agendas. Further, it is not the case that economic success will necessarily generate more inclusive politics in the foreseeable future. Thus, both the long-term economic and political outcomes of a strategy of centralisation remain uncertain.

5

Challenges of the Civil Service

Rwekaza S. Mukandala[*]

I INTRODUCTION

The civil service affects the economic development of a country in many ways: first because its general function is to set the institutions of state power into operation; second, and most important for our purpose, because history has shown that the success since the late nineteenth century of what Gerschenkron (1962) called 'late industrialisers' is partly attributed to the role of the state in general and the civil service in particular. For example, in his excellent study on Japanese industrialisation, Chalmers Johnson (1981, 1999) demonstrated how the Ministry of International Trade and Industry spearheaded 'Japan's extraordinary and unexpected post-war enrichment' (Johnson, 1999, pp. 33–4). In certain circumstances, however, the civil service may be detrimental to economic development through incompetence, corruption, or being too huge, and thus requiring a large amount of material resources for its maintenance. Whether the civil service plays a positive or negative role in a particular country's quest for economic development is a hypothesis whose determination or verification depends on concrete material forces and dynamics, in particular the nature of the regime and its expectations regarding the role of the civil service, the capacity of the civil service, and the enabling environment.

In colonial Tanganyika, for example, the scope of state activity was narrow, as the main preoccupation of the colonial state was maintenance of law and order and general administration of the colony. Following the defeat of the Germans in the First World War, Tanganyika became a trusteeship colony under the British in 1918 until her independence in 1961. During that period,

[*] Rwekaza Mukandala is grateful to Dr Parestico Pastory and Dr Jesper Katomero for their assistance in preparing this chapter. He is also grateful to Professor François Bourguignon, Samuel Mwita Wangwe, and Jan Gunning for their very useful comments on earlier drafts of the chapter.

state administration was informed by Sir David Cameron's policy of indirect rule, first introduced in the country in 1926. The state relied on 'agents' to run its affairs. The colonised population, regarded as subjects rather than citizens (Mamdani, 1996), were ruled through native authorities anchored by chiefs. Most of the social services were provided by faith-based organisations, though their services were subsidised by the government. Investment in key social sectors was very minimal and was almost surpassed by that of religious institutions (Jamhuri ya Muungano wa Tanzania, 2011; Mukandala, 2015).

Economic activities were dominated by private companies based either in London or Nairobi, which was the regional centre for British East African colonies. Marketing boards and cooperative unions handled the production and marketing of major agricultural crops including cotton, coffee, and pyrethrum. For cotton, for example, the Lint and Seed Marketing Board handled marketing while the Victoria Federation of Cooperative Unions handled the production and purchase from farmers. Necessary economic service was provided by regional outfits. These included managing the currency as well as air, rail, marine, and road transportation; postal services; harbours; cargo handling; power supply; and school examinations.

The colonial civil service played a minimal function of law and order, guaranteeing economic extraction and exploitation of resources including supply of forced labour, and overseeing the operations of colonial state corporations and private companies. According to Nyerere (1974, p. 263), 'it was designed for the administration of a nation, not for its development'. Its administrative capacity, though, was low. Therefore, at independence, the civil service faced serious challenges. It was small relative to the size of the country and was dominated by expatriates who constituted 71 per cent of the senior officials. This was mainly because of an acute shortage of qualified indigenous Tanzanians. At independence, the country had twenty-one graduates, out of whom eleven were indigenous Africans. Most of the civil servants were concentrated in the few urban areas, with vast rural areas left unattended.

The colonial state left the country not only with an enormity of sociopolitical, economic, and development challenges, but also the lack of a strong indigenous capitalistic class to spearhead the development effort. Therefore, after independence in 1961, there was no viable option other than the state becoming a central actor in the social and economic development of the country.

We address three questions in this chapter. To what extent has the civil service contributed to economic development in Tanzania? What have been the constraining factors to effective civil service performance? And, finally, what are the necessary and most promising directions for reforms to maximise civil service contribution to economic development?

The chapter draws heavily on documentary evidence, specifically government publications and reports, press reports, scholarly literature, assessments, and surveys carried out by national and international organisations including the World Bank, the National Bureau of Statistics (NBS), and the

World Economic Forum. In addition, select interviews with senior government officials at central, regional, and district levels were conducted. While there is extensive literature on the role of the state in development (Gerschenkron, 1962; Johnson, 1982; Wade, 1992), the economic literature on the role and the evaluation of the contribution of civil service to development is extremely scant and weak. This is partly because there is no simple way of summarising its activity by a few indices that can be compared across countries and overtime. It is also difficult to delineate the contribution of the civil service to phenomena that are outcomes of inextricably linked actors and forces, such as economic development. Under these circumstances, as Bourguignon put it in his comments on an earlier draft of this chapter, 'expert intuition and a systematic review of the main aspects of the way civil service delivers its mission is the only effective approach'. This is not to say or imply that the civil service was solely responsible for any achievements (Johnson, 1999, p. 33).

The chapter is organised into five sections, including this introduction. Section II describes and assesses the civil service contribution to economic development. Section III draws from the preceding sections and looks at the constraints on the effective contribution of the civil service. Section IV explores promising directions for civil service reforms and their sustainability. Section V concludes.

II THE ROLE AND POLITICAL CONTEXT OF THE CIVIL SERVICE IN ECONOMIC DEVELOPMENT

Given the limitations and challenges of the colonial civil service, the post-independence state embarked on a serious state- and nation-building project. Practically, the idea of state building meant constructing effective public authority, establishing viable state institutions, and creating responsive and legitimate agents of governance (Hyden, 1983; Chazan et al., 1999). Next to state building was the daunting task of nation building, which entailed forging a unified political community. This was because of the arbitrary basis of colonial boundaries, where newly independent states inherited diverse populations that often became fractious as disparate groups contended for power, resources, and identity (Hyden, 1983; Nnoli, 2002). This was reinforced by the colonial policy of indirect rule mentioned in the introduction, which in effect resulted in exacerbating and enhancing ethnic and racial identity differences. As a central institution of the state, the civil service took centre stage in engineering change. Tanzania's civil service has been an integrated departmental system anchored by ministries, whose numbers have varied from the initial 11 in 1961 to the current 23.[1] Permanent secretaries working under ministers are the professional heads of ministerial organisations.

---

[1] Commenting on the change, then-President Mkapa wondered whether it had 'become less civil or more public'.

They generate policy proposals and alternatives for politicians to make deci-sions (singly in ministries or collectively in the Cabinet), implement the pol-icies decided by the executive in all areas, and produce the public services needed for the good functioning of the economy and society. The inherited colonial civil service was transformed through Africanisation and localisa-tion policies to reflect the national character; its role changed from being simply extractive and administrative to become developmental, thus spear-heading the country's socioeconomic development. Its role in development can be meaningfully assessed in three phases: the transitional years after independence, 1961–6; the socialist phase, 1967–85; and the liberalisation phase, 1986 to date.

A The Transitional Phase, 1961–1966

The civil service in the early years of post-independence was charged with a role in policymaking and execution. The inherited model of policymak-ing was based on the traditional dichotomy of politics and administration. It assumed that civil servants would generate ideas and draft policy proposals, which would then be presented to politicians for deliberation and approval. Immediately after independence, external consultants took a centre stage in policy drafting. The first planning document for independent Tanganyika – the Three-Year Plan, 1961/2–1963/4 – was drawn up by the World Bank mission. Regarding agriculture, for example, the government emphasised that

The Government policy for developing rural production is guided by recommendations formulated in 1961 by a World Bank Mission [...]. This policy consists of following a twofold approach in agriculture via the improvement approach and the transformation approach (United Republic of Tanganyika, 1964, p. 14).

Civil servants were charged with plan execution. The first Five Year Plan, 1964/5–1968/9, was drawn up by French consultants. Sidelining the civil service from policymaking prevented it from bringing important inputs into consideration, before final decisions were made by politicians. As a result, some of the policy decisions were context insensitive and therefore difficult to implement. In the early 1960s, for example, the 'Ministry of agriculture tried to resist the transformation approach which they regarded as foreign inspired, ill-conceived and ill-advised' (Mukandala, 1992, p. 67). The transformation approach was abandoned by 1966 (Coulson, 2015). In the same vein, the first Five Year Plan proved difficult to implement because its forecasts were based on statistical assumptions that were weak, population growth was seriously underestimated, and outside advice from the Food and Agriculture Organization and the World Bank regarding crop prices proved to be wrong. In any case, there was a serious manpower shortage to implement the plan, as already noted. Van De Laar (1973, p. 72) estimates that only about one-third of targets regarding government investments were realised.

B The Socialist Phase, 1967–1985

The Arusha Declaration, published on 5 February 1967, marked a major watershed in Tanzania's history in general and in her development efforts in particular. Several decisions and actions had a direct impact on the civil service role in economic development. First, it was declared that 'The policy of TANU is to build a socialist state, the state must have effective control over the principal means of production and it is the responsibility of the state to intervene actively in the economic life of the nation' (Nyerere, 1968, pp. 230–2). As a result, the government formulated and implemented interventionist policies, including nationalisation of the means of production and provision of free social services. The state formally became the major engine of economic development. Consequently, many private companies were nationalised and transformed into public corporations. In the meantime, new corporations were created in other economic activities. Together with the decision that the state must control the commanding heights of the economy, it was also evident that the preferred state instrument would be the public corporation (also called parastatal or state enterprise). Thus, a lot of economic development activities and initiatives were implemented through the public enterprise sector. The number of such enterprises exploded from nine in 1966 to around 420 in 1980. The Second Five Year Plan (1969–74) projected 'a fast rate of expansion in productive capacity through the agency of the parastatal organisations' (Second Five Year Plan (1969), vol. 1, p. 223). The civil service was thus sidelined from direct operations of these critical economic development activities.

The civil service, however, retained the role of control and supervision over this budding sector. The exercise of that role, though, proved difficult to say the least. Parastatals proved to be too many, some of them too big and sensitive, and too complex to control. The control structure itself was a complex spaghetti maze involving the president and *Ikulu*, central ministries led by finance and development planning; parent ministries of particular parastatals; holding corporations, for example the National Development Corporation and Tanzania Textile Company; regulatory parastatals, for example the National Price Commission or the Tanzania Bureau of Standards; various committees, for example the Committee on Parastatal Management Agreements; the party branch at the workplace and the political commissar (beginning 1975); the party, trade unions, workers' councils, and so on. In addition to size and complexity, many parastatals had vague objectives, areas of responsibilities were largely undefined, and there were no specialised control units in ministries. A government official concluded that 'both the parastatal [...] and the systems of the controls are beset by some of the least desirable features of bureaucratic inefficiency' (Coulson, 1978). In the meantime, state scope and functions continued to expand, further overextending the civil service.

Secondly, it was decreed that: 'it is the party which guides the government by providing directives which shall be implemented by government during a definite period' (Nyerere, 1967). From then onwards, the civil service role was limited to supposed policy implementation under the watchful eye of the party. All major subsequent basic policies were initiated by the party. Even in implementation, according to Pratt (1979, p. 226):

The party, far from meekly ratifying the policy proposals of a conservative civil service, has tended instead to be resistant and unsympathetic towards those who talk the language of priorities, of moderation, of bottlenecks and of shortages.

This practice continued until the beginning of the 1980s, when the civil service took part in preparing the National Economic Survival Programme (1982) and the Structural Adjustment Programme (SAP) (1983). Their implementation stalled because of lack of resources and support from donors. In 1984, changes were initiated to make the civil service more relevant in policy initiation. Prime Minister Edward Sokoine issued '*The Ministerial Circular No. 1 of 1984*'. This decreed that, in addition to the party, the government could also initiate basic policy. The civil service thus played a role in all subsequent policy initiatives, although they had heavy donor influences.

Thirdly, in the 1970s, the government undertook several other grand decisions that had a serious impact on the civil service. For instance, in 1972, following a consultancy report by McKinsey and Co., there was a massive reorganisation of regional administration. This included the abolition of local authorities and their replacement by state structures all the way to village level, through a policy that was formally called decentralisation but was in fact deconcentration. This policy move entailed extension of civil service responsibilities from the centre through the regions, districts, and divisions all the way to the grassroots. There was a consequent absorption of all local government employees into the civil service. During the 1973–4 intensification of villagisation, civil servants were appointed as village managers throughout the country. This resulted in a massive recruitment of new functionaries into the civil service. Civil service numbers increased by 28.31 per cent in 1973 and a further 29.13 per cent the following year. This move also involved the transfer of senior and experienced administrators and professionals from the centre to the regions and districts. During 1971–2, cooperative unions, which had been the pillars of agriculture production, were supplemented by newly created Crop Authorities. Finally, in 1976, cooperative unions were abolished. All these decisions and others resulted in the expansion of state scope and functions without proper planning and sequencing. They spread the civil service and its resources too thinly for effective performance.

The civil service also did not fare very well in economic development activities under its direct supervision. Hasty policymaking without professional technical information, poor implementation mechanisms, and a poorly motivated staff all led to very poor performance. In agriculture, for example, between 1967 and 1977 there were several major policy initiatives, all of which were failures. The Socialism and Rural Development policy (1967), which called for villagisation and communal agriculture, entailed moving the rural population into *Ujamaa* villages, where they were to engage in communal farming and other economic activities including transportation and trading. It would also be easy for people to access social services. The implementation of the policy contributed to famine in the early 1970s, destruction of people's housing as they were forced to move, and even deaths in some cases. The policy was eventually abandoned. The 'Politics is Agriculture' policy (1972) was aimed at achieving national food self-sufficiency. People were to be encouraged to abandon traditional farming methods and practices, and to use modern farming equipment, methods, and management systems. Implementation proved very difficult. Following massive food shortages, large quantities of maize (600,000 metric tons), wheat (170,000 metric tons), and rice (130,000 metric tons) were imported (Lofchie, 1989, p. 110).

After the failure of the 'Politics is Agriculture' policy of 1972, and the subsequent food shortages, the party attributed the problem to drought. Irrigation was deemed to be the answer. A new policy, 'Agriculture: Life or Death', was adopted by a hastily conveyed party National Executive Committee (NEC) meeting in 1974. It was aimed at mobilising people to complement rain-fed agriculture with irrigation. According to Sokoine (1984), the decision was taken hurriedly by the party without professional and technical advice from civil servants. No organisational arrangements for implementation were made. According to Sokoine (1984, p. 53), 'The running and management of irrigation schemes in most cases had been practically no one's responsibility.' Sidhu (1981, p. 8) adds that there was no reliable information on the irrigation potential of the country and on prior irrigation projects. While the Ministry of Agriculture statistics indicated that there were 55,792 hectares under irrigation in 1975, the party headquarters indicated that there were 133,245 hectares. According to the Ministry of Agriculture (1980), there were, for example, no proper surveys and investigations, no serious studies on soil and topography, no economic appraisals, nor hydrological studies, no studies on cropping patterns and other agroeconomic considerations.

Throughout the socialist phase, the civil service was heavily involved in several ways in the country's economic development. Its support role in policymaking was minimal. The party was supreme and all major policy decisions of the time were made by the party's NEC, which had a powerful secretariat. The civil service was charged with policy implementation. Here, too, the party had its fingers in the pot. According to Prime Minister Sokoine (1984, p. 4), after 1977, the party also 'acquired the power and role of supervision of the implementation process'. With the exception of social service provision, especially education and health, as well as law and order, most state initiatives in production and distribution had very low success rates. Agricultural productivity and output either stagnated or declined, industrial productivity declined, and most parastatal enterprises registered losses and required massive state subsidies to stay afloat (Moshi, 1995; Mukandala, 1998). Since the civil service was not a lone or even the key player in economic development, it can only assume limited responsibility.

Tanzania experienced rapid economic growth in the years after 1966, but this was short lived. The economy started experiencing difficulties in the early 1970s, which grew into a crisis by the late 1970s. The official position attributes this problem to falling crop prices in the world market, the 1978–9 oil crisis, the war with Uganda, and the 1973–4 drought (Jamhuri ya Muungano wa Tanzania, 2011). The explanations contain elements of truth as these tragedies wiped out national foreign reserves and thus weakened the capacity of the state to deliver services, let alone undertake investment projects. However, the official position underplays the fact that economic difficulties were also nourished by economic and administrative policies the government had engaged in. In time, such grand policy decisions as nationalisation of the commanding heights of economy, pan-territorial pricing, abolition of local governments, and disbanding of cooperative unions proved to be unfavourable to economic growth. Under President Nyerere's leadership, the country underwent serious extensive administrative reorganisations. The civil service lurched from one reform initiative to another, including Africanisation, localisation, increase in scope and functions, decentralisation, retrenchment, salary squeeze, and so on. Implementation was the main problem, partly because of the nature of the initiatives: many were ideologically driven policies, poorly thought out, and lacking full information. Knowledge and expertise were subordinated to ideology and politics. Most of the policies that were aimed at consolidating the political base of workers and peasants, broadly defined, also generated opposition from a broad range of actors at times, including civil servants. Most of these policies were beyond the control of parliament, let alone the civil service, since the NEC of TANU had self-appointed itself as a supreme decision-making organ in the country. According to Shivji et al. (2020, p. 220) for example, 'NEC adopted the Arusha Declaration, bypassing all the organs of the state, the national assembly included'.

C The Liberalisation Phase, 1986 to Date

The cumulative failures discussed here led the International Monetary Fund (IMF) to conclude that there was a structural failure of the Tanzanian economy. The recommended solution was a small government and an increased role for market forces. By the mid-1980s, the economic situation forced the government to accept the IMF's SAPs to meet the conditions for accessing international lending from international financial institutions and bilateral aid agencies. SAPs were accompanied by stringent measures for reforming the public sector. These policies called for cutbacks in state scope through such mechanisms as retrenchment, employment freeze, and withdrawal of the state from production and business sectors, as well as reducing the level of state intervention in key social sectors. As far as the civil service was concerned, the Civil Service Reform Programme (CSRP) was launched in the early 1990s to give effect to the structural adjustment endeavour. Available evidence indicates that the SAPs were successful in terms of reducing state scope and controlling budget deficits, but unsuccessful in driving economic growth, which stagnated at 1.8 per cent of gross domestic product (GDP) between 1991 and 1995 (IMF, 2016). For instance, public service employment was reduced from 355,000 in 1992 to about 270,000 in 1999 (Ntukamazina, 2000). While many public enterprises were privatised, a good number of these were abandoned, cannibalised for parts and spares, or converted into something else. There were cutbacks in investment in social services, especially education, health, and water. Cost sharing in education was introduced in 1986. User fees were introduced in health in 1993.

President Mwinyi, however, given the serious economic problems when he assumed power, and under tremendous pressure from donors, was forced to govern effectively. Hard choices could not be avoided, as the harsh economic realities demanded implementation of economic and social policies, which entailed hardships for the population in the short term. He dismantled many pillars of the Arusha Declaration, imposed a pay and employment freeze, removed subsidies, and imposed cost sharing. President Mwinyi relented on the eve of presidential and parliamentary elections in 1990. He reinstated the annual salary increases and introduced a new salary structure, increasing the minimum salary by 26.14 per cent and the top salary by 38.53 per cent (Kiragu and Mukandala, 2005b, p. 240).

Several allowances were also reintroduced. In July 1991, the CSRP was launched. Following the reintroduction of competitive multiparty politics in 1992, with reinvigorated trade unions going on strike in 1993 and 1994, and elections looming in 1995, President Mwinyi wavered. The party was worried. In 1994, the civil service average nominal wage was raised by 74 per cent. A year later, in July 1995, it was raised by a further 75 per cent. In the meantime, several agreed reformed benchmarks were missed and a stand-off with donors ensured.

The civil service was very involved in the preparation of various economic recovery policies and programmes together with the IMF and World Bank. These included the Economic Recovery Programme (ERP I and II), the Priority Social Action Programme, and later on the Poverty Reduction Strategy Paper (PRSP). The civil service also managed the privatisation of hundreds of parastatal enterprises, and the divestiture from ownership of other business concerns. It also oversaw the re-establishment of local government authorities (LGAs) in January 1984, as well as cooperative unions, liberalisation of imports and export trade, and devaluation of the currency.

The enactment in 1990 of the National Investment Promotion and Protection Act, which was reviewed in 1997, underlined the recognition of the private sector as the engine of growth. Various private sector institutions, including the Tanzania Private Sector Foundation and the Tanzania Business Council, chaired by the president, were established to give voice to private sector concerns and challenges.

President Mkapa came into power vowing to clean up the mess of corruption and the allowances mania. Assured of an overwhelming control of parliament, though he supported a consolidation of allowances into salary, which led to a pay increase, and supported the Selective Accelerated Salary Enhancement Scheme (SASE), he abandoned the planned pay increase for the year 2001 (elections were over). He also abandoned plans to raise the wage bill ratios. Under his leadership, many reform measures were initiated and partly implemented.

President Kikwete took power after a fractious election within the ruling party, and his majority shrank further after the 2000 elections. His rule was marred by frequent crisis following revelations of corruption and embezzlement deals by politicians and civil servants. He thus pursued populist policies to shore up the base, which allowed reform doubters to intensify their efforts to neutralise and reverse technocratic reform initiatives. His bold reform initiative 'Big Results Now' (BRN) was expensive, unpopular outside the six select areas, attempted to short-circuit the formal civil service, and was abandoned by his successor.

All the measures taken to spur economic growth, including introduction of VAT in 1995, rated at 50 per cent, promotion of exports (especially non-traditional), exploitation of minerals, especially after enactment of the Tanzania Investment Act in 1997, and the ensuing foreign exchange availability after the mid-1990s, led to clear signs of improvements. Real GDP improved – after a dismal 3.3 per cent growth in 1997, it averaged 4.8 per cent for the period 1996–2003. Inflation reduced from 21.0 per cent in 1996 to 4.4 per cent in 2003, and there was an increase in foreign direct investment flows, from USD 148.5 million in 1996 to USD 247.8 million in 2003. This positive growth has continued. Average growth of real GDP averaged 6.5 per cent during the ten-year period 2006–15.

The IMF data show that, although Tanzania recorded increases in average growth (GDP) from 2.3 per cent (1981–5) to 5.8 per cent (1985–90), which was not really significant growth given that this was a post-crisis period, average growth for 1991–5 fell to 1.8 per cent (IMF, 2016). One of the reasons for the decline was that the 1980s/90s World Bank- and IMF-engineered reforms concentrated on cost containment and not on strengthening institutional capacity of the civil service. In short, the quantity and ultimately quality of the civil service was highly eroded. As Fukuyama correctly put it, 'while the optimal reform path could have been to decrease scope while increasing strength [...] many [sub-Saharan African] countries actually decreased both scope and strength' (Fukuyama, 2005, pp. 21–2). Highlighting the impact of SAPs on Africa's civil service, studies revealed that the capacity of the civil service to provide basic services declined (Adepoju, 1993). African governments lost the capacity to hire, retain, and motivate the best talents. The migration of Africa's best talents for greener pastures abroad resulted in a shortage of highly skilled human resources, while those who remained in the service resorted to all kinds of legal and illegal methods, including corruption, to survive.

1 The Civil Service in the Post-SAP Period

The unintended consequences of SAPs on the economy in general and the civil service in particular created lessons and grounds for re-examination of donor development policy. By the mid-1990s, both development partners and the government had come to the realisation that cost-containment measures were inadequate reform strategies for addressing economic crises. Therefore, at the turn of the millennium, the focus of the reform path began to shift slightly, from cost containment to increasing institutional effectiveness. This widening of scope was formally recognised with the launch of the PRSP in the year 2000. This prioritised six areas: education, health, water, judiciary, agriculture, and roads. Later on, in the Medium-Term Economic Framework, the government expanded the priority areas and added the police and prisons. It also added new categories of key areas, including energy, manufacturing, industries, lands, mining, and tourism. With support from the World Bank, a new reform programme, the Public Service Reform Programme-I (PSRP-I) was launched in 2000 and implemented for seven years thereafter, giving way to PSRP-II, which ended in 2011.

President Magufuli's style was somewhat different from his predecessors, probably owing to a changed political environment. He came into power at a time when his ruling party had lost its heyday of high popularity. The last tenure of his predecessor experienced mounting grudges from almost every section of society, which translated into increased acceptability of and popular support for the opposition. For the first time in multiparty history, the opposition increased its seat share in the parliament from 26 per cent in 2010–15 to about 31 per cent after the 2015 general elections. It also scored victory in local government elections in major towns and cities. Votes for CCM's presidential candidate dropped from 80 per cent in 2005 to 58 per cent in the 2015 elections. In the move to restore legitimacy and popular support for his party and government, President Magufuli came into power promising to launch a war against embezzlement, corruption, and misbehaviour among public officials. His early years in office witnessed a number of top officials in the civil service being held to account, removed from their positions, or sued in court. His early and consistent actions toward the civil service seem to have shaped both public and media opinion that the conduct of the civil service had improved. Furthermore, this was a time when civil servants became real political scapegoats for government mistakes. The words and actions of top political executives and party stalwarts were increasingly succeeding in turning the public against the civil service. The improvement of public employees' welfare almost seemed to be a non-agenda in current government priorities, and there was mounting resentment that their efforts were less appreciated.

Generally, the two PSRPs aimed to improve the administrative capacity of the civil service through strengthening of systems and processes with the view to enhancing civil service efficiency, effectiveness, and accountability. Similarly, a plethora of sector-specific reforms were implemented with the

TABLE 5.1 *Post-SAP Tanzania public sector reforms*

Institutional Reforms	Duration
i. Public Service Reform Programme (PSRP) I and II	2001–2
ii. Public Financial Management Reform Programme	1998–2017
iii. Local Government Reform Programmes I and II	1998–2014
iv. Legal Sector Reform Programme (LSRP)	2000–13
v. Business Environment Strengthening	2003–13
vi. National Anti-Corruption and Action Plan	2001–11
vii. Second Generation Financial Sector Reform Programme	1990–2013
Service Delivery Reforms	
i. Health Sector Reform Programme	1994–2017
ii. Education Sector Development Programme	1997–2015
iii. Agricultural Sector Development Programme	2005–
iv. Roads Sector Development Programme	–
v. Water Sector Development Programme	2009–17

Source: Construct by authors

purpose of improving services in key social and economic sectors (Table 5.1). These reform interventions were accompanied by a series of capacity-building training programmes geared at enhancing the capacity of civil servants. For a detailed account of the reforms, see Mutahaba et al. (2017).

Specific reform interventions under the PSRP included installation of public service management (PSM); restructuring the civil service, including introducing executive agencies; improving civil service pay systems and incentives; strengthening leadership and management; strengthening information management systems, including adoption and use of information and communication technology (ICT); building policy development and management capacity of ministries, departments, and agencies; and improving service delivery systems and accountability. Follow-up assessments regarding programme implementation have revealed the following positive developments as far as the quality of the civil service is concerned (Kariuki, 2017):

• Improvements in policymaking and regulatory capacity –79.4 per cent of ministries, departments, and agencies were making evidence-based policies using the standard guidelines.
• Improved use of performance management systems (PMSs) by ministries, departments, and agencies and their linkages to service delivery; for example, 85 per cent of ministries, departments, and agencies and 80 per cent of LGAs were using a total of eleven core tools.
• Improved management of public servants: for example, 99.5 per cent of civil servants were on the Human Capital Management Information System; and 82 per cent of the population reported satisfaction with central government services, up from 74 per cent in 2004, although below the target of 85 per cent.

Tanzania has been recording encouraging economic growth during the last seventeen years. For instance, for ten years from 2001, the country sustained an average annual growth rate of 6.7 per cent compared with 3.0 per cent in the preceding decade. Similarly, from 2011 to 2016, the economy continued to expand at an average of 6.9 per cent and has maintained a 7 per cent growth for the last four years, putting Tanzania among the fastest growing economies in Africa.

To conclude this section, the preceding historical analysis reveals that from independence until towards the end of the 20th century, the civil service had minimal contribution to Tanzania's economic development. In the earlier period, the inherited civil service from the colonial state supervised a mixed economic model while undergoing rapid expansion through new recruitment and localisation. The civil service played a traditional role in policy initiation, advice, and implementation. It also resisted some policy initiatives, as already noted in the case of agriculture. The year 1967 was a watershed moment for the civil service as well as the size of its role in economic development. Not only did it usher in the policy of socialism and self-reliance, but it also removed the civil service from a meaningful role in policymaking. Policymaking was now the preserve of the party, and the role of the civil service became confined to policy implementation under the watchful eye of the party. As already noted, things went severely wrong, culminating in a crisis that ended with the abandonment of the *Ujamaa* project. The civil service was now empowered to once again play its traditional role in policymaking and implementation, though now under the watchful eyes of the IMF and World Bank. Though initially constrained by cost-containment measures and removed from direct production and commercial activities, it nevertheless participated in many policy decisions and carried out their implementation. The new millennium was ushered in with reforms geared at improving the quality of the civil service. Together with investments and economic promotion policies, an encouraging growth in the last seventeen years cannot be disconnected from increased state administrative capacity, in this case, the civil service.

III CONSTRAINTS TO EFFECTIVE CIVIL USHER SERVICE PERFORMANCE

Civil service performance in economic development has had highs and lows, as indicated in the preceding section. It performed relatively well after the Arusha Declaration in 1967, before falling to very low performance levels throughout the 1970s, 1980s, and early 1990s. Performance has improved since the late 1990s, reaching more satisfactory levels in the decade and a half since the year 2000. This section explores the factors behind this performance. Four factors explain civil service performance: civil service capacity; motivation and conduct; the policy cycle and environment; and resources and tools.

A Civil Service Capacity

In this section, capacity refers to staffing levels, and their educational, professional, and technical skills and competence. Other capacity issues, for example, systems, tools, and resources, will be discussed in subsequent sections. The issue of staffing levels has varied from too few staff members at independence in 1961 and during the decade of the socialist project 1966–76, through a perception of having too many, leading to retrenchments in 1976 and after 1996, to a 'truce' situation of having fairly adequate numbers but with neither the right nor adequate mix of educational, technical, and professional competencies and skills in the period after the year 2000.

Bureaucratic expansionism in Tanzania is a historical phenomenon because, since independence, the civil service has been characterised by rapid expansion in its size. For instance, according to the Survey of Employment and Earnings (SEE), the number of civil service posts increased from 65,708 in 1966 to 191,046 in 1976, and 295,352 in 1980. By 1976, the annual growth rate was 16.2 per cent and the cumulative increase over the same period was almost fivefold. However, the overall increase in total employment was only 28.4 per cent. The reasons for the increases in earlier periods include recruitment of necessary human resources after independence, the expanded scope and functions of the civil service, decentralisation measures and villagisation campaigns that led to more employees being brought in, and, finally, patronage and corruption that took its toll in terms of bringing unwanted people into the service. However, the increase in numbers was not matched by an increase in production. The cumulative growth of GDP at 1966 constant prices over the same period was 38 per cent, with an average annual increase of 3.2 per cent. Clearly, this was a phenomenal growth in the size of the civil service, with a consequent increase in the size of the wage bill.

Efforts made to check the increase included retrenchments. It was concerns over the wage bill that fuelled the perception that the civil service was too large, leading to several bouts of retrenchments. A total number of 9,466 staff was retrenched in 1976, and 16,109 ghost workers were identified and purged from the payroll in 1980. A further 50,000 civil servants were retrenched in 1994. The size of the workforce was reduced by 25 per cent from 355 in 1992 to 270 in 1997. There was also a ten-year employment freeze as part of SAP conditionality throughout the 1990s.

Concerns over the size of the wage bill continued in the period after 2001 and are discussed fully in Appendix A.1. Up to the year 2010, the increase in size was probably roughly on a par with the growth in GDP. As shown in Appendix A.1, there was a notable increase between 2010 and 2015, largely because of massive recruitment of teachers and health workers. Yet efforts to keep the wage bill in check have continued, including a tight centralised control and monitoring of the payroll, a two-year freeze on employment, suspension on salary adjustments, and increments. All these have been aimed at holding the public service size in check; consequently, not only do many public needs remain unmet, but also even established posts remain unfilled in the civil service, as will be discussed in the next section.

Moreover, at least for the last fifteen years, growth in civil service size does not seem to have had negative implications for the economy. As shown in Figure 5.A.1 in Appendix A.1, the fast rate of growth in public sector employment (of which the civil service constitutes 89.7 per cent) expanded at an average annual rate of 8.1, slightly above formal private employment. This did not prevent GDP from growing at the rate of 6.3 per cent of GDP in the same period. Still, about 50 per cent of government revenue was spent on the civil service wage bill, a figure that has risen since 2012.

B Staffing Levels

The trend noted in civil service size has always been accompanied by high vacancy rates in middle and senior levels, and in professional, science, and technical fields. The vacancy rate was 10 per cent at independence in 1961, increasing to 29 per cent by 1972, and averaged 36 per cent throughout the 1970s (Wily, 1981; Mukandala, 1983). The situation got worse during the difficult years of the 1980s and 1990s. The employment freeze did not help, as those who left for greener pastures could not be replaced. This shortage of critical skills has meant that the civil service has been unable to perform certain critical functions. In the education sector, while there is reportedly over employment, there is also a shortage of over 20,000 science and mathematics teachers, as this interviewee revealed:

We have 7,000 arts teachers who are in excess in our schools. This means paying for civil servants who do not deliver, expanding the wage bill without returns. You may find between three to four teachers teaching one subject in secondary schools. And because their number exceeds the required threshold (teacher–student ratio), they have to coordinate themselves to teach topics in a subject. For the science teachers, we have a shortage of about 20,000 teachers. This number is huge and means a lot if we want to seriously move forward as a nation. There is an urgent need for the government to train and hire science teachers to address this shortage. (Interview, President's Office Public Service Management (PO-PSM) I, 12 October 2017)

In spite of these claims, a study by Twaweza (2015) reveals that the Secondary Education Development Plan target of 1:30 teacher–student ratio is far from being met. Twaweza reports that, on average, the teacher–student ratio in the schools studied was 1:88. Similarly, there is a worsening staff shortage in health, public administration, and other sectors. According to a recent employment and earnings survey:

The results reveal that there were 135,694 job vacancies in the formal sector in 2014/15, of which Technicians and associate professionals had the largest number of 72,950. Professionals had the second largest number of vacancies which was 30,880 followed

TABLE 5.2 *Staffing profile in Bunda district, Mara region*

S/N	Department	Staff requirement	Available staff	Shortage	Future recruitment plans 2017–18
1	Administration	182	113	69	15
2	Finance and commerce	25	12	13	3
3	Water	23	12	11	5
4	Construction	21	7	14	3
5	Land, natural resources, and environment	33	8	25	3
6	Hygiene and environment	5	2	3	0
7	Agriculture, irrigation, and cooperatives	81	59	22	10
8	Livestock and fishery	51	35	16	10
9	Primary education	1,56	1,13	430	100
10	Secondary education	479	366	113	104
11	Health	542	182	360	80
12	Planning and statistics	6	2	4	4
13	Community development	29	11	18	10
14	Legal affairs	3	2	1	1
15	Internal audit	6	3	3	3
16	Information and communication technology	2	1	1	1
17	Procurement	6	6	0	0
18	Election	3	0	3	3
19	Bees and honey	3	1	2	2
	Total	3,06	1,952	1,108	357

Source: Field Data (2017)

by Service workers and shop sales workers with 14,472 vacancies. Education industry (47,256 vacancies) had the largest number of vacancies followed by public administration and defence; compulsory social security with 46,067 vacancies. Human health and social work activities industry was third and had 23,668 vacancies. (NBS, 2015)

Inadequate staffing is also a challenge in LGAs where real social-economic activities take place. A more recent and often cited reason has been the freezing of government employment pending the verification exercise of the qualifications of civil servants. For instance, in one of the districts that we visited in Mara region in June 2017, we found that only the Procurement Management Unit out of nineteen departments/units was staffed to the appropriate level (Table 5.2). The overall district staff requirement is 3,054, but presently there are only 1,952.

The shortage of staff in certain critical areas in the public service has been increased by the recent termination of staff with inappropriate educational qualifications or forged academic certificates. For instance, addressing the media, the permanent secretary of the PO-PSM reported that by May 2017, a total of 9,932 staff had been terminated on the grounds of forging academic certificates and 1,538 with questionable certificates were being investigated (IPP Media, 4 May 2017). Health and education were the sectors most affected by this exercise.

C Competences and Skills

The civil service capacity to administer effectively not only depends on the numbers, but also on the quality of the labour force employed by the civil service: does the labour force have the requisite skills and competencies to administer effectively? The answers to this question may not be affirmative and there may well be variations between sectors or job cadres. For example, using the health sector as a case study, and as indicated in Table 5.3, Service Delivery Indicators (SDIs) show that public service health providers could correctly diagnose 59.9 per cent of case conditions compared with 65.9 per cent of health providers in the private non-profit sector. However, they did better than the private for-profit sector. Thus, the problem may not be a public sector one, although the public sector is the main employer of health care professionals. Adherence to critical guidelines is low, at below 50 per cent, and this is also the case in both the profit and non-profit sectors. Clinicians' ability to manage maternal and neonatal complications is extremely low, as public sector providers adhered to only 31.3 per cent of clinical guidelines in that area, while it was even lower for the two groups of private providers.

The same situation exists in the education sector. For instance, results from educational sector SDIs show that primary school teachers lack the necessary academic and pedagogical skills to teach. Teachers score extremely low in content knowledge. SDI tests show that only one out of five teachers scored more than 80 per cent (minimum knowledge cut-off point) on the combined mathematics and English test, while 1.1 per cent of teachers scored above the 80 per cent cut-off in English. Respectively, the average scores in English, mathematics, and pedagogy were 42 per cent, 63 per cent, and 36 per cent. The SDIs also reveal that, although teachers seem to have done better in mathematics, only 26 per cent were above the 80 per cent cut-off point (World Bank, 2015b). Evidence from these two critical sectors serves to reveal a broader picture with regard to the skills and competence levels of the civil service. As revealed elsewhere in this chapter, the poor abilities among school and college graduates indicate that the skills and levels of competencies of the civil servants in other sectors cannot be exceptional.

Apart from poor training, this low level of skills and competence in Tanzania's civil service is partly a consequence of recruitment and promotion practices. Recruitment and the civil service career path into middle- and higher-level positions are critical factors in determining the quality of the

TABLE 5.3 *Basic health service delivery quality*

SDI	Tanzania	Public	Private (non-profit)	Private (for-profit)
Case load (per provider per day)	7.3	7.1	5.7	10.8
Absence from facility (% providers)	14.3	13.9	17	12.8
Diagnostic accuracy (% clinical cases)	60.2	59.9	65.9	54.2
Adherence to clinical guidelines (% clinical cases)	43.8	43.7	45.5	42.1
Management of maternal and neonatal complications (% clinical cases)	30.4	31.3	30.1	26.4

Source: World Bank (2015a, p. 10)

civil service. Experience from other countries indicates that, if one is to hire the best candidates, recruitment into the civil service should involve competitive examinations. Similarly, promotions into middle cadre and higher levels should involve competitive training and performance evaluation (Bhatt and Kim, 2000). The quality of the civil service is also improved through rigorous evaluation of the performance of civil servants' contribution to organisational goals.

Historically, recruitment into Tanzania's civil service has been conditioned by varying factors. Recruitment into the colonial bureaucracy was not only based on education and professionalism but also on race and ethnicity. Soon after independence, there was a preference for indigenous Africans, in other words, Africanisation, and thereafter localisation. Clearly, given the shortage of qualified Tanzanians, there was a liberal interpretation of merit in order to get people into available positions. Up to the early 1980s, all graduates from the university and other tertiary institutions were recruited into public service. Interviews were for placement purposes only. Relatedly, a decision was made to hire many of the former members of the militia who fought in the war against Idi Amin.

There was also a notable hiring of friends and relatives by senior civil servants to compensate for low pay, higher taxes, high costs of living, and shortages, especially in the late 1970s and early 1980s. All these factors severely challenged the application of the principle of merit in recruitment. Following several reform initiatives, in 1999 the government launched a public service management and employment policy, subtitled 'In Pursuit of Public Services through Merit and Result Oriented Management'. Informed by new public management theories, the policy attempted to adopt good practices from the private sector to improve the quality and process of recruitment. Some of these practices included open competitions for jobs, advertisements in the media, formal selection criteria including balancing academic and professional qualifications, non-discrimination, and so on. Three years later, a Public Service

Employment Secretariat was established. Available data do not permit us to determine and compare the employment structure of the public sector with the rest of the formal sector.

The recent push for utilisation of explicit meritocratic criteria in recruitment has also been challenged by the nature of the available eligible pool of applicants. These are the products of an education system that has been in crisis for a long time. Extensive expansion and disorganisation, poor infrastructure, inadequate human resources, and low morale and motivation have affected all levels of education in Tanzania with few exceptions. As revealed previously, many graduates are therefore of low ability and poorly trained. Concerns for equality dictate that graduates from all institutions, no matter how unworthy, be treated equally. When some of these have found their way into the interview panels, the results have been disastrous.

Our findings reveal that the ability of the civil service in terms of hiring the best and brightest, and motivating, retaining, training, developing, and promoting them has declined in relative terms. One of the reasons for this is the absence of an incentive structure that attracts and retains the best minds. In most cases, however, declining civil service quality is closely related to the nature of recruitment and promotion. The practice has shown that recruitment into the civil service is still short of rigorous screening and vetting. Simply for illustration, until 2015 and after increasing public outcry, it was not uncommon to find that positions into prestigious public institutions were filled up with big 'country surnames'. Whether that was/is an outcome of competitive screening is beyond the scope of this chapter to establish. Rather, it questions the level of coincidence. Similarly, although the government's commitment to hire all university graduates was abandoned a long time ago, all trained teachers and health professionals continued to be hired until around 2010.

Promotion into middle- and senior-level positions depends on seniority/longevity in service and in certain cases one's connections and partisan attachment, rather than performance. Although over the past few years the government has introduced the Open Performance Appraisal System (OPRAS) as a performance management tool to be used for guiding promotion decisions, its utility is highly questionable. The traditional three years' automatic promotion system remains in force. Although there are schemes of service, complaints abound of their not being followed. Similarly, in recent years, recruitment into management positions has undermined a basic ethos of the civil service, its political neutrality. In demonstration of this, an interviewee revealed:

We are witnessing a new phenomenon of partisan cadres from political parties invading the civil service, ascending to the ranks of Regional Administrative Secretary, District Administrative Secretary, and District Executive Director. This is not a good gesture for an efficient civil service. We need to professionalise instead of politicising the civil service... (Interview, PO-PSM II, 12 October 2017)

Traditionally, promotion into such positions would require not less than ten years of experience in the civil service as well as rigorous performance evaluation and vetting. The Public Service Commission, which stands to defend the autonomy of the civil service and at least insulate it from the mounting political surge, is rather indifferent. This lack of rigorous screening and vetting hinders the civil service from hiring the right personnel not only in terms of skills but also in terms of ethics. One of the interviewees shared his/her experience on how things used to be conducted, which deserves to be quoted at length:

After the probation period expired, the newly employed civil servant was taken to the Public Service College, Magogoni Dar es Salaam, and trained on economics, administration, taxation minutes writing, government stores, standing orders, government finance etc. After this three-month dose, an examination would be administered and once you passed you would be vetted by government security organs and receive training on how to handle government information. Not everybody was required and/or qualified to work in the civil service. The reason why we have ethical issues in the current civil service is because we abandoned this rigorous procedure of screening, vetting and training civil servants... (Interview, PO-PSM-III, 12 October 2017)

Connected to recruitment is the question of employee training and development, as the interviewee quote here suggests. Tanzania has an array of instruments that provide guidelines on training of civil servants, including the Public Service Management and Employment policy of 2008; the Public Service Act No. 8 of 2002 (Cap. 298), the Public Service Standing Orders of 2009, and the 2013 training policy. However, these instruments have failed to translate into effective vehicles for guiding and coordinating training programmes for civil servants. This comes at a time when the skill levels of civil servants and potential recruits are under serious criticism.[2] Coupled with coordination and resource constraints, civil service training is somewhat chaotic. Interviews were relatively illustrative of this:

Despite the institutional, policy, and legal strength that the ministry has, training programmes offered to civil servants have not been efficient. This is because of inadequate resources for the training of civil servants; training programmes not being structured to address different levels, cadres, responsibilities, and attitudinal transformation of civil servants; lack of systemic training geared to prepare public servants to occupy higher positions in the public service; limited training infrastructure in the public service; proliferation of training institutions whose training contents do not satisfy the needs of the public service both in terms of quality and relevance; inadequate management and coordination of training opportunities in the civil service; civil servants terminating their service after competing training sponsored by the government. (Interview, PO-PSM IV, 10 October 2017)

---

[2] See Section III C, which provides some data on skill levels.

Political appointments into management and top leadership civil service positions are at times presented as necessary in order to keep the bureaucracy under close political control and thus guarantee democratic accountability. However, this has weakened the civil service autonomy in fulfilling its obligations professionally. The ring of political patronage has operated at the expense of civil service professionalism, such that the art of administration is overshadowing the science. A recent study has revealed that it is safer for the civil servant to trade the law for a political directive (Pastory, 2017). These findings suggest a re-examination of the system of civil service recruitment, promotion, and appointments to higher-level positions.

D Civil Service Motivation and Conduct

Motivation is a complex concept but can simply be defined as anything that influences employees' commitment to and delivery of the job. This complexity arises from the fact that there is a complex web of factors that promote positive work behaviour, and a significant number of motivational theories exist to that effect (Kanfer, 1990; Clark, 1998). In short, motivation is explained as an intrinsic, extrinsic, cognitive, and environmental/contextual phenomenon. Because of this complexity and since, invariably, some of the issues have been discussed elsewhere in this chapter, this part concentrates on extrinsic and intrinsic motivation, civil service compensation, and moral incentives in particular.

1 *Compensation*

Compensation has been a contentious issue in the civil service. In the early years after independence, the civil servants' pay package was considered too generous. It was one of the grievances that led to the university students' protest in 1966 as well as trade union strikes. President Nyerere's slashing of civil service salaries including his own was followed by more drastic action after the Arusha Declaration. Thereafter, the civil and public service compensation in general was guided by three types of policies. The first type included policies that reduced and froze the incomes of higher officials while restricting their capacity to earn income from other outside engagements. These policies included a policy of 'The top to stand still until the gap between the lower and higher salaries is narrowed', increased progressive taxation of high income, and a leadership code that forbade leaders from outside earnings and property ownership, especially houses. The second type of policies entailed increasing lower incomes. This involved raising the minimum wage; paying special allowances to those in the lowest two salary scales; and several salaries increases that favoured the lowest earners. The third type of policies included abolishing some of the privileges enjoyed by senior officials while extending other privileges to everybody in the civil service. As a consequence, real wages went down after the Arusha Declaration in 1967, and in the crisis period between 1979 and 1984.

According to an International Labour Organization (ILO) study (1989), Tanzania experienced a 65 per cent drop in real wages from 1979 to 1984. It was one of the sharpest declines in real income in Africa (Ghai, 1987). The compression of wages within the public sector, from 33:1 in 1967, to 5:1 in 1981 (Kiragu and Mukandala, 2005b) has been a disincentive for senior servants and professionals, hence the brain-drain, corruption, and non-monetary compensation of all types. This spiral would continue until the hefty pay increases in the late 1990s. A series of further salary increases have continued to be made, which, combined with low inflation, have made the lot of civil servants tolerable.

According to the available studies, public wages in real terms seem to have improved since 2001, outcompeting those in the private sector (Leyaro et al., 2014, p. 10). There was no change in private wages between 2001 and 2006, while there was a 50 per cent increase for central government employees. There was also a 20 per cent drop in private sector wages between 2010 and 2015, while there was no change in public sector wages. Public sector employees also had a wage advantage of 25 per cent due to education, age, and tenure during 2001–6 (Leyaro et al., 2014, p. 10). It thus seems that public sector employees are better off after the public sector reforms referred to than in the past, especially when one also takes into account their non-monetary income.

For the two years since 2015, earnings in the civil service have, however, stagnated. This is because there has not been any salary increments for two consecutive years since the fifth-phase government came into power. Similarly, promotions and employment in the civil service have been frozen pending verification of civil servants' qualifications and cleaning of ghost workers. The freeze of promotions and salary increments, as well as changes in the salary structure, has left many civil servants demoralised. Concerns have been raised that the verification exercise has now turned into a government excuse for evading its human resource compensation responsibility. Most of the civil servants interviewed at the ministries, regions, and districts expressed their dissatisfaction as they were not certain of their compensation prospects. Expressing this dissatisfaction, one of them put it this way:

I and my colleagues were promoted early 2016; six months later a directive came from the PO-PSM that our promotion was revoked pending verification of our education qualifications. I had planned to use my salary increment from my promotion to finish my house and pay school fees for my children. This dream vanished, and I am not sure when I will get my right. Under this kind of work environment, why should I be motivated to work, why should I be committed to serving my country if my employer does not care about my rights? (Interview, local government authority I, 16 October 2017)

A related issue is the absence of an attractive incentive structure. Stagnant real wages, wage compression, especially for middle and senior grades, and a promotion and reward system loosely based on merit are working against the morale of middle and senior officials in the civil service. Wage compression for middle and senior officials has continued to characterise public service pay (Kiragu and Mukandala, 2005b). In this regard, one of the interviewees hinted:

[T]he fifth-phase government is striving hard to ensure equity in compensation of civil servants in order to cut down the gap between the highest paid and lowest paid. The president already hinted that he wants a civil service that is fairly remunerated but in practice this has not translated into real gains. Most middle- and lower-cadre civil servants have lost hopes of having their salaries raised. Promotions have been frozen, cutting down the morale of civil servants. (Interview, PO-PSM III, 12 October 2017)

Additionally, there has been a problem or failing to follow through and achieve some of the reform targets. Salary differentials are still lower than the pay reform targets; the salary structure is still highly compressed; some professionals are relatively underrated. Plans to implement annual salary adjustments have not been followed through; the wage bill to GDP ratio, which was expected to rise progressively, has been declining. Relatively, consolidation and rationalisation of the public service has not been realised. Related to this, compensation is still diverse and unequal even among people carrying out the same functions. On 18 October 2017, and also as recently as 5 January 2018, the Minister for Public Service expressed his disgust at the situation and called for an overhaul of the salary system (*Daily News*, 2018). As has been the case historically, this emerging government's drive to address pay inequities across government institutions does not seek to do so by adjusting low income upwards but by lowering top pay levels. Such a move had been started by the President back in 2016 when some heads of parastatal organisations were forced to choose between reduced pay levels and vacating their positions. This newly emerging trend suggests that the morale of the civil service is likely to continue declining.

Apart from wages, civil servants enjoy other incentives such as paid leave, opportunities for personal development, pensions, health insurance, loan guarantees, and job security. Most of these incentive schemes are not offered by the majority of private sector employers. The top-cadre civil servants (at the level of chief executives, heads of divisions, and other cadres that report directly to the chief executive) enjoy top-up allowances in terms of housing, transport, communication, and duty allowances. The majority of lower-cadre personnel are, however, less motivated by both pay and the job. For instance, in the education sector, one study revealed that more than two-thirds of teachers who were surveyed would not choose the teaching profession if they could choose again (Mkumbo, 2013). Similarly, in 2008, a survey of 448 health care workers at Muhimbili National Hospital found that almost half of both doctors and nurses were not satisfied with their job, and this was also the case for 67 per cent of auxiliary clinical staff and 39 per cent of support staff (Leshabari et al., 2008). This level of dissatisfaction was explained as the result of low salary levels, unavailability of necessary equipment and consumables to ensure proper patient care, and improper management of employees' welfare.

Nevertheless, a recent comparative study revealed an improvement. Carried out in 2013, it reported that 82.6 per cent of health workers in Tanzania were satisfied with their jobs, compared with 71 per cent in Malawi and 52.1 per cent in South Africa (Blaauw et al., 2013).

This improvement is probably one of the outcomes of health sector reforms.

2 Moral Incentives and Ethics

In addition to these material incentives, in the period after independence and during the socialism phase, there was also a reliance on moral incentives. More specifically, appeals were made for people to be nationalistic, to love their country and make sacrifices for her independence and development. Everybody was urged to work hard. Combined with socialist slogans of equality and justice, these appeals were very effective and encouraging. This was more so when they were made by Mwalimu Nyerere, given his charisma and honesty. These appeals to people's moral commitment to the country helped civil servants cope with emerging hardships in the 1970s. The climax of these moral appeals was during the Tanzania–Uganda war of 1978–9. The following economic hardships colluded to undermine these appeals. The liberalisation phase, with its emphasis on individualism and market forces, further undermined the effectiveness of moral incentives. Since then, civil servants have expected material returns for their labour. When they decline or stagnate, commitment and productivity is bound to suffer.

Civil service conduct plays a significant portion in economic development. Not only is an undisciplined civil service that is characterised by shirking, corruption, and misappropriation of public resources less productive, but it also diverts public resources to private gains. Lessons from Japan and other advanced economies have shown that a highly disciplined and committed civil service plays a crucial role in economic growth (Bhatt and Kim, 2000). An ethical civil service has a sense of duty, and it can serve as a deterrent to opportunistic behaviour from politicians. Generally, the findings indicate that, since the late years of *Ujamaa*, Tanzania's civil service has been characterised by work misbehaviour such as shirking of responsibilities (absenteeism and negligence) and corruption and misappropriation of resources (e.g. through procurement and creation of ghost workers), and generally it has failed to regulate opportunistic politicians and even colluded with them, at the expense of the economy.

The civil service as an institution of service delivery is integrated in society. Thus, any analysis regarding how the civil service conducts itself has to be embedded within the values, culture, and norms that guide a particular society. The Tanzania public service ethics code emphasises equity, probity, integrity, moral conduct, and political neutrality. In theory, the values, culture, and norms that guide the conduct of the civil service encourages enhancing employee involvement, rewarding teamwork, recognising individual effort, and incorporating the needs of the clients, in this case delivering critical outputs to the citizens. However, our findings on this issue suggest that ethical values such as honesty, integrity, impartiality, and fairness, among others, have been in constant decline in the civil service. As a result, these declining values have encouraged inefficiencies and thus have likely affected the productivity of the civil service. Recounting the heyday of the Arusha Declaration and the leadership code of conduct of 1967, a respondent in the PO-PSM elucidated:

When I joined the civil service in 1978, there was a clear ethical strategy to shape the conduct of civil servants. Upon joining the service, one had to fill in the Arusha Declaration form, ethical form, and commitment to party ideals form. These forms had put massive restraints on civil servants from engaging in corrupt behaviour and other forms of pathologies. The next step was a two-year probation pending confirmation... (Interview, PO-PSMIII, 12 October 2017)

Moreover, there is a growing decline in the spirit of volunteerism among civil servants in particular and the public in general. While in the past it was common for the civil servant to sacrifice for the common good, that heyday died with Ujamaa in 1985. As one of the interviews revealed, a majority of civil servants in middle- and higher-level positions are unlikely to commit their efforts without expecting individual returns. This lack of commitment to public duty is aggravated by an ethical crisis.

The civil service absenteeism rate is reportedly especially high in the education sector. Civil servants are reportedly either absent from their workstations or present but doing job-unrelated businesses. For instance, in the education sector alone, a study by Twaweza (2015) reveals that 31 per cent of teachers were absent from workstations during the period of study in 2015, while 34 per cent were present but not teaching, and only 35 were teaching. Respectively, the findings for 2016 were 27 per cent, 32 per cent, and 41 per cent. The 2016 report on Tanzania's SDIs show students received roughly 39 per cent of the scheduled teaching time, which is equivalent two hours and forty-six minutes per day instead of the official five hours and fifty-six minutes (World Bank, 2015b). Twaweza estimated that a classroom absenteeism rate of 50 per cent costs the country TZS 862 billion per year through paying people who have not produced anything. This amount equals roughly 1 per cent of GDP, and is 63 per cent of the total budget for the Ministry of Education, Science, and Technology in the financial year 2017/18. The absenteeism rate in the health sector was reported at 14 per cent, which is lower than African and Asian standards. Although no data on absenteeism for other sectors were available, anecdotal evidence suggests that the situation may not be very dissimilar, especially for civil servants who attend but work fewer than expected official hours. All these suggest that the productivity of civil servants is still low. Corruption is also one of the major ethical issues constraining efficiency in the civil service, slowing down the pace for social and economic development. Both grand and petty corruption increase the cost of public service delivery and cripple the effectiveness of the civil service.

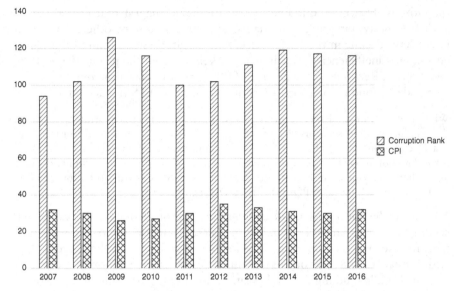

FIGURE 5.1 Tanzania's CPI and rank, 2007–16 Trading Economics/Transparency International (2016). (Accessed: 1 November 2017)

Understanding this fact, the Tanzanian government has, over time, put institutional arrangements in place to curb corruption. Various anti-corruption campaign programmes have been waged to complement the institutional strengthening as well. However, the anti-corruption crusade efforts have not delivered significant results. Available data indicate that Tanzania is ranked 116th least corrupt nation out of 175 countries (Transparency International, 2016). The data also show that the corruption rank in Tanzania averaged 98.37 from 1998 until 2016, reaching an all-time high of 126 in 2009 and a record low of 71 in 2002, for reasons that are not clear (Trading Economics, 2003). Tanzania's average rank for the past decade stood at 110, while it scored an average 30.6 out of 100 points in the Corruption Perception Index (CPI) (Figure 5.1). CPI ranks countries and territories based on how corrupt their public sector is perceived to be.

Other reports also paint a gloomy picture regarding corruption in the Tanzanian civil service. For instance, *The Global Competitiveness Report, 2015–2016*, which assesses the competitiveness landscape of 140 economies, providing insight into the drivers of their productivity and prosperity, notes:

Indeed, gifts and other bribes are perceived to be widespread when applying for public utilities and permits. In fact, businesses (presumably multinationals, as national firms could not make the comparison) consider the prevalence of irregular payments and bribes within public utilities in Tanzania as one of the worst in the world. Likewise, more than a third of households' report paying a bribe to obtain public utilities in Tanzania. (World Economic Forum, 2016)

Notably, anti-corruption initiatives in the past have not registered progress because there has not been a serious commitment by the government to punish ethical violators, especially those involved in big corruption scandals. Equally, the anti-corruption institutions are under-resourced in terms of finances and human resources, and lack the requisite autonomy and will to spearhead the fight. Parliament, which could exert pressure for intensified anti-corruption efforts, is reportedly toothless and worse still suffering from ethical problems brought about by some of its members (Pastory, 2017). In addition, the lack of impartiality and public support necessary to steer the process ahead has been another constraining hurdle. Corruption is likely to stall the efficient delivery of critical outputs, stalling the social and economic development of the country as it diverts public resources to private ends. For instance, available evidence indicates that in the last ten years more than TZS 813 billion is known to have been expropriated through the four famous corruption scandals alone: External Payment Arrears, Bank of Tanzania Twin Towers, Richmond, Tegeta Escrow, Tanzania (AfriMAp, 2015; The Citizen, 24 June 2015). There are no reliable estimates of how much the country has lost through other corruption schemes.

The corruption and embezzlement phenomenon in Tanzania's civil service dates back to the late years of *Ujamaa* and emerged as a response to a real fall in income. Initially, civil servants resorted to inventing all kinds of fringe benefits. These included bonuses, subsidised shops, canteens, and cafeterias at workplaces, transport, dispensary and/or private-practitioner medical services, housing, clothing, farming plots, transport services to ease access, and a host of recreational facilities. These were supplemented by extensive allowance claims (sometimes fraudulent and/or inflated) for travel, prolonged conferencing, and so on. As the economic situation got worse, the demand for fringe benefits blossomed into outright racketeering, or *Ulanguzi*, as it was commonly called. This was one of the most phenomenal haemorrhages of public resources in Tanzania. Corruption reigned supreme and everybody was a seller and a buyer. The undisputed climax of the phase was the burning of the Bank of Tanzania building in 1984, the precise cause of which has never been made clear. The prime minister launched a large military-style operation against racketeers in 1984. He died in a road accident on 12 April 1984.

This clampdown was followed by a phase of projects (*Miradi*). To survive, one simply had to have a project and dab in the informal sector. In July 1987, Party Chairman Nyerere advised Tanzanian experts to 'involve themselves in gardening, poultry keeping and other activities which could enable them to augment their meagre incomes'. The assumption was that civil servants would maintain the separation between official and private activities and income. That was not the case. Official positions and resources were used for private gain as officials tried to make ends meet. The replacing of the leadership code by the Zanzibar Declaration in 1992, allowing leaders to accumulate wealth, legitimised what was already taking place. Various components in the economic reform programmes, including support to the private sector, created further opportunities for civil servants. Privatisation, the promotion of decentralisation, operational autonomy for various entities, and outsourcing and subcontracting of the supply of various goods and services have all created opportunities for civil servants to make 'deals' and make money. If President Mwinyi's period was properly known as a time of *Ruksa* (everybody could do anything), Presidents Mkapa and Kikwete's times are known as the years of deals, or *Dili*. The years 1995 to 2015 were a time when Tanzania fell into costly dubious contracts, some of which have already been mentioned. It was also the period when the country adopted legislation, such as mining laws, that turned out to be economically hazardous. Although the misappropriation was in part engineered by the politicians, a thoughtful analysis would not isolate the civil service from these ills.

E Policy Cycle and Environment

One of the main constraints to an effective and efficient role for civil servants has been the nature of policymaking and the consequent policy decisions. In May 1965, Tanzania become a *de jure* one-party state. Combined with the Arusha Declaration and the socialist project in 1967, the party assumed supreme policymaking powers. The role of civil servants as advisers and facilitators in policymaking was reduced. Their role remained policy implementation under the watchful eye of the party. This fact in the context of the ideological thrust of 'state-led development', as well as wanting to 'run while others walked' (Hyden, 1975), changed the traditional mode of policymaking characterised by studies, policy drafts, deliberation, recommendations, and decisions. Many policies were made in haste without full consideration of all available alternatives and their consequences. The resulting policy decisions were poorly considered, including lack of consideration of the mechanisms of implementation and their possible consequences. Many policies were impossible to implement. Nationalisations, irrigation, decentralisation, politics in agriculture, pan-territorial pricing, and price controls are cases in point. This trend continued until the mid-1980s, when Tanzania succumbed to internal and international pressure, abandoned the socialist project, and adopted the SAP. More generally, the position and contribution of the civil service was also constrained and minimised by several factors. The whirlwind of the rapid policy changes, massive state and political reorganisations, transfer of personnel, and expansion of civil service functions while at the same time moving other functions to other entities created confusion in action and at times outright resistance on the part of the civil service.

From 1985 onwards, the country experienced the implementation of what Stiglitz (2003, p. 34) has called a 'one-size-fits all' approach, anchored by economic management by fiscal austerity, privatisation, and market liberalisation. The state (civil service) role was to maintain law and order, to provide an enabling attractive environment for business and investments, to generate economic and social policies, and to provide important social and economic services. The civil service was caught in a pincer movement. The pendulum swung from one extreme, where the civil service and the state were expected to be the engine of growth, to the other extreme, where they were now expected to make room for market forces. Both extremes were fuelled by ideological fervour. The socialist ideology informed the *Ujamaa* project, while liberalisation was driven by a blind belief in the magic of market forces. According to Stiglitz (2003, pp. xiii–xiv),

Decisions were made on the basis of what seemed a curious blend of ideology and bad economics, dogma that sometimes seemed to be thinly veiling special interests. When crises hit, the IMF prescribed outmoded, inappropriate, if 'standard' solutions. There was a single prescription [...] ideology guided policy prescription and countries were expected to follow the IMF guidelines without debate.

During this period, after 1980, according to Green (1995, p. 102),

The Fund and Bank were rapidly building up gatekeeper and coordinator roles so that they significantly influenced all official transfers not just their own [...] they sought to provide or impose overall economic policy prescription.

Constrained by conditions and conditionality, the civil service once again had very little room for manoeuvre as the policy of adjustment took its toll, and growth stagnated.

Several changes were brought about by a general rethink of the World Bank approach to development after the World Bank's 1999 annual meeting and the introduction of the PRSP approach to engaging with developing countries (Mallaby, 2004, p. 254). The IMF/World Bank and western donors made more commitment to consultations, participation, and empowerment. Coupled with the launch of the PSRP already alluded to, the civil service was strengthened and its role in policymaking appreciated. The policy cycle and environment has had an impact on civil service performance. Its policymaking advisory role within the context of political neutrality of the post-independence period was replaced by a restricted role in policymaking facilitation, resulting in hastily made and poorly considered policies that were difficult to implement. The resulting economic crises led to the liberalisation phase during which the state and civil service were confined to the so-called core functions carried out under conditionality. A workable equilibrium seems to have stuck since the year 2000, with a reformed civil service trying to facilitate market forces for economic development.

F Resources and Working Tools

In order to be efficient and effective, a civil service has to convert inputs (policies, plans, priorities, ideas, labour) into outputs (tangible outcomes such as service delivery in the form of water, health care, and education). Conversion of the inputs into outputs requires working tools that can facilitate the process. Working tools, in this case, may involve both hard and soft infrastructure. The hard infrastructure may include physical buildings, such as office building, vehicles, ICT, and so on. The soft infrastructure may involve computer software programmes for managing human or financial resources and filing systems, for example.

It is fair to note that a lack of resources, critical tools, and infrastructure has been a continuing challenge for the civil service. Lacking enough budgetary outlays to acquire the necessary tools, facilities, and equipment, it has had to improvise and/or abandon implementation plans. All the years that the government's budget had serious deficits, for example 1976–2000, meant that there were limited resources for the civil service.

Recognising the importance of equipping the civil service with working tools, the CSRP, which spanned 1991–9, PSRP I, 2000–7, and PSRP II, 2008–12, had specific reform packages geared at strengthening the working tools within the civil service. For instance, ICT is one of the critical tools that had to be introduced in government to facilitate government processes under the rubric of e-government. Here, the focus was on building the capacity of government institutions to use ICT in running government operations. The interventions involved installation of ICT tools and facilities, training, development of management information systems, and steps to establish e-government infrastructure and e-government agency (Mutahaba et al., 2017).

While significant progress was achieved in equipping the civil service with relevant tools, it is mainly the central government institutions in urban settings that enjoy this progress. Some LGAs have also registered some progress, but generally institutions that are peripheral to the central government and the urban districts are trailing behind. The general working environment is not conducive: office buildings are dilapidated and poorly furnished. In some areas, private homes of government officials at grassroots level become public offices. ICT infrastructure is in short supply and, where it is available, there are problems with internet connectivity and power outages.

This general observation is supported by findings from the key social sectors. For instance, Table 5.4 shows that public health facilities are less equipped in terms of equipment, drugs, and infrastructure than both the profit and non-profit private sectors.

The education sector has its share of challenges as well, particularly in regard to student–textbook ratio. This ought to be 1:1, but in practice this target is very far from being realised. For instance, a recent survey by Twaweza (2016) indicates that the student–textbook ratio was 26:1 in Tabora region, and 3:1 in Mtwara, Kilimanjaro, Njombe Katavi, and Ruvuma. Similarly, reporting the situation in secondary schools, a baseline study report by a team of experts on a similar matter concluded: 'For most students in the sample schoolbooks are not available or only available when shared with several other students' (Barrett et al., 2014).

TABLE 5.4 *Availability of working tools and resources*

SDI	Tanzania	Public	Private (non-profit)	Private (for-profit)
Drug availability (% drugs)	60.3	58.9	66	62.8
Equipment availability (% facilities)	83.5	81.7	92.5	84.5
Infrastructure availability (% facilities)	50	40.6	66.9	91.2

Source: World Bank (2015a, p. 10)

Generally, these findings show that the civil service is yet to be sufficiently equipped with the necessary tools required for performing the work. This has negative implications for the effectiveness of the civil service and its performance, thus precluding its ability to make an effective contribution to the country's development.

IV MAXIMISING THE CIVIL SERVICE ECONOMIC POTENTIAL: FUTURE REFORM DIRECTIONS

Tanzania has sustained relatively stable growth for the past ten years. This achievement, however small, cannot be explained without appreciating the role of public service reforms undertaken since 2000 to strengthen the administrative capacity of the public service in general and the civil service in particular. Notwithstanding, the civil service has not contributed enough to driving economic development. Its capacity to effectively implement policies and laws, to make available the necessary means of administration and to deliver critical outputs is still limited. Besides, staff work morale is declining, unethical conduct remains, and its administrative autonomy, which is limited, seems to be under constant pressure. Although staffing levels have been expanded, critical posts in the civil service remain unfilled. While praising the reform efforts carried out in the past fifteen years, a sympathetic evaluation study has also noted that reforms implemented by the government so far have not been institutionalised and have not been made part of the organisational culture (Mutahaba et al., 2017, p. 75). In view of all this, what are the necessary and most promising directions for reforms to maximise the civil service contribution to economic development? How can the proposed reforms be sustained, and what are the forces and dynamics that need to be in place to ensure a sustained and successful reform effort? These questions are addressed in turn.

A Reform Dynamics

A major study of the dynamics of public sector reform in eight African countries identified five major actors that have determined the success or failure of reforms, either by their actions or inaction (Kiragu and Mukandala 2005a).

These are the executive, donors, market institutions, representative institutions, and civil society.

Civil servants, as part of the executive, have played a major role in implementing many of the reform initiatives, but have also resisted and reversed those that reduced their power, authority, status, and especially their incomes. Their constant battles with parastatal enterprises have been alluded to. Efforts to decentralise either by deconcentration (1972) or devolution (1984) have also been resisted. Measures to compress the salary structure and the continuous salary freezes have been neutralised by recourse to allowances and outright bribery and corruption. Their advice to political leadership has often self-serving, for example the introduction of SASE and the sale of the substantial public residential houses to themselves.

Donors (and consultants) have played a key role in the reforms, especially since the mid-1980s. They pressed for the introduction of SAP in the 1980s, made public service reforms one of the conditionalities that culminated in the CSRP in July 1991, and were also involved in PSRP-I and II. They have been equally involved in follow-up implementation and financing through either project or basket arrangements. Donors' involvement has been limited by their being outsiders. Their frequent resort to conditionalities and threats has often led to resentment, reverse donor fatigue, and even resistance. In addition to consideration of issues of sovereignty and independence, politicians have followed their advice when their survival was not threatened. Civil servants have done the same when their incomes were not at risk.

Market institutions and the private sector in general have been relevant for a number of reasons. First, they have served as a reference point for levels of income and compensation in general. Thus, salary and allowance proposals have often made reference to what is earned in the private sector. Imitations of compensation levels in the private sector have contributed to the enormous disparities in pay in the public sector. Efforts have been made to reach comparable private sector pay levels either through salaries in the case of parastatal enterprises and executive agencies or through allowances for civil servants. The private sector has also served as a reference point in the search for appropriate management tools, processes, and systems. For example, permanent pensionable tenure has been abandoned for some posts in favour of contract employment, and appointment through internal evaluation has been supplemented by extensive advertisements of posts in an effort to attract outside applications in line with the tenets of new public management.

Secondly, the private sector has also been a competitor for the very highly qualified personnel and also at the very level of the civil service, thus applying pressure on the civil service to pay higher salaries. Thirdly, market dynamics, especially supply and demand, and the rise in prices have equally generated pressure on the civil service to raise salaries, and also served as an incentive for civil servants to engage in all kinds of legal and illegal activities to make ends meet. The large informal sector has provided an economic avenue for civil servants to augment their incomes. Finally, the private sector has been part of an unholy alliance involving politicians and civil servants in carrying out major corruption scams. These scams have bent or broken civil service rules and set back efforts to institutionalise an effective merit-based civil service.

Representative institutions including parliament and local government councils have played a limited role. This is for two main reasons. First, reform efforts have been initiated and designed by the executive or donors (and consultants) as technical issues outside the scope of parliament. Secondly, parliament has been weak, dominated by the dominant party and a dominant executive. Occasional enquiries into scandals and scams and their exposure, which have increased in recent years, have helped to improve governance in general. The strengthening of parliamentary committees has helped in this regard.

Civil society organisations including the media, non-governmental organisations, political parties, and trade unions have suffered a similar fate to representative institutions. A suffocating political climate, marked by bureaucratic laws, secrecy, and intimidation, has limited space for investigation and expression. In some cases where the media and civil society have been critical of government performance, the reaction by government has not been good, mostly labelling critics as seditious. Thus, the entire reform process has been top-down, and supply driven by the executive and donors. The demand, or popular, side has been absent or too weak to have a viable impact in sustaining reforms.

All reform initiatives in Tanzania since independence have been supply driven. Early reforms until 1984 were initiated by the executive. Subsequent reforms until the 1990s were initiated by donors as a conditionality. Later reforms, PSRP I and II, were formally initiated by both government and donors. BRN was an executive adventure. Financially wholly supported by donors, it was aimed at transforming Tanzania's public service delivery systems in six key ministries (later increased to eight). Citizen (bottom-up) demands have targeted broader governance reforms, specifically constitutional reforms, but these have either been thwarted or frustrated in the process.

Early reforms including changes brought about by the Arusha Declaration were inspired by political objectives seeking to consolidate political power, strengthen the state and its institutions, and deliver fast equitable economic development. By 1980, it was obvious that they could not and did not work. Many of the civil service reforms during that period were poorly conceived, ill-informed, top-down, poorly funded, took on too much, and were poorly implemented. Post-1985 reforms were once again top-down based on doubtful assumptions, and sought to reduce state scope, functions, employees, and costs. The civil service emerged a weakened organisation. These reforms generated resistance and political opposition and had to be changed, as already noted. The 2001–11 period experienced the most successful reform efforts. The reasons behind the success of these reforms include strong political will and commitment made possible by a strong political organisation, strong presidents, a weak opposition, and the resultant political stability. These reforms had the shared involvement of donors, the executive, and civil servants. Their Achilles heel was their top-down character. Representative institutions and civil society were not involved.

Executive watchdog institutions, especially the Prevention of Corruption Bureau and the Control and Auditor General, were relied upon to play the oversight role, which they did up to a point. But they were part of the system reporting to the executive and they could not replace the role of parliament, councils, civil society, trade unions, political parties, and the media.

There is little doubt that the reform initiatives undertaken during the 2000–12 period have positively impacted on the administrative capacity of the state in general and the civil service in particular. However, the reform initiatives have not all been successful since there are still various constraints that continue to preclude the civil service from making a more effective contribution to economic development. Recent initiatives by the World Bank to introduce PSRP-III are still at a nascent stage. Previous reform experiences and existing conditions suggest a need for new direction to focus the reforms and ensure their suitability. This is discussed next.

B Reform Areas and Directions

The foregoing analysis suggests that the future direction of the civil service rests in strengthening its institutional capacity, respecting its operational autonomy, rehabilitating its ethical conduct, and strengthening its morale. This would entail improving recruitment and selection systems, introducing rigorous competitive performance- and merit-based evaluation and promotion systems, and improving on-the-job training and development systems to sharpen civil servants' skills. Recruitment into the civil service has gone through several stages, starting with taking in everybody who was educated in the early years of independence. This was initially necessitated by the absence of an available pool of qualified candidates. It was later reinforced by a commitment to full employment during the socialist phase. The years of hardships and an employment freeze resulted in the emergence of a pool of qualified people who were unemployed. The expansion of tertiary institutions in the country has resulted in adding thousands of unemployed Tanzanians to this pool. There is therefore every reason to recruit the best and brightest on the basis of merit. There is also a need to undertake a human resources audit in the civil service to determine posts that can be scrapped to open up space for critical positions. The civil service needs to be kept as lean as possible but without affecting its efficiency. Continuous checking on civil service size while observing its staffing needs is essential, as freezing recruitment without addressing staffing gaps is likely to lead to more harm. Current shortages may be addressed by undertaking job analysis and design, and taking stock of institutions and re-examining their mandate to identify those with diminished relevance or duplicate functions. Excess staff would have to be transferred to areas with extreme needs.

Performance evaluation was greatly compromised during the socialist phase. Management feared attracting the wrath of workers if they were strictly evaluated. Low pay for civil servants necessitated routine promotions for them to increase their take-home pay (Jamhuri ya Muungamo wa Tanzania, 1994). OPRAS, which was piloted more than ten years ago, has now been made mandatory throughout government. Its implementation has hit several snags, including unfamiliarity with its use, but these can be gradually sorted out to maximise its usefulness. Coupled with competitive appointments to middle and senior cadres, constitutional protection of civil service autonomy is essential in order to curtail the overbearing political influence and patronage networks.

The civil service incentive structure needs to be improved and attached to performance. Although, according to Mtei (2009, p. 158), the Adu Salaries Commission of 1961 had prescribed lower salaries for Tanganyika than those obtained in Kenya and Uganda, all salary review commissions since then have called for a raise in civil service salaries, especially the minimum wage (Kiragu et al., 2005, pp. 217–19). Surely, 'if you pretend to pay people, they will also pretend to work'. A comprehensive pay review is important to establish realistic pay levels, establish relativism in the pay system by addressing extreme pay inequalities especially between various parts of the public service, devise attractive packages for rare professionals, and tie it all to verifiable individual performance. Therefore, the current PMSs and practices would need to be reviewed to make sure that a robust system is adopted and effectively implemented. Moreover, internal and external accountability mechanisms need to be strengthened and immediate and strenuous actions taken against misbehaviour.

Successful reform implementation requires proper time management. In this, the leaders are faced with the challenge of fostering a new work culture that gives value to time. There is need for close supervision and enforcement of civil service rules and procedures regarding punctuality, absenteeism, strict separation of private and official issues, and maximum attention to one's duties during official hours. For civil servants, there must be real transformation away from the 'business as usual' attitude, which puts emphasis on inputs, to a results orientation, which focuses on measurable outputs, outcomes, and impacts.

In the recent past, the government has introduced cost-cutting measures in the civil service, including curbs on meetings, workshops, and conferences, suspension of travel except where it is absolutely necessary and beneficial to the country, prohibition of renting private facilities including offices and hotel services, and preferring use of the civil service's own facilities and services. Other measures that have been undertaken include limits on office perks such as refreshments, lunch, or dinner except where necessary, and even then choosing the least expensive option. At a broader level, this has gone hand in hand with reduced recurrent spending. These cost-containment measures are important and need to be sustained, provided that an assessment is undertaken to evaluate their impact on private sector development.

Finally, ICT adoption and use has a greater role in the performance of the civil service now and in the future. Significant tractions are already being registered in the area of e-government, and e-decision-making in the civil service. However, future ICT endeavours will need to be oriented toward solving service delivery problems affecting citizens and facilitating business processes across all government institutions. Together with ICT adoption, there is an urgent need to retool civil servants, in terms of skills as well as the equipment and infrastructure needed to carry out work.

C Reform Sustainability

The sustainability of civil reforms requires that reform initiatives are accepted and supported by key stakeholders outlined in the previous section, particularly the ruling political elite. Since politicians wish to maximise their tenure in political office, reforms that are likely to end up in political power realignment or pose threats to the *status quo* are likely to be resisted. Such reforms are those that seek to erode patronage potential by introducing merit-based competitive recruitment and promotion to higher-level positions in the civil service, as well as reforms aimed at insulating civil servants from overbearing political influence. Similarly, reforms that aim to reduce the operational autonomy of central bureaucracy, such as transferring powers and resources to the private sector, executive agencies, or local governments, are likely to be resisted by central government bureaucracy at national level. Breaking the ring of vested interests is always a difficult task and reform reversal is something to be expected. The dangers of stagnation and reversals have often been anticipated by the government itself. In 2004, Prime Minister F. Sumaye (2004, p. 13) said:

The risk of reversing the gains that have been made faces Tanzania because there are still amidst us those who are either complacent, sceptical or resistant to the changes that the Third Phase Government has vigorously and persistently pursued since it came to office.

Sumaye saw four levels of resistance: political leadership, bureaucrats and technocrats, the general population, and workers. It can be noticed that political leadership was placed at the top level of resistance. Education is very important for demonstrating the folly and impact of continued bad practices. It is also important to demonstrate the benefits of reforms to maximise the efficiency and effectiveness of the civil service.

Conventional approaches to sustainability of reforms/changes, such as involvement of key actors in the reform process from the early stages of conceptualisation, are also recommended here. This is likely to increase a sense of ownership and commitment to reforms. In general, reform initiatives have tended to be a government-donor phenomenon, sidelining other key actors, such as representative institutions and civil society organisation. As a result, these institutions make little follow-up on reform implementation, while the government becomes insulated from those questioning aspects of the reforms.

Reforming the civil service has to be a continuous process. In this regard, every reform initiative has to be backed up with a robust system of monitoring to identify potential challenges and emerging trends that require government attention and action. For example, a continuous or periodic check of civil service size, performance, and productivity, a review of operational rules, procedures, and systems, and monitoring of behavioural patterns of civil servants must become institutionalised government processes.

V CONCLUSION

The civil service is a crucial institution to a country's economic development. In the case of Tanzania, its contribution to economic development since independence has been both positive and negative. Throughout the period under review, it has played an instrumental role in maintaining a peaceful environment for economic activities to take place. Its performance in the delivery of critical social and economic services has varied and faced many challenges of quantity, quality, and capacity. Its delivery of critical government development programmes, especially during the socialist phase, was revisited, and room was created for the private sector to play a role for reasons dealt with within the various sections of this chapter. Civil service operational autonomy was a contested terrain and was continuously challenged. As already pointed out, poor policy choices by politicians; made without extensive and careful consideration of context, doomed most of these policies to fail. Factors related to civil service limited involvement in policy making, capacity, organisational resources, motivation, and ethics have been advanced in explaining the difficulties that the civil service had in contributing to economic development. A hostile external environment was an added barrier.

There have, however, been various reform initiatives aimed at improving the efficiency and effectiveness of the civil service, and there is little doubt that the capacity of the civil service to administer them has relatively improved. However, this study's findings have shown that a lot is yet to be done to maximise the potential of the civil service to contribute effectively to economic development. One of the areas that requires immediate attention is the relationship between civil servants and politicians. A critical element in this regard is to empower the civil service by unplugging links of political patronage while at the same time ensuring democratic accountability. This could be done through introducing a competitive and transparent system of performance evaluation and promotion to senior positions in the civil service. This should go hand in hand with strengthening the role and the power of the Civil Service Commission over recruitment, promotion, and disciplinary matters. This kind of reform undertaking is unlikely to succeed unless supported by the top political executives. Sustainability of these reforms would therefore depend on the efficiency of the overall governance system of the country. Therefore, successful civil service reforms have their future in constitutional reforms.

APPENDIX

A.I PUBLIC AND PRIVATE FORMAL EMPLOYMENT
AND WAGES

Tanzanian statistics do not permit the construction of a complete annual series of employment, and they are still weaker on wages. This appendix presents what are probably the best estimates available.

Employment

The Integrated Labour Force Surveys (ILFS) and household surveys provide a complete picture of employment at several points in time. The ILO and World Bank World Development Indicators (WDI) series are based on these observations and the interpolation between them. For the formal sector, the Survey of Employment and Earnings (SEE) should give annual information on employment and wages by the government, parastatals, and private formal firms. That survey indeed covers the whole public sector (general government, parastatals, and public agencies), all private formal establishments with more than fifty employees, and a representative sample of private formal establishments with fewer than fifty employees.

The SEE has been taken annually since 2001, although it was not taken in 2008 and 2009. Moreover, the definition of employment statistics may have changed during that break, as public employment figures show a 15 per cent drop between 2007 and 2010, which corresponds to no known drastic cut in the civil service. The SEE consistently reports a drop in the real wage bill of the public sector comparable with that of employment. Yet such an evolution does not fit the 9.6 per cent annual change in the real government wage expenditures reported by the Bank of Tanzania for the 2007–10 period. Some figures are given in the text for public employment prior to the SEE series. They are supposed to also come from the SEE but it was not possible to go into more detail. This is the reason the series prior to 2001 may not be comparable with later data.

The employment data for the public sector in Figure 5.A.1 is thus broken down into three partial series. A few observations for the period before 2001, 2001–7 and 2010–15. To correct for the statistical gap between 2007 and 2010, the figures for 2007 and before were scaled down to be consistent with the most recent data, under the assumption that, contrary to the SEE, public employment would have grown as GDP – that is, roughly 5 per cent annually, between 2007 and 2010. Observations of private formal employment are only available for the last two periods. The figure also shows the evolution of GDP and total employment.[3]

---

[3] The source for employment is the ILO for the period 1991–2015, a series based on the ILFS and econometric estimates in between. Estimates before 1991 are based on the evolution of the population aged fifteen and above in WDI.

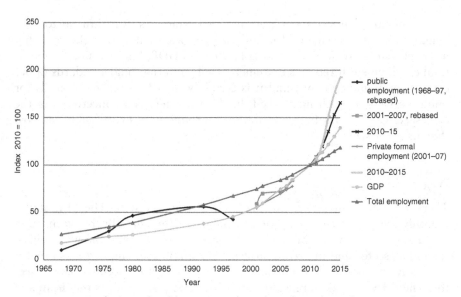

FIGURE 5.A.1 Evolution of public, private formal, and total employment and GDP, 1968–2015 (2010 = 100)
Source: Trading Economics/Transparency International (2016). (Accessed: 1 November 2017)

An important institutional issue concerning public employment is whether it tends to over-grow, as is the case in countries where the public sector is used to distribute rents, buy votes, or shelter unemployment, especially among skilled workers. Such motives were clearly not relevant during the socialist era, when the growth in public employment was due to the increasing role of the state in a socialist economy. They could be relevant during President Magufuli's government in view of the noted growing divergence with GDP, taken as an indicator of the need for public services.

Yet GDP may not be a good indicator of the need for public services in a low-income country where many of these needs are not satisfied. It is true that, across countries and over time, the relative size of the public sector tends to grow more than proportionally with GDP. That the growth in public employment over recent years corresponds in Tanzania to a massive recruitment of teachers is indeed evidence of unsatisfied needs. But the large number of ghost workers uncovered some years ago is evidence in the opposite direction.

That the need for public service may be increasing faster than GDP is also supported in Figure 5.A.1 by the very clear formalisation of the Tanzanian economy over recent years. Private formal employment has doubled between 2010 and 2015, growing five times faster than total employment, even though it still represents a minor share of total employment (roughly 7 per cent). Increasing formality implies an increasing administrative burden.

In summary, based on available aggregate statistics, it is difficult to infer whether the civil service in Tanzania is plethoric or not. It is the case that it has grown lately at a rate that is faster than GDP, but as a proportion of total employment it remains extremely low by international standards (4 per cent of total employment), and it is certainly the case that many needs for public services are still unsatisfied. In short, if there is a concern about the civil service, it would be more about its productivity or, possibly, its cost than its sheer size.

Wages

There are two sources of information on formal wages. The SEE shows monthly average earnings by private/public sector annually between 2005 and 2015. Presumably, this statistic is obtained by dividing the wage bill in the public sector and in private firms by the number of employees, so that it is sensitive to changes in the structure of employment by occupation and sector. The ILFS was taken in 2001, 2006, and 2014. It provides the mean and median monthly income of paid employees by sector of employment – that is, central/local government versus private sector (non-agriculture). It covers a broader ground than SEE since paid employees are not necessarily all in the formal sector, this difference being more important for the private than for the public sector.

The evolution of real earnings by sector according to the two sources is summarised in Table 5.A.1.

Given the differences in coverage between the two sources, it is difficult to draw firm conclusions on the evolution of wages over time, except that wage growth seems to have slowed down in the public sector since 2010, after growing fast previously. In the private sector, it is hard to believe that real wages have gone down so much, as shown by the SEE, at a time when growth of GDP per worker was more than 3 per cent a year. Growth rates seem more reasonable with the ILFS, and it seems unlikely they are sizeable exclusively because of wages in the informal sector.

A common feature of the two sources of data is the rather high differential between the public and the private sector, which might have been increasing since 2005, according to the SEE, or has peaked in the mid-2000s, according to the ILFS. Using the ILFS 2001–6, Leyaro et al. (2014) have shown that the public/private earning differential is maintained when controlling for the education and the age of the employees. The remaining differential was estimated to be 40 per cent in 2001 and 60 per cent in 2006.

An important conclusion of this brief review of employment and wage data is the need to improve the collection of data, or maybe simply to get more precision from existing data.

TABLE 5.A.1 *Evolution of mean monthly real earnings in the public and formal private sectors according to the SEE (2005–15) and the ILFS (2001–14)*

Year	Mean real monthly earnings (2015=10 TZS)		Annual growth rates		Public/private ratio	Share of government's wage bill in revenues	Share of government's wage bill in GDP
	Private	Public	Private	Public			
SEE							
2005	604	801			133	30.8	4.1
2010	486	986	-4.2	4.2	203	40.5	5.3
2015	350	1007	-6.4	0.4	288	47	7.2
ILFS							
2001	137	224			164		
2006	169	413	4.3	13.1	245		
2014	359	648	9.9	5.8	181		

Source: Construct by authors using the SEE (2005–15) and the ILFS (2001–14)

Discussion of 'Challenges of the Civil Service'

Discussion by Jan Willem Gunning

I THE IDEA OF A CIVIL SERVICE

We can think of the civil service simply as the people employed in the public sector, with the task of providing public services. This corresponds to the every-day use of the term. The public administration literature, however, is much more restrictive: it requires both *independence* and *meritocracy*. Independence implies that the civil service consists of career bureaucrats who advise their political masters and faithfully execute their programmes, irrespective of whether or not they share their views. In return, they are secure in their position: they cannot be fired for their political views and remain in position when the government changes. Meritocracy means that the hiring, firing, and career advancement of civil servants are determined solely by their professional competence and performance, not by any payments they make or by their religion, political allegiance, ethnic affiliation, or social class.[4] The meritocratic civil servant in this model is incorruptible. While he must be paid well, so as not to be led into temptation, his main motivation is the esteem (and self-esteem) acquired through his contribution to the public interest.

It is worth stressing that such a civil service is not a Western invention. For example, imperial China had already instituted a system of selecting civil servants on the basis of merit some 1,400 years ago: henceforth, prospective mandarins had to pass a famously difficult entrance examination. Once they had been admitted to the civil service, their independence was encouraged by not

---

[4] The Wikipedia article on the civil service (accessed 25 April 2018) begins as follows: 'The civil service is independent of government and composed of career bureaucrats hired on professional merit rather than appointed or elected, whose institutional tenure survives transitions of political leadership.' While this is a rather clumsy sentence, it clearly attempts to define the civil service on the basis of the two criteria of independence and meritocracy.

stationing them in their region of origin and by frequently transferring them to another part of the empire during their career. When Marco Polo described the mandarin system, it had already functioned in China for some 700 years, while at that time in Europe the public sector was still basically an unprofessional extension of the court, serving at the whim of the prince and his entourage.

In Europe, there was no independent and meritocratic civil service until 1800. In Great Britain it dates from the late nineteenth century. Pressure to replace patronage by selection on the basis of merit had already mounted in the 1850s when the disastrous British experience in the Crimean War revealed that the civil service was almost as chaotic and incompetent as the military.[5] The resulting public outcry led to the famous Northcote–Trevelyan report of 1854, which proposed drastic reforms. However, no action was taken for a very long time. Only in 1870 did Gladstone as prime minister adopt its recommendations for an independent, politically neutral civil service, selected on the basis of merit and paid well enough to resist corruption. Most other Western countries adopted similar innovations.

But notable exceptions remain to this day. In the United States, political appointments are still quite common: an incoming president is entitled to replace some 4,000 civil servants. One result is that many American ambassadors are millionaires who have distinguished themselves with campaign donations rather than as career diplomats.

Independence has an obvious implication for any study of the impact of the civil service: consequences (good or bad) of policies cannot be attributed to the civil service that has implemented them. For example, if policy choices made by politicians result in economic growth or stagnation, then that in itself says nothing about the quality of the civil service. It is after all possible that bad policies are implemented by a high-quality civil service, or indeed vice versa.[6] Similarly, if educational outcomes are very poor, as they are in Tanzania, then this may be due to policies (e.g. bad teacher training programmes, low salaries) or to their implementation by civil servants (e.g. teacher absenteeism).

This represents, of course, a problem for empirical analysis. There now exists a booming literature (which uses experimental methods) on how the functioning of the civil service can be improved. This provides evidence on,

---

[5] In the army, commissions and promotions (up to colonel) in the infantry and cavalry regiments could be bought. (This often required a fortune. The infamous 7th Earl of Cardigan, for example, paid the modern-day equivalent of some £3 million for the colonelcy of a prestigious cavalry regiment. He later led the Charge of the Light Brigade, the greatest military blunder in the Crimean War.) As a result, high rank typically reflected wealth rather than competence. This purchase system survived for 200 years, from its origin in the corrupt Restoration period of Charles II until it was finally abolished in 1871.

[6] This is relevant for Tanzania. In my view, the economic disaster of the early 1980s largely reflected the policies of the 1960s and 1970s rather than the weak quality of the civil service.

for example, what incentives can reduce teacher absenteeism. But there is no established methodology for establishing the past impact of the civil service; any attempt to do so faces the daunting task of disentangling the effect of the policies themselves from the way they were implemented.

In many African countries, the civil service tradition left by the colonial powers quickly crumbled after independence. That system was hardly meritocratic to begin with (since it involved racial discrimination) and a purely meritocratic system would have been very difficult to set up at the time: educational attainments were still quite low. (In 1962, Tanganyika – as it then was – had only a handful of people with Masters degrees; President Nyerere was one of them.) More importantly, in many countries the civil service was seen, not primarily as the provider of public services, but as the key channel for patronage. The ruling group used its control over the state to provide benefits to its supporters, notably in the form of public sector jobs, which provided income, security, and prestige. The provision of public services was therefore in itself of limited importance; it mattered mainly to the extent that it guaranteed or threatened the survival of the regime.

An important implication of the use of the civil service as a tool for patronage was that real wages in the public sector were fixed far in excess of market-clearing levels. This induced massive migration from rural to urban areas.[7] Excess supply in the urban labour market required mechanisms for allocating the scarce jobs. The mechanisms that were adopted typically favoured particular regional or ethnic groups.

Patronage was not the only reason why a civil service in the strict sense, that is independent and meritocratic, disappeared or failed to emerge in many African countries. Under many regimes, notably those we would now call developmental states (Adam and O'Connell, 1999). Weberian independence was not considered necessary or desirable: political leaders and their civil servants were seen as jointly involved in nation building; a strict separation of their roles (choosing policies and implementing them) would have been considered counterproductive.

II TANZANIA 1962–1982

Tanzania's experience in this period was exceptional. After having gained its independence in December 1961, it initially followed a familiar path: indigenisation of the civil service combined with continued heavy reliance on expatriates who wrote all the key planning documents. The Arusha Declaration marked the end of that period. Tanzania became exceptional in Africa in at least two ways: by embarking on a far-reaching attempt, unique in Africa, to

---

[7] The famous Harris–Todaro model of rural–urban migration was inspired by the experience in East Africa, notably in Kenya (Harris and Todaro, 1970, pp. 126–42).

build a socialist economy,[8] and by adopting strict policies designed to keep civil servants honest.

In Tanzania, the key economic policies of that period – import controls, production in parastatals, price controls, communal farming, and pan-territorial agricultural pricing – led to a balance of payments crisis and economic stagnation. This was temporarily veiled when Tanzania benefited from a huge term of trade improvement, the beverages boom of 1975–9, but it became clear in the early 1980s when exports collapsed, serious shortages emerged, and people reverted to barter trade (Bevan et al., 1990). It would, of course, be absurd to attribute this disastrous outcome to the quality of the civil service. In fact, in my view, prior to the collapse, the Tanzanian civil service did a remarkable job of carrying out an almost impossible task.

Notably, Tanzania had in the 1970s one of the least corrupt civil services in Africa, in spite of the huge opportunities for corruption created by the system of controls. In the 1960s, Nyerere had already introduced the 'leadership code', a set of rules that prohibited middle- and senior-ranking party members and civil servants from holding shares in, or being a director of, a private company; renting out houses; receiving more than one salary; or employing others. Pratt comments:

He did not see the leadership rules as the imposition of a morality which was not accepted. They were the enforcement of an ethic that was still part of the values of society. It was an ethic that was being rapidly replaced in the towns, amongst the leaders and within the civil service by an aggressive acquisitive individualism. (Pratt, 1976, pp. 235–6)

Nyerere saw clearly that if people in powerful positions were allowed to maximise their own income, then his vision of a socialist economy could not be realised. He and his advisers, such as Reginald Green and Justinian Rweyemamu, both Harvard PhDs, failed to see, however, that the system of controls erected in the 1960s and 1970s created enormous incentives for 'acquisitive individualism', for example in the form of the very large gap that emerged between the official and the black-market exchange rate. The control system therefore helped to undermine the very ethic that Nyerere hoped to enforce.

This chapter on the Tanzania civil service addresses three questions:

- How much has the civil service contributed to economic development?
- What constrained its performance?
- How can it be reformed so as to maximise its contribution to economic development?

I will consider these three questions in turn.

---

[8] Many newly independent African countries, for example Ghana and Kenya, adopted 'African socialism', but few really practised what they preached. Price control in Kenya, for example, was not seriously enforced, and hence did not lead to great deviations from market-clearing price levels.

III THE CONTRIBUTION OF THE CIVIL SERVICE TO
ECONOMIC DEVELOPMENT

Regrettably, how much the civil service has contributed to economic development is not an empirical question that can be answered rigorously. The reason is
that it is impossible to build a convincing counterfactual: one cannot make comparisons over time (did outcomes differ between periods with or without a civil
service?) or across space (did outcomes differ between areas with and without a
civil service?).[9] One can, of course, determine whether changes in the size or the
functioning of the civil service were followed by changes in outcomes. Strictly
speaking, this establishes, of course, only correlation, not causation. Interpreting
the outcomes as causal effects would amount to the *post hoc ergo propter hoc*
fallacy, since economic outcomes have many determinants other than the quality
of the civil service. In fact, an 'omitted variable' may well be responsible for both
a change in the civil service and a change in economic outcomes. Concluding
that the one causes the other would then clearly be a mistake.

This is a common and fundamental problem in economic history. As usual,
the best one can hope to do to explain economic outcomes at the national level
is to arrive at a *plausible* account of causal effects.[10]

Nevertheless, Mukandala does arrive at conclusions regarding causal effects.
He notes, 'Its support role in policymaking was minimal. The party was supreme
and all major policy decisions of the time were made by the party's NEC, which
had a powerful secretariat.' The party (TANU, later CCM) was powerful both in
the design of policies and in the supervision of their implementation. In fact, but
this is not in the chapter, there was next to the civil service a powerful parallel
party structure that reached from the top down to the very lowest levels. (Under
the ten-cell system there was a party official for every ten households, much as
in China. The ten-cell leader conveyed party instructions to the households and
reported on their activities.) Mukandala writes: 'Since the civil service was not a
lone or even the key player in economic development, it can only assume limited
responsibility' for the poor success rate of a long series of policies initiated in the
Nyerere period. He concludes, and I agree, that the 'grand policy decisions' then
taken were detrimental to economic growth. Mukandala adds:

Most of these policies were beyond the control of the civil service since the NEC of
TANU had self-appointed itself as a supreme decision-making organ.

---

[9] I am not sure what Mukandala's position is on this methodological issue. At one stage, he concludes that 'at least for the last fifteen years, growth in civil service size does not seem to have
had negative implications for the economy' since it grew at 5.7 per cent compared with a GDP
growth rate of 6.5 per cent. This is a *non sequitur*.

[10] At lower levels there is, of course, more scope for empirical analysis: one can exploit policy differences between various administrative units. There is a rich literature that uses this approach.
The key problem such studies face is that policies are usually not randomised over administrative units so that differences in outcomes need not be caused by policy differences.

Here I disagree, for three reasons. First, that policy decisions were taken by politicians should not be seen as an aberration, but rather as the normal state of affairs.[11] That the civil service was excluded from the policymaking process tells us little on its contribution to development. At best, the exclusion of professional advice may have contributed to poor policy choices.

Secondly, that the party also played a major role in what is properly the arena for a civil service, policy implementation, is a major confounder for the analysis of the civil service's contribution. Mukandala mentions it only in passing. In my view, while assessing the impact of a civil service rigorously would be extremely difficult in the best of circumstances, TANU's role in policy implementation makes such an analysis impossible: there simply is no independent civil service in this period, so, for better or worse, outcomes cannot be attributed with any confidence to the way the service functioned.

Thirdly, in line with this, the chapter first seems to argue that the outcomes were very bad but cannot be attributed to the civil service. However, the chapter also argues:

Generally, the findings indicate that, since the late years of Ujamaa, Tanzania's civil service has been characterised by work misbehaviour such as shirking of responsibilities (absenteeism and negligence) and corruption and misappropriation of resources (e.g. through procurement and creation of ghost workers), and generally it has failed to regulate opportunistic politicians and even colluded with them, at the expense of the economy.

You cannot have your cake and eat it too: either the contribution of the civil service was '*minimal*', and it had only '*limited responsibility*' for what went wrong, or 'it has failed to regulate opportunistic politicians and even colluded with them, at the expense of the economy'. By seemingly trying to have it both ways, the chapter leaves unclear what its answer is to the first of the three questions.

IV CONSTRAINTS ON THE PERFORMANCE OF THE CIVIL SERVICE

What constrains the civil service depends of course on what it is supposed to do: a lack of qualified candidates, for example, is a constraint for a Gladstonian civil service but not for a service that is meant to provide patronage.

Within the Gladstonian framework, there are three issues to consider. First, what are the incentives for people to join (and remain in) the civil service? Incentives can include pay, security, prestige, and opportunities for corruption. The issue is whether the package offered by the civil service (officially

[11] That these decisions were not taken in the cabinet but by the party's executive committee is something else.

or not, including the opportunities for engaging in bribery) is attractive compared with an alternative, for example employment in the private sector. In other words: can the civil service attract and retain high-quality candidates? Secondly, is the civil service's independence guaranteed or is its functioning hampered by political interference? Thirdly, are hiring, promotion, and firing based exclusively on merit, or do non-meritocratic criteria such as ethnicity or party membership play a role?[12]

Regarding the first issue, there are several indications in the chapter that incentives are indeed problematic. Mukandala shows, for example, that there are (and have been) major staff shortages, notably in health and education. He explains that these reflect a freeze on public sector employment, but he also refers to 'those who left for greener pastures'.[13] In what way these other pastures were greener is not discussed. This is a pity since an analysis of the incentives for joining or leaving the civil service must be the basis for any proposed reform.

Table 5.3 presents very interesting evidence from a recent World Bank study, comparing quality indicators in the public and private sector. Perhaps surprisingly there appear to be *no* large differences. If the public and private sectors do not really differ in terms of workload or absenteeism, then what makes the civil service relatively attractive or unattractive, and how has this changed over time? Real wages in Tanzania fell dramatically from the late 1960s until the mid-1980s; they rose again in the mid-1990s. Unfortunately, there is no evidence in the chapter on changes over time in the *relative* attractiveness of the two sectors, public and private.[14] Apparently, the situation in 2015 was such that public wages were 'outcompeting those in the private sector' (Mukandala is quoting Leyaro et al., 2014, p. 10). However, the chapter stresses that two major problems remain: intrinsic motivation has drastically declined since the days of Nyerere, and, while incentives are quite attractive in the higher ranks, motivation is quite low for those in lower ranks, the majority of civil servants. Corruption has become a major issue, and the chapter makes it plain that this has a long history, going back to the late *Ujamaa* years.

On the other two issues, the chapter is very clear. In the 1960s and 1970s, politicisation severely undermined the civil service's neutrality: it could no longer freely use its professional expertise. The party had no time for the setting of priorities or for moderation. Since that time, the civil service has become more independent. However, the relationship between civil servants and politicians remains linked by patronage; in that sense, the civil service is not completely independent. There was a period when all university graduates were recruited by the public sector and patronage (in the form of hiring friends and relations) was a

---

[12] Tanzania has a very large number of ethnic groups. Ethnicity has therefore never played a major role as it has in countries with a few large ethnic groups, such as Nigeria or Kenya.

[13] See Section 3.2 in Mukandala (2018).

[14] Mukandala writes that his findings reveal that incentives have 'relatively declined'. This would have been very important, but he does not present evidence of this.

major issue. However, from 1999 there have been meritocratic reforms, including the introduction of open competition and non-discrimination. Forged or questionable academic certificates used to be accepted, but have now become the basis for a large number of dismissals.[15] The discussion of these reforms is tantalising but very brief. I would have liked to know more about how they were designed and, most importantly, how they survived in spite of the fact that they must have run into opposition from vested interests. Did Tanzania find ways to overcome this problem that are relevant for future reforms or for reforms in other countries?

The recent changes seem to be in the direction of greater independence and meritocracy. The chapter makes abundantly clear that there still is a long way to go. For example, Mukandala describes that candidates from different institutions must be treated equally in spite of large quality differences and wryly notes 'the results have been disastrous'. Moreover, connections still matter, most promotions are still automatic, and party membership can still trump qualifications. There is clearly scope for deeper reforms.

V REFORMING THE CIVIL SERVICE

Recall that the third question asked how the civil service can be reformed so as to maximise its contribution to economic development. The chapter suggests numerous improvements: better recruitment, rigorous competition, merit-based evaluation, scrapping unnecessary posts, continuous checking, an improved incentive structure with pay tied to verifiable performance criteria, stronger accountability, action against misbehaviour, better time management, and improved ICT use. It is hard to disagree with this list.

Reform must, of course, be selective: an attempt to address all these issues simultaneously would be a recipe for failure. The standard approach to setting priorities in civil service reform is largely technocratic: it focuses on the low-hanging fruit and postpones reforms that are costly or aimed at less urgent problems. Essentially, this amounts to ordering reform measures in terms of cost–benefit ratios.

Mukandala correctly notes that this approach is unlikely to lead to sustainable reform. Measures intended to reduce political influence on the civil service or aimed at eliminating the scope for patronage will be resisted by politicians, who will quickly recognise that they undermine their position. This is, of course, the central issue in any political economy analysis of reform, whether it be of the civil service, trade policy, decentralisation, taxation, or industrial policy. In all such cases, the challenge is to design reforms that will not be blocked by a set of agents in a position to do so, notably, but

---

[15] Indeed, this is one of the reasons for the current staff shortages in health and education.

not necessarily, those in power. Essentially, the ruling class must perceive a reform package as an improvement of their position in spite of the fact that the reforms themselves directly threaten their position. Typically, this will require some form of compensation.

This issue of making the unacceptable acceptable is at the heart of the political economy of reform. I note, not as a criticism but with some regret, that the chapter does not address this. Given the importance of this issue, this makes the discussion similar to Hamlet without the Prince of Denmark. I had hoped to learn what the key sensitivities were that would generate opposition to reform and in what way that resistance might be overcome. That hope was disappointed, but I recognise, of course, that these are extremely difficult questions to answer, even in a speculative way.

6

Fiscal Decentralisation as an Example
of Institutional Ineffectiveness

Servacius Likwelile and Paschal Assey

I INTRODUCTION

Decentralisation involves political, administrative, and fiscal reforms aimed at increasing the decision-making capacity and development efficiency of local administrations through the redistribution of powers and resources between administrative levels. The different dimensions of decentralisation can vary in importance and can be rolled out in different sequences. Decentralisation reforms very often target public service delivery (such as health, education, transport, water, and sanitation) in ways that may relate primarily to the administrative or the fiscal dimension. This may be because of technical and pragmatic concerns about appropriate sub-national government functions, but it may also reflect powerful political and institutional dynamics (Eaton et al., 2010).

Decentralisation has been the objective of important reforms in many developing countries and a major focus of the considerable support provided by development partners. Such reforms have swept across the world since the mid-1980s a trend seen by some observers as being influential for good governance and for improving the lives of ordinary citizens. African governments and international donors alike have indeed embraced the idea that decentralisation can promote development and good governance as local governments are more likely to be responsive to local needs, even though the record is mixed on several fronts. In any case, local governments' share of public expenditure has more than doubled in many countries, and they now often play the leading role in the delivery of local public services. Academics are increasingly interested in evaluating the consequences of the change this evolution entails for the institutional relationship between levels of government, particularly for fiscal transfers (Falleti, 2005).

The focus of this chapter is on fiscal decentralisation, dwelling mainly on the administration of local revenue mobilisation given the centrality of financial resources in empowering local authorities to deliver on their mandate and improve their performance. Effective mobilisation of local revenues calls for a proper coordination of the local/central government mechanism and an administrative system with sufficient capacity to collect and analyse information, and plan and execute such proposals. In the case of Tanzania, this fiscal dimension was chosen to demonstrate the weaknesses of state coordination and the critical challenges involved in setting up an institutional arrangement addressing such weaknesses.

The chapter begins with an overview of the theoretical considerations behind the growing global trend towards decentralisation. It then summarises how the relationship between central and local government has evolved in Tanzania since pre-colonial times. It explains why, despite a recent reform programme, the current legal framework remains complex and confusing, impacting negatively on efficiency.

The capacity to collect revenue at local level is extremely limited in Tanzania. Expanding on previous studies (in particular Tanzi, 2000; Fjeldstad, 2001; Fjeldstad et al., 2010; Fjeldstad and Semboja, 2011; Masaki, 2018), the chapter identifies five key reasons for this: ambiguity in defining the roles and responsibilities of different state organs, leading to overlaps and conflicts of interest; arbitrariness, inconsistency, and unpredictability in government decisions and actions; weak institutional capacity for effective fiscal decentralisation; overdependence on the central government for financial transfers; and transparency and accountability asymmetry, with institutions reporting mostly to the central authorities. Practical consequences in terms of revenue are dramatic, including frequent cases of tax evasion, corruption, and even embezzlement of revenues, and constant political tension between local and central governments.

At a more general level, the chapter also considers how important fiscal decentralisation is for the success of decentralisation overall, and concludes by identifying three key directions for future reform in Tanzania.

II THE THEORY OF CENTRAL–LOCAL GOVERNMENT RELATIONSHIPS

Every country has different layers of government with different functions, based on their particular circumstances and experiences (van der Dussen, 2008). Consequently, decentralisation processes are initiated for different reasons. Some countries want to make the public sector leaner and more efficient. Others are motivated by disenchantment with the performance of centralised policies. Decentralisation may be motivated by a desire to contain or appease local demands for greater cultural and political autonomy. It may reflect an awareness of the global trends in institutional reform and a desire to not be left behind. Governments do not generally decentralise with the aim of pursuing greater macroeconomic stability and growth, though this may be an outcome (Martinez-Vazquez and Vaillancourt, 2011).

Decentralisation generally refers to the devolution of decision-making powers from the central government to local or sub-national governments. A related idea is de concentration, in which central governments retain decision-making power but diversify and customise the provision of public services to lower levels of government. According to the sequential theory of decentralisation, the extent to which decision-making power is devolved in practice depends on the sequencing of political, administrative, and fiscal decentralisation (Falleti, 2005).

Regarding fiscal decentralisation, there are four basic approaches: empowering local governments to set up their own tax systems; central retention of all taxes, with proceeds shared with local governments through intergovernmental transfers; assigning selected taxes exclusively to local governments; and sharing revenue from specific centrally collected sources with local government. Many systems are hybrids of these approaches, with the choice depending on considerations that may be technical, historical, demographic, economic, geographic, or political (Martinez-Vazquez and Vaillancourt, 2011).

In principle, decentralisation is often considered to be a desirable aim. Economists such as Oates (1972), who first developed the theory of fiscal federalism, argue that decentralisation should increase citizens' welfare because service providers will have better information about diverse needs and preferences, and greater flexibility to address them. While such theories assume that governments are benevolent, a growing literature on public choice theory – which assumes that officials are selfish – also often favours decentralisation. A branch of this literature known as market-preserving federalism holds that decentralisation can incentivise good behaviour among government officials, control the intrusiveness and expansiveness of the public sector, and support effective private markets (Weingast, 1995; McKinnon, 1997).

It is theorised that decentralisation should reduce corruption, as accountability, information, and transparency should be greater at the local level; so should possibilities to encourage collective action and build social capital, which would lead to a higher probability of corruption being detected and punished (Boadway and Shah, 2009). If individuals and businesses are mobile, fiscal decentralisation should also help to constrain government misbehaviour by opening up the possibility of competition among jurisdictions.

There are counter-arguments, however. Decentralisation could create opportunities for rent-seeking by weakening central agencies' scope for monitoring, control, and audit. By involving a larger number of officials in dealing with potential investors and revenue sources, political decentralisation can also create more opportunities for corruption and clientelism. The risks are especially high when elites dominate the local political scene. Incentives for corruption at the local level may also be higher owing to poorer compensation, lower career prospects, and lower morale (De and Prud'homme, 1994).

What does the evidence say? Based on cross-country comparisons, Huther and Shah (1998) find that fiscal decentralisation is associated with greater citizen participation, more political and democratic accountability, social justice, and improved economic management and operational efficiency; it is also found to have a positive effect on institutional quality and the quality of government (De Mello, 2011). There is strong evidence that fiscal decentralisation increases the share of education and health expenditures in total government expenditures, especially in developing countries (Shelton, 2007). Working on Bolivia, Faguet (2004) finds evidence that fiscal decentralisation increases investment in social sectors, such as education, urban development, water and sanitation, and health care.

Based on case studies, decentralisation has also been found to positively impact education outcomes such as literacy rates, years of schooling, dropout rates for primary and secondary education, public school enrolment, and test scores (Faguet, 2004; Peña, 2007, among others). In the health sector, positive impacts include decreasing infant mortality. Decentralisation has been found to increase access to water and sewage services and deliver better quality infrastructure at lower costs than in centralised settings, mainly where a community-driven development approach is used.

While generally positive, however, the evidence is mixed and incomplete – not least because it is difficult to isolate the effect of decentralisation on development from other processes such as economic growth and institutional changes in the public sector. There remain open questions about how diversity, complexity, proximity of local officials, political constraints, accountability, incentives, corruption, rent-seeking, and state capture by local elites affect the success of decentralisation – and about whether deconcentration can be as efficient as decentralisation.

Capacity may be the key factor in determining the extent to which decentralisation succeeds: services may improve when decentralised to high-capacity local governments and deteriorate when decentralised to low-capacity local governments. For instance, theories of public finance often tend to assume that local governments will have fiscal capacity, defined as the ability to raise tax revenues 'given the structure of the tax system and its available powers of enforcement' (Besley and Persson, 2013). However, in practice local governments in low-income countries tend to lack fiscal capacity. Africa has performed particularly poorly compared with the rest of the world in terms of the level of local revenue generation and service delivery, with local governments depending heavily on central government grants to finance their budgets.

The diverse and complex political economy challenges that underlie lack of capacity at the local level rarely receive sufficient attention (McLure, 1998). They include the incentives and behaviours of national-level politicians and bureaucrats, who shape the rules of the intergovernmental fiscal game and how they are implemented, and the local-level political economy dynamics among elected local councillors, local government staff, and citizens. When local governments lack capacity, an appropriate balance needs to be found between central oversight and local autonomy.

III THE EVOLUTION OF LOCAL GOVERNMENT IN TANZANIA

Tanzania's history of local government dates back to the chiefdoms of the pre-colonial era, as summarised in Table 6.1. During the first decade of independence, 1961–71, the government replaced native authorities with local officers who were democratically elected, in common with other newly independent African states, with the aim of improving the delivery of public goods and services. This was partly the result of the independence euphoria, but also reflected the genuine determination of the new government to bring fundamental changes to the citizens. The leadership's reflection on a strategy for national social and economic development led to the Arusha Declaration of 1967 that committed Tanzania to a development strategy based on 'socialism and self-reliance'. The emphasis of the Second Five Year Development Plan (1969–74) was on rural development, which required further administrative reforms – at the local level – in order to improve the capacity and effectiveness of the machinery of government in carrying out the new rural development effort (Collins, 1974). However, local governments remained closely supervised by, managed by, and accountable to the central government. This reflected in part the British system of government the country inherited, in part the aim of strengthening national unity, and in part the fear – not publicly acknowledged – that local authorities, just like the independent cooperative unions, could become a source of opposition (Mnyasenga and Mushi, 2015).

It quickly became clear that local authorities were failing to achieve the expected results owing to, among other factors, expansion of services that did not match the available financial resources, lack of competent personnel, and rampant mismanagement of funds (both local and grants from the central government), leading to poor social and economic performance. The period also witnessed an ascendancy of politics and politicians over the bureaucracy that led to a loss of consistency in policies and operations at both central and local government level.

In 1972, local governments were abolished, and the government created new regional and district committees (in place of district councils), which were given responsibility to coordinate both economic and social development activities while reporting to the Prime Minister's Office. By then, Tanzania had thus opted for a deconcentration rather than a devolution type of decentralisation. In effect, the central government started to directly manage the local development process and provision of social services.

There was, however, a lack of preparedness in the implementation of this reform that showed up in low human capacity, lack of resources, and inherent disincentives for task compliance in the whole administrative system. The social services infrastructure collapsed in the severe economic crisis of the late 1970s and early 1980s, which, under the strong pressure of the donors, led a few years later to a complete change of development strategy, from a socialist to a market economy. Notable at that time was the overextension of the state,

TABLE 6.1 *The evolution of local government in Tanzania*

Period	Type of local governance
Pre-colonial era	Chiefdoms, and councils of elders.
German era (1884–1917)	Mainly direct rule but also limited urban authorities.
British era (1917–61)	Native authorities encouraged since 1926 (indirect rule); township authorities for large urban areas; Municipalities Ordinance 1946; Local Government Act 1953.
First decade of independence (1961–71)	Chiefdoms abolished; inclusive local authorities encouraged; local governments overwhelmed by duties, with limited resources; rural authorities abolished 1972, urban authorities abolished 1973.
Deconcentration (1972–82)	A system of deconcentration of central government replaced the comprehensive local government system that had existed for a decade.
Reinstitution of local government (1982–95)	Urban Councils (Interim Provisions) Act 1978 required that town and municipal councils be re-established from 1 July 1978; 1982 comprehensive local government legislation passed; 1984 comprehensive system of local government re-established.
Local government reform (since 1996)	Comprehensive programme of reforming local governments to make them efficient, effective, transparent, and accountable.

Source: History of Local Government of Tanzania by United Republic of Tanzania President's Office, Regional Administration and Local Government

which placed great pressure on its capacity, while the heightened ideological content and politicisation of the government decision-making process eroded the authority and self-confidence of the bureaucracy. Faced with that erosion in the capacity to carry out the economic management tasks of government, donors increasingly pressed for administrative reforms, including the reinstitution of local government institutions. The reintroduction of urban authorities had taken place in 1978. Then a series of laws on local government were passed in 1982 and there was a constitutional amendment in 1985.

These measures proved to be flawed. They did not clearly define the relationship between central and local government – in practice, the centre retained strong powers of control and supervision, and the structure of local government authorities (LGAs) overlapped with that of the ruling party (Mnyasenga and Mushi, 2015). LGAs were given only limited power to mobilise their own human resources, implement their own plans and strategies, and raise revenue, borrowing, and spending. From the early 1990s, various studies, commissions, workshops, and seminars pointed out the complexity, ambiguity, and fragmentation of the legal framework, with overlaps and conflicts among legislation, circulars, standing orders, and other regulations from ministries responsible for health, education, extension services, water supply, and rural roads. At a higher level, it also became evident that fundamental political, administrative, and economic reforms were imperative for the government to improve economic efficiency and effectiveness. Several far-reaching economic and political reforms were thus introduced during this period, including macroeconomic stabilisation and fiscal restraint, market liberalisation, and privatisation on the economic side, and also the establishment of multiparty democracy in 1992 on the political side.

Tanzania consequently embarked on a new Local Government Reform Programme (LGRP) in 1996, accompanied by the decentralisation by devolution (D by D) strategy, in which LGAs were supposed to be largely autonomous institutions, free to make policy and operational decisions consistent with the country's laws and policies, and with the power to possess both human and financial resources. Reforms were aimed at downsizing central government, reforming local governments, and decentralising more powers to them. It was expected that the D-by-D strategy would yield, among other outputs, the delivery of quality services to the people in a participative, effective, and transparent way. There was, however, little analysis and documentation of the implementation challenges at both national and local authority levels. The LGRP was to be implemented in two phases – a stand-alone programme from 1998 to 2008, and integration into the government system from 2009 to 2014. It set out to address five dimensions:

1. *Financial*: giving local authorities more sources of revenue, including conditional and unconditional grants from the central government;
2. *Administrative*: de-linking centrally controlled personnel from sectoral ministries and integrating them in the local government system;
3. *Central–local relations*: limiting the roles of central government to policymaking, support and facilitation, monitoring, and quality assurance;
4. *Service function*: decentralising the management and provision of public services, with the aim of enhancing their quantity and quality; and
5. *Democratic*: strengthening local democratic institutions, enhancing public participation and bringing control to the people.

By the end of the first phase in 2008, however, only four pieces of legislation had been partially amended,[1] and a legal harmonisation task force had only

---

[1] The Local Government (District Authorities) Act, 1982 [CAP 287 R.E. 2002]; the Local Government (Urban Authorities) Act, 1982 [CAP 288 R.E. 2002]; the Local Government Finance Act, 1982 [CAP 290 R.E. 2002], and the Regional Administration Act, 1997 [CAP 97 R.E. 2002]. The Regional Administration Act was amended by Act No. 6 of 1999 and further amended in 2006 by the Local Government Laws (Miscellaneous Amendment) Act No. 13 of 2006.

just started to review sector laws and policies (Mnyasenga and Mushi, 2015). Rather than clarifying overlaps in responsibility, some of these amendments actually exacerbated ambiguity: for example, Act No. 6 of 1999 and Act No. 13 of 2006 introduced a provision that the central government could do 'any such other acts and things as shall facilitate or secure the effective, efficient and lawful execution by the District Authorities of their statutory or incidental duties'. By the end of the second phase in 2014, neither a comprehensive local government law nor harmonised central and sector legislation were in place. This remains the case today (April, 2023).

In summary, government decentralisation in Tanzania has gone through four phases: first, active decentralisation was pushed by the national-level bureaucratic elite that swiftly emerged following independence; second, the consolidation of that process was impeded by the major disruption that followed the Arusha Declaration and the increasing state control over the whole economy, at a time most able civil servants were transferred to manage the new parastatals, spreading available talent very thinly (Van Arkadie, 1995); third, an attempt at reverting the process took place some ten years later, with the major institutional adjustment process that followed the crisis of the early 1980s and led to the re-establishment of a market economy, but, for various reasons, the economy remained *de facto* essentially centralised; and, fourth, under the pressure from donors using economic arguments, including the need to reduce the role of the central government (World Bank, 2004) and improve the delivery of public services as well as the participation of citizens (Smoke, 1994; Manor, 1999; World Bank, 1999; Olowu, 2000), decentralisation, in its devolution definition, is again posted as a major reform objective (LGRP laws). How far has this reform gone?

IV LOCAL AND CENTRAL GOVERNANCE IN TANZANIA TODAY: A COMPLEX AND CONFUSING LEGAL FRAMEWORK

The legal framework governing relationships between central and local government in Tanzania is complex and confusing. For example, local authorities are legally mandated to make and implement their own development plans, finding their own sources of revenue – but central ministries are also legally empowered to determine the sources of local government revenue, and can veto decisions made at the sub-national level. Sector ministries are also legally empowered to intervene in the functions of LGAs.[2]

The overwhelming power of the minister responsible for local government is suggested by the sheer number of mentions in the relevant legislation: according to Mnyasenga and Mushi (2015), the minister is mentioned 95 times in the 156 sections of the Local Government (District Authorities) Act, 1982 [CAP 287 R.E. 2002]; 80 times in the 111 sections of the Local Government (Urban Authorities)

---

[2] By S174A (2), as amended by s.10(c) of Act No. 13 of 2006.

Act, 1982 [CAP 288 R.E. 2002]; and 60 times in the 65 sections of the Local Government Finance Act, 1982 [CAP 290 R.E. 2002]. Most of these mentions are concerned with the control and supervision of local government powers, functions, and finance through approval powers; appellate power; issuance of guidelines, regulations, directives, orders, and direct interventions; appointment and transfer powers of local government staff; disciplinary powers over local government staff; variation of local government functions; and powers to dissolve local government councils. Most of these powers are discretionary and can be delegated by the minister to any public officer.

In practice, research indicates that the central government indeed exercises tight control over LGAs. Studies carried out by REPOA (2008), Tidemand and Msami (2010), and Kunkuta (2011) reveal the most frequently used mechanisms: issuing policy statements and guidelines; giving directives and commands that direct the LGAs to perform or not to perform certain activities; issuing circulars; discipline and transfer of local government staff; and setting budget ceilings. In the opinion of 87.4 per cent of those asked by the researchers, the minister's power negatively influences the autonomy of LGAs.

The same studies also observed that Regional Administrative Secretariats negatively affect the autonomy of LGAs. In theory, these regional authorities should play a facilitating role, providing technical advice, support, and supervision.[3] In practice, they put heavy pressure on local authorities, frequently issue directives, and veto development plans and programmes that are deemed to be inconsistent with national policies. While this can sometimes be justified, experience suggests these powers are exercised excessively – in particular, political tensions emerge in constituencies dominated by opposition parties when LGAs are pressured to prioritise implementing the party manifesto above their own plans.

Figure 6.1 depicts how LGAs receive directives, guidelines, circulars, memoranda, codes of conduct, and so on from a wide variety of other governmental bodies: the Ministry of Finance and Planning; the President's Office – Regional Administration and Local Government; sector ministries, such as education and health; and regional and district authorities. LGAs lack the capacity to implement them efficiently, or to comply with these varied stakeholders' different reporting requirements and formats. This results in data being unreliable: there are, for example, substantial variations between budget figures presented to local councils and to the parliament, information on expenditure compiled by the Prime Minister's Office Regional Administration and Local Government (PMO-RALG), and what appears in the audited final accounts (Fjeldstad et al., 2010).

Overall, the general feeling about the 1998 reform of the functioning of LGAs and their relationship with the central government is that it is

---

[3] Section 12 of the Regional Administration Act, 1997 [Act No. 19 of 1997].

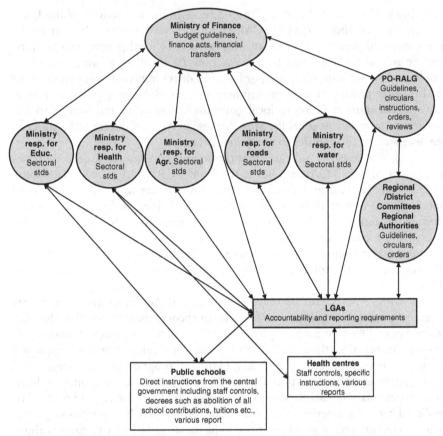

FIGURE 6.1 Interactions between central and local government
Source: Construct by authors

unfinished business. Progress seems to have taken place in the volume of services delivered and in their quality. It is also the case that LGA expenditures and employment weigh more in public spending and the civil service today (April 2023). Yet the control of LGAs over their staff and their total spending is limited, owing to what two evaluators call a 'dual level of authority'. The same evaluators concluded that, up to 2008, the end of the first stage of the reform, LGAs were not more powerful than they were in 2000. To date (April 2023), the situation remains more or less the same, or may have slightly deteriorated with the increased control by the central government under the fifth phase, with the recent decision to transfer key staff in departments of land and water to the central government, including further transfer of local government sources of revenue. Thus, despite the significant devolution of authority and resources to sub-national levels of government, persisting capacity deficits, increased financial dependence on the central government, and political and institutional constraints impact negatively on the pace of reforms, and also mean that the achievements have fallen short of the intentions of the reform agenda.

Among the weaknesses underscored by observers, the issue of fiscal decentralisation ranks high. We now turn the spotlight on it.

V FISCAL DECENTRALISATION: THE CHALLENGES OF REVENUE COLLECTION

The LGRP aimed to ensure discretionary powers for local councils to levy local taxes and fees and pass their own budgets, reflecting their own priorities alongside the obligation to meet nationally mandated standards in the delivery of the public services for which they are responsible. The bulk of the funding for these services – which include primary education, primary health, local roads, potable water, sanitation, and agricultural extension – comes from central government, as do the salaries and emoluments of council civil servants. Transfers are allocated according to a formula that takes into account socio-economic factors such as the size of population, area, poverty, and access to health facilities.

There is ample evidence that the reforms have not been effective in increasing LGAs' fiscal autonomy. Only a few large urban councils in Tanzania can finance a substantial share of their expenditure from their own revenue sources. Between 2000 and 2007, revenue collected in urban LGAs increased by 36 per cent, but declined by 4 per cent in rural LGAs; this is attributed to the central government abolishing certain 'nuisance taxes' in 2003/4, inappropriate tax design and poor collection systems (REPOA, 2007; Fjeldstad et al., 2010). In the 2006/7 financial year, LGAs collected about TZS 60 billion in local taxes, representing only about 7 per cent of total LGA expenditure (Tidemand and Msami, 2010). In 2012/13, transfers from the central government accounted for 85 to 90 per cent of local budgets – on a par with corresponding numbers from other African countries, such as Lesotho (90 per cent), Uganda (88 per cent), and Ghana (69 per cent). The share of total national tax revenues collected by local governments – about 6 per cent – remained almost unchanged since 1996 (Fjeldstad, 2003).

Table 6.2 lists the main sources of revenue for local governments. The most important are classified as non-tax, including produce taxes, market fees, service levies, licences and permits, property tax, and fines and penalties. Collecting such revenues creates opportunities for rent-seeking; doing so efficiently requires robust monitoring and enforcement systems to ensure transparency and accountability, along with skilled staff who are costly to employ and maintain at the local level (Besley and Persson, 2013). Guidance from central and sectoral ministries is lacking; indeed, political interference with local revenue collection is prevalent.

TABLE 6.2 Revenue sources for local governments

Taxes on property	Other taxes on permission to use goods
• Property rates	• Forest produce licence fees
	• Building materials extraction licence fee
Taxes on goods and services	• Hunting licence fees
• Crop tax (maximum 3% of farm gate price)	• Muzzle-loading guns licence fees
• Forest produce tax	• Scaffolding/hoarding permit fees
Taxes on specific services	*Turnover taxes*
• Guest house levy	• Service levy
Business and professional licences	*Entrepreneurial and property income*
• Commercial fishing licence fee	• Dividends
• Intoxicating liquor licence fee	• Other domestic property income
• Private health facility licence fee	• Interest
• Taxi licence fee	• Land rent
• Plying (transportation) permit fees	
• Other business licence fees	
Motor vehicle and ferry licences	*Other local revenue sources*
• Vehicle licence fees	• Administrative fees and charges
• Fishing vessel licence fees	• Fines, penalties, and forfeitures

Source: Construct by authors

Political economy reasons, or more exactly unaligned incentives and disincentives, are among the critical forces that help to maintain such a complex and inefficient system. Important stakeholders, including bureaucrats and politicians, as well as powerful taxpayers, resist changes in an attempt to protect their influence and control of the local tax system. In the case of Tanzania, Fjeldstad (2001) maintains that such an environment offers informal incomes for civil servants and their social network members and provides a visible arena for local councillors to play out their political aspirations *vis-à-vis* their constituents. It also provides incentives for some powerful taxpayers, in particular businesspeople, landowners, parastatals, and the cooperative unions, to seek to retain the *status quo*, since it facilitates evasion.

A Property Tax: A Case Study

Property tax provides a case study of the challenges. While property valuations are based on the number of storeys and type of floors, walls, and roof, there is no clear and consistent methodology: more accurate valuations would require financial skills, infrastructure, and documentation, which are generally lacking. Valuations are often arbitrary and highly disputed, and in 2017 the central government proposed to replace them with flat lump sums depending solely on the number of storeys and urban or rural location.

Responsibility for collecting property tax has changed three times in a decade. Before 2008, when it lay with municipalities, revenue collection was poor, corruption was rife, and local politicians often interfered (Fjeldstad et al., 2010; Fjeldstad, 2015). As a result, the system was partially centralised: in 2008, the Tanzania Revenue Authority (TRA) was given the responsibility of collecting property tax on behalf of municipalities in Dar es Salaam, which retained the power to declare an area rateable, set rates, and grant exemptions.

However, mutual mistrust impeded cooperation between the TRA and municipal authorities. Imperfect information flowing to central operators created opportunities for corruption, contrary to what was expected from this re-centralisation decision, and negatively impacted revenue collection. The World Bank became concerned that the move indicated lack of government commitment to the decentralisation process, and temporarily stalled funding of the valuation and assessment of properties in Dar es Salaam. In February 2014, the system was thus re-decentralised. An elected councillor in one of the municipalities said:

Re-decentralisation of property tax administration is a perfect move. From the time TRA started to collect property tax, revenue deteriorated. I strongly believe that the collection by municipality will be far better than that of TRA. First and foremost is that the municipality knows that it is collecting the money to finance its budget, so all efforts will be instituted to meet the target. (Fjeldstad et al., 2019, p. 14)

The TRA, in contrast, reacted with resignation and frustration. A senior officer argued:

All municipalities are very happy about re-decentralisation of property tax collection because right from the start when TRA took over they were disappointed [...] [they] have been trying to make tricks so that TRA is perceived inefficient. For example, when TRA took over, all municipalities set larger targets to TRA year after year despite the fact that the tax base remained the same. (Fjeldstad et al., 2019, p. 14)

In July 2016, the central government again made collection the responsibility of the TRA – a decision that took municipalities by surprise, as it appeared not to have been based on a comprehensive assessment of the challenges experienced between 2008 and 2014 or the performance of municipalities since 2014 (Fjeldstad et al., 2017). Yet the failure to establish a stable and predictable regime is reflected in a significant proportion of potential revenue going uncollected: Budget Execution reports for the past three fiscal years indicate an average collection of local revenue of between 47 and 53 per cent of projections.

B Lack of Local Capacity for Revenue Collection

The vacillation on property tax collection indicates a more general dilemma: while decentralising tax collection makes sense in principle, LGAs in Tanzania have always lacked the administrative, institutional, and fiscal capacity to collect local taxes. This is a problem common to most African countries, particularly in rural areas (Fjeldstad et al., 2014). A study conducted by REPOA for the PMO-RALG found that executive officers at the ward and village levels in Tanzania are typically educated only to primary- or secondary-school level and have minimal skills to handle the functions their posts require (REPOA, 2007).[4] Although there are many unemployed graduates, they are not attracted by the status, remuneration package, and working environment at ward and village level. The councils studied did not have sufficient staff trained to collect, process, and manage fiscal data or conduct quantitative analyses to guide policymaking.

Some local governments tried to improve capacity by outsourcing revenue collection to private agents: property taxes, bus stand and parking fees, forestry levies, and market fees. However, arrangements were often poor owing to a lack of knowledge about the local tax base or clear methods of establishing charge rates. Assessment of revenue potential was generally *ad hoc* and based on outdated figures, suggesting corruption and inefficiency. For example, collection of fees at the Ubungo Bus Terminal in Dar es Salaam was outsourced to a private agent owing partly to concern about fraud among council officials – but the private agent then retained most of the revenue collected. A conservative estimate by the Chr. Michelsen Institute and REPOA researchers is that the city council received only about 44 per cent of revenue collected between 2002 and 2006.

Local government capacity is usually augmented by staff from central government institutions. However, these institutions themselves have shown limited capacity for designing, developing, and implementing measures to strengthen local government. Most of the staff are not accountable to the LGAs but to the Local Government Service Commission and/or parent sectoral ministries such as education and health in central government. Their effectiveness is limited by lack of knowledge of local conditions, with fragmented management of staff at the local authority level exacerbated by under-financing and subterfuge. Asymmetries in reporting and accountability create significant potential for overlaps and inefficiencies.

These problems are compounded by limited use of technology for planning and reporting, particularly fiscal planning and accountability. The International Monetary Fund considers Tanzania to have one of the best public financial management systems in sub-Saharan Africa (Nord et al., 2009), and most district councils have computerised budget and accounting systems – but the REPOA research team found that limited staff capacity means these systems are often not actually used. Most councils still carry out budgeting and accounting manually, with huge implications for fiscal management and operational efficiency in general.

When weak capacity at the local government level leads to inefficiency, as planned activities cannot be properly implemented, this fuels perception of

---

[4] In six councils – Bagamoyo, Ilala, Iringa, Moshi, Kilosa, and Mwanza – between 2002 and 2013.

corruption: survey data indicate that 72 per cent of citizens viewed corruption as a serious problem in councils in 2013, up from 59 per cent in 2003 (Fjeldstad et al., 2008).

C Can Central Transfers Be Used to Build Fiscal Capacity?

Local revenue collection is important for fiscal autonomy. It creates a compelling sense of *local ownership* of resources and builds a strong basis for local oversight of resource use. It is thus considered important as it increases public officials' accountability to their constituents, even though this is not the only way of making progress on that account.[5] It also incentivises efficiency and limits the pressure for ever more central transfers and public debt (McLure, 1998). A study of local budgets in East African countries found that collecting more local revenue led to a higher share of expenditure on service delivery, while dependence on intergovernmental transfers and development aid was associated with a higher budget share for administrative costs and employee benefits (UN-HABITAT, 2015).

However, decentralising revenue collection creates high potential for mismanagement and corruption: local governments may be better at eliciting people's preferences, but they have a higher chance of being captured by local elites and politically powerful groups. When enforcement and monitoring systems lack capacity, the cost of collecting local revenue can be a significant proportion of the revenue collected – sometimes even exceeding it. It can be argued that when levels of administrative capacity are low, it makes sense to entrust the collection of sub-national taxes to the central tax administration and establish an elaborate arrangement for provision of capacity-enhancing fiscal transfers to LGAs. Almost twenty years ago, Fjeldstad (2001) observed that it was unrealistic to expect that the administration in many local governments in Tanzania would have adequate capacity and the required integrity to manage increased fiscal autonomy. He concluded that '*In fact, there is a real danger that, in the absence of substantial restructuring of the current tax system combined with capacity building and improved integrity, increased autonomy will increase mismanagement and corruption.*' The situation has barely changed.

Is it possible for grants from the central government to build capacity to collect revenue at the local level? Some have argued that grants from the central government crowd out local revenues, sapping the incentive for LGAs to collect their own dues (Shah, 2006; Masaki, 2018). However, the evidence mainly comes from studies in countries with sound fiscal institutions: analysis by Masaki (2018) strongly suggests that intergovernmental transfers can help

---

[5] This was one of the goals of the Community Driven Development projects, through allowing community members to decide about the allocation of external funds among various local public goods. Results were not unambiguous, though. See Mansuri and Rao (2004, 2013).

expand local revenues in Africa, especially in rural areas. In urban areas, the marginal positive effect is lower as there tend to be more robust fiscal institutions and higher political costs associated with increasing taxes (Resnick, 2012). Evidence also shows that when fiscal transfers facilitate the provision of public goods, this improves voluntary tax compliance (Masaki, 2018).

The question is how long it will take for central government transfers to build and strengthen local capacity so that they can have sufficient capacity to mobilise and manage their own revenue collection. And what incentives will be needed to enable LGAs to build such capacity? There is a genuine issue of capacity at the local government level, which necessitates continued central government support and balancing of the central government role at that level if there is genuine desire to see fiscal autonomy take root. The most important thing is to have the proper incentives in place and effective monitoring from the central government and its agencies. The Tanzania Social Action Fund programme has been able to build capacity of local communities through engagement of local citizens in direct implementation of local projects in the health, water, education, and roads sectors. On the other hand, it should be stressed that some local communities in Tanzania exhibit fairly satisfactory performances in terms of local governance and financial management, suggesting that capacity building in other communities might indeed achieve much (see Boex and Muga, 2009; King, 2014).

As earlier noted, efforts to build local capacity to collect revenue need to be accompanied by measures to ensure that citizens have the information on local government revenue, budgets, and accounts that they need to hold their leaders to account. This challenge is most acute when formal accountability institutions, such as audits and legislative reviews, are weak owing to limited knowledge of what is happening at the local level, as is common in most local authorities in Tanzania (Msami, 2011). LGAs publish the financial information required by the central government and development partners, but researchers have found that much of this information does not reach the public. Only a small minority of people are aware of basic budget information (Fjeldstad, 2004, 2006), and public notices are often too technical for ordinary citizens to understand (REPOA, 2007).

Given the objectives of decentralisation reforms of fiscal autonomy for local government, measures should be taken to build the necessary capacity and create the necessary environment for expenditure efficiency and accountability of local officials – promoting more effective coordination, stability of the system, policy consistency, and predictability of the decision-making process.

VI CONCLUSION: DIRECTIONS FOR REFORM

The centre has an important role to play in the quest for local autonomy. Future reforms in Tanzania should address the complex and confusing administrative relationship between central and local government, along with limited fiscal capacity at the local level and the frequency of centrally imposed changes in revenue regimes, which make it harder to develop sustainable fiscal capacity at the sub-national level.

A Revisit the Fiscal Decentralisation Agenda

Effective collection of non-tax revenue hinges on a constructive working relationship between central and LGAs to create sound fiscal institutions and accountability to local taxpayers. There are certainly costs to local taxation as its administration needs more tax evaluators and collectors, and greater capacity to monitor and penalise non-compliance. Given limited fiscal capacity at the sub-national level, it makes sense, as an assured way to build the requisite institutional capacity at that level, to have the central government collect revenues and establish clear legal mechanisms to transfer part of those revenues to LGAs based on recognised resource endowment, the need in terms of public services to be provided, and a fiscal capacity-building component.

B Address Institutional Set-Up to Create Efficiency

The profusion of conflicting laws leads to haphazard influence on LGA operations from central and sectoral agencies and regional and district leadership. This is counterproductive. A reform agenda should address harmonisation of laws and create a framework for centre–local interactions on policy and revenue mobilisation that prevents abuse and promotes efficiency.

C Address Unpredictability of Government Decisions

There has always been the question as to what motivates the central government officials to give up powers and resources to sub-national governments. Any decentralisation measure tends to reduce the power and authority that national politicians enjoy relative to sub-national actors. Yet the same political personnel recognise at the same time the efficiency and governance gains to be expected from decentralisation. This could be the basis for unpredictable reform behaviour as the incentive schedule changes over time and context. Unpredictability of government decisions and actions deters investment, slows economic activity, and has negative implications for decentralisation reforms. A reform agenda should rationalise the conduct of discretionary decisions and actions by the central government and set up a consultative forum to engage local authorities in policy discussions, with the Association of LGAs in Tanzania playing a role.

Tanzania's government has already expressed the desire, through the LGRP, for full-fledged fiscal decentralisation – but there has, as yet, been limited realisation. A renewed reform agenda is needed, with central transfers allowing for smooth operations at the LGA level until the requisite fiscal capacity is built.

Discussion of 'Fiscal Decentralisation as an Example of Institutional Ineffectiveness'

Discussion by Jan Willem Gunning

I THE CONCEPT OF DECENTRALISATION

Decentralisation is a rather vague term, used to denote quite different concepts: political, administrative, fiscal, and market decentralisation.[6] While these concepts overlap, they also differ in major ways. To start with the most radical of these four concepts, market decentralisation shifts authority and responsibilities out of the government to the private sector. Typically, under such privatisation the government retains considerable power as a shareholder (sometimes with special powers as holder of a 'golden share'), or as regulator of the private firms providing public services. The central issue with this type of decentralisation is that the two agents, the government and the private provider, do not have the same objectives or information. This gives rise to a principal–agent problem.[7]

Fiscal decentralisation is in my view best thought of not as a form of decentralisation in its own right, but rather as a necessary complement of the three other types of decentralisation. After all, whenever central government functions are shifted to regional or local governments or to private providers, these must be enabled to fulfil their function. At a minimum, they must have an adequate source of revenue: local taxes, user charges, or a transfer of central government revenue.

---

[6] This section owes much to *The Online Sourcebook on Decentralization and Local Development*, notably to the useful taxonomy in the section entitled 'What is Decentralization?'. My own taxonomy is different in two respects: I have classified devolution as a form of political rather than as a form of administrative decentralisation, and I have demoted fiscal decentralisation from its independent status, making it a necessary complement to political, administrative, or market decentralisation.

[7] The modern economics literature on regulation is concerned with how, given these two differences, contracts can best be designed. A good example for developing countries is Laffont (2005).

Administrative decentralisation transfers authority and responsibility for the planning, management, and provision of public services to a lower level of government or to a special agency. In its weakest form, *deconcentration,* authority and responsibility remain with the central government but are shifted from civil servants based in, for example, the capital to those based at a regional centre. In a stronger form, delegation, the central government surrenders some of its control over planning and execution to an agent that has considerable autonomy while remaining accountable to the central government.[8]

Political decentralisation shifts political control over public decision making to representatives of those directly affected. Typically, control is transferred to an elected body at a lower level, such as a city council or regional legislature. (When political decentralisation is far reaching, it is sometimes called *devolution.* But the difference is only one of degree: there is no clear boundary.)

II THE RATIONALE FOR DECENTRALISATION

What are the pros and cons of decentralisation? There are at least four different rationales, related to scale, externalities, preferences, and rent-seeking.[9] First, economies of *scale* in some aspects of public services provision obviously favour centralisation. Secondly, decentralisation is problematic if decisions taken locally have effects outside the jurisdiction. Such *externalities* will lead to underprovision if the spillover effects are positive or overprovision in the case of negative effects. In this case, centralisation to a sufficiently higher level has the advantage that the externalities are internalised: the effects in other jurisdictions that would be ignored at the local level are taken into account when the decision is transferred to a higher level. (The subsidiarity principle implies that decisions should be taken at the lowest possible level, but not lower. This in itself is too vague to be helpful, but defining the appropriate level in terms of externalities gives the concept teeth.)

Thirdly, if *preferences are heterogeneous* across space, then public services must be provided in different forms in different locations, and this calls for at least administrative decentralisation. This is likely to work only if complemented with some form of political decentralisation so that local preferences can be articulated at the political level and policymakers are held accountable for the way they respond to those preferences. Decentralisation then has the advantage that it generates better information on the demand for public services and (through political accountability) strong incentives for the public sector to tailor provision to that demand.

---

[8] The concepts overlap should be clear by now: if, for example, a public service is provided by a regulated monopolist then this involves privatisation, a form of market decentralisation, but also delegation, a form of administrative decentralisation.

[9] Some of these arguments are mentioned in the theoretical section in the chapter; however, Section III adopts a much narrower view of the possible motivations for decentralisation.

Finally, decentralisation may increase the scope for *rent-seeking*. Hence, public sector functions are sometimes centralised in order to reduce this.[10] However, it is important to note that the direction of the effect of decentralisation on rent-seeking is not clear. Rent-seekers who try to influence decisions at higher government levels may face more countervailing power there (either from competing rent-seekers or from public sector agents who oppose them) than those who operate at lower levels. On the other hand, at the local level their actions may be easier to observe and therefore to resist. The net effect of these two forces, countervailing power and asymmetric information, is not clear.[11]

III THE REASONS FOR DECENTRALISATION IN TANZANIA

This brief review of the nature and rationale for decentralisation will help to structure my discussion of this chapter by Likwelile and Assey.

The chapter clearly shows how special the Tanzania case is. Local government was weakened dramatically after the 1967 Arusha Declaration. The LGAs were revived in the early 1980s but were given remarkably little power: the central government and the party remained firmly in control. The law even entitles the central government to do anything that 'shall facilitate or secure the effective, efficient, and lawful execution by the District Authorities of their [...] duties'.

Likwelile and Assey give a clear and very useful account of the evolution of local government in Tanzania. (This is neatly summarised in Table 6.1.) But they say very little about the reasons for the various changes they document. The centralisation in the late 1960s clearly had very little to do with the rationales I have listed: scale economies, externalities, heterogeneous preferences, or rent-seeking.[12] Instead, it was mainly driven by ideology. The subsequent decentralisation is more puzzling. Why did it happen? Because donors pressed for it? Because rent-seekers felt it would give them new opportunities? Because the leadership believed in it? What then did they think it would achieve? Why did reforms oscillate between centralisation and decentralisation?

---

[10] Centralisation is, of course, not the only option. The history of imperial China offers a famous example of an alternative response: mandarins were regularly rotated so as to reduce the probability that they would succumb to corruption at the local level. A relative stranger was apparently considered immune to corruption, at least for some time.

[11] These two effects form the centrepiece of the analysis of the World Development Report 2004, World Bank (2003).

[12] There is one important exception. The original justification for villagisation was that public services could be better provided if the scattered rural population was concentrated in villages. This idea was prominent in many of President Nyerere's speeches. At least implicitly this argument appeals to economies of scale in service provision. Voluntary formation of *Ujamaa* villages proceeded frustratingly slowly. This eventually led to the forced villagisation of 1974, which involved considerable violence and created much resentment.

The chapter is almost silent on these questions. There are very brief references to the economic crisis of the early 1980s,[13] the collapse of public services provision at that time, and 'pressure' from donors. We are not told what the objectives of the reforms were. Hence, the chapter offers a fascinating factual account of the reforms, but no political economy analysis of the changing incentives for the various agents involved, nor an empirical analysis of the results of the reforms.

Reading between the lines, the real story appears to be that the central government, while often describing decentralisation as a way to promote good governance (perhaps even a panacea), has in fact never fully accepted decentralisation. Its ability and desire to resist in practice what it preached waxed and waned over time, for reasons that are unfortunately not discussed. As a result, Tanzania has moved back and forth between centralisation and decentralisation, responsibilities have often been unclear, and fiscal decentralisation has seldom been in line with political and administrative decentralisation. If this interpretation is correct, then the incentives for the central government to push for or to resist decentralisation should be at the centre of the story. Focusing instead on fiscal decentralisation, as the chapter does, amounts to studying the symptoms rather than the disease.

IV FISCAL DECENTRALISATION AND LOCAL REVENUE COLLECTION

At the outset, in Section I, the authors indicate that their focus is '*on the administration of local revenue mobilisation given the centrality of financial resources in empowering local authorities to deliver on their mandate and improve their performance*'. This suggests that to understand decentralisation and development in Tanzania the key process to study is fiscal decentralisation.

This seems hard to justify, for two reasons. First, as the authors themselves stress, local authorities do not have the capacity and integrity required for a successful decentralisation. Therefore, fiscal autonomy may lead to mismanagement and corruption. Secondly, fiscal decentralisation is a process that makes political or administrative decentralisation possible. That *may* lead to better governance and thereby to better service provision. Whether it actually did so in Tanzania is an important empirical question, but that question is not addressed in the chapter.

In Tanzania LGAs are almost exclusively financed through transfers from the central government: these account for more than 90 per cent of their revenue.[14]

---

[13] The chapter refers to the 'economic crisis' of the late 1970s and early 1980s. However, in the late 1970s Tanzania benefited hugely from the beverages (coffee and tea) boom (1975-9), the greatest terms of trade bonanza in the country's history. That boom enabled the government to resist the pressure of some donors for radical economic reforms. Reforms were postponed until the crisis became manifest in the early 1980s (Bevan et al., 1990).

[14] Masaki (2018, Table 1) gives intergovernmental transfers in 2012/13 as 91.47 per cent of total local government revenue.

The authorities are allowed to raise their own revenue but usually lack the capacity to do so.[15] Possibly, this heavy reliance on transfers undermines horizontal accountability.[16]

It is worth stressing that local taxation is neither necessary nor sufficient for horizontal accountability. It is not necessary since, contrary to what the chapter suggests, effective accountability can be achieved without fiscal decentralisation. Reinikka and Svensson (2004) show in a famous study of the use of government transfers for education in Uganda that posting news in the village about the transfer was sufficient to trigger a powerful process whereby villagers held teachers accountable. In this case, accountability was achieved without any institutional change, simply by empowering people with information. Similarly, in Tanzania, villagers in Mkenge (Bagamoyo District) learned in a non-governmental organisation training programme about their rights. They then proceeded in 2010 to throw out the village council with a vote of no confidence for failing to account adequately for public expenditure. Tanzania has also practised an innovative system of village meetings in which spending priorities are discussed.[17] While local leaders predictably try to capture these meetings, they are often overruled so that government transfers are spent on, say, education rather than roads. These examples suggest that the absence of local revenue mobilisation does not preclude effective accountability.

There is a third point to consider, made by Besley and Persson (2013): local taxation requires highly qualified staff for assessment, monitoring, and enforcement.[18] This may make fiscal autonomy very costly.

In summary, there is a trade-off to consider, which involves three effects. The traditional argument is that local taxation will lead to better accountability and hence to better public services delivery, in line with local preferences. These benefits have to be weighed against the cost of local taxation, which may be relatively high if economies of scale are important: the Besley and Persson point. But it may be possible to avoid this trade-off, namely by achieving accountability without relying on the scrutiny of expenditure by taxpayers. The village

---

[15] Transfers are usually seen as crowding out local revenue mobilisation (just as aid may undermine domestic taxation), but for Tanzania there is some evidence of crowding in Masaki (2018). I will return to this evidence later.

[16] In the aid effectiveness literature, it is used to explain a negative effect of aid on governance: aid recipients are accountable to donors rather than to domestic taxpayers. The same reasoning applies here: if LGAs rely largely on locally raised revenue, then they will be held to account by the local population rather than by the central government. If preferences are heterogeneous, this is an important advantage.

[17] This is to be distinguished from the village assemblies, which, while legally supreme, have little power in practice (REPOA, 2008, p. 27).

[18] Of course, central taxation also requires such staff. Whether economies of scale in taxation offset the disadvantage of central staff lacking local knowledge is, again, an empirical issue.

meetings are one way of doing this.[19] An optimal policy that takes these three effects into account clearly cannot be identified without empirical analysis. But it is important to point out that the desirability of fiscal autonomy – taken for granted in much of the chapter – is by no means obvious.[20]

V INSTITUTIONAL WEAKNESSES

Likwelile and Assey argue that raising local revenue faces several institutional weaknesses, including discretion, arbitrariness, unpredictability, and inconsistencies in decisions by the central government. One of the examples they discuss is the oscillation between centralisation and decentralisation in the collection of property taxes. In the pre-2008 phase of decentralised collection, corruption was rampant. This suggests that centralisation may be needed to reduce rent-seeking. But the chapter also mentions that in the subsequent centralised phase, 'Imperfect information flowing to central operators created opportunities for corruption'. This leaves the reader with a puzzle: if corruption, arguably due to different causes, could flourish in both regimes then what, if any, is the effect of decentralisation on corruption? Apparently, there is no empirical work on this. Clearly, there is a need for an empirically based study that compares corruption under decentralisation and centralisation.

VI REFORMS

The chapter's section on reform (Section VI) is quite brief but lists a whole series of possible reforms.

First, the authors argue that the fiscal decentralisation agenda should be revisited so as to develop a set of rules for local and central governments and ensure predictability. While this is vague, they also take a clear position: given the poor fiscal capacity of the lower-level governments, 'it makes sense [...] to have the central government collect revenues and establish clear legal mechanisms to transfer part of those revenues to LGAs based on recognised resource endowment, the need in terms of public services to be provided, and a fiscal capacity-building component'. This is probably the key statement in the chapter, and I will return to it.

Secondly, predictability should be ensured by 'rationalis[ing] the conduct of discretionary decisions and actions by the central government'. This sounds like motherhood and apple pie: it is hard to see how one could disagree. Predictability is, of course, a good thing, but how the central government's scope for discretionary actions should be rationalised is not at all clear. This

---

[19] There are many other ways, discussed extensively in the 2004 *World Development Report*.
[20] That dependence on transfers from the central government is denoted as the weakness of 'overdependence' is revealing. But the authors are not consistent: later in the chapter, they see fiscal decentralisation as problematic.

would require a thorough analysis of the pros and cons of centralisation, culminating in a convincing diagnosis of the problem.

Returning to the key statement about the desirability of the reliance on transfers from the central governments, a few comments are in order. First, this statement seems somewhat contradictory with the authors' advocacy elsewhere in the chapter of the desirability of fiscal autonomy, unless it is understood as referring to a temporary measure motivated by lacking local capacity. Fiscal autonomy, of course, requires a drastic reduction in the reliance of the LGAs on transfers from the central government. Secondly, one reason for their favouring transfers appears to be the evidence they cite from Masaki (2018) that transfers crowd in local revenue. There is a technical reason to be somewhat sceptical of this result.[21] More importantly, while Masaki finds a large elasticity of crowding in (0.6), given the very low share of local revenue in total revenue this translates in fact into a very weak effect. Since transfers finance 91.5 per cent of domestic expenditure, an extra government transfer of TZS 1.00 crowds in only about TZS 0.06 of domestic revenue. Therefore, while the effect is statistically significant, it is in economic terms almost trivial. Thirdly, the acute need for 'more tax evaluators and collectors, and greater capacity to monitor and penalise non-compliance' are good arguments (following Besley and Persson, 2013) for relying on central tax collection and transfers to LGAs. However, and this is my main objection, this does not clinch the case: these disadvantages of local fiscal autonomy must, as noted before, be weighed against the advantage of fiscal autonomy leading to improved accountability, taking into account the scope for achieving accountability in other ways. Finally, clearly the *status quo* cannot continue indefinitely. The authors see, if I understand them correctly, continued heavy reliance on transfers as a temporary measure.[22] Local capacity must be built up (largely financed by these transfers) so that eventually local revenue can be substituted for transfers. This is sensible but, as the authors recognise themselves, raises the question of how long this will take and, crucially, what incentives LGAs have to use the transfers for such capacity building.

VII CONCLUSION

The experience of decentralisation in Tanzania is of special interest for two reasons. First, the starting position was an extreme one: the central government

---

[21] Masaki (2018) regresses own revenue of local governments (excluding agricultural taxes) on transfers and uses rainfall as an instrument for central government transfers. The exclusion restriction is that rainfall should not directly affect own revenue since agricultural taxes have been excluded. I am not fully convinced by this reasoning: in rural areas the revenue from many sources will be higher in a good rainy season, not just the revenue from agricultural taxes. Hence, the exclusion restriction would be violated.

[22] See the final sentence of the chapter.

and the party exercised a degree of control that was unique in Africa. Secondly, the subsequent decentralisation quickly turned into a bewildering oscillation between more and less central control. That this back-and-forth process was possible, was in part due, as the chapter rightly stresses, to ambiguities in the law. In this respect too, Tanzania seems to be a special and instructive case. The chapter gives an excellent description of this strange Echternach procession (three steps forward, two steps back). However, we learn what happened, but not the reason why.

The effects of decentralisation (political, administrative, or fiscal) on welfare, notably through the provision of public services, are the outcomes of a very complicated process. There are changes in formal power, in the opportunities and incentives for rent-seeking, in corruption, in the scope for holding officials accountable, and in the information available at different levels of government. Since there are many opposing effects in this tangled process, theory is of little help to decide on the desirability of centralisation or decentralisation. The chapter makes almost no use of evidence. There is some evidence for Tanzania, but empirical work is an urgent priority. Ideally experimental methods should be used to estimate the effects of decentralisation. When randomisation is not feasible, comparing outcomes across locations with different levels of decentralisation can still generate very useful information. Even less formal evidence can be helpful. Anecdotal evidence, for example on the effects of decentralisation on corruption or on the circumstances that enable village meetings to hold officials accountable, can begin to build a body of evidence.

In the absence of firm evidence there is little that can be concluded. Is fiscal autonomy desirable? Early in the chapter, the authors appear to take this for granted. However, they later argue that it would lead to corruption and to poor management because of the weak capacity of LGAs. If this is correct, should we then consider Tanzania's incomplete and half-hearted fiscal decentralisation as a blessing in disguise? This seems to be a corollary of the authors' conclusion that reliance on central government transfers should continue until the LGAs have built sufficient capacity for raising their own taxes.

Most importantly, the end of the chapter narrowly focuses on the need for capacity building. The political economy issues, including the incentives for corruption, are discussed in the earlier parts but slowly disappear over the horizon.

I have argued that the chapter's focus on fiscal decentralisation amounts to studying the symptoms rather than the disease. The central issue is what incentives the agents involved – the central government, local authorities, and various groups of rent-seekers – face. These incentives will in part determine what groups will push for decentralisation or will resist it. Theoretical analysis cannot take us very far here. An empirically based study that compares the effects of, and the incentives for, rent-seeking under decentralisation and centralisation is an urgent priority.

7

Through the Maze of Land Right Laws

Sist J. Mramba

'If markets do not exist in areas such as land, then they must be created [...] state intervention in markets beyond creation must be kept at bare minimum.' Harvey (2005)

I OVERVIEW

It is widely recognised that the fuzziness of land rights is a constraint on Tanzania's development. In rural areas, land is the main resource of a large population of poor farmers and cattle herders – as well as of modern production units that can exploit a source of comparative advantage. Conflicts could be avoided for as long as land was abundant, but since the 1980s there has been growing pressure on land. With an expanding urban population, unclear land rights also constrain development in urban areas.

Private ownership of land is a concept that has always been ideologically foreign to Tanzanian society. Instead, ownership of land is vested in the president, who is supposed to use it for the public good. Laws define various *occupancy rights* for land users, which are meant to be substitutes for formal *property rights* in other economies. These occupancy rights have to allow for various local customary rules of land allocation and transmission, which apply to much of the country's land.

Because of this – and various flaws in the existing formal laws and their implementation – the present system is far from offering the security that is required for an efficient and productive economic use of land. There is a heavy administrative apparatus, which is commonly judged as inefficient and the source of rent-seeking opportunities. As noted by Fischer, many developing countries are characterised by poor policies and weak institutional settings, which create opportunities for corruption and embezzlement by privileged interest groups (Fischer, 2005).

The next section of this chapter gives a brief historical perspective on land tenure issues, tracing continuity from colonial times through the 'villagisation' era to the recommendations of the Presidential Commission of Inquiry into Land Matters, Land Policy and Land Tenure Structure, which resulted in the 1995 National Land Policy and 1999 Land Acts. During this time the pendulum has swung between the desire to protect customary small-scale landholders and the desire to give investors the security they need to develop long run and large-scale projects.

Despite many critiques and partial reforms, the system established in 1999 still provides the basis of land management in Tanzania. Section III explores that system, which categorises land in three ways: *village land*, which is under the jurisdiction of village councils, and accounts for around 70 per cent of all land in Tanzania; *reserved land*, which includes forest reserves, beaches, and game parks, and accounts for 28 per cent of all land in Tanzania; and *general land*, which accounts for only 2 per cent of land but is economically crucial because it includes urban land and large-scale agricultural projects.[1]

Different rules of occupancy apply to village land and general land, and disputes commonly involve attempts to reclassify village land as general land, which is necessary for it to attract external investment. When proposed changes to village land involve over 50 hectares, they need to be approved by the Commissioner for Land. The process is slow, cumbersome, and subject to various costs. The law provides for compensation for the people who previously occupied the land, but in practice this is typically inadequate and delayed.

The situation is complicated by the fact that the formal rights of occupancy defined by the 1999 Act coexist with various informal ones, and the administrative process of surveying land to grant formal rights has been progressing slowly – indeed, a large majority of rural Tanzanians, and about half in urban areas, still do not have formal rights over the land they use. Section IV explores these informal rights, completing a description of the actual situation regarding land tenure in Tanzania.

Section V provides an overview of the institutional arrangements for land administration in Tanzania, which are complex. It sets out the ways in which land rights can be granted, and the mechanisms for selling rights over land or using them to raise credit – although it is sometimes said that land in Tanzania has no value because it is formally owned by the state, there are actually various ways in which the right of occupancy is transferable for value. This section also explores the mechanisms for resolving disputes over land, of which there is a large and growing backlog.

Section VI draws on the preceding discussion to identify the eight main institutional issues and challenges with the system. Although proposals for

---

[1] Section 5(12) of the Land Act 1999 on the transfer of village land to general land.

revising the National Land Policy are currently being discussed, these seem unlikely to be fully resolved:

- *Duality of tenure*: The handling of the distinction between general land and village land is the main source of friction and inefficiency, combining often inadequate protection for villagers with disincentives for investors that may lead to missed economic opportunities. Better defined, better implemented, and fairer administrative procedures for land transfers would provide efficiency gains on both sides.
- *Immense powers of eminent domain*: Land is deemed to be akin to state property, and the state has not always used its resulting powers judiciously or in the public interest – indeed, what constitutes the public interest is a matter of debate. Customary landholders are not protected by fair information and consultation procedures, and the losses they endure can be very great.
- *Limited formalisation*: Procedures for formalisation are bureaucratic, unrealistic, expensive, and time-consuming. Registry records are often unclear and automated systems are rare.
- *Gender discrimination*: Although discriminatory practices under customary law are illegal, in practice it remains a serious problem that women's access to and control of land often depends on the will of male relatives, making it harder for them to obtain loans or invest in improving their land.
- *Institutional overlaps*: Multiple and diverse institutions are involved in implementing land-related laws and policies. The resulting overlaps can create inefficiency and undermine accountability.
- *Corruption and inefficient land administration*: While the government discourages informal payments, they are widely used. This indicates the need for further institutional reform and efforts to make people more aware of their legal entitlements and to create incentives to report rent-seeking behaviour.
- *Ineffective land dispute settlement framework*: Dispute resolution mechanisms are often hard for ordinary people to access, whether because of the need to travel, the fees involved, language barriers, delays, or lack of clarity about authority.
- *Inadequate resources*: Shortfalls in human, material, and financial resources exacerbate problems with the legal and institutional framework.

The chapter concludes by summarising areas in which reform is a priority, including tackling corruption, improving coordination, scaling up programmes to formalise occupation rights, and streamlining procedures to demarcate land available for occupation and investment.

II A BRIEF HISTORICAL PERSPECTIVE ON LAND TENURE ISSUES

There is some continuity in matters of land tenure between colonial times and post-independence Tanganyika, and later the United Republic of Tanzania, with some basic principles of the colonial era retained but with disorderly and sometimes contradictory additions. What was kept from the colonial era is essentially the view that land, whatever its type and its use, is formally the property of the government. It is now formally in the hands of the president, considered as the 'trustee' of the national land.

Since colonial times, however, the sensitive issue has been the status of all the land under customary law and the alienation of that land for use by non-indigenous or foreign investors, notably for export-oriented large-scale agricultural production (Tenga and Mramba, 2014, p. 55). The explicit rejection of full private property – and consequently the necessity to rely on rights of occupancy somewhat akin to long-run leases – was strongly reaffirmed by Nyerere in the mid-1960s, often against the advice of foreign advisers. Nyerere expressed his view on that issue before independence (Nyerere, 1958, pp. 55–6):

[I]n a country such as this, where, generally speaking, the Africans are poor and the foreigners are rich, it is quite possible that, within eighty or a hundred years, if the poor African were allowed to sell his land, all the land in Tanganyika would belong to wealthy immigrants, and the local people would be tenants. But even if there were no rich foreigners in this country, there would emerge rich and clever Tanganyikans. If we allow land to be sold like a robe, within a short period there would only be a few Africans possessing land in Tanganyika and all others would be tenants.

This view has not been debated since. In essence, it was realised during this time that – as recommended by the East African Royal Commission of 1953–5 – market mechanisms had to enable willing sellers to make land available to willing buyers (Shivji, 1998), but market freedom could not be left to price alone. It had to be further regulated.

Modifications to colonial rules related to the ways in which land could be alienated from customary users: from total discretion in colonial days (see Box 7.1) to the official protection of small farmers under customary law. The strength of this protection, however, fluctuated somewhat over time. Cases demonstrate a clear struggle between the need to protect customary small-scale landholders and statutory large-scale farmers. Indeed, the whole period after independence was characterised by an ongoing debate about the space to be given to customary laws and the way to give investors, including public entities, the security on the use of land they need to develop long run and large-scale projects.

In some cases, the government used statutory instruments to frustrate customary land tenure in favour of statutory land tenure.[2] The situation was

---

[2] Consider the enactment of the Range Development and Management Act, No. 51 1964, which once applied in areas where pre-existing customary rights were extinguished. The Nyarubanja Tenure Enfranchisement Act, No. 1 1965 and the Customary Leaseholds (Enfranchisement) Act, No. 47 1968 abolished the Nyarubanja form of feudal system in Karagwe and customary tenancies respectively. The Rural Farmlands (Acquisition and Regrant) Act 1966 and the Urban Leaseholds (Acquisition and Regrant) Act 1968 granted land to tenants in rural and urban areas respectively. See also the Coffee Estates (Acquisition and Regrant) Act 1973 and the Sisal Estates (Acquisition and Regrant) Act 1974, which enable the government to take over land.

Box 7.1: Pre-independence land cases

The 1953 case of *Mtoro Bin Mwamba* v. A.G (*2TLR*, 1953, 327) decided that the Washomvi law, or customary law, did not recognise individual ownership to land except for an individual's usufructuary rights – and that where land was held by a native, the inference was that the possession was permissive and not adverse. In that case, the interest of the small-scale natives was merely right to the growing trees and not ownership of the land itself. In the cases of *Descendants of Sheikh Mbaruk bin Rashid* v. *Minister for Lands and Mineral Resources* (*EA 348*, 1960) and *Muhena bin Said* v. *Registrar of Titles* (*16 EACA*, 1948, 79) it was established that land occupation by natives was none other than the admitted general permissive occupation by all inhabitants of the territory.

---

complicated by the creation of the *Ujamaa* villages in Nyerere's socialist era, the massive population resettlement operations undertaken under that programme, and the objective to improve agricultural productivity and the country's export potential. The alienation of customary land was rather common during the 'villagisation' period, whether at village level in order to reorganise production and increase productivity through mechanisation, or through parastatals being given the right to alienate large swaths of customary land.

Mpofu argues that villagisation marked the apex of the state bourgeoisie's efforts to put rural production under its hegemony. He sees resettlement of peasants in chosen localities as a vehicle to facilitate state supervision and control of smallholding producers (Mpofu, 1986, p. 120). Tenga and Mramba note that the relocation of peasants, during operation *vijiji*,[3] caused massive land tenure confusion and legal disputes (Tenga and Mramba, 2014). As a result, peasants whose land had been acquired sued in courts of law for restoration of such lands, and when they won their cases, the government reacted by issuing notices to extinguish their customary tenures (Mchome, 2002, p. 70; Tenga and Mramba, 2014, pp. 61–2).

The general trend away from peasants' control in the 1970s was evidenced in the overhaul and abolishment of local institutions that had grassroot-level participation, and their replacement with more bureaucratic ones directly controlled by the central government.[4] This is reflected in Shivji's view that *Ujamaa* served the interests and ideological hegemony of the state bourgeoisie (Shivji, 1986, p. 3), as *Ujamaa* remained a variant of petty bourgeois socialism and the official ideology of the state (Mpofu, 1986, p. 122).

---

[3] Swahili word for villages (plural); the singular is *kijiji*.
[4] Consider Mpofu on the abolishment of district and town councils with assumption of their functions by regional authorities (Mpofu, 1986, p. 122).

The liberalisation period in the mid-1980s reverted to the dual land system with the development of large-scale plantations and better-protected customary land: a relative shortage of food products reinforced the weight given to farmers and cooperatives under customary law. Cases that witnessed the unavoidable tension between the two types of agricultural exploitation during this time include *National Agricultural Food Corporation (NAFCO)* v. *Mulbadaw Village Council and sixty-seven others* (see Box 7.2) (Tanzania Law Report, 1985, Case No. 88).

Box 7.2: *NAFCO* v. *Mulbadaw Village Council and sixty-seven others*

About 26,000 acres of land in Basotu ward, Hanang district, including 8,125 acres in dispute between the litigants in this case, were occupied by the Kilimo department from 1968–9. NAFCO succeeded Kilimo, entering into occupation of 22,790 acres of the land in 1969. NAFCO was offered a ninety-nine-year right of occupancy in January 1973. No wheat was planted on the land until 1979. The Mulbadaw Village Council, and another sixty-seven villagers of the same area, filed a case in the High Court against NAFCO, claiming damages for trespass over their lands and destruction of their crops and huts during the time of its occupation. The High Court awarded the Mulbadaw village TZS 250,000 as general damages, all the other claimants a global sum of TZS 1,300,000 as general damages, and TZS 545,600 as special damages.[5] The judge also declared that the 8,125 acres in dispute belonged to the claimants, and ordered NAFCO to cease its trespass forthwith.

However, after NAFCO appealed, the Court of Appeal stated that:

An administrative unit did not necessarily imply that the land within its administrative jurisdiction was land belonging to it. The village council could acquire land only by allocation to it by the District Development Council under direction 5 of the Directions under the Villages and Ujamaa Villages (Registration, Designation and Administration) Act, 1975 [...] those villagers who had testified had customary tenancies or what are called deemed rights of occupancy [...] had to establish that they were natives before a court could hold that they were holding land on a customary tenancy. The 4 villagers [who] had not established that they were in occupation on the basis of customary tenancies were thus not 'occupiers' in terms of the Land Ordinance. (Court of Appeal of Tanzania, 1985)

---

[5] TZS 250,000 was equivalent to USD 29,070 (1 USD = TZS8.6 in 1975), TZS 1,300,000 was equivalent to USD 151,163, and TZS 545,600 was equivalent to USD 63,442, all according to the Bank of Tanzania (2011, p. 115).

Little progress was achieved in trying to codify this complex relationship between formal and informal, or modern and traditional, land tenures and agricultural farms. This led to the aforementioned Presidential Commission on land matters under the direction of Professor Shivji, and the passing of the National Land Policy in 1995 and the Land Act in 1999. Despite many critiques and partial reforms, this system still provides the basis of land management in Tanzania.

III LEGAL LAND TENURE IN TANZANIA ACCORDING
TO THE 1999 LAND ACT

Section 4 of the Land Act reiterates the basic public property principle of land tenure in Tanzania:

[A]ll land in Tanzania shall continue to be *public land* [*our emphasis*] and remain vested in the President as trustee for and on behalf of all the citizens of Tanzania [...]. The President and every person to whom the President may delegate any of his functions under this Act, and any person exercising powers under this Act, shall at all times exercise those functions and powers and discharge duties as a trustee of all the land in Tanzania so as to advance the economic and social welfare of the citizens.

It categorises land in three ways:

(4) For the purposes of the management of land under this Act and all other laws applicable to land, public land shall be in the following categories: (a) general land; (b) village land; and (c) reserved land.

Village land is under the jurisdiction of *village councils* (*Village Land Act* 1999, sections 7 and 8) and therefore governed by statutory law (*Village Land Act* 1999) and customary law.[6] The councils, elected by *village assemblies* (*Local Government (District Authorities) Act, No. 7* 1982, section 57) are in charge of the management of all land in their perimeter (*Village Land Act* 1999, section 8). Village land mostly comprises rural land and peri-urban areas.[7] Village land accounts for around 70 per cent of all land in Tanzania, supporting around 80 per cent of the population – many being farmers and pastoralists (Tenga and Kironde, 2012, p. 17; *Draft Land Policy,* 2016).[8]

---

[6] See the *Village Land Act* 1999, sections 18(1)(d) and 20, which provides for the application of customary law to regulate customary rights of occupancy.

[7] Under section 3 of the Land Act, peri-urban area means an area which is within a radius of 10 kilometres/6 miles outside the boundaries of an urban area or within any larger radius which may be prescribed in respect of any particular urban area by the minister. See *the Local Government (District Authorities) Act, No. 7 1982,* section 28(2), which allows the minister for local government to provide for the inclusion of neighbouring villages in the area over which a township authority is established, for the purposes only of provision by the authority of any specified services to those villages.

[8] The figures could have changed – for instance, general land is assumed to be between 3 and 5 per cent, while village land is considered to have decreased to between 67 and 65 per cent.

Reserved land is set aside for special purposes, including forest reserves, beaches, game parks, game reserves, land reserved for public utilities and highways, and hazardous land (*Land Act 1999*, sections 6 and 7). It is administered under different legislation: for example, forestry reserves are administered under the Forest Act (Sundet, 2005). Reserved land accounts for 28 per cent of all land in Tanzania.

General land covers all the land that is not either village land or reserved land. It is administered by the Commissioner for Land on behalf of the president (*Land Act* 1999, sections 9 and 10). Although it accounts for only 2 per cent of land, it is economically crucial, supporting 20 per cent of the population (Tenga and Kironde, 2012, fn. 28): it includes urban land and agricultural land granted to investors for large-scale operations (Tenga and Kironde, 2012, fn. 28).

The distinction between village land and general land is a potential source of dispute when attempts are made to free village land for external investors, a frequent case that is found not to be satisfactorily handled in the Land Act. The official definition of general land – 'all public land which is not reserved land or village land and includes unoccupied or unused village land' (*Land Act* 1999, section 2) – creates an apparent ambiguity, as there is no provision in the Act to clarify what is exactly meant by 'unoccupied or unused village land'. The process for non-villagers to access land under the control of villages is slow and cumbersome, as villages are limited in the amount of land they can allocate: any amount above a maximum of 50 hectares must be approved by the district council or Commissioner for Land (Tenga and Kironde, 2012).

The distinction between the types of land is of utmost importance and justifies the division of the Land Act 1999 into two parts. The Village Land Act deals with customary land occupancy rights in rural areas, while the Land Act deals with all the other land, including agricultural investment and urban development as well as reserve land.

A Rights of Occupancy

Under the Land Acts, village and general land are ruled by different rules of occupancy (Tenga and Kironde, 2012). A 'Right of Occupancy' is defined as 'a title to the use and occupation of land and includes the title of a Tanzanian citizen of African descent or a community of Tanzanian citizens of African descent using or occupying land in accordance with customary law' (The Village Land Act, 2006, np).

The definition has two vital parts: the meaning, that is the title, to the use and occupation of land; and who shall qualify to occupy such land, including tribal communities that profess customary law. While the provision is a typical remnant of the British land policy, its retention in the law carries less weight, as various laws – including the United Republic of Tanzania (United Republic of Tanzania) Constitution 1977 as amended – recognise the rights of tribal communities. People who do not profess customary law can alternatively acquire a

Granted Right of Occupancy (GRO) upon conversion of the land from village land into general land, even if they are not of the stated descent such as whites or those of Asiatic origin such as Indians. Moreover, under the British Land Ordinance, natives in the context of land occupation included Swahilis and Somalis, while the Land Act 1999 only requires membership of a tribal community to hold land under customary law.

Two types of rights of occupancy apply, respectively, to general and village land: the GRO reasserts the pre-existing system of formal land titles on general land, while the Customary Right of Occupancy (CRO) refers to informal land rights granted by village councils on village land.

1 Granted Right of Occupancy

This right, granted on general land, is deemed to be the main form of landholding in urban areas. It is granted by the commissioner on behalf of the president for a maximum of ninety-nine years. The cost involves application fees, the cost of preparing the certificate of title, registration fees, survey fees, deed plan fees, stamp duty on the certificate and a duplicate, and a premium (Kironde, 2014; World Bank, 2014b, p. 27). Tenga and Kironde note that government efforts to generate funds to acquire and service land, by charging a premium based on some formula of cost recovery, makes it difficult for low-income households to access land registration services (Tenga and Kironde, 2012, p. 28).

The premium has been 7.5 per cent of the land value since 2015, but a budget speech delivered by the Minister of Lands, Housing and Human Settlements Development (MLHHSD) expressed the ministry's intention to reduce it to 2.5 per cent of the land value (United Republic of Tanzania, 2018, p. 18). This will mean a huge decrease in the amount of premium and relief to land title applicants. Section 31 of the Land Act provides that, in determining the amount of a premium, the minister shall have regard to:

a. The use of the land permitted by the right of occupancy which has been granted;
b. The value of the land as evidenced by sales, leases, and other dispositions of land in the market in the area where the right of occupancy has been granted, whether those sales, leases and other dispositions are in accordance with the Act or any law relating to land which the Act replaces;
c. The value of land in the area as evidenced by the price paid for land at any auction conducted by or on behalf of the government;
d. The value of the land as evidenced by the highest offer made in response to a request made by or on behalf of the government, a local authority or parastatal for a tender for the development of land in the area;
e. Any unexhausted improvements on the land; and
f. An assessment by a qualified valuer given in writing of the value of land in the open market.

TABLE 7.1 *Current official costs of first-time registration of a government grant (in TZS)*

Fee	Amount	Comments
Premium	2.5% of land value	Application for a right of occupancy – 20,000
		Preparation of certificate of title – 50,000
		Registration fees – 80,000
		Survey fees – 300,000
		Deed plan fees – 20,000 (0–1 hectare varying with increase in size)
		Stamp duty on certificate and duplicate – 1,000
Land rent for one year	Paid per annum	Per m² depending on category, locality, and use

Source: United Republic of Tanzania (2015)

In addition, as for the land rent, section 33 of the Land Act provides that:

Rent is determined by the Minister depending on factors such as: (a) the area of the land; (b) the use of land; (c) the value of land; (d) where there is insufficient evidence of value in that area from which an assessment of the value of land may be arrived at, an assessment by a qualified valuer of the value of land in the open market in that area which may be developed for the purpose for which the right of occupancy has been granted; and (e) the amount of any premium required to be paid on the grant of a right of occupancy.

Table 7.1 shows the estimated cost to be incurred as premium and land rent to be granted land. It assumes that the land is acquired from previously unsurveyed land that has been made the subject of planning followed by survey, parcelling, titling, and certification.

If the land has occupiers, a process of compensation will be followed: it was stated in the cases of *Mwalimu Omary and another* v. *Omari Bilali (TLR 1990, 9) Suzana Kakubukubu and two others* v. *Walwa Joseph Kasubi and the Municipal Director of Mwanza (TLR 1989, 119)*, and *James Ibambas* v. *Francis Sariya Mosha (TLR 1999, 364)* that pre-existing rights to land can be extinguished only upon payment of compensation. The amount of compensation paid to original occupiers follows criteria in the Land Act and the Land Acquisition Act. However, concerns remain as the amount is not necessarily dependent on prevailing market rates and the payment is not always prompt.

Efforts by the government to ensure availability of surveyed plots is unsatisfactory. For instance, the number of registered titles, transfer documents, and certificates of unit titles issued in the financial year 2017/18 is below what was originally intended. In the stated financial year, the MLHHSD registered 79,117 titles, of which 32,178 were certificates of title (from the initial plan of 400,000 titles) and 46,939 transfer documents (from the initial plan of 48,000 documents) (United Republic of Tanzania, 2018, p. 27). The capacity of the ministry to deliver is low, since issuance of new titles is not more than 35,000 titles per year.

The GRO can be likened to a 'term of years' or lease granted by a superior landlord. In the case of *Abualy Alibhai Aziz* v. *Bhatia Brothers Ltd* (2000), it was stated that:

A right of occupancy is something in the nature of a lease and a holder of a right of occupancy occupies the position of a sort of lessee *vis-a-vis* the superior landlord. It is a term and is held under certain conditions. One of the conditions is that no disposition of the said right can be made without the consent of the superior landlord. [Since] [...] there is now no freehold tenure in Tanzania all land is vested in the Republic. So, land held under a right of occupancy is not a freely disposable or marketable commodity like a motor car. Its disposal is subject to the consent of the superior or paramount landlord as provided for under the relevant Land Regulations.

The implication is that the government exercises oversight powers over land dispositions under the custodial duty of the president (*Land Act 1999*, section 4). Under that mandate, he not only approves dispositions, but also receives notifications on any dispositions that are about to take place. Although this may seem unnecessary control over the freedom of disposition, it remains a regulatory mechanism, especially in cases of fraud, tax avoidance, breach of conditions, and transfer irregularities.

Sometimes the land for grants may include reserved land, where the president so permits. The grant is generally subject to the payment of rent,[9] although the commissioner has power to grant the land without rent.[10] The use of this power is less common, although it can be used as an incentive to attract investment in land. The grant has to be mandatorily registered under the Land Registration Act if it is for more than five years. The GRO may be acquired compulsorily in the public interest subject to prompt, reasonable and fair compensation, as provided under the Constitution and the Land Acquisition Act, Cap. 118.

Under section 19 of the Land Act, the GRO can be granted to citizens or non-citizens. Non-citizens can get it for investment purposes when they are registered with the Tanzania Investment Centre (TIC) or the Export Processing Zones Authority (EPZA).[11] The section created debate in the recent past when foreign investors became much more interested in agricultural investments in Tanzania and were accused of 'land grabbing'.

A major area of concern, further explored later, is that investors cannot get village land unless it has first been transformed into general land. Boudreaux remarks that, to attract investors, the government has stated its intent to transfer

---

[9] See the *Land Act 1999*, section 33: the holder of a right of occupancy shall pay an annual rent.
[10] See the Land Act 1999, section 33(7).
[11] See the 4th Written Laws Misc. Amendment 2016, which amends section 19 of the Land Act.

a significant portion of village land to the general land category, with arguments that plenty of land in Tanzania is freely available and unoccupied (Boudreaux, 2012, p. 3).

In urban areas, which are general land, GROs coexist with other types of occupancy, including private individual semi-formal occupancy through derivative rights in the form of residential licences; private individual informal occupancy, where land is used informally with no or limited involvement of public authorities; communal or collective occupancy under the Unit Titles Act;[12] and informal occupation owing to encroachment of public land. In all these types of urban tenure, occupancy is formal or informal, individual or collective, and legal or illegal. From a governance point of view, the regulation of these different types of land occupancy is very dependent on a resilient, effective, institutional framework to avoid disputes.

In a survey done by Land Matrix (2016) to provide the average land market demand and scale of land acquisitions in Tanzania, it was noted that, overall, thirty-two investors from seventeen countries were engaged in large-scale land investments in Tanzania. Investors from the United States had the largest size under contract, while investors from the United Kingdom (UK) had the highest number of concluded deals. African investors did not play a significant role in land deals in Tanzania. Most of the land involved in these deals is customary land, which must undergo conversion into general land before it is granted to the investors. Owing to inadequate compensation paid and delays in the payment, discontent arises with the government and between investors and local communities.

2 Customary Right of Occupancy

The CRO bears all the attributes of a GRO except that it only applies in a customary tenure setting and on village land. The Village Land Act provides room for both individual and collective land rights (*the Village Land Act* (1999), sections 12 and 13). Village land can thus be used by an individual occupier or by a community, such as a pastoral community as grazing land, for forest reserve, water dam, and so on. These options provide flexibility for occupiers to enjoy the preferred rights of occupancy.

The Act allows village councils to issue *Certificates of Customary Rights of Occupancy* (CCROs) upon application.[13] In effect, these formalise customary tenures; but their issuance depends on regularisation of the village land.

---

[12] The Unit Titles Act No. 16 of 2008 was enacted to provide for the management of the division of buildings into units, clusters, blocks, and sections owned individually and designated areas owned in common; to provide for issuance of certificate of unit titles for the individual ownership of the units, clusters, or sections of the building, management and resolution of disputes arising from the use of common property; to provide for use of common property by occupiers other than owners; and to provide for related matters.

[13] See *the Village Land Act* 1999, sections 18(1)(a) and 22–5, on procedures for application of CRO and the issuance of the CCRO by the village council thereof, under section 25.

In essence, the Village Land Act provides room for a village to have its outer boundaries surveyed, demarcated, and registered by the MLHHSD in order to obtain a Certificate of Village Land (CVL). The individual villagers could then apply to have their private parcels surveyed and registered. Only at the end of that process can villagers receive their CCRO document. It is also necessary that the village has issued a land use plan identifying what part of the village land could be individually titled, what part could be used communally, and what part could be reserved for further as-yet undefined uses. In the absence of such regularisation, landholdings on village land are based on the 'deemed right of occupancy', which may result from inheritance or clearance of unset-tled land.[14]

The CCROs are meant to provide land occupiers on village land with the same advantages and protection as the owners of GROs in general land. This is not completely the case because of some specific constraints in the case of the CCROs. One such constraint is the impossibility of transmitting CCROs, through sales, donation, or bequest, to somebody *outside* the village community without the approval of the village council.[15] Of course, this is to make sure that the land of a village does not end up being controlled by people for-eign to the village. Yet it seriously reduces the collateral value of the CCROs for potential lenders, undermining one of the objectives of CCROs – to allow holders to access the credit market.

B Land Transformation by the State and the Issue of Compensation

The Village Land Act allows for the transformation of village land into gen-eral land.[16] The initiative may come from the government needing to acquire land for some public purpose, in which case a standard expropriation proce-dure is followed, including compensation of evicted people. Askew suggests that determining what land can be transferred to the general land category is

---

[14] The Land Act provides that CRO includes deemed right of occupancy. 'Deemed right of occu-pancy' is defined under section 2 as meaning the title of a Tanzanian citizen of African descent or a community of Tanzanian citizens of African descent using or occupying land under and in accordance with customary law. Customary law under the Interpretation Act 1996 Cap 1 R.E. 2002 means any rule or body of rules whereby rights and duties are acquired or imposed, established by usage in any African community in Tanzania and accepted by such community in general as having the force of law, including any declaration or modification of customary law made or deemed to have been made under section 9A of the Judicature and Application of Laws Ordinance.

[15] See section 18(1)(g) and (h) on the attributes of the CRO, which includes transferable, inherit-able, and transmissible by will; however, section 31(3) requires that, unless otherwise provided for by the Act or regulations made under the Act, a disposition of a derivative right shall require the approval of the village council having jurisdiction over the village land out of which that right may be granted. See factors to be considered by the village council before approval in section 33.

[16] What follows draws extensively from Makwarimba and Ngowi (2012).

one motivation for mapping and certifying village land areas, which necessarily raises the spectre of widespread dispossession among the native communities in the wake of commercial agricultural expansion (Boudreaux, 2012, p. 3; Askew et al., 2017).

The rights of people whose land has been expropriated or acquired and the procedures for expropriation are provided for by the Land Acquisition Act 1967, Land Act Cap. 113,[17] Village Land Act,[18] and the Land Acquisition Act Cap. 118.[19] The right to compensation is assessed according to the concept of opportunity, which takes into account the market value of the real property, relying on land transactions within the neighbourhood (excluding use being made of land, crops being grown, yields, and prices); disturbance allowance; transport allowance; loss of profits or accommodation; cost of acquiring the land; and any other loss or capital expenditure incurred in development of the land. Interest at the market rate is charged for delay in payment exceeding six months (*Land Act 1999*, section 3(1)(g); *Land (Assessment of Compensation) Regulations*, 2001).

In practice, compensation is usually inadequate and rarely paid on time. There have been many cases in urban Tanzania where the payment of compensation has been affected many years after the assessment, without reflecting the decline in the value of money. As Shivji (1998, p. 35) puts it:

Compensation is hardly ever paid before dispossession. The amounts are paltry and have long been overtaken by inflation resulting in universal dissatisfaction with compensation.

The distribution of compensation also often ends up being inequitable within the households. Displacement often disturbs cultural and social values and norms as well as the composition and bonds of families, who may be dispersed in different locations, in opposition to human rights ideals. The far-reaching socio-economic impacts of compulsory land acquisition include income levels, land utilisation, land ownership structure, and farming practices.[20]

It should be borne in mind that when the government is acquiring land, it both sets the rules for determining and paying compensation and actually determines and pays the compensation. This could be seen as violating legal rights, as landowners expect to have their land assessed by a non-interested party.

1 Compensation and Market Value Dichotomy

Generally, compensation and market value for land have continued to be incongruent. Msangi, citing Ndjovu, argues that since there is no freedom of transaction in compulsory acquisition, there is no market as such for

---

[17] Section 3(1)(g).
[18] See, for instance, sections 3, 4, 6, 14(2), and 18(1)(i).
[19] Sections 6–18 of the Act.
[20] For a study of Kenya, see Syagga and Olima (1996).

the compulsorily acquired property and that just compensation cannot be the same as market value (Ndlovu, 2003; Kironde, 2006; Ngama, 2006; Msangi, 2011, p. 20). He considers market value as the estimated amount for which an asset should exchange on the date of valuation between a willing buyer and a willing seller in an arm's-length transaction after proper marketing wherein the parties had each acted knowledgeably and without compulsion, which is not the case for compensation (Msangi, 2011, p. 20). In compulsory acquisition, where the transaction is not based on willingness from the seller in a free exchange, the market value cannot be said to have been attained because sellers have been compelled to sell against their will (Msangi, 2011).

As far as obtaining land market value based on crops is concerned, the government employs a formula for both perennial and seasonal crops. For a seedling crop it pays 30 per cent per stem, for mature crop 60 per cent, for optimum producing crop 100 per cent, and for aged crop 15 per cent. The price of an acre would stand at roughly between USD 180 and 1,500, depending on the age of the trees/plants (United Republic of Tanzania, 2013a).

Under the Land Acquisition Act, vacant land is not to be considered in assessing compensation, but this situation changed under the Land Act (1999). The National Land Policy (1995) recommended an improvement to the compensation package. The Land Act 1999, under section 3(1)(g), generally clarifies and improves on the nature and manner of the compensation package to be paid.

The government may give alternative land of the same value in the same local authority area in lieu of or in addition to compensation, if this is practicable (s. 11(1)(2); s. 12(3) of the Land Acquisition Act 1967). Under section 3 of the Land Acquisition Act 1967, where land is compulsorily acquired the minister is required to pay compensation *as may be agreed upon* or as determined according to the provisions of the Act. In practice, however, the government has preferred to determine compensation rather than to negotiate.

In urban areas declared to be planning areas, where a grant of public land is made the value of land is not paid. Previous landowners may be asked whether they should be paid compensation in cash, in land of equivalent value, or a bit of both. In order for this to work, the market for land needs to be transparent and not administratively determined, as is the case.

As for village land, it has been argued that despite the supposed protection of village certificates (which constitutes the first stage of formalisation), villages are undergoing state-directed re-surveying of their boundaries for the purposes of cutting off large parcels for farmers and investors (International Work Group for Indigenous Affairs (IWGIA), 2015). In Kilombero, state-directed re-surveying, branded re-formalisation, has permitted the acquisition of large tracts of land for the purposes of accommodating agriculture and rendering pastoralism untenable (Boudreaux, 2012, p. 3).

2 TIC-Led Commercial Land Operations

The initiative to acquire land may come from the TIC, responding to the demand of local and foreign investors who are granted certificates of incentives (*the Tanzania Investment Act* 1997, section 17) for the right to use land for specific purposes – cultivation, factories – judged to be in the Tanzanian public interest.[21] Formally, the decision is validated by the Commissioner for Land, but the centralisation of the decision-making process depends on the size of the operation. Up to 50 acres/20 hectares, the village assembly and village council are the final decision makers (*Village Land Regulation GN No. 86*, 2001). Above that limit, the process is in the hands of the district council, Commissioner, and Minister for Lands, with consultation of the village councils concerned (*Village Land Regulation GN No. 86*, of 2001, Reg. 76(2) and Reg. 76(3). Under section 5(12) of the Land Act, the land will have to be transferred to the general land category, upon which the Commissioner for Land will have general mandate.[22]

There are also less formal procedures in use. For instance, investors may identify the suitable land directly or through intermediaries. They then approach the relevant district council,[23] which in turn deals with village councils and assemblies. Minutes of the meetings where the land acquisition is approved by those bodies are then submitted to the TIC, thus *ex post* rather than *ex ante* as in the official procedure, or the Commissioner for Land, for the effective transfer procedure to be launched.

Compensation is due to people whose CROs are extinguished. Although there is no uniform resettlement policy, there have been efforts at resettlement when the acquisition emanates directly from the government.[24] For large operations, however, the evaluation of the Tanzanian public interest in the projects that require land acquisition by foreign investors plays a huge role in the decision-making process. Not surprisingly, despite the detailed procedures included in the law, land acquisition operations do not go without frictions and disputes. Examples of successful and unsuccessful land acquisitions can be seen in Boxes 7.3 and 7.4.

---

[21] See the context of public purposes under section 4(1) of the Land Acquisition Act, Cap. 118 R.E. 2002, which includes uses of general public nature such as land for mining minerals or oil, exclusive government use, for general public use, for any government scheme, for the development of agricultural land or for the provision of sites for industrial, agricultural or commercial development, social services, or housing.

[22] See the power of the commissioner under section 10(1) of the Land Act that the commissioner is the principal administrative and professional officer of, and adviser to, the government on all matters connected with the administration of land and is responsible to the minister for the administration of the Act and matters contained in it.

[23] The district is a local administrative layer above the village.

[24] See, for instance, United Republic of Tanzania, Ministry of Agriculture and Food Security (2003); United Republic of Tanzania, Bank of Tanzania (2014); United Republic of Tanzania, Ministry of Energy and Minerals (2015); United Republic of Tanzania PMO-RALG (2014).

Box 7.3: Examples of success stories of land acquisition

NEW FOREST COMPANY LTD (UK AND TANZANIA)

The New Forest Company engaged in agroforestry in the Kilolo-Ihemi cluster of the Southern Agricultural Growth Corridor (SAGCOT) area in Iringa region. The company was incorporated in 2006. It faced the challenge that, although the land was available, it was not in a single lot but in fragments owned by separate individuals. The company initially asked for 30,000 hectares of land for pine forest plantation, and succeeded in obtaining 8,000 hectares through the following steps:

Step 1: Land Identification

- The investor consulted TIC on the intended investment.
- The investor complied with the statutory requirement of capital threshold and obtained a certificate of incentives.
- The investor visited the Kilolo District Executive Director (DED) for possible investment in his district.
- The DED contacted prospective village councils with potential land.
- Notice was sent to the village council of the intention of the investor to inspect the available land.
- The investor was introduced by the DED to the village council for a site inspection.
- The investor and the village council discussed options for investment.
- The village council convened to discuss the investor's request. The village assembly was convened to approve the village council's decision.
- The amount of land that could be allocated was considered, bearing in mind land disposal limitations.
- For occupied land, the investor negotiated with the occupiers on terms of surrender and compensation. The district council worked out the property valuation for the land that would be offered: an acre of land was compensated for TZS 100,000 (approximately USD 45). In addition, the investor was required to pay statutory compensation as per the Land Acts.

Step 2: Land Transfer Process (Conversion of Land from Village Land to General Land)

- The village council informed interested parties as to the content of the notice.
- Affected persons made representations to a village assembly meeting attended by the Commissioner for Land.
- The Commissioner for Land/Authorised Officer attended negotiations on the terms of compensation.
- The Land Officer submitted the agreements and the intention to transfer village land to general land to the Commissioner for Land (Form 8).
- The commissioner prepared a notice of transfer and submitted it to the minister.
- The minister submitted the notice for transfer to the president.
- The minister issued a transfer permit.

- The transfer of village land notice was gazetted and posted on places in the village for thirty days before it took effect.
- After the lapse of the notice period, the land was surveyed, and preparation for a certificate of GRO followed.

Step 3: Grant of Right of Occupancy to TIC

- The TIC applied to the commissioner for a GRO for investment purposes.
- The commissioner granted title to TIC for ninety-nine years.
- The commissioner forwarded the title to the Register of Titles for registration.

Step 4: Issuance of Derivative Right and Registration of Leasehold Title

- The TIC prepared a leasehold agreement for the investor, incorporating conditions and covenants, for ninety-eight years.
- The TIC sent the leasehold agreement and the right of occupancy to the registrar for registration of the leasehold title (derivative right).
- The Registrar of Titles issued a leasehold title as an encumbrance to the GRO on 1 July 2011.

Currently, ten villages are involved in the project: Kidabaga, Magome, Ndengisirili, Isele, Kisinga, Kiwalamo, Idete, Makungu, Ipalamwa, and Ukwega. The transfer of the land from the village and villagers was relatively smooth. There were some complications: although the company made promises, such as support for school renovation, local health services, and road maintenance, these were not put in enforceable contracts. Nevertheless, at present, there are no conflicts between the investor and the host communities.

Rungwe Avocado Project (Tukuyu, Mbeya Region)

Where land acquisition is not possible owing to scarcity or tenure issues, there is room for contract farming or out-grower schemes. This has been the case for part of Rungwe (in Tukuyu district, Mbeya region), where an avocado project is being implemented.

The Rungwe avocado project is considered a success story. No land was taken from the community, avoiding the complex procedure of compensation, and a contractual agreement was reached quickly for the investor to provide farmers with seedlings and an assured market for their produce. The investor shares modern technology with farmers and conducts market research for the farmers.

Some weaknesses have been pointed out. In interviews, some of the farmers voiced concern that there was no room to verify the accuracy of the prices given or the possibility of suing in the case of losses attributable to market variations. Some complained that the seeds cannot be replanted, as can those of indigenous species. Nonetheless, relationships between the investor and the host communities are generally good.

Box 7.4: Example of unsuccessful story of land acquisitions

SUN BIOFUELS AFRICA LTD (SBF) (UK)

SBF was set up in September 2005 and wanted to acquire land for agribusiness. The process – which involved identifying a suitable area of land; meeting villagers; issuing letters to the government gazettes; engaging a consultant to carry out valuation on the land; identifying, mapping, and valuing areas that were occupied, farmed or otherwise utilised by the villagers; and satisfying the TIC that the whole process had been done – took four years (Kitabu, 2011, pp. 7–10). In January 2009, the village land was gazetted as general land and title granted to TIC. In May 2009, the TIC issued a leasehold title to SBF for ninety-eight years.

SBF negotiated with village authorities with the support of local politicians. According to district officials, twelve villages in five wards gave part of their land, totalling about 20,000 hectares. The process involved village council and village assembly meetings, but villagers complained that it was not participatory. The SBF had no formal contract with villagers in Kisarawe, for example: the only document the village had was minutes of the village council, which contained promises by the investor – but no timeframe for implementation or legal mechanism to ensure delivery. These promises included helping with the drilling of wells; providing modern farming implements, seeds, fertilisers, pesticides, and a milling machine; jobs; constructing buildings for a dispensary, extension officers, and teachers, classrooms, pit latrines, a technical school, student dormitories, secondary schools, library, sports facilities, and a land registry office; solar energy for schools; and compensation for those adversely affected.

Land officers from the district land office started the process of surveying and mapping the area to be acquired before discussions at the village level were concluded. The modality for determining the amount of compensation to be paid was not made open. The villages had no land use plans, which made it hard for village authorities to know the size of the land acquired. It was difficult for villages to prove ownership of some land because it was deemed unoccupied, although clearly it was being used and formed part of the village land that was not allocated to individual occupiers. The acquisition did not take into account prospects of future village population growth.

Eventually, the investor decided that his initial biofuel project was not viable, and sold the project to another private firm. However, the operation ultimately left many local farmers with no land and no job.[25]

See Carrington et al. (2011). The collapse of SBF has left hundreds of Tanzanians landless, jobless, and in despair for the future. Consider also the case of a Dutch firm called Bioshape in the southern Tanzanian district of Kilwa, where a large jatropha plantation went bankrupt, leaving locals complaining of missing land payments and the land not being returned to its owners.

IV THE DISTRIBUTION OF ACTUAL LAND TENURE STATUS IN TANZANIA

The previous section's description of the law governing the rights of land occupancy in Tanzania might suggest that the absence of private ownership has been fully compensated for by an alternative system of essentially public land leases. However, there are other land tenure statuses than the granted rights of occupancies, customary rights of occupancies, and the derivative rights – that is, subleases – in Tanzania. This is essentially because of the administrative burden of delivering granted rights and customary rights of occupancies, and also because of the difficulty of establishing precisely the boundaries of the land that could be concerned by the delivery of additional formal titles. Surveying land occupation develops at a very slow pace.

It follows that informal land tenure statuses coexist with formal ones. In 2012, a large majority of Tanzanian citizens lived without a formal land occupancy status.[26] So far, in urban areas, roughly over 50 per cent of inhabitants have no formal title. In rural areas, most villages now have village land certificates, meaning their boundaries have been surveyed, only a few of them have elaborated their land use plan and are in a position of issuing certificates of customary rights. In 2020, it was estimated that 200,000 certificates of granted rights and 520,000 certificates of customary rights would be issued between 2020 and 2021, but by 15 May 2021, only 56,390 and 34,869 respectively had been issued, representing roughly 5 per cent of the rural population.[27]

The tenure typology in urban areas as reviewed by the World Bank in its 2012 Study includes formal private use, semi-formal private use, informal private use, communal use, and informal occupation of state urban land.[28] In the rural sector, the tenure types are also diverse. They range from individual private use under GRO to private individual land use, communal use of rural land, reserved lands, and informal occupation of reserved land (legal squatting).

The government's expected land use changes in both urban and rural areas may imply intensification of certain forms of tenure: in particular, there is expected to be a substantial shift to general land from village land. This calls for clear strategies such as restructuring of the areas for cultivation, especially conversion of land from village land to general land, which may impact rural tenure typologies; restructuring the settlement areas, especially village land, where transfer to general land is involved; and restructuring areas for conservation for ecological and ecosystem maintenance.[29]

---

[26] See Deininger et al. (2012)
[27] See United Republic of Tanzania, MLHHSD Budget Speech (2021/2). See also Schreiber (2017).
[28] See Deininger et al. (2012).
[29] Consider United Republic of Tanzania MLHHSD (2011a, p. 48).

V INSTITUTIONAL FRAMEWORK FOR LAND ADMINISTRATION

As the Land Act provides, all land in Tanzania is public land vested in the president, who is required to manage the land for the benefit of the citizens. The president can acquire land for public purposes or transfer land from one category to a different category (*Land Act 1999*, section 4(7)). Aspects of this custodial duty are legally mandated to others, as summarised in Figure 7.1, including the MLHHSD, the Commissioner for Land, supported by various authorised officers, land allocation committees, LGAs, and the National Land Advisory Council (*Land Act 1999*, sections 8–14 and 17).

The MLHHSD is responsible for sector management including policy, regulatory, support, and capacity building, as well as national functions such as national mapping, land use planning, and record keeping that cannot be fragmented into district and village functions (*Land Act 1999*, section 8). The National Land Advisory Council, whose chairperson is appointed by the president, reviews and advises the minister on all aspects of land policy (*Land Act 1999*, section 17). The Commissioner for Land reports to the permanent secretary of the MLHHSD and is mostly responsible for operations of land acquisition, transfer, disposition, and revocation (*Land Act 1999*, sections 9, 10, and 11).

The regional restructuring and local government reforms have also assigned much of the responsibility for land administration, particularly the interaction with land users, to LGAs, which are under the authority of the President's Office – Regional Administration and Local Government (PO-RALG)(*Land Act 1999*, section 14) Yet land allocation is ratified by the land allocation committees (*Land Act 1999*, section 12).[30] These committees deal with land other than village land.[31] They consist of local representatives of the commissioner – or the commissioner himself at the national level – and local officers responsible for various tasks, including land surveying (*Land Act 1999*, section 12(2)).

---

[30] See also the functions of the *Land Allocation committees* under the Land (Allocation Committees) *Regulations, GN No. 72* (2001).

[31] At the district authority level (excluding land within boundaries of an urban authority) in respect of plots for central/local government offices; plots for residential, commercial/trade, and service purposes; plots for hotels, heavy and light/small industries; plots for religious and charitable purposes; farms not exceeding 500 acres subject to the approval of the minister; and land for other purposes not specified here. At the urban authority level in respect of plots for central/ local government offices; plots for residential, commercial/trade, and service purposes; plots for hotels, heavy and light/small industries; plots for religious and charitable purposes; land for urban farming; land for other purposes not specified here. At the ministry's headquarters or central level in respect of land for creation of new urban centres; plots for foreign missions; beach areas and small islands; plots for housing estates exceeding an area of 5 hectares; land for allocation to the TIC for investment purposes under the Tanzania Investment Act (1997); land for use of activities which are of national interest.

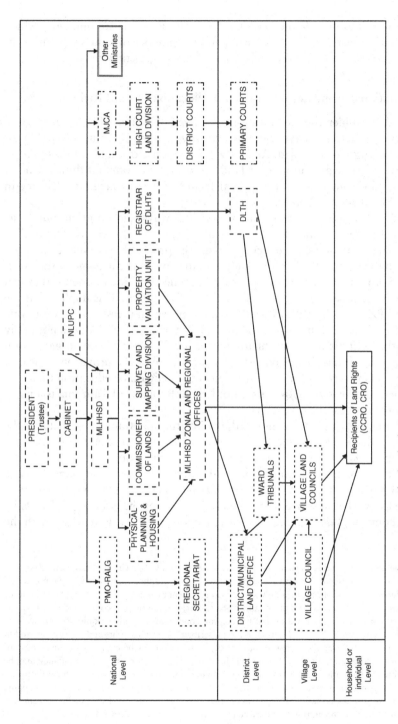

FIGURE 7.1 Institutional arrangements for land administration in Tanzania
Source: United Republic of Tanzania, Strategic Plan for the Implementation of the Land Laws (SPILL), 2013b

Other entities include the National Land Use Planning Commission, which advises the minister on land use issues and the practice of land use planning at local, regional, and national levels (*Land Act 1999*, section 12(2)).

A Institutional Mandates on Grant and Allocation of Land Rights

As provided under the Constitution of United Republic of Tanzania (1977 as amended), citizens have the '*right to own property*' (United Republic of Tanzania (1977 as amended, Art. 24(2)) in the sense of 'rights of occupancy'. The laws regulate and administer land rights and concomitant duties. One of the core functions of the institutional framework is to facilitate delivery in terms of land acquisitions.

Land in Tanzania can be acquired in various ways, such as grant, purchase, and gift. For general land, the law provides that land rights can be acquired by both citizens and non-citizens. For citizens, the procedure is to make an application to the Commissioner for Land, who may grant in the name of the president.[32] For non-citizens, the Act provides that the only kind of interest they can acquire is for investment approved by the TIC or EPZA. This implies that the TIC or EPZA are the authorities that can approve an investment and/or issue derivative right to an investor. The mandate of TIC and EPZA does not apply where the entity is a non-profit foreign or local corporation or organisation with the aim of the relief of poverty or distress, the public provision of health, or other social services for the advancement of religion or education under an agreement to which the Government of United Republic of Tanzania is a party (*Land Act 1999*, section 19(3)(a)).

As far as village land is concerned, the institutional framework includes the minister, who is responsible for policy formulation (*Land Act 1999*, section 8; *Village Land Act* 1999, section 8(11)), and the Commissioner for Land, who is the principal administrator of all land including village land (*Village Land Act* 1999, section 8(7); *The Land Act* 1999, sections 9, 10, and 11). Village assemblies approve village land allocation or the granting of CROs by village councils (*Village Land Act* 1999, section 8(5)). The latter deals with the

---

[32] Section 22 of the Land Act provides for the application for a GRO. The application must be: submitted on a prescribed form and accompanied by a photograph; accompanied by the prescribed fee; signed by the applicant or a duly authorised representative or agent of the applicant; sent or delivered to the commissioner or an authorised officer; contain or be accompanied by any information that may be prescribed or that the commissioner may in writing require the applicant to supply; accompanied by a declaration in the prescribed form of all rights and interests in land in Tanzania which the applicant has at the time of the application; where any law requires the consent of any local authority or other body before an application for a right of occupancy may be submitted to the commissioner, accompanied by a document of consent, signed by the duly authorised officer of that local authority or other body; if made by a non-citizen or foreign company, accompanied by a Certificate of Approval granted by the TIC under the Tanzania Investment Act, and any other documentation that may be prescribed by that Act or any other law.

management of the village's land (*Village Land Act* 1999, section 8). The ward development committee, the ward being the administrative level just above the village (*Village Land Act* 1999, section 8(6)(b)) can require reports from the village council on the management of the village's land. (*Village Land Act* 1999, section 8(6)(b)). At the next level, the district council provides advice and guidance to any village council within its jurisdiction on the administration of its land (*Village Land Act* 1999, section 9).

Where the boundaries of the village's land are not in dispute, that is after surveying, the Commissioner for Land is required to issue a CVL certifying the boundaries of the village land and giving a mandate to the village council to manage the village land (*Village Land Act* 1999, section 7(6)). The CVL is granted in the name of the president, affirming the occupation and use of the land by the villagers in accordance with the customary law applicable to land in the area.[33] For pastoralists, the CVL affirms the use of land for depasturing cattle in a sustainable manner in accordance with the highest and best customary principles of pastoralism practised in the area (*Village Land Act* 1999, section 7(7)(c), section 7(7)(d) and section 29). Together with the Land Use Planning Act, the Act also provides for the establishment of land use plans for villages and the creation of village-level committees under the village council that would oversee the implementation of the land use plans.[34]

A study on how 90 per cent of the citizens of Tanzania in rural areas acquire, hold, and dispose their lands has confirmed that customary landholding is still the prevalent mode (Kironde, 2009) for medium and smallholder farmers. Not all land in villages is allocated by village councils, since the Village Land Act generally recognises other forms of acquiring land such as purchase and inheritance. As a result, both the Land Act and the Village Land Act acknowledge 'deemed rights of occupancy', which emanate from occupation by villagers from time immemorial and allocations made by village councils upon application from villagers or non-villagers. Allocations by village councils are mainly on the land reserved for future use to needy applicants upon complying with certain formalities.[35]

Since the deemed rights are not compulsorily registrable,[36] they remain more precarious against the GROs (which are preferred by large-scale farmers) owing to their weak protection and lower competitive market status. Correcting these calls for pragmatic land use plans and issuance of CCROs to all landholdings on village land. There are also debates on uniform certificate of title for granted rights and customary rights in order to do away with the

---

[33] On conditions of the CCRO see *the Village Land Act* 1999, section 7(7)(c) and section 29.
[34] See generally on village land administration: Wily (2001); Geir (2005); Josefsson and Aberg (2005); Larsson (2006); The National Land Use Planning Commission (2011).
[35] See the power of the village councils to allocate land to applicants (*Village Land Act* 1999, sections 22–2).
[36] Case of *Methusela Paul Nyagwaswa supra*.

stigma associated with CROs. In the financial budget 2016/17, the MLHHSD planned to prepare land use plans for five districts comprising 1,500 villages. By 15 May 2017, however, the ministry and various stakeholders had managed to prepare land use plans for only ninety-one villages in twenty-three districts (United Republic of Tanzania, MLHHSD, 2018, pp. 49–50). This lack of success reflects that the plans were prepared unsystematically.

Village councils are constrained in various ways. They are supposed to seek approval of the village assembly for various decisions, in particular the portions of village land that can be set aside as communal village land and other purposes. They must consult with the district council on the exercise of their functions. To ensure proper record keeping, they are required to maintain a register of communal village land in accordance with any rules that may be prescribed. And, of course, they are constrained by the customary law in their area.

The Village Land Act provides that customary law governs CROs (*Village Land Act* 1999, sections 18 and 20). Yet any rule of customary law and any decision taken in respect of land held under customary tenure must take into account the fundamental principles of national land policy and of any other written law (*Village Land Act* 1999, section 20(2)) such as the United Republic of Tanzania Constitution. Any rule of customary law, customs, traditions, and practices of the community that conflicts with the fundamental principles or written law shall be deemed to be void and inoperative and shall not be given effect by any village council or village assembly or court of law (*Village Land Act* 1999, section 20(2)).

Despite such a clear legal position, it is intriguing that some customary norms still disregard fundamental principles – including equality over land, which results in dispossession of women through customary inheritance rules.[37] In particular, some discriminatory statutory laws conflict with the well-intentioned principles of the Land Act and the United Republic of Tanzania Constitution

---

[37] Various judicial decisions have been registered on this, such as *Ephrahim* v. *Holaria Pastory and Another* (2001) AHRLR 236. In this case a woman, Holaria Pastory, had inherited some clan land from her father by a valid will. Finding that she was getting old and senile and had no one to take care of her, she decided to sell the clan land to one Gervazi Kaizilege, a stranger and non-member of her clan. One Bernado Ephrahim, a member of the clan, filed a suit in the Primary Court at Kashasha, Muleba district, praying for a declaration that the sale of the clan land was void under the Haya Customary law – for females have no power to sell clan land. This was in accordance with the Haya Customary Law (Declaration) (No. 4) Order of 1963; specifically, its paragraph 20, which was to the effect that 'women can inherit and acquire usufruct right but may not sell'. The Primary Court granted the prayer. She appealed to the District Court at Muleba. Here the decision of the Primary Court was quashed on the basis of the Bill of Rights in the Constitution that guaranteed equality for both men and women. Bernardo Ephrahim was not satisfied and appealed to the High Court of Tanzania at Mwanza. At the High Court, the decision of the District Court was upheld on the ground that the relevant Haya Customary Law was discriminatory on the basis of gender, thus inconsistent with Article 13(4) of the Constitution.

on equality on land rights. One such law is the Customary Law Declaration Order, Order No. 4 of 1963, which classifies heirs into three degrees with women holding the third position.

B Institutional Mandates on Disposition

The Land Act defines disposition as follows:

Disposition means any sale, mortgage, transfer, grant, partition, exchange, lease, assignment, surrender, or disclaimer and includes the creation of an easement, a usufructuary right, or other servitude or any other interest in a right of occupancy or a lease and any other act by an occupier of a right of occupancy or under a lease whereby his rights over that right of occupancy or lease are affected and an agreement to undertake any of the dispositions so defined. (*Land Act 1999*, section 2)

In other words, land can be exchanged, transferred, and subject to a variety of market transactions. This is important as agribusiness investors need tools to raise capital, for example mortgages. If the right of occupancy were not fungible, the raising of credit for modern agriculture would be extremely limited (Tenga and Mramba, 2018, p. 10).

This is not always appreciated, as suggested by the antiquated phrase 'land in Tanzania has no value' – in fact, there are various ways in which the right of occupancy is transferable for value. That phrase often meant that since a right of occupancy is a grant for 'use and occupation', the value to the landholder would only be value that is generated through his investment on land – that is, 'bare land' has no value *per se*. But this kind of statement is fraught with danger as it has led to a lot of negative sentiment, which necessitated the amendment of the Land Act to state clearly that land has value (Tenga and Mramba, 2018, p. 10).

The Land Act, for instance, provides for the disposition of the GRO in three separate parts. First, it provides for the administrative oversight, where one can make the necessary applications to the Commissioner for Land or his authorised officers to approve and register a disposition of land. Second, it deals with what one may consider to be a theory of land transfers – the legal assumptions that underlie each disposition of land, such as that the need for each disposition must be in writing and that certain conditions are implied in every transfer, including that there are no latent defects in the land that have not been disclosed to a purchaser. These 'consumer protection' provisions are essential in modern property transactions; in the old days, the concept of *caveat emptor* or 'buyer beware' gave little protection to the unwary purchaser.

Third, there are detailed regulations for certain major forms of dispositions, such as the sale, mortgage, or lease of the GRO. The Land Act contains separate parts for each form of disposition. Previously, consent to any kind of disposition was mandatory, but under the Land Act (1999) there are many exceptions – only for specific kinds of disposition is official approval mandatory, otherwise a notice to the Commissioner for Land will suffice.

The president is the highest authority in the regulation and control of disposition of land in Tanzania. His mandate includes overseeing transfers of land. Practically, however, this function has been under the responsibility of the Commissioner for Land, assisted by authorised officers, as detailed in sections 36–41 of the Land Act. These sections have been referred to as mandate for oversight of the dispositions of GRO on general lands: disposition that has not obtained the requisite approval from the Commissioner for Land is rendered ineffectual, unless it is of a kind that requires only the furnishing of notice to the commissioner (*Land Act* 1999, sections 36 and 37). The cost is considered high, and it can take from two to four months to get a registered title.[38]

The amendment of section 41 of the Land Registration Act, Cap. 334 on registration of disposition calls for disposition of land to be subject to registration with mere notification to the commissioner, mainly to facilitate disposition by way of mortgage. The initial position was that no disposition could be registered unless the registrar received a certificate in writing from the Commissioner for Land signifying his approval, and only registered dispositions could create, transfer, vary, or extinguish any estate or interest in any registered land. Under the amended section, the applicant can now simply submit for registration all relevant documents accompanied by a prescribed fee, and the registrar then registers the disposition and notifies the commissioner.

For village land, the disposition of customary rights of occupancy requires approval of the village council. This is intended to protect village land against acquisition by non-villagers, but it is debatable if it has succeeded. A village council has exclusive decision power only if the land does not exceed 20 hectares. Where it exceeds 20 hectares, the approval of the district council is needed. If it exceeds 50 hectares, the approval of the Commissioner for Land is required (United Republic of Tanzania, MKURABITA Report, 2005). Such a provision seems to challenge the freedom of village councils and go against the principles of devolution and subsidiarity as expressed in the United Republic of Tanzania Constitution,[39] and reflected in Local Government Authorities Acts.[40] Powers seem to be legally granted to the village council by one hand only to be taken away by the other.

There is thus a kind of dualism in the land disposition system: centralisation of control and management of general land, with devolution of control to customary law at the village level. Such dualism cannot go without frictions and incidents likely to affect the economic efficiency of the whole land sector and to produce social frustration, such as those detailed in Box 7.5.

[38] See the United Republic of Tanzania, MKURABITA Program on Formalization of the Assets of the Poor in Tanzania and Strengthening the Rule of Law Report (2005d).

[39] See Articles 145 and 146, that the purpose of having LGAs is to transfer authority to the people. LGAs shall have the right and power to participate, and to involve the people, in the planning and implementation of development programmes within their respective areas and generally throughout the country.

[40] See *the Local Government (District Authorities) Act, No. 7 1982*, sections 26 and 142.

Box 7.5: Control of mandate of village councils

LUHANGA VILLAGE, MBARALI DISTRICT

The government in Mbeya returned 5,000 hectares of village land in Luhanga village Mbarali that had been taken from more than 200 villagers belonging to the Luhanga community for an investment project. The government directed the district council to take action against all village government officials who were involved in the process of allocating the land without respecting the legal procedure.

When handing back the land to the Luhanga community, the Regional Commissioner, Amosi Makala, said:

The government had made such decision after discovering that the process of allocation contravened procedures under the Village Land Act and its Regulations [...]. Act No. 5 of 1999 makes it clear that village councils have no mandate to allocate more than 20 or 50 hectares but, in that case, they allocated more than 5,000 without even consulting the district council [...]. [Furthermore,] apart from the allocation lacking procedural compliance, the investors did not seem to be genuine due to their failure to honour their promises to facilitate socio-economic issues in the area.

Lukenge Village, Kibaha District

In January 2018, the government, through the Kibaha District Commissioner, ordered an investor who had taken 5,000 hectares from the village government without following legal procedures to return it to the community within ninety days. The investor had failed to develop the land for eight years, contrary to the contract of disposition agreed with Lukenge village, Magindu ward.

The District Commissioner took action after villagers complained to her about the land transfer. According to the commissioner, the investor took the land for the purpose of investing in livestock and fish farming, but failed to commence the project. Instead the investor was using the land for other projects and did not support community socio-economic activities.

Data on the amount of land transfer in Tanzania are sketchy. Sule (2016), for instance, while cautious of the data, considers that:

There [have been over] 34 deals with about 1,000,000 ha owned by foreign investors (and joint ventures between the Tanzanian and foreign investors), whether announced, ongoing or concluded land acquisition processes. Out of these deals, only deals with a total of around 555,000 ha are reported by at least two different sources and can thus be considered as verified with certain reliability. Of the verified deals, only ten deals with a total area of 145,000 ha can be considered as concluded deals. The remaining reported area of 410,000 ha derives from deals that are so far only announced or

---

Box 7.6: Centralisation of land management

In September 2006, the minister of MLHHSD banned sale of land by villagers to foreigners. The minister gave the stern directive in a public meeting in Magu district, Mwanza, when resolving a land dispute that had lasted for thirty years between villagers and an investor. He said that 'there is a habit by a majority of villagers of allowing the so-called investors to come in to buy land from separate villagers, resulting in the investor occupying land which exceeds the statutory limit. Worst still, instead of developing it, the investor uses it as collateral to borrow money from banks and afterward sell it by surveying and creating plots.' He directed that it was prohibited for the district council or officers in his ministry to approve any such transactions.

---

that have land acquisition ongoing, but not concluded (including the contested AgriSol Energy deal with an area of 325,000 ha). [It is appreciated that] since these data are three years old, a number of new projects are likely in place and some projects have either ceased or become dormant. (Sule, 2016, p. 112)

In its assessment of investment in commercial agriculture, the MLHHSD found that out of 121 commercial farms in the country – amounting to 223,443 hectares – in Tanga, Morogoro, Pwani, Njombe, and Kagera regions only 63 (about 52 per cent) had been developed, while 58 (about 48 per cent) had been abandoned (United Republic of Tanzania, MLHHSD, 2018, p. 22). This is quite alarming and could point to a problem with the investment conditions or failure to closely monitor investors' compliance with investment plans. An example is given in Box 7.6.

C Institutional Mandates on Dispute Settlement

The Land Acts provide for the establishment of a land dispute settlement mechanism in Tanzania. They assert the need for structures to be instituted at the lowest local level with room for accessing higher levels in case of no resolution. In 2002, the Land (Disputes Courts) Act was enacted. It provides for a dispute settlement system with five levels of hierarchy.

The lowest level is the village land council, followed by the ward tribunal, where procedures are mostly informal as advocates are not allowed and decisions are taken by lay judges. The next level is the District Land and Housing Tribunal (DLHT), where advocates are allowed so procedures are more formal. There are too few tribunals, so some serve an entire zone rather than a single district. In regions where DLHTs are scarce, citizens face high travelling costs to get their case settled in a tribunal. This renders the principle of equality before the law somewhat illusory.

TABLE 7.2 *Land disputes in DLHTs*

Total number of pending land disputes by 30 June 2016	Total number of land cases filed from July 2016 to 15 May 2017	Total number of land cases decided from July 2016 to 15 May 2017	Total number of pending cases on 15 May 2017
13,89	26,245	18,571	21,564

Source: United Republic of Tanzania, MLHHSD (2018)

The upper levels of the land judiciary hierarchy are the High Court (Land Division) and the Court of Appeal. Procedures in these courts may be cumbersome. For instance, a person whose dispute was first handled in the ward tribunal cannot appeal from the High Court to the Court of Appeal unless (s)he receives certification from the High Court that there is a point of law involved. Moreover, an appeal from the High Court for a matter that originated in a DLHT, or High Court must seek leave before appealing to the Court of Appeal. These restrictions have been deemed to be challenges in the settlement of land disputes. Overall, it is an intricate institutional structure of land administration, the complexity of which reflects somewhat antinomic basic principles.

When presenting the MLHHSD budget in the financial year 2016/17 in parliament, the minister of MLHHSD outlined the status of land disputes in DLHT in the country from 30 June 2016 to 15 May 2017. Table 7.2 summarises.

It would appear that the stock of pending cases is increasing at a vertiginous rate: up 60 per cent in a year, equating to more than a full year of new cases. This clearly unsustainable if the judiciary capacity is not improved or the causes for disputes reduced.

VI INSTITUTIONAL ISSUES AND CHALLENGES

The Land Acts were passed in 1999 and began to be implemented in May 2001. Although they represented an improvement, they were quickly found to be unsatisfactory on several grounds. Major challenges are still present, as evidenced by the impressive number of reports that have since been produced on the persistent institutional weaknesses of the land rights system and land administration, and several partial reforms that have attempted to improve the situation. For example, only four years after implementation, the law was amended to repeal and replace Chapter 10 related to mortgages, under pressure from financial institutions, which found that it inhibited bankable projects. Another amendment in 2005 changed provisions related to leases, followed by one in 2008 to promote mortgage financing.

More fundamentally, reports including the MKURABITA (Property and Business Formalisation Programme) Report (2005), BRN (2013), and the Land Governance Assessment Framework (LGAF) (2009 and 2015) pointed to major institutional challenges. The 2009 LGAF report proposed a systematic review of the National Land Policy of 1995 to explore the extent to which expected gains had materialised and what could be done to improve the performance of land management. Issues touched upon include: land surveying, mapping, and registration; affirmative action to address gender issues; redefining institutional mandates; strengthening of decentralisation; making land use planning more participatory; changing expropriation practices; and improving conflict resolution mechanisms. The same institutional issues were again stressed in the 2015 LGAF report. The government reacted by commissioning in 2016 a review of the National Land Policy 1995. A draft policy is presently under consideration.

The implementation of the Land Acts was sufficiently difficult that it gave rise to two Strategic Plans for the Implementation of Land Laws, the first in 2005 (SPILL-I) and the second in 2013 (SPILL-II). A SWOT (strengths, weaknesses, opportunities, and threats) analysis undertaken in the latter pointed out positive but also numerous negative sides of land policies in Tanzania. The negatives are summarised in Table 7.3.

Clearly, the weaknesses listed in Table 7.3 result both from unsatisfactory institutional arrangements and limited state capacity – aspects that it is not really possible to completely disentangle. Despite the SPILL's well-conceived analysis, and despite some, though unsatisfactory, progress over recent years, the main difficulties affecting the functioning of the land sector have not been resolved. The 2016 draft National Land Policy proposes to introduce some substantial changes in the National Land Policy 1995 and its implementation instruments. As the Policy is not finalised at the time of writing, the next sections describe the main present shortcomings of land management in Tanzania without consideration for the reforms considered in this new version of the Policy. The few debates organised about the draft of the National Land Policy 2016 do not suggest most challenges listed here will disappear, as the focus of these debates seems mostly to concern the protection of smallholders against large-scale investors.[41]

A Duality of Tenure

There is little doubt that the duality of tenure introduced by the key distinction between general land and village land, and the associated difference between GROs (and derivative rights) and CROs, is the main source of friction and inefficiency in the institutional setting of land rights in Tanzania. Transforming

---

[41] See, for instance, The Citizen (2017).

TABLE 7.3 *Weaknesses and threats in land policies*

Weaknesses	Threats
Inefficient and ineffective land administration	Massive growth of irregular settlements
Institutional arrangements uncoordinated	Unregulated land markets
Land administration services concentrated in limited parts of Tanzania	Limited housing/building mortgage market
Shortage of staff, particularly in land disputes	Underfunding of the land administration infrastructure
Implementation of new land law is slow	Oversight of land dispute mechanisms questioned
Key mechanisms (National Land Advisory Council, village land councils, tribunals, etc.) not in place	Increasing land conflicts
Shortage of planned, surveyed, and serviced land	Lack of harmony with laws in other sectors
Poor enforcement of rules and planning regulations	Growing marginalisation of the poor
Dispute settlement machinery not empowered	
Lack of maps	
Tarnished image of the land sector in the eyes of the public	

Source: United Republic of Tanzania, MLHHSD, SPILL (2013b)

village land into general land to facilitate large-scale investments, in agriculture as well as in other activities, is often an uneasy and unpopular operation, to such an extent that it may act as a disincentive for investors and lead to missed economic opportunities.

One of the objectives of the present land management system is clearly to protect indigenous smallholders from their land being acquired by large-scale operators who might use the land more productively but with lower employment, a different output mix, and insufficient compensation for evicted people. This objective – so clearly expressed in Nyerere's quotation at the beginning of this chapter – is justified, even though it implicitly means some strategic choices about agricultural development have been made that may not have been fully analysed; for example, how much land for food crops in smallholdings and cooperatives and how much for commercial crops in large-scale plantations.

It is estimated that by 2017, more than 11,000 of Tanzania's approximately 12,500 villages had mapped their outer limits, but only about 13 per cent had adopted land use plans. Of the approximately 6 million households located in rural villages, only about 400,000 had obtained individual title documents (Schreiber, 2017, p. 1). This implies that more than half of Tanzania's 12,500 villages still do not have CVLs and very few rural citizens hold occupancy certificates to secure their individual land parcels.

The problem is that, within the present institutional setting, this protection is often elusive. This has two consequences. On the one hand, smallholders feel insecure and may not take the necessary steps to improve their land, increase yields, and respond to market incentives. On the other hand, large-scale operators may be discouraged from acquiring land by endless procedures and high transaction costs. Better defined, better implemented, and fairer administrative procedures for land transfers would provide efficiency gains on both sides.

From a sociological or political science point of view, however, there is much more to land than economics. At all levels, the choice of an institutional structure through which land rights are managed has major implications for the distribution of power in society and ultimately on control over land.

The frequency of incidents about rights of occupancy is high and rising. These incidents arise from the perceived violation of the principle of equality behind the intended comparable status of the GROs on general land and the CROs on village land (*The Village Land Act* (1999), section 18(1)). Although one could assert that the attributes of the CRO under section 18(1) of the Village Land Act are not realistic, since they depend on the administrative inclination of relevant authorities and judicial interpretation, they remain important features in the protection of customary right holders. Judicial trends before the enactment of section 18(1) of the Village Land Act relied on inquiries called upon by the Minister of MLHHSD in the case of land conflict that had shown disregard for customary right and the mandate of village councils, as exemplified in Box 7.7.[42]

Many incidents have also arisen from the acquisition of customary land rights for the public interest. Since 98 per cent of land in Tanzania is village land or reserved land, village land is the main source of land acquisition for other purposes, where there are particular development needs. Nonetheless, conflicts may also be brought about by overlaps between individual villages' land and reserved land (parks, game reserves, conservation areas). Schreiber, for instance, notes that villagers have faced pressure from government officials and conservationists, who wanted more land allocated to conservation and lucrative tourist lodges (Schreiber, 2017, p. 2). Within villages, there have also

---

[42] See cases such as *Methusela Paul Nyagwaswa v. Christopher Mbote Nyirabu* (1985), *Suzan Kakubukubu and two others* v. *Walwa Joseph Kasubi and the Municipal Director of Mwanza* (1988), *AG v. Lohay Akonaay and Joseph Lohay* (1995), and *Mwalimu Omary v. A. Bilali* (1990), in which the CRO was in dispute against the GRO.

Box 7.7: Interference over mandate of village councils

In Mabwegere, village authorities had to defend their village boundaries all the way to the Court of Appeal, where they had won in September 2011. However, the regional and district authorities refused to implement the court order to respect the village boundaries, and instead maintained their intention to redraw the village boundaries to reallocate land to the neighbouring rice farming village of Mbigiri. On 30 May 2015, the Mabwegere village chairman was arrested and ordered to publicly announce his support for the redrawing of his village boundaries in order to be released. As he refused to do so, he was jailed for a month. This was followed by a ruling of the Morogoro DLHT on 3 June 2015 to rescind the village certificate of Kambala village and reduce the village land from 48,650 to 16,104 hectares – a reduction of 66 per cent (ITV, 2015).

---

been many disputes between pastoralists and farmers, with pastoralists often removed from their habitual or traditional grazing lands, as for instance in Kilosa-Morogoro.[43]

B Immense Powers of Eminent Domain

The concept of public land has given the state immense power, because land is deemed to be controlled by the state and thus akin to state property.[44] Yet the power of eminent domain, and the state's policing and managing capacity – which allow it to regulate land use in the public interest through planning and granting of planning permission – have not always been used judiciously and in the public interest.

What constitutes public interest has remained a matter of contention. In the recent history of Tanzania, for instance, public interest included acquiring land for private investors. On the management side, large-scale allocation of land by the state was often undertaken with no consultation of the affected communities. In effect, customary landholders are not protected by fair information and consultation procedures. Free, prior, and informed *consent* for the allocation of customary lands is not obligatory when the public interest is involved. There is also no assurance that evicted customary landholders or those deprived of parts of their lands will be able to find jobs or other livelihoods to compensate for their losses. Needless to say, the losses endured by local communities can be very great, including the commercial value of the

---

[43] See Mkomazi Game Reserve in the case of *Lekengere Faru Purut and 52 others* v. *Minister for Tourism, Natural Resources and Environment and three others.*

[44] 'Eminent domain' formally refers to the power of the state to take private property for public use while requiring 'just compensation' to be given to the original owner.

land or, in the absence of well-functioning markets, its recurrent-use value and its potential for a commercial enterprise.

Commons in communities under customary tenure have been particularly vulnerable, on the argument that they are unowned, or idle, or simply that they belong to the state. Often the most valuable land assets of rural communities are targeted by commercial investors, leaving these communities sinking deeper into poverty (Songela and Maclean, 2008; Action Aid, 2009; Chijoriga, 2009; Mwamila et al., 2009; Sulle and Nelson, 2009; Kaarhus et al., 2010; Oakland Institute, 2011). Such cases include land acquired by Bioshape in Kilwa for Biofuel, Sun Biofuel in Kisarawe, and SEKABBT in Bagamoyo.

Occasionally, compensation has been paid to evicted communities, but they complain it is grossly inadequate. Promises made about employment opportunities and the improvement of rural infrastructure often do not materialise (LEAT, 2012). Expected tax revenues at the local level also fail to be realised as investors demand and get exemptions. This has the effect that host communities rise up against investors. It has been suggested that the government should adopt alternative models that engage more of the existing producers, such as contract farming and out-grower schemes, rather than displacing them (Vermeulen and Cotula, 2010; Tenga and Kironde, 2012).

C Limited Formalisation

In rural areas, land surveys and issuance of CCROs are still done sporadically and on an *ad hoc* basis. In most cases land CCROs have depended on pilot projects that have not managed to cover a large part of the country. As also noted in Section IV, informal urban tenure outpaces formal tenure – a clear indication that unplanned settlements are increasing fast. This is because of a high rate of urbanisation and arbitrary expansion of city boundaries, which has even eaten into self-governing villages.[45]

Even when land occupancy rights have been granted at one level or another, procedures and standards for formalisation are characterised by being bureaucratic, unrealistic, expensive, and time-consuming. Only a minority of land records are found in the land registers. Registry records are often unclear and cases of multiple titles for the same piece of land are not uncommon. Automated land recording and documentation systems are rare. Land administration is often centralised. Possibly because of this, it is characterised by non-transparency and lack of accountability. This scares low-income households, as well as potential investors.

---

[45] See, for instance, Gastorn (2003).

D Gender Discrimination

Gender inequality in access to and control of land remains a serious problem. As noted by Shivji, while people can have access to land through various means including allocation and purchase (Shivji, 1998, p. 84), control of the proceeds from the land is another matter. The Food and Agriculture Organization notes that rural women in particular are responsible for half of the world's food production and produce between 60 and 80 per cent of the food in most developing countries, but they lack effective decision-making power as individuals under traditional law (Food and Agriculture Organization, 2002, p. 26). Often, women are left holding whatever rights they have at the will of male relatives (Food and Agriculture Organization, 2002, p. 26).

One of the major remaining obstacles to increasing the agricultural productivity and incomes of rural women is insecurity in their land tenure, reflected in rules of access and control. Traditional or customary systems that might protect women's access to land have failed to promote their full control over the land they operate. While land may be considered valuable collateral by credit institutions, the marginalisation of women excludes them from obtaining loans and making important investments.

Although the Village Land Act provides for the illegality of discriminatory practices in customary law (in section 20), there are still complaints about the mistreatment of women in terms of land rights. Improving access and security for women will require changes in cultural norms and practices.

E Institutional Overlaps

Land administration is affected by potential overlaps in implementation of land-related laws and policies owing to the multiplicity and diversity of land-related institutions. Overlap of responsibilities, and the complexity of the relationships between the various public entities in the land management system, undermines efficiency and sometimes threatens basic principles such as the separation of powers.

For example, land officers in the LGAs – village, ward, and district – are under the responsibility of the MLHHSD. While they are paid by and report to superiors in the ministry, they execute functions for local governments, which are themselves under the responsibility of the PO-RALG. Another example is that sectoral ministries have their say on swaths of land under the MLHHSD – the Ministry of Natural Resources and Tourism deals with reserved lands, for instance.

Problems of overlap and lack of coordination are also acute in the land dispute settlement system. At the lower level of the system, the village land councils and the ward tribunals are under local government authority responsibility, which falls under the PO-RALG. Right above them, the DLHTs are under the MLHHSD. At the top, however, the High Court (Land Division) and the Court of Appeal are under the judiciary. This institutional set-up creates problems of accountability and contravenes the principle of separation of powers (Gastorn, 2009, pp. 583–4; Kironde, 2009). It also creates unnecessary problems in the delivery of justice, hence the need for reform.

F Corruption and Inefficient Land Administration

Much as institutional framework is crucial in land governance, Askew notes that:

[W]eak land governance and property rights systems can lead to opaque land deals, which facilitate corruption and undercut responsible actors seeking access to land for productive investment. Weak governance [...] allows unproductive land speculation and undermines agricultural productivity. (Askew et al., 2017, p. 5)

Kironde points out that corruption challenges in the land sector are partly blamed on lack of an efficient land records system. Falsifying or hiding land information has led to long delays in getting approvals for land use plans, land surveying, and change of use (Kironde, 2014, p. 12). He notes that although the government discourages informal payments, through public notices in offices and public education campaigns, they are paid all the same. Mechanisms to detect and deal with illegal staff behaviour exist in some registry offices, such as use of the Prevention and Combat of Corruption Bureau, but it has proved difficult to eliminate rent-seeking, and the general public does not have the incentive to report it. Indeed, rent-seeking is condoned through intermediaries as it seems to speed up delivery.

Transparency International (2017) has indicated a slight overall improvement in the fight against corruption: from 2016 to 2017, the country's score increased from 32 to 36, and it climbed by three places from a global rank of 106 to 103. In a more focused study, Afrobarometer noted some likelihood of corruption-related practices to facilitate land registration, with rich people very likely to offer bribes (Afrobarometer, 2017, p. 7). Ordinary people also seem to be used to making informal payments, which indicates that institutional practices still need further reform (Afrobarometer, 2017, p. 7). See Figure 7.2 for an overview of the likelihood of corruption on land transactions for ordinary and rich individuals. It could also demonstrate that many people are not aware of their entitlements, and there is need for more efforts on awareness raising on land rights. The Information Land Management Integrated System is expected to minimise the avenues of corruption and fast-track land delivery.

G Ineffective Land Dispute Settlement Framework

The dispute settlement machinery is complex, straddling the judiciary and the executive, and disputes are on the rise. The nature of the disputes varies: some result from conflicting land uses such as agriculture and pastoralism, agriculture and conservation, or pastoralism and conservation, and others result from

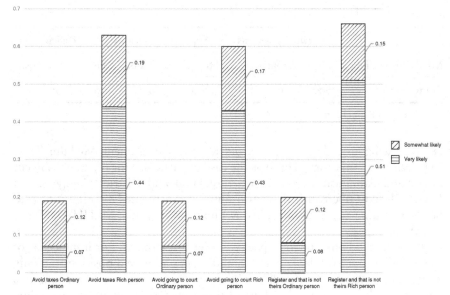

FIGURE 7.2 Corruption Index on Land Transactions
Source: AfrobBarometer (2017)

transfer of village land to general lands or dubious land deals by investors on village lands.

Despite some government efforts to improve both formal and informal mechanisms, weaknesses persist. As seen earlier, most DLHTs are located far away from local communities. On top of that, filing fees and legal representation are expensive; there are language barriers, as the language used in legal matters is English; jurisdictions may be limited; DLHTs' chairpersons may lack independence; there is an excessive multiplicity of land disputes settlement authorities; and, because of ineffective voluntary mediation, most matters end up in full trial (Massay, 2013, pp. 167–82).

A report by the Law Reform Commission acknowledges that the legal system governing settlement of land disputes has not met the desired standard. Problems such as delay in settlement of land disputes, backlog of cases, inaccessibility of institutions, inadequate financial and human resources, and multiplicity of institutions contribute to a huge degree of inefficiency and ineffectiveness (United Republic of Tanzania, Law Reform Commission, 2014).

H Inadequate Resources

Even if existing policy and laws were fully satisfactory, inadequate human, material, and financial resources would frustrate their successful execution. For instance, there was little progress on many of the actions set out in SPILL

TABLE 7.4 *MLHHSD staffing by March 2013*

MLHHSD staffing	Filled positions		Approved positions		Deficit	
	HQ	Outposts	HQ	Outposts	HQ	Outposts
Total	707	379	1,093	1358	386	979

Source: United Republic of Tanzania, MLHHSD, SPILL (2013b)

(2005) owing to a lack of funds outside the Government Medium Term Expenditure Framework. This was the case in particular for the establishment of a Land Administration Infrastructure Fund and District Compensation Funds. The cost of creating these institutions was estimated in SPILL (2005) to be roughly USD 300 million (United Republic of Tanzania, MLHHSD, SPILL, 2013b, p. 20).

Addressing administrative capacity is a lengthy process. For instance, as of March 2013, the MLHHSD had a total of 2,451 approved positions but only 1,086 were budgeted for and filled. The remaining gap was 386 in headquarters and 979 in the outposts. The filling of these positions is irregular, depending on the state of the economy and available budget. In one report, the MLHHSD mentioned that the government's attention was focused on the education and health sectors, leaving much of the land sector's manpower needs unfilled (United Republic of Tanzania, MLHHSD, SPILL, 2013b, p. 20) The staffing figures noted in Table 7.4 make it obvious that the MLHHSD is operating below capacity. Although these figures relate to 2013 and efforts to fill positions are being made, until 2018 the situation had not changed substantially, owing to attention focusing more on immediate socio-economic demands.

As for training capacity, it has been considered that the output from Ardhi University and other institutions can go a long way to satisfying the staffing requirements for high-level land sector professionals. Ardhi Institute Tabora (ARITA), and Ardhi Institute Morogoro (ARIMO), which are under the MLHHSD, have been useful in training manpower at technician and certificate levels. ARITA offers certificate courses in Cartography, Land Management, Valuation and Registration, and Graphic, Arts and Printing, as well as a Diploma Course in Cartography. ARIMO offers certificate and diploma courses in Geomatics (United Republic of Tanzania, MLHHSD, SPILL, 2013b, p. 30).

These two institutions can play an important role, working with Ardhi University, in outputting staff suitable for manning the land sector at district, ward, village and *mitaa* levels (United Republic of Tanzania, MLHHSD, SPILL, 2013b).[46] Since there are some 12,000 villages, 3,337 wards, and 2,651 *mitaa* in the country, which may go up in the near future, it would be necessary to train 20,000 land administration auxiliaries in at least one cadre in

---

[46] A *mitaa* is a sub-location.

support of the land sector for about five years (United Republic of Tanzania, MLHHSD, SPILL, 2013b). Enrolment at the Morogoro and Tabora land institutes in 2015–16 was 495, and in 2016–17 it rose to 559 (United Republic of Tanzania, MLHHSD, SPILL, 2013b, p. 65).

Although the ministry through SPILL projected training of 474 staff at a total estimated cost of TZS 803.99 million (about USD 0.5 million) (United Republic of Tanzania, MLHHSD, SPILL, 2013b), funding has remained a challenge. In the 2017/18 budget speech by the Minister of MLHHSD, it was established that in the financial year 2016/17, the ministry had planned to build the capacity of 150 employees, and by 15 May 2017, it had supported training to 491 employees. In the financial year 2017/18, the ministry planned to provide training to 70 employees and employ 291 new employees, besides improving working facilities (United Republic of Tanzania, MLHHSD, 2018, p. 64). This is a positive trend, but it remains to be seen whether the kind and level of training offered is adequate to meet the current demands.

VII CONCLUDING REMARKS AND RECOMMENDATIONS

This chapter has assessed the land tenure system, the way it is implemented, and how it is supposed to work. It has analysed how the administrative and judiciary apparatus may help the economy exploit its comparative advantage in agriculture. It has shown that while the legal framework has put in place essential principles for land governance, these principles are not self-executing – their success depends on a vibrant and capable institutional framework.

Among the key recommendations which emerge from this chapter, it has been noted that there is a need for more effective coordination, collaboration, and capacity building at the various governance levels; procedures for large-scale investment in land need to be streamlined; there is a need to scale up land use programmes in rural areas to address village land conflicts and demarcate land available for occupation and investment; in urban areas, also, large-scale regularisation schemes need to be rolled out; and more efforts are needed to raise awareness on land rights to tackle corruption.

The existing political economy situation is a source of conflict between large-scale farmers holding CROs and small-scale farmers holding CCROs. The gaps in the land registration system for village land, that is CCROs, make it difficult for smallholder farmers to access credit. CROs are not accepted as collateral by banks. Moreover, the slow and complicated process of transferring village land into general land undermines investment in agriculture. If one is lucky, it takes three to five years to complete the process and receive the CCRO from the MLHHSD. The powers of the commissioner to grant the transfer could be on paper only, but applicant investors are often told that their certificates could not be issued in time because of the awaited approval from the President's Office.

TIC approval is also complex, largely because it does not have a land bank. It therefore has to go through the same process of transferring village land. It has proved to be very difficult for the TIC to establish its own land bank, for whatever reason. Better institutional arrangements between village councils and the TIC could solve this. How to protect indigenous smallholders' land from acquisition by large-scale farmers has surfaced over time. This can, however, be addressed by identifying vacant land and demarcating it for use by large-scale operators. Contract farming and out-grower schemes are a good approach to address the problem, as is currently being demonstrated in the SAGCOT area. The establishment of a Tanzania commodity market could address the price-fixing issues.

Discussion of 'Through the Maze of Land Right Laws'

Discussion by Klaus Deininger

The legal basis for land ownership and access in Tanzania is provided by the Land Act and the Village Land Act, both passed in 1999 as the result of a process involving a Presidential Commission in 1991 and formulation of a national land policy in 1995.[47]

When they were passed, these laws were lauded as among the most advanced in Africa (Alden-Wily, 2003). Yet for several reasons, many laid out in this chapter, Tanzania failed to realise this potential and, with a ranking of 132 in the World Bank's 'Doing Business: registering property' indicator, is close to the bottom of this indicator globally.

Four elements illustrate the gaps in Tanzania's land registration system and the costs these impose on the broader economy. First, Tanzania has not computerised even the textual part of its land administration system and relies on a manual paper-based system that offers few advantages but provides ample opportunity for processes to get delayed and documents to be 'lost' or forged. Second, there is no integration between spatial and textual records, something that not only increases the costs of registering, but also reduces the security provided by land documents. Third, the system for formalising transfers is inefficient and cumbersome, with some of the associated requirements (such as official consent) unnecessary, so that even formal properties risk falling back into informality. Finally, coverage is extremely limited, with the number of new CROs created annually likely to be less than the number of new plots created so that in percentage terms coverage is decreasing rather than increasing.

At the time Tanzania was debating its land policy, Rwanda, one of its neighbours, experienced one of the most traumatic periods in its history. A desire to

[47] The views expressed in this note are those of the author and do not necessarily represent those of the World Bank, its Board of Executive Directors, or the member countries they represent.

never again let the state's failure to secure land rights for all trigger violence at this scale led that country to develop a set of land laws and policies and subsequently implement the most comprehensive land regularisation programme in Africa so far, which, by 2013, had registered all of the country's 11.5 million parcels (Ali et al., 2014) at a total cost of about USD 6 per parcel. With 86.6 per cent of land formally registered in the name of women (either jointly or individually) and rapid activation of mortgage-based credit (Ali et al., 2017), this allowed realisation of tangible social and economic benefits. It also provides the basis for land valuation to ensure fairness in case of expropriation, for raising revenue through land taxes, and for forward-looking land use planning including urban expansion.

Here, we suggest several concrete next steps that could allow Tanzania to improve land tenure security at a scale similar to that in Rwanda without giving up some of the distinctive characteristics of land tenure in Tanzania.

I IMPROVING LAND TENURE IN URBAN AREAS

Improve registry efficiency and integration: Despite efforts to modernise the system, most of Tanzania's land registry is still paper-based and not integrated with the cadaster or land-related databases maintained by local governments. To address this, action will be needed in four areas, as follows:

- Make digitisation of records mandatory to reduce petty corruption, generate audit trails, and allow workflow monitoring. Experience with digitisation projects globally suggests that the key to success is to get buy-in from the mid-level bureaucracy and experience in how to do so can be drawn on from several successful cases.
- Agree on time-bound targets and measurable outcome indicators for system improvement (including the level of digital coverage) that can be routinely generated from administrative data available to the MLHHSD (possibly linked to other administrative datasets) and regularly report to the public and to high-level decision makers on progress.
- Provide banks with online access to an authoritative and fully electronic register to allow them to verify the absence of competing registered claims to the same land, a piece of information that will have far-reaching consequences for their ability to repossess the land in case of default. Similarly, establish online links to tax administration, courts, the national ID, and the civil registry to ensure that every change in a person's civil status automatically triggers a change in all parcels to which this person has a right.
- Empower local government by ensuring that parcel data from the land registry can be used by them for the processes they are responsible for, such as planning, permitting, and property taxation and that information already contained in databases maintained by local government is systematically taken into account in efforts to expand coverage with CROs.

Adjust regulations for low-cost first-time registration: First-time registration in Tanzania is unaffordable owing to three factors, namely:

- An emphasis on upfront payment of a premium that is unaffordable to poor credit-constrained households who, as clearly demonstrated in the literature (Ali, 2016; Manara and Regan, 2022), could benefit from secure land documentation and are interested in obtaining and willing to pay for it.
- A requirement for highly accurate boundary demarcation that transfers large rents to surveyors (who often operate using outdated technology rather than making use of advances that allow acquisition of highly accurate imagery via drones or satellites as survey regulations have not been updated). Global experience demonstrates that, while a spatial description that allows any parcel to be identified unambiguously on a map is essential for a public registry to function, high-precision surveys are a private good and should be treated as such.
- A complex paper-based and manual process that involves numerous formal and informal steps with opportunities for rent extraction and hold-up that led to emergence of intermediaries to help landowners navigate the process.

Regulatory action will be needed to collect revenue for titled properties on an ongoing basis rather than the current focus on prohibitive upfront fees that just increase informality; open the door for use of modern low-cost surveying methods as the norm and allow land owners to acquire high-precision surveys at their own cost; and streamline and digitise the workflow for first-time registration to reduce the amount of time and resources required, and define parameters for workflow management for any efforts to expand coverage with land title to make an impact.

Complete CRO issuance in urban areas: Pilot experience in Dar es Salaam (Ali et al., 2016) suggests that even poor slum-dwellers are interested in and willing to pay for documents to provide them with secure tenure. The potential benefits from doing so, in terms of investment and credit access as well as planning and effective service provision, are undisputed. Therefore, once the steps outlined already are completed (which, on the basis of initial steps having been accomplished, could be done in the context of pilots with the explicit goal of refining workflows together with software to implement them), efforts to expand coverage with CROs to all urban areas will be a high priority. Counts of all built structures in Tanzania that have recently been produced using machine learning together with high-resolution imagery can indicate the overall volume of work to be covered and should be used to set milestones in terms of monthly targets, and the cost of doing so must not exceed USD 10 per parcel.

II IMPROVING RURAL LAND TENURE

While the government spent considerable resources on issuance of CCROs to rural dwellers, the literature suggests that the impact of such documents remains limited (Stein et al., 2016). This is not too surprising as village land cannot be transferred to outsiders. As long as this restriction remains in place, CCROs offer little increment in terms of tenure security. Demarcating village land, together with establishment of clear rules of how to manage land internally in the village, would, in such a situation, be a lower-cost option to guarantee tenure security. Introduction of CCROs has many parallels to unsuccessful attempts to introduce a lower level of tenure (in the form of residential licences) in urban areas. While these were promoted with great fanfare, they provided no tangible benefits and thus fell into disrepair (Ali et al., 2016). To move forward with rural land tenure, the following steps would be desirable:

Complete issuance of CVLs: The fact that, some twenty years after the coming into force of the Village Land Act, only a fraction of villages have received a CVL is puzzling. It not only undermines the basis for Tanzania's rural land tenure system, but also raises questions about the government's seriousness in implementing its stated policy. Complete issuance of CVLs based on boundaries surveyed using modern low-cost technology – with disputes that cannot be resolved in the process marked on the record – and publicly accessible through a web portal would be a fundamental step towards ensuring that external support to Tanzania's rural land sector will have the desired impact.

Clarify content and status of village land use plans: Conceptually, village land use plans should be the main instrument to address informational asymmetries between villages and potential investors, providing a basis for villages to attract investors with a profile that would most effectively contribute to local development. The de facto prohibition of direct deals between villagers and investors precludes this and undermines villages' incentives to systematically identify investment opportunities and put them on public notice using village land use plans. It is thus not surprising to find that, despite large amounts of resources invested in establishing such land use plans, a lack of clarity regarding their status and level of publicity prevails.

To address these issues and improve clarity in land management for investors and local government, a regulatory framework to clarify the status of village land use plans is urgently needed. It should contain provisions regarding responsibilities and standards for elaboration, approval, and public availability of relevant documents to prevent plans being changed at the whim of local officials; ensuring compliance with such land use plans or for aggrieved parties (including herders) to seek redress in case of violation; and resolving inconsistencies with higher-level plans and the modality and frequency with which such plans should be updated (as well as the resources available for doing so).

Allow local decisions on transferability of CCROs: Experience in other countries suggests that a one-size fits all approach to indiscriminately restricting transferability without considering local conditions or allowing ways for villages to adjust these by weighing local opportunities and risks may fail to contribute to greater equity and instead lead to widespread informality and underuse of land. As Tanzania has decision-making structures at village level available, it would not be difficult to allow village assemblies transferability of land (with or without restrictions in terms of either the size of individual land transactions to prevent landlessness or the amount of land that can be acquired by any individual to prevent concentration) to outsiders, similar to what has been done in Mexico with great success (Deininger et al., 2002; Valsecchi, 2014; de Janvry et al., 2015), though at some political cost (de Janvry et al., 2015). This should be contingent on a parcel-level land information system being in place, and thus could also help to direct resources for CCRO demarcation in the right direction.

Mandatory conversion to general land: The conceptual basis for the mandatory conversion from village to general land in case of investment is typical of an enclave approach to agricultural investment that is not consistent with the need for such investment to benefit local farmers through market- or technology-related spillovers (Ali et al., 2018) or social services. Given that most successful agricultural investments started rather small and expanded subsequently, and that success is often contingent on collaboration between locals and investors to achieve shared benefits, the fact that land given to investors would permanently be removed from village control (including in case an investment fails) pitches each against the other. It thus creates strong incentives for stakeholders to use the many opportunities provided by the complex and duplicative process for land conversion to slow down transfers, in the process frustrating (or bankrupting) investors who attempt to acquire land in the legally prescribed way. If options are in place for villages to decide on transferability of land as suggested earlier, there is no need for such conversion to general land, as villages can make land available to investors directly in ways that ensure such investment is undertaken gradually and generates local benefits.

Use rural land taxation to discourage speculative landholding: Anecdotal evidence suggests that owners of holdings who managed to get their land converted to general land are very large, with many using only a small fraction of the land they own. Land taxes at a meaningful rate that would be levied on, say, all holdings above the 50-hectare limit those villagers are currently allowed to acquire would provide a strong incentive to either use such land more productively or transfer it to those who may be able to do so, thereby activating rental or sales markets.

8

Power Sector Reform and Regulation

Catrina Godinho

I INTRODUCTION

The power sector has long been singled out as a major obstacle to development in Tanzania. Despite abundant and diverse natural resources, sustained donor support in building technical capacity, and favourable macroeconomic conditions since the early 2000s, the sector continues to act as a bottleneck. In 2011, the lack of adequate and reliable supply of electrical power was identified as one of the most binding constraints to growth in the Partnership for Growth diagnostics report (Partnership for Growth, 2011).

The troubled development of the power sector in Tanzania may be attributable, to some extent, to the complex technical and steep financial imperatives involved in system expansion, including implementing various policies and best practice reforms. However, a retrospective sector analysis suggests that there are also considerable institutional blockages and entrenched dysfunctional (informal) institutional dynamics and processes that have played a determining role. Yet because these dynamics are often beyond the public purview, they are poorly understood or charted. This makes strategic interventions that may alter systemic challenges all the more difficult.

This chapter will thus focus on the institutional evolution of the Tanzanian power sector and will be directed towards providing a comprehensive review of the sector's extended, and ongoing, developmental challenges. The basic question to be answered is whether government's failure to implement the structural reforms that it has repeatedly committed to is due to institutional blockages or to purely technical, and possibly financial, factors. The author examines *why it has not been possible for Tanzania to move from an institutional equilibrium that does not bring about the desired sector outcomes (investment, system expansion, and improved technical performance) to one that does.*

In order to answer this question, an extensive, desk-based, analytical literature review of academic research, news reports, and primary documents was undertaken. In addition, a number of high-priority in-depth interviews were conducted with key stakeholders. This approach allowed for a methodical analysis of key features in the sector's development trajectory.

The chapter is structured in five main parts, beginning with an overview of the current structure and status of the Tanzanian power sector. A narrative account of the institutional development of the power sector is then provided, which is followed by an exploration of some of the resultant underlying political economy dynamics. In the final section, a number of conclusions are considered in parallel with potentially strategic reform interventions.

II THE TANZANIAN POWER SECTOR: STRUCTURE AND PERFORMANCE

A Institutional Structure

Despite over two decades of attempted institutional reforms, the structure of the power sector continues to most resemble that of the traditional industry model – a model that has largely been dysfunctional in Tanzania and across the region for decades.[1] Despite a period under private management contract (2002–6) and repeated policy commitments to unbundling and some privatisation, the Tanzania Electric Supply Company (TANESCO) continues to operate as a vertically integrated, state-owned de facto monopoly. Tariffs remain below cost recovery, planning has not translated into timely initiation of procurement of new power generation capacity, procurement has mostly not been transparent or competitive, and TANESCO's technical and financial performance is poor. Some so-called standard model reforms,[2] however, have been implemented – most importantly, the troubled introduction of private sector participation in generation and the establishment of an independent regulator. Tanzania is thus an exemplar of what has become known as a hybrid model, where private and public investment coexist in a sector that continues to be state dominated (Victor and Heller, 2007; Gratwick and Eberhard, 2008).

---

[1] A state-owned, vertically integrated (generation, transmission, and distribution) monopoly, regulated by the government (i.e. not an independent regulator), is considered to be the simplest form of the traditional industry model, which was the international norm from the early twenty-first century through to the 1980s (Eberhard and Godinho, 2017).

[2] At the most general level, the standard model includes the following steps: the corporatisation and commercialisation of national utilities, the introduction of competition through restructuring, privatisation, and allowing for the entry of private power producers and distributors, the establishment of independent regulatory institutions, and the creation of power markets (Bacon, 1999; Williams and Ghanadan, 2006; Victor and Heller, 2007; Gratwick and Eberhard, 2008; Jamasb et al., 2015).

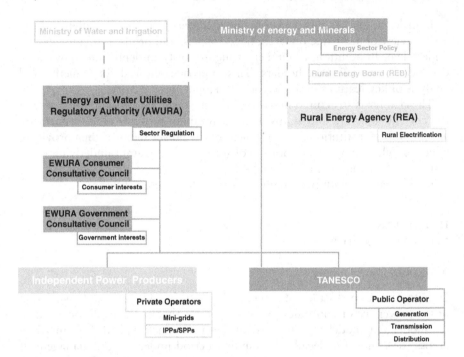

FIGURE 8.1 Tanzania power sector structure
Source: Construct by author

In this structure, depicted in Figure 8.1, the Ministry of Energy and Minerals (MEM) is responsible for policy and planning in the sector, as well as governance of TANESCO.[3] As the single buyer, TANESCO has power purchase agreements (PPAs) with independent power producers (IPPs) – including Songas, Independent Power Tanzania Ltd (IPTL), small power producers (SPPs), emergency power producers (EPPs), and the Mtwara Energy Project (formerly an off-grid generation and distribution concession). Responsibility for scaling up rural electrification was designated to the Rural Energy Authority (REA) in 2007, which also reports to MEM. Since June 2006, the Energy and Water Utilities Regulatory Authority (EWURA) has been responsible for sector regulation. It is part of the Ministry of Water and Irrigation (MWI), which gives the regulator a greater degree of (but still far from full) independence from political interests active in the energy sector. Owing to

---

[3] In October 2017, President Magufuli split MEM into two parts and appointed ministers to each. Mining was highly politicised under the Magufuli administration, with a major corruption scandal involving the previous Minister of Energy and Minerals – regarding underreporting on export volumes – leading to his dismissal earlier in 2017. In July, a new law was passed to increase mining taxes, force companies to renegotiate their contracts, and allow the state to own up to 50 per cent of mining firms.

capacity constraints in MEM and the generalised permeability of *de jure* institutional boundaries, both EWURA and TANESCO advise and play a technical support role to the ministry.

The institutional governance of the Tanzanian power sector is also shaped by national-level legislative arrangements that confer significant power on the president and those directly appointed by him. Sector planning, operation, and management are as a result highly political – rather than techno-bureaucratic – in nature. This has contributed to the disempowerment of ministry, utility, and – at the time of writing in 2017 – regulator technical staff. Most decisions relating to sector planning, capital expenditure, and structural reforms have to be ratified by various ministers and/or the president according to the law. Though legislation related to the regulator, EWURA, provides for significantly greater independence when compared with TANESCO – there are no formal provisions in the law under which a ministry or other government body can overturn any of its decisions – higher-level institutional arrangements allow this to be subverted. For example, in 2017, the prime minister, presumably under the direction of the president, reversed an EWURA-approved tariff increase and later suspended its director general.

The *de jure* institutional relationships between the political executive and other sector entities have contributed to certain norms being established, including a fairly authoritarian culture that has undermined decision-making capacity and the necessary delegation of powers to make the implementation of various policies, plans, and best practice procedures possible. This is especially true in MEM and TANESCO, though perhaps less so in EWURA and REA (Box 8.1).

Box 8.1: Authority of appointment across key entities in the power sector

MEM

The Minister, Deputy Minister, and Permanent Secretary of MEM are appointed by the president and hold office 'during the pleasure of the President' (Constitution of the United Republic of Tanzania, 1984). They can be suspended, dismissed, or reassigned at any point.

TANESCO

TANESCO is 100 per cent state owned, governed under the Public Corporations Act of 1992 and the Companies Act of 2002. A board of nine directors is responsible for the corporate governance and financial management of the company, including the appointment of management and officers. The President of the United Republic of Tanzania is responsible for appointing the chairman of the board and the chief executive, while the remaining eight board members are appointed by the Minister of Energy and Minerals. Of these eight board members, the Treasury Registrar represents the shareholder (government) and another represents MEM. The remainder are typically government officials, independent businessmen, or professionals.

EWURA

In June 2006, an independent regulator – EWURA – became operational, reporting to MWI. EWURA's chairman is appointed by the president, with the remaining six board members appointed by the Minister of MWI. Before this, MEM – in coordination with TANESCO – was responsible for tariff setting, licensing, and the regulation of the sector.

REA

REA, which became operational in 2007, is governed under the Rural Energy Act (2005) by the Rural Energy Board (REB). The Minister of Energy and Minerals is responsible for selecting the REB's board members and the board chairman, from recommendations provided by recognised organisations and the board, respectively. The REB's members are representative of sector stakeholders, with strict rules around representation set out in the 2005 Act. The REB is responsible for appointing the REA's Director General and the management and oversight of the REA.

However, it is not only hierarchical and somewhat authoritarian norms that have contributed to a lack of efficacy among staff in MEM and TANESCO. Undue political influence and involvement in planning and procurement, unchecked by a disempowered technical and managerial staff, has also allowed for corruption in the sector on a grand scale (Gray, 2015). Most notoriously, the procurement of (and ongoing contract with) IPTL, the Richmond (later Dowans, then Symbion) EPP in 2006, and other EPP contracts in 2011 were allegedly brokered between top public officials and their patrons. At the time of writing in 2017, several moves against regulatory independence provide a warning against assuming that strong legislation is enough to withstand deep institutional dynamics and powerful political economy interests.

B Power Sector Performance

The stunted institutional evolution of the power sector since the 1990s is mirrored by its performance and development trajectory, which has not been able to keep up with economic growth and demand. While net generation capacity has tripled to reach a current scale of just over 1.3 GW (gigawatts), high population and economic growth rates have meant that per capita capacity has only increased marginally (from 19.6 to 24.2 MW (megawatts) per capita – lower even than regional averages). Meanwhile, consumption per capita has increased at a slow and steady rate of 2.4 per cent annually since 1990, just passing the 100 kWh (kilowatt hour) per capita mark by 2014. Even if recent reports of a substantial uptick – to 137 kWh per capita in 2016 – are confirmed, current consumption rates still fall far short of the upper bound for lower-income countries – 490 kWh per capita – with real implications for Tanzania's ambitions to achieve middle-income status by 2025.

Electricity supply in Tanzania is persistently unstable, often inadequate, and insecure. In addition to the challenges of attracting sufficient investment at the necessary pace and stubbornly optimistic system expansion planning, Tanzania's continued (though reduced) reliance on hydropower leaves the country vulnerable to severe droughts that have recurred with some regularity, in 1994–5, 2005–6, and 2011–13. This has necessitated contracting (at different times) over 300 MW of short-term oil based EPPs during times of supply crisis, at significant cost to the power utility and government balance sheet.

Owing to the high coping costs associated with drought periods, the sector's financial equilibrium has remained precarious. The IPP IPTL, along with private EPPs Richmond/Dowans/Symbion and others running on imported liquid fuel, has undercut improvements in supply security by financially debilitating TANESCO at times of drought or under the pressure of peak demand. Dependence on liquid fuel imports and gas (which is denominated in USD) has also brought greater currency and fuel price shock exposure. Political pressures around tariff increases have also been a challenge, especially considering TANESCO's dependence on external sources of finance for system expansion – by 2013, 80 per cent of TANESCO's total assets was financed by liabilities (loans, grants, trade payables), having increased from 40 per cent in 2007 – and the government's policy ambivalence on private sector participation. This has made it difficult for the beleaguered utility to invest in system expansion or offer a risk profile favourable to investors. This has only been exacerbated by TANESCO's difficulty in implementing utility management and operations best practice – in part owing to political conflicts and weak accountability mechanisms.

Given the prevalence of supply-side crises, the weak financial standing of the utility, and general governance challenges, it is perhaps not surprising that progress in advancing electricity access has been slow. As will be discussed later, access rates remained stagnant between the early 1960s and 1990 – at between 5 and 7 per cent. Since the 1990s, grid access rates have gradually increased, reaching between 14 and 16 per cent in 2014. This figure was around 20 to 25 per cent in 2017, with 30 to 40 per cent living in proximity to the grid.[4] Urban users have been the primary beneficiaries. Recent advances can be attributed to institutional reforms in the mid-2000s, increasing interest from the donor community in funding electrification programmes, technological developments offered by solar power for off-grid and mini-grid solutions, and growing political demands from citizens.

Yet, for Tanzanian electricity consumers, persistent supply insecurity has meant that load-shedding is an everyday occurrence, which – when the supply–demand balance is pushed to the brink, as at the outset of the 2011–13 drought – can reach up to eighteen hours a day. Unsurprisingly, many businesses and private consumers that can afford to do so have backup generators to bridge the gap. The cost of supply insecurity to the economy, as well as individual households and businesses, thus goes beyond unserved demand or even the costs associated with emergency supply. Mitigating its persistence is critical to sector development.

From a technical perspective, the disappointing development of Tanzania's power sector reflects planning and procurement failures over the longer term, including inadequate strategies to attract investment or affordable finance, and poor management of external shock events and supply-side crises. Critically, Tanzania has made little progress in introducing and enforcing best practice models of institutional restructuring as relates to the separation of planning, procurement, and investment functions, applying least-cost planning principles, or implementing transparent and competitive procurement processes.

The structural, institutional, and performance characteristics of Tanzania's power sector are indicative of a hybrid or dual market. According to Victor and Heller (2007, p. 30), this is 'not a waystation to the standard textbook model but, rather, a stable equilibrium outcome'. They go on to explain that 'while not the most economically efficient outcome, the dual market arises and is held in place by strong political forces that favour a system in which parts of power generation and delivery are profitable even as other parts are plagued by non-payment, inadequate investment, and economically inefficient operation' (Victor and Heller, 2007, p. 30). In order to understand, and possibly address, those challenges identified from the technical perspective, it is thus imperative to go further to the institutional and political economy core of the current dysfunctional equilibrium. The remainder of the chapter turns to this task, beginning with an overview of the institutional evolution of the sector, before moving to a political economy analysis of key features and outcomes.

---

[4] It should be noted that Tanzania typically uses the following equation for calculating access, which provides an overestimation of access rates – such as the 41 per cent reported in the 2016 Power Sector Master Plan or the 67 per cent reported by REA.
- Power accessible population= Σ accessible village * Population in the village
- Electrification rate = Power accessible population / Total population * 100

III THE TANZANIAN POWER SECTOR'S INSTITUTIONAL DEVELOPMENT

When charting the institutional development of the Tanzanian electricity supply industry – from its inception during the colonial era, through independence and the nationalisation of electricity assets and industry, a period of extended structural adjustment and attempted market-oriented reform, to the return of more centralised governance in the present day – certain institutional features and patterns emerge.

The spatial distribution of electricity continues to reflect colonial/extractive interests, with most of the population still without access to power. Despite numerous attempts at commercialisation, including rationalising tariffs, staff numbers, and establishing the financial viability of TANESCO, the sector continues to place pressure on the national budget, while TANESCO accumulates debt and arrears. Supply is insecure, as disconnected policy, planning, and procurement have undermined timely system expansion and the exploitation of natural gas reserves – meaning that poorly maintained and balanced network infrastructure, volatile liquid fuel prices, and variable hydrological conditions persistently threaten availability. According to the World Bank enterprise surveys, businesses report nine outages per month (on average), lasting around six and a half hours. The situation is likely worse in rural areas. The pervasion of certain (African) socialist ideological tenets in policy discourse has been more or less constant since independence, specifically around the public good attributes of electricity, the need for state intervention and governance in the sector to ensure social and developmental objectives, deep concern around private sector involvement and 'foreign' interference, and a certain leaning toward statist models. Corruption, rent-seeking, and patronage have been present at least since the mid- to late 1970s. However, this is a politically sensitive issue and blame is typically shifted away from the dominant ruling party to 'aberrant' individuals acting in the sector, corrupting private sector interests, or to international actors. This has impacted human resource capacity development in the sector, as a number of high-level corruption scandals have led to rounds of dismissals, especially in government.

In this section, a chronological narrative account considers the development of some of these features – with special attention to the more recent period of attempted market-oriented power sector reforms and the political economy of sector outcomes.

A Early Institutional Infrastructure in the Power Sector – The Colonial Period

Electric power was first introduced in Dar es Salaam, Tanzania (then Tanganyika) in 1908 by German colonialists in the service of the railway workshops there, as well as predominantly European parts of the city. Following the transition to British rule in 1920, the electricity supply industry was governed by the colonial Government Electricity Department. It was then privatised in 1931, with the establishment of the private Dar es Salaam and District Electric Supply Company and TANESCO utilities. Over the decades that followed, these utilities grew, with TANESCO exporting power to neighbouring Kenya. The legacy of the colonial export crops and mineral extraction in the region is still evident in the national grid, which correlates with the colonial railway system in East Africa. From a technical standpoint, this imbalance could stress the system as it expands. From a political standpoint, the persistent differences in services provided in different regions could become a political issue if they push internal migration patterns that are difficult to navigate socially.

B From Ujamaa to Structural Adjustment – 1960s–1980s

After gaining independence in 1961, Tanzania became a one-party socialist state under the leadership of President Julius Nyerere (1962–85) and his political party, the TANU (later CCM). The new regime set out to nationalise industry and commercial enterprise, which became national policy with the 1967 Arusha Declaration, and to establish a socialist command control economy. In the lead up to this, the government began the process of nationalising both power utilities in 1964 through an agreement to buy the East African Power and Lighting Company's TANESCO shares over a period of ten years. Over the same time, TANESCO was established as the sole national power utility, responsible for generation, transmission, and distribution in Tanzania.

The Tanzanian power sector became a favoured recipient of financial and development aid in the form of official development assistance (ODA) from the World Bank and the International Monetary Fund (IMF), as well as from bilateral institutions such as the Swedish International Development Cooperation Agency (SIDA), the Norwegian Agency for Development Cooperation, the Japan International Cooperation Agency, and others. This assistance was substantial when compared with other countries in the region, with the total ODA received in 1980 being double the regional average – a significant proportion of which went to the power sector (Edwards, 2012). In addition to the provision of financial and technical support in various system development projects, sponsored training programmes were advanced to foster local expertise in the sector. Generation capacity increased steadily into the early 1970s (reaching 266 MW in 1975),[5] and sales increased at around 10 per cent per year. Despite the socialist agenda, electricity access remained low, at around 7 per cent.[6]

---

[5] Compared with other Least Developed Countries (LDCs) with similar populations in the 1970s, Tanzania's installed capacity was dwarfed. For example, Venezuela's installed capacity was already above 16,000 MW and Malaysia above 3,000 MW.

[6] Access rates were on a par with much of the rest of the sub-Saharan Africa region (barring a few outliers, such as Senegal – 36 per cent), but lower than LDCs in the rest of the world, such as India (16 per cent), Mexico (~50 per cent), or Korea (95 per cent).

However, external factors, including the 1973 and 1979 oil shocks, the 1979 Ugandan War, commodity price volatility, and hydrological variability, put undue strain on the economy and power sector. In addition, ODA decreased dramatically in the early 1980s, primarily in response to an emerging divergence in views on Tanzania's socialist development policies and what was seen to be excessive public spending.

The state and many state-owned enterprises (SOEs) became increasingly inefficient owing to a lack of accountability, inadequate incentives, and the resultant pervasion of rent-seeking behaviour and corruption. The formal command economy began to collapse, progressively supplanted by informal and black-market economies. The institutions built in the first decades of independence had depended on the centralisation of political and economic power in the state and the party, through which resources (including jobs in government and SOEs) were distributed to the population. However, lacking sufficient state income, formal checks and balances, political competition, transparency, and certain civic freedoms, the system was vulnerable to external shocks and internal inefficiencies and malfeasance. By the early 1980s, Tanzania was rated as one of the poorest countries in the world, and corruption was becoming a national issue (World Bank, 1998; Heilman and Ndumbaro, 2002; Gray, 2015).

Around this time, there was a shift in donors' lending policies. Led by the Bretton Woods institutions, the provision of aid, loans, and other forms of development assistance became increasingly conditional on meeting a set of market-oriented macroeconomic policy prescriptions. These policies stood in opposition to the *Ujamaa* model, while because they were externally driven, they provoked overt hostility from President Nyerere and many in the ruling CCM party. In a bid to access financial support without losing independence, Nyerere launched the National Economic Survival Programme (NESP) in 1981, followed by NESP II in 1982, and then a local version of the IMF's Structural Adjustment Programmes (SAPs) in 1983. These programmes, however, failed to satisfy donor conditions.

In 1985, Nyerere stepped down as president – preserving his legacy of *Ujamaa*, by not publicly acquiescing to market reforms. His preferred successor, Ali Hassa Mwinyi (1985–95), was considered to be a moderate supporter of the liberalisation policies that the country would need to implement to regain access to aid. Once in power, he initiated structural adjustment reforms under the IMF's Economic Recovery Programme (ERP) (1986–9) and the Enhanced Structural Adjustment Facility Programme (ESAF, 1989–92) with some success, initially renewing donor confidence. However, considerable resistance to reforms continued behind the closed doors of the CCM, where those with vested economic or political (including ideological) interests pushed against or subverted interventions, specifically privatisation.

In the power sector, these crises further impaired the underperforming traditional industry model. Unable to capitalise on economies of scale, reduce investment costs through securing low-interest long-term bonds, or steadily expand the system to meet demand, TANESCO's financial and operational performance deteriorated rapidly. Generation capacity and sales were especially affected, with TANESCO's financial ills further compounded by the mounting debts owed to the utility by the government (including SOEs) and rampant power theft (with system losses above 20 per cent). The initiation of macroeconomic stabilisation policies in 1986 pushed the utility into an even more dire situation, as currency devaluation vastly increased the burden of foreign-denominated loans, as well as operational and investment costs. As the Tanzanian government fell further behind the Weberian ideal of a techno-bureaucratic modern state, which underlies the traditional model, vested political and economic interests took advantage at every level.

C Power Sector Reforms – On Again, Off Again

1 Conditionality and Standard Model Reforms

By the beginning of the 1990s, generation capacity stood at only 300 MW,[7] access had remained almost unchanged at between 5 and 7 per cent (according to the Ministry of Water, Energy and Minerals (1992) and the World Bank (2020), respectively), and technical and non-technical losses were above 20 per cent.[8] The sector was not self-financing and suffered substantial commercial losses. The institutional equilibrium – the rules governing tariff setting, collection, operations, planning, procurement, governance, management, and oversight – had become thoroughly dysfunctional. In Tanzania, the 'basic sectoral problem' identified in the seminal 1993 policy paper *The World Bank's Role in the Power Sector*, in which what has become known as the 'standard reform model' was first iterated, seems cogent (World Bank, 1993).

The basic sectoral problem relates to undue government interference in those day-to-day organisational and operational matters that should be under utility control. Such interference undermines the accountability of those responsible for day-to-day management functions. It has influenced procurement decisions, mitigated against least-cost fuel choice, resulted in an inability to raise power tariffs to meet revenue requirements, restricted utilities' access

---

[7] Where some LDCs were growing at an average rate of between 5 and 16 per cent a year between the early 1970s and late 1980s (e.g. Malaysia ~10 per cent p.a., South Korea ~13 per cent p.a., India ~8 per cent p.a., Venezuela, Pakistan, and Brazil at ~9 per cent p.a.), Tanzania only managed to increase generation at a rate of less than 1 per cent p.a.

[8] Losses refer to the amounts of electricity injected into the transmission and distribution grids that are not paid for by users. Total losses have two components, technical and non-technical. Technical losses occur naturally and consist mainly of power dissipation in electricity system components such as transmission and distribution lines, transformers, and measurement systems. Non-technical losses are caused by actions external to the power system, and consist primarily of electricity theft, non-payment by customers, and errors in accounting and record-keeping (World Bank, 2009).

to foreign exchange, mandated low managerial and technical salaries that are tied to low civil service levels, and promoted excessive staffing and political patronage. These problems have in turn, in many cases, brought about generally inadequate utility management and organisation; lack of accountability; flight of experienced and capable staff owing to uncompetitive employment conditions; weak planning; inefficient operation and maintenance; high technical and non-technical losses; and weak financial monitoring, controls, and collection (World Bank, 1993, p. 33).

As in many countries in the region, loans and grants in the power sector soon became conditional on the implementation of standard model institutional and structural reforms that were being prescribed as the solution to this problem. The primary components of standard model reforms include the commercialisation and corporatisation of electricity utilities, the introduction of independent regulation, unbundling vertically integrated utilities, and liberalising the sector to allow for private sector participation (Bacon, 1999; Hunt, 2002; Williams and Ghanadan, 2006; Victor and Heller, 2007; Gratwick and Eberhard, 2008). Through such reforms, the traditional industry model in developing countries would be supplanted with a model that allowed for competition, institutionalised checks and balances, alternative sources of investment, separation of and specialisation in sector functions, greater transparency, and transfer of private sector commercial expertise and resources.

Figure 8.2 presents an overview timeline of reform interventions. In the remainder of this section, we consider different phases in the reform agenda and some of the determinants of the outcome of various components of standard model reforms.

2 First Steps towards Standard Model Reforms

Needing to re-contextualise the role of the energy sector in national development and reconcile sector-level policy with the macroeconomic policy shifts of the SAPs and the thrust of the then-emergent standard model, the 1992 National Energy Policy was produced. The policy opened the sector to private participation, stating that 'private electricity generation and distribution will be encouraged' in areas where TANESCO had not yet developed power infrastructure (Government of Tanzania, 1992). It also provided for the establishment of a rural electrification fund, which – it was envisioned – would be supported by community involvement in the style of *Ujamaa*. Already in the midst of the first drought-related power shortages and load-shedding, significant emphasis was put on resource diversification away from hydropower. Like many of the later policies and legislation, the 1992 policy tentatively opened the door for market-oriented and governance reforms without actually providing a comprehensive set of actionable next steps and without reducing the scope for political interference in the sector.

Of course, weak or absent policy commitments in developing countries had informed the basis of the conditional lending agenda behind standard model

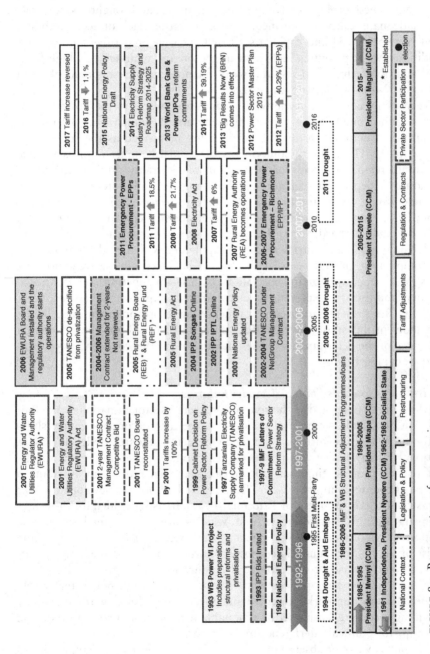

FIGURE 8.2 Power sector reform experience
Source: Construct by authors

Box 8.2: Songas – Tanzania's first competitive and transparent IPP

Gas-based power generation at the Songo Songo gas field had been identified as a least-cost option in the 1991 Power Sector Master Plan. However, neither the government nor TANESCO had the necessary funds or expertise to develop gas-to-power generation alone. In 1993, MEM invited sixteen companies to bid for the 60 MW gas project at Songo Songo under a build, own, operate, and transfer arrangement – thus initiating the first competitive IPP process – with support from the World Bank. However, no credit enhancement was provided (despite the poor investment environment), bidders were only given six months to submit their bids, and the plant size was small by international standards. As a result, only two bids were submitted and Over-the-Counter Market – a joint venture between Ocelot Energy Inc. and TransCanada Pipelines – was awarded the tender in 1994 and established the project company Songas. Negotiations were protracted, with additional equity partners coming on board in 1995 (Tanzania Petroleum Development Corporation and TANESCO) and then again in 1996 (Tanzania Development Finance Company Ltd, International Finance Corporation, Deutsche Investitions und Entwicklungsgesellschaft, and Commonwealth Development Corporation).

---

reforms. Unsurprisingly, the World Bank's Power VI project thus not only provided for the construction of the 180 MW Kihansi hydroelectric power plan, but also included sector reforms in its objectives. Explicit objectives included supporting the utility in preparing for and initiating restructuring and privatisation, and the development and operation of private gas generation at Songo Songo. The 1993 International Development Association (IDA) loan agreement for the Power VI project was made conditional on TANESCO entering into a subsidiary loan agreement with the government and committing to the conditions set out in the loan – this could be considered the first instance where the government committed to standard model reforms (International Development Association and United Republic of Tanzania, 1993). These included adhering to specific financial covenants and to the principles of international, competitive, and transparent procurement practices, the corporatisation and commercialisation of TANESCO's operations, undertaking an asset evaluation study and a tariff study, implementing the recommendations thereof and regularly updating both thereafter, and enforcing a plan of action for the recovery of overdue accounts from government agencies and parastatals. In addition, the government committed to undertaking and then implementing the recommendations of a privatisation study and to the development of a gas-to-power IPP at Songo Songo (Box 8.2).

In order to mitigate the severe effects of drought-related load-shedding while the Songo Songo IPP was being negotiated, SIDA provided TANESCO with the funds to procure two 18 MW Open Cycle Gas Turbine (OCGT) plants at Ubungo and committed to covering operational (mainly fuel) costs for two years – with the expectation that Songas would be online by the end of that period. The government was able to procure a further two 35 MW OCGT plants through the World Bank facility. With this additional support, and a focused Songas procurement process, it might have been possible to emerge from the drought with improved capacity at competitive costs. Yet, although these plants mitigated the effects of drought-related shortages and provided much-needed space for strategic sector planning, specifically the Songas procurement process, it did not allay the sense of emergency that load-shedding had brought about.

There is evidence to suggest that certain interested parties seized upon this sense of panic to advance a specific agenda,[9] interrupting efforts to rationalise the sector by entertaining unsolicited bids – most prominently, a proposal for the procurement of 100 MW from a plant that would be built by IPTL (Box 8.3).

Box 8.3: IPTL – the dark horse IPP and the subversion of procurement best practice

The IPTL project was not planned for or necessary. According to the Power Sector Master Plan, it was based on hugely overstated investment costs and expensive, outdated technology. Nonetheless, it was defended as 'South–South cooperation', a politically shrewd cover as it played on Tanzanian's discomfort with Western (capitalist) interest's involvement in the country since the initiation of the SAPs. It was also packaged as an 'emergency' supplier, allowing for a direct and opaque procurement process. Despite serious doubt being cast on the economic and financial viability of the PPA by some concerned state officials, TANESCO's board – under the sway of key government officials – signed the twenty-year PPA in May 1995 (ahead of the national elections). This was done without the consent or knowledge of the World Bank, breaking a covenant of the Power VI project.

---

[9] Like later controversial deals in the energy sector, IPTL exposed 'similar patterns of contention within the ruling party and links between senior party figures and domestic and international business' (Gray, 2015, p. 389). According to Brian Cooksy (2017), the IPTL deal hinged on the brokering efforts of local businessman, James Rugemalira (IPTL's local partner and 30 per cent shareholder), who forged a path for the unsolicited bid from Merchmar (a Malaysian company piggybacking on former Malaysian Prime Minister Mohamed's campaign of 'South–South' cooperation) – using whatever means necessary to sway public officials, including through paying bribes. It should be noted that this deal, again like later instances of grand corruption, was negotiated ahead of a national election where a new CCM president would be elected to run.

Creating a rift with the World Bank, the signing of the IPTL PPA resulted in delays in the Songas deal – which ironically proved to be one of the most cost-effective gasses IPPs on the continent, in large part owing to the competitive negotiation process of its PPA. IPTL, meanwhile, is one of the most expensive and has been detrimental to the financial sustainability of TANESCO and the sector as a whole.

While the costs of corruption and maladministration now widely associated with IPTL are substantial, the derailment of planning, management, and procurement processes is considered by some to be the more detrimental casualty of the fallout that ensued. The opaque, uncompetitive, and corrupt deal-making pioneered in the IPTL deal would be repeated in later procurement processes in the power sector – to the detriment of its financial sustainability and developmental mandate.

The IPTL deal was one of many incidences where the government diverged from national plans and policies in the early to mid-1990s and where evidence pointed to behind-the-scenes politicking. The implementation of conditions set out in the IMF's ERP (1986–89) and the ESAF (1989–92) had led to fundamental changes in the political economy landscape. Rent-seeking opportunities had opened in areas where the flux of new liberalisation and privatisation policies had created the space for vested or emerging interests to intervene directly in the processes of government. At the same time, the reintroduction of multiparty politics in 1992 created a more competitive environment for clientelism, as a larger and less cohesive group of political and economic interests vied for power in the lead up to the first multiparty elections in 1995. These developments led to a withdrawal of donor support in 1994.

3 Standard Model Reforms after Embargo

Benjamin Mkapa was elected as the CCM presidential candidate in the lead up to elections. A relative party outsider seen to be untainted by scandal, Mkapa's campaign promised change, decisive action against corruption, and economic growth and development. Upon winning the 1995 elections, the Mkapa administration prioritised rehabilitating relations with donors, anti-corruption interventions, and refocusing reforms. At the time, development assistance accounted for 20–30 per cent of GDP – there was no alternative.

In the power sector, this meant committing to more concrete steps to structural reform in line with donor conditions. According to the 1996 IMF ESAF, the restructuring and privatisation of public utilities would be accorded the highest priority over the 1996–9 ESAF loan period. In 1997, the government explicitly committed to restructuring and privatising TANESCO in a letter to the IMF and specified TANESCO for privatisation under the Parastatal Sector Reform Commission (PSRC) – meaning that TANESCO was no longer exempt from the law governing the transformation of other parastatals. This move irrevocably tied reforms to the ultimate privatisation of a public sector utility, a concept that was not only ideologically incongruent with the still-dominant socialist paradigm, but was also well on the way to becoming synonymous with corruption. This had a damaging effect on the feasibility of later reforms.

Over the following years, these commitments would be reiterated in IMF letters of intent while policy and legislation were in draft. In 1999, a Policy White Paper on the Restructuring and Divestiture Strategy for the Electricity Sector was submitted to and approved by Cabinet. Though the policy document and Cabinet decision are not publicly available, the policy commitments were articulated in a 1999 IMF ESAF policy paper: they included the vertical and horizontal unbundling of TANESCO and the establishment of a neutral system and market operator, a centralised purchasing agency, and an independent regulator (IMF, 1999). According to the policy paper, the strategy would be implemented by year-end 2000.

This, however, was thoroughly undermined by the government's failure to fulfil important covenants designed to improve the financial, management, and institutional development of the sector in preparation for reforms. Crucially, the government consistently failed to support TANESCO on the issue of non-payment by preventing the utility from cutting power to defaulting customers – a subsequent report on the issue found that the problem was 75 per cent political (World Bank, 2003). In addition, no new legislation or policy was introduced, little stakeholder engagement was conducted, and there was little else that would suggest that the government intended to implement the ambitious strategy laid out in the ESAF paper.

After seven years of attempted (including internal) reforms, which were initiated in 1992, TANESCO was still an overstaffed, poorly managed, and financially insecure utility that, despite having strong technical capacity by Tanzanian standards, lacked commercial culture and autonomy. Toward the end of the Power VI project, World Bank supervision missions thus recommended that a new management team be recruited for TANESCO during the transition to privatisation, to which the government – at the level of the president – committed in late 2000. In addition, a number of 'next step' interventions were pressed for through the IDA Programmatic Structural Adjustment loan, as well as a number of other donor programmes. Two studies by international consultants were initiated – the first by Mercados (released in 2001) and the second by Stone and Webster (released in 2003). In 2001, the government passed the EWURA Act, providing the basis for the establishment of the independent regulator. In the same year, the PSRC initiated a competitive and transparent recruitment process for a two-year management contract for TANESCO.

4 Privatisation: One Step Forward – TANESCO under Private Management

In January 2002, the PSRC awarded the two-year TANESCO management contract to NET Group Solutions – a firm from South Africa. The lack of genuine political and public support surfaced almost immediately, when the start of the contract was delayed owing to push back from the general public and TANESCO staff. The Minister for Energy and Minerals and TANESCO board openly cast doubt on the selection process and forty-six MPs called for clarification on the issue in parliament – undermining the legitimacy of the contract (BBC, 2002; Kapika, 2013). Tanzanians also viewed the contract as the first step towards the privatisation of a strategic public sector utility, which was an ideologically fraught issue. Meanwhile, TANESCO staff unions threatened sabotage unless a labour agreement was secured before the initiation of the contract, fearing the inevitable staff rationalisation process. Despite this push back, the NET Group management team – consisting of only four resident managers – took over operations in May 2002. They required a police escort onto TANESCO premises.

Upon assuming management, the team first prioritised gaining the support of staff: a labour agreement was developed by TANESCO and accepted by the union later that year. From this point, staff relations were secure. In their activities, the management team focused on improving revenue collection and utility information systems, enforcing collections from sensitive public offices, and rationalising staff. In these activities, the management team was successful – monthly revenue increased from USD 10–12 million to USD 16 million per month by 2004, approximately 20 per cent of the staff were amicably retrenched, and reporting systems were improved. The first contract was viewed as a categorical success by the donor community. However, broad-based political and public support was still lacking despite high-level, somewhat behind the scenes, backing from President Mkapa.

Under pressure from the World Bank, the management contract was renewed for a further two years in 2004. In the contract extension, the team was more explicitly tasked with translating revenue gains into improvements in performance. Monthly revenue doubled during the second contract, increasing to USD 22–4 million. This was driven by improved collections – especially from large, politically sensitive customers such as the national police, post office, and Zanzibar – as well as increased tariffs. The tariff structure was rationalised by removing the cross-subsidisation between consumers, with industrial tariffs at −28 per cent and residential/light commercial tariffs at +39 per cent. The lifeline tariff was also reduced from 100 kWh to 50 kWh.

A significant portion of the increased revenue, however, was absorbed by the IPPs coming online – IPTL was commissioned in 2002 and Songas in 2004.[10]

---

[10] TANESCO began to purchase power from the IPPs, with per unit costs higher than their older plants.

With the onset of the 2005–6 drought, the utility was compelled to use IPTL and Songas as baseload plants, both of which were more expensive than originally anticipated at the start of the contract in 2002. This put the utility back into a dire financial situation. The management team was thus not able to invest much in network infrastructure and, critically, did not pay sufficient attention to customer service and connections. This meant that private sector participation was not translating into better quality or more reliable electricity services for most Tanzanians. When the management team reaped substantial 'success fees' for its interventions, it only added to public and political distaste.

These shortcomings were in part attributable to the management team itself, the misaligned incentive structure of the contract, and external conditions. However, political interference played a role as well, compounded by tenuous lines of accountability between the TANESCO board, MEM and other ministries, the PSRC, President Mkapa, consumers, the public and the media, and donors. There have been reports that politically connected members on the TANESCO board actively sabotaged the contract (through exercising their veto power, stalling decision-making processes, or providing misleading information to the political executive) in order to then be able to prove that the management contract, or privatisation more broadly, was a bad idea. The management team was certainly not operating in a wholly supportive political environment, and tensions began to mount.

5 Privatisation: Two Steps Back – TANESCO's Despecification and Return to Public Governance

In 2005, just ahead of the elections, President Mkapa despecified TANESCO – backtracking on plans to privatise the utility. In 2006, acting against the recommendations of a 2005 report conducted by the Presidential Privatisation Review Committee, incoming President Kikwete decided against renewing the management contract. It is clear that, under this contract, many of the informal institutional arrangements had been challenged – including political involvement in tariff setting, staffing, collections, and procurement. With these two steps, the sector and utility governance reverted to its previous institutional structure.

Coincidentally, this recreated a situation where crisis (drought) conditions created an opening for corrupt political and economic interests to again craft an IPP deal around the time of national elections, bypassing power sector development plans and the principle of competitive and transparent procurement. Many suspect that the 2005 election – won by CCM's candidate, Jakaya Kikwete – was funded by faction benefactors that orchestrated the infamous Richmond IPP deal. Like the IPTL deal in 1995, it had disastrous and long-lasting consequences for TANESCO and the stability of the sector as a whole. It is worth noting that the management team actively resisted the Richmond deal (Box 8.4).

Box 8.4: The Richmond EPP IPP – another scandal

The Richmond Development Company was awarded an expensive 100 MW power deal during the 2006 power shortages under controversial circumstances. It then turned out that the company had neither the technical expertise nor the capacity to meet its contractual agreements. In late 2006, Dowans Holdings took over the contract and eventually provided the agreed 100 MW – after drought conditions had abated.

Despite Richmond, and then Dowans, not being able to supply the agreed amount of power in the agreed timeframe, TANESCO had to pay a steep daily 'take-or-pay' capacity charge to the company (Kapika, 2013). This caused acrimony in the media and parliament. Toward the end of 2007, a Select Committee was established to investigate the deal. In February 2008, the committee's report was presented in parliament and broadcast on live TV. This led to the resignation of the prime minister at the time, Edward Lowassa (2005–8), as well as the current and previous Ministers of Energy and Minerals, Msabaha and Karamagi, who were implicated in the scandal. President Kikwete then dissolved Cabinet. In addition to the predictable disruption following the December 2005 elections and a change in the presidency, the Richmond scandal saw three different ministers serving between 2006 and 2009, as well as multiple shuffles among technical staff. This thoroughly destabilised the sector.

This matter was not dealt with in the courts, but rather internally by the government and within the CCM party. Lowassa would later compete as a opposition presidential candidate in 2015. The lack of policy continuity between regimes, compounded by the shuffling of ministers and technical staff (including permanent secretaries), has been a near insurmountable obstacle to maintaining momentum in sector development and reform interventions. Relations with development partners – especially those such as the World Bank which were supporting reforms – also suffered over this period.

---

6 Some Positive Developments – Policy, Regulation, and Rural Energy
Notwithstanding the circumstances noted here, this period did see some other important reform steps implemented. To begin with, the second National Energy Policy was released in 2003. This commits to the principles of competitive, private sector involvement, and efficiency, and to establishing a new governance system by 'differentiating the roles for (a) policy making and legislative functions carried out by Government and the Parliament; (b) the regulatory functions carried out by an independent regulator; and (c) other functions carried out by public and private operators' (Ministry of Energy and Minerals, 2003). Once again, however, much of the policy was far from actionable, and sticking to the principles has been a challenge.

Rural energy was also given special attention in the 2003 policy, leading to the enactment of the Rural Energy Act in 2005, which established the REB and the Rural Energy Fund. Rural energy, however, did not benefit from much political interest or budgetary support in at least the first five years following these interventions. On the one hand, this reflects a similar state of affairs to that in neighbouring countries – where grid-extension was viewed as too expensive, off-grid was not yet attractive, and rural electrification had not become a politically salient issue. On the other hand, CCM was also doing very well when it came to public opinion polls and at the ballot box – meaning that the political pressures behind issues such as rural electrification were not yet determining national policy priorities.

EWURA – the independent regulator – finally became operational in June 2006. Intriguingly, this was the same month that the Richmond deal was signed. While delays were likely by default rather than design for the most part, in the case of EWURA and other components set out in policy or law, certain interests benefited from the regulatory gap and may have contributed to holding up processes at key junctures. TANESCO (an unregulated *de facto* monopoly) certainly had an interest in delaying the effective functioning of EWURA, as did those involved in the IPTL and Richmond deals.

7 Public Governance, Independent Regulation, and Political Interference – An Incomplete Reform Model

Having repealed the management contract and backtracked on privatisation, the new Kikwete administration had a clear interest in 'proving' that the state-owned model could work if it was to maintain control over the sector. When TANESCO reverted to local management in 2007, the more than capable Dr Idris Rashidi, formerly involved in reforms in the banking sector, was appointed managing director. During his three-year contract, Rashidi built capacity in the utility, creating and filling three new positions with competent staff – chief financial officer, chief internal auditor, and chief information officer. Remaining senior management positions were filled through competitive recruitment processes. Together with the senior management team, Rashidi introduced performance measurements into the human resources system with balanced score cards, launched a staff development programme, and amended relationships with energy-intensive users (anchor customers). He also arranged a USD 300 million syndicated loan, with the support of the government, which allowed TANESCO to clear the debt backlog, introduce performance-based staff remuneration, and improve billing and metering systems. Hydrological conditions were also in TANESCO's favour over this period, which reduced the cost of generation. In 2008, TANESCO registered a profit. Other metrics of utility performance, however, worsened. Transmission and distribution losses peaked in 2009, collection rates – which had improved considerably under the management contract – decreased dramatically (from ~95 to ~56 per cent) as politically connected customers forced to pay during the management contract slipped into old patterns of politically condoned non-payment, and access rates, which had increased from 10.5 to 12.6 per cent under the management contract, actually dipped back down to 11.2 per cent in 2009 (World Bank, 2020).

This mixed performance underscores the vulnerability of public governance to political interference in a country where the political economy system is prone to using publicly owned companies for rent-seeking and patronage, even where corporatisation efforts attempt to 'ring-fence' such interests. Three different ministers served between 2006 and 2009. Rashidi has said that it was difficult for him to understand the 'special rights and interests' the ministry and the board had in management decisions. Though there have rarely been public confrontations between different factions operating in TANESCO and the government, the period when Rashidi was managing director proved an exception. Despite a stellar performance, his contract was not renewed, and more 'politically suitable' candidates were appointed from 2010.

While these tensions played out at the utility, EWURA was steadily building capacity and authority as regulator. The five-year delay in operationalising EWURA had involved a dispute between development partners and the government about where the regulator should be placed. Eventually, it was agreed that it would fall under MWI, as advised by the World Bank. This allowed the regulator a greater degree of autonomy from MEM and distance from undue political influence. The pace of EWURA's development reflects the soundness of the 2001 EWURA Act, significant support from development partners, the realisation of existing technical capacity, and a suitable degree of independence from the government.

8 The Resurrection of the Reform Agenda

In June 2008, it seemed as if reforms would be resurrected when the Electricity Act was passed, replacing the 1957 Electricity Ordinance Amendment. The Act was preceded by a Power Sector Reform Strategy in 2007, which is not publicly available. In relation to regulation, the 2008 Electricity Act further delineated policy and regulatory roles between MEM and EWURA. It also placed renewed emphasis on the issue of rural electrification, including certain provisions of support to the REA. Critically, the Act also provides a legislative foundation for sector restructuring – albeit a weak one. According to the Act, the minister may, in consultation with the Minister of Finance and the Authority (EWURA), restructure the electricity supply industry in order to foster competition for increased efficiency, enhance the development of private capital investment, and promote regional electricity integration – giving full power to the minister and, behind the minister, the president (The Parliament of the United Republic of Tanzania, 2008). The Act also stipulates that the minister shall within one year of the Act coming into force prepare and publish a policy for the reorganisation of the electricity market, though it also specifies that the minister can amend this policy at any time.

Though commitments to standard model reforms were made anew in 2008, it is important to note that there was a general movement away from 'privatisation' and toward public–private partnership (PPPs) during this period. The PSRC was dissolved in 2007. In 2009, the government launched a PPP policy, which was followed by the PPP Act in 2010 and the publication of PPP regulations in 2011. The idea of publicly owned projects that allow for private sector participation certainly gained traction and provided an alternative frame for reforms – one that was more compatible with the Tanzanian socialist ideology and, in the case of the power sector, vested political and economic interests. While the policy components remain similar, this shift provided reforms with a new and improved frame. Yet concrete reform interventions have yet to follow, in part because of the onset of another electricity sector crisis, triggered by another drought and exacerbated by exchange rate volatility and political instability.

In 2010, Tanzania was again hit by devastating drought. By 2011, customers could experience load-shedding of up to eighteen hours a day. As had been the case in previous periods of supply crisis, the government launched an Emergency Power Plan – adding 331 MW through short-term, emergency contracts that were neither transparent nor competitive. Under emergency procedures, EWURA approved a tariff increase of 40.29 per cent starting in January 2012. Even with the tariff increase, TANESCO was not able to bear the extra financial pressure of expensive thermal generation. By the end of 2012, accumulated arrears to IPPs, EPPs, and fuel suppliers were estimated at USD 276 million – and were forecast to increase.

9 Another Crisis, Another Election Season

The crisis prompted a bold policy response, a critical action in the lead up to the 2015 elections. The reform agenda seemed to again be resuscitated in 2013, with the politicised Big Results Now (BRN) initiative. Part policy, part party manifesto, BRN focused on bridging the gap between policy planning and effective implementation in key sectors, including energy and natural gas. BRN recommended redefining the sector strategy and structure, including the gradual restructuring of TANESCO to bring about viability to the entire system. Tanzania also mended relations with some of the bigger development partners, including the World Bank. The World Bank Power and Gas Sector Development Policy Operation programmatic loans offered financial and technical support for the government's sector reform and development policies.

At the start of 2014, a second tariff increase of 39.19 per cent was approved by EWURA in order to lift tariffs closer to cost-reflective levels, and the government agreed to retire two-thirds of EPP capacity, bringing costs down so that they could meet somewhere in the middle. TANESCO's 'financial gap' reduced slightly, though the utility was still in a precarious position. In the same year, a number of policies were approved – including the Natural Gas Policy, Petroleum Policy, and the Electricity Supply Industry Reform Strategy and Roadmap 2014–25 (ESIRSR) (Box 8.5).

Box 8.5: ESIRSR, 2014–25

In the ESIRSR, the government sets out an explicit timeline of structural reforms for the first time, including the unbundling of TANESCO's generation segment and allowing IPPs to sell directly to bulk off-takers (though paying wheeling costs) in the short term (by December 2017), the vertical unbundling of transmission and distribution in the medium term (by June 2021), and the horizontal unbundling of both distribution and generation in the long term (by June 2025). Together, BRN and the ESIRSR set the following targets for 2025: generation capacity of 10,000 MW (up from 1,500 MW), connections at 50 per cent (up from 24 per cent – this number is likely lower than reported in the ESIRSR), and the reduction of system losses to 12 per cent (from 18 per cent – though losses have been volatile in the past, soaring above 35 per cent in 2009–10).

Despite various interventions and numerous bailouts, TANESCO's financial situation remained dire while internal accounting remained relatively opaque, obscuring the impact of the injection of funds and limiting advances made in eradicating (official) operational subsidies and improving the transparency of government transfers. Planning was clearly characterised by short-term politics, rather than technically sound, long-term processes, and the lines between planning, policy, and procurement were frequently transgressed. Despite repeating commitment to the tenets of transparent and competitive processes, as well as attracting and facilitating private sector participation and investment, power projects initiated over this period lacked transparency and were bent towards publicly funded and owned models. Though EWURA's role in overseeing procurement and advising on policy and planning mitigated this to some extent, TANESCO's complex relationship with the government limited the scope of EWURA's influence. TANESCO is often treated as an extension of government – especially when it comes to procurement. While EWURA can regulate some of the formal processes, the informal processes between TANESCO and government are beyond the regulator's purview and reach. An example of this can be found in the letters between EWURA and the Ministry of Energy, which show how the government propagated an unwritten policy, according to which all future generation projects were to be PPPs (Eberhard et al., 2016, p. 196), highlighting the politics behind *de facto* policy and the weakness of *de jure* policy and regulation.

As 2015 was an election year, with the CCM again competing with a new president and facing stiff competition, the political drive behind BRN and other policies, especially those providing the basis for increased public expenditure, juxtaposed with the procurement of various power projects (such as the 308 MW Kilwa, introduced by retired public servants and a foreign investor, and the 600 MW Symbion Mtwara plant), should be interpreted with care. Political anxiety around another IPTL-related scandal – the Escrow scandal – also coloured this period, with funds pilfered through the Central Bank of Tanzania and distributed to government officials and politically connected persons in the lead up to elections. The scandal also cost Tanzania hundreds of millions of dollars of donor funding, just as the country was heading into a new administration.

10 A New Regime – Magufuli's Power

Tanzanians talk of a 'regime change' when referring to elections – despite the fact that the CCM (formerly TANU) party has been in power since independence (1961) and the fact that the country has operated as a multiparty democracy since 1992. However, this is not really a misnomer, considering the discontinuity in official policy between governments, the change in executive and technical staff following elections (even when the same president is in power), and the significant power that presidents wield when in office.

This pattern has certainly been evident in the most recent elections. In the two years that John Magufuli had been president, at the time of writing in 2017, there have been significant changes across government – indicating that long-term policy frameworks may shift considerably. Specifically, there has been a distinct movement towards more centralised governance and a state-led growth model, alongside a commitment to attracting private sector investment and industry. Whether Magufuli will be able to balance the increasingly autocratic dominant-developmental politics with the government's dependence on external sources of investment and funding is yet to be seen – especially as the natural gas economy develops. Partnerships with Chinese investors might make this possible.

Given the 'regime change', it is somewhat unsurprising that many have relegated BRN to politics and expect that the timelines and objectives of the ESIRSR will be reviewed. With a return to the idea of big government and Magufuli's reinterpretation of Nyerere's self-reliance, many doubt that TANESCO will be unbundled under the current administration. Key steps to unbundling, as set out in the ESIRSR, have already been delayed. PPP development will most likely continue to be prioritised in the generation segment, with the government maintaining a stake in (and influence over) all future projects through TANESCO. This shift is concerning given the state of the utility, which had accumulated arrears to IPPs, EPPs, and fuel suppliers to the tune of USD 490 million as of May 2016 – despite financial injections in previous years, increased tariffs, and the retirement of around two-thirds of EPP capacity.

Some actors have been able to ride recent political waves in the sector, while others have not. REA has benefited from the politicisation of access, attracting general budget support of TZS 534 billion (USD 239 million) for 2016–17 (up 50 per cent from 2015–16 and about fifty times the original budget of TZS 11 billion in 2007 – more in real terms). There are some concerns, however, over the likely inflated reporting of recent improvements in access – suggesting the influence of political (and potentially economic) interests.

EWURA, meanwhile, has managed to steadily build technical capacity. In addition to licensing and tariff adjustment, EWURA has played an important role in procuring SPPs (Odarno et al., 2017).[11] According to a recent report by the World Resources Institute (WRI), the number and installed capacity of mini-grids in Tanzania has nearly doubled since 2008, when the government introduced the SPP framework (Odarno et al., 2017). EWURA is seen to have brought sanity back into the sector, resurrecting investor confidence through the technically adroit execution of its regulatory duties. However, political pressures are mounting.

The financial standing of TANESCO has improved somewhat, and steady capacity additions are beginning to reduce supply-side risks that have plagued the utility since the 1990s. However, it is poised to fall back into old patterns as President Magufuli learns to hold the reins. Since the beginning of 2017, President Magufuli has tightened his grip – sending shockwaves through the sector. In January, he reversed the EWURA-approved 8.53 per cent tariff increase, and then fired the TANESCO managing director and demoted the deputy managing directors of transmission, distribution, and generation for implementing it. In May, he then fired the Minister of Energy and Minerals for his alleged involvement in a mining sector corruption scandal. Breaking with his predecessors, Magufuli launched criminal proceedings against individuals implicated in the IPTL deal and related Escrow scandal through the criminal system. However, his dismissal of the EWURA director general following EWURA's non-renewal of IPTL's licence suggests that his motives may not have been based on curbing corruption, but perhaps reflected some internal conflict within CCM around the IPTL deal. Then, in October, he split MEM into two separate ministries, appointing new ministers and staff to each.

With interventions in other key sectors and dramatic clampdowns on civil liberties to match, Magufuli is driving an alarmingly autocratic agenda in Tanzania. His agenda may transmute into a true developmental state model – which, as seems to be the case in Ethiopia, would depend on funding from China or similarly oriented states. This might disrupt the political economy system enough to allow for institutional development. For the time being, this

---

[11] 'Tanzania has at least 109 mini-grids, with installed capacity of 157.7 MW (exact figures are not known, because some small systems may not have registered). They serve about 184,000 customers. Sixteen of these plants are connected to the national grid; the remaining 93 operate as isolated mini grids. Not all the installed capacity goes to customer connections; some is sold to the national utility, the TANESCO. Hydro is the most common technology (49 mini-grids), although the 19 fossil fuel systems account for 93% of customer connections and almost half of total installed capacity. Mini-grid owners and operators in Tanzania include the national utility, private commercial entities, faith-based organizations, and communities' (Odarno et al., 2017, p. 7).

seems unlikely. Instead, it is likely that Tanzania will see more continuity than discontinuity in the short to medium term as the key features of the dysfunctional institutional equilibrium in the sector do not seem incongruent with Magufuli's leadership.

VI INSTITUTIONAL STRUCTURE OF THE TANZANIAN POWER SECTOR

A Political Economy of Institutional Reform and Power Sector Development

Having presented a narrative account of the institutional development of the power sector, we now turn to consider the underlying political economy dynamics – including various institutional characteristics – that have shaped the sector's development trajectory and its current dominant features. This section identifies and builds upon a few thematic areas: policy and legislation, transparency and accountability, stakeholder engagement, politics and patronage, and dominant party politics.

1 Policy and Legislation

One of the most interesting aspects of Tanzania's reform experience has been the disconnect between stated policy and implementation. The government has produced numerous policies on power sector reforms – including internal policies, which are not publicly available – but, with the exception of the 2001 EWURA Act and 2005 REA Act, policy has not been suitably translated into robust legislation. Policy is often vague, leaving the door open to interpretation, as is the legislation that follows. Considerable discretionary powers for political executives, most notably the Minister of Energy and Minerals, are maintained – making little in legislation ultimately binding. There are too few accountability mechanisms built into legislation that could really bring key directives into force. Lacking continuity in sector leadership, with a revolving door in place of committed governance in TANESCO and the ministry, this type of policy and legislation makes implementation unlikely. In addition, there is a more general pattern of miscommunication and weak coordination between ministries, departments, the utility, and the regulator – meaning that internal accountability within the sector is also low. As a result, the president and other members of the political executive continue to wield considerable power over policy implementation, including in areas such as planning, procurement, utility management, and tariff setting.

Assuming that dominant political and economic actors do not have a genuine interest in reforms – implementation would likely disrupt the privileges and resources that the current institutional equilibrium distributes to the already powerful – why does the Government of Tanzania perennially resuscitate the reform agenda?

In this analysis, two explanations emerge. The first relates to the consistent politicisation of the power sector. There are a number of reasons for this, including the (co)incidence of drought, load-shedding, and associated scandal in the years before elections. The second relates to the donor communities' interest in the sector, which has for over thirty years been identified as a primary impediment to development.

Retrospectively, it is interesting to note that publicly available policy has been released in the years before an election when the CCM will compete with a new presidential candidate (policy 1992 – election 1995, policy 2003 – election 2005, policy 2014 – election 2015), while the non-publicly available variety emerges shortly after elections (1999, 2007). It seems that publicly available policy has functioned as a campaign tool locally, while internal or non-public policy has allowed the government to access aid and loans from external actors, such as the IMF and World Bank – possibly providing new administrations with essential general budget support following elections.

Understood in this way, policy has allowed the incumbent CCM government to reap some of the benefits of reforms without actually implementing them, while continuing to reap the benefits (including those related to rent-seeking) that their effective control over the sector and utility affords. The fact that there is often policy discontinuity between 'regimes' (presidents) is a natural outcome, as CCM's staying power is at least in part dependent on the party's ability to appear to be evolving in response to the public's needs and international policy trends. Publicly available/official policy has not provided an adequate base for strong legislation (both in terms of the lack of specificity in policy proposals and the persistence of unresolved ideological discrepancies) and, as a result, the policy–legislative basis for reform has been weak – ultimately undermining implementation. In gauging commitment to reforms, internal policies are certainly not indicative of genuine intentions and public policies need to be understood in the political context.

2 *Transparency and Accountability*

An important component of the overall rationale behind standard model reforms is that of transparency and accountability. It may not feature prominently, yet most aspects of the model – independent regulation, commercialisation and corporatisation, unbundling and separation of functions – are associated with greater transparency of information and a more dispersed system of accountability. Independent regulators typically provide a bridge between the utility, government, and consumers, and are bound to make information public – whether it be on performance, licensing procedures, or tariff setting. As soon as part of the sector is privatised, as may be the case following an initial public offering, additional laws apply, specifically around accounting and financial reporting, and a more diverse shareholding protects against capture. In an unbundled system, where consumers have a choice of who their power providers are, distribution or retail utilities are held accountable. Meanwhile, IPPs – perhaps in competition with government-owned and operated generation – are held to a certain standard in order to gain a share of dispatch. Increasing the number of actors in the sector means that governance and accountability should improve in general, with diversity in represented interests and more decentralised power dynamics.

In Tanzania, standard model reforms would clearly undermine the *status quo* – in which, at almost every level, power is centralised, and certain interests predominate, whether they are financial/economic (linked to rent-seeking and clientelism) or political (the government's desire to maintain power and control over the sector). By resisting reforms, or implementing them only partially, levels of transparency and accountability are kept low. Current institutional rules do not provide enough protection against this. Instead, vertical appointment structures, strict guidelines on sector information and lines of communication, and the frequent application of *de facto* power by political actors work against the development of decision-making capacity, accountability, and trust in governance structures.

3 Stakeholder Engagement

Stakeholder engagement, or the lack thereof, has been a serious impediment to reforms, and is one of a number of indicators that suggest that genuine political interest in or will to implement reforms has been absent. Though there are examples of stakeholder engagement and public education drives, including public lectures and seminars, engagement has been inconsistent, and political statements around reforms have been contradictory at key junctures, undermining other forms of stakeholder engagement. In the chronological narrative presented, public engagement and discourse around the management contract provides an example of this. At the time of writing in 2017, President Magufuli made inconsistent statements on the issue of IPPs – in some instances stating that private sector participation in generation would be actively supported and then, in others, that all new generation would be publicly owned.

In the short term, inconsistent stakeholder engagement impedes the smooth implementation of reform steps. Over the long term, however, inconsistent stakeholder engagement has undermined the viability of reforms as the possibility of building support for the rationale behind reforms has been eroded. This inconsistency is a common feature of hybrid or dual markets, of which Tanzania is an example, where uncertainty benefits those who are able to use political connections and power to determine key policy, procurement, and planning decisions.

Actors in the sector become disoriented, unsure of which direction could or should be taken. If the ESIRSR or another reform strategy is to be implemented, continuous and consistent stakeholder engagement with a clear message – ideally backed by government and driven by a reform champion – will be crucial in making reforms politically and socially feasible, in addition to strong legislation.

4 Politics and Patronage

Tanzania's failure to restructure and privatise TANESCO seems inconsistent with the country's success in privatising the majority of SOEs and implementing other components of SAP-styled market liberalisation policies. This inconsistency can be understood to indicate a number of underlying factors.

The first is that the power sector is of national strategic importance and technically complex. This means that reforms are more politically sensitive and resource intensive than, for example, privatising state-owned hotels.

The second is that the sector is highly politicised and holds a special position in the socialist paradigm, where electricity is considered a public good that the government should provide – both as an input into economic growth and as a social service.

The third is the type of opportunity that the sector provides for rent-seeking and patronage. While privatising certain manufacturing or agriculture SOEs, especially those that were commercially viable, provided an opportunity for the establishment and/or strengthening of an existing economic and political elite class (especially after the strictures on the accumulation of wealth/capital were loosened post-Nyerere), increasing private sector ownership and participation in the power sector would do the opposite. In the current structure, politically connected actors are able to influence decisions in procurement and operations that benefit certain business interests (including shielding business from non-payment of electricity bills or tariff increases) – allowing political actors to 'buy' support and/or accumulate resources for political campaigning or to otherwise influence political processes. However, there are other businesses that would want to see change/reform. For the moment, these actors are largely excluded from political spheres, while a small and closely related (often overlapping) group of political and economic actors works together to maintain the *status quo*. This, to some extent, mirrors the difference in opportunities for rent extraction in the economy, which typically load onto trade, construction, and communication – with industry potentially more competitive and thus more difficult to extract rents from. While everyone has an interest in improving power supply, those with the greatest interest – competitive industry – have less influence and less to offer the clientelistic networks that 'make things happen' in Tanzania.

While there is no self-declared anti-reform coalition, it seems likely that a lobby against reforms does exist that coordinates at higher levels, beyond public purview. One example might be found in the 'reform narrative' that is presented more or less consistently in the media. When compared with neighbours such as Kenya and Uganda, which have each had their own battles with power sector reforms, the Tanzanian narrative is decidedly more anti-reform in general and there is a lot of misinformation – for example, on the private management contract or Songas – that is repeated across platforms. Given that the press is only considered partly free in Tanzania (scoring 50–60 per cent in the Freedom House Press index, with 100 being least free) and that the government and political parties are seen to use the press media to advance political interests, the persistent anti-reform narrative might be one example of coordinated lobbying. The soft power of controlling the reform narrative and the public's understanding of reforms (e.g. private sector corruption, foreign interference, pro-profit/anti-poor) is then matched by the political executives' use of *de facto* power over decision-making processes. Excepting those that have been exposed in corruption scandals, this lobby acts behind a veil.

Without a dramatic change in government or a change in power between private sector insiders and outsiders, existing patronage networks present a steep barrier to reforms.

5 Dominant Party Politics

Tanzania's political economy is characterised by the dominance of CCM and its socialist legacy. While the country has progressively adopted a more neoliberal economic stance since the mid-1980s, the political legitimacy of the state and of the ruling party is dependent on the continuation of first President Julius Nyerere's legacy of African Socialism or *Ujamaa*. Despite the apparent failure of Nyerere's model and the economic ideological shift following his abdication in 1985, socialist political ideology has remained embedded in the dominant political culture and paradigm, with the core components of self-reliance and state-led development providing the basis of political identity, along with the practice of paternalistic leadership and autocratic government. Maintaining this legacy is one part of CCM's strategy in maintaining power.

The other part is also to an extent a legacy issue. Under the stain of economic contraction and the strictures of socialist policies, a shadow culture of rent-seeking, low public service accountability, and clientelism emerged in the later years of Nyerere's government. This culture became entrenched as economic and then political competition spread following early economic liberalisation interventions and the introduction of multiparty politics in 1992. The incumbent CCM was able to use the state apparatus for rent-seeking in the lead up to the first elections, providing the necessary resources and patronage networks to ensure that the party stayed in power. The political and economic elites were thus intertwined, and their fates have been interdependent since. Patronage plays a critical role in maintaining the current political economy system.

The development of these parallel but antithetical cultures spurred a third culture – one of cognitive dissonance and a common suspension of disbelief around the socialist model of government. While neoliberal economic ideology has been adopted, it has not permeated the political system. And though corruption scandals have exposed patronage networks at numerous points, the paternalistic CCM has been able to undercut formal punitive institutions, using internal disciplinary processes to circumvent the law. This is not to say that the CCM has not encountered opposition. Rather, the socialist legacy and strong patronage networks have – thus far – insulated the party considerably.

Looking at the issue of power sector reforms, it is clear that genuine political will has been lacking. Acknowledging the close relationship between economic and political interests, what makes unbundling and privatisation – among other interventions – undesirable?

First, key components of standard model power sector reforms are antithetical to the legacy of African socialism. The ideal of state-led development stipulates those certain essential industries are government owned or controlled – the power sector is such an industry. The ideal of 'self-reliance' is of particular relevance to policy choices – the unbundling and privatisation of the state-owned power utility are seen to be 'foreign' ideas. The idea of public goods is pervasive: electricity is considered a public good that should be provided by the government.

Unbundling and privatisation would thus undermine the legitimacy of CCM by eroding the ideological foundation of government. Implementing reforms in the power sector would be like admitting that the government could not provide for its citizens or lead economic development or live up to the legacy of its, and the country's, founding principles. While full unbundling and privatisation is no longer viewed as a feasible or suitable model for Tanzania, anxiety about these steps – and the expected implications for CCM's legitimacy – means that structural reforms in general are highly complex policy issues.

Secondly, as explored earlier, the current structure of the power sector provides the best opportunity for rent-seeking and patronage, through centralised and un-transparent procurement processes run between TANESCO and the government. If competitive procurement processes, facilitated by a restructured sector, replaced the current system, there would be little room for the still-underdeveloped local private sector or political rent-seeking.

Standard model reforms would thus limit CCM's ability (or that of factions within CCM) to use the state apparatus for rent-seeking and/or to establish and maintain patronage networks, which – with the increasing competitiveness of elections – is an important component in maintaining political power. Conversely, if you look at the issue of rural electrification – which has been bolstered by the 'unbundling' of rural electrification functions from TANESCO – REA has been able to attract significant resources, create jobs, and benefit certain actors through connecting villages and households (feeding into patronage networks), while at the same time bolstering the government's socialist image and winning the CCM votes. Institutional change in this area may create new incentives and opportunities in others and has the potential to open the sector to more reforms.

B Political Economy of Institutional Equilibrium in Hybrid Markets

When one approaches the issue of power sector development and reform from a techno-economic standpoint, Tanzania seems to be in a state of disequilibrium. The power utility is financially unsustainable and inefficient, recurrent

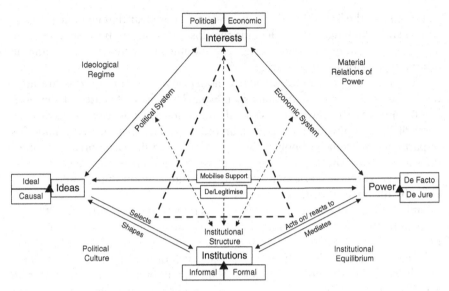

FIGURE 8.3 Political economy diamond
Source: Construct by authors

drought-related crises seem to precipitate reckless short-term decision making with dire consequences for longer-term planning, and sector outcomes are
poor – less than 30 per cent of the population has access to electricity, supply is inadequate and unreliable, and a perennial investment crisis undermines
already-unrealistic system expansion and maintenance plans. Furthermore,
pendular policy, inconsistent political signalling around reforms, institutional
weakness, and evident capacity constraints seem to mirror (and thus confirm)
a state of institutional disequilibrium.

Yet, from a political economy perspective, there are certain features of the
current system that might indicate that this is a distortion – that the very indicators of economic disequilibrium may constitute a feature (and outcome) of
a relatively stable institutional equilibrium. Recent work in institutional economics pays a good deal of attention to dysfunctional institutional equilibria –
specifically that of Acemoglu and Robinson (2012), as well as exploring the
political economy foundations thereof – such as the work on political settlements, led by the work of Mushtaq Khan (2010). Taking this further, we argue
that institutional equilibrium might be conceptualised as a constituent part of a
larger political economy equilibrium – understood as the relatively stable and
mutually reinforcing structural relationships that exist between institutions,
interests, ideas, and power, and the dynamic interactions that maintain them.
In Figure 8.3, this is captured in the 'political economy diamond', which provides a concept map of political economy equilibrium.

According to this model, systemic change (i.e. a shift in equilibrium) – which is represented by the central green triangle – requires change at each of the core nodes: institutions, interests, ideas, and power. Significant change at just one of the nodes could bring about a situation of disequilibrium, which is indicated by unpredictable outcomes and can catalyse change at other nodes. However, without change at all nodes, equilibrium will likely be restored – often through the see-saw effect, whereby an effective reform is undercut by countervailing interventions that maintain the overall balance in the system (Acemoglu et al., 2008). A classic example is the intractability of subsidies, which has shown the multiplicity of distortionary instruments that can be thought up to satisfy the same politically powerful constituencies – maintaining power dynamics and incentive structures, often through the utilisation of ideational touchstones (e.g. state-led development through public investment).

The institutional equilibrium identified in the Tanzanian power system is consistent with the experience and outcomes of power sector reforms in many other developing countries, what Victor and Heller (2007) term a 'dual market' (also known as a hybrid market model). According to Gratwick and Eberhard (2008, p. 3958), 'most developing countries [...] now have hybrid power markets, with elements from both the old and new industry', characterised by 'contested policy and institutional space[s]'. Understood this way, the introduction of standard model reforms, along with the initiation of SAPs from the 1980s and the reintroduction of multiparty democracy in 1992, created 'new organisations and [interests] that favour an alternative equilibrium – a type of "dual market" that combines elements of a state-centred and market-centred' system (Victor and Heller, 2007, p. 260). This 'market' – and the evolving, accompanying institutional (and political economy) equilibrium – might not be the 'most desirable in terms of efficient or good governance', but is a 'remarkably stable' outcome (Victor and Heller, 2007, p. 261).

As the literature on hybrid markets would suggest, TANESCO is best positioned to 'hold' the weakest parts of the system. The utility's access to concessional loans and government support (when need be) allows it to do so very differently from the private sector. In the past, this has been to the benefit of those with access to power who were indirectly or directly subsidised by government, for example through suppressed tariffs or politically condoned non-payment (especially for SOEs and government entities). The benefits have been more widely distributed through TANESCO's support of electrification. While TANESCO is not profit making, it allows for a certain type of rent extraction (procurement) and rent distribution (including jobs and contracts), which is favourable for dominant political and economic interests. The fact that TANESCO enjoys *de facto* soft budgets and can access state bailouts means that it can be used in this way, while incentives for greater efficiency are relatively weak. Because political power is highly centralised and cadre deployment is part of CCM's own patronage system, it is unlikely that the government will cede its control over TANESCO. This is true also of planning and policy functions, as well as top-down procurement norms. Meanwhile, TANESCO is likely to obstruct reforms that could disrupt its monopolistic position in the power sector.

In comparison, profit-making IPPs have provided an opportunity for rent extraction on a grander scale – made grander still by the supply-side crises that have been used as opportunities for the political executive's involvement in procurement. The only IPP that was transparently and competitively bid for, Songas, has been mired in corruption scandals and in the negative narrative promulgated by the government and the media. PPPs, especially those with China, are likely to have provided similar opportunities made easier through some institutionalisation: transparency remains low and there is room for direct political involvement.

EWURA has been one of the most positive reform interventions in terms of improving sector performance. However, there are many challenges raised by the hybrid model. First, EWURA has to contend with the 'public good' characteristics of electricity – designated in political rhetoric, policy, and legislation. This makes it difficult to regulate tariffs and state entities, including TANESCO and REA, where their actions are justified by socio-political considerations. Secondly, a key feature of the hybrid model is continued political influence, whether it be in procurement with a view to rent-seeking or tariffs with a view to appeasing voters – which makes reg-ulation highly politicised and the regulator vulnerable to censure. Thirdly, there are extreme asymmetries of information between the regulator, market actors, and TANESCO – making it difficult to gauge true costs and calculate appropriate tariffs. These tensions are well captured by Victor and Heller (2007, p. 296), who describe how 'regulators pressured from multiple sides in pursuit of multiple goals with limited access to reliable information are highly unlikely to produce stable or predictable rules' that can withstand political pressures.

The hybrid power market is also consistent with other hybrid features of the institutional, and greater political economy, system. Tanzania is considered to have a hybrid political regime (an illiberal democracy), where regular elec-tions are not necessarily accompanied by the civil liberties that would translate into real political competition and accountability. Looking at ideology and policy discourse, Tanzania occupies a 'transitional' space between socialism and market-liberalism, except that the direction of transition seems to change frequently. The institutional space is similarly fraught, when one considers the tensions between fundamental institutions, such as the economic institutions fundamental to market-oriented development models (e.g. property rights), and the state-oriented nature of political institutions (e.g. the constitutional designation of far-reaching powers to the president). Much like the hybrid model in the power sector, many of these features are seemingly stable – if dynamic – and have been present since at least the 1990s.

V POLITICAL ECONOMY, REFORM, AND DEVELOPMENT – CONCLUDING COMMENTS

This chapter investigates why it has not been possible for Tanzania to move from an institutional equilibrium that does not bring about the desired sector outcomes (investment, system expansion, and improved technical performance) to an institutional equilibrium that does.

It has been argued that the select standard model reforms that have been implemented in Tanzania – the removal of TANESCO's *de jure* monopoly, the procurement of IPPs, the establishment of an independent regulator, and the unbundling of rural electrification functions to REA (and SPPs), alongside the political and macroeconomic reforms of the 1980s and 1990s – created a dynamic hybrid model that is supported by and informed by the broader political economy system. Some of the features of this system seem, at face value, to be examples of disequilibria. Yet at a system level there is an unexpected stability – one that has been able to keep CCM in power since the 1960s, perpetuates a deep political culture tied to the ideology of African socialism, and where the tension between informal and formal institutions creates a sort of balance that serves the interests of a highly centralised political and economic elite. Indeed, in terms of predictability and continuity, Tanzania is actually an outlier in the region.

The argument has been made quite strongly that the current hybrid model in the power sector is also relatively stable and, having survived twenty-plus years, may continue to do so. Tanzania provides an example of how such systems do survive – with both positive and negative developmental outcomes. The question is then what sort of interventions or policy options might tip the balance of the outcomes in favour of development and institutional evolution. Regarding insights for policy options, there are a number of standout messages from the literature.

The first is that the effectiveness of policies depends on the matching of instruments with institutional weaknesses and political economy realities. Much of the debate on power sector reforms and development tends to focus on increasing the role of the private sector, on the degree of independence of regulators, on the design of procurement rules, and on the quality of contracts as a key tool to stimulate performance in the sector. These are certainly relevant, but theory and experience also suggest that there might be room for other options which decrease the consequences of the current dysfunctional institutional equilibrium for sector development and work within the political economy system to fast-track its evolution and facilitate positive institutional development cycles. For instance, the potential role of local authorities in the design, selection, implementation, and monitoring of more local solutions to make faster progress in achieving rural access targets or secondary cities targets seems to have been underestimated in the past. However, Tanzania's experience with SPPs (and enabling regulation) shows that this is a policy option that mitigates the lack of incentives for TANESCO to expand into rural areas and corresponds to the more general pressures of decentralisation currently facing the CCM and government, as well as the long-standing ideological legitimacy of decentralised socialist governance.

The second insight of direct use to the policy debates in the Tanzanian power sector may be that when the institutional equilibrium generates systemic uncertainty in the choice of options, the best is often the enemy of the good. Picking options that limit regulatory failures, initially at least, rather than focusing on the adoption expected to deliver an uncertain high payoff, may be the most effective way of building up institutional capacity, credibility, and accountability. EWURA's slow and steady development is an example of this. In general, smaller, simpler scale approaches tend to work better in this context, as they are easier to implement and to monitor locally. Moreover, simply trying to adopt solutions designed for other contexts, similar only in technical dimensions but quite dissimilar in terms of political economy, tends to be quite counterproductive. Increasingly, evidence suggests that designing options that recognise local contextualities – political culture, institutional norms, power dynamics, ideology, and interests – is critical to the success of interventions (Eberhard and Godinho, 2017).

A third insight is that, just as there are out of sector determinants of the feasibility and outcomes of various reforms, there are also out of sector interventions that can be leveraged to kick-start, support, or sustain sector interventions. Much of the literature indicates that the most important reforms lie in finance – specifically the application of hard budget constraints on state-owned companies such as TANESCO. Hard budget constraints are typically made possible by increased transparency on subsidies and transfers – which can create political demand and will for financial accountability. Corporate governance is another important area, but should be designed with an eye to political channels of communication and authority. In general, moving the governance of power utilities and state-owned companies to the Ministry of Finance – away from minerals and energy ministries – can support the realisation of 'better' corporate governance, as can the partial unbundling or partial listing of a state-owned company. Many of these out of sector interventions, such as standard model reforms, are decidedly against the grain – but, in opportune moments, can make more progress than sector-level interventions.

A fourth insight, for which a case does not need to be made in the Tanzanian context, is building and protecting regulatory institutions. This is especially relevant given the recent transgressions against regulatory independence in Tanzania.

A fifth insight to be considered is that the assessment of the institutional context of the sector needs to account for all actors – not just local actors. For instance, investors will push for short-term returns in negotiations, while politicians are likely to be concerned with the next election and users with their own well-being rather than that of the country. The main point here is that an analysis of the political economy of the sector needs to help the government and other actors understand core features of the local system, but should also consider the political economy of donors and other foreign actors (McCulloch et al., 2017). Over-optimism was mentioned as an issue in the design of the Master Plans earlier, but it is difficult not to wonder why donors are so keen to share this optimism and to continue choosing solutions that do not seem to address local institutional limitations and opportunities. McCulloch et al. (2017) make the case that donors, specifically, have not really been keen or able to internalise the role of political constraints in their own diagnostics and most importantly in their support programmes. These concerns had already been raised by others such as Tripp (2012), Faustino and Booth (2014), and Piron et al. (2016), but McCulloch et al. (2017) add that donors also underuse the margin they have to do so within the new aid modalities, such as the possibility of engaging groups outside government in favour of support. While donors continue to play a big role in policy design in the Tanzanian power sector, this is an issue that has to be addressed.

A final concluding insight is that the political economy lens allows one to identify obstacles *and* opportunities for reform, evolution, and development. Institutional reform has received special attention in the development literature and praxis because of the way in which institutions shape incentives and determine interests, mediate power dynamics, and give shape to – and reshape – political culture and ideas. However, it is equally important to identify other possible entry points, such as the building of coalitions around certain issues in order to alter power dynamics, or the use public education drives to change the way people understand electricity services. Making the most of such opportunities can drive positive adaptations in the sector, as well as supporting, legitimising, and reinforcing institutional reforms. Indeed, it is the absence of many such complementary interventions – stakeholder engagement, coalition building, mechanisms to increase transparency and accountability, support of free media and speech, strong legal imperatives, and consequences – that helps us to understand the challenges to reform and development in the Tanzanian power sector.

Discussion of 'Power Sector Reform and Regulation'

Discussion by Antonio Estache

The main purpose of this chapter is to conduct an assessment of the difficulties observed in Tanzania's power sector as part of a global diagnostic of Tanzania's institutional constraints on its ability to deliver economic policies.[12] To do so, the author provides an historical perspective on the sector's institutional evolution, highlighting governance and financing challenges as well as recurring political hesitations on key policy decisions. The diagnostic is extremely detailed, lucid, and honest, and provides enough details to anchor a discussion of additional reform needs.

The diagnostic is also quite humbling in terms of how much can be done at policy design level with 'standard or imported' policy solutions. The country suffers from a lasting record of imperfect political and technical accountability for failures to deliver, and these are unlikely to be addressed under highly centralised and standardised 'business-as-usual' approaches to sector reform. Tanzania's political preferences and current institutional constraints do not seem to be consistent with large standard reforms, delivering fast improvements more transparently.

This note argues that the diagnostic presented here implies that unless alternative, possibly unusual, institutional and reform strategies are at least piloted on a reasonable scale, progress is likely to continue to be slower than stated in the Master Plans (including the 2016 plan). It is also unlikely that the sector will achieve the financial autonomy required to finance the needs of the 62.3 per cent of the population without access to electricity (75.5 per cent in rural areas) and of the many businesses rationed in quantity and in quality. To help in the identification of alternatives, the following comments on the chapter provide some suggestions to follow up analytical, policy, and political work.

---

[12] I am grateful to F. Bourguignon, D. Camos, and R. Schlirf for useful discussions. Any mistake or misinterpretation is entirely my responsibility.

I MARKET CONTEXT: THE UNDERESTIMATED
DEMAND AND SUPPLY BOTTOM LINE

Before discussing broad institutional options to address market and government failures in the design and implementation of energy policies in Tanzania identified by the General Electric Company, it seems useful to highlight the outcome of these failures at the very basic quantitative level. This helps to indicate a sense of the size of the challenge and the specific issues to address, as well as possibly anchoring the recognition of the scope for innovative rather than standardised solutions.

Very concretely, for an observer unfamiliar with the country, the data suggest that the investment *level* is not the only problem. Investment *speed* is just as important. Supply has hardly been catching up with a fast-growing demand. Worse yet, the growth of this demand may actually be underestimated. Current consumption is at around 108 kWh/capita. This is only 20 per cent of the sub-Saharan African average.[13] This is a capacity development and management issue, a major weakness of Tanzania, hinting at a mismatch between the institutional choices and the capacity of the country to design and implement a policy in this sector.

The size of the capacity gap continues, indeed, to be huge. As of 2017, Tanzania had less than 1,500 MW of installed grid generation capacity running at 70 per cent load on average to serve a population of 58.2 million with one of the fastest growth rates in the world (3.1 per cent in 2016).[14] In recent times, demand has been growing at an average annual rate close to 10 per cent, and since investment has not followed, about two out of three Tanzanians do not have a chance of seeing their needs met in the short term under the current technological characteristics of the sector.

It will take ten to fifteen years to close the gap, at least.[15] Since the early 2010s, the successive Master Plans have converged towards estimates of investment needs sufficient to cater to a peak demand of 4,000–4,700 MW by 2025–30. The latest plans focus on rapidly developing gas-fired and coal-fired generation in the short to mid-term (2017–19), while focusing on hydrogeneration capacity in the long term (2019–25) – in a region with a record of droughts.[16] The plans

---

[13] In 2014, this consumption per capita was 1,931 kWh in low- and middle-income developing countries, 745 kWh in lower middle-income countries, and 2,060 kWh in middle-income countries.

[14] Transmission and distribution losses (18 per cent) in Tanzania are standard for the region, but significantly higher than in other countries around the globe.

[15] Note that the new Rural Energy Master Plan 2022–30 provides a roadmap to reach 100 per cent energy access by 2030.

[16] More specifically, the government plan under the BRN initiative to be implemented by 2020 is to generate 1,500 MW from gas, 160 MW from oil, 100 MW from wind, 60 MW from solar, 11 MW from small hydropower, and 200 MW from coal, as well as 650 MW from estimated geothermal potential. The strategy is partially anchored in the recent discoveries of 55.08 trillion cubic feet of natural gas reserves off the coast of Tanzania. For now, Tanzania is a net importer

appear to be realistic in theory, but the details available to casual observers do not seem to internalise the lessons from the recurring delays observed in Tanzania for large-scale power projects and the factors driving demand growth. This is a process-related issue that needs to be addressed in the design of reforms.

Progress has mostly benefited urban users. According to the 2016 Energy Access Situation Report, about two-thirds of urban areas have access to electricity. The main beneficiaries of access rate improvements have been the capital city and the upper-income classes and businesses.[17] Technically, they also benefit from the lowest-cost solutions. Cost-effective grid electricity prevails in urban areas, with 96.4 per cent of the households with access to electricity connected to the grid.[18] Grid connection is only available to 34.5 per cent of households in rural areas and, in many cases, the technological choices deliver a load level inconsistent with the willingness and ability of populations to pay.[19]

The outcome is a heterogeneity of costs faced by users and a somewhat regressive investment plan timing. Currently, the poor, the majority of the rural population, spend about 35 per cent of their household income on energy, two and a half times what the rich spend.[20] This distributional issue linked to both investment costs and timing should be a much larger concern to the various sources of financing supporting the transformation of the sector, given that there is now enough evidence that the decision-making process needs to be revamped to speed up the delivery of energy at a reasonable cost consistent with the preferences of the majority of the population outside of the major cities.

Timing and technological choices drive the investment financing capacity and options. Irrespective of any institutional or policy issue, the physical challenge boils down first to a financial challenge in the short run. The continued backlog, the slow investment speed, and the significant financing gaps are recognised in the 2016 Master Plan update. Various sources mention investment needs of around USD 40 billion investment under current technological preferences.[21]

---

of petroleum products, although over 30 per cent is re-exported to landlocked neighbouring countries (Zambia, the Democratic Republic of Congo, Rwanda, Malawi, and Burundi).

[17] Only 16.9 per cent of areas enjoy this service in environments in which efforts are being made to reduce poverty and improve standards of living.

[18] As of 2016, in Dar es Salaam, 99.3 per cent of households are connected to grid electricity. Another region with a high number of grid electricity is Kilimanjaro (88.0 per cent). The least-connected regions to grid electricity are Lindi (24.5 per cent), Njombe (36.6 per cent), Mtwara (38.9 per cent), and Katavi (41.1 per cent).

[19] As of 2016, according to the United States Agency for International Development (USAID, 2018), a connection charge to the TANESCO grid in a rural area costs at least USD 200, and this is for an unreliable service.

[20] Most of the rural population relies on expensive, hazardous, and low-quality fuels such as kerosene for lighting and charcoal for cooking.

[21] For example, Peng and Poudineh (2016).

If this were to be spread over ten years, the high case scenario, it would roughly mean 10 per cent of GDP. This is unrealistic. It means that closing the gap will have to be slower and that the sector needs to consider ways of cutting costs to make the most of the fiscal envelopes to be allocated to the sector. It also means that, unless technological choices are adjusted, it is hard to see how Tanzania will be able to produce enough electricity fast enough to meet its objective of becoming a middle-income country by 2025.[22] And this should matter to the assessment of the location and nature of investment decisions in the sector and to growth expectations.

How much scope is there to adjust technological options? Tanzania's successive Master Plans have long recognised that there are alternatives to the traditional energy sources, and that these are expected to help during the transition to the 2025 access rate goals. In 2016, of the electrified households, about 25 per cent are not connected to a grid – 24.7 per cent with solar power and 0.3 per cent through individual electricity generated from sources such as small generators. But these technological approaches could also be considered for the medium to longer run to cater to the rural population as a way of managing both cost and time preferences. This is a serious option in an environment in which new low-cost technology relying on local renewable options is emerging fast and providing reliable, affordable service.[23]

So far, progress in making the most of the alternatives has been slow considering the potential they offer – even if it has been high by sub-Saharan African standards. According to a WRI (2017) report, Tanzania has at least 109 mini-grids (93 operating as isolated), with installed capacity of at least 157.7 MW, but they only serve about 184,000 customers, a far cry from meeting the needs of the 35 to 40 million living in rural areas.[24]

[22] Kichonge et al. (2014) show the dominance of hydro, coal, natural gas, and geothermal as least-cost energy supply options for electricity generation in all scenarios. Under a dry weather scenario, they argue for a shift to coal and natural gas to replace hydroenergy, with little scope for solar thermal, wind, and solar photovoltaic (PV), but this ignores the discount rate/rate of time preference dimension. Lower values favour wind and coal-fired power plants, while higher values favour the natural gas technologies.

[23] USAID (2018) explains that Devergy, one of the providers of alternatives to TANESCO catering to rural areas of western and eastern Tanzania, relies on an adaptive mini-grid system controlled by a wireless communication system allowing the monitoring of individual meters working with a pay-as-you-go system. Its mini-grids use distributed, networked solar PV with battery storage delivering reliable (99 per cent) 24-volt direct current electricity to between 60 and 400 households. Each household receives up to 250 watts of electricity, and compatible appliances can be purchased at local kiosks. The initial connection fee ranges from USD 6 to USD 12 per customer; this covers the meter, wiring, installation costs, and two bulbs. This is less than 5–10 per cent of the connection fees charged by TANESCO for connections to their grid. The recurring cost is based on consumption on a standard tariff structure allowing the recovery of operational expenditures.

[24] Hydro is the most common technology (forty-nine mini-grids), although the nineteen fossil fuel systems account for 93 per cent of customer connections and almost half of total installed

The growing interest in these alternative technological options has been matched and stimulated by the development of pay-as-you-go solar companies supported by mobile phone companies (MKopa, Zola, and Mobisol). This has smoothed cost recovery through mobile payment systems such as Airtel, Tigo-Pesa, or M-Pesa. Mobile operators have become essential drivers of the growth potential of these alternative providers in rural regions.[25]

In the short run, these solutions may be seen by some observers as a niche to be exploited to deliver faster in areas unlikely to see the benefits of the investment programmes before the end of the plan period.[26] But it is not unreasonable to argue that these solutions should be considered as more than a short-term niche. And the scope to make the most of this option should be included in the assessment of the potential changes in the design of institutions in the sector.

How much are current choices biased by the insufficient analytical support to decisions? For a newcomer to Tanzania going through the recent literature and policy documents available on the sector, it is difficult not to think that there may be a recurring optimism bias in the sector diagnostics used to anchor policy decisions.

First, on the demand side, needs may be regularly underestimated. They seem to ignore the expected change in the purchasing power of the population, which implies much higher income elasticity than recognised by the Master Plan. They also underestimate important details of the consequences of the ambitious economic growth and diversification targets aimed at by the authorities in their strategic development plan. This implies that it may be useful to take a more precise look at the data anchoring the Master Plan. It would be beyond the main purpose of this note to go through a data and methodological diagnostic, but an independent audit of these basic quantitative dimensions would not be an unusual exercise in an environment in which institutional and governance weaknesses may reduce the incentives to take a cold look at the facts. This is what countries such as Vietnam and Laos have been doing since the early 2010s as part of the sector-restructuring efforts, for instance.

Second, on the supply side, there is a common bias in favour of the lowest-cost technologies. This is fine if the assessments are not biased by a reliance on standard financial discount rates rather than rates accounting for

capacity. Tanzania has twenty-five biomass mini-grids and thirteen solar mini-grids (ten of them small donor-funded, community-owned demonstration projects). There are no wind mini-grids in Tanzania.

[25] Ohio State University (2017).

[26] This is not an irrational option under tight financing constraints, considering that the cost of grid extensions ranges from about USD 6,500 per kilometre in densely populated regions to as much as USD 20,000 per kilometre in regions with dispersed populations. This high cost of grid extension in remote areas and the slow speed at which these extensions tend to take place are two of the main reasons for considering opportunities for off-grid electrification more rigorously.

the relevance of the time preferences of users. The rate of time preference is relevant to reflect the sense of urgency of regions otherwise expected to stay unconnected for a while. Over two-thirds of Tanzanians seem to have a much higher discount rate than is reflected in standard project evaluations. This matters for the choice of technology since this choice impacts the time of delivery. The relevance of this time preference in Tanzania is actually quite clear from the craving for mini-grids, which reveals a willingness to go for more expensive marginal costs as long as delivery is faster. It would seem useful to consider the differences in investment costs accounting for these differences to see whether the resources allocated to the sector are going to the most cost-effective technology once more realistic discount rates have been accounted for. If the preference for alternative faster options is confirmed in the Tanzanian case, the next challenge is to see how best to internalise these in the institutional design, as discussed in the next section.

II TOWARDS AN ACTIONABLE INSTITUTIONAL DIAGNOSTIC

Walking through the history of the sector as we do in this chapter is both fascinating and depressing as it highlights the recurring character of some of the mistakes and the high degree of politicisation of decisions in the sector. In countries with stronger sector governance, these decisions are usually handled through simple administrative processes designed to cut the risks of capture and distortions, ultimately sustaining and increasing accountability. A few of the issues identified in the chapter, and rephrased here to deal with them more conceptually, are:

- An inability to establish credibility: the repetition of promises unmet for over twenty-five years should simply have been internalised long ago in the design of reforms and institutions and has largely been ignored in successive reform waves.
- The excessive margin given to some agents, both public and private, to bias and/or capture processes and officials/authorities, or to be opportunistic in exploiting policy failures and random weather shocks (most notably in the award of IPPs).
- The inability of authorities to minimise the risk of cream-skimming in the preparation of PPPs, allowing private actors to take the rents from low-hanging fruits, leaving the government with the unmanageable fiscal and bureaucratic burden of dealing with the high-cost items – most notably in the preparation of service obligations and entitlements as well as in the distribution of cost and revenues in the design of IPPs.
- The misuse of tariff reforms, notably when they ignored the fiscal limits on efforts to rely on direct subsidies, or the lack of continuity in the staffing and rules, which tends to be important for key technical and contractual dimensions, even if too much continuity may sometimes increase the risks of capture and corruption.

TABLE 8.A.1 *Impact of institutional weaknesses on key sector service performance indicators*

	Quantity	Quality	Costs	Prices
Limited technical, human, regulatory capacity	?/-	-	?	+
Limited commitment capacity	?/-	-	+	+
Limited accountability	-	?	+	?
Limited fiscal capacity	?/-	-	+	?

Source: Adapted from Estache and Wren-Lewis (2009)

In sum, conceptually, each of these examples fits into the usual main characterisations of institutional weaknesses: non-benevolence, non-commitment, non-accountability, non-technical, regulatory, or human capacity, and non-fiscal capacity problems.[27]

The consequences of these weaknesses have been quite well documented empirically.[28] They all imply a lower welfare for the country and each has somewhat predictable consequences for the key dimensions of interest in any sector diagnostic – that is, the quantity of service delivered (both in terms of volume and coverage), its quality (which can be either insufficient or excessive), its cost (which can be influenced by the quantity and quality choices), and its price (which is related to costs but may also be linked to the specific regulatory regime adopted).

Table 8.A.1 summarises the likely impact of institutional weaknesses as identified in the academic literature. These are quite consistent with the evidence available on Tanzania. Coverage (i.e. quantity) has been lower than it should be as a result of a combination of the various types of institutional weaknesses (there is no question mark for Tanzania on this dimension). Quality is lower on average, even if it may be better for some users, such as in the large cities. Costs have all been higher than needed in Tanzania as well. Finally, prices may appear to be too low to cover costs, but they are all higher than they should be given the margin there is to cut cost through alternative technological choices and improvements in management approaches. Tanzania does not appear to be different in terms of the institutional weaknesses characterising the sector, based on the evidence available.

Of course, this characterisation largely focuses on very basic correlations between institutional weaknesses identified and outcomes. Causality often runs both ways. For instance, high costs may limit the capacity to do more with the

[27] See Estache and Wren-Lewis (2009) for a detailed discussion of this classification and for its implications for the restructuring of a sector and its regulation.
[28] See, for instance, Estache and Wren-Lewis (2010) for a non-technical survey.

fiscal resources allocated to the sector. Moreover, interactions between the various types of weaknesses are relevant.

For instance, a lack of accountability is often a good predictor for lack of commitment and hence lack of credibility, which tends to slow down the interest of the average private investor or lender. This may make specific deals in the sector easier in the short run because they focus on the easy transactions, or, worse, governments have to come up with packages that guarantee the low-cost high margins are passed on to private investors while the high-cost, high-risk low margins are left to the public sector without any room for cross-subsidies or risk of mitigation opportunities. But these 'cream-skimming' deals tend to be disproportionately more in the interest of specific public and/or private actors than in the longer-run country interest. This is why it is crucial to internalise in the design of procurement practices that the accumulated evidence shows that the tolerance for cream-skimming allowed by weak capacity and weak accountability tends to favour the few and penalise the majority. The biases in favour of Dar es Salaam and of targeted private actors provide good illustrations of this risk.

Note that theory and empirical evidence also explain some counterintuitive observations. For instance, the fact that prices may need to be higher may be consistent with the fact that the various types of institutional weaknesses imply higher than needed risk levels. This implies a high cost of capital, which in turn implies a high average tariff to allow the private investors to recover their risky investment. This is not an easy sell politically, but it can be addressed by making the most of tariff structure adjustment to minimise the social consequences of higher average tariffs, even when the ability to subsidise is limited.[29]

This conceptualisation of Tanzania's problems does not simply serve to show that the consequences of the institutional weaknesses identified in this chapter are and were predictable. It is also useful because it allows the identification of institutional adjustments suggested by theory and supporting evidence to reduce the importance of these weaknesses and of their consequences. Once more, it would go beyond the scope of these comments to review the list of possible solutions, but a few of them seem to be particularly relevant to the Tanzanian context.

A first relevant insight is that the effectiveness of policies depends on the matching of instruments with institutional weaknesses. Much of the debate tends to focus on increasing the role of the private sectors, on deregulating, on the degree of independence of regulators, on the design of procurement rules, and on the quality of contracts as a key tool to stimulate performance in the sector. All are of course relevant. But theory and experience also suggest that other

[29] See, for instance, Peng and Poudineh (2016) to see the scope for tariff adjustment available in the Tanzanian case.

institutional dimensions, such as decentralisation or the extent to which mandates are shared within government or across government, may offer additional options. A decentralised energy system is characterised by locating energy production facilities closer to the site of energy consumption.[30] In many contexts, this makes it easier to optimise the use of local renewable energy, and, from an institutional viewpoint, easier to reduce the consequences of institutional weakness inherited from history (including legal and constitutional history) or built-in culture, for instance.[31] This is because decentralised energy systems tend to put power sources closer to the end user. This increases the accountability of the local decision makers and gives them the option of reducing their need to wait for network expansions decided nationally. Whether the local managers are named by the local authorities or are simply local representatives from the national government, the pressure they will face to deliver faster is likely to be stronger than it currently is in Tanzania.[32] While these options seem to be realistic and have been adopted by other countries, this chapter suggests that they may not have been considered thoroughly enough in the Tanzanian case. And indeed, based on the information available publicly, it seems that the potential role of local authorities in the design, selection, implementation, and monitoring of more local solutions to make faster progress in achieving rural access targets or secondary cities targets may have been underestimated.

A second relevant insight from the theory and supporting evidence is that when there are multiple sources of institutional weaknesses, a ranking in terms of urgency may be needed. Moreover, particular attention needs to be paid to the impact of any policy across institutional weaknesses because solutions to one problem may make things worse in another dimension. For instance, regulatory capacity limitations argue for higher-powered incentive regulation (i.e. price or revenue caps), while commitment or credibility problems argue for low-powered incentive regulation (i.e. cost plus/rate of return). In the Tanzanian context, a casual observer of the evidence available thanks to the diagnostic presented in this chapter would be more concerned with the commitment issue than with the regulatory capacity problem.

The third insight that is of direct use to the policy debates in the Tanzanian power sector may be that when institutional weaknesses imply systemic uncertainty in the choice of options, the best is often the enemy of the good. Picking

---

[30] Decentralised generation facilities may be connected to a grid (national or mini) or simply serve a particular site without feeding potential excess generation into the grid. As the regions develop, mini-grids can become more common and eventually be upgraded to form a distribution network that is connected to a larger transmission network. This sequential approach has the advantage of increasing the system's reliability in the longer run (in particular when intermittent sources are used), while allowing consumption in the short run.

[31] For more details, see Estache (2017b).

[32] And, of course, this will require developing new regulations. For instance, an evaluation of the need to adapt ownership and pricing rules for off-grid and mini-grid services is likely to be needed.

options that limit regulatory failures initially at least, rather than focusing on the adoption expected to deliver an uncertain high payoff, may be the most effective way of building up institutional capacity, credibility, and accountability. Smaller, simpler-scale approaches tend to work better in this context as they are easier to implement and to monitor locally, for instance. Moreover, simply trying to adopt solutions designed for other contexts, similar only in technical dimensions but quite dissimilar in terms of institutional weakness intensity or nature, tends to be quite counterproductive. Increasingly, evidence suggests that designing options that recognise local traditions and norms is the way to go, as seen in research on the role of religious norms in the incentive to deliver in infrastructure.[33]

A fourth insight to be considered here is that the assessment of the institutional context of the sector needs to account for *all* actors. Each has its own agenda and each of these agendas is likely to overlap with the others only partially. For instance, investors will push for short-term returns in negotiations, while politicians are likely to be concerned with the next election and users with their own well-being rather the country's well-being. This chapter nicely illustrates the multiplicity of players, both local and foreign as well as both public and private. However, it may not do justice to the relevance of both national and sub-national players as well as to the potential role of civil society. The main point here is that the analysis of the political economy of the sector needs to help the government look into its strengths and weaknesses, but it also needs to get donors and other foreign actors to do the same. Over-optimism is mentioned as an issue in the design of the Master Plans, but it is difficult not to wonder why donors are so keen to share this optimism and to continue going for solutions that do not seem to address the local institutional limitations and opportunities.

A final insight is that politics is the main determinant of many of the relevant outcomes. This has also been documented in various overviews of experiences of reform in the sector, in sub-Saharan Africa (Eberhard et al., 2016) and elsewhere (Scott and Seth, 2013). The relevance of the political economy of the sector is quite obvious in the overview presented here, and it is perhaps even more brutally stated in McCulloch et al. (2017). What they add is how surprising it is that donors have not really been keen, or able, to internalise the role of political constraints in their own diagnostics and most importantly in their support programmes. These concerns had already been raised by others such as Tripp (2012), Faustino and Booth (2014), and Piron et al. (2016); but McCulloch et al. (2017) add that donors also underuse the margin they have to do so within the new aid modalities, such as the possibility of engaging groups outside government in favour of support. This is perhaps more relevant to donors than to the Tanzanian authorities, but it is certainly relevant to the effectiveness of institutional reforms to improve the power sector performance in Tanzania.

---

[33] See, for instance, Pal (2010) and Pal and Wahhaj (2016).

III SO WHERE CAN TANZANIA GO FROM HERE?

It would be inappropriate for this note to try to make specific suggestions to address the many issues raised in this chapter, since I did not have the opportunity to conduct detailed fieldwork. But it may be helpful to conclude the discussion by arguing that the analysis makes a strong case to support the consideration, in much more detail than the available information suggests, of one specific institutional reform that may be of relevance in the debates on power sector reform in Tanzania. It addresses the underuse of both technological and institutional options (Ahlborg and Hammar, 2014; AfDB, 2015; Ahlborg and Sjöstedt, 2015; Grimm et al., 2015; Moner-Girona et al., 2016; Peters and Sievert, 2016; World Future Council, 2017; WRI, 2017).[34] The REA has already been working on its development (e.g. REA, 2016). These insights need to be matched with those produced by the analysis of the potential roles of local communities in the development of Tanzania's power capacity (e.g. Kaundinya et al., 2009; Goldthau, 2014; Alstone et al., 2015). Experience suggests that decentralisation of power sector decisions can fail to deliver, but it also shows that it can work if homework is carried out to match technology, regulatory tools, institutional options, and institutional constraints (e.g. Peters and Sievert, 2016).

The challenges to get decentralised options implemented in Tanzania are unlikely to be minor given the current political context. But getting ready to make things happen and to go further than simply thinking through the fine tuning of regulation to allow renewable sources to grow seems like a desirable option. In doing so, WRI (2017) argues that it may be a good idea to take a look at success stories such as the one experienced by Bangladesh, for instance. Box 8.A.1 summarises the lessons for Tanzania from Bangladesh's increased decentralisation of decision processes sustained by national financial and technical assistance used to speed up rural access rates. It illustrates the long checklist of dimensions that need to be taken into account. All of them seem realistic in the Tanzanian context.

The adoption of a much more decentralised approach to cater to the needs of rural areas, combined with a large role for local stakeholders and civil society, would not be unusual in sub-Saharan Africa. Equivalent approaches have been adopted by many sub-Saharan African countries in the water sector. Over 80 per cent of the countries in the region have

---

[34] The World Future Council argues that by deploying 100 per cent renewable energy, Tanzania could provide reliable universal access to the level of industrialised countries by 2050. The study also argues that renewable sources are about 30 per cent cheaper than fossil resources. This can be seen in the 2017 financing agreements for the West Lunga project under Zambia's first Scaling Solar mandate. It was signed between Bangweulu Power Corporation Limited (sponsored by Neoen/First Solar and Zambia's Industrial Development Corporation), the International Finance Corporation, and the Overseas Private Investment Corporation. This PV plant will bring a capacity of 47.5 MW of reliable solar energy for a 6.015 cent/kWh tariff, fixed for twenty-five years. This is much lower than the current price of a kWh in the country.

Box 8.A.1: Learning from Bangladesh?

The recent WRI (2017) report argues that Tanzania could adapt the Bangladesh experience with the fast development and adoption of renewable alternatives in rural areas. The main insights may be that the policy framework and long-term strategy need to address not only policy and regulation, but also financing, maintenance, and technical assistance commitments.

At *the institutional level*, it requires a more decentralised vision of the implementation of energy policy in the country than currently considered by Tanzania. This implies local leader and stakeholder involvement and the management of synergies across local stakeholders, including local businesses, parliamentarians, media, and civil society groups.

At *the technical level*, to diminish the variability of intermittent renewable sources, several renewable energy sources will have to be connected. This implies that Tanzania would be willing to facilitate and adopt the technical and structural changes needed for an energy system only fed by renewable energy. This could be done regionally at least initially as part of a pilot.

At *the financial level*, Tanzania would have to develop a comprehensive national finance mechanism for individuals, households, and possibly smaller businesses to access funds to invest in local renewable sources. This implies a willingness to develop dedicated affordable credit lines, for instance, as well as monitoring systems to ensure the transparency of funding. It also demands regulatory adjustments to link funding to performance.

At *the human level*, the approach also implies a commitment to invest in education and awareness of technological and financial options to make sure that the financial options and subsidies find takers, and that the beneficiaries of these support mechanisms are those who need them. This may require some nudging to help local communities make the right decisions rather than wait for options that are unlikely to come fast enough to meet their needs.

Ultimately, *at the political level*, the approach demands a willingness to adopt a national vision endorsing an unbundling and delegation of some responsibilities as part of an institutional reform of the sector. This may be the most important challenge to achieve the necessary improvements in autonomy and accountability. According to WRI, the challenge is unlikely to be met.

Source: Adapted from WRI (2017)

implemented at least some form of shift of responsibilities in the sector to sub-national authorities, although often more in the form of devolution rather than full decentralisation.[35] For instance, an increasingly standard element of the institutional framework of the water sector in many countries of sub-Saharan Africa is the requirement for local public participation in water planning, management, and regulatory decisions, as well as consultation with local stakeholders. The role of local authorities in the design and implementation of policies has also increased.

Besides an increased role for local authorities, there are other options that Tanzania could consider in its efforts to accelerate the efficient, equitable, and financially sustainable delivery of electricity in the country. But their discussion would demand a much more technical diagnostic of financial, planning, and regulatory tools than can be covered in this chapter. For now, there may be enough food for thought in addressing the institutional and political issues already identified and possibly arguing for a more thorough follow-up audit or diagnostic of the sector processes and tools available to address institutional weaknesses. More and better analysis is not only possible. It is needed.

---

[35] See, for instance, Estache (2017a) for a longer discussion and additional sources and, in particular, Jaglin et al. (2011) for a useful and relevant discussion of decentralisation implementation challenges in the water sector.

PART III

INSTITUTIONS AND DEVELOPMENT
IN TANZANIA

Based on the five preceding analyses of key thematic areas, and the more general description of the political, economic and institutional features of Tanzania's development in the first part of the volume, this last part tries to synthesise what has been learned. This exercise leads to an articulated view of the main institutional problems hindering progress in various areas, their negative consequences for development, and, most importantly, their causes, proximate or more distant, as well as their susceptibility to reforms. This is the essence of the 'diagnostic' this whole volume has endeavoured to produce.

9

An Institutional Diagnostic of Tanzania's Development

François Bourguignon and Samuel Mwita Wangwe

This final chapter has two goals. First, it aims to synthesise what has been learned from the previous chapters, emphasising the institutional challenges that have been identified. Second, it seeks to identify the main common factors behind those challenges, as well as the policies and reforms most able to weaken their effects. Indeed, it appears that most of the identified instances of institutional challenges in the Tanzanian economy result from a small number of basic institutional weaknesses, which logically form the core of our final diagnostic. The reflection on the ways to remedy them, while taking into account the political economy context, including the structure of political power, leads to a set of recommendations for reform that follow two key principles about the way to approach reform of the legal and administrative apparatus in Tanzania. The first principle is to allow for more competition and market mechanisms both within the economy and in the way it is managed. The second principle emphasises the need for a continuous rigorous, independent, and transparent evaluation of the functioning of the public sector at all administrative levels, of policy outcomes, and of the socioeconomic progress being achieved. Whether these principles may be applied mostly depends on political economy factors.

I THE IDENTIFIED INSTITUTIONAL CONSTRAINTS ON TANZANIAN DEVELOPMENT

This first part of the chapter summarises the conclusions drawn from the seven preceding chapters. Organising them within an integrated and coherent framework is undertaken in the second part of the chapter.

A The Uncertain Growth Engine of Tanzania's Economic Development

Tanzania's development since independence has been deeply affected by major institutional changes that took place during this period – from a market economy and import substitution industrialisation just before and after independence, to a socialist economy after the 1967 Arusha Declaration, to a market economy again after the economic crisis of the late 1970s and early 1980s that led to the Economic Survival Strategy (1981–2), a home-grown Adjustment Programme (1982–5), and the Structural Adjustment Programme (SAP) driven by the International Monetary Fund (IMF) and the World Bank after 1985. Such a major institutional oscillation is bound to have left some deep imprints on the way today's economy works.

If the severe slow-down that characterised the difficult shift from a socialist to a market economy during the 1980s and the first half of the 1990s has now given way to solid growth, several concerns can be expressed about its long-run sustainability.

First of all, there is uncertainty about what is and what could be the growth engine of Tanzania in the future. Such an engine must necessarily relate to the tradable sector. This is because final demand constraints related to domestic income are absent in foreign trade and also because production for the domestic economy does not produce foreign currency resources. Relying on non-tradable activities thus requires some growing exogenous source of outside revenues. Yet agricultural output has grown less rapidly than gross domestic product (GDP) since the mid-2000s, and manufacturing has been roughly on a par growth with GDP. It is therefore unlikely they played a leading role in the overall growth of the economy, especially in view of the relatively modest GDP share of manufacturing – that is, 9 per cent. Favourable terms of trade as well as foreign capital and aid flows were more important explanatory factors of the satisfactory growth performances observed since the turn of the millennium. They raised aggregate domestic demand, fostering production and investment in goods and services that could not be imported. This may not last. The emphasis put on industrialisation, including the agroindustry and therefore agriculture, by the present administration and its predecessors is thus most justified. So far, however, results have been limited, and identifying whether institutional constraints are responsible for this lack of dynamism is of great importance.

Three other sources of concern come out of our review of Tanzania's development. The first is the slow, and in some cases negative growth of productivity throughout most sectors of the economy, except in agriculture, where GDP share grew despite a falling share of employment. This seems in contradiction to the rather high observed rate of investment and suggests the latter may not be well allocated, with possibly a deficit in productive factors complementary to private investment, infrastructure, and power in particular. A second concern is the excessive dependence of the economy on foreign financing, including official development assistance. This means that the high level of investment of the last decade or so may not be sustainable in the long run, unless domestic savings can progressively substitute for foreign fund inflows.

The final concern is about the slow reduction of poverty, despite relatively high aggregate growth per capita performances, indicating that growth has not been particularly inclusive. This may be because of the nature of growth or essentially a lack of integration of agriculture and the informal, predominantly rural sector in the growth process, another key institutional characteristic of Tanzanian society. This bias is reinforced by the low quality of public services delivered to poor people. The low quality of education in particular reduces the future ability of the poor segment of the population to integrate within the modern economy.

B Tanzania Compares Well with Peer Countries in International Governance Rankings

There are a number of governance indicators that aim to summarise in a simple multi-dimensional scale the various dimensions of countries' governance. It is not clear whether such a complex system as the governance of a country can really be summarised through a few summary indicators. Moreover, the significance of most available indicators in terms of symptoms or causes of institutional challenges is often very ambiguous. However, they convey information that is worth examining.

Two approaches have been used in the present study. First, use has been made of the six aggregate indicators of the well-known Worldwide Governance Indicators (WGI) database. They are themselves based on a large number of sub-indicators, which were classified into six categories, and then a 'common factor' was statistically extracted from each of the categories. The second approach was developed for this study, with a statistical procedure being used to classify all individual indicators in the extremely rich Quality of Government (QoG) database according to the proximity of their cross-country variations rather than imposing an arbitrary grouping. Then, a common factor was extracted from all indicators within each of these endogenous categories to characterise how a country performs within a category. This endogenous categorisation yields results slightly different from the WGI. In addition to these two sets of indicators, use was also made of the investment climate surveys conducted by the World Bank based on a sample of firm managers.

The main governance challenges according to WGI are 'control of corruption', 'government effectiveness', and 'regulatory quality', in that order. The procedure based on QoG data points first to 'administrative capacity', then to 'competitiveness', which is similar to 'regulatory quality' in WGI, and finally to the 'control of corruption and the rule of law'. Within that approach, however, corruption is high in Tanzania but not worse than in neighbouring countries (Kenya, Malawi, Uganda, Mozambique, and Burundi), except Rwanda, or in better performing developing economies such as Bangladesh, Vietnam, and Cambodia.

We draw from this statistical exercise that 'government effectiveness' or 'administrative capacity' to manage the economy seem to be the most serious weaknesses in Tanzania, even though what these generic titles cover and what is primarily responsible for the lack of effectiveness is not very precise.

'Regulatory quality' or 'competitiveness' include the impact of taxes, business regulation, and the quality of public infrastructure and services on the ease of doing business in general. 'Doing business' and 'competitiveness index' rankings released respectively by the World Bank and the World Economic Forum confirm the negative expert appraisal included in the preceding indicators.

Corruption is widespread, or even ubiquitous, in the developing world, whether in sub-Saharan Africa, Asia, or Latin America. This does not necessarily hamper all aspects of development. Some aspects of corruption may even facilitate economic development, as when it permits the relaxing of administrative constraints that divert the allocation of resources from their efficient use. Yet it is noteworthy that, substantially more than with the WGI indicators, Tanzanian business managers find corruption to be particularly detrimental to the economy.

C How Tanzania's Decision Makers Evaluate Its Institutions

Two surveys were launched to ask decision makers in different positions in society what they felt were the most economically constraining institutional challenges in Tanzania. The first was a questionnaire survey administered to a sample of about 100 decision makers from the public and private sectors, at various hierarchical levels and in different areas of the country. The second survey consisted of open-ended interviews with top decision makers and politicians within different areas of expertise and from different horizons. This second group of respondents comprised sixty people, including two past presidents, the Chief Justice, and the Controller Auditor General, as well as top civil servants, businesspeople, and academics.

For the most part, these surveys and in-depth interviews were conducted mostly in 2016 and early 2017. As this was the first year of the Magufuli administration, one can wonder whether respondents were referring to the previous or the new administration when they were interrogated. The formal survey asked the respondents to refer to the medium- to long-term past (described as the past five to ten years) when answering the questions. This timeline was given in recognition that institutions take time to change, and therefore it would be more informative to understand long-standing patterns than any perceived changes that may come with a new administration. To capture the perceived direction of change with respect to the past, respondents were later asked whether they thought things were changing with the new administration. The same principle applied informally to the open-ended interviews. The evaluation of Tanzanian institutions by decision makers thus essentially focused on the pre-Magufuli era.

The most frequently cited institutional challenges that came out of the questionnaire survey and the open-ended interviews were the political institutions, the way politics is done in Tanzania, the public administration, and the business environment.[1] More precisely, the following domains were singled out as particularly problematic:

- land law, whose complexity and slow implementation entail social conflicts, numerous court cases, corruption, and frustration among both smallholders and investors;
- corruption in general, between government or administration and business, between the administration and people, and between government and citizen (patronage);
- a lack of transparency in state operations and the weakness of check-and-balance institutions;
- poor regulation of business activity, referring to the operations of big businesses or to the general investment climate;
- poor regulation of utilities, especially electricity; and
- the inefficiency of the civil service: low capacity, absenteeism, corruption, overlapping responsibilities, and patronage in recruitment practices.

Of course, this list is a mixed bag in the sense that it includes institutions *per se* (e.g. the land law or the executive's checks and balances) but also the causes (e.g. lack of capacity in civil service) and the symptoms (e.g. absenteeism of civil servants, corruption), and the consequences of these weaknesses (e.g. land conflicts or investment climate). Yet the general picture these surveys consistently draw of economically relevant institutional challenges in Tanzania is instructive, and parallels the conclusions drawn from governance indicators.

Identifying the causes of institutional weaknesses and differentiating symptoms and consequences was undertaken in the second part of the study, by focusing on specific thematic areas thought to be of critical importance both for the functioning of the economy and for our understanding of the nature of institutional challenges.

D Institutions and Development in Some Critical Areas

Five areas were chosen based on the information collected from decision makers in the preceding stage of the study, which were thought to exemplify the way particular institutions may obstruct or slow down development. Each area gave rise to an in-depth analysis, generally, by a Tanzanian scholar, and was then discussed by a foreign expert so as to put the issues at stake in an international perspective. A summary of each study is given in what follows.

---

[1] Note that questions related to this particular area in the questionnaire differed substantially from questions in the 'doing business' survey of the World Bank or in the competitiveness index of the World Economic Forum.

1 Business and Politics: An Ambiguous Relationship

In Tanzania, as in most developing countries, big modern firms, or conglomerates, contribute a sizeable part of GDP growth and are the main employers in the modern private sector. Because of this, there are good reasons for governments to support them, presumably in a fully transparent way. But because of both positive and negative externalities and/or market failures more frequent in developing economies, their activity should also be regulated, again in the most transparent way. The relationship between big business and the government, or the ruling party, is particularly opaque in Tanzania and frequently subject to scandals of corruption uncovering anti-developmental policy decisions. This is contrary to a well-thought policy framework that would establish clear reciprocal behavioural rules for business and government agencies in the interest of the community. This absence of a transparent and effective industrial policy – in the broad sense of regulating, monitoring, and possibly supporting big as well as medium-sized business – appears to be a major institutional challenge with major implications for Tanzania's development.

This key institutional issue has been analysed in depth in Chapter 4, 'Politics and Business: An Ambiguous Relationship' by Samuel Mwita Wangwe, and in Hazel Gray's comments. Various factors explain the current state of play and the relative inefficiency of industrial policies and strategies. Three of them seem particularly important. In some cases, they point themselves to other structural weaknesses of the politico-economic apparatus.

First, regime changes in recent history may not have left very much time for market rules and industrial policy principles to settle down in the national community. The economy went from markets subject to colonial rule before independence, to more open markets just after independence, to limited and mostly hidden market operations during the socialist period, and back to markets with rules progressively being set but still incomplete or largely ineffective during the liberalisation period and in some cases until the late 2010s.

Going back and forth across regimes also implies that there is no full political consensus in the Tanzanian political elite about what regime to favour, whether full market capitalism or a mixed economy with substantial weight given to the state. This absence of clear consensual principles with respect to the relationship between the state and the market, or private firms, may be considered as an institutional failure *per se* as it introduces uncertainty among economic actors about the attitude of the state with respect to private firms. This ideological ambiguity may be a second reason why no clear strategy with respect to big business and the private sector in general is yet fully explicit. Almost forty years after the end of the socialist era, the Magufuli administration exhibited such ambivalence with respect to private investment. However, the Suluhu administration now reverted to a more business-friendly approach.

A third reason has to do with the ethnicity of the owners and managers of big business. It turns out that a majority of large firm owners are Tanzanian Asians or Tanzanian Arabs. Several Asian businessmen were present in Tanzania just before or just after independence. Starting from trade businesses at the local or regional level, they invested in manufacturing behind the protection barriers erected, on their own advice, by the young independent state. Behind the scenes, or sometimes as managers of parastatals, they continued to have influence during the socialist era. After liberalisation, they progressively built economic empires, soon joined by Tanzanian Arabs. A majority of big business leaders thus belong to ethnic minorities that have tended to dominate economic life outside agriculture, practically since independence, with less strength, of course, during the socialist era. These ethnic groups are not fully integrated with the indigenous African population, which tends to see them as 'exploiters' (Fouéré, 2015), and considers them today as running a large part of the Tanzanian economy. Because of this, any policy that would openly favour business might meet popular opposition if the main beneficiaries were perceived to be Asian and Arab big businesspeople. Successive governments may have refrained from developing this kind of policy, even though it was possibly beneficial for development, explicitly because of this often-unacknowledged ethnic division.

It is unclear why there are few indigenous Africans among top chief executive officers, especially in industry, even though things may be progressively changing. At the time resentment against Asian business was at its highest, indigenous African entrepreneurs complained that an Asian monopoly prevented them from raising funds from banks or hiring people with the required know-how to get into big business. Such a complaint is not necessarily justified. Yet today, only two indigenous Africans are among the fifteen top business leaders in Tanzania. Younger indigenous African businessmen have recently been in the news, though.[2]

Another reason for the lower weight of indigenous in comparison with non-indigenous Tanzanians among business leaders might be found in the clear comparative advantage, because of ethnic proximity with the people, of the former's presence in political or public service careers rather than in business, although this could be compensated for by their much larger population size. On the other hand, it is true that Asian and Arab business leaders have sometimes moved openly into politics to reinforce business's position in general, rather than acting from behind the scenes. In any case, this ethnic division in Tanzania, which is found with comparable features in other African countries,[3] is clearly an important determinant of the functioning of economy and politics.

[2] A twenty-eight-year-old Tanzanian was ranked among the top thirty young African entrepreneurs by *Forbes* in 2017 (www.forbes.com/sites/mfonobongnsehe/2017/03/13/30-most-promising-young-entrepreneurs-in-africa-2017/).

[3] The same issues with Asian business arose in other East African countries and with the Lebanese in West Africa. In the case of East Africa, Ranja suggests that there is some strong path dependence as Asian business was dominant just before and after independence, when indigenous Africans were involved mostly in politics and agriculture. Because of family business background, it has been easier for Asians than indigenous Africans to launch new businesses (Ranja, 2003).

A fourth and last reason can be invoked to explain the difficulty of establishing clear rules for industrial and regulation policy. This is the fragmentation of political power within the dominant CCM party as well as the existence of groups within the party with diverse economic interests in big business. Divergent interests and views, including ideological, across CCM factions themselves linked to diverse business interests make it impossible to get an agreement on policy decisions involving big business interests, or to prevent party members colluding with business, or even to expel them when caught in corruption scandals.[4] A centralised power within the ruling party would probably eliminate this obstacle, and this may indeed be the strategy that was initially followed by President Magufuli, formerly a second-tier personality within CCM, who was elected on a strong anti-corruption mandate in 2015.

If the lack of explicit and effective industrial and business regulation policies is to be considered as a key institutional weakness of the Tanzanian economy, caused by, and leading to, corruption, clientelism, and cronyism, two important questions must be considered.

First, if no explicit industrial policy favouring some specific sector through protection, infrastructure development, fiscal exonerations, or subsidies seems possible or desirable, then why not adopt a neutral policy that would favour business in general – that is, the World Bank 'doing business' approach? Why wouldn't big businesspeople themselves be asking for such an industrial policy, sometimes referred to as 'horizontal' industrial policy? After all, a better investment climate would dynamise investment, foster the development of small and medium-sized enterprises, accelerate growth, and finally benefit big businesspeople too. As long as such a policy would not change their own arrangements and the support they get from government people, they should not oppose such an improvement of the investment climate. The difficulty here is that it would be difficult to improve the business climate by fighting civil servants who are taking bribes for delivering a licence or a permit to new investors or operating firms, when bribes from big business are known to be cashed higher up in their hierarchy. The same would be true when deciding about public infrastructure investments, big firms managing to have them serve their own interest rather than that of the collective. Corruption is contagious. It cannot be stopped for some operations when it continues elsewhere. Without powerful control measures, big business's grip on parts of the political elite thus trickles down to a deleterious general business climate.

---

[4] Edward Lowassa, prime minister, and several of his ministers had to resign after the Richmond scandal in 2008, a private power provider that failed to deliver and charged onerous fees with the support of the government. Yet they were not expelled from the CCM party. Lowassa himself competed to be the party's presidential candidate in 2015, before moving to the opposition when Magufuli was chosen.

Second, isn't it the case that the Tanzanian economy does well, so that business–politics collusion may not be a big problem after all? Maybe, but is it doing well sustainably? The review of Tanzanian development in this volume points to the relative weakness of growth in tradable sectors, especially agriculture and manufacturing. Could it be that the big business–politics connection has some responsibility for this? Wangwe indeed suggests that imports are often given some advantage over domestic production through supporting the 'traders'. Sugar and rice producers have complained that imports make domestic production barely profitable. Is such an industrial policy in the interest of the country – in other words, the consumers and industrial transformers of these products – or in the private interest of traders? Transparency about the goal pursued with such a policy and its consequences is lacking. Public statements are made about policies to be pursued or reforms to be undertaken, but they are generally weakly motivated and not, or poorly, evaluated *ex post*. This is what Wangwe refers to as transparency without accountability.

2 State Coordination: Fluctuating Stances about Decentralisation
Development requires an efficient government sector that is able to produce and manage public goods, monitor and regulate the private sector, collect taxes to finance these activities, and redistribute across social, geographic, or income groups. The way the government organises its activity is essential for its efficiency. A key organisational issue in this respect is the allocation of decision power among the various decision and monitoring units of any government, from the centre (president or prime minister), to ministries, to local governments and various types of public agencies.

It would have been too unwieldy to analyse the efficiency of the Tanzanian government apparatus by reviewing all its dimensions. Cases of responsibility overlaps, competition across units, and rent-seeking seem to be present in many areas and at various levels of the public sector's vertical structure. Instead, the approach to the issue of state coordination in this volume has focused on the relationship between two levels of government, the central and the local, on the way it has evolved over time and a practical aspect of it, namely the collection of local taxes.

The dominant fact in the fascinating account that Servacius Likwelile and Paschal Assey give of decentralisation in Tanzania in Chapter 6 is the constant vacillation of the government since independence about the decision power that should be granted to local government authorities (LGAs), both in terms of local service delivery and tax collection, that is between decentralisation taken as deconcentration, with centrally appointed civil servants in charge of local affairs, or devolution of decision-making power to local governments and their democratically elected decision-making entities. The central–local government relationship went from decentralisation, inherited from the colonial period, in the first decade after independence, to full centralisation during the early socialist period, back to weak decentralisation in 1972, and then to centralisation again whereas an ambitious local government reform was voted in 1998 that had to be progressively implemented over a rather long period. As of 2014, the end of that period, however, neither a comprehensive local government law nor a harmonised central and sector legislation was in place. This is presumably still the case today, although the Suluhu administration has recently shown signs of willingness to implement the National Decentralisation Policy, which has been on hold for two decades or so.

In the field of fiscal decentralisation, the oscillation was still more pronounced. The responsibility for the collection of the property tax changed three times in the last decade: decentralised before 2008, centralised, and then re-decentralised in 2014, and apparently centralised again in 2016.

Such back-and-forth movement would not be a concern if it simply corresponded to a trial-and-error process, the aim of which was to find the most efficient arrangement. This does not seem the case, however, as the periodicity of changes does not permit rigorous evaluation of the various regimes. As well acknowledged in Chapter 6 and in the comments by Jan Willem Gunning, capacity is clearly missing at the local level for the assessment, the monitoring, and the enforcement of taxation. For the time being, it is thus the case that tax collection should optimally be in the hands of the central government, while local governments rely on conditional central government grants to finance local operations not centrally managed. On the other hand, local tax revenues account for a very minor part of the total budget of local governments. Together, these two arguments logically lead to the hypothesis that oscillating responsibilities reflect either some hidden rent-seeking competition between local or regional politicians, central government tax collectors, and possibly ruling party members, or the views of some external decision maker, such as donors or a new leader.

Likwelile and Assey recognise that corruption was rampant both with the centralised and the decentralised tax collection arrangement. They also mention that the World Bank had apparently been pressing for decentralisation to be re-established in 2014, a decision that was cancelled in 2016 under the Magufuli presidency, thus showing a consistent, and probably justified, opposition of the central government to decentralising tax collection. Even in that case, however, the issue of corruption remains open.

Fiscal decentralisation is often justified by resorting to the argument that it is an incentive for the accountability of local governments with respect to their constituency. Gunning is right in stressing that fiscal decentralisation is in fact neither necessary nor sufficient for local government accountability. Sharing information about the actual grants received from the central government and the accompanying conditionality with local constituencies could be effective too, as well illustrated by the positive effect of advertising central government grants to local schools on the management of schools in Uganda (Reinikka and Svensson, 2005, 2011). Existing studies in Tanzania suggest, however, that not much of the publicising of local financial information reaches the public – see Chapter 6 by Likwelile and Assey.[5] Studies also show that there is an overlap or confusion of responsibilities between local government executives and centrally appointed civil servants working with them or monitoring them at higher district or regional level, but often applying the central government's agenda (Venugopal and Yilmaz, 2010; Hulst et al., 2015).[6] None of this is contributing to local accountability.

The preceding mostly anecdotal evidence indicates that decentralisation is not very effective in Tanzania. This means that local preferences for local public goods and constraints in creating and managing them may not be satisfactorily taken into account in the overall public decision-making process, thus reducing the overall efficiency of the public sector.

Should decentralisation be made more effective in Tanzania, and more efficient in view of its potentially high current cost? As noted by Gunning, this is an empirical question, but there is unfortunately little evidence to answer it, in Tanzania or in developing countries in general.[7]

Yet the chapter by Likwelile and Assey, as well as Gunning's comments, raise an important question for our reflection. It concerns the issue of capacity, and consequently of capacity building. An obvious limit to an enhanced decentralisation strategy in Tanzania is the capacity of local executives to produce local public goods and manage budgetary issues as well as the relationship with their constituency and with central government. This is very clear in the issue of tax collection but probably applies to other dimensions of local governance, even though centrally appointed local administrators or monitoring agents may not always have more capacity themselves. Under these conditions, would a central government resist enhancing decentralisation because it is not in its political interest, or simply because local executives don't have the necessary management capacity? If decentralisation is essentially a good policy, with adequate local capacity, then it would be important to facilitate capacity building at the local level, a point stressed by Likwelile and Assey. This would probably be the most efficient first step towards a more ambitious decentralisation policy.

In summary, it is difficult to say whether limited decentralisation has been a handicap for Tanzanian development. That it is a desirable long-run goal is not debatable. Yet conditions and, most importantly, the local capacity for a strong effective decentralisation are presently absent in a substantial part of the country.

---

[5] See also the interesting survey undertaken by Twaweza on public knowledge of local economic management, where 70 per cent of the people were unaware of budget issues in their local government, despite the information being duly disseminated (Twaweza, 2013).

[6] Note that, though they appeared five years apart, both articles describe the tension between village council members and administrators, essentially created by a system of public administration that remains extremely centralised.

[7] See Mansuri and Rao (2013) for a cautious synthesis of the literature.

The real handicap, however, lies in the succession of contradictory policy regimes, which has prevented learning taking place over time. Of concern is also the fact that corruption seems to have been present under the various regimes.

3 The Civil Service

The smooth and transparent functioning of modern states relies on the quality of the civil service. Several constraints interfered with the satisfactory working of the civil service in Tanzania in the past and hampered its economic development. Some of them tend to be less severe today, but serious challenges remain.

In Chapter 5, Rwekaza Mukandala lists four such weaknesses: capacity, motivation and conduct, politicisation – or political interference – and resources and tools. Capacity and resources clearly depend on the level of development and the availability of human capital and public funds. From an institutional point of view, motivation and political interference play the most important role because they ultimately define the rules according to which the civil service, the political apparatus – that is, government, parties, parliament – and the private sector interact in the economic development process, and which possibly deviate from official rules.

Initially extremely limited but fast growing after independence, the Tanzanian civil service expanded still faster but, in a first stage, in an orderly way during the socialist era. Needs were enormous because of the expansion of services such as health and education, the centrally controlled management of local communities, and the need to coordinate the multiple nationalised and newly created public companies. Collective motivation was great, and strict rules preventing high-level civil servants doing business or enjoying hidden material advantages were enforced. Unwise decisions at political level, the multiplication of parastatals, the quasi-impossibility of coordinating them, and external events, rather than a dysfunctional civil service, were responsible for the chaos and the severe crisis of the early 1980s.

Before then, however, and still worse during the crisis, the functioning of the civil service had severely deteriorated. Not only had it been completely disorganised, but also initial rules of conduct had been dismantled, partly to compensate for the effects of the crisis. High-level civil servants and parastatal executives obtained huge non-monetary compensation for declining real wages, whereas they were making deals with the private sector to further increase their income. A huge wave of corruption settled in.

Things became worse at the time of the transition back to a market economy. The process of privatisation and the lack of a civil service able to efficiently manage this new economic system opened the door still more widely to all sorts of deals involving civil servants, politicians, and businesspeople. A culture of corruption permeated the whole economy and the public sector in particular. At the same time, the civil service was decimated by the SAP and its focus on market mechanisms as a substitute for state intervention.

It took time before the situation came back to a more normal position. At the turn of the millennium, when donors started to weaken their market bias, the civil service could at last fill its role as a policymaking facilitator and the manager of public goods and services. Yet corruption, political patronage, and the pre-eminence of politics in policymaking were entrenched. This is still the situation today, even though President Magufuli broke away from his predecessors in showing political will and energy to reduce corruption.[8]

Mukandala gives many examples of the way in which corruption and the lack of motivation of civil servants are costly for the economy and the society. For instance, the cost of teacher absenteeism has been evaluated at 1 per cent of GDP. Assuming that other civil servants display equivalent behaviour, showing up at work but not working the legal number of hours or shirking, the cost would rise to 2.5 per cent of GDP. Add to this tax evasion, over-invoicing of contracts, and other corrupt practices, and the cost to the economy becomes sizeable. Patronage is another issue. The size of the public sector increased by 50 per cent between 2012 and 2015, with a net addition of 70,000 employees every year. Questions arise whether all these employees fill real needs; whether the newly recruited employees are friends or relatives of politicians – or civil servants; whether it is possible to expand at such a pace while maintaining the same level of productivity; and whether recruitment criteria had to be substantially lowered for these new employees to be appointed. Likewise, it turns out that civil servants are better paid – a 30 to 40 per cent premium on average – than private sector workers, even controlling for educational level and age.[9] Although the difference may be smaller for top positions, is this wage premium justified by efficiency arguments or is it a political gift to a pivotal part of the electorate?

Even though Tanzania's level of corruption seems comparable with its neighbours and even better growth performers, this is certainly not a reason for not doing anything to improve the quality of Tanzania's civil service. It is unfortunately not possible to give a precise estimate of how much income is being lost or diverted because of a weak civil service. Available evidence is too partial to permit such estimates. Likewise, as emphasised in Jan Willem Gunning's comments, it is not possible to evaluate how much growth has been missed. Yet absenteeism, the excessive number of civil servants, and their inadequate skill are doubtlessly detrimental to efficiency and growth.

It remains to be seen whether civil service reform can be done and how. As emphasised by Gunning and Mukandala, any reform has its own political economy context. In the present case, the countervailing forces to a reform would be civil servants themselves, the politicians who use the civil service for patronage or as a channel to cash bribes, and those private agents who benefit from bribing

---

[8] Once elected, he launched a campaign to eliminate ghost employees and check the qualification and degrees of public employees.

[9] See Leyaro et al. (2014, Table 7).

civil servants and politicians. All of them have power, including the civil servants themselves. Yet introducing more discipline in the areas where absenteeism and shirking are strong does not seem impossible. A lot of experiments have been run lately in various countries involving the kind of carrot to offer and the kind of stick to use.[10] Improving the quality of recruitment, devoting more resources to capacity building, and avoiding the recent oscillation in the number of new hires cannot do any harm and will not meet very much opposition either.

4 The Tanzanian Land Management System: Complex, Inefficient, and Conflictive

Land has been the subject of intense debate and dispute in Tanzania as it is the main resource of a large population of poor farmers and cattle herders as well as an essential input for commercial investment in rural and urban areas.

Chapter 7 by Sist J. Mramba sets out to analyse the existing system of land occupancy rights and its effectiveness in managing multiple sources of conflicts, and proposes how the system could be reformed. It is shown that there is some continuity in matters of land tenure (such as government ownership of land) between colonial times and post-independence Tanganyika, and later the United Republic of Tanzania, whereby some basic principles of the colonial era were kept after independence. An important modification that was made is in respect of the way the land could be alienated from customary users so as to protect small farmers. Indeed, the whole period after independence has been associated with a permanent debate about the space to be given to customary laws in handling interests of public and private large investors. The creation of the semi-collective *Ujamaa* villages in Nyerere's socialist era impacted on the alienation of customary land in the process of reorganising production. The liberalisation period in the mid-1980s reverted to the dual land system, with the development of large-scale plantations and better protected customary land rights. Nevertheless, land conflicts persisted unabated.

The Land Act (1999), a major piece of legislation, reiterates that all land in Tanzania shall continue to be public and remain vested in the president as trustee for and on behalf of all the citizens of Tanzania. This is of course a key institutional principle. A second principle is the recognition of the customary law through a categorisation of land. For the purposes of management, land is categorised into 'general land', 'village land', and 'reserved land' directly managed by the state. On general land, officially agreed users are given an extended lease, or granted right of occupancy, governed by statutory law. On village land, occupancy is governed by local customary law. The corresponding rights can be formalised by Certificates of Customary Rights of Occupancy (CCROs), with the land under the jurisdiction of the village itself being certified. However, these certificates cannot be delivered as long as the village has not had a its land surveyed and issued a land use plan, which leads to the release of a Certificate of Village Land (CVL).

---

[10] See for instance the section on State Capacity in Dal Bo and Finan (2020).

While the Tanzanian Land Act was associated with much optimism in Africa,[11] Klaus Deininger points out in his comments that in practice four elements illustrate the gaps in Tanzania's land registration system for small-holders, which impose costs on the broader economy. These four elements are: (1) low level of computerisation of land administration; (2) lack of integration between spatial and textual records; (3) high fees for formalising transfers; (4) and limited number of new CCROs created annually. In this regard, Deininger proposes action on improving registry efficiency and integration, adjusting regulations for low-cost first-time registration, and completing CCRO issuance in urban areas.

Land for investment is a major challenge. While large-scale land investment by foreigners has continued to be welcomed, in practice acquisition of land for investment has been complex, especially where the land is village land. In this case, village land has first to be transformed into general land, which presently represents only 2 per cent of total land, and the procedure is cumbersome. Consequently, land investments are limited with consequences on economic growth.

Although the Land Commissioner, acting on behalf of the president, has power to grant general land, the use of this power is not common, and the process is long. Challenges of valuation have attracted frequent land conflicts. The initiative to acquire land may also come from the Tanzanian Investment Centre responding to the demand of investors. However, there are also less formal and less centralised procedures used in the acquisition of land, but these are not necessarily less complex.

Encouraging investments is one of the objectives of the present land management system. Another, possibly more important but also potentially conflictive, is to protect indigenous smallholders from acquisition by a large-scale operator. Transforming village land into general land to facilitate large-scale investments, in agriculture as well as in other activities, has been perceived as a threat to smallholder farmers rather than an opportunity to complement their activities with large-scale investors. A further disempowering mechanism has been exhibited in the way the commons in communities under customary tenure are managed. The village communities have been particularly vulnerable, given the argument that commons are unowned or idle, or simply that they belong to the state. On the agricultural side, the issue is clearly that of the trade-off between modern high-productivity large-scale production process and traditional low-productivity farming and herding. No clear answer has been given to this socially hypersensitive question.

Alternative models of empowerment have been used that engage more of the existing producers, such as contract farming and out grower schemes. These do not displace smallholder farmers, but there are no institutional mechanisms to provide them with some capacity over price fixing. As a result, farmers often

---

[11] See Alden-Willy (2003), for instance.

perceive that they are underpaid for the crops they supply to the large factories. On the other hand, the institutional framework for using smallholders' land as equity for facilitating participation in large-scale investments is not functional. The fact that this has been functional in other countries such as China suggests that this option deserves further scrutiny to find how it could be an option in Tanzania.[12] The dichotomy between traditional and modern agriculture and the tensions owing to the absence of a well-functioning land market are likely to continue.

Institutional mandates for granting land rights and ruling on disposition and dispute settlement do exist, but these are overshadowed by a multiplicity of actors and entities that overlap, have no effective coordination or collaboration, and often lack administrative capacity. In effect, capacity building at the various governance levels is needed. In practice, land management and administration has been faced with challenges of efficiency and effectiveness as well as shortage of staff and rent-seeking.

The question of the balance between centralisation and decentralisation arises in the case of land in the form of dualism in the land disposition system: centralisation of control and management of general land on the one hand and devolution of control to customary law at the village level. The oft-cited cases of overlap of responsibilities and the complexity of the relationship between the various central and local public entities in the land management system are a sign of struggles for power over resources and over rent-seeking between these levels of government. Some of the conflicts and difficulties in managing land issues have in part been attributed to this dualism, which affects the economic efficiency of the whole land sector.

In this regard, Deininger provides useful insights into the alternative of providing space for village governments to integrate the investment activities of large-scale investors with village-level land use plans. He makes a case for complete issuance of CVLs – which, today, only a fraction of villages possess – using modern low-cost surveying technology, and proposes clarifying the content and status of village land use plans as a basis for attracting potential investors with a profile that would most effectively contribute to local development. This option would provide villages with the incentives to systematically identify investment opportunities that are consistent with their own land use plans. This provides a strong case for empowerment of local governments in land management for investors.

Weak land governance and property rights systems, including limited capacity to generate clear records, provide information on time, and process titles, lead to opaque land deals, and have contributed to facilitating corruption and undercutting responsible actors seeking access to land for productive investment. As very well shown by Mramba, the same is true of the land judiciary system, which does not have the capacity to deal rigorously with the numerous

---

[12] See Zhou et al. (2021).

cases put to it. Nowadays, the ongoing awareness campaigns and computerisation through the Information Land Management Integrated System are expected to bring more transparency and minimise the opportunities of corruption. This is an opportunity that remains to be harnessed.

A finding worth emphasising in Tanzania is the complementarity between local governance in land matters and the impact of land titling, even through rather informal CCROs, on agricultural investment and productivity. Thus, Kassa (2018) shows that the effects of titling on agricultural investment is generally positive and sizeable, but the investment return is either negative or non-existent when there is a higher level of disapproval of the local governing units by plot owners. Likewise, Hombrados et al. (2015) find no significant effect of land titling once the characteristics of farm households are taken into account, and suggest that the capacity of local civil servants in charge of land issues and the enforcement of property rights may be determinant.

Over the last fifteen years or so, several major reports have been mandated by parliamentary commissions or the executive to evaluate the present legislative land occupation right system and suggest possible reforms. As of 2018, no legislative change had been made to the 1999 Land Act.

5 The Power Sector: An Example of De Facto Weak Regulation

The power sector has long been singled out as a major obstacle to development in Tanzania. In her in-depth analysis of the institutional evolution of the Tanzanian power sector (Chapter 8), Catrina Godinho addresses this issue. She considers the underlying political economy factors that have made it so difficult for Tanzania to move from an institutional equilibrium that does not bring about the desired sector outcomes in terms of power supply (investment, system expansion, and technical performance) to one that does.

Notwithstanding attempted institutional restructuring and ambitious reform policies, the structure of the power sector continues to most resemble that of the traditional industry model, which is a state-owned, vertically integrated (generation, transmission, and distribution) monopoly, regulated by the government (i.e. not an independent regulator).[13] This model has largely been dysfunctional in Tanzania and across the region for decades. Yet TANESCO the state-owned electricity company, continues to operate as a vertically integrated utility with considerable monopoly power. The (difficult) introduction of private sector participation in generation and the establishment of an independent regulator, the Energy and Water Utilities Regulatory Authority (EWURA), has not changed the situation substantially. Electricity supply in Tanzania is persistently unstable, often inadequate, and insecure. Owing to the high coping costs associated with drought periods and political pressure around tariff increases, the sector's financial standing has remained precarious.

---

[13] This model was the international standard from the early twentieth century through to the 1980s (Eberhard and Godinho, 2017).

Tariffs remain below cost recovery, planning has not translated into timely initiation of procurement of new power generation capacity, procurement has mostly not been transparent or competitive, and TANESCO's technical and financial performance is poor.

Political interference in the sector and its institutions has been a constant feature of Tanzania's power sector. For example, the president's obstruction of regulator-approved tariff increases in 2016, followed by the dismissal of several executives at TANESCO, and finally the removal of EWURA's Director General all constitute rather problematic interventions. These and similar decisions on the part of the executive seem to bely a strong short-run bias considering that, in the long run, suppressed tariffs and unstable governance reduce the capacity of TANESCO to invest in sector maintenance and expansion, discourage private investment in the sector, and increase the cost of doing business. While these decisions are often justified by protecting the (urban) poor, low electricity access rates and risk-inflated costs of supply do not benefit those who need modern energy services the most; nor do they benefit businesses in general, who frequently cite poor electricity services as a primary development constraint; nor do they contribute to the reduction of poverty through economic growth.

There have also been a number of high-level corruption scandals. These were related to deals made with independent power producers to enlarge the power generation capacity of the country or to respond to emergency needs. The Independent Power Tanzania Ltd and Richmond deals resulted in much delayed and absurdly overpriced power supply, which led to huge financial losses at TANESCO. Those deals were authorised by the government, which suggests that high-rank executives were involved. A prime minister had to resign in 2008 after the Richmond scandal broke out.

The problematic experience with corruption in both public and private deals underscores the vulnerability of sector governance to political interference in a country where the political economy system is prone to using publicly owned companies and their links to the private sector for rent-seeking and patronage, even where corporatisation efforts attempt to ring-fence such interests. However, much of the blame has been laid at the feet of the private sector, strengthening the ideological bias against private participation in the sector – especially against private energy providers that could function as least-cost suppliers to a publicly owned system operator. These outcomes reflect a lack of capacity in the government and/or political will in the executive to ensure transparent and accountable governance in the sector. This is confirmed by recent moves against the independent regulator, which had emerged as an island of excellence in terms of technical expertise in the region.

There are too few accountability mechanisms built into existing legislation, specifically the 2008 Electricity Act, that could really bring key directives into force. This leaves the political executive with considerable power over policy implementation. Reforms have been resisted or at best implemented only partially, a situation that has contributed to checking (keeping low) levels of transparency and accountability. While potentially an improvement, the ESIRSR 2014–25 roadmap to reform has not been suitably translated into robust legislation. In effect, the status quo is maintained through institutional rules that include vertical appointment structures, archaic guidelines on sector information and lines of communication, and the frequent application of *de facto* power by political actors. In his discussion, Antonio Estache summarises well the state of play by stressing that the partial or biased implementation of past reforms, the repeated scandals about the attribution of private power deals, and their limited efficacy and ill-managed tariff policy have together made future reforms essentially 'non-credible'. Under these conditions, it will be difficult to attract private investors in order to expand the capacity of the sector to the extent needed by industrialisation and development.

Interestingly, Tanzania has emerged as a leader in the region when it comes to decentralised options – primarily because of EWURA's adroit regulation and lower levels of political interest or rent-seeking opportunities in smaller power projects. Urban and rural access rates have significantly increased in recent years. After a slow start, the Rural Energy Agency (REA) – established in 2005 – has begun functioning satisfactorily and rural electrification progress has considerably accelerated over the past five years, even though Estache suggests that it could move faster with support from the government and development partners. This is an interesting case, which highlights the benefits of effective regulation. However, the fact that it is sometimes perceived as a threat to the monopoly power of TANESCO and the special relationship between the executive and the utility could become a challenge. Even as it stands, REA hands over much of the distribution infrastructure to TANESCO after construction – which has placed further financial strain on the utility, but more power in the hands of those who control it. There have also been some allegations of corruption, as government funding has flowed to REA at unprecedented levels in recent years.

From a political economy perspective, Godinho argues that the situation of the power sector may be interpreted as an institutional equilibrium that might be conceptualised as the relatively stable and mutually reinforcing structural relationships that exist between public organisations, private interests, economic beliefs, and political power. The energy requirements of development will continue to rise rapidly as industrialisation takes root. Increased investment in the energy sector will prove determinative, yet institutional constraints remain immense, and the public sector is not in a position to finance the state-led model that is championed politically. Hence, there is a need to rely on the private sector without the guarantee that this will be politically acceptable, unless the executive moves toward greater transparency, accountability, and independence of sectoral institutions. The Suluhu administration has recently come with signs of more private sector tolerance, as indicated by the composition of the new board of TANESCO, which is dominated by members with a private sector background. This suggests that the type of inter-ference witnessed in the Magufuli administration might be reversed by the new administration.

E Conclusion of Part 1: Five Basic Institutional Weaknesses

In trying to classify the most often cited institutional weaknesses throughout the various chapters of this volume and the preceding summary synthesis, the following general headings become clear:

- ill-defined structure of public decision-making;
- selective distrust of market mechanisms and private sector;
- under-performing civil service;
- rent-seeking and corruption; and
- patronage and weak business regulation.

These themes were not only dominant in the in-depth studies of particular aspects of the Tanzanian economy but, rather remarkably, in the more general approach to institutions and development adopted in the first chapters of this volume. They indeed fit well the economic diagnostic that pointed, *inter alia*, to the lack of dynamism of the tradable sectors, excluding natural resources: agriculture being handicapped by an inefficient and partly ineffective land rights allocation system, and industrialisation being slowed down by a badly managed power sector and a weak regulation of the business sector. The slow develop-ment of these sectors and the poor delivery of public services such as education and skills development also explain the lack of inclusiveness of recent economic growth. The five institutional weaknesses noted here also fit the conclusions obtained from the analysis of the international databases on governance indica-tors as well as the results from our own survey of opinions among Tanzanian decision makers. There, the dominant themes were corruption, government ineffectiveness, and regulatory quality (or the investment climate). The general picture obtained from these diverse approaches to the relationship between institutions and development in Tanzania is thus consistent.

It is by choice that the preceding taxonomy has been limited to five items. Some of them could easily be broken down into autonomous sub-themes. For instance, the ill-defined structure of public decision-making comprises an often-mentioned overlap of responsibilities across different units of the public administration, but it also includes a centralisation bias of decision-making by which the central power may discretionarily intervene at all levels in the public sector, imposing decisions or changing the decisions taken at a lower admin-istrative level. This may be considered as a special case of overlap of responsi-bilities with absolute priority given to central power's objectives and rationale. In situations of asymmetric information and objectives between the executive and the decentralised administrative unit, this is bound to lead on occasion to economically inefficient decisions.

Another sub-theme under the 'ill-defined structure of public decision-making' heading is the gap between the passing of laws and reforms, or the recommendations emanating from publicly appointed expert commissions and their entry into force. A related issue is the succession of reforms in the same area. Examples of such situations were seen in relation to the management of the power sector, the reform of the civil service and the decentralisation law, multiple reports on the dysfunction of the land laws and the decentralisation law, with a particular situation in the latter case being a law that had not been fully brought to force, and parliamentary reports. These occasional gaps in the implementation of the law are also related to the centralisation bias, as they clearly emanate from the will of the executive, delaying the application of democratically grounded decisions.

It should be clear from this example that the identified institutional weaknesses in the list are generic in the sense that they may include deficiencies of a different nature. They will be analysed in more detail later. Before doing so, however, it must be emphasised that, although ubiquitous in the functioning of the Tanzanian economy, the five weaknesses are only the symptoms or the consequences of institutions that are working in a way that is not as favourable to long-run inclusive development as it could be. As such, they do not say much about the underlying causes of this unsatisfactory functioning, even though some of these causes have been mentioned on several occasions throughout the preceding chapters. It is now time to regroup them into a consistent framework to help us to understand the origins of institutional challenges for the development of Tanzania, and how to address them.

II THE INSTITUTIONAL DIAGNOSTIC

The preceding list of institutional weaknesses corresponds to the symptoms of institutional dysfunctions. A diagnostic must go beyond the symptoms to uncover the causes behind them and envisage possible remedies. This is what is done in the second part of this chapter.

A Institutional Weaknesses, Proximate Causes, and
Deep Factors: A Conceptual Framework

Table 9.1, presumptuously termed 'The diagnostic table', tries to relate the basic institutional weaknesses identified in this study with their general consequences on economic development on the one hand, and what may be their proximate causes on the other. These causes, which are amenable to changes through policies and reforms are then related to 'deep factors', which may be responsible for whether those policies and reforms could be undertaken or not.

In examining Table 9.1, it is quite important to realise that there is no one-to-one relationship between the elements of the various columns. One institutional

TABLE 9.1 *The diagnostic table*

Deep factors	Proximate causes	Basic institutional weaknesses	Economic consequences
Political game (joint structure of political and economic power)	Under-capacity of State apparatus (skills, resources, technology)	Ill-defined structure of public decision-making (Responsibility overlap, centralisation bias, law implementation gap)	Ambiguous growth engine and long-run growth perspectives (slow productivity gain, slow industrialisation)
Social structure (ethnicity, rural-urban, education...)	Misaligned incentives (high and low levels of civil service)	Under-performing civil service	Poor investment climate
Donors' views and leverage	Imprecision and complexity of the law	Rent-seeking and corruption	Low quality public services
Historical legacy (Ideology, government credibility, trust, ...)	Type of leadership (transparency and accountability) (state–business relationship)	Patronage and weak business regulation	Regressive distribution and redistribution
		Selective distrust of market mechanisms (Power sector, Land)	Occasionally inefficient public decision-making (e.g. power sector, local communities, land investments)

weakness does not have a unique general consequence and has more than a unique proximate cause. The relationship between the four columns is essentially multivariate. The important point is essentially the chain of causality. The whole set of institutional weaknesses is the consequence of the whole set of proximate causes, which depend themselves on the whole set of deep factors, even though, in both cases, the relationships may be stronger between particular items. On the other side, the set of institutional weaknesses affects how the economy works.

The relationships described here are complex and need some explanation. The right-hand side is fairly clear. Indeed, it has been seen throughout this volume that identified institutional weaknesses played a determinant role in affecting economic policies and economic outcomes in Tanzania and ultimately its long-run development path. Only some general implications of these weaknesses are mentioned in Table 9.1, but more detailed consequences could have been picked from previous chapters.

The items that appear under the 'proximate causes' column of Table 9.1 need more explanation. Considering institutions as a set of rules imposing tasks or behavioural constraints on the various economic actors, why would the latter not follow the rules? A first possibility is that they do not have the skills or knowledge to perform these tasks or to manage the constraints they are subject to. In the same vein, they may not have the equipment or resources to perform their tasks or deal with the constraints. In short, laws, administrative rules, and tasks may not be fully adapted to the level of development of a country. This lack of administrative capacity has been pointed to repeatedly in the preceding chapters, in particular in connection with the management of land rights and the civil service in general. It has also been emphasised both in the opinion survey and the analysis of governance indicators completed in the first part of this volume.

A second cause of the identified institutional weaknesses is the misalignment of incentives for economic and civil actors to fulfil the task asked of them and/ or comply with the various institutional rules they are subject to. Incentives may be of the carrot or the stick type, rewarding those who behave well in the first case and punishing those who do not in the second. The main point here is that rewarding and punishing require that the evaluation of behaviour be properly conducted, with the appropriate skill and economic resources. It also requires that evaluators be themselves monitored to prevent transgressors and evaluators colluding.

Transgressing rules may also be unavoidable when rules are ill-adapted, inconsistent, or too complex. Several identified institutional weaknesses in Tanzania were thus due to ambiguities, imprecisions, or too much complexity of the law and administrative rules. We shall return to this point in more detail, but we may note here that this issue was found to be highly relevant in the case of the Land Act and recognised as such in the multiple official reviews of that piece of legislation.

The final set of proximate causes of institutional weaknesses may also come from the type of leadership, or more precisely the nature of the government, the strength of the supervision it exerts on the public administration, its transparency, and its accountability. The underperformance of the civil service, its rent-seeking behaviour, or major corruption scandals involving high-ranking political personnel may be the result of lax supervision and a weak obligation to accountability by the executive. Even when evaluation entities do exist, an example being the Comptroller Auditor General in Tanzania, they may be under the thumb of the executive or may deliberately not be given the resources they need to perform their task. An authoritarian leadership is not necessarily efficient if authority is used inappropriately, as may be the case with the centralisation bias mentioned earlier.

Of special importance is the nature of the relationship between the state and the business sector, as repeatedly emphasised in previous chapters. Does the government have the power to decide and implement policies that may constrain the private sector? Or does the latter enjoy an effective leverage on the government, through the strategic importance of some firms for the whole economy, so that their own interest prevails over that of the community? The absence of a well-articulated industrial policy suggests that the second situation is more likely in Tanzania, but this may not be true of all activities, and bargaining may take place leading to intermediate solutions. Of course, the possibility also exists that big business bribes government members or influential people within the dominant CCM party for personal enrichment or political survival.

It remains to be seen more precisely how these proximate causes apply and how they combine in the case of Tanzania to produce the identified institutional weaknesses, and which policy or reform could remedy them. Before doing so, however, a word must be said about the 'deep factors' column of Table 9.1. Deep factors have to do with the feasibility of policies that could remedy the proximate causes of institutional weaknesses.

The political game, that is to say the process by which a policy is actually put to work or stopped, is ultimately the main factor that makes a reform aimed at correcting institutional weaknesses possible or not. In this respect, the de facto structure of political power is essential. But, because some reforms also need the agreement or cooperation of non-political actors as well, for example big business, it is the joint distribution of political and economic power within society that matters. In the case of Tanzania, the presence of a dominant party, the CCM, tends to enhance the decision power of the government. Yet factions within the party and their links with economic interests may well hinder particular action and reforms intended by the executive.[14]

---

[14] On the 'factionalisation' of the dominant party CCM, see Cooksey (2013) and Gray (2015). On the 'change of regime' pushed by Magufuli within CCM, see Andreoni (2017, 41) who, following Khan's (2010) political settlement taxonomy, sees the Tanzanian regime as having moved from 'Competitive clientelism' to '(vulnerable) Authoritarian coalition', possibly *en route* towards a 'Potential Development Coalition'.

For instance, the long and continuing indeterminacy about the private or public status of power generation and distribution resulted from the inability to align interests of political and economic powers along one option. In several instances, the executive's will to sue high-rank politicians for corruption has been stopped in ways that have never been elucidated, or at least made public. Likewise, industrial development policies have remained undecisive and opaque because of power conflicts between business-linked political powers within the dominant party.

To be sure, the joint structure of political and economic power may change over time. This certainly happened at the time of the transition back from socialism to a market economy and more recently under the Magufuli administration, whose anti-corruption goal may have led to an unexpectedly strong authoritarian shift in the exercise of power. Further changes may now be expected with the Suluhu administration.

The social structure of society may also be an obstacle to institutional reforms. For instance, the demographic importance of peasants in the population might block reforms that would affect their autonomy because this would substantially reduce the electoral support of the party in power. Such factors combine with the political game to make some reforms possible or impossible. In the case of Tanzania, this remark certainly applies to the difficulty of reforming land laws as well as the implicit struggle between local and central governments in tax collection.

The historical legacy may also create a context that affects the capacity and the effectiveness of institutional reforms. The role of ideology and the attachment to the socialist past that leads to some distrust of market mechanisms and the private sector in some areas is a clear example of such a legacy. The trust that citizens may have that political personnel and the public administration can effectively implement a reform may also be an important factor for facilitating or, in its absence, for blocking it or making it inoperative. There is indeed an issue of government credibility. Reforms that have repeatedly been promised but unsuccessfully implemented become non-credible and become unable to change the behaviour of people and firms. Something of this type may have happened in Tanzania with the fight against corruption. Things may have changed under President Magufuli, but it is still too early to know whether this has really been the case.

Donors are also mentioned among the deep factors, essentially because their contribution to the public budget and therefore their leverage on Tanzania's government is sizeable. They reacted to several major corruption scandals by suspending aid disbursements, and they also directly imposed their own views on institutional reforms, as was seen in the case of decentralisation, and of course at the time of the shift back to the market economy in the 1980s.

Deep factors logically appear as the ultimate causes of basic institutional weaknesses. But, as mentioned earlier, they may change over time, so that reforms that were not possible may become possible. Because of this, an institutional diagnostic needs to be explicit about how the proximate causes for institutional weaknesses may be reformed, and on the gains and losses of all actors who would be involved in this process, so that all are aware of the consequences of exerting the power at their disposal.

This is what the next sections of this chapter intend to do.

B The Reform Potential for Correcting Tanzania's Institutional Weaknesses

The preceding conceptual framework for drawing an institutional diagnostic of Tanzania is now applied to the generic institutional weaknesses identified in the first part of this chapter. For each generic weakness in turn, available evidence is briefly summarised, before reflecting on their proximate causes, possible directions of reform, and potential political economy obstacles. These various considerations aim to show the potential for mitigating or correcting identified institutional weaknesses, or, in other words, what would need to be done to reduce them and what would prevent this from happening.

1 More Efficiency in Public Decision-Making

In any economy, the structure of public decision-making is complex. Efficiency requires that, for most operations, information gathering, analysis, decision-making, and implementation occur in a precise place in the functional structure of the public sector. The thematic studies have shown that Tanzania's decision-making system is set in such a way that it is not always clear who makes decisions and that the number of procedures needed to reach a decision may be burdensome. Law simplification and skill enhancement could be one way to straighten public decision-making.

Land transactions are a good example of this. In practice, investors must deal with many different actors before a final decision is made, from village councillors to district commissioners, to bureaucrats in the Land Commissioner's office in the Ministry of Agriculture, not to mention several technical services. This complex procedure is likely to disincentivise investors, as already observed on some occasions – see Chapter 7.

There are many examples of lack of coordination and overlapping responsibilities among administrative units in charge of closely related operations. This is the case, for instance, for the National Land Use Planning Commission and the Director of Urban and Rural Planning in the Ministry of Agriculture, and in the absence of a clear line of communication between the Tanzania Revenue Authority, a public agency responsible for tax collection, and the Ministry of Finance, responsible for tax policy. Decentralisation raises the same kind of coordination challenge, with some confusion of mandates between local government executives and central government appointed officers advising on or controlling local decisions, and with an intricate set of relationships between LGAs, the prime minister's office, the Minister of Finance and various sectoral ministers. That a decentralisation reform approved by parliament in 1996, and supposed to be entering into full force by 2008, is not fully implemented more than ten years later is symptomatic of the shortcomings in the structure of public decision-making. Together with the sudden decision by the executive to recentralise the management of local taxes in 2016, this is an example of both the inherent difficulty of coordinating various levels of government and a centralisation bias.

This gap between the passing of laws and effectively implementing them, or the ineffectiveness of government-commissioned expert reports on the land laws, also reveals not only a centralisation bias, but also governing dysfunctions. No fewer than six reviews and reports on the land laws have been produced since 2004.[15] Yet little progress was achieved, and there are still serious difficulties in implementing the law.

Another telling example of the lack of coordination and centralisation bias can be found in the power sector. After decades of delay, a clear decision-making structure has been put into place with well-defined functions for the state-owned company TANESCO and the regulatory authority EWURA, whose technical competence is widely praised. Yet the central authority can veto decisions taken within that structure, as was the case during the Magufuli administration when a tariff rise was cancelled by central government and the managers of the two entities were simply demoted, their appointment, and demotion, being by law under the sole competence of the president. The argument put forward was that such a rise would have increased poverty, whereas not raising tariffs would have meant loss to TANESCO and a need for subsidy in order to operate without accumulating debts. Whatever the argument for or against the rise, such an event suggests either that the regulatory authority ignored some key social welfare aspects of its decision, which means something is wrong in the composition of the group of experts making tariff recommendations, or that it is indeed the expression of a very centralised power possibly acting under political motives. The same can be said about procurement decisions in the power sector. The multiple past corruption affairs linked to the choice of private power providers, which ended up both ineffective and exorbitantly expensive, and involving top government members are clear evidence that, even though well-organised on paper, the decision structure can be short-cut at a high level of the state.

The proximate causes for these institutional failures differ according to the issue being considered. In the cases of both land rights management and decentralisation, there is little doubt that the complexity of land laws and the ambiguity of the laws that rule the relationship between LGAs and the central

---

[15] Two SPILLs (Strategic Plan for the Implementation of the Land Laws, 2007 and 2013), the MKURABITA (Property and Business Formalisation Programme, 2004), the land leg of the BRN programme (2005), the Land Tenure Support Programme (2016) and the current Land Policy Review and draft National Land Policy (2016).

state play an important role. An obvious direction of reform is therefore the simplification and the rationalisation of these laws and administrative rules. The lack of adequate skills, particularly at the local level, is another handicap to the efficient application of the law, which calls for serious efforts in recruitment and training.

Of course, some people gain from the complexity of some laws and the administrative organisation as they generate multiple rent-seeking opportunities. This is the reason reforms as simple as the previous ones – that is, legal simplification and skill enhancement – are not necessarily consensual. It has been seen that repeated changes in task allocation between local and central governments reflected a struggle between local elites and the dominant central party in capturing local rents. The involvement of the state in major decisions concerning the power sector may also be analysed as too much *de facto* power to the executive, and also in terms of hidden personal interest by powerful politicians who short-circuit decision making by the power company and the regulatory authority, for instance in procurement decisions. Finally, the delay observed in implementing laws such as the decentralisation laws or the limited responsiveness of various administrations to reform proposals of the land law is likely to reflect more a lack of consensus and possibly incompatible views because of conflicting interests by powerful political actors, rather than a practical difficulty in implementing reforms.

Reforms that would enhance state capacity may not be consensual in the short and medium term. Yet it bears emphasis that, in the long run, they will be beneficial to whoever is in power.

2 Overcoming Distrust of Market Mechanisms and the Private Sector

Distrust of market mechanisms and the private sector was observed in two areas in the course of this study: the allocation of land rights and the attempts at restructuring the power sector. In both cases, it was shown to have a heavy economic cost.

As in many other sub-Saharan African countries, the Tanzanian government faces a dilemma in the agricultural sector. On the one hand, it wants to foster the development of the sector with modern technology applied on large-scale farms and productivity gains among smallholders. On the other hand, it wants to protect traditional farmers from being displaced by private investors. This objective is all the more important since traditional farming areas are where most poverty is found. Unsettling that sector could thus have adverse consequences on poverty, as it did in the 1970s during the attempt at collectivising land, leading virtually to famine.

Based on the principle of public ownership of land, the Tanzanian land laws intend to combine these two objectives by distinguishing between village land for traditional farming and general land for modern productive uses of land, the former being governed by customary laws and the latter by statutory law. The difficulty is in the transformation of village land into general land for investment purposes.

Even though they were designed long after the end of the socialist planning period, the land laws very much retain the feel of a planning system. It seems as if it was attempted to move land management away from a market system as much as possible. However, there is no contradiction between the public ownership of land and the functioning of a land market if what is priced and exchanged is not the ownership but the right to use land, that is through long-term leases. To be sure, market operations for land rights take place today both in urban and rural areas, but the key operation that enables investors, or even the state, to access village land remains cumbersome, long-winded, sometimes uncertain, and possibly costly because of the multiple opportunities for rent-seeking by land officers at various levels of the hierarchy. The community's wish to protect traditional farmers from being expelled from their land by commercial investors or speculators has led to a labyrinthine administrative system that is considered by many observers to be a major obstacle to development.

The current system has also led to some *a priori* antagonising of village communities with respect to agricultural investors because of the complexity and the frequent ineffectiveness of many of the deals between them, most often engineered by public intermediaries involving bribes, or sometimes signed by corrupt village leaders who are acting without consulting their villagers. Compensation packages that involve promises of employing villagers or building village infrastructure, such as schools or roads, are indeed more difficult to enforce than a simple transfer of resources to village communities.

The proximate causes for the inefficiency of the land allocation process lie in the complexity of the land laws, ineffective public operators, particularly at the local level, and weak control of corruption. To this must be added the incomplete mapping of the land, which makes the task of processing and recording land operations particularly difficult. The important point is that both the lack of capacity and the rent-seeking behaviour are themselves to a large extent brought about by the complexity of the law and the extremely slow mapping process. Improving things thus involves correcting those two weaknesses.

Simplifying the complex administrative procedure to transfer land from villages to investors might work through more reliance on market mechanisms, such that village communities and investors, rather than numerous public intermediaries, would be the main actors of the transactions. They would have to agree on the size of the land to be transferred, its location, and the price and nature of the compensation – including through shares in the investment venture – to the community, with the village being fully responsible for managing the reallocation of land that might be needed among villagers. Full publicity of transactions conducted elsewhere in the region or in the country, as well as of the consequences of the corresponding deals among smallholders, would be absolutely necessary to guarantee full information and market transparency. National interest would be taken into account only in the very final steps of the procedure, with some veto power in the hands of the government in case the deal related to very large swaths of land and was thought to be harmful for the national or regional economy.

Information on transactions and their consequences for village communities is essential. Knowing the price at which transactions took place in the region is a guarantee that no side will feel cheated if an agreement is reached. More importantly for the villagers, knowing whether smallholders elsewhere were ultimately harmed or benefited from the deal, possibly through the public goods the village could acquire thanks to the deal, is key to avoid social disasters or to obtain the right compensation.

Arrangements other than cash transaction for the unconstrained use of the land are sometimes made with investors: contract farming, smallholders acquiring equity in the investor's venture and continuing to work their land, compensation in kind, and so on. Except maybe for contract farming, suitable only in specific cases, all these arrangements are bound to result in conflict at some stage, either at the time of sharing profits or when deciding on payment to labourers. Previous experience is not encouraging. Such contracts are simply too complex and cannot take into account all contingencies. However, considering that forms of equity arrangements have been working elsewhere (e.g. China), there is a case for exploring further possibilities. In the meantime, cash deals between an investor and a village, with redistribution or the acquisition of farm-productivity enhancing public goods being left to the local authority, could be promoted, as they are more transparent and make village authorities fully accountable.

Of course, for such a market-like solution to be possible, it is necessary that the whole land has been mapped so that precise limits to the land being transferred can be established. This requires resources to be made available for that purpose, although there seems to be some disagreement on the actual cost of this operation. Within villages, land management could remain as it is, with some possible land reallocation under the control of the village council in case the land transferred to investors impinges on the farms of smallholders. The titling process (CCROs) would keep developing, accelerating the extension of within-village and across-village transactions.

The preceding discussion refers to land transfers from small scale, near subsistence farmers in traditional rural communities and large-scale domestic or foreign commercial investors. But land consolidation is also needed within communities to increase yields. Progress has recently been made through the extension of medium-scale farms – 5 to 10 hectares – in some regions where land is still abundant. This has resulted from informal transactions that have led to the regrouping of small plots, with these transactions generating economies of scale and creating positive spillovers.[16] Such a spontaneous restructuring or reform of village land and accompanying productivity gains would be quicker and stronger if market mechanisms were encouraged and made easier at the local level.

---

[16] See World Bank (2019b).

A larger role for market mechanisms in land right transactions should strengthen the potential and incentives for investors, medium-scale farmers, smallholders, and village communities to exploit the clear comparative advantage of Tanzania in agriculture and agro-industry, and reforms in that direction would probably meet some resistance. Civil servants and politicians, who are currently able to extract economic or political rents from the present unclear decision-making structure, would oppose them, as would possibly peasants and village communities, given their attachment to tradition. The structure of political power matters here. To the extent that village communities would retain some control of land transactions on their territory, they could probably be persuaded that these reforms were in their favour.

The proximate causes for a distrust towards the market and private actors in the power sector are of a different nature. Historical legacies matter, but so do the rent-seeking opportunities for politicians who are close to the central power to control the operations of a big public company, most importantly the procurement process.

History matters here because of the socialist past of Tanzania and the primacy of public companies in the socialist era, especially in the delivery of such a critical good as electricity. But history matters also because of several huge corruption scandals linked to subcontracting power generation to private firms. Keeping the electricity company as a vertical public monopoly is seen as a kind of guarantee against such corruption cases. But, of course, doing so also provides rent-seeking opportunities to influential politicians in all procurement operations made by the public company, including with private providers when the capacity of the company is overly constrained – as has been the case in the past.

Correcting the situation requires actions on two fronts. The first of these is re-establishing credibility in the procurement process. This means better supervision of procurement operations, but more importantly a composition of the contract-awarding commissions guaranteeing its objectivity. Allowing one or two reputable foreign experts to sit on this kind of commission may be a way of getting closer to that objective. Second, unbundling the public electricity company into power generation and distribution and then enhancing the current limited private providers to sell power to the public company would mean competition, and therefore more transparency and fewer rent-seeking opportunities in power provision. After all, this kind of reform was repeatedly recommended by expert reports and explicitly considered in the Electricity Act passed in 2008 that is presumably still in force today.

3 Enhancing the Civil Service's Performance
In one of the first evaluations of governance in Tanzania in the mid-1990s, the civil service was found to be one of the key weaknesses of the public sector.[17] Things have changed enormously since then. The skill of civil servants

---

[17] According to the 1994 Helleiner report as cited by Edwards (2012, p. 42).

has substantially increased, and several reforms of the civil service have been undertaken, introducing a more rigorous recruitment process and a performance-based career management system. Yet the draft of a new wave of reforms explicitly acknowledges various problems faced by the public service, including staff demotivation and indiscipline, inadequate accountability, widespread corruption, underskilled staff, lack of meritocratic incentives, and weak and passive leadership.

Without anticipating the actual measures to be included in this new reform, improvements are certainly still needed in the civil service. Judging from the absenteeism among teachers and, to a lesser extent, health personnel, there is no reason for productivity to be much higher in other occupations in the government sector. Presumably, supervision is not stronger than in education, so that shirking is probably as frequent as teachers' absenteeism. The estimate of the aggregate loss owing to absenteeism and shirking is high – roughly 2.5 per cent of GDP, not including the weak performance of schoolchildren or the low quality of other public services.

Besides the organisational inefficiencies analysed earlier in the public sector, an important proximate cause for this state of affairs has to do with incentives. In this respect, a first possibility is that salaries are insufficient to compensate for the efforts and time that teachers would spend in school if they were indeed there full time. Teachers and, by extension, other civil servants tend to shirk, moonlight, or rent-seek so that their standard of living is equivalent to what they could get with another (private) employer. On average, however, it has been seen that, other things being equal, salaries in the public sector are substantially higher than in the private sector, even though this may be more the case for low- rather than high-skilled workers.[18] In short, some salary adjustment may be needed in some parts of the civil service – for instance, for graduate secondary school teachers or to attract candidates in maths and science – but, overall, the compensation of civil servants does not seem to be a major disincentive to effort. The same seems to be true of career prospects, which have supposedly been improved in the last programme of public service reform.

The alternative cause for weak incentives could be the ineffectiveness of the performance management system (PMS) and monitoring and evaluation (M&E) function. Shirking may be easier in the public than in the private sector because not enough resources are allocated to PMS and M&E activity in the former and the supervision structure of the civil service may be poorly

---

[18] The starting teacher salary is TZS 420,000 gross. Such a salary level is far from being infrequent in the private sector among starting young workers with a bachelor degree, presumably higher than grade A teacher degree, which presently requires a single year of training at the end of high school. Under-compensation seems to be more a problem among secondary school teachers. Evidence of this is the extremely high attrition rate for this category. On these aspects, see Ministry of Education and Vocational Training and UNESCO (2014).

organised. It may also be the case that PMS and M&E agents and supervisors are shirking themselves, or tend to side with the public-sector employees they are supposed to evaluate because of the public sector status they share with them. In both cases, they are not performing the task entrusted to them.

There is a huge body of literature on how to incentivise teachers.[19] Experiments in this area have been conducted in many countries. In Tanzania, the need to improve the performance of the education system has been duly recognised, and much reflection and experimentation has been undertaken.[20] Reforms in that sector could take advantage of that knowledge in the educational sector. See the recent survey of this area by Dal Bo and Finan (2020).

Less is known about incentivising other civil service jobs. To the extent that supervision is closer than in the educational area and that both work intensity and outcomes can be more easily observed, a first step may be in the disciplining of public sector employees. Understanding why supervisors do not enforce better discipline on their subordinates and why PMS and M&E do not function better is thus essential for designing the measures most able to remedy that situation. As with other developing countries, Tanzanians have a long tradition of seeing a civil service job as a perk with essentially low expectations of the productivity of civil servants at all levels of the hierarchy. Formally, introducing performance-based remuneration as done in the recent reform of public service is undoubtedly going in the right direction, but is clearly bound not to work if performances are not properly evaluated because of evaluators' lack of capacity or motivation.

Other proximate causes for the underperformance of the public sector are the lack of resources and the insufficient skill of civil servants in some crucial areas. Here, again, the education sector is a good example. The performance of the primary education system is low not only because of the scarcity of teachers and increased school enrolment – of course this is huge progress, in part brought about by the abolition of tuition fees – but also because of teacher absenteeism and because their training is recognised as inadequate. Things are possibly even worse now that basic teacher training has been reduced to a single year in teacher training colleges with a second 'hands on' year in school, with limited supervision. The situation may be particularly serious in teaching because of the need to increase the number of teachers to comply with a targeted student–teacher ratio at a time of fast-growing school enrolment. Indeed, a large part of the very fast increase in the size of the civil service over recent years has taken place because of a massive recruitment of teachers, and one may thus understand that the quality of recruitment, including teacher training, has gone down.[21] Recruitment in other public activities has also been fast, with possibly the same effect on quality.

---

[19] See for instance Ganimian and Murnane (2016).
[20] See, for instance, the Kiu Funza experiment led by Twaweza and Innovations for Poverty Action, or the Roads to Inclusion and Socioeconomic Opportunities Tanzania programme.
[21] On all these issues of teacher pay and teacher training, the interview with the head of the Tanzanian Teacher Union, Ezekiah Oluoch, in *The Citizen* (2014), is extremely informative.

Remedies for these causes of the lack of effectiveness of civil service are obvious: the compensation system has to be re-examined to make sure that it is adapted to the reality of the labour market, especially in areas where the supply side seems short; PMS and M&E must be scaled up and made more effective at all levels, in particular by making sure there is no collusion between those who evaluate and those who are evaluated; and recruitment and training must be improved.

It is unlikely that such measures would meet any real opposition within the Tanzanian political elite, except maybe from workers' unions complaining of excessive supervision and therefore workload. The main constraint here is resources. The Tanzanian budget is already extremely tight and relies extensively on foreign aid and foreign loans. Improving the quality of the civil service may thus require difficult trade-offs within the public budget. Of course, this does not lessen the need for more discipline.

4 Addressing Rent-Seeking and Corruption

Rent-seeking activity and corruption may be the clearest symptoms of weak-performing institutions. They arise from situations where a public sector agent with some autonomous decision-making power grants to a private sector agent an advantage in a way that is openly illegal or bypasses official operational rules. The cost of such behaviour is twofold. On the one hand, it biases the economic allocation process in comparison with what the institutional rules are expected to produce, which may not necessarily be economically efficient. On the other hand, it redistributes resources in a way that may be regressive, as when poor people find themselves forced to pay bribes to access a supposedly free public service.

The proximate cause for rent-seeking and corruption lies first in the incentives for agents to adopt such a behaviour. As with absenteeism or shirking, it may be due to an inadequate compensation system and agents compensating for it through extracting rents from others, and to weak PMS and M&E. However, as was clear from the discussion on land, rent-seeking may also be the consequence of ill-conceived institutions that grant too much de facto unchecked decision power to potentially untrustworthy agents, lack transparency, or impose rules that are unduly restrictive for economic activity. In the latter case, it is even possible that corruption is economically efficient, in the sense that it improves the lot of the briber, of the one who pays the bribe, and of the whole community if it helps to cut red tape.[22] Another cause of widespread corruption is the lack of transparency of public decision-making in connection with the private sector.

Yet there is also an externality dimension in rent-seeking and corruption that must be stressed because it conditions the way to fight it. If this

---

[22] This 'corruption greases the wheel' argument was first made by Leff (1964) and Huntington (1968).

behaviour were limited to a few public officers, it is likely that they would soon be confounded with enough discipline on the part of the executive, a policy that would probably be accepted by most political actors. The difficulty appears when this behaviour becomes so widespread that everybody may hold everybody else under the threat of being denounced, thus neutralising this basic anti-corruption tool. Those uncorrupted people paying a rent will not denounce their rent-seeker either, as long as the institutional constraint that makes a bribe mutually advantageous has not been corrected. A true culture of corruption may then develop, where everybody acts under the expectation that none of the people aware of the corrupt action will denounce participants. Informal bilateral rules substitute for formal collective rules. This practice is most widespread in political elections, where most voters and seekers of political positions participate in corruption activities. From that point of view, and despite Magufuli's general anti-corruption action, it is believed that the level of corruption in political elections in 2020 was higher than that in previous elections. The main challenge lies in political commitment to fight corruption, considering that the route to political positions is not free from corruption.

Economic theory provides an interesting representation of this phenomenon under the form of a multiple equilibrium. There is an equilibrium where most agents are corrupt, asking for or paying a bribe.[23] For this to be the case, the probability of denunciation must be low, meaning there are few 'clean' people. In the other equilibrium, a large proportion of people are clean, which makes corruption dangerous because of the high probability of being caught.[24] Most observers tend to believe that Tanzania is in the former equilibrium, with corruption so widespread that it is indeed 'a way of life', as a journalist wrote in view of the repeated corruption scandals at the end of the Kikwete mandate.[25]

Although very crude, this model shows the enormous difficulty in fighting corruption when it is widespread. This is because the preceding equilibria are 'stable', in the sense that small departures from the original equilibrium with a slight change in the probability of corrupt people to be sanctioned cannot prevent the system from going back to the original equilibrium. This is what has been observed in Tanzania with various past attempts at curbing corruption. Moving to the clean equilibrium requires a 'big push', with a sufficiently large group of people above any suspicion of corruption leading the fight against corruption.

---

[23] This equilibrium resembles the inferior 'prisoner's dilemma' equilibrium. The existence of another 'clean' equilibrium corresponds to another game called the coordination game or 'assurance game' (see Nichols, 2003). A more complete model has been proposed recently by Dixit (2017).

[24] See the argument in Wydick (2008).

[25] Cited in Policy Forum (2017, p. 8).

There are few examples of countries that have successfully combated corruption, or at least reduced it to sporadic cases, starting from a culture of corruption. Singapore and Hong Kong may be the most famous cases. In both countries, a big corruption scandal moved public opinion. A politically powerful leader then put together an anti-corruption team made up of police personnel and judges who were above suspicion, whose mission was to sue corrupt civil servants and businesspeople with maximum publicity. It took time, but it worked. In the case of Singapore, interestingly enough, the strategy also included redesigning the law so as to eliminate situations that would provide rent-seeking opportunities, as well as making sure that civil servant salaries were well aligned with remunerations in the private sector.[26]

There are many more examples of countries where anti-corruption policies and agencies have been unsuccessful or short-lived, including Tanzania. The main difficulty is forming the 'above-suspicion' anti-corruption core team, giving it all the resources it needs, politically supporting its decisions, and maintaining the fight for long enough.

Corruption seems to be sufficiently severe in Tanzania that such policies should be seriously considered. This was the position of the Magufuli administration, which launched an aggressive anti-corruption campaign based on a solid team around the president and on re-establishing discipline in the upper tiers of civil service. After some apparent early progress, doubts have been expressed about whether fundamental change had been obtained at the time he passed away, six years later. His noticeably rigged re-election in 2020 would seem to confirm those doubts.

It should not be forgotten that, as mentioned in the case of Singapore, simplifying the law, making the administrative apparatus more transparent, reducing the monopoly power of civil servants in particular decisions, and aligning their compensation with the private sector are an equally important side of the fight against corruption. Most importantly, such measures are much less likely to be resisted by those political forces that would be under threat in a direct attack against corruption.

5 Strengthening Business Regulation and Competition

The relationship between the government or the political elite and big companies hides another aspect of corruption and rent-seeking through economic favouritism. Practically, politicians in power, or with influence on the executive, offer advantages to a company, in exchange for their economic support. This is legally reprehensible in some cases, as with vote-buying, but economic support may take other forms, for instance through contributions to electoral campaigns, grants to regional development, or employment creation in particular localities.[27] Even though such practices are close to lobbying, the difference

---

[26] See Quah (2011). The cases of Singapore and Hong Kong are also discussed in Dixit (2016).
[27] See Babeya (2011).

from straight corruption is small, especially when the political support granted by companies is hidden, as it is most often the case.

Because electoral support mostly comes from business, this patronage system is equivalent to the latter extracting a rent, under the form of a competitive advantage or otherwise, from the government or, more exactly, from citizens. They are able to do so for three major reasons. First, they have the resources to support the electoral campaigns of their political allies. Second, as economic growth relies to a large extent on big business, no government would take the risk of antagonising them. Third, major firms are often in monopolistic positions, which limit the leverage the government may have on them. Such a state of affairs is certainly not a guarantee of economic efficiency since the interest of big groups is not necessarily that of the nation. Pursuing an economic development strategy that would be collectively beneficial but would hurt the interest of some major firm would be a risky bet for governments, as the firm might retaliate by favouring rival political groups or, when in partial control of the media, campaigning against the government's decisions. The institutional weakness here is the lack of independence of the government or public decision-making process with respect to the interests of major private companies and the opacity of that relationship. The joint structure of political and economic power is thus what determines policies that affect big business.

The Magufuli administration faced this problem, as its predecessors did. Shortly after taking power, President Magufuli stated that he would not let businesspeople 'play with his government'. He then took vigorous action in that direction by fighting tax evasion and intervening in several corruption cases that involved big companies. Without really releasing the pressure, he nevertheless made clear a year later that he was open to signing agreements with them provided they contributed to the industrialisation agenda.[28]

This was probably the right strategy by then. However, even though the relationship with the executive improved, big firms retain considerable power, including of course that of influencing the political game. As the dominant political party, CCM, is somewhat fragmented in various political factions; there has always been room for large companies to play one faction against another and potentially unsettle the executive. As seen earlier, this might change if the leadership were able to exert more control on the party.

The other effective way of reducing the power of big businesses is to weaken their monopoly position both as leading economic actors and in their areas of specialisation. This requires the fostering of competition on two levels. First, the emergence of new economic leaders should be favoured, which includes making sure that promising business managers will not be ostracised because of their ethnic origin or other personal characteristics. In other words, there

---

[28] See Andreoni's (2017) distinction between 'Magufuli the bulldozer', a nickname he inherited from his time as Minister for Public Works, and 'Magufuli the builder'.

should be no glass ceiling, most notably when raising funds, for entering the business elite other than talent. Second, it should be checked that incumbent firms are not restricting competition in their area of activity by raising barriers of entry, including through artificial business regulation obtained from the government. In short, this would mean empowering the Fair Competition Commission and sectoral regulatory authorities, for example the Sugar Board,[29] so that they are more proactive and more rigorous, this being particularly important in the financial sector. Foreign investment and trade policy, in particular the dismantling of various types of non-tariff barriers since base tariffs are set at the level of the East African Community, should also be used to check domestic monopoly power and foster the development of new activities. At the same time, trade and tax authorities should be encouraged to tighten the control of counterfeit imports and the levy of legal tariffs. Transparency of the long-run industrial policy pursued by the government is also a necessary condition for resisting the political influence of local big business.

In relation to big domestic companies and the design of industrialisation strategies, the development of South Korea bears some lessons. Although industrial development was based on big companies, the *chaebols*, the Korean government managed not to become their hostage, at least during the years during which development took off, and to develop its own strategy. This was done by creating competition between *chaebols*, especially in export markets where they would not be constrained by domestic demand, never granting support to one group that would not be granted to at least one other and, most importantly, making those grants conditional on successfully meeting precontracted objectives.[30]

Promoting competition among leading companies in Tanzania would not bear fruit in the short run, and it may well be the case that it would be partly neutralised through their political leverage. Coupled with an authoritarian stance on corruption and an adequate communication policy on the government's industrialisation strategy, it could nevertheless progressively improve the competitive landscape, restrict the *de facto* political power of the business elite, and allow for more effective and more open collaboration between the government and business.

C The Need for More Transparency and Accountability of Central Government

Summarising the preceding sections, the proximate causes for the institutional weaknesses identified earlier in this volume are clear. They can be

---

[29] This is mentioned in reference to the kind of collusion that has been observed in the past between big import companies and this particular regulatory authority, to the detriment of local producers.

[30] See Amsden (1989) and the chapter on South Korea in Bourguignon and Platteau (2023).

divided into two groups. The first comprises three basic causes for economic actors not behaving according to institutional rules: lack of capacity or skills to apply the rules, weak incentives not to deviate, and rules that are too complex together with an ill-adapted administrative organisation. Several types of remedies have been mentioned, depending on the institutional weakness being considered. Some of them essentially require more resources and capacity building among civil servants in various positions. Implementing them should not raise any opposition. The same is true of the cases where the compensation of public officers is thought to be inadequate, this being an incentive for absenteeism and rent-seeking. Another type of remedy is to enhance the PMS and M&E function in public service in terms of frequency and effectiveness. This is most likely to raise some resistance from unions and to reinforce political opposition to the government. Finally, top civil servants would oppose administrative reorganisation that would terminate their source of rent. In all these cases, however, central power should be able to impose those remedial policies. Political will is what is needed. The Magufuli administration took measures that went in that direction, even though these were not ambitious enough.

The second group of causes is much more difficult to resolve. Hidden political opposition is likely to be strong when attacking grand corruption, a key institutional weakness now deeply rooted in Tanzanian society, or trying to regulate big business to enhance its contribution to development. Institutional improvement in these areas touches upon deep political factors. The success of such reforms depends on the political game and to a large extent on another deep factor that has been little alluded to before, the *trust* that citizens may have in the government and the president. In this respect, the transparency and accountability of the government play a key role because, through the clarity of public decision-making and of the evaluation of the executive's actions, they deeply affect the structure of political power. A government that is trusted by the public may take key decisions in some areas that would otherwise be blocked by particular interests. Conversely, lack of transparency and accountability feed suspicion by the public and make governments weaker in the face of vested interests.

Asked about transparency in Tanzania, a former Minister of Justice and Constitutional Affairs, said a few years ago: 'It's something that is not in our culture!', adding: 'Our government has always been run on confidentiality.' It is difficult to say whether Tanzania does better or worse than other countries on that account because of the ambiguity of available cross-country indicators for governance. However, in view of the thematic studies conducted in this project and of the general challenges discussed in this chapter, it seems fair to say that Tanzanian governance is barely transparent and, when transparent, barely accountable.

Of course, governing a country cannot be done in full sight of everyone. That is not the point. Transparency and accountability essentially require government objectives and intended policy reforms to be publicly set out, and, *ex post*, properly and publicly evaluated and debated, so that lessons are drawn from experience.

In the case of Tanzania, it is sometimes argued that the representation of the dominant party, CCM, in parliament is so overwhelming that debates do not have much content. This was the case with the preceding legislature where CCM held 72 per cent of the seats. Things are much worse today, since the opposition has been muted through the 2020 election – which is widely believed to have been rigged – and the violent repression of political opponents by the Magufuli administration. The question of transparency thus became completely irrelevant, and the public debate was simply shut down. Magufuli's successor, Samia Suluhu Hassan, may hopefully prove less authoritarian, but she will run the country practically unopposed until a new election in 2025, except maybe for diverging factions within what has become again the 'single party'.

In a perceptive analysis of governance in Tanzania, Lawson and Rakner (2005) show how the institutions in place and the presence of a dominant party were preventing the legislature from really holding the executive to account. Formerly, this has not always been the case, though, as could be seen at the time of the Escrow scandal – when several hundred million dollars were siphoned from the Central Bank, and the Public Accounts Committee of the parliament, chaired by a member of the opposition, exposed those members of the government whose carelessness had permitted it to happen and obtained their resignation. It turns out, however, that this was made possible because of one faction of CCM working against another, which was supportive of those party members involved in the scandal.[31]

Party fractionalisation is not a substitute for a lively opposition, as differing views tend to dissolve within party unity with respect to the electorate. It does not provide any incentive for transparency, except when it cannot be avoided as in extreme cases such as grand corruption scandals, as revealing within-party clashes would be electorally counterproductive. Note also that, even in front of publicised corruption scandals, central power is not necessarily held to account, as culprits within the party are not even sacked or properly sued.

Transparency and accountability are also missing in areas other than corruption and big business patronage. As stressed earlier in this chapter, not enough efforts are being devoted to the evaluation of the functioning of public services or to specific policies. The decentralisation reform has apparently not been fully implemented. Why is this the case? With respect to land laws, there have been multiple official assessment reports over the last ten years or so, yet little has been done. Is this because of inefficient governance or because of hidden vested interests? In the first case, there would be pure

[31] See Gray (2015, p. 392).

advantages in the government openly drawing the lessons of these reports and taking appropriate action.

It may also be stressed that none of these reports was a true evaluation, in the sense of attempting to quantify the economic and social losses due to the difficulty of implementing the laws or to the law itself in comparison with alternative rules. It is striking, for instance, that no fully reliable database showing the number and general features of land transactions is available to evaluate the present system of land transfers. This lack of evaluation and data gap is also observed in the educational sector, despite public knowledge that it does not function well, or in other activities of the public sector.

Only systematic evaluations of policies allow progress to be measured and adequate decisions to be taken. This is true at all levels of the governance of a country and irrespective of the structure of political and economic power. Generating the data for such evaluation, even internally within the executive, is a necessity and, of course, a step towards transparency, and possibly accountability. There might be capacity constraint in producing such evaluations, but this could easily be remedied if the political will is present. The path towards public management efficiency and, at a later stage, transparency, accountability, and citizens' trust, starts with producing the adequate data, and allowing public access to them – unlike some laws passed during Magufuli's rule.[32]

D Three Key Principles for Action

The basic institutional challenges singled out in the thematic chapters of this study can be traced back to proximate causes that take different forms depending on the challenge being considered, but they result from a few basic mechanisms analysed in the preceding sections. Likewise, when examining the various remedies that have been suggested to overcome the main causes of basic institutional weaknesses, it is striking to realise that, assuming that the political will for reform does exist, they rely on essentially three principles for action.

The first principle is the necessary improvement of state capacity on the one hand through the rationalisation of laws deemed too complex for easy implementation and the structure of public decision-making, and, on the other hand, both equipment and skill enhancement of the civil service.

The second principle is to allow for more *competition and competitive market mechanisms* to play their role as much as possible but under adequate and strict supervision and regulation. This in no way should be taken as the blind promotion of ultra-liberal dogmatic economic principles in favour of fully competitive markets. Their limits are well known. This recommendation

---

[32] The 2015 Statistics Act criminalised the publication of statistics without government approval. It was somewhat amended in 2019 but is apparently still applicable.

must be interpreted exactly in the other way as the need to *avoid unchecked monopoly situations in all possible decision-making areas*, whether in the administration, the delivery of public services, or indeed in the market. This 'more competition' – or 'fewer monopoly situations' – principle applies to land management with decentralised cash transactions between village communities and potential investors, to power generation with competition among providers, and to sectors of activity dominated by big business. But it also applies to the public sector with reforms that would reduce the monopoly power enjoyed by some operators – for instance, by allowing users to use alternative paths to obtain a licence, permit, or official document, and rewarding the most effective and expeditious ones. The extreme case is, of course, the use of information and communications technology facilities that simplify procedures and keep records of the performance of public officers. Making public service more competitive also brings about the right alignment of compensation with labour market conditions and individualises careers by relying more heavily on performance evaluation, assuming of course personal performance evaluation is properly, that is independently, conducted and based on objective criteria rather than on personal relations or cronyism.

The third principle is the systematic, *regular, and rigorous evaluation of the functioning of the public sector, policy outcomes, and socioeconomic progress*. Concerning the functioning of the public sector, this goes beyond applying results-based management principles based on a few indicators that can more or less easily be manipulated. The same applies to policy and social progress. In all these cases, evaluation is often performed *ex ante* on the basis of stated objectives and intended inputs rather than *ex post* on observed outcomes. Performance evaluation should be part of the evidence that measures the outcome of government actions, and its results, as quantitative as possible, should be made public.

Several countries have now made the proper independent evaluation of policies and reforms in some specific areas a constitutional obligation.[33] This could be an example to follow in Tanzania. Note, however, that this requires substantial progress to be made on the collection and analysis of statistical material and for the evaluation to be conducted by teams of independent analysts, which could possibly include foreign experts or observers who could guarantee the quality and impartiality of the evaluation.

At the political level, this principle of evaluation includes the checks and balances principle that defines, together with a few others, the functioning of democracy. Together with a strong and dominant party, the Tanzanian constitution gives extensive power to the president, to such an extent that the first president, Julius Nyerere, was known for joking about the constitution

---

[33] Mexico may have been a frontrunner in this field. The evaluations of the effectiveness of public spending and, by extension, of a broad set of policies is also close to being a constitutional obligation in France.

potentially allowing him to behave like a dictator. Strong central power, within reasonable limits, may be a good thing if wisely exerted. It is sometimes necessary to encourage reforms that are fundamentally good despite wide opposition by the elite, including within the dominant party. This is the case in Tanzania with corruption. Strong central power is not an advantage if it means that the executive is able to avoid its actions being properly evaluated by popular representation and public opinion, and to ignore the recommendations on key subjects that emanate from official expert commissions. The centralisation bias and the law implementation gap found to be key institutional challenges in Tanzania may be the result of such a concentration of power, a concentration that dangerously increased under Magufuli's presidency. Strengthening checks and balances, in particular by introducing plurality in the filling of key positions presently under the sole control of the president and institutionalising the public evaluation of policies by independent experts, possibly including foreign observers, could contribute to improving the institutional context that conditions Tanzanian development. In this respect, it bears emphasis that properly publicised, evaluations emanating from donors and international organisations and conducted in collaboration with local experts may be extremely valuable.[34]

Applied to specific sectors, such reinforcement of independent policy evaluation capacity and open reliance on expertise might in some cases greatly help the central power, even when it is close to being autocratic, by publicly exposing the forces that go against development and justifying policies. On the contrary, opacity or purely self-conducted evaluations lead to public distrust and, with time, risk adverse political turnarounds in case of a major exogenous shock.

E Conclusion

Following the medical metaphor, a diagnostic should be a statement about what disease is possibly causing observed symptoms of dysfunction. It is accompanied by a prescription describing the cure that is suggested to eradicate the disease. It is an illusion to believe that we can be as rigorous and effective in our institutional diagnostic. We have identified a list of symptoms caused by underlying institutional problems in Tanzania and the way they affect economic development, our institutional diagnostic exercise shedding light on the proximate causes of these dysfunctions, and general directions for reform being suggested. However, emphasis has also been placed on several 'deep factors', most often of the political economy type, which may prevent reforms from taking place or being effective. It is hoped that these

---

[34] As long as they are not censored, as with the IMF report whose publication was blocked by the Magufuli administration in 2019. Inter alia, the report expressed doubts about the government's policies and about GDP growth estimates.

reflections and conclusions will be of some help for thinking about long-run growth in Tanzania.

Given the use of the word 'diagnostic', some readers might have expected to find at the end of this volume a long prescription of things to do in most areas of public intervention. We have made such a list and mentioned in it several of the policy suggestions made throughout the volume – see the Appendix. However, the real contribution of this study is elsewhere: it is in the deep analysis provided in relation to the basic institutional weaknesses, including the political economy factors that may prevent effective reforms, and in the few fundamental principles of reform stated at the end of the preceding section. These principles should guide the reflection of policymakers in elaborating reforms and monitoring the progress made.

Economists are expected to quantify the effect of all possible reforms on the level of economic activity, the rate of growth, and the reduction of poverty. This is not an easy task when reaching beyond purely economic issues. In the field of institutions, this is simply impossible because of the extraordinary complexity of the way in which institutions affect development and the not-less extraordinary complexity of the mechanisms, including economic development, that could make institutions evolve. Economists regularly produce cross-country analyses that address these deep issues, but they are much too rough and aggregate to describe the reality of a specific country. Progress can be made only through detailed analysis of real cases, which has been attempted in this volume.

The reason why the relationship between development and institution is so complex is because it cannot be analysed without explicitly accounting for the structure of political power. It has been shown that this is of primary importance in Tanzania, as in any other country. Our discussion of corruption is a case in point. It would clearly make no sense for an institutional diagnostic of Tanzania to simply conclude that 'corruption is damaging and should be eradicated'. Such a statement is certainly true, but useless for two obvious reasons. First, it is difficult to know how damaging corruption is to the economy, and what kind of corruption exists. Second, even if it can be shown that it is indeed very damaging, effectively eradicating it is not a simple policy decision. It requires the political determination for doing so, a huge political power, as well as the possibility of committing to such a policy for a sufficiently long time. Not all governments are in such a position.

An institutional diagnostic cannot get into the detail of the political economy of some of the pertinent reforms that could address institutional weaknesses. Yet it may be hoped that making the political actors aware of existing weaknesses and possible cures will also make them face up to their own responsibilities, whatever their political leanings. This is the reason why, irrespective of the political economy context, it is essential to show the nature of the institutional constraints that must be relaxed to enhance development, and the nature of the instruments that can be used to eliminate particular institutional weaknesses. This is what we hope this study has contributed in the case of Tanzania.

APPENDIX

A.I SUMMARY OF RECOMMENDED
GOVERNANCE-IMPROVING POLICY REFORMS
AND ACTIONS IN THIS VOLUME

Public Service

- Enhanced capacity building through training.
- Improvement of recruitment process (skills and motivation).
- Revisit the public service compensation package by type of occupation relative to alternative employment (e.g. a teacher compensation evaluating commission).
- Generate and publish annual indicators of public service delivery quality (education,[35] health, etc.).
- In education and health, rely on huge international experimental literature on improvement of providers' incentives and service delivery.
- Strengthen internal PMS and M&E – that is, the Open Performance Appraisal System type, but rely more systematically on *external evaluations* by independent observers of the functioning of administrative entities.
- Develop a cadre of transformative leadership in order to make performance evaluations objective and meaningful.
- Restructure public administration to reduce the number of positions with close to personal monopoly power in decision-making at all levels.

Land Management

- Give more autonomy to village communities in dealing with investors and full ownership of cash compensations and rents.
- Explore options of using village land as equity by collaborating with investors.
- Ensure full publicity of village-general land transfer operations (size, compensation, rents, impact on village smallholders).
- Maintain full record of all land operations.
- Complete land surveying and the delivery of Certificates of Village Land.
- Accelerate delivery of CCRO holders and allow for contracting with non-villagers.

Central Government's Transparency and Accountability

- Systematic use of independent *ex post* evaluation, possibly including foreign observers, of the functioning of the public sector and policy reforms.

---

[35] Original performances rather than Southern and Eastern Africa Consortium for Monitoring Educational Quality scores based on average of countries participating in this programme.

- Regular publication and public discussion of a set of economic and social progress indicators – that is, 'beyond GDP'.
- Transparency of appointment at high-responsibility positions (regulatory agencies -for example, EWURA, Fair Competition Commission, Sugar Board – procurement commissions, Chief Justice, Controller Auditor General, and so on.); appointment commissions including sectoral experts, and short-listing process, with publication of short-listed personalities.
- Reporting on the implementation of voted reforms and follow-up on expert commission reports.

Legal Framework

- Necessary revisiting and simplifying of the legal set-up in several areas, such as land and decentralisation.

Competition

- Unbundling of TANESCO (generation-distribution, allowing competitive private providers).
- Independent expert reporting on protection – outside East Africa Community rules.

Afterword

François Bourguignon and Samuel Mwita Wangwe

The Tanzania Institutional Diagnostic was mostly completed in 2017 and 2018, at a time when it was too early to detect structural changes attributable to the Magufuli administration that had come to power in November 2015. Five years later, at the time of publishing this volume, many changes took place during the last two years of Magufuli's first mandate and during the first year after his re-election, including his unexpected death and his vice president, Samia Suluhu Hassan, succeeding him in March 2021. One could have expected some continuity in this transition from a president to his deputy. The elements of discontinuity one can observe – treatment of COVID, freedom of speech, private sector development, foreign relations including with foreign companies – suggest that, indeed, either she did not agree with everything Magufuli did or she may have learned from experience that some reversals, adaptations, and improvements were necessary. As far as the present study is concerned, it also means that some of the disruptive measures taken by Magufuli might be about to be reversed, so that institutional changes since the core of the present study was completed might be less than could have been expected a few years ago, for instance at the time of the electoral campaign for Magufuli's re-election, when a clear authoritarian drift in Tanzanian institutions was evident.

Under these conditions, the question arises of whether, with more visibility over the recent years, the main conclusions of the Institutional Diagnostic should be revised.

Some institutional aspects of the way both Tanzanian society and its economy function have been subject to change, and have been profusely commented on. Some changes were in the right direction, in the sense that they address or mitigate some institutional weaknesses emphasised in the Diagnostic. This is the case regarding the implementation of new anti-corruption strategies, even though it is still too early to evaluate what is, or what will be, their actual impact. Some other changes are more debatable but, for them too, it is difficult to identify the effect they are likely to have on development, especially in view of the fact that they may be in the process of being reversed. In what follows, therefore, we only identify the changes or decisions that are the most salient and we ask whether they aggravate or possibly attenuate the institutional weaknesses identified in the Diagnostic.

Referring to the five basic weaknesses that were singled out there, we ask the following question: how would major events, policy, strategies, and reform decisions observed over the last three or four years modify the Diagnostic?

Ill-defined structure of public decision-making was the first weakness. It is difficult to say whether progress has been made about the overlapping of responsibilities, an important point that was underscored in the Diagnostic, without surveying insiders. On the other hand, the 'centralisation bias' that was also emphasised has not weakened; indeed, quite the contrary given the numerous presidential interventions on detailed aspects of the functioning of the economy, from the export of cashew nuts to the management of the Dar es Salaam Port Authority, to regulating mining companies and to the formation of agencies taking over some functions of local government authorities such as the Rural Water Supply Agency and Tanzania Rural and Urban Roads Agency. It may also be recalled that the centralisation bias diagnostic was also partly based on the early overruling by Magufuli's regime of decisions made by the agency supposedly responsible for the regulation of the electricity sector, the EWURA. Finally, the point made in the Diagnostic about the long implementation delays of laws and reforms still seem to apply. No progress has been made on adjusting the land laws and a recent report on decentralisation (Ewald and Mhamba, 2019), meaningfully entitled 'Recentralization', similarly suggests there is no noticeable progress in pushing forward the Local Government Reform Programme. However, there are indications that the so-called Samia administration is reviving the operationalisation of National Decentralization Policy and statements are made in support of local economic development such as building industrial parks. However, it is too early to discern the significance of this change.

Concerning *selective distrust of market mechanisms and the private sector*, the numerous statements of President Magufuli against the private sector – including both national and foreign firms operating in Tanzania – lead one to think that this institutional weakness has been aggravated for a while. Nonetheless, this opinion must be nuanced. On the one hand, these presidential critiques and actions were probably not directed to the operations of the private sector *per se* but rather to their consequences in the area of corruption. Reducing corruption, which was the absolute priority of President Magufuli, has entailed not only sacking ministers and top civil servants earning illegal income but also exposing the private firms providing it. Since the beginning of his mandate, he stated on many occasions that it was that aspect of the behaviour of private firms that he was criticising, certainly not their key role in economic growth, employment, and industrialisation. On the other hand, most indicators referring to the business climate have deteriorated in recent years. Tanzania has dropped 13 places in the World Bank Doing Business global ranking in a few years.[1] Furthermore, its 'regulatory quality' score, which includes business environment, in the Worldwide Governance Indicators significantly worsened between 2013 and 2018, after improving over the previous period.[2]

Of course, this worsening of the business climate may only reflect the fight against corruption and tax evasion resulting in many private firms being the victims of some harassment by tax people. Business managers at some stage expressed their frustration to the President, who then demoted the Commissioner General of the tax collection agency – the TRA. The President took this opportunity to castigate the approach TRA was adopting to harass businesspeople, which was leading to the closure of some businesses. He thus expressed a wish that the TRA would exert more effort to collect taxes without undue harassment. However, the formation of a task force parallel to TRA to collect tax, which threatened some firms of being charged of money laundering, with no bail, if they did not pay tax as estimated by the task force did not really go in that direction. In addition, attachment of tax obligations to bank accounts became common causing uncertainty to private sector operations.[3]

On the contrary, some other reforms have been undertaken to improve the business climate, like the easing of administrative procedures and approval of the blueprint for easing the business environment in May 2018 and its implementation from 2019 onwards. They may be seen as a move in the direction of reversing the backsliding trend on the business climate indices and global rankings. Overall, however, the approach Magufuli adopted towards the private sector was perceived as hostile while favouring the public sector institutions to perform functions that were usually performed by the private sector. This bias towards public sector operations was most explicit in sectors such as insurance and construction.

The Samia administration is reversing the negative perceptions on the private sector. She has held meetings with the private sector associations culminating in the meeting of the TNBC three months of her coming into

---

[1] See the World Bank's *Doing Business* reports, from 2015 to 2019, on the *Business Enabling Environment* website.

[2] See WGI-Interactive Data Access on *WorldBank.org*.

[3] Relevant for the preceding argument is the fact that the worsening of Tanzania's rank in *Doing Business* is very much influenced by the 'paying tax' and 'trading across borders' component of the overall doing business score.

office, has travelled abroad with private sector delegations, and has accelerated the implementation of the Blueprint. Improvements have been made in registration of businesses, permitting engagement of foreign experts and easing immigration procedures for investors. President Samia's attitude towards the private sector is a reversal of Magufuli's. It is too early to discern the results of the new direction but there are indications that the Samia administration is reversing the negative stance towards trust in markets and the private sector.

The *underperformance of the civil service* was found to be a third institutional weakness. Because this is to a large extent the consequence of a limited availability of skills and resources as well as putting in place performance management systems, changes in this area are necessarily slow. Incentives matter too, however. From that point of view, action was apparently taken to dynamise parts of the civil service and public agencies. At the same time, however, fiscal austerity led the executive to freeze promotion and salaries of civil servants, thus severely reducing their incentives. In addition, the fight against corruption in the public sector, as well as efforts to increase revenues, has led the executive to shake up the TRA several times. This crackdown has also affected other parts of the public sector. However, it is difficult to know whether it addressed the basic functioning of the sector or was limited to sacking managers. New managers were supposedly uncorrupted and expected to undertake efficiency-enhancing reforms. These efforts need to be reinforced by structural and institutional reforms to ensure sustainability, though, while re-establishing incentives throughout the civil service hierarchy, including performance management systems.

The Samia administration has now reversed the ban on promotions and the freeze on salary increments and has made promises about improving incentives for the civil service and about enhancing civil service reforms. In fact, salary increases have been announced to take effect from 1 July 2022. The style of micromanagement into the affairs of civil service has changed to one of greater autonomy. President Samia has instructed the Ministry responsible for civil service to review all regulations, update them, and then make sure they are followed. The tone is that of institutional reform and application of the rule of law. However, it is too early to make a judgement about what will have been the change in the efficiency of the public sector over the last few years. Moreover, the data that are needed to evaluate progress are most often missing.

The last two institutional weaknesses identified in the Diagnostic were *rent-seeking and corruption* and *patronage and weak business regulation*. These have clearly been the top priority of President Magufuli's mandate, based on the personal commitments he made during the 2015 electoral campaign. The rigorous anti-corruption policy that was launched right from the start of the Fifth Phase Government focused on two sides of corruption: on the one hand, civil servants, especially at the top of the scale, and on the other hand big business. Action was taken against many people in top positions in the public sector, including ministers, top managers, and board members of public agencies who were either suspected or found guilty of corruption. Also, several firms were sued, and their operations suspended for evading taxes, most often with the complicity of top civil servants and influential politicians. Famous cases include a row with the Canadian Acacia mining company, which was accused of under-reporting the gold content of the ore it was exporting and then forbidden to ship it abroad. The company had to cease operations before an agreement, which is more favourable to Tanzania, was found. Another notable regulatory dispute took place with Aliko Dangote, the Nigerian businessman, about a cement factory for which the government wanted to renege on promises made by the previous administration. Here too, the plant was closed for some time until an agreement was reached.

These affairs had a demonstration effect to other investors that is likely to have contributed to worsening the business climate and, as mentioned above, reinforced the feeling that the government has an anti-private sector bias, particularly against foreign companies. In more recent times, President Magufuli had made pronouncements inviting investors including foreign investors to create or expand their businesses in Tanzania. It must also be stressed that the target of government's attacks may not have been the companies themselves but rather the politicians and civil servants covering their illegal operations and benefiting from their largesse. If the objective was officially to make the operations of these companies more transparent, some observers also think that there may have been a political strategy behind it. Indeed, restricting companies' ability to bribe powerful politicians, who are most likely to belong to some faction of the dominant party, could have helped the President to better control that party.[4] This assertion is given credence by the observation that no action was taken against his close associates who were perceived to be corrupt.

In effect, there is a perception that double standards were applied in the fight against corruption during the Magufuli era, and that corruption may not have declined as much as claimed. On the other hand, corruption accusations may have been used as a way of getting rid of some opponents. Among the many people who were accused of corruption, some of them stayed in custody for one, two, or more years without being taken to court. When President Samia came to office many of these people were released and the Director of Public Prosecution was removed. This signalled the respect of the rule of law. However, the Prevention and Combating of Corruption Bureau, which had been very much strengthened during the Magufuli administration, continued to function as before in the Samia administration. Yet, one point that is

---

[4] This argument was made by Dan Paget (2017) on *African Arguments*.

relevant to this study is the emphasis she has placed on institutional capacity building in fighting corruption.

Effectively fighting corruption in a country where it has become a culture, of course, comes with some collateral economic costs, such as antagonising investors and the business community. To be sure, affairs like the Acacia–government row and the hassling of domestic and foreign firms by the tax authority have received widespread coverage by the national and international business media. Yet this reputational cost may be worth incurring if the expected impact of such a strategy on corruption and long-run economic growth is large enough. It is, however, too early to make any judgement on growth. As far as corruption is concerned, it is true that most indicators have improved. Tanzania's rank in Transparency International's 'perception of corruption index' went up from 130 in 2015 to 99 in 2018. Likewise, the Worldwide Governance Indicator for the control of corruption improved somewhat in 2018 as compared to previous years, without the change being enormous either. The same is true of the World Bank Country Policy and Institutional Assessment index for corruption.[5] It must be realised, however, that those indicators reflect intended policies more than their outcomes, the problem in the case of corruption being that outcomes are extremely difficult to apprehend in the short and medium terms and that it may take a long time before changes in actual behaviour are observed.

Probably the greatest challenge of corruption is political corruption as demonstrated in the general elections of October 2020. That election was marred with a high level of corruption. Magufuli had threatened that corruption within the ruling party would not be tolerated and that any candidate who was discovered of engaging in corruption would be dropped from the race. In reality, it is believed that the level of corruption turned out to be higher than in previous instances. This reveals two further challenges. First, it is unlikely that such a magnitude of corruption could have been possible without candidates themselves making use of huge amounts of corrupt money. Second, as the pool of political leaders is selected from that group, the commitment of political leadership to the fight against corruption is seriously challenged. The ruling party won all parliamentary seats except a couple. Opposition parties cried foul, but their voices did not make a difference. Usually those who are dissatisfied with the results are allowed to petition This time there were no election petitions, a sign of loss of confidence in the objectivity of 2020 General Elections under President Magufuli's watch as well as a sign of loss of people's trust in the impartiality of the judiciary.

In summary, the fight against corruption by both subsequent administrations is without a doubt addressing one of the major institutional weaknesses of Tanzania. This represents a major change compared to preceding

[5] See, respectively: Corruption Perception Indexes on *Transparency International*, the WGI-Interactive Data Access on *WordBank.org*, and the World Development Indicators on *WorldBank.org*.

administrations. Nevertheless, some time will be needed to ascertain whether this really modifies the institutional diagnostic conducted in the present study. Experiences in other countries suggest that beating corruption takes a long time and undiminishing efforts accompanied by institutional reforms. In this regard, corruption is likely to still remain a pertinent problem in Tanzania for some time.

Putting things together, it seems that, although positive from several points of view, the action led by the two subsequent administrations (Magufuli and Samia) over the last three or four years has not modified the basic institutional weaknesses identified in the Diagnostic. There is an improvement in some areas, but there are signs of deterioration and possibly new weaknesses in others. This is the case of *transparency and accountability*, the two general principles of action recommended in the Diagnostic to help improve other institutions. The kind of departure from these principles seems to have changed, but the overall goal is still distant. While the Diagnostic found there was 'some transparency with little accountability' in previous administrations, the last three years during the Magufuli administration seem to point rather to greater accountability with less transparency. Formerly, many cases of misconduct were detected without much action being taken. In comparison, fewer cases have been exposed recently but action has been taken, that is, accountability is now upheld without delay. Overall, however, the transparency of the government in relation to its citizens seems to have been reduced, in some cases threatening the sense of democracy that has characterised Tanzanian society ever since independence, a quality that the Diagnostic considered, albeit perhaps not explicitly enough, as a major institutional strength.

Deliberate opacity of policies and outcomes, infringement on individual freedom, and rising authoritarianism during the Magufuli era were largely underscored and commented in the international press, whereas the national media found it increasingly difficult to raise these issues domestically. The list is long of events and decisions that contribute to this judgement. A few examples will suffice here.

The amendment to the Statistics Act tabled in Parliament in September 2018 that made it a criminal offence to publish statistics both 'to disseminate or otherwise communicate to the public any statistical information which is intended to invalidate, distort or discredit official statistics released by the National Bureau of Statistics without authorisation'. This is one example of the opacity the government attempted to impose on the debate on policies and policy outcomes. To be sure, this decision was reversed in 2019 after bowing to pressure from the World Bank. Even so, however, the Statistics Act of 2018 restricted the debate on policy, in a direction opposite to the 'evaluation culture' recommended in the Diagnostic. It also cast doubt on the accuracy of published statistics, a doubt that was apparently shared by the World Bank, which estimates 2018 GDP growth has been noticeably lower than officially announced (World Bank Group, 2019, 11). In this vein, the vetoing by the government of the publication of the IMF Article IV statutory 2019 report, which suggested growth was slower than reported and was also critical of some of the government's policies, inspired the same doubts. Because of such issues, it is hard to be convinced that efforts were truly being made under Magufuli towards more transparency and accountability in the economic policy sphere.

Beyond economics, several events and government decisions by the Magufuli administration, which also pertain to transparency, have led several international NGOs of repute to raise some concern about the treatment of human rights in Tanzania. It is not the place here to go into any detail on issues that are largely outside the scope of the Diagnostic. Yet the fact that an NGO like Human Rights Watch expressed concerns about the freedom of expression and the freedom of assembly in Tanzania, or that 30 civil society organisations called the attention of the United Nations Human Rights Councils to their perception that 'the space for human rights defenders (HRDs), civil society, journalists, bloggers, the media, LGBTI persons, and opposition and dissenting voices' was 'shrinking' are to be underscored.[6] Also, a bilateral donor like the EU temporarily recalling its ambassador in November 2018 or suspending some aid programmes a little later, in both cases due to human right concerns, is not to be taken lightly, even though the crisis was quickly resolved.[7]

Since she assumed power in March 2021, the Samia administration seems to have reversed these trends of erosion of transparency and the treatment of human rights in Tanzania. Freedom of the press and other media has been restored and the threats to democracy have been mitigated.

In summary, the conclusion of this brief review of the way accounting for the recent past might lead to a revision of the Diagnostic is threefold. First, among the institutional weaknesses identified in the Diagnostic, progress may have been achieved on the corruption front, although it will probably take time before evidence of a real improvement is available. In this respect, it is fair to say that the resurgence of political corruption at the time of the 2020 presidential election is not a positive signal. There is no reason to modify the Diagnostic on other weaknesses, as President Samia seems to be decided to correct the most unfavourable institutional changes introduced by her predecessor.

The second conclusion is that a new weakness may have appeared. Unlike as was recommended in the conclusion of the Diagnostic, it seems the Magufuli administration was moving away from the pursuit of transparency

---

[6] See the Human Rights Watch Report 2019 (Human Rights Watch, 2019) or the letter to the UN HRC (Human Rights Watch, 2020).
[7] See press news from Niba (2018) on *RFI* and Baynes (2018) on *The Independent*.

in many ways. Such an attitude might have been part of a political strategy meant to ensure more authority rests with the President, possibly to win the anti-corruption battle. Most developing countries need 'strong' heads of state to push collective development rather than letting private interest rule. However, getting too strong without corresponding strong institutions may be dangerous if it means policymaking becomes less and less transparent. Besides mounting political discontent, the risk is that no countervailing opinion and correcting force would then prevent the country from heading in a wrong direction. This trend is being reversed in the Samia administration which is apparently restoring transparency and democracy. However, the ease with which this is being done is reinforcing the point made in the Diagnostic of weak institutions.

This is our third conclusion, namely the institutional weakness revealed by the flexibility of Tanzanian institutions depending on the president. There is a fundamental flaw in political institutions that permit the excesses observed during the Magufuli era to take place and eventually to be corrected by the next administration. What was stated as a joke by Nyerere that the Tanzanian constitution allowed him to rule as a dictator is in fact true. The constitution does not protect against a President who would strongly deviate from democratic principles.

A possible explanation of the Magufuli's authoritarian shift was his need to take full control of the various factions within the CCM ruling party in order to launch his anti-corruption strategy. This initial fragmentation of the ruling party into distinct groups of interest was a key feature of the political economy of Tanzania before Magufuli, and a potential obstacle to the adoption of some development-friendly reforms. He apparently succeeded in controlling them, as shown by the results of the 2020 general election. There is full uncertainty about what would have happened next: would he have moved back to a less authoritarian leadership or not? Samia's leadership of the CCM so far has shown two types of changes. First, she appointed new leaders in the Secretary General and Vice-chairman positions. Second, she has demoted or removed from their positions leaders who were identified as aspirant for presidency in 2025, which implicitly means that she does not have her hands free from CCM factions.

The Magufuli era may have been a kind of parenthesis in the political history of Tanzania, during which a disruptive president attempted to impose a tough anti-corruption strategy, seen as essentially advantageous for development, which required exerting authoritarian power over various political factions. However, the negative attitude towards the private sector was not favourable to long-term private investment that is crucial for development. Such a state of affairs had been unseen in Tanzania over the last 30 years, and maybe since independence, and certainly was a major change over preceding administrations. President Samia took over, reverted to a more democratic and decentralised rule, but is now probably facing re-built factions within the ruling party which aspire to power in the next general election, and may represent obstacles to the conduct of policy by the new administration.

Even though there is some continuity with the previous administration, it cannot be discarded that the situation is back to what it was under Magufuli's predecessor. All in all, there is no evidence of need or reason to change our diagnostic.

References

Acemoglu, D., and Robinson, J. (2012). *Why Nations Fail: The Origins of Power, Prosperity and Poverty.* Crown Business, New York.

Acemoglu, D., Johnson, S., Robinson, J. A., and Yared, P. (2008). Income and democracy. *American Economic Review*, 98(3), 808–42.

ActionAid (2009). Implications of biofuels production on food security in Tanzania. *Report, Dar-es-Salaam: ActionAid International Tanzania.*

Adam, C. S., and O'Connell, S. A. (1999). Aid, taxation and development in Sub-Saharan Africa. *Economics and Politics*, 11, 225–53.

Adepoju, A. (ed.). (1993). *The Impact of Structural Adjustment on the Population of Africa.* Heinemann, London.

AfDB (African Development Bank) (2015). *Renewable Energy in Africa: Tanzania Country Profile.* Retrieved from: www.Afdb.org/fileadmin/uploads/afdb/Chapteruments/Generic-Chapteruments/Renewable_Energy_in_Africa_-_Tanzania.pdf (Accessed: 1 February 2018).

AfriMAp (2015). *Effectiveness of Anti-Corruption Agencies in East Africa.* Open Society Foundations, New York.

Afrobarometer (2017, December 6). AD178: In Tanzania, anti-corruption efforts seen as paying dividends, need citizen engagement. Afrobarometer Dispatch No. 178.

Ahlborg, H., and Hammar, L. (2014). Drivers and barriers to rural electrification in Tanzania and Mozambique: Grid-extension, off-grid, and renewable energy technologies. *Renewable Energy*, 61, 117–24.

Ahlborg, H., and Sjöstedt, M. (2015). Small-scale hydropower in Africa: Socio-technical designs for renewable energy in Tanzanian villages. *Energy Research and Social Science*, 5, 20–33.

Alden-Wily, L. (2003). *Community-based land tenure management: Questions and answers About Tanzania's new Village Land Act, 1999.* IIED Issues Paper 120, International Institute for Environment and Development, London.

Ali, D. A., Collin, M., Deininger, K., Dercon, S., Sandefur, J., and Zeitlin, A. (2016). Small price incentives increase women's access to land titles in Tanzania. *Journal of Development Economics*, 123, 107–22.

Ali, D. A., Deininger, K., and Duponchel, M. (2017). New ways to assess and enhance land registry sustainability: Evidence from Rwanda. *World Development*, 99, 377–94.

Ali, D. A., Deininger, K., and Goldstein, M. (2014). Environmental and gender impacts of land tenure regularization in Africa: Pilot evidence from Rwanda. *Journal of Development Economics*, 110, 262–75.

Ali, D. A., Deininger, K. W., and Harris, C. A. P. (2019). Does large farm establishment create benefits for neighboring smallholders? Evidence from Ethiopia. *Land Economics*, 95(1), 71–90.

Alstone, P., Gershenson, D., and Kammen, D. M. (2015). Decentralized energy systems for clean electricity access. *Nature Climate Change*, 5(4), 305–14.

Aminzade, R. (2014). *Race, Nation and Citizenship in Post-Colonial Africa: The Case of Tanzania*. Cambridge University Press, Cambridge.

Amsden, A. (1989). *Asia's Next Giant: South Korea and Late Industrialisation*. Oxford University Press, Oxford.

Andreoni, A. (2017). *Anti-corruption in Tanzania: A Political Settlements Analysis*. Anti-Corruption Evidence, University of London.

Andreoni, A., Mushi, D., and Therkildsen, O. (2020). The political economy of scarcity in East Africa: A case study of sugar production, smuggling and trade in Tanzania. *ACE Working Paper, 31*.

Arndt, C., Leyaro, V., Mahrt, K., and Tarp, F. (2017b). Growth and poverty: A pragmatic assessment and future prospects, in Tanzania. In Adam, C., Collier, P., and Ndulu, B. (eds.), *The Path to Prosperity*, p. 190. Oxford University Press, Oxford.

Arndt, C., Mahrt, K., and Schimanski, C. (2017a). On poverty–growth elasticity. *Working Paper 2017/149*. UNU-WIDER, Helsinki.

Askew, K., Maganga, F., and Odgaard, R. (2017). *Dispossession through formalization: The plight of pastoralists in Tanzania*. Paper prepared for presentation at the 2017 World Bank Conference on Land and Poverty, World Bank, Washington, D.C., 20–24 March 2017.

Atkinson, A. B. (2011) Evidence on top incomes in Tanzania 1948–1970. *Working Paper, 11/0070*. International Growth Centre, London.

Atkinson, A. B., and Lugo, M. (2014). Growth, poverty and distribution in Tanzania. *Working Paper 10/0831*. International Growth Centre, London.

Ayee, J. R. A. (2005). Public sector management in Africa. *Economic Research Working Paper No. 82*. Africa Development Bank, Legon.

Babeya, E. (2011). Electoral corruption and the politics of elections financing in Tanzania. *Journal of Politics and Law*, 4(2), 91–103.

Bacon, R. (1999). *A Scorecard for Energy Reform in Developing Countries*. Public Policy for the Private Sector, World Bank, Washington, D.C.

Bahl, R., and Martinez-Vazquez, J. (2008). The property tax in developing countries: Current practices and prospects. In *Making the Property Tax Work: Experiences in Developing and Transitional Countries*. Lincoln Institute, Kentucky, USA.

Baland J. M., Bourguignon, F., Platteau, J. P., and Verdier, T. (2020). *Handbook of Institutions and Development*. Princeton University Press.

Bank of Tanzania (2011). *Tanzania Mainland's 50 Years of Independence: The Role and Functions of the Bank of Tanzania*. Dar es Salaam.

Bank of Tanzania (2017, August). *Monthly Economic Review*. Dar es Salaam.

Bank of Tanzania (BOT) (1982). *Tanzania: Twenty Years of Independence (1961–1981). A Review of Political and Economic Performance.* Dar es Salaam.

Barker, C. E., Bhagavan, M. R., Mitschke-Collande, P. V., and Wield, D. V. (1986). *African Industrialisation: Technology and Change in Tanzania.* Gower Publishing Co.

Barker, J. S., and Saul, J. S. (1974). *The Tanzania Elections in Post-Arusha Perspective, in Socialism and Participation: Tanzania's 1970 Elections.* Tanzania Publishing House Ltd, Dar es Salaam.

Barrett, A. M., Mtana, N., Osaki, K., and Rubagumya, C. (2014). *Language Supportive Teaching and Textbooks in Tanzania: A Baseline Study Report.* Mimeo Ministry of Education, Dar es Salaam.

Barro, R. J., and Lee, J. W. (2013). A new data set of educational attainment in the world, 1950–2010. *Journal of Development Economics,* 104, 184–98.

Baynes, C. (2018, November 6). *EU recalls ambassador to Tanzania over 'deterioration of human rights' amid crackdown on gay people.* The Independent. Retrieved from: www.independent.co.uk/news/world/africa/tanzania-anti-gay-crackdown-arr ests-eu-recalls-ambassador-dar-es-salaam-a8620546.html

BBC (2018, July 11). *Tanzania research group threatened over Magufuli survey.* The East African. Retrieved from: www.Theeastafrican.Co.Ke/news/ea/Tanzania-research-group-threatened-over-Magufuli-survey/4552908-4657646-mynsnjz/index .html.

Belghith, N. B. H., Lopera, M. A., Ndip, A. E., and Karamba, W. (2018). Analysis of the mismatch between Tanzania Household Budget Survey and National Panel Survey Data in poverty and inequality levels and trends. *Poverty and Equity Global Practice Working Paper 145.* The World Bank, Washington, D.C.

Benin, S. (2016). *Agricultural Productivity in Africa: Trends, Patterns, and Determinants.* International Food Policy Research Institute, Washington.

Bertho, F. (2013). *Présentation de la Base de Données "Institutional Profiles Database 2012".* Les Cahiers de la DG Trésor – n° 2013-03 – Juillet 2013.

Besley, T., and Persson, T. (2013). Taxation and development. In Auerbach, A. J., Chetty, R., Feldstein, M., and Saez, E. (eds.), *Handbook of Public Economics* (5). Elsevier, Amsterdam.

Bevan, D., Collier, P., and Gunning, J. W. (1990). *Controlled Open Economies: A Neoclassical Approach to Structuralism.* Oxford University Press (Clarendon), Oxford.

Bhatt, V. V., and Kim, H. (2000). Japanese civil service system: Relevance for developing countries. *Economic and Political Weekly,* 35(23), 1937–43.

Bienen, H. (1970). One-party systems in Africa. In Huntington, Samuel P., and Moore, Cement H. (eds.), *Authoritarian Politics in Modern Society. The Dynamics of Established One-Party Systems.* Basic Books, New York.

Bigsten, A., and Danielsson, A. (1999). *Is Tanzania an Emerging Economy? A Report for the OECD Project "Emerging Africa".* Department of Economics at Lund University and Department of Economics at Goteborg University, Sweden.

Bigsten, A., and Danielson, A. (2001). *Is the Ugly Duckling Finally Growing Up?* Nordiska Afrikainstitutet, Uppsala.

Blaauw, D., Ditlopo, P., Maseko, F., Chirwa, M., Mwisongo, A., Bidwell, P., et al. (2013). Comparing the job satisfaction and intention to leave of different categories of health workers in Tanzania, Malawi, and South Africa. *Global Health Action,* 6(1), 19287.

Boadway, R., and Shah, A. (2009). *Fiscal Federalism*. Cambridge Books, Cambridge University Press, UK.

Boex, J., and Muga, M. C. (2009). What determines the quality of local financial management? The case of Tanzania. *IDG Working Paper No. 2009–02*, Urban Institute Centre, Washington, D.C.

Boudreaux, K. (2012). An assessment of concerns related to land tenure in the SAGCOT region. *Unpublished Report for USAID Tanzania*.

Bourguignon, F. and Platteau, J. P. (2023). *Institutional Challenges at the Early Stages of Development: Lessons from a Multi-Country Study*. Cambridge University Press, Cambridge.

Bryceson, D. F. (1993) *Liberalizing Tanzania's Food Trade*. James Currey, London.

Carrington, D. (2011). *UK firm's failed biofuel dream wrecks lives of Tanzania villagers*. The Guardian. Retrieved from: www.Theguardian.com/environment/2011/oct/30/africa-poor-west-biofuel-betrayal

Carrington, D., Paul, J., Maurayi, T., and Sprenger, R. (2011). *Sun Biofuels have left us in a helpless situation: They have taken our land*. The Guardian. Retrieved from: www.guardian.co.uk/environment/video/2011/nov/09/biofuel-tanzania-video (Accessed: 16 August 2018).

Catterson, J., and Lindahl, C. (1999). *The Sustainability Enigma: Aid dependency and the phasing out of projects, the case of Swedish aid to Tanzania*. Expert Group on Development Issues.

Chande, J. K. (2005). *A Knight in Africa: Journey from Bukene*. Penumbra Press.

Chandra, V., Kacker, P., and Li, Y. (2008). Fostering growth, export competitiveness and employment. In Utz, R. J. (ed.), *Sustaining and Sharing Economic Growth in Tanzania*. World Bank Publications.

Chavent, M., Kuentz, V., Liquet, B., and Saracco, L. (2011). ClustOfVar: An R package for the clustering of variables. *Journal of Statistical Software*, 50(13).

Chazan, N., Lewis, P., Mortimer, J., Rothchild, D., and Stedman, S. J. (eds.). (1999). *Politics and Society in Contemporary Africa*. 3rd edition, Lynne Rienner, Boulder, CO.

Cheeseman, N., Matfess, H., and Amani, A. (2021). Tanzania: The roots of repression. *Journal of Democracy*, 32(2), 77–89.

Clark, R. E. (1998). Motivating performance: Part 1 – Diagnosing and solving motivation problems. *Performance Improvement*, 37(8), 39–47.

Cliffe, L., and Cunningham, G. L. (1973). Ideology, organisation and the settlement experience in Tanzania. In Cliffe, J. S., and Saul, L. (eds.), *Socialism in Tanzania* 2. East African Publishing House, Nairobi.

Collier, P., and Wangwe, S. (1986). *Labour and Rural Poverty in Tanzania*, Collier, P., Radwan, S., and Wangwe S. (eds.). Clarendon Press.

Collins, P. (1974). Decentralization and local administration for development in Tanzania. *Africa Today*, 21(3), 15–25.

Cooksey, B. (2013). *Public goods, rents and business in Tanzania*. Background paper 1, Africa Power and Politics Programme, Overseas Development Institute, London.

Cooksey, B. (2017). *IPTL, Richmond and "Escrow": The Price of Private Power Procurement in Tanzania*. Africa Research Institute, London.

Cooksey, B., and Kelsall, T. (2011). *The political economy of the investment climate in Tanzania*. Africa Power and Politics Series No.1, Overseas Development Institute, London.

Coulson, A. (1978). Agricultural policies in mainland Tanzania. *Review of Africa Political Economy*, 10, 74–160.

Coulson, A. (1982). *Tanzania: A Political Economy*. Oxford University Press, London.

Coulson, A. (2013). *Tanzania: A Political Economy*. Oxford University Press, Oxford.

Coulson, A. (2015). 'Small' or 'Large' Farm: Which Way for Tanzania, Lucian, A. Msambichaka, J. K. M., Selejio, O., and Mashindano, O. J. (eds.). Dar es Salaam University Press, Dar es Salaam.

Coulson, A. (ed.). (1979). *African Socialism in Practice*. Spokesman, Nottingham.

Court of Appeal of Tanzania. (1985, June 21). *National Agricultural and Food Corporation vs Mulbadaw Village*. TLR 88 (TZCA).

Daily News (2018, January 6). *Dar es Salaam*. Tanzania.

Daima Associates Limited Development Consultants and Policy Analysts and the Overseas Development Institute, Joint Evaluation of General Budget Support Tanzania 1995–2004 (2005, April). *Revised final report: Report to the Government of Tanzania and the Poverty Reduction Budget Support (PRBS)*. Development Partners Tanzania.

Dal Bo, E., and Finan, F. (2020). At the Intersection: A Review of Institutions in Economic Development, in Baland et al. (Eds.), *The Handbook of Institutions and Development*, Princeton University Press.

De, C., and Prud'homme, R. (1994). On the dangers of decentralization. *Policy Research Working Paper Series*.

de Janvry, A., Emerick, K., Gonzalez-Navarro, M., and Sadoulet, E. (2015). Delinking land rights from land use: Certification and migration in Mexico. *American Economic Review*, 105(10), 3125–49.

de Janvry, A., Gonzalez-Navarro, M., and Sadoulet, E. (2014). Are land reforms granting complete property rights politically risky? Electoral outcomes of Mexico's certification program. *Journal of Development Economics*, 110, 216–25.

De Mello, L. (2011). Does fiscal decentralization strengthen social capital? Cross-country evidence and the experience of Brazil and Indonesia. *Environment and Planning C: Government and Policy*, 29, 281–96.

Deaton, A. (2013). *The Great Escape: Health, Wealth, and the Origins of Inequality*. Princeton University Press, Princeton, NJ.

Deininger, K., Lavadenz, I., Bresciani, F., and Diaz, M. (2002). *Mexico's second agrarian reform: Impact on factor markets and household welfare*. Discussion Paper. World Bank, Washington, D.C.

Deininger, K., Selod, H., and Burns, A. (2012). *The Land Governance Assessment Framework: Identifying and Monitoring Good Practice in the Land Sector*. World Bank, Washington, D.C.

Dixit, A. (2016). *Anti-Corruption Institutions: Some History and Theory*. Revision of a paper presented at the International Economic Association Roundtable on Governance Institutions and Corruption, Montevideo, Uruguay. Retrieved from: www.Princeton.Edu/~dixitak/home/IEAConf_Dixit_Rev.pdf

Dixit, A. (2017). *Fighting Corruption by Altering Equilibrium in an Assurance Game*, Preliminary draft. Retrieved from: www.Princeton.Edu/~dixitak/home/AssurAntiCorr.pdf

Easterly, W. (2006). *The White Man's Burden: Why the West's Efforts to Aid the Rest have Done so Much Ill and so Little Good*. The Penguin Press, London.

Eaton, K., Kaiser, K., and Smoke, P. (2010). *The Political Economy of Decentralization Reforms: Implications for Aid Effectiveness.* World Bank, Washington D.C.

Eberhard, A., and Godhino, C. (2017, February). A review and exploration of the status, context and political economy of power sector reforms in Sub-Saharan Africa, South Asia and Latin America. *MIR Working Paper.* Graduate School of Business, University of Cape Town.

Eberhard, A., Gratwick, K., Morella, E., and Antmann, P. (2016). Independent power projects in Sub-Saharan Africa: Investment trends and policy lessons. *Energy Policy,* 108 (2017), 390–424.

Economic and Social Research Foundation (2016). *Education foundations of the development of skills and productive capabilities.* THDR 2017: Background Paper No. 10, ESRF Discussion Paper 71, Dar es Salaam, Tanzania.

Edwards, S. (2012). Is Tanzania a success story? A long-term analysis. *Working Paper 17764.* National Bureau of Economic Research, Cambridge, MA.

Edwards, S. (2014). *Toxic Aid: Economic Collapse and Recovery in Tanzania.* Oxford University Press, Oxford.

Eichengreen, B. (2008). The real exchange rate and economic growth. *Working Paper 4. Commission on Growth and Development.* World Bank, Washington D.C.

Estache, A. (2017a). Successes and failures of water and sanitation governance choices in Sub-Saharan Africa (1990–2017). *ECARES Working Paper, 2017–32.* Université libre de Bruxelles, Brussels.

Estache, A. (2017b). Institutions for infrastructure in developing countries: What we know and the lot we still need to know. In Bourguignon, F., et al. (eds.), (forthcoming). *Frontiers in Development Economics.* OUP. Retrieved from: https://ideas.Repec .org/p/eca/wpaper/2013-230527.Html (Accessed: 1 February 2018).

Estache, A., and Wren-Lewis, L. (2009). Toward a theory of regulation for developing countries: Following Jean-Jacques Laffont's lead. *Journal of Economic Literature,* 47(3, September), 729–70.

Estache, A., and Wren-Lewis, L. (2010). Regulation in developing economics: A survey of theory and evidence. In Baldwin, R., Cave, M., and Lodge, M. (eds.), *Oxford Handbook of Regulation,* pp. 371–406. Oxford University Press, Oxford.

Evans, P. (1995). *Embedded Autonomy: States and Industrial Transformation.* Princeton University Press, Princeton, NJ.

Ewald, J., and Mhamba, R. (2019). *Recentralization: Interrogating the state of local democracy, good governance and development in Tanzania.* Swedish International Centre for Democracy, Research Report No. 13.

Faguet, J. (2004). Does decentralization increase government responsiveness to local needs?: Evidence from Bolivia. *Journal of Public Economics,* 88(3–4), 867–93.

Falleti, T. G. (2005). A sequential theory of decentralization: Latin American cases in comparative perspective. *American Political Science Review,* 99(3), 327–46.

Farole, T. (2011). *Special Economic Zones in Africa: Comparing Performance and Learning from Global Experiences.* World Bank Publications.

Faustino, J., and Booth, D. (2014). *Development entrepreneurship: How donors and leaders can foster institutional change.* Working Politically in Practice Series. Overseas Development Institute, London.

Fischer, P. (2005). *Rent-seeking, institutions and reforms in Africa: Theory and empirical evidence from Tanzania.* PhD thesis submitted to the University of Konstanz, Germany.

Fjeldstad, O. H. (2001). Fiscal decentralization in Tanzania: For better or for worse?, *CMI Working Papers WP 2001:10*. Chr. Michelsen Institute, Bergen.

Fjeldstad, O. H. (2003). Fighting fiscal corruption: Lessons from the Tanzania Revenue Authority. *Journal Public Administration and Development. The International Journal of Management Research and Practice*, 23(2), 165–75.

Fjeldstad, O. H. (2004). What's trust got to do with it? Non-payment of service charges in local authorities in South Africa. *Journal of Modern African Studies*, 42(4), 539–62.

Fjeldstad, O. H. (2006). Local revenue mobilization in urban settings in Africa. In Millet, K., Olowu, D., and Cameron, R. (eds.), *Local Governance and Poverty Reduction in Africa*, pp. 105–26. Joint Africa Institute, Tunis.

Fjeldstad, O. H. (2014). Tax and development: Donor support to strengthen tax systems in developing countries. *Public Administration and Development*, 34(3), 182–93.

Fjeldstad, O. H. (2015). When the terrain does not fit the map: Local government taxation in Africa. Journal Perspectives on politics, production and public administration in Africa. In Kjær, A. M., Pedersen, L. E., and Buur, L. (eds.), *Perspectives on Politics, Production and Public Administration in Africa. Essays in honour of Ole Therkildsen*. Copenhagen: Danish Institute for International Studies.

Fjeldstad, O. H., and Kater, L. (2017). Theory and practice of decentralization by devolution: Lessons from a research programme in Tanzania (2002–2013). In Mmari, D., and Wangwe, S. (eds.), *Perspectives from Twenty Years of Policy Research in Tanzania*. Mkuki na Nyota Publishers, Dar es Salaam.

Fjeldstad, O. H., and Semboja, J. (2011). Dilemmas of fiscal decentralization: A study of local government taxation in Tanzania. *Forum for Development Studies*, 27(1), 205–14.

Fjeldstad, O. H., Ali, M., and Goodfellow, T. (2017). Taxing the urban boom: Property taxation in Africa. *CMI Insight 1: 2017 (March)*. Chr. Michelsen Institute, Bergen.

Fjeldstad, O. H., Ali, M., and Katera, L. (2019). Policy implementation under stress: Central-local government relations in property tax administration in Tanzania. *Journal of Financial Management of Property and Construction*, 24(2).

Fjeldstad, O. H., Katera, L., and Ngalewa, E. (2008). Outsourcing revenue collection: Experiences from local government authorities in Tanzania. *REPOA Brief*. Dar es Salaam, Tanzania.

Fjeldstad, O. H., Katera, L., and Ngalewa, E. (2010). Local government finances and financial management in Tanzania: empirical evidence of trends 2000–2007. *REPOA Special Paper No. 10–2010*. Mkuki na Nyota Publishers, Dar es Salaam.

Fjeldstad, O. H., Ngalewa, E., and Katera, L. (2008). *Citizens demand tougher action on corruption in Tanzania*. Research on Poverty Alleviation, 11. Dar el Salaam, Tanzania.

Food and Agriculture Organization (2002). *Land Tenure Studies: Land Tenure and Rural Development*. Rome.

Fouéré, M. A. (2015). Indians are exploiters and Africans idlers! The production of racial categories and socio-economic issues in Tanzania. In Adam, M. (ed.), *Indian Africa*. Mkuki na Nyota Publishers, Dar es Salaam.

Fukuyama, F. (2005). *State-Building: Governance and World Order in the Twenty-First Century*. Profile Books, London.

Furukawa, M. (2014). Management of the international development aid system and the creation of political space for China: The case of Tanzania. *Working Paper No 82*. JICA Research Institute.

Gaddis, I., Morisset, J., and Wane, W. (2013). *Law and order: Countering the threat of crime in Tanzania.* Retrieved from: http://blogs.Worldbank.org/africacan/law-and-order-countering-the-threat-of-crime-in-tanzania (Accessed: 6 November 2017).

Ganimian, A. and Murnane, R. (2017). Improving Education in Developing Countries: Lessons From Rigorous Impact Evaluations, *Review of Educational Research*, 86(3), 719–55.

Gastorn, K. (2003). *Scheme of regularisation of land rights. Old package in a new approach?*. Paper prepared to commemorate 60th birthday anniversary of Prof. Gamaliel Mgonga Fimbo PhD on 8 August 2003, Faculty of Law, University of Dar es Salaam.

Gastorn, K. (2009). *The dynamics and continuity in land dispute mechanisms in mainland Tanzania: The jurisdictional debate, 583–584.* Paper presented at the Workshop on Land Governance in Support of MDGs: Responding to New Challenges, Washington, D.C., 9–10 March 2009.

Geddes, B. (1994). *Politician's Dilemma: Building State Capacity in Latin America.* University of California Press, Berkeley.

Geir, S. (2005). The 1999 Land Act and Village Land Act: A technical analysis of the practical implications of the Acts. In *Report of the Symposium on the Implementation of the 1999 Land Acts, Courtyard Hotel.* Dar es Salaam, 1 and 2 March 2005. Organised by Oxfam Ireland Trocaire, and Concern, funded by Development Cooperation Ireland.

Gerschenkron, A. (1962). *Economic Backwardness in Historical Perspective.* Harvard University Press, Cambridge.

Ghai, D. (1987). *Economic growth, structural change and labour absorption in Africa: 1960–85.* Discussion Paper No. 1 URRISD. Geneva, Switzerland.

Gibbon, P. (1995). Merchantisation of production and privatisation of development in post-Ujamaa Tanzania: An introduction. *Liberalised Development in Tanzania*, 9–36.

Gibbon, P. (1999). *Privatisation and Foreign Direct Investment in Mainland Tanzania, 1992–98.* Danish Institute for International Studies, DIIS.

Global Integrity Report (2016). Retrieved from: www.Globalintegrity.org/research/tanzania/ (Accessed: 8 November 2017).

Global Peace Index (2017). *Institute for Economics and Peace.* Retrieved from: http://economicsandpeace.org/reports/ (Accessed: 8 November 2017).

Goldthau, A. (2014). Rethinking the governance of energy infrastructure: Scale, decentralization and polycentrism. *Energy Research and Social Science*, 1, 134–40.

Government of Tanzania (2013). *Tanzania Development Vision 2025. Big Results Now! Roadmap – National Key Result Area: Energy 2013/14–2015/6.* Retrieved from: www.Pdb.Go.Tz/Chapteruments/energy.pdf (Accessed: 1 February 2018).

Gratwick, K. N., and Eberhard, A. (2008). Demise of the standard model for power sector reform and the emergence of hybrid power markets. *Energy Policy*, 36(10), 3948–60.

Gray, H. (2013). Industrial policy and the political settlement in Tanzania: Aspects of continuity and change since independence. *Review of African Political Economy*, 40(136), 185.

Gray, H. (2015). The political economy of grand corruption in Tanzania. *African Affairs*, 114(456), 382–403.

Gray, H. (2018). *Turbulence and Order in Economic Development.* Oxford University Press, Oxford.

Gray, H., and Khan, M. H. (2010). Good Governance and Growth in Africa: What can we learn from Tanzania?. In Padayachee, V. (ed.), *The Political Economy of Africa.* Routledge, London.

Gray, H. S. (2015). The political economy of grand corruption in Tanzania. *African Affairs*, 114(456), 382–403.

Green, R. H. (1995). The vision of human-centered development: A study in moral economy. In Legum, C., and Mmari, G. (eds.), *Mwalimu. The Influence of Nyerere*. James Currey, London.

Grimm, M., and Peters, J. (2016). Solar off-grid Markets in Africa – Recent dynamics and the role of branded products. *Ruhr Economic Paper n. 619, RWI, Essen*.

Grimm, M., Munyehirwe, A., Peters, J., and Sievert, M. (2015). A first step up the energy ladder? Low cost solar kits and household's welfare in rural Rwanda. *Ruhr Economic Paper n. 554, RWI, Essen*.

Hampton, W. (1987). *Local Government and Urban Politics*. Longman, London and New York.

Han, C., and Peirolo, S. (2021). *Time to Teach, Teacher Attendance and Time on Task in Primary Schools*. Tanzania Mainland UNICEF Office of Research, Florence.

Harris, J. R., and Todaro, M. P. (1970). Migration, unemployment and development: A two-sector analysis. *American Economic Review*, 60, 126–42.

Harvey, D. (2005). *A Brief History of Neoliberalism*. Oxford University Press, Oxford.

Hausmann, R., Rodrik, D., and Velasco, A. (2005). *Growth Diagnostics*. The Growth Lab, Harvard University. Retrieved from: https://growthlab.Cid.Harvard.Edu/files/growthlab/files/growth-diagnostics.pdf

Havnevik, K. J. (1993). *Tanzania: The Limits to Development from Above*. Nordic Africa Institute.

Heilman, B., and Ndumbaro, L. (2002). Corruption, politics, and societal values in Tanzania: An evaluation of the Mkapa Administration's anti-corruption efforts. *African Association of Political Science*, 7(1), 1–19.

Helleiner, G. (2002a). Emerging relationships between poor countries and external sources of finance: The case of Tanzania. *International Journal, Spring*, 2002, 57(2), 227–32.

Helleiner, G. (2002b). Local ownership and donor performance monitoring: New aid relationships in Tanzania. *Journal of Human Development*, 3(2), 251–61.

Henstridge, M., and Rweyemamu, D. (2017). Managing hydrocarbon resources. In Adam, C., Collier, P., and Ndulu, B. (eds.), *Tanzania, The Path to Prosperity*, p. 49. Oxford University Press, Oxford.

Hombrados, J. G., Devisscher, M., and Herreros Martínez, M. (2015). The Impact of land titling on agricultural production and agricultural investments in Tanzania: A theory-based approach. *Journal of Development Effectiveness*, 7(4), 530–44.

Hoogeveen, J., and Ruhinduka, R. (2009). *Poverty reduction in Tanzania since 2001: Good intentions, few results*. Paper prepared for the Research and Analysis Working Group.

Hulst, R., Mafuru, W., and Mpenzi, D. (2015). Fifteen years after decentralization by devolution: Political-administrative relations in Tanzania local government. *Public Administration and Development*, 35(5), 360–71.

Human Rights Watch (2019, March 21). *Tanzania. Events of 2018*. Human Rights Watch. Retrieved from: www.hrw.org/world-report/2019/country-chapters/tanzania-and-zanzibar

Human Rights Watch (2020, October 28). *UN Human Rights Council Should Address Tanzania Crackdown*. Human Rights Watch. Retrieved from: www.hrw.org/news/2019/05/13/un-human-rights-council-should-address-tanzania-crackdown

Hunt, S. (2002). *Making Competition Work in Electricity*. John Wiley and Sons, Inc, New York.

Huntington, S. P. (1968). *Political Order in Changing Societies.* Yale University Press, New Haven.

Huther, J., and Shah, A. (1998). Applying a simple measure of good governance to the debate of fiscal decentralization. *Policy Research Working Paper Series No. 1894.* World Bank, Washington, D.C.

Hyden, G. (1975). "We must run while others walk": Policy making for Socialist Development in Tanzanian-Type of polities. In Kim, K.S., Mabele, R., and Schultheis, M. (eds.), *Papers on the Political Economy of Tanzania,* p. 5. Heinemann Educational Books, Nairobi.

Hyden, G. (1976). Decentralization and the government staff. *Decentralization Research Project Working Paper No 76.1.* Dar es Salaam.

Hyden, G. (1983). *No Shortcuts to Progress: African Development Management in Perspective.* University of California Press, Berkeley and Los Angeles.

Ibbott, R. (2014). *Ujamaa: The Hidden Story of Tanzania's Socialist Villages.* Crossroad's Books, London.

IMF (1999). *Letter of Intent.* Retrieved from: www.Imf.org/external/np/loi/1999/071499.Htm (Accessed: December 2017).

IMF (2014). *Government Finance Statistics Manual 2014.* Washington, D.C.

IMF (2016). *United Republic of Tanzania: Selected Issues.* Washington, D.C.

IMF (2017, June 26). *Commentary by IMF Deputy Managing Director Tao Zhang.* Reuters. Retrieved from: www.Reuters.com/article/tanzania-economy-imf-idUSL8N1JN47R

International Development Association and United Republic of Tanzania (1993, 26 July). *Development Credit Agreement (Sixth Power Project) between International Development Association and United Republic of Tanzania.* Credit Number: 2489 TA.

International Labour Organisation (1989). *World Labour Report,* 4, Geneva.

International Work Group for Indigenous Affairs, IWGIA (2015). *Ethnic violence in Morogoro Region in Tanzania.* IWGIA Briefing Note, March 2015, Copenhagen, Denmark. Retrieved from: www.Iwgia.org/publications/search-pubs?publication_id=714

IPP Media (2016, February 7). *Poor Skills in Graduate Who's to Blame?* Retrieved from: www.Ippmedia.com/en/news/poor-skills-graduates-who-blame (Accessed: 25 October 2017).

IPP Media (2017, May 4). *Civil Workers in Fake Certificates Saga can now Appeal, Says Government.* Retrieved from: www.Ippmedia.com/en/news/civil-workers-fake-certificates-saga- can-now-appeal-says-govt (Accessed: 6 November 2017).

ITV (2015, June 2). *Mvutano wa wakulima na wafugaji umeibuka mahakamani baada ya kufuta cheti cha kijiji cha wafugaji, Morogoro.* Retrieved at: www.itv.co.tz/news/local/1617-20182/ Mvutano_wa_wakulima_na_wafugaji_umeibuka_mahakamani_baad a_ya_kufuta_cheti_cha_kijiji_cha_wafugajiMorogoro.html

Jacob, T., and Pedersen, R. (2018). New resource nationalism? Continuity and change in Tanzania's extractive industries. *The Extractive Industries and Society,* 5(2), 287–92.

Jaglin, S., Repussard, C., and Belbéoch, A. (2011). Decentralization and governance of drinking water services in small West African towns and villages (Benin, Mali, Senegal), The arduous process of building local governments. *Canadian Journal of Development Studies / Revue canadienne d'études du développement,* 32(2), 119–38.

James, R. W., and Fimbo, G. M. (1973). *Customary Land Law of Tanzania: A Source Book.* East African Literature Bureau, Nairobi.

Jamhuri ya Muungano wa Tanzania (1994). *Taarifa ya Kamati ya Kurekebisha Muundo na Bajeti ya Serikali.* Dar es Salaam.

Jamhuri ya Muungano wa Tanzania (2011). *Tarrifa ya Miaka Hamsini ya Uhuru wa Tanzania Bara 1961–2011*. Ofisi ya Rais, Dar es Salaam.

Jamasb, T., Nepal, R., and Timilsina, G. R. (2015). A quarter century effort yet to come of age: A survey of power sector reforms in developing countries. *World Bank Policy Research Working Paper*, (7330).

Jansen, E. G. (2009). Does aid work? Reflections on a natural resources programme in Tanzania. *U4 Issue*, 2009(2).

Jedruszek, J. (1978). *Development in Employment and Productivity in Tanzania, 1967–77*. Economic Research Bureau, University of Dar es Salaam.

Johnson, C. (1982). *MITI and the Japanese Miracle: The Growth of Industrial Policy, 1925–1975*. Stanford University Press.

Johnson, G., Snoek, H., Elborgh-Woytek, K., Kourelis, A., Davoodi, H., and Kanaan, O. (1999). *Tanzania: Recent Economic Developments*. International Monetary Fund, Washington, D.C.

Josefsson, E., and Aberg, P. (2005). *An evaluation of the land laws in Tanzania*. Master's thesis, SHU, Sweden.

Joshi, A. R., and Gaddis, I. (eds.). (2015). Preparing the Next Generation in Tanzania: Challenges and Opportunities in Education. World Bank Publications.

Kaarhus, R., Haug, R., Hella, J., and Makindara, J. (2010). Agro-investment in Africa – Impact on land and livelihoods in Mozambique and Tanzania. *Noragric Report No. 53*, Norwegian University of Life Sciences.

Kanfer, R. (1990). Motivation theory and industrial and organizational psychology. *Handbook of Industrial and Organizational Psychology*, 1(2), 75–130.

Kapika, J. (2013). *Power-sector Reform and Regulation in Africa: Lessons from Kenya, Tanzania, Uganda, Zambia, Namibia and Ghana*. HSRC Press, Cape Town.

Kariuki, E. (2017). *Government of the United Republic of Tanzania: Presentation of PSRP III White Paper*. A presentation delivered at the Joint National Workshop on Public Service Improvement and Decentralization-by-Devolution 2 and 25 October, Dodoma.

Kassa, W. (2018). Land titling, local governance and investment: An empirical investigation in Tanzania. *Journal of Sustainable Development*, 11(1), 56–66.

Kaufmann, D., and Kraay, A. (2002, November). *Growth Without Governance*. Available at SSRN: https://ssrn.com/abstract=316861

Kaundinya, D. P., Balachandra, P., and Ravindranath, N. H. (2009). Grid-connected versus stand-alone energy systems for decentralized power – A review of literature. *Renewable and Sustainable Energy Reviews*, 13, 2041–50.

Kessy, A. T., and McCourt, W. (2010). Is decentralization still recentralization? The Local Government Reform Programme in Tanzania. *International Journal of Public Administration*, 33(12–13), 689–97.

Khan, M. (2010). *Political settlements and the Governance of Growth-Enhancing Institutions*. Research Paper Series on Governance for Growth, School of Oriental and African Studies, University of London, London.

Kichonge, B., Mkilaha, I. S. N., John, J. R., and Hameer, S. (2014). Modelling of future energy demand for Tanzania. *Journal of Energy Technologies and Policy*, 4(7), 16–32.

Kim, H. (1994). *The civil service system and economic development: The Japanese experience*. Report on an international colloquium held in Tokyo, 22–25 March 1994, World Bank, Washington, D.C.

Kimambo, N., Maddox, G. H., and Nyanto, S. S. (2017). *A New History of Tanzania*. Mkuki na Nyota Publishers.

King, N. A. S. (2014). Transparency enhancement in Tanzania: A focus on local government administration in Mbeya district. *International Journal of Humanities, Social Sciences and Education*, 1(6), 34–9.

Kiragu, K., and Mukandala, R. (2005a). *Politics and Tactics in Public Sector Reforms: The Dynamics of Public Service Pay in Africa*. Dar es Salaam University Press, Dar es Salaam.

Kiragu, K., and Mukandala, R. S. (2005b). *Public Service Pay Reform: Tactics, Sequencing and Politics in Developing Countries: Lessons from Sub-Saharan Africa*. Dar es Salaam University Press, Dar es Salaam.

Kironde, J. M. (2006). The regulatory framework, unplanned development and urban poverty: Findings from Dar es Salaam, Tanzania. *Land Use Policy*, 23(4), 460–72.

Kironde, L. (2009). *Improving land sector governance in Africa: The case of Tanzania*. Chapter presented at the Workshop on Land Governance in Support of MDGs: Responding to New Challenges, Washington, D.C., 9–10 March 2009.

Kironde, L. (2014). *Public land Information: Registry and cadastre*. Paper prepared for the LGAF, Country Report.

Kitabu, G. (2011). *Investigative Report on Biofuel Investments*. HAKIARDHI, Dar es Salaam.

Krueger, A. O. (1974). The political economy of the rent seeking society. *American Economic Review*, 64(3), 291–303.

Kunkuta, G. E. A. (2011). *Responsiveness and Accountability of Urban Government: Experiences from Provision of Water and Sanitation in Temeke Municipality in Dar es Salaam, Tanzania*. Unpublished PhD thesis, Mzumbe University.

Kweka, J. (2004). *Transport Cost and Trade Policy in Tanzania*. Economic and Social Research Foundation, Dar es Salaam.

Laffont, J. J. (2005). *Regulation and Development*. Cambridge University Press.

Land (*Allocation Committees*). (2001). Regulations, GN 72, published on 4 May 2001.

Land (*Assessment of the Value of Land for Compensation*). (2001). Regulations, 2001, GN 78, published on 4 May 2001.

Land (*Compensation Claims*). (2001). Regulations, 2001, GN 79, published on 4 May 2001.

Land (*Conditions of Rights of Occupancy*). (2001). Regulations, 2001, GN 77, published on 4 May 2001.

Land (*Dispositions of Rights of Occupancy*). (2001). Regulations, 2001, GN 74, published on 4 May 2001.

Land Act (1999). Parliament of the United Republic of Tanzania.

Land Matrix (2016). *Large scale land acquisitions profile Tanzania*. Retrieved from: https://landmatrix.org/media/filer_public/cc/7b/cc7b6743-8bdf-4c50-9927-33dbcbb3fd2b/tanzania_country_profile.pdf (Accessed: 24 August 2018).

Larsson, P. (2006). *The challenging Tanzanian land law reform: A study of the implementation of the Village Land Act*. MSc dissertation, Swedish Royal Institute of Technology, Sweden.

Lawry, S., Samii, C., Hall, R., Leopold, A., Hornby, D., and Mtero, F. (2016). The impact of land property rights interventions on investment and agricultural productivity in developing countries: a systematic review. *Journal of Development Effectiveness*, 9(1), 61–81.

Lawson, A., and Rakner, L. (2005). *Understanding Patterns of Accountability in Tanzania*. Final Synthesis Report. Oxford Policy Management, Chr. Michelsen Institute and REPOA.

LEAT (2012). *Land Grabbing for Agribusiness in Tanzania: Challenges and Prospects*. Dar es Salaam.

Leff, N. H. (1964). Economic development through bureaucratic corruption. *American Behavioral Scientist*, 8, 8–14.

Leo, H. (2017, July 10). *Dar es Salaam*. Tanzania.

Leshabari, M. T., Muhondwa, E. P., Mwangu, M. A., and Mbembati, N. A. (2008). Motivation of healthcare workers in Tanzania: A case study of Muhimbili National Hospital. *East African Journal of Public Health*, 5(1), 32–7.

Leyaro, V., Twumasi Baffour, P., Morrissey, O., and Owens, T. (2014). Determinants of Urban Labour Earnings in Tanzania, 2000/01-06. *Research Paper 14/03*. CREDIT, University of Nottingham.

Lindner, S., and Transparency International. (2014). *Tanzania: Overview of corruption and anti-corruption*. U4. Retrieved from: www.U4.No/publications/ tanzania-overview-of-corruption-and-anti-corruption (Accessed: December 2017).

Liviga, A. J. (1992). Local government in Tanzania: Partner in development or administrative agent of central government?. *Local Government Studies*, 18(3), 211–15.

Lofchie, M. (2014). *The Political Economy of Tanzania: Decline and Recovery*. University of Pennsylvania Press, Philadelphia, PA.

Lofchie, M. F. (1989). *The Policy Factor. Agricultural Performance in Kenya and Tanzania*. Lynne Rienner, Boulder and Nairobi.

Longo, F. (2001). Modernizar la gestión pública de las personas: los desafíos de la flexibilidad. *Reforma y Democracia*, 19(19), 1–14.

Makwarimba, M., and Ngowi, P. (2012). *Making Land Investment Work for Tanzania: Scoping Assessment for Multi-stakeholder Dialogue Initiative*. REPOA, Dar es Salaam.

Maliyamkono, T. L., and Bagachwa, M. S. D. (1990). *The Second Economy in Tanzania*. James Currey, London.

Mallaby, S. (2004). *The World's Banker*. Penguin Press, New York.

Mamdani, M. (1996). *Citizen and Subject in Contemporary Africa and the Legacy of Late Colonialism*. Princeton University Press, Princeton, NJ.

Manara, M., & Regan, T. (2022). Ask a local: Improving the public pricing of land titles in urban Tanzania. *The Review of Economics and Statistics*, 1–44.

Manor, J. (1999). *The Political Economy of Democratic Decentralization*. World Bank, Washington, D.C.

Mans, D. (1994). Tanzania: Resolute action. In Husain, I., and Faruqee, R. (eds.), *Adjustment in Africa: lessons from Country Case Studies*, pp. 352–426. World Bank, Washington, D.C.

Mansuri, G., and Rao, V. (2004). Community-based and -driven development: A critical review. *The World Bank Research Observer*, 19(1), 1–39.

Mansuri, G., and Rao, V. (2013). *Localising Development: Does Participation Work. World Bank Policy Research Report*. World Bank, Washington, D.C.

Martinez-Vazquez, J., and Vaillancourt, F. (eds). (2011). *Decentralization in Developing Countries: Global Perspectives on the Obstacles to Fiscal Devolution*. Edward Elgar, Cheltenham.

Masaki, T. (2018). The impact of intergovernmental transfers on local revenue generation in Sub-Saharan Africa: Evidence from Tanzania. *World Development*, 106, 173–86.

Massay, G. E. (2013). Adjudication of land cases in Tanzania: A bird's eye overview of the District Land and Housing Tribunal. *Open University Law Journal*, 4(2).

Mbowe, G. (1993). Parastatal sector reform and privatisation in Tanzania. In Ramanadham, V. V. (ed.), *Constraints and Impacts of Privatization*. Routledge, New York.

McCluskey, W., and Franzsen, R. (2005). An evaluation of the property tax in Tanzania: An untapped fiscal resource or administrative headache?. *Property Management*, 23(1), 45–69.

McCulloch, N., Sindou, E., and Ward, J. (2017). The political economy of aid for power sector reform. *Green Power for Africa: Overcoming the Main Constraints*, 48(5–6), 165–84.

Mchome, S. E. (2002). *Evictions and the Rights of People in Conservation Areas in Tanzania*. Faculty of Law, University of Dar es Salaam.

McKinnon, R. I. (1997). The logic of market-preserving federalism. *Virginia Law Review*, 1573–80.

McLure, C. E., Jr. (1998). The tax assignment problem: Ends, means, and constraints. *Public Budgeting and Financial Management*, 9(4), 652–83.

McMillan, M., Page, J., and Wangwe, S. (2017). Unlocking Tanzania's manufacturing potential. *Tanzania: The Path to Prosperity*, 3, 151.

McMillan, M., Rodrik, D., and Verduzco-Gallo, I. (2014). Globalization, structural change, and productivity growth, with an update on Africa. *World Development*, 63, 11–32.

Miller, T., and Holms, K. (2011). *Index of Economic Freedom: Promoting Economic Opportunity and Prosperity*. The Heritage Foundation, Washington, D.C.

Ministry of Agriculture (1980). *Policy Proposals for the Institutional Arrangement for Irrigation Development Programme*. Mimeo, Dar es Salaam.

Ministry of Education and Vocational Training and UNESCO (2014). *Enhancing Teacher Education for Bridging the Education Quality Gap in Africa: The Case of Tanzania*.

Ministry of Energy and Minerals (2003). *National Energy Policy, 2003: The Energy Sector in Tanzania*.

Ministry of Energy and Minerals (2014). *Electricity Supply Industry Reform Strategy and Roadmap 2014–2025*. Retrieved from: www.Tanesco.Co.Tz/index.Php/media1/downloads/announcements/12-electricity-supply-industry-reform-strategy-and-roadmap-2014-2025 (Accessed: 1 February 2018).

Ministry of Energy and Minerals (2014). *United Republic of Tanzania: Electricity Supply Industry Reform Strategy and Roadmap 2014–2025*. Dar es Salaam.

Ministry of Energy and Minerals (2016). *Power System Master Plan 2016 Update*. www.Ewura.Go.Tz/wp-content/uploads/2017/01/Power-System-Master-Plan-Dec.2016.pdf (Accessed: 1 February 2018).

Ministry of Water, Energy and Minerals (1992, April). *The Energy Policy of Tanzania*. The United Republic of Tanzania.

Mkapa, B. (2005). Foreword. In Chande, J. K. (ed.), *A Knight in Africa: Journey from Bukene*. Penumbra Press.

Mkenda, A. F., Luvanda, E. G., and Ruhinduka, R. (2010). *Growth and distribution in Tanzania: Recent experience and lessons*. Interim Report to REPOA, Dar es Salaam.

Mkumbo, K. A. (2013). Factors associated with teachers' motivation and commitment to teach in Tanzania. *Journal of Educational Sciences & Psychology*, 3(1).

Mmuya, M. (1998). *Tanzania: Political Reform in Eclipse: Crises and Cleavage in Political Parties*. Friedrich Ebert Stiftung.

Mnyasenga, T. R., and Mushi, E. G. (2015). Administrative legal framework of central-local government relationship in mainland Tanzania: Is it tailored to enhance administrative devolution and local autonomy. *International Review of Management and Business Research*, 4(3), 931–44.

Moner-Girona, M., Ghanadan, R., Solano-Peralta, M., Kougias, I., Bódis, K., Huld, T., and Szabó, S. (2016). Adaptation of Feed-in Tariff for remote mini-grids: Tanzania as an illustrative case. *Renewable and Sustainable Energy Reviews*, 53, 306–18.

Moshi, H. (1995). Parastatal Sector Reforms and Private Sector Development in Tanzania. In Msambichata, L.A., Kilinds, A.A.L., and Mjema, G. (eds.), *Beyond Structural Adjustment Programmes in Tanzania*, pp. 171–90. Economic Research Bureau, Dar es Salaam.

Mpofu, H. (1986). The state and the peasantry. In Shivji, I. (ed.), *The State and the Working People in Tanzania*. CODESRIA.

Mramba, E. F. (2015). *Tanesco Overview*. Tanesco Overview Supply Company Limited, Tanzania.

Msami, J. (2011). *Transparency in local finances in Tanzania, 2003–2009*. REPOA Brief No. 25, REPOA, Dar es Salaam.

Msangi, D. E. (2011). *Land acquisition for urban expansion: Process and impacts on livelihoods of peri urban households*. Dar es Salaam, Tanzania, Licentiate thesis, Swedish University of Agricultural Sciences, Uppsala.

Mtei, E. (2009). *From Goatherd to Governor*. Mkuki na Nyota Publishers, Dar es Salaam.

Mukandala, R. S. (1983). State enterprise control: The case of Tanzania. In Grosh, B., and Mukandala, R. S. (eds.), *State-Owned Enterprises in Africa*, pp. 25–147. Lynne Rienner, London.

Mukandala, R. (2018). *The civil service and economic development in Tanzania*. Final version, March 2018.

Mukandala, R. S. (1992). Bureaucracy and agriculture policy: The experience of Tanzania. In Asmeron, H. K., Hope, R., and Jani, R. B., (eds.), *Bureaucracy and Development Policies in the Third World*. University Press De Boelelaan, Amsterdam.

Mukandala, R. S. (1998). Trends in civil service size and income in Tanzania, 1967–1982. *Canadian Journal of African Studies*, 17(2), 253–63.

Mukandala, R. S. (2015). The state and the provision of public services. In Mukandala, R. S. (ed.), *The Political Economy of Change in Tanzania: Contestations Over Identity, the Constitution and Resources*, pp. 298–315. Dar es Salaam University Press, Dar es Salaam.

Mutahaba, G., Bana, B., and Mallya, E. (2017). *Reforming Tanzania's Public Sector: Assessment and Future Directions*. Mkuki na Nyota Publishers, Dar es Salaam.

Mwamila, B., Kulindwa, K., Kibazohi, O., Majamba, H., Mlinga, R., and Charles, D. (2009). *Feasibility of large scale biofuel production in Tanzania*. Study report sponsored by the Swedish Embassy in Tanzania, Dar es Salaam.

Nyerere, J. K. (1958). *Mali ya Taifa*, cited by G. Sundet, The formalisation process in Tanzania: Is it empowering the poor?. Note prepared for the Norwegian Embassy, December 2006.

National Bureau of Statistics (2016). *Formal Sector Employment and Earnings Survey*. Dar es Salaam.

NBS (2002). *Household Budget Survey 2000–2001*. Report, Dar es Salaam.

NBS (2009). *Household Budget Survey 2007*. Final Report, Dar es Salaam.

386

References

NBS (2014). *Household Budget Survey Main Report 2011–2012*. Technical Report, Dar es Salaam.

NBS (2015). *Tanzania Investment Report: 2014, Foreign Private Investments*. Dar es Salaam.

NBS (2020). *Household Budget Survey 2017/18*. Dodoma.

Ndjovu, C. E. (2003). *Compulsory Purchase in Tanzania: Bulldozing Property Rights*. Royal Institute of Technology, Department of Infrastructure, Division of Real Estate Planning and Law, Stockholm, Sweden.

Ndulu, B., and Mwase, N. (2017). The building blocks towards Tanzania's prosperity: Lessons from looking back, and the way forward. In Adam, C., Collier, P., and Ndulu, B. (eds.), *Tanzania, The Path to Prosperity*, p. 9. Oxford University Press, Oxford.

Nellis, J. R. (1998). Public enterprises in Sub-Saharan Africa. In Grosh, B., and Mukandala, R. S. (eds.), *State-Owned Enterprises in Africa*, pp. 3–24. Lynne Rienner, London.

Ng'eni, F. B., and Chalam, G. V. (2016). Fiscal decentralization and fiscal autonomy in Tanzania local government authorities: A review of existing literature and empirical evidence. *European Journal of Business and Management*, 8(28), 28–36.

Ngama, R. (2006). *Effects of 20,000 plots project on surrounding neighbourhoods in Dar es Salaam: The case of Bunju and Boko in Kinondoni municipality*. BSc thesis, Department of Land Management and Valuation, University College of Lands and Architectural Studies, University of Dar es Salaam.

Niba, W. (2018, December 31). *World Bank, EU suspend aid to Tanzania*. RFI. Retrieved from: www.rfi.fr/en/africa/20181231-worldeu-tanzania-sanctions

Nichols, P. (2003). Corruption as an assurance problem. *American University International Law Review*, 19(6), 1308–40.

Nnoli, O. (2002). *Introduction, Nnoli, O. Editor, Government and Politics in Africa –A Reader*. AAPS Books Harare, Zimbabwe.

Nord, R., Sobolev, Y., Dunn, D., Hajdenberg, A., Hobdari, N., Maziad, S., and Roudet, S. (2009). *Tanzania: The Story of an African Transition*. International Monetary Fund, African Department, Washington, D.C.

North, D. (1990). *Institutions, Institutional Change and Economic Performance*. Cambridge University Press, Cambridge.

North, D., Wallis, J., and Weingast, B. (2009). *Violence and Social Orders: A Conceptual Framework for Interpreting Recorded Human History*. Cambridge University Press, New York.

North, D., Wallis, J., Webb S., and Weingast, B. (2012). *In the Shadow of Violence: Politics, Economics and the Problems of Development*. Cambridge University Press, Cambridge.

Ntukamazina, D. A. (2000). Civil service reform in Tanzania: A strategic perspective. In Mukandala, R. S. (ed.), *African Public Administration: A Reader*, pp. 524–36. AAPS, Harare.

Nyerere, J. (1967). *The Arusha Declaration and TANU's policy on socialism and self-reliance*. Retrieved from: www.Marxists.org/subject/africa/nyerere/1967/arusha-declaration.html

Nyerere, J. (1977). *The Arusha Declaration Ten Years After*. United Republic of Tanzania, Government Printer, Dar es Salaam. Retrieved from: www.Tzonline.org/pdf/thearushadeclarationtenyearsafter.pdf

Nyerere, J. K. (1968). *Freedom and Socialism*. Oxford University Press, Dar es Salaam.

Nyerere, J. K. (1974). *Freedom and Development*. Oxford University Press, Dar es Salaam.

Nyerere, J. K. (1958). *Mali ya Taifa*, cited by G. Sundet, The formalisation process in Tanzania: Is it empowering the poor?. Note prepared for the Norwegian Embassy, December 2006.

Nyerere, J. K. (1967). *After the Arusha Declaration. Presidential Address to the National Conference of TANU*. Mwanza, 16 October.

Nyerere, J. K. (1968). *Freedom and Socialism*. Oxford University Press.

Oakland Institute (2011). *Understanding Investment Deals in Africa*. Oakland, CA.

Oates, W. (1972). *Fiscal Federalism*. Harcourt Brace Jovanovich, New York.

Odarno, L., Sawe, E., Swai, M., Katyega, M. J., and Lee, A. (2017, October). *Accelerating Mini-Grid Deployment in Sub-Saharan Africa: Lessons in Tanzania*. World Resource Institute. Retrieved from: www.Wri.org/publication/tanzania-mini-grids (Accessed: December 2017).

OECD (2013). *OECD Investment Reviews: Tanzania*. OECD, Paris.

Ofisi ya Rais Ikulu (2017). *Taarifa kwa vyombo vya habari Jamhuri ya Muungano wa Tanzania Kurugenzi ya Mawasiliano ya Rais Ikulu*. Dar es Salaam.

Ohio State University (2017). *Small scale solar power systems for rural Tanzania: Market analysis and opportunities*. Retrieved from: http://globalwater. Osu.Edu/files/Solar-Power_Tanzania_web.pdf (Accessed: 1 February 2018).

Olingo, A. (2017, September 28). *Uncertainty Clouds Tanzania Gas Investment as Low Prices Persist*. The East African. Retrieved from: www.Theeastafrican.Co.Ke/business/Uncertainty-clouds-Tanzania-gas-investment/2560-4115452-v2ch52/index.html

Olowu, D. (2000). Bureaucracy and democratic reform. In Hyden, G., Olowu, D., and Ogendo, H. (eds.), *African Perspectives of Governance*, pp. 153–79. Africa World Press, Trenton/Asmara.

Paget, D. (2017, November 5). *Two Years on, How Magufuli Changed TZ*. The Citizen. Retrieved from: www.Thecitizen.Co.Tz/News/Two-years-on-how-Magufuli-changed-TZ/1840340-4173716-tql9g/index.html

Paget, D. (2017, July 17). Tanzania: Magufuli's mining reforms are a masterclass in political manoeuvring. *African Arguments*. Retrieved from: https://africanarguments .org/2017/07/tanzania-magufulis-mining-reforms-are-a-masterclass-in-political-man oeuvring/

Pal, S. (2010, September). *Social norms, culture and local infrastructure*. Discussion paper, Brunel Economics and Finance, London.

Pal, S., and Wahhaj, Z. (2016). Fiscal decentralization, local institutions and public goods provision: Evidence from Indonesia. *Journal of Comparative Economics*, 45(2), 383–409.

Partnership for Growth (2011). *Tanzania Growth Diagnostic: A joint analysis for the Governments of the United Republic of Tanzania and the United States of America*.

Pastory, P. (2017). *Regulatory compliance in local government procurement in Tanzania: Institutions and context*. PhD dissertation, University of Dar es Salaam.

Peña, S. (2007). Evaluation of the effects of decentralization on educational outcomes in Spain. *Working Papers in Economics No. 228, Espai de Recerca en Economia*. Universitat de Barcelona.

Peng, D., and Poudineh, R. (2016). *Sustainable Electricity Pricing for Tanzania*. Paper EL 20, Oxford Institute for Energy Studies, Oxford. www.oxfordenergy.org/wpcms/wp-content/uploads/2016/07/Sustainable-electricity-pricing-for-Tanzania-EL-20.pdf (Accessed: 1 February 2018).

Peters, J., and Sievert, M. (2016). Impacts of rural electrification revisited – The African context. *Journal of Development Effectiveness*, 8(3), 327–45.

Piron, D. (2016). *Enforcing austerity through a discreet calculative infrastructure: The evolving definitions of PPPs in the ESA*. Interpretive Policy Analysis. Online: http://hdl. Handle. Net/2268/200545 (Accessed: December 2017).

Piron, L. H., Baker, A., Savage, L., and Wiseman, K. (2016). *Is DFID getting real about politics? A stocktake of how DFID has adopted a politically-informed approach (2010–2015)*. Discussion paper, Governance, Open Societies and Anti-Corruption Department, Department for International Development, London.

PMO-RALG (2013). *A study on LGAs own source revenue collection*. Tanzania.

PO-RALG (2017). *PO-RALG local government revenue collection dashboard*. Tanzania.

Policy Forum (2017). *Tanzania Governance Review 2015–2016*. Policy Forum, Mikochni, Dar es Salaam.

Ponera, G. E., Mhonyiwa, J. E., and Mrutu, A. S. (2011). *Quality of primary school inputs in Tanzania mainland*. Policy Brief 2, SACMEQ Gaborone, Botswana.

Power Africa (2015). *What Power Africa means for Tanzania*. Tanzania.

Pratt, C. (1975). Nyerere on the transition to socialism. *African Review*, 5(1), 63–76.

Pratt, C. (1976). *The Critical Phase in Tanzania 1945–1968. Nyerere and the Emergence of a Socialist Strategy*, pp. 235–6. Cambridge University Press, Cambridge.

Pratt, C. (1979). Tanzania's transition to socialism: Reflections of a democratic socialist. In *Towards Socialism in Tanzania*, pp. 193–236. University of Toronto Press.

Quah, J. S. T. (2011). *Curbing Corruption in Asian Countries: An Impossible Dream?*. Emerald Group Publishing.

Ranja, T. (2003). Success under duress: A comparison of the indigenous African and East African Asian entrepreneurs. *ESRF Globalization Project Paper Series*.

REA (2016). *First call: Invitation to submit applications for results-based financing (RBF). Grants for renewable energy investments in green mini and micro grids*. Ministry of Energy and Minerals, Dar es Salaam. Retrieved from: www.Ewura.Go.Tz/wp-content/uploads/2016/09/RBFONLINE-APPLICATION-GENERAL-INFORMATIONS-.pdf (Accessed: 1 February 2018).

Regional Centre on Small Arms and Light Weapons (n.d.). *A Report of Analysis on Armed Crimes in East Africa Community Countries (Burundi, Kenya, Rwanda, Tanzania and Uganda)*. Nairobi.

Reinikka, R., and Svensson, J. (2004). Local capture: Evidence from a central government transfer program in Uganda. *Quarterly Journal of Economics*, 119(2), 679–705.

Reinikka, R., and Svensson, J. (2005). Fighting corruption to improve schooling: Evidence from a newspaper campaign in Uganda. *Journal of the European Economic Association*, 3(2/3), 259–67.

Reinikka, R., and Svensson, J. (2011). The power of information in public services: Evidence from education in Uganda. *Journal of Public Economics*, 95(7–8), 956–66.

REPOA (2007). *Framework for Downward Accountability in Local Government Authorities*. Prime Minister's Office, Regional Administration and Local Government (PMO-RALG), Tanzania.

REPOA (2008). *The oversight processes of local councils in Tanzania*. Final Report, July 2008, Tanzania, p. 27.

Resnick, D. (2012). Opposition parties and the urban poor in African democracies. *Comparative Political Studies*, 45(11), 1351–78.

Rodrik, D. (2008). The real exchange rate and economic growth. *Brookings Papers on Economic Activity*, 2008(2), 365–412.

Root, H. L. (2016). *Capital and Collusion: The Political Logic of Global Economic Development*. Princeton University Press.

Rweyemamu, J. (1973). *Underdevelopment and Industrialization in Tanzania*. Oxford University Press, New York.

Rweyemamu, R. (1979). The historical and institutional setting of Tanzanian Industry. In Kim, K. S., Mabele, R. B., and Schultheis, M. J. (eds.), *Papers on the Political Economy of Tanzania*. East African Publishers.

Schreiber, L. (2017). *Registering Rural Rights: Village Land Titling in Tanzania, 2008–2017. Innovation for Successful Societies*. Princeton University, Princeton, NJ.

Scott, A., and Seth, P. (2013). *The Political Economy of Electricity Distribution in Developing Countries – A Literature Review*. Overseas Development Institute, London.

Shah, A. (2006). *Local Governance in Developing Countries*. Public Sector Governance and Accountability. World Bank, Washington, D.C.

Shao, J. R. (1978). *Some features of Tanzanian manufacturing industry*. Master dissertation, University of Dar es Salaam.

Shelton, C. (2007). The size and composition of government expenditure. *Journal of Public Economics*, 91(11–12), 2230–60.

Shivji, I. (1986). The transformation of the state and the working people. In Shivji, I. (ed.), *The State and the Working People in Tanzania*. CODESRIA.

Shivji, I. (1998). *Not Yet Democracy: Reforming Land Tenure in Tanzania*. Dar es Salaam University Press, Dar es Salaam.

Shivji, I. (2021, June 21). *The Dialectics of Maguphilia and Maguphobia*. CODESRIA Bulletin, online, n. 13.

Shivji, I., Yahya-Othman, S., and Kamata, N. (2020). *Development as Rebellion. Julius Nyerere*, A Biography. Mkuki na Nyota Publishers, Dar es Salaam.

Sidhu, H. S. (1981). *Problems of Irrigation Development in the Regions of Tanzania and Some Suggested Solutions*. Ministry of Agriculture, Dar es Salaam.

Silver, M. (1984). *Enterprise and the Scope of the Firm*. Martin Robertson, London.

Skinlo, T. E. (2007, May). *"Old" and "new" authoritarianism in Tanzania – theoretical, methodological, and empirical considerations*. Master's thesis, Department of Comparative Politics, University of Bergen.

Smoke, P. (1994). *Local Government Finance in Developing Countries. The Case of Kenya*. Oxford University Press, Nairobi.

Smoke, P., and Lewis, B. (1996). Fiscal decentralization in Indonesia: A new approach to an old idea. *World Development*, 24(8), 1281–99.

Sobhan, R. (1996). *Aid Dependence and Donor Policy. The Case of Tanzania*. University Press Limited, Dhaka, Bangladesh.

Sokoine, E. M. (1984). *Public policy making and implementation in Tanzania*. Draft Master thesis, University of Dar es Salaam.

Songela, F., and Maclean, A. (2008). *Scoping Exercise (Situation Analysis) on the Biofuels Industry within and Outside Tanzania*. Energy for Sustainable Development report for the WWF Tanzania Programme Office.

Stein, H., Maganga, F. P., Odgaard, R., Askew, K., and Cunningham, S. (2016). The formal divide: Customary rights and the allocation of credit to agriculture in Tanzania. *The Journal of Development Studies*, 52(9), 1306–19.

Stiglitz, J. E. (2003). *Globalisation and Its Discontents*. W. W. Norton and Company, New York.

Sule, E. (2016). Land grabbing and agricultural commercialization duality: Insights from Tanzania's transformation agenda. In Chinigo, D. (ed.), *The New Harvest*. Agrarian Policies and Rural Transformation in Southern Africa.

Sulle, E., and Nelson, F. (2009). *Biofuels, Land Access and Rural Livelihoods in Tanzania*. IIED, London.

Sumaye, F. (2004). *United Republic of Tanzania. Reforming Tanzania's public administration: Status and challenges*. Report of a stakeholder workshop held on 8 October 2004 Mimeo, Dar es Salaam, Tanzania.

Sundet, G. (2005, February). *The 1999 Land Act and Village Land Act: A Technical Analysis of the Practical Implications of the Acts*. REPOA, Dar es Salaam.

Sutton, J. E. G. (1969). The peopling of Tanzania. *A History of Tanzania*, 1–13.

Sutton, J., and Olomi, D. (2012). *An Enterprise Map of Tanzania* (Vol. 3). International Growth Centre in association with the London Publishing Partnership.

Svendsen, K. E. (1986). The creation of macro-economic imbalances and a structural crisis. In Boesen, J., and Koponen, J. (eds.), *Tanzania: Crisis and Struggle for Survival* (No. 77). Nordic Africa Institute.

Syagga, P., and Olima, W. (1996). The impact of compulsory land acquisition and displaced households: The case study of the third Nairobi Water Supply Project, Kenya. *Habitat International – A Journal for the Study of Human Settlements*, 20(1).

Szirmai, A., and Lapperre, P. (2001). *The Industrial Experience of Tanzania*. Palgrave Macmillan, London.

Tangri, R. (1999). *The Politics of Patronage in Africa*. James Currey, London.

Tanzania Growth Diagnostics (Partnership for Growth) (2011). *A joint analysis for the Governments of the United Republic of Tanzania and the United States of America*.

Tanzania Law Report (1985). Case No. 88.

Tanzania Private Sector Foundation (2015). *Business Leaders' Perceptions of the Investment Climate in Tanzania – 2015*. Dar es Salaam.

Tanzi, V. (2000). Fiscal federalism and decentralization: A review of some efficiency and macroeconomic aspects. In Tanzi, V. (ed.), *Policies, Institutions and the Dark Side of Economics*. Edward Elgar, Cheltenham.

Tanzi, V., and Davoodi, H. R. (2000). Corruption, growth and public finances. *IMF Working Paper No. 00/182*. Washington, D.C.

Tenga, W. R., and Kironde, L. (2012). *A Report for the WB on Study of Policy, Legal and Institutional Issues Related to Land in the Southern Agricultural Growth Corridor of Tanzania (SAGCOT)*. Dar es Salaam.

Tenga, W. R., and Mramba, S. J. (2014). *Theoretical Foundations of Land Law in Tanzania*. Law Africa, Nairobi.

Tenga, W. R., and Mramba, S. J. (2018). *Conveyancing and Disposition of Land in Tanzania: Law and Procedure*. Law Africa, Nairobi.

Teorell, J., Sundström, A., Holmberg, S., Rothstein, B., Alvarado Pachon, N., and Mert Dalli, C. (2022). *The Quality of Government Standard Dataset, Version Jan 22*. University of Gothenburg: The Quality of Government Institute. Retrieved from: www.Gu.Se/en/quality-government. https://doi.org/10.18157/qogstdjan22

Tidemand, P., and Msami, J. (2010). *The impact of local government reforms in Tanzania 1998–2008*. Research on Poverty Alleviation, Special paper 10/1, Dar el Salaam, Tanzania.

The 2015–16 Demographic and Health Survey and Malaria Indicator Survey (TDHSMI). Retrieved from: https://dhsprogram.com/pubs/pdf /FR321.pdf (Accessed: 10 March 2018).

The Citizen (2015, June 24). *How corruption rocked Kikwete's government in the past decade*. Retrieved from: www.Thecitizen.Co.Tz/News/How-corruption-rocked-Kikwete-s-govt-in-the-past-decade/1840340-2763268-rd1y4yz/index.html (Accessed: 8 December 2017).

The Citizen (2017, September 7). *Land policy 2016 attracts criticism*.

The Constitution of the United Republic of Tanzania (1984). CAP. 2, Terms of office of Ministers and Deputy Ministers Act No.15 of 1984 Art.9.

The Land Acquisition Act (2002). No. 47 of 1967 [Cap. 118 R. E. 2002].

The Land Act (2002). No. 4 of 1999 [Cap. 113 R. E. 2002].

The Land Registration Act (2002) [Cap. 334 R. E. 2002].

The Local Government (*District Authorities*) (2002). Act, No. 7 of 1982 (1982) [Cap 287 R. E 2002].

The National Land Use Planning Commission (2011).

The Parliament of the United Republic of Tanzania. (2008). *The Electricity Act*.

The Tanzania Investment Act (2002). No. 26 of 1997 [Cap. 38 R. E. 2002].

The United Republic of Tanzania (2002). Constitution 1977 as amended [Cap. 2 R. E. 2002].

The Village Land Act (1999). Parliament of the United Republic of Tanzania. Cap114. Page 6.

The Village Land Act (2002). Act No. 5 of 1999, [Cap. 114 R. E. 2002].

Therklldsen, O., and Bourgoin, F. (2012). Continuity and change in Tanzania's ruling coalition: Legacies, crises and weak productive capacity. *DIIS Working Paper*. Denmark.

Thoburn, J. (2013). Vietnam as a role model for development. *Achieving Development Success: Strategies and Lessons from the Developing World*, 99–118.

Thompson, G., and Bazilian, M. (2014). Democratization, energy poverty, and the pursuit of symmetry. *Global Policy*, 5(1), 127–31.

Tilley, H. (2011). *Beyond rationality: A new theory of accountability and foreign aid for Tanzania*. PhD thesis, Department of Economics, School of Oriental and African Studies, University of London.

TRA (2017, May). *Report of Tanzania Revenue Authority*. Domestic Revenue Department, Dar es Salaam.

Trading Economics Retrieved from: https://tradingeconomics.com/ (Accessed: 1 November 2017).

Transparency International (2016). *Corruption Perception Index 2016*. Retrieved from: www.Transparency.org/cpi2016 (Accessed: 7 November 2017).

Transparency International (2018). *2018 Corruption Perceptions Index – Explore the results*. Retrieved from: www.transparency.org/en/cpi/2018

Tripp, A. M. (2012). Donor assistance and political reform in Tanzania. *Working Paper 2012/37*. United Nations University–World Institute for Development Economics Research, Helsinki.

Twaweza. (2013). *KiuFunza: The Thirst to Learn Baseline Database*. Twaweza, Dar Es Salaam. Retrieved from: http://twaweza.org/go/kiufunza-launch1.

Twaweza (2015). *Education: Schooling or fooling*. Retrieved from: www.Twaweza .org/uploads/files/Education%20Tamasha.pdf (Accessed: 10 March 2018).

Twaweza (2016, September 1). *Press release*. Retrieved from: www.Twaweza.org/ uploads/files/UwezoTZ-2014ALA-PressRelease-EN- FINAL.pdf (Accessed: 10 March 2018).

UN-HABITAT (2015). *The Challenges of Local Government Financing in Developing Countries*. United Nations Human Settlements Programme, Nairobi.

UNDP (2014). *Tanzania Human Development Report: Economic Transformation for Human Development*. ESRF, Dar es Salaam.

UNIDO (1988). *Regenerating Africa Manufacturing Industry: Approach and Programme. Studies of the Rehabilitation of African Industry*. No. 1 PPD 101, 29 December.

UNIDO (1990). *Rehabilitation of African Industry*. No. 12. PPD 168, 10 July.

UNICEF (2017). *Tanzania 2017 Education fact sheet*. Retrieved from: www.Unicef .org/tanzania/media/681/file/UNICEF-Tanzania-2017-Education-fact-sheet.pdf

United Republic of Tanganyika (1964). *Five Year Plan for Economic and Social Development*. Government Printers, Dar es Salaam.

United Republic of Tanzania (1967). *Arha Declaration: Answers to Questions*. Dar es Salaam.

United Republic of Tanzania (1968). *Second Five-Year Development Plan 1*. Government Printers, Dares Salaam.

United Republic of Tanzania (1987). *Public Expenditure Review Vol II*. Dar es Salaam.

United Republic of Tanzania (1992). *The Public Corporations Act*.

United Republic of Tanzania (1993). *The Public Corporations Act*. Public Corporations Act Amendment No. 16.

United Republic of Tanzania (1999). *The Public Corporations Act*. Public Corporations Act Amendment No. 17.

United Republic of Tanzania (2001). *Agricultural Sector Development Strategy (2001)*. MAFS, Dar es Salaam.

United Republic of Tanzania (2002). *The Public Service Act*. No. 8 of (Cap.298). Dar es Salaam.

United Republic of Tanzania (2005a). *National Strategy for Growth and Reduction of Poverty (NSGRP)*. Vice-President's Office, Dar es Salaam.

United Republic of Tanzania (2005b). *Privatization Impact Assessment – Infrastructure*.

United Republic of Tanzania (2005c). *Rural Energy Act*.

United Republic of Tanzania (2005d). MKURABITA Program on Formalization of the Assets of the Poor in Tanzania and Strengthening the Rule of Law Report.

United Republic of Tanzania (2007, July). *Report of the Sub-committee on Matters Required to be Accomplished to Enable Tanzania Revenue Authority to Collect Property Rates on Behalf of Local Government Authorities in Mainland Tanzania*. PMO-RALG and TRA, Dar es Salaam.

United Republic of Tanzania (2008). *Public Service Management and Employment Policy*. Dar es Salaam.

United Republic of Tanzania (2009). *The Public Service Standing Orders*. Dar es Salaam.

United Republic of Tanzania (2010). *Public Service Pay and Incentive Policy*. Dar es Salaam.

United Republic of Tanzania (2013). *Public Service Training Policy*. Dar es Salaam.

United Republic of Tanzania (2014). *Electricity Supply Industry Reform Strategy and Roadmap 2014–2025*.

United Republic of Tanzania (2015). MLHHSD Budget Speech.

United Republic of Tanzania (2016a). *Speech by the Minister for Finance and Planning, Estimates of government revenue and expenditure for fiscal years 2016/17*. Dodoma.

United Republic of Tanzania (2016b). *Tanzania Demographic and Health Survey and Malaria Indicator Survey 2015–2016*. Final Report, Dar es Salaam.

United Republic of Tanzania (2017a). *Tanzania Human Development Report*.

United Republic of Tanzania (2017b, June 8). *Speech by the Minister for Finance and Planning, Estimates of government revenue and expenditure for 2017/18*. Dodoma.

United Republic of Tanzania (2021, February). MLHHSD Budget Speech.

United Republic of Tanzania Survey of Employment and earnings (1966–1980). Government Printer, Dares Salaam.

United Republic of Tanzania, MLHHSD Budget Speech (2021/2)

URT, Bank of Tanzania (2014). *Resettlement Policy Framework*. For the Proposed Additional Financing for the Housing Finance Project in Tanzania, Dar es Salaam.

URT, Law Reform Commission (2014). *Report on the Review of the Legal Framework on Land Dispute Settlement in Tanzania*. Dar es Salaam.

URT, Ministry of Agriculture and Food Security (2003). *Resettlement Policy Framework for the Participatory Agricultural Development and Empowerment Project*. Dar es Salaam.

URT, Ministry of Energy and Minerals (2015). *Resettlement Policy Framework Updated for the Additional Financing for the Sustainable Management of Mineral Resources Project*. Dar es Salaam.

URT, MKURABITA (2005). *Report on Property and Business Formalization in Tanzania*. MLHHSD, Dar es Salaam.

URT, MLHHSD (2011). *National Land Use Framework Plan 2009–2029*. Dar es Salaam.

URT, MLHHSD (2013a). *Guidelines for Valuers and Strategies for Property Valuation in Tanzania*. Dar es Salaam.

URT, MLHHSD (2013b). *Strategic Plan for the Implementation of the Land Laws (SPILL)*. MLHHSD, Dar es Salaam.

URT, MLHHSD (2015). *Rules and Regulations for Amendment of Land Rent Rates*. Fees and Charges from 1 July 2015, Dar es Salaam.

URT, MLHHSD (2016). *Draft Land Policy*. Dar es Salaam.

URT, MLHHSD (2018). *Minister of Land Housing Human Settlements Development*. Budget Speech, Financial Year 2017/18, Dar es Salaam.

URT, National Land Use Planning Commission (2011). *Guidelines for Participatory Village Land Use Management in Tanzania*. 2nd edition, Dar es Salaam.

URT, PMO-RALG (2014). *Resettlement Policy Framework for Dar es Salaam Metropolitan Development Project*. Dar es Salaam.

USAID (2017). *Maternal and child health in Tanzania*. Retrieved from: www.Usaid .Gov/sites/default/files/Chapteruments/1860/Maternal_and_Child_Health_Fact_ Sheet_2017_FINAL.pdf (Accessed: 10 March 2018).

USAID (2018). *Adaptive Solar PV Mini-Grids in Tanzania*. Retrieved from: www .Usaid.Gov/energy/mini-grids/case-studies/tanzania-smart-solar (Accessed: 1 February 2018).

Valentine, T. (1985). *Government Wage Policy and Labour Related Trends in Developing Countries: The Case of Tanzania*. Mimeo Dar es Salaam, Tanzania.

Valsecchi, M. (2014). Land property rights and international migration: Evidence from Mexico. *Journal of Development Economics*, 110, 276–90.

Van Arkadie, B. (1995, September). *Economic strategy and structural adjustment in Tanzania*. PSD Occasional Paper No. 18, World Bank, Washington, D.C.

Van der Dussen, J. W. (1992). Financial relations between central and local government in the Netherlands: Why are they different?. *Local Government Studies*, 18(4), 94–105.

van der Dussen, J. W. (2008). Financial relations between central and local government in the Netherlands: Why are they different?. *Financing European Local Governments*, 18(4), 94–105.

Van De Laar, A. J. M. (1973). Tanzania's second Five Year Plan. In Cliffe, L., and Saul, J. S. (eds.), *Socialism in Tanzania. An Interdisciplinary Reader 2 Policies*. East Africa Publishing House, Dar es Salaam.

Venugopal, V., and Yilmaz, S. (2010). Decentralization in Tanzania: An assessment of local government discretion and accountability. *Public Administration and Development*, 30(3), 215–31.

Vermeulen, S., and Cotula, L. (2010). *Making the Most of Agricultural Investment: A Survey of Business Models that Provide Opportunities for Smallholders*. FAO, Rome; IIED, London.

Victor, D., and Heller, T. C. (2007). *The Political Economy of Power Sector Reform*. Cambridge University Press, Cambridge.

Vilby, K. (2007). *Independent? Tanzania's Challenges since Uhuru: A Second Generation Nation in a Globalized World*. Nordiska Afrikainstitutet, Uppsala, Sweden.

Village Land Regulations (2001, May 4). *GN 86*.

Wade, R. (1992). *Governing the Market*. Princeton University Press, Princeton.

Waigama, S. (2008). *Privatization process and asset valuation: A case study of Tanzania*. Doctoral dissertation, KTH.

Wane, W., and Gaddis, I. (2015). An educational service delivery scorecard for Tanzania. In Joshi, A. R., and Gaddis, I. (eds.), *Preparing the Next Generation in Tanzania: Challenges and Opportunities*, pp. 65–86. World Bank Group, Washington, DC.

Weber, M. (1978). *Economy and Society: An Outline of Interpretive Sociology (Vol. 2)*. University of California Press.

Weingast, B. R. (1995). The economic role of political institutions: Market-preserving federalism and economic development. *The Journal of Law, Economics and Organizations*, 11(1995), 1–31.

Wydick, B. (2008). *Games in Economic Development*. Cambridge University Press, Cambridge.

Williams, J. H., and Ghanadan, R. (2006). Electricity reform in developing and transition countries: A reappraisal. *Energy*, 6(7), 815–44.

Wily, B. (1981). *A Profile and Analysis of Government Manpower in Arusha Region*. Mimeo Dar es Salaam Tanzania.

Wily, L. A. (2001). *Community-Based Land Tenure Management: Questions and Answers About Tanzania's New Village Land Act, 1999*. International Institute for Environment and Development, London.

World Bank (1961). *The Economic Development of Tanganyika*. Johns Hopkins University, Baltimore, MD.

World Bank (1967). *Appraisal of the Development Program of the Tanganyika Electric Supply Company Limited Tanzania*. Washington, D.C.

World Bank (1976). *Report and recommendation of the President of the International Bank for Reconstruction and Development to the executive directors on a proposed loan to the United Republic of Tanzania for the Kidatu hydroelectric project – Second stage, Tanzania.* Washington, D.C.

World Bank (1981). *Accelerated Development in Sub-Saharan Africa: An Agenda for Action.* Washington, D.C.

World Bank (1987). *Industrial Development in Tanzania: An Agenda for Industrial Recovery.* Washington D.C.

World Bank (1993). *The World Bank's Role in the Electric Power Sector: Policies for Effective Institutional, Regulatory, and Financial Reform.* The World Bank.

World Bank (1993). *Tanzania – Sixth Power Project (English).* Washington, D.C.

World Bank (1998). *Support to the Government of Tanzania's Anti-Corruption Program.* World Bank, Washington, D.C.

World Bank (1999). *Beyond the Centre: Decentralizing the State. World Bank Latin America and Caribbean Studies.* Washington, D.C.

World Bank (2000). *Reforming Public Institutions and Strengthening Governance.* Washington, D.C.

World Bank (2003). *World Development Report 2004: Making Services Work for Poor People.* Washington, D.C.

World Bank (2004). *Fiscal Decentralization and Subnational Expenditure Policy.* Washington, D.C.

World Bank (2008). *The Growth Report: Strategies for Sustained Growth and Inclusive Development.* Commission on Growth and Development, Washington, D.C.

World Bank (2013). *Enterprise Surveys.* Retrieved from: www.Enterprisesurveys.org/ (Accessed: 10 November 2017).

World Bank (2013). *Project Performance Assessment Report: The United Republic of Tanzania Public Service Reform Project (IDA-33000-TZ AND IDA 3300A-TZ).* Washington, D.C.

World Bank (2014a). *Tanzania: Productive Jobs Wanted, Country Economic Memorandum.* Washington, D.C.

World Bank (2014b). *Service Delivery Survey, Tanzania.* Washington D.C.

World Bank (2015a). *Tanzania 2014 Service Delivery Indicators: Health Technical Report.* Washington, D.C.

World Bank (2015b). *Tanzania Mainland Poverty Assessment.* Washington, D.C.

World Bank (2016). *TZA Third Power and Gas Sector DPO (1st of the new series).* Washington, D.C.

World Bank (2017). *Implementation completion and results report (IDA-52150 and IDA 53170).* On a series of two credits in the total amount of SDR 130.1 million (US$200 million equivalent). To the United Republic of Tanzania for the first and second power and gas sector DPO, Africa Region: Macroeconomics and Fiscal Management Global Practice, Washington, D.C.

World Bank (2017a). *Doing Business 2018: Tanzania.* World Bank Group Flash Report. Retrieved from: www.Doingbusiness.org (Accessed: 15 February 2018).

World Bank (2017b). *Governance and the Law. World Economic Report.* Washington, D.C.

World Bank (2017c). *Monitoring Global Poverty: Report of the Commission on Global Poverty.* Washington, D.C.

World Bank (2017d). *United Republic of Tanzania, Systematic Country Diagnostic.* Report No. 110894-TZ, Washington, D.C.

World Bank (2019a). *Tanzania Mainland Poverty Assessment, Executive Summary.* Washington, D.C.

World Bank (2019b). *Tanzania Update: Transforming Agriculture, Realizing the Potential of Agriculture for Inclusive Growth and Poverty Reduction.* Africa Region Macroeconomics Trade and Investment Global Practice, Issue No. 13, Washington, D.C.

World Bank (2020). Global Electrification Database from *Tracking SDG 7: The Energy Progress Report.* World Bank. Retrieved from: https://data.worldbank.org/indicator/ EG.ELC.ACCS.ZS?locations=TZ

World Bank (2021). *The World Bank in Tanzania: An Overview.* March 23, 2021, updating, Washington, D.C.

World Bank (2022). *Business Enabling Environment.* World Bank. Retrieved from: www.worldbank.org/en/programs/business-enabling-environment

World Bank (2022). *WGI-Interactive Data Access.* World Bank. Retrieved from: http:// info.worldbank.org/governance/wgi/Home/Reports

World Bank Group Macroeconomics, Trade and Investment Global Practice, Africa Region (2019). *Tanzania Economic Update: Human Capital: The Real Wealth of Nations.* World Bank, Washington D.C.

World Economic Forum (2016). *The Global Competitiveness Report 2016–2017.* Geneva.

World Economic Forum (2017). *The Global Competitiveness Report 2017–2018.* Geneva.

World Future Council (2017, May). *Policy roadmap for 100% renewable energy and poverty eradication in Tanzania.* Retrieved from: www.Worldfuturecouncil.org/ file/2017/05/Policy-Roadmap-Tanzania.pdf (Accessed: 1 February 2018).

World Resources Institute (2017). *Accelerating mini-grid deployment in Sub-Saharan Africa: Lessons from Tanzania.* Retrieved from: www.Wri.org/publication/ tanzania-mini-grids (Accessed: 1 February 2018).

World Trade Organisation (2019). *Trade Policy Review: East African Community (EAC).* 2019, 238–40.

Zhou, C., Liang, Y., and Fuller, A. (2021). Tracing agricultural land transfer in China: Some legal and policy issues. *Land,* 10(1), 58.

Index

Footnotes are indicated by n. after the page number.

Printed in the United States
by Baker & Taylor Publisher Services